The Chair of Verity

Alexander Webster preaching from the 'Chair of Verity' in 'Haddo's Hole', St Giles' Church, Edinburgh (John Kay).

The Chair of Verity

Political preaching and pulpit censure
in eighteenth-century Scotland

Ronald Lyndsay Crawford

humming earth

Published by
humming earth
an imprint of
Zeticula Ltd
Unit 13
196 Rose Street
Edinburgh
EH2 4AT
Scotland

http://www.hummingearth.com
admin@hummingearth.com

Text Copyright © Ronald Lyndsay Crawford 2017

Front Cover image:
David Allan, "The Black Stool (The Stool of Repentance)"
National Galleries of Scotland

ISBN 978-1-84622-053-1 hardback
ISBN 978-1-84622-054-8 paperback

All rights reserved. No part of this publication may be reproduced, stored in a retrieval system, or transmitted in any form or by any means, electronic, mechanical, photocopying, recording or otherwise, without the prior permission of the publishers.

To the ministers,
office-bearers and members
of the congregation,
past and present, of
Netherlee Parish Church, Glasgow,
where Evelyn and I have listened contentedly
to the chair of verity since 1962.

Alexander Carlyle depicted as the scourge of the Popular party of the Church of Scotland. John Erskine is shown as the head with the black wig (John Kay).

1. Timoth. 4. ¶*The time is come that men can not abyde the Sermon of veritie nor holsome doctrine.*
John Knox (c. 1514-72).
From the title page of a sermon preached in Edinburgh on 19 August 1565 (London? 1566).

*

I never yet esteemed the Pulpit a fit Place for Slander and Defamation, and I hope shall never be left to prostitute it to so base a Purpose.
Reverend John Erskine (1721?-1803).
The People of God Consider'd as All Righteous In Three Sermons preach'd at Glasgow,
April 1745. (Glasgow, 1745), 'Advertisement', iv.

*

In this country, by the moderation and good behaviour of the clergymen, they have acquired the general esteem and good-will of the laity; their character and office are both held sacred; and, as their profession is very different from that of spreading injurious calumnies against their neighbours, so their practice is in general believed to correspond with it, whence the pulpit has been emphatically termed the Chair of Verity.
Charles Hay (later Lord Newton) (1740?-1811).
'Petition of John Snodgrass Sheriff-clerk of Paisley; Robert Hunter Merchant in Paisley; William Wilson, Son to John Wilson in Cumberland-factory; James and David Chalmers, late Weavers in Orchyard-street of Paisley; and Robert Cross junior, Merchant in Walneuk of Paisley' to the Court of Session, dated 25 November 1775, in the process *Snodgrass and others v The Rev. John Witherspoon*, 14.

*

The pulpit has been well termed the chair of verity, and certainly nothing should be delivered from it, but what is consistent with the great objects to which the use of it is appropriated. Nothing could be more derogatory to the honour of the church and its members, and more destructive of the peace of society, than the [sic] *suffering the pulpit to become a vehicle for propagation of private scandal and defamation, or to be made an engine for gratifying private revenge or resentment. ... The influence which every minister has, or ought to have, over the minds and opinions of his hearers; the faith due to any thing asserted by him, especially in such a place; and the number of people present on such an occasion, all concur to add an infinite weight to any accusation or aspersion delivered from the pulpit.*
David Rae (later Lord Eskgrove) (1729-1804).
'Petition of John, Robert, and David Scotlands [sic], Merchants in Dunfermline', to the Court of Session, dated July 14 1775, in the process *Scotlands v The Rev. James Thomson*, 9.

*

The Liberty of the Pulpit was our great ground of defence. ... The Court of Session, however, the fifteen judges, who are at the same time the Jury, decided against the minister, contrary to my humble opinion ... .
James Boswell, advocate (1740-95).
The Life of Samuel Johnson, LL.D (London, Charles Dilly), 2v. 1791.
[Penguin Classics, ed. David Womersley, London, 2008, 548.]

Acknowledgements

This is my opportunity to thank a range of people, many of them good friends, who have gone the extra mile in rendering assistance to me in a variety of contexts.

I owe a lasting debt to Rick Sher. Rick was my PhD external examiner some years ago; we have remained in touch ever since and I remain massively indebted to him for his continuing support and encouragement.

In equal measure I remain indebted to Emeritus Professor Andrew Hook of the University of Glasgow, a distinguished authority on eighteenth-century Scottish-American ties whose work inspired my own early interest in the subject; Andrew was kind enough to read some of the drafts of specific chapters and was sufficiently helpful and complimentary to encourage me in my determination to see the work through to the end.

To my principal mentor at the time of my PhD research, Professor Richard Finlay, professor of modern history at Strathclyde University and head of the School of Humanities there, I shall always be grateful; I owe Richard a real debt of gratitude not just for his many acts of kindness to me generally, but also for providing quick and sound advice in answer to an email or a phone call.

Similarly, my sincere thanks go to

Professor John Finlay (no relation to Richard), head of legal history at the University of Glasgow, for reading an early draft of chapter 3 and making valuable comments thereon,

Professor John W. Cairns of the chair of civil law at the University of Edinburgh who generously shared with me some of the fruits of his remarkable and sustained research into slavery which I was able to make good use of in chapter 10,

Jim Caudle, Associate Editor of the Yale Boswell Editions, for answering queries in relation to an early draft of Appendix B, and

Professor Colin Kidd, Head of the School of History at the University of St Andrews, for patiently helping me unravel some bibliographical difficulties I encountered in my draft of chapter 5.

To my good friend Jim Green of the Library Company of Philadelphia whom I continue to trouble unconscionably from time to time with bibliographical conundrums I felt sure only he could help resolve, aided by the vast resource that is the LCP,

James Hamilton of the Signet Library and Andrea Longson of the Advocates Library for expertly helping me locate arcane legal documents; similarly to

Dr David Brown and Dr Alison Lindsay of the National Records of Scotland for whom, as in the case of my Witherspoon book, nothing ever seemed too much trouble.

Once more, to my American 'guru' and helpmate, Kate Mearns Ohno of the Franklin Papers at Yale, who was always there to unscramble my befuddled brain when the occasion needed; and to my old chum from my early Strathclyde days, Dr Andrew Noble, who read drafts and shared eighteenth-century thoughts (and jokes) with me over innumerable cappuccinos in the Avenue at Newton Mearns.

I am also indebted to Aberdeen University Press for generously allowing me to reproduce in chapter 2 extracts from my book *The Lost World of John Witherspoon – Unravelling the Snodgrass affair, 1762 to 1776* (2014).

I apologise sincerely and unreservedly to anyone I have failed to notice here and ought to have done.

Last but never least, I have once more in a published work of mine to make clear that this study would probably have never seen the light of day without the loving help and encouragement of my wife Evelyn who has had to put up with far too many of my 'black dog' moments in the long hours of researching and writing a book as large as this inevitably represents. But I promise her that since all good things must come to an end it is unlikely that she will have to put up with another of the same: *tempus terit* and all that.

Ronald Lyndsay Crawford
University of Strathclyde

Glasgow:
March, 2017

Contents

Acknowledgements	ix
Illustrations	xv
Preface	xvii
Abbreviations	xxi

Introduction   Political preaching and pulpit censure   1

The pulpit as the 'chair of verity'	7
Reformation ideas of church governance, morality and discipline	9
Calvin as preacher and the changing role of the sermon	12
John Knox's special brand of pulpit censure	16
'Liberty of the pulpit' in eighteenth-century Scotland	20
Postscript	22

1   Patronage and secession   25

The evolution of parties in the Church of Scotland	28
'Spiritual Vassalage' : perceptions of church patronage in Scotland	29
Disputed settlements: the deposition of Thomas Gillespie and its consequences	33
Pulpit ideas of patronage	42

2   Profaneness   55

The crime of 'profaneness'	56
The sermon *Seasonable Advice to Young Persons*	57
The Snodgrass affair(s)	62
Kirk Session, Presbytery and General Assembly	64
Court of Session process: 1762 to 1776	69
The Snodgrass affair considered as a factor in Witherspoon's decision to quit Scotland for America	73

3   Bribery and corruption   77

James Thomson's sermons of 16 and 30 October 1774   78
Corruption in burgh and parliamentary elections – the
    'Nabob of the North'   82
Scotlands v The Reverend James Thomson (1775-76)   86
Court of Session Decreet of 8 August 1776   94
James Thomson's appeal to the House of Lords   94
Samuel Johnson's 'oral essay' on pulpit censure   95
Colonel Campbell and his Trustees v Robert Scotland (1778)   97
Postscript   99

4   The Stage   103

The Kirk, the stage and moral corruption   104
Allan Ramsay and the Edinburgh theatre   107
The Reverend George Anderson and pulpit censure of the stage   112
Douglas, a tragedy (1756) – a 'poppy that would fain pass as a rose'   118
Adam Ferguson and John Witherspoon join the debate   123

5   'Heresy'   129

John Adam's debt to John Anderson and John Witherspoon   130
'A.B.'s letter to John Adam: the *Scots Magazine* correspondence   137
Reactions to Fergusson's letter and the heresy case   144
Postscript   152

6   Reform   155

The Kirk and 'the people'   156
William Dunn's synodical sermon of 9 October 1792   160
The case against William Dunn   169
Dunn's role in the trial of Thomas Muir   174
James Lapslie: minister of Campsie and government informer   176
Postscript   181

7   Patriotism   183

Bibliographical note   185
Religious doctrine and social stability   185
Hugh Blair: a reluctant political preacher   189
Alexander Carlyle's brand of Moderate conservatism   198
Carlyle's brand of pulpit censure and the Friends of the People   202
Postscript   207

8 America	**209**
Scots loyalists and American patriots	211
The Scottish Enlightenment and the American crisis	217
William Thom: advocate of emigration to America	221
Thom's trilogy of American war sermons	227
Fast day responses to the events of 1776	234
9 Popery	**241**
The Church of Scotland's perceived role in the identification and persecution of Catholics	243
Anti-popery and the device of the re-cycled sermon: Hugh Blair, John Willison and James Fordyce	247
Popery and the enigma of Dr John Erskine	256
Patrick Grant's sermon of moderation and reconciliation	263
10 Slavery	**269**
Enlightenment ideas of liberty, equality and enslavement	270
Pulpit censure of slavery: 1. William Robertson (1755)	280
Pulpit censure of slavery: 2. Thomas Hardy (1794)	287
The Kirk joins the abolition debate	294
Postscript	297
Endnote	**299**
Appendices	303
Notes	335
Bibliography	405
Index	429

The Wrath of Man praising GOD.

A
SERMON

Preached in the

High Church of *Edinburgh*,

May 18th, 1746.

Before His GRACE the

Lord High Commiſſioner

TO THE

General Aſſembly of the CHURCH of SCOTLAND.

By HUGH BLAIR, A. M.
One of the Miniſters of *Canongate*.

Publiſhed by Deſire of the Lord High Commiſſioner.

EDINBURGH,
Printed by R. FLEMING: For A. KINCAID.
M.DCC.XLVI.

Title page of the original printed version of Hugh Blair's post-Rebellion sermon of 1746 which he re-worked 30 years later.

Illustrations

(*Note*: for 'John Kay', see the Bibliography)

Alexander Webster preaching from the 'Chair of Verity' in 'Haddo's Hole', St Giles' Church, Edinburgh (John Kay)	ii
Alexander Carlyle depicted as the scourge of the Popular party of the Church of Scotland. John Erskine is shown as the head with the black wig (John Kay)	vi
Title page of the original printed version of Hugh Blair's post-Rebellion sermon	xiv
Title page of John Knox's only published sermon, preached in Edinburgh	17
Title page of John Erskine's first published pamphlet while a young minister in Kirkintilloch (1742)	26
John Witherspoon, painted in the year of his death, 1794, by Rembrandt Peale, after Charles Willson Peale	54
James Boswell of Auchinleck by Sir Joshua Reynolds, 1785	75
Chalk on paper drawing of Allan Ramsay (1684-1758), poet and playwright, sketched by his son and namesake (1713-84) in 1729	102
'Dr Tail's Faithometer', from William Thom's satire on the Kilwinning heresy	152
Thomas Hardie (sic) (John Kay)	154
Hugh Blair by Sir Henry Raeburn (detail)	182
Alexander 'Jupiter' Carlyle in old age, by Archibald Skirving	208
Title page of Charles Elliot's edition of Thomas Paine's *Common Sense* (1776)	231
Title page of John Willison's *Popery another Gospel* (1746)	237
John Erskine (John Kay)	240
Principal William Robertson by Sir Henry Raeburn, painted in 1792	268
Title page of 'the Edinburgh Montesquieu' of 1750, v.1	292
Advertisement from the *Edinburgh Evening Courant* of 4 May 1756 relating to the runaway slave baptized in Beith by John Witherspoon	293
Title page of Hugh Latimer's *Fruitfull Sermons* (1635)	311
Theodorus completed by David Fordyce but published posthumously in 1752	387

Preface

It will, I suggest, be obvious from chapter 2 that the idea for this study emerged out of research for my book on the Scottish career of John Witherspoon, the Church of Scotland minister who left Scotland behind in 1768 to become an American, a College president and, as a 'signer' of the Declaration of Independence and an active politician throughout the revolutionary war, a founding father of the United States. But my book has also been inspired by Richard Sher's *chef d'oeuvre*, first published in 1985 and recently re-issued (2015), *Church and University in the Scottish Enlightenment*.

When I was immersed in the original documentation relating to the fourteen-year long Court of Session action for defamation that John Snodgrass and others had initiated against Witherspoon it struck me forcefully that this long-forgotten and almost totally overlooked legal process had originated in a sermon Witherspoon had preached from his Laigh Church pulpit in Paisley. Orally, and later in print, the Paisley minister had unsparingly censured his seven individual 'targets' on the ground of their alleged conjoint 'profaneness', a serious crime according to the accepted rules of the time governing church discipline. His mistake was that in a rapidly changing and increasingly sceptical age he failed to have regard for the limits to which his notions of ecclesiastical authority might be challengeable in a different court, to which all the king's men and women were ultimately subject and where the Kirk had no controlling authority.

The oral performance that was provoked by the scandal at the core of this great crisis in Witherspoon's life belongs to a minor category of sermons that, when I reflected on it further, has, I submit, been seriously neglected: sermons, that is, whose 'application' is concerned with contemporary issues in society on which the preacher has resolved to make public comment. Sermons of this *genre* are characterised by their preachers contributing to an on-going debate that, they sense, involves not just their own congregation but the wider world. They were devised by their preachers for the purpose of offering comment on, and criticism (in the broadest sense of the term) of specific issues they believed required *public* comment and, if appropriate, *public* censure leading, they dared hope, to condign punishment.

It also became clear to me that pulpit censure itself was properly a sub-group within an altogether larger class of *political* sermons, a division of homiletics that has its origins far back in the spontaneous sermons of the itinerant preaching friars of the later middle ages, and pre-eminent much later, of course, in many of those articulated by several of the greatest names of the Protestant Reformation. It was only when I enlarged my reading on the subject that I became aware of the full extent to which the idea of politics in the pulpit had its protagonists and, more commonly, its opponents, a clash of view that in some ways persists to this day in the modern church. It seems not so long ago when 'Keep politics out of the pulpit' was the common catchphrase of numerous politicians who refused to condone what they regarded as unwarranted encroachment on their sacred turf; interestingly, and perhaps significantly, such views are nothing like so strident now as formerly.

In due course, my wider reading on the subject not only astonished me by the scope and sheer volume of political sermons matching my adopted criteria but, above all, by the possibilities they offered for a fresh and original way of approaching, individually, the huge variety and range of topics they covered. The modern mind may find it hard to conceive of churchmen as scene-stealers and pacesetters but the historian knows otherwise. For centuries, after all, the pulpit was palpably, in Calvin's memorable description, the *chair of verity* and, remarkably, has only ceased to be so regarded within my own lifetime. So far as I am aware, this study is the first to suggest that within the context of the Scottish enlightenment new ways of approaching familiar topics – including patronage, (political) reform, popery, heresy, patriotism, slavery and 'America' – are capable of being opened up anew through the medium of the spoken sermon, even though, to point out the obvious, all that we have left to go on (with one exception – James Thomson's 'virtual' sermon as discussed in chapter 3), are published, and thus inevitably *edited* versions of the spoken originals.

It's also worth pointing out that few if any of the sermons discussed in this book can be regarded as 'stand alone' pieces. The obvious exceptions are the two extreme examples of the Paisley and Dunfermline legal cases (chapters 2 and 3) which, so far as I know, are genuinely unique examples of their kind. By and large, however, by conscious design of the preacher the substance and content of most of the political sermons I discuss here represent his personal contribution to on-going public debate of the 'big' issues which he has chosen to address from his pulpit. These men were deliberately setting a scene, adopting a pose, introducing what they genuinely construed was original intellectual comment on matters of societal concern that, subjectively, they held as deserving of both congregational and, proleptically, much wider attention. Since my own academic interest as a historian lies in the eighteenth century it was natural for me, I plead, to identify sermons of that fascinating but complex period that seemed to me not only to engage important contemporary public debate, but to cast new light on often well-worn topics.

All the sermons represented here are by Scottish authors, partly because I would have been uncomfortable attempting to grapple with the output of preachers and writers outside my immediate area of academic expertise, but less subjectively on account of the quite different ecclesiastical traditions prevailing in England, Ireland and elsewhere in the United Kingdom. The Church of Scotland had its own massive issues to confront from the first to the last decades of the period we call the age of the Enlightenment, some of the most important of which I have chosen to illustrate in what follows; apart from lying at the heart of the highly idiosyncratic pulpit censure cases discussed in chapters 2 and 3, chapters 1, 4, 5, and 9 deal in particular with some of these momentous and recurrent church concerns.

By its nature, I have found this is not an easy or straightforward subject and potentially complex in an often dense and gritty kind of way. The dominant force of provenance is, naturally, the Protestant Reformation, including the particular homiletic contributions of the twin *colossi* of those times, John Knox and Jean Calvin. It is their influence within the Reformation that must ultimately, I think, command the high ground in any treatment of subsequent political preaching in its broader historical context.

Abbreviations

ALSP	Advocates Library, Session Papers
BL	British Library
Crawford	Crawford, Ronald L. 'Checklist of books and pamphlets printed in Paisley 1769-1799' (*Appendix A* of unpublished University of Strathclyde PhD thesis (2011), 351-403). A much earlier version is included in the NLS Scottish Book Trade Index (SBTI) from the same author's Glasgow BLitt thesis, v. 2, of 1965.
DOST	*Dictionary of the Older Scottish Tongue* (Scottish National Dictionaries/Oxford University Press)
ESTC	English Short Title Catalogue (online)
EUL	Edinburgh University Library
Gaskell	Gaskell, Philip, *A Bibliography of the Foulis Press* (London, Rupert Hart-Davis, 1964).
GUL	Glasgow University Library
Fasti	*Fasti Ecclesiae Scoticanae*, 'The Succession of Ministers of the Church of Scotland from the Reformation', by Hew Scott, New Series, volumes 1-7, 1915-1928.
LWJW	Crawford, Ronald L. *The Lost World of John Witherspoon Unravelling the Snodgrass affair, 1762 to 1776* (Aberdeen, Aberdeen University Press, 2014).
Morison	Morison, William Maxwell, *The Decisions of the Court of Session, from its first institution to the present time, digested under proper heads, in the form of a Dictionary* 22v. (Edinburgh, for John Anderson, 1815).
NLS	National Library of Scotland, Edinburgh
NRS	National Records of Scotland, Edinburgh (formerly National Archives of Scotland)
OSA	'Old' *Statistical Account of Scotland* drawn up by Sir John Sinclair from material supplied by ministers of parishes (Edinburgh, Creech, 1791-99)
SSPCK	Society in Scotland for Propagating (occasionally 'for Promoting') Christian Knowledge
SL	Signet Library
SND	Scottish National Dictionaries
State Trials	Howell, *A Complete Collection of State Trials* (London, 1809-26)
Walker	Walker, David M., *A Legal History of Scotland* 7v.(1988-2004), v.5 *The Eighteenth Century* (Edinburgh, T. and T. Clark, 1998).
WJW	*The Works of The Rev. John Witherspoon*, 4v., with an introduction by L. Gordon Tait, (Bristol, Thoemmes Press, 2003), based on the four-volume set (Philadelphia: William W. Woodward, 1800-1802).

Introduction

Political preaching and pulpit censure

The time is come that men can not abyde the Sermon of veritie[1] *nor holsome doctrine.*
                                    Second Epistle of Paul to Timothy, 4, v. 3 [2]

[The scriptural text cited by John Knox on the title page of his only published sermon, London [?], 1566. The sermon was preached in the 'Church of Edenbrough' on Sunday, 19 August 1565 in the presence of Henry Stewart, Lord Darnley, just three weeks after his marriage to Mary Stuart in the chapel of the Royal Palace of Holyrood. The translation cannot be identified and (which in itself is significant) is probably Knox's own.]

Whatever criteria one chooses to adopt, it cannot be doubted that one of the greatest preachers who ever lived was the co-founder of Methodism, John Wesley. This was a man, we are told, who from the age of thirty-six onwards, 'travelled 225,000 miles and preached more than 40,000 sermons, some of them to more than 20,000 people'.[3] In his classic study *Enthusiasm* (1950) Ronald A. Knox wrote of Wesley:

> Continually on the road, continually in the public eye, engaged oftener than not in such controversies as would have sapped the nervous strength of a man ordinarily vigorous, he lived to the age of eighty-eight as a prophet would live who was determined to *reproach his contemporaries with their decadence.*[4] [italics added]

But not all responded to his message of good news. Scotland, in particular, turned a deaf ear. Wesley famously said of the good folk of Glasgow that 'they hear much, know everything, and feel nothing.'[5] Yet, for all that, in Glasgow he did find some roses among the thorns:

> My spirits were moved within me at the sermons I heard both morning and afternoon. They contained much truth, but were no more likely to awaken one soul than an Italian opera.[6]

At Perth, when he offers to start a Society there, 'only four men and four women come up to discuss the project with him, and towards the end of his life Edinburgh is only producing five converts in five years.'[7] Ireland was much the same, only more difficult. Knox comments: 'If Scotland was the wayside, Ireland was the stony ground.'[8] Almost in despair, Wesley records that 'at least ninety-nine in a hundred of the native Irish remain in the religion of their fathers.'[9]

For all his brilliance, Wesley could on occasion be wilful, headstrong and even unscrupulous. In his sermon *A Calm Address to our American Colonies* (1775) he resorted (not for the first time) to blatant plagiarism when he 'borrowed' heavily without acknowledgment from Samuel Johnson's *Taxation no Tyranny; an Answer to the Resolutions and Address of the American Congress* (published earlier in the same year), a pamphlet commissioned by the British government, the anti-American pose struck in it seriously upsetting Johnson's biographer, James Boswell.[10] The point is that for all his many faults Wesley was a political preacher of the highest order.

I first stumbled on the term 'pulpit censure' in course of researching the remarkable legal process involving the Reverend Dr. John Witherspoon and the protracted action for damages and defamation he was forced to defend, and ultimately lost, in the Court of Session in Edinburgh from 1762 until 1776. By the time the process was finally determined Witherspoon had become an American and a committed member of the second Continental Congress, the bureaucracy set up not only to co-ordinate and manage the war with Britain, but effectively also to govern the emergent nation in waiting. The results of my research were published in *The Lost World of John Witherspoon*,[11] a title that, unsubtly, was meant to imply a kind of *double entendre*: that is, that the facts of the case had to all intents and purposes been shrouded in mystery since Witherspoon's day. But I also wanted to get across the point that the real wonder (or so it seemed to me) was that modern Witherspoon scholars had either been unaware of the case, or, if they knew of its barest essentials, had given up on it. Yet, the 'Paisley case', as it came to be known to lawyers who regarded it as a precedent for a subsequent action that was believed to hold certain parallels, is one of the great monuments of pulpit censure; it was set in motion by a sermon and set alight by the subsequent publication of that same sermon, resulting in the Court action against the minister, initiated by the men whose characters and reputation he was accused of having defamed.

As I delved more deeply into the case what came to surprise me more and more was the extent to which pulpit censure — especially in a Scottish context — appeared to have been completely passed over in any survey of the history of the sermon whether as 'literary, political, religious and controversial performances.'[12] This book, then, concerns a particular subset of sermons falling within the category of 'pulpit censure' or 'pulpit rebuke'. Almost all the sermons represented in this book — and the determinant for their inclusion here — conform to the requirement that the men who originally preached them were, for one reason or another, 'determined to reproach' *either* aspects of contemporary society that troubled them *and/or* (though much more rarely) individuals within society whose behaviour in a given context had earned their public rebuke. The more general idea I try to get across here is not, I freely acknowledge, my own but ultimately derives, I suppose, from Alexander Broadie, whose hypothesis mirrors my own conclusion that the voice of the pulpit is in some measure indivisible from the story of the Scottish Enlightenment. I am still a little in awe of Broadie's conclusion that 'in presenting his ideas on society and morality within a theological context, [Hugh] Blair is more representative of the ethos of the Scottish Enlightenment than is the sceptic Hume.'[13] Blair, we should recall, as the archetypal Moderate and the most commercially successful of our eighteenth-century sermonisers, is remembered for anything but his (palpably few) sermons containing any hint of political content.

The Scottish Enlightenment is sometimes portrayed as a movement of ideas *simpliciter*, whereas Broadie reminds us that this is looking down the wrong end of the telescope (my words) and that it was much more than that. Like any other expression of 'enlightened' ideas, the Scottish Enlightenment manifested new ways of regarding human progress, thought and culture and, in doing so, was often inconsistent, rarely if ever self-defining and, above all, paradoxical. One of the greatest paradoxes lying at the heart of the Enlightenment as it evolved in eighteenth-century Scotland is the more or less constant presence within it of powerful contrary voices, articulating sentiments we may find difficult to reconcile with our traditional understanding of an enlightened approach to anything. I have certainly found that among the most powerful (though hardly the only) examples of such enigmatic contrary voices are those articulated by representatives of the Popular party of the Church of Scotland. Yet, as Thomas Ahnert has reminded us, some of these are often legitimate 'Enlightened' voices.[14] They manifest themselves in pulpit sermons, in many cases still available to us in their published (that usually means, to a greater or lesser degree, *edited* and often much supplemented) mode. Such writings, as uncompromising as they are prolific, convey a wholly different voice of Enlightenment Scotland, and it is foolish to ignore them. Occasionally, the voice that comes across from that quarter is inventive and original. We may not think of Kirk ministers as contributing much to an 'enlightened' world – though Hugh Blair, as Sher and Broadie insist, certainly did – but even opponents of Moderatism such as John Witherspoon, Robert Walker, John Erskine and William Thom all, paradoxically, deserve to be considered as authentic Enlightenment voices.

If the eighteenth-century Church of Scotland can be said to have been characterised by any factor distinguishing it from how it might have seemed to outsiders looking in from earlier times, it is surely this: that it bore all the hallmarks of deep division, resulting from events and/or processes that, in themselves, and quite literally, were without precedent. In the face of an unusually potent mix of (internal) epistemological and (external) sociological change which the Kirk faced throughout the greater part of the eighteenth century, discord thrived. Weathered by population growth, town and city squalor, industrialisation, rebellions, wars, two revolutions and all the attendant human deprivation consequent on them – not to mention the impact on itself of the Scottish variant of the Enlightenment and the frequent lively scepticism at its core – the Kirk, corporately (as well as many of its ministers individually) felt it simply had no choice but to speak out.

The Glasgow orthodox satirist and champion of the Academy movement, William Thom of Govan, for example, longed for the 'days of antient simplicity' when men were 'not yet civilized into atheism'.[15] Similarly, when ministers attack 'popery' we can be sure that they do so because they regard it as a threat to their own security and that of the reformed church to which they belong. When they condemn the 'illiberal' and immoral tendencies they perceive as rampant in the nation at large – evidenced, for example, by the contemporary appetite for the theatre and the stage – they do so in the belief that if the sparks of decadence should be allowed to develop into a raging fire, religion itself will be scorched to an extent that can only *in extremis* foster a kind of pagan anarchy. 'How dreadful', cries Thom, 'if ever the pulpit should be debased in this manner!' –

> One had better never preach at all, or cry in a desert, as be guilty of any such gross and criminal prostitution.[16]

To add to an already alarming list of external threats to the established Church there was the palpable, complex and ever-present threat *from within*: a divided, even decadent clergy, heated disputes over the persistently vexatious issue of patronage, the rise and continuing popular attractiveness of secessionism, not to mention the gathering storm observable in all manner of 'heresies' and the toxic threat they were held to represent. Never black nor white, enlightened evangelicals vied with extreme Moderates, just as Calvinists with hard-nosed Erastians.

Additionally, from around the middle of the century the church found itself increasingly immured in disputes relating to the issue of censure itself. Moderate ministers, in particular, began to turn a blind eye not just to the tediously repetitive catalogue of personal immorality cases 'delated' day and daily to their kirk sessions, but were reluctant to get involved in much more serious offences against all the rules of Kirk discipline, such as 'profaneness' and, even, on occasion, what was perceived as outright heresy. For the minister of Dundonald in Ayrshire, Thomas Walker, a Calvinist evangelical hardliner, it was all too much. Disgusted with what he saw as the excessively mild treatment of Kames and Hume at the General Assembly of 1755 [17] Walker published an anonymous pamphlet in Glasgow in the following year, timed to be on the streets just before the Assembly sitting. He hit out at the '*dastardly pusillanimity*' he detected on the part of too many of his fellow ministers of the gospel who failed to confront the problem, and went on to protest that in the absence of ministerial censure irresolute individuals

> betray a very considerable and important part of their trust, and will have to answer to the King of the church, for the *external* purity, the purity of profession, in that society whose spiritual interest was committed to their care.

Specifically, with regard to the works of men like David Hume, 'all that is demanded' is, according to Walker,

> that infidel writings be not suffered to retain this advantage which they have from the Christian character continued with the authors. That they be not allowed the sanction of a Christian licence, or permission to spread such infectious poison, and circulate such counterfeit coin.[18]

In the event, however, the Assembly Committee of Overtures' two-day debate on the issue simply fizzled out. Led by Hugh Blair and other like-minded Moderates in opposing the 'transmission' of the overture for formal censure to the Assembly, the Committee finally agreed to abandon the proposal on the grounds that censure 'would not serve the purpose of edification'. A vote was taken on whether or not to transmit the overture; the move to do so was overwhelmingly defeated by 50 votes to 17.[19]

In the closing decades of the 'long' century, and in the wake of the two greatest revolutions the world had yet experienced, the need as articulated from the pulpit for some ministers – much more often, it has to be said, those aligned with the Popular party and, frequently also, dissenting secessionist preachers operating outside the national church – to go on the offensive and, unremittingly to 'continue to reproach', becomes ever more insistent. On the one hand, for example, there was (at least hypothetically) the huge issue of abolition of the slave trade in Britain to contend with and, on the other, serious pitfalls lying in store in the form not just of a creeping popular scepticism, but, with increasing regularity, assaults on personal belief and ministerial 'priestcraft'. In response to these issues, as it seemed to many, an increasingly out of touch Kirk could offer only fawning displays of uncritical loyalism to a regressive, repressive government in London and Edinburgh, determinedly bent on extinguishing the last vestiges of serious (though generally localised) popular unrest, triggered by allegedly seditious political ideology. William Moodie, minister of St. Andrew's Church in the New Town, Edinburgh, and a loyalist anti-reformer who became Moderator of the General Assembly in 1799, was indignantly moved to preach a sermon in May 1797 on the theme that 'we have lived to see our government traduced as a system of oppression and tyranny'.[20]

Moodie had specifically in mind the sentiments of another Kirk minister, the Reverend William Dunn of Kirkintilloch, a Popularist in whose parish the advocate Thomas Muir had actively canvassed his radicalism with particular vigour. Dunn was cited as a Crown witness at Muir's trial in August 1793 and he was also cited by Muir himself in his defence. In the event, neither side called him to give evidence. As chapter 6 discusses, Dunn had preached a synodical sermon the year before in which he unambiguously took the side of political reform and, his passion getting the better of his judgment, came close to aligning himself with sentiments that might easily have passed muster in the eyes of the authorities as technically 'seditious', according to the prevailing government interpretation formulated on the initiative of Pitt's autocratic Home Secretary, Henry Dundas. In doing so, Dunn had, it seemed, crossed the boundary of accepted convention. For his crime, he would be imprisoned in the Tolbooth.

As the Reverend John Erskine (also affiliated to the Popular party and acknowledged as one of its champions) had put it just four years before, in a sermon he preached before the magistrates in Edinburgh on 2 September 1792, but not published until the following year:

> Some may ask, Should the pulpit canvass the propriety of political measures, about which the wise and good think differently? – No. It would be as foolish and impious, as to preach on the method of fencing or improving a farm; on the validity of a claim for an estate; on plans for building or repairing a house; or on the evidence of a pannel's innocence or guilt. Such, who have inclination, leisure and ability, lawfully may; and such, whose authority must determine these matters, ought, from a sense of duty, carefully to examine them: but, the place for teaching or learning them, is not the house of God.

But then Erskine appears to concede that there could be circumstances where a minister might contradict that code of conduct, in a responsible way:

> Yet, though these questions have nothing to do with the pulpit, general maxims of virtue and prudence, which should guide in considering and determining them, are an important branch of moral instruction. ... The teacher who keeps back from his hearers nothing profitable, but declares to them the whole counsel of God, will sometimes illustrate these portions of the sacred volume: and surely, their applicableness to questions, which excite general attention, renders not this the less reasonable.[21]

Several decades before Erskine's thoughts on the subject of politics in the pulpit were published, his friend and fellow Evangelical, John Witherspoon of Paisley, had made much the same observation. Witherspoon, too, found it difficult to reconcile a natural opposition to political preaching with the need to take the side of 'the people' as the miserable victims of man's greed and folly. On the one hand, Witherspoon is in no doubt that

> ... ministers [ought to] take care to avoid officiously inter-meddling in civil matters ... [22]

Yet, on the other hand, we find, Witherspoon says, a palpable need on the part of ministers to get involved in day-to-day issues, affecting ordinary mortals, who need spiritual sustenance more than ever. And if that requires condemnation from the pulpit of harmful state policies, then so be it:

> Is not this nation, once in a manner the arbitress of the fate of Europe, now become the scorn and derision of her neighbours and all that are round about her? What weak and divided councils among those that preside? Instead of any genuine public spirit, a proud and factious endeavour to disgrace each other's measures, and wrest the ensigns of government out of each other's hands. How numerous and expensive, but how useless and inactive have been our fleets and armies? And how deplorable is the condition of our colonies abroad? They are the chief theatre of the war, because, indeed, they are the subject of the contest.[23]

For centuries sermons have been regarded as a legitimate vehicle for the transmission of a preacher's *'determination to reproach his contemporaries with their decadence.'* In the reign of Henry VIII, for example, the Bishop of Hereford, John Skip [or Skyppe], from the pulpit of the Chapel Royal on Passion Sunday 1536, used the biblical story of Haman and Ahasuerus[24] as backdrop to his sermon criticising Thomas Cromwell and his ministers over their policies towards the reclamation of church lands and property for the Crown. In doing so no one present missed the obvious direct censure of the king himself. More than a hundred years later, on 8 May 1650, James Graham, Marquis of Montrose, on his journey to the scaffold, was brought a prisoner in ropes to the village of Keith in Banffshire where, next day, he and his captors attended morning service in the local church. The minister, William Kininmonth,[25] preached a sermon 'into his face', choosing his text from *1 Samuel* 15, verses 32-35, the chilling story of the prophet Samuel hewing Agag, the Amalekite, 'in pieces before the Lord in Gilgal', uttering the words as he did so: 'As thy sword hath made women childless, so shall thy mother be childless among women.' Montrose, legend has it, shouted out defiantly: 'Rail on, Rab-shakeh!' and 'turned his back on the minister.'[26]

And in my own lifetime, on Sunday 3 August 1941, Bishop (later Cardinal) Clemens von Galen (1878-1946) preached a sermon from the pulpit of St. Lambert's Church, Münster in which he roundly condemned the on-going Nazi euthanasia programme:

> I am reliably informed that lists are being drawn up in the asylums of the province of Westphalia of those patients who are to be taken away as so-called 'unproductive national comrades' and shortly to be disposed of. The first transport left the Marienthal institution near Muster during the past week. ...
> Have you, have *I* the right to live only so long as we are 'productive', so long as we are recognised by others as 'productive'?[27]

Pulpit censure may, therefore, be said to occur when a minister of the gospel uses the vehicle of his sermon to condemn practices he regards as unseemly or, in a Christian ethical context, immoral and corrupting. Setting aside the numerous cases of disciplinary public penance exercised by Church of Scotland ministers and their Kirk Sessions on named parishioners within the context of the ordinary Sabbath service – the kind of thing made notorious by frequently grotesque misconceptions of the sexual adventures of the poet Burns – it does seem that it was only rarely that ministers indulged in pulpit attacks upon individuals who, in the judgment of the Session, had infringed accepted standards of moral behaviour expected from followers of Christ. *Both* kinds of public censure – the condemnation of objectionable practices and the extreme of resorting to rebuke of individuals, whether kings or commoners – were always exercised in circumstances where ministers regarded it as not only their right, but their duty to speak out. Affirmation of their duty in that regard derived from their personal subscription to the *Confession of Faith* and from the Kirk's corporate code of disciplinary procedures known as the *Form of Process*. Above all, scriptural provenance for the legitimate use of sermons as an instrument of ministerial censure had its roots in the words of Paul's first letter to the *Thessalonians*, 5, verses 14-15:

> Now we exhort you, brethren, warn them that are unruly, comfort the feebleminded, support the weak, be patient towards all men.
> See that none render evil for evil unto any man; but ever follow that which is good, both among yourselves, and to all men.

John Knox, on the other hand, drew his inspiration for his own fearless and unexcelled brand of pulpit censure from the Second Letter of Paul to *Timothy*:

> The time is come that men can not abyde the sermon of veritie nor holsome doctrine.

Alongside these texts, chapter 4 of Melville *et al*'s *Second Book of Discipline* was sometimes cited in tandem where it describes the duty of a pastor or minister:

> He ought also to watch above the manners of his flock, that the better he may apply the Doctrine to them, in reprehending the dissolute persons, and exhorting the Godly to continue in the fear of the Lord.

The pulpit as the 'chair of verity'

My decision to base the core of this study on sermons preached in the eighteenth century by Scottish ministers, though not necessarily all by ministers of the established Church of Scotland, is not capricious. One of these sermons, possibly the most consequential of all, was preached outside Scotland. All the sermons chosen for commentary in the pages that follow deal with important contemporary issues, viewed by their preachers against an analogous scriptural backcloth. Individually, they may be found to shed important new light on each of the arbitrarily selected issues comprising the chapter headings, set in the context of their contemporary background.

Sermons of this period meeting the criteria of pulpit censure are, it is suggested, of considerable interest to the historian for two reasons: first, their content is consistent with post-Reformation ideas of the re-affirmation of 'real' preaching. They were assumed, that is, to have originated from the so-called 'chair of verity' (*chaire de verité*), a term used by Calvin himself to indicate the substance and purity of the message and the honour due the man in orders preaching it. Secondly, from Calvin's day on, censure from the pulpit was seen as an essential element of the denunciatory obligations of a minister of the reformed Christian church. Jane Dawson asserts, for example, that in his final years Knox assumed that 'when he was preaching he was six feet above contradiction, and carried that pulpit immunity with him when delivering pronouncements elsewhere.'[28]

To state the obvious, in their original oral form sermons are, of course, irrecoverable. Sermons by their nature are oral compositions, whereas all that we have to go on in what has come down to us are printed literary productions, often substantially extended and expanded by the addition of prefaces, dedications, introductions, authors' footnotes and other critical apparatus, supplemented after (in some cases, considerably after) the originals were first preached before a church congregation. At the same time, we need to recognise that there was nothing new in authors 'editing' sermons that publishers, with an eye to the main chance, saw as good commercial propositions, likely to be in popular demand and to sell well. After all, even Calvin himself (who, we are told, possessed 'extraordinary abilities as a preacher'), and his successors in the Genevan church, needed their printer/publisher. They found him in Robert Estienne ('Robertus Stephanus')[29] who came to Geneva in search of Calvin in 1551 and is credited with the system of adding verses to chapters of books of the Bible to make them easier to locate, with the aim of aiding the people in their devotions.

In the long history of the Church of Scotland, even ministers themselves were not spared censure in circumstances where they consciously refrained from censuring others from their pulpits according to the exigent spirit of the times. At the General Assembly of August 1648 an Act was passed 'for censuring Ministers for their Silence, and not speaking to the Corruptions of the Times'. These same words from the 1648 Act would be cited by the Reverend Gabriel Wilson, minister of Maxton in the Presbytery of Selkirk, in support of a controversial synodical sermon he preached in October 1721, later published in a much expanded form under the title *The Trust* (1723). In his preface to the published version Wilson claimed that the 'unaccountable treatment' [30] he had met with since his sermon was preached had been the result of malicious enmity on the part of daydreamers who were accustomed to 'turn dull and heavy-headed in Time of Sermon.' Wilson's general point is that if he had chosen to remain silent in the face of what the Act had decreed, he would risk placing himself in breach of the trust ministers had entered into with God and the people, one of the cardinal articles of that trust according to the Act being that they were directed to face up to and confront head-on the 'Corruptions of the Time':

> What would our worthy and zealous Reformers say, if they were to see this Sermon brought in a Pannel [Sc. law = the accused in a trial] before a General Assembly of the Church of Scotland, and the Preacher accused for Heresy and Slander?[31] What would these honest Men say, who made that Act, August 3.1648, for censuring Ministers for their Silence, and not speaking to the Corruptions of the Time?

Wilson, and others of similar view, had in the forefront of their minds the kind of sermons that the 1648 Act decreed ministers ought to preach:

> That the main current of applications[32] in sermons may run along against the evils that prevail at home, and namely, against the contempt of the word, against all profaneness, against the present defection from the league and covenant, ... against the plots and practices of malignants, and against the principles and tenets of Erastianism, which spread among divers in this kingdom ... .

Ministers are warned that failure to comply with the directive – or even a half-hearted compliance – would have the gravest of consequences, with deposition from their charge reserved for the most recalcitrant:

> ... if any [ministers] be found too sparing, general, or ambiguous in the foresaid applications and reproofs, that they be sharply rebuked, dealt with, and warned to an end, under the pain of suspension from their ministry ...; but if there be any, who do neglect and omit such applications and reproofs, and continue in such negligence, after admonition and dealing with them, they are to be cited; and after due trial of the offence, to be deposed, for being pleasers of men rather than servants of Christ ... .

Reformation ideas of church governance, morality and discipline

To the scholar of the Reformation, this is all, of course, very familiar. The directive to ministers, for example, ultimately derives from Calvin's *Ecclesiastical Ordinances* (1541) in which he laid down how the Genevan church would be governed, just as his much better known *Institutes of the Christian Religion*[33] is Calvin's monument – not only his greatest theological statement, but the cornerstone of Reformation faith, doctrine and practice. The Ordinances prescribed two ruling authorities: the Venerable Ministry and the Consistory. The first consisted of the pastors 'examining those who felt themselves called to ordination, afterwards presenting those whom they had passed to the Council for their approval, studied the scriptures, listened to sermons on doctrine and acted as moral censors.' The Consistory, a council of six ministers and twelve elders, was, however, easily the most significant of Calvin's instruments of government. Green tells us that 'the Consistory took cognisance of every form of activity, dealing with the gravest vices and the most trivial of offences':

> Its discipline was strict and the sentences it passed were often but not invariably harsh. Adultery, gambling, swearing, dancing, drinking, sleeping in sermon times and any practice that could be conceivably described as Roman, all came within its purview.[34]

Relevant sections of the Church of Scotland's 1648 Act of Assembly echo and owe much to Calvin's 1541 *Ordinances*. Without mentioning Calvin by name, an English translation of the Ordinances by Robert Fills had been published in London in 1562: *The Lawes and Statutes of Geneva as well concerning ecclesiastical discipline*. Fills included not only the complete ('worde for worde') text of the *Ordinances* ('Ordonnances') 'translated out of Frenche into Englishe', but also that of the *Edicts* (civil constitution) of 1543. Fills – or *Fillet*, as, in November 1557, his name was entered in the Swiss city's

Livre des Habitants, with the designation 'Un Anglois' – was an English member of John Knox's Genevan congregation. The bibliography is important:[35] Fills's book was printed and published by Rowland Hall, printer of the 1560 'Geneva Bible', the first bible in English to employ verse-division, a system invented by Robertus Stephanus (*aka* Robert Estienne, or 'Robert Stephens').[36] It clearly shows the extent to which the Genevan system of reformed church discipline anticipated the same uncompromising approach of the Scottish Kirk nearly a hundred years later in expressing a similar intolerance of weak ministers who duck out of their obligations of pulpit censure, as well as a near-identical form of punishment for backsliders:

> Concerning Crimes they ought in no case to be borne with, if they be evyll Crimes, that is to saye, yf they oughte to be punished by the laws. And if any of the mynisters doe faile, then the Seniorye oughte to put to their bandes, and over and besides the ordinarie punyshement with whiche they be accustumed to punishe other offe[n]ders, to take him, punishe him, & depose him, from his office.[37]

Both in terms of its historic significance and contemporary effect the Reformation amounted to nothing less than an explosive religious revolution. In common with all revolutions, the Reformation involved just as much of an upheaval in the grittier matter of governance as it surely did in the more ethereal flights of theory and doctrine – in this case, naturally, Protestant Christian theology. In the Protestant revolution one of the most ground-breaking innovations of all was lay involvement in church courts; translated into Scottish terminology, that meant at all levels from kirk sessions, presbyteries (but, in their case, only later) and synods, to the supreme authority of the General Assembly itself. Calvin's ideas of church governance – which, as we have seen, he (with the help of others) first set out in the form of the 1541 *Ordinances* for the authorities in Geneva – were the ultimate inspiration for Knox, Melville and their followers when formulating their own ideas of church 'discipline' (in the broader sense of the term, meaning roughly 'regimen').

These ideas extended to the notion of lay elders being elected by congregations themselves. In the reformed Scottish church, kirk sessions first made their appearance in the 'privy kirks' of the late 1550s, but it was not for more than a generation later until they were present in every parish. While the concept of the synod had its origin in the supervision of clergy and congregations by superintendents, commissioners and bishops who presided over synods twice a year – consisting of a minister with an elder or deacon from every parish of the diocese – presbyteries, by contrast, 'formed no original part of the Scottish reformed polity', but from 1578 onwards their creation was 'advocated as one feature of the anti-episcopal programme.'[38]

In time, elders could (and did) speak in church courts in the knowledge that their contributions would not just be listened to, but recorded (often verbatim) in minutes that were scribed by fellow elders. Frequently elders would challenge their ministers in particular matters [39] (at times, though rarely, even in doctrinal issues) and ministers could not rely on 'their' elders supporting them on issues that came before a higher church court. Of course, the ultimate provenance of all Christian discipline is to be found in the words of Christ himself – from *Matthew's gospel* (§18, v. 15-22). McCulloch explains:

[It should be] hardly surprising in an organization which was in its first generation both small and self-consciously separate from ordinary society, [that] the method described is personal and private. 'If your brother sins against you, go and tell him his fault, between you and him alone. If he listens to you, you have gained your brother.' So two people should sort out their own dispute; if they cannot, then other Christians should be involved, and if remedy still fails, the whole Church should intervene. Discipline should thus come from within, both individually, and within the Church's community, and should as far as possible, avoid any secular system of law – if [the offender] refuses to listen even to the Church, let him be to you as a Gentile and a tax collector, Jesus commanded only as a last resort.[40]

In Calvinist Scotland, therefore, the kirk session became the primary agent of discipline in church and parish, a role that persisted well into the last decades of the eighteenth century, and, in a few instances, into the early nineteenth century. Despite serious divisions inside the church that reached deep down into its theological roots – combined with the unwelcome parallel emergence of seceding congregations from the 1730s onward – the national Kirk robustly continued to justify its function as judge, jury and executioner in moral and other 'crimes' allegedly committed by its members and parishioners. It did so in the conviction that if its judicatures failed to act, no one else would or should step into the breach. If, as argued by ministers in their sermons, such a state of inanimate and unacceptable torpor were to go unnoticed, the town, parish and, without exaggeration, potentially even the entire nation was doomed to irremediable collapse under the consequentially insupportable burden of sin resulting from apathy and inactivity.

In support of that argument, the Kirk as body corporate had a powerful ace up its sleeve: the manifest evidence and undeniable presence of seriously deteriorating moral standards in Scotland's burgeoning industrialising towns and cities. Concomitant with urban expanding workforces possessing, in good times, much more money to spend was the opportunity presented many of weak will to advance down heedlessly the primrose path of dalliance. In the face of grossly declining standards of morality, the Kirk's response to this potential crisis was, in the memorable words of Iwo Clark, the development and rise of 'an ecclesiastical system of moral espionage.' Clark has especially in mind that in by far the majority of cases brought before a kirk session, the whistle-blower was an elder who had 'delated' the offence, either direct to the session, or to the session via the minister. Consequently, many elders were effectively unpaid spies and informers, precisely as Clark suggests.

What Calvin would have made of all this is fairly clear. Using as his authority the words of Christ in the same passage in Matthew's gospel just cited, he reveals his thoughts on discipline and retribution in the pages of the *Institutes*. It is a graduated response that Calvin favours: the first step consists of 'private admonition by a fellow church member', which he trusts will result in repentance.[41] If that fails, the second step is to admonish him or her with two or three witnesses present. If the sinner still persists in refusing to acknowledge the sin and repent, then he or she is brought before the church, 'which Calvin understands to be the assembly of the elders.' The sinner is then 'gravely admonished by the public authority of the church.' If that, too, fails to awaken repentance, the person concerned is 'removed from the fellowship of the church by excommunication.' Excommunication has the effect of disqualifying the stubborn sinner from participating in the Lord's Supper, and his/her children are denied baptism. In cases of 'open, notorious and flagrant sin', Calvin allows for the third, extreme measure to be proceeded to, omitting resort to either of the intermediate steps.

Of key importance to an understanding of how discipline was practised by his later followers in Protestant churches outside the boundaries of Switzerland, Calvin held that exercising discipline was the clear responsibility of every believer and that 'every man should endeavour to admonish his brother.'[42] In particular, pastors and elders have to be diligent in this since 'their duty is not merely to preach and teach', but also to 'warn and exhort in every home.' He exhorts believers to 'use whatever means they possess to return the excommunicated to Christ and to the unity of the church.' Above all, the church should 'exercise gentleness, and should confirm its love, to those separated from the body, while continually praying for them.' [43]

The early Scottish reformers had written, re-written and codified their own rules of procedure culminating in the *First* and *Second Books of Discipline*,[44] the prime movers of which were, respectively and successively, John Knox and Andrew Melville who had borrowed heavily from the Swiss and French models favoured by Zwingli, Bullinger and, of course and especially, from Calvin himself who had been trained as a lawyer.[45] In 1707, the year of parliamentary union in Britain, the General Assembly of the Church of Scotland adopted what it called its *Form of Process*, regulating, codifying and updating its systems for the detailed conduct of disciplinary procedures at all hierarchical levels. The *Form of Process* remained the standard text in guiding and shaping Kirk discipline, and stood broadly unaltered until the early years of the twentieth century, by which time, ironically, the Kirk had long opted out of its former role in such matters.[46]

The Reformation did not invent preaching; it merely re-discovered its power and effectiveness in the spreading of the word:

> The old papal popular sermons had gone off like a charge of gunpowder, producing only a fright, a bustle, and a black face: but those of the *newe learning*, as the monks called them, were small hearty seeds, which being sown in the honest hearts of the multitude, and watered with the dew of heaven, softly vegetated, and imperceptibly unfolded blossoms and fruits of inestimable value.
>
> These eminent servants of Christ excelled in various talents, both in the pulpit, and in private. Knox came down like a thunder-storm, Calvin resembled a whole day's set rain, Beza was a shower of the softest dew.[47]

Calvin as preacher and the changing role of the sermon

In 1539 Jean Calvin was charged with the task of responding on behalf of the citizens and magistrates of Geneva to Cardinal Jacopo Sadoletto's invitation[48] that they re-embrace the Catholic faith. Sadoletto was bishop of Carpentras in south-eastern France, frequently the summer residence of the Avignon Popes and once the see of the great Boethius himself.[49] Indignantly yet coolly, Calvin in his response proceeds to enumerate the list of points defining the gulf between the 'old' and the 'new' Christian religions. The three most basic that stood out from the rest were, he claimed, 'doctrine', 'discipline' and 'the sacraments'. To these, Calvin added a fourth which he called 'ceremonies', defining these as effects of which 'you have more than enough, but for the most part so childish in their import, and vitiated by innumerable forms of superstition, as to be utterly unavailing for the preservation of the Church.' He then turns to the issue of 'sermons'. In the former days of the church, before people began to question its beliefs, practices and procedures, Calvin asks the rhetorical question:

> ... what sermons in Europe then exhibited that simplicity with which Paul wishes a Christian people to be always occupied? Nay, what one sermon was there from which old wives might not carry off more whimsies than they could devise at their own fireside in a month? For as sermons were then usually divided, the first half was devoted to those misty questions of the schools which might astonish the rude populace, while the second contained sweet stories, or not unamusing speculations, by which the hearers might be kept on the alert. Only a few expressions were thrown in from the Word of God ... .[50]

But, argues Calvin, 'as soon as our [reformers] raised the standard, all these absurdities, in one moment, disappeared from amongst us.' And a little later in his letter, while conceding that 'those over which you preside are churches of Christ', Calvin harangues Sadoletto over the hierarchies of Catholicism, beginning with the Pope himself:

> ... we maintain that the Roman Pontiff, with his whole herd of pseudo-bishops, who have seized upon the pastor's office, are ravening wolves, whose only study has hitherto been to scatter and trample upon the kingdom of Christ, filling it with ruin and devastation.
> ... For in all places where the tyranny of the Roman Pontiff prevails, you scarcely see as many stray and tattered vestiges as will enable you to perceive that there churches lie half buried.[51]

It is, however, Calvin's next comment that is of greatest moment in the general context of this study. Answering Sadoletto's injunction in the closing sentences of his letter to the Genevans 'not to have a hatred for our faith and doctrine, for it is written '*What they say, do*', Calvin testily replies:

> ... iniquity has reached its height, and now those shadowy prelates, by whom you think the church stands or perishes, and by whom we say that she has been cruelly torn and mutilated, and brought to the very brink of destruction, can bear neither their vices nor the cure of them. ...
> But whatever the character of the men, still you say it is written, 'What they tell you, do'. No doubt if they sit in the chair of Moses. *But when from the chair of verity, they intoxicate the people with folly, it is written, 'Beware of the leaven of the Pharisees'*, (Matt. xvi. 6). [italics added][52]

Calvin's way of effectively demolishing Sadoletto's argument is to insist that far from the people being exhorted to fall in with all that the 'old' preachers taught, when it was known that they had abused their place of privilege in the pulpit – the *chaire de verité* – reformed pastors, by contrast, were 'not sent forth by Him to rule the Church with a licentious and lawless authority', but instead were bound 'to a certain rule of duty which they must not exceed, so the Church is ordered' (*1 Thess.* v. 21; *1 John* iv, 1). The argument as well as the terminology – especially the issue surrounding the significance of the phrase, chair of verity, as a metaphor for the evangelical pulpit – are crucial and will figure prominently later in this study when lawyers acting for aggrieved parties, in the setting of the supreme civil court in Scotland, successfully contested that inherited Calvinist 'right' which they presumed to call '*liberty of the pulpit*'.[53]

In relation to preaching more generally, the reformed churches were if anything even more revolutionary in their approach to the denser matters of organisation and discipline. MacCulloch is particularly helpful in defining the extent to which the reformers felt it necessary to physically transform not just the furniture inside churches when they set about the task of adapting them to changed Protestant priorities, but also the literal orientation of ministers in their preaching mode, and consequently of congregations in *listening* to God's word:

> The size and grandeur of newly built Protestant pulpits were permanent reminders of the paramountcy of the sermon, and led to the drastic restructuring of Reformed church interiors from Ireland to Lithuania. This dramatically canopied wooden preaching-turret now became the chief focus of the congregation's eyes rather than the altar or communion table. Commonly in the existing long, narrow medieval church buildings, the furnishings were turned around through ninety degrees, pulling the congregation away from the old climax of the altar at the east end and facing them either on to the long northern wall, where sunlight could fall on the preacher's face as he brought his people to struggle with God's word, or on the south, where in dramatic silhouette he could scan the eyes of his flock as he spoke.[54]

The pulpit had now become the cynosure of the act of worship and the sermon its liturgical epicentre. Reformation historians of both the older and younger generations concur that the centrality of the sermon in the new Protestant liturgy offered unusually attractive possibilities in preaching. Most obviously, sermons began to represent easily the most important vehicle by means of which the tenets of Protestantism could most directly be conveyed to the people.[55] Not all of this was a good thing. At first, liberated theology was confused and bewildered by various interpretations of a kind of '*d.i.y*' religion and, inevitably, all manner of rogues and buffoons felt encouraged to try their hand at preaching. Chadwick tells the story of ignorant tipplers occupying the pulpit in 1620 in the village church of Eaton Constantine in Shropshire, named and shamed as local schoolmasters half of whom led scandalous lives. Sermons went on seemingly endlessly until hour-glasses were provided in an effort to limit their length. One hourglass that has survived from this period was found to have been (probably deliberately) wrongly calibrated so that it completed its hour in forty-eight minutes![56]

All of this, of course, was dramatically different from medieval attitudes to preaching which older scholars like Jusserand, Owst and Coulton skilfully recreated in writing about the preaching friars of Chaucer's England – men like Father John Ball and the Wycliffite Lollards of the Peasants' Revolt. Modern scholars such as D. L. D'Avray, Bernadette Paton, Anne Thayer and others have researched the traditions and ways of life of the great medieval preachers of the towns and cities of Europe before the watershed that was set to evolve, over a remarkably short period of years, into the Protestant Reformation. According to these modern scholars what is often overlooked is the extent to which censure of morals and of socio-economic malpractice of every description did not escape the Friars, intent as they were on painting pictures of Hell awaiting the fornicator and the cheat, while at the same time busily peddling their indulgences to a largely guileless, unsuspecting public thereby guaranteeing the purchasers temporary immunity from the fires of hell and the worst that the syphilitic demons and the blackest imps might conjure up. Also, modern scholars stress, the tendency in medieval Christianity was emphatically towards specialist preachers; for example, itinerant mendicant monks delivering sermons to crowds of curious onlookers. Of special relevance to this study perhaps is Carolyn Muessig's research into '*sermones ad status*', the practice of tailoring model sermons to particular types of audience, including such as merchants and money-changers, pilgrims, lepers and other sick people, city and town dwellers, married persons, widows, virgins and young girls and so on.[57]

The essential point is, of course, that in these distant days the sermon, often informal and usually infrequent, rarely came into liturgical prominence and never occupied the central ground in the mass. It was simply not the Catholic way. All of this was swept away with the onset of the Reformation when the role of the sermon was transformed. Once again it was Calvin who led the way. Extraordinarily Calvin is reckoned to have climbed into the pulpits of the churches of Geneva – St. Pierre, St. Madeleine and St. Gervais – more than four thousand times. His successor, Theodore Beza, wrote that 'apart from preaching every day from week to week, he preached twice on Sundays as often as he was able ..., [and] kept up this pace without interruption until his death, and he never missed once except when he was very ill.' We learn elsewhere (from his biographer, Colladon) that Calvin preached ten different sermons in two weeks 'whenever he did not have obligations outside of Geneva or when he was laid up with illness.' Thanks in great measure to Denis Raguenier, a French refugee from Bar-sûr-Seine, who could take notes in an early form of shorthand, more than 2,300 sermons of Calvin are thought to have been recorded, but (for a variety of reasons) by no means all of these have survived. While Calvin himself was actively involved in the publication of his lectures (*praelectiones*), the sermons were never subjected to his pen before they were published. Indeed, it seems that (like John Knox) he was positively luke-warm about publishing his sermons, being of the view that as they were originally meant for Genevans they could be considered unsuitable for circulation outside Geneva.

While Calvin's theology acknowledged that the word of God and the preaching of it were closely integrated and that preaching was the means of leading people to salvation – the preacher, if you like, as both *messenger* and *intercessor* – he acutely recognised, we are told, the 'tension between the task to which he knew he had been called and the reality of the congregation of Geneva'. To put it a different way, he had a lively awareness of the need to point out from the pulpit sins and abuses 'in a brutally honest fashion, so that the listeners would ask God humbly for forgiveness and to renew their lives.' That approach did not always go down well. Prominent free citizens of Geneva became hot about their collars and some are on record as refusing to be hectored from the pulpit. Calvin's use of generalised pulpit censure clearly annoyed them and their adverse comments are recorded in the minutes of the Consistory of Geneva.[58]

John Knox's special brand of pulpit censure

Paradoxically, the sermons of John Knox offer perhaps the greatest examples of pulpit censure in English of any age, even though, astonishing as it may seem, we have only one complete printed example to rely on. Of course, numerous other sermons by Knox are available to us in extract but we cannot regard the majority of them as entirely reliable. In 'The Life and Death of John Knox', prefacing the London edition of Knox's *History of the Reformation of the Church of Scotland* [sic] of 1644,[59] his capricious editor David Buchanan (a direct descendant of George Buchanan) wrote of Knox's sermons:

> In his Sermons he was powerful and persuasive, and so assisted with the irresistible Power of God's all-sufficient Grace, that when he spoke but Ephphatha (desiring the Lord's People to lift up their everlasting Doors, that the King of Glory might enter in)[60] presently there was such a Piercing and Opening in the Hearts of his Hearers, that they were forced to cry out, Doubtless God is here, God is with the Preacher.

According to David Buchanan, and, as we have seen, like Calvin before him, Knox could simply not be bothered to arrange his sermons for publication: 'altho' he was both learned and eloquent, he not being willing to busy himself much with the Press'.[61] As he himself put it, Knox regarded his primary vocation to 'instruct the ignorant, comfort the sorrowful, confirm the weak, and rebuke the proud, by tongue and lively voice, in these most corrupt days, than to compose books for the age to come'.[62]

In Book I of his *History*, writing of his exploits as usual in the third person, Knox narrates the background to 'The first publick Preaching of *John Knox*, made in the Parish Church of *St. Andrews*'[63] at Easter 1547, just ten weeks after the death of Henry VIII. Knox had come to St. Andrews ostensibly to resume his tutoring of 'some gentlemen's children, whome certaine yeares he had nourished in godlines.' At 'a certaine houre' he proceeded with his friends Francis and George Douglas and Alexander Cockburn to the Castle chapel where he read a lecture.[64] His few auditors, including Henry Balnaves and the Castle chaplain John Rough,[65] 'perceaving the maner of his doctrine', tried there and then 'earnestly to travell [travail] with him, that he would take the preaching place [Buchanan = 'the Function of Preacher'] upon him.' Knox 'utterly refused', excusing himself on the grounds that 'he would not run where God had not called him.' Spearheaded by Sir David Lindsay of the Mount,[66] Knox's friends and followers in his absence contrived to make it difficult for him to opt out of the preaching ministry and they soon concluded that Rough should be entrusted with the task of setting him up. Accepting the commission, Rough's charge to Knox was as follows:

> Brother, ye shall not be offended, albeit that I speak unto you, that which I have in charge even from all those that are here present, which is this: In the name of God, and of his Son Jesus Christ, and in the name of these that presently call you by my mouth: I charge you, that ye refuse not this holy vocation, but as ye tender [have regard to] the glory of God, the increase of Christ his kingdom, the edification of your brethren, and the comfort of

A SERMON
preached by Iohn Knox,
Minister of Christ Iesus in the Publique audience of the Church of Edenbrough, within the Realme of Scotland, vpon Sonday, the. 19. of August. 1565. For the which the said Iohn Knoxe was inhibite preaching for a season.

1. Timoth. 4.
¶ The time is come that men can not abyde the Sermon of veritie nor holsome doctrine.

To this is adioyned an exhortation vnto all the faythfull within the sayde Realme, for the reliefe of suche as faythfully trauayle in the preaching of Gods worde. Written by the same Iohn Knoxe, at the commaundement of the ministerie aforesayd.

Imprinted Anno. 1566

Title page of John Knox's only published sermon, preached in Edinburgh, 19 August 1565 me, whom ye understand well enough to be oppressed by the multitude of labours, that ye take upon you the public office and charge of preaching, even as ye look to avoid God's heavy displeasure, and desire that he shall multiply his graces with you.[67]

Rough then turned to face the small company assembled before him, and asked them two questions: '*Was not this your Charge to me?*' and '*Do ye not approve this vocation?*' They answered with one voice: '*It was* [Buchanan, 'is'] *and we approve it.*' This was all too much for Knox. The narrative – and we need to pinch ourselves at this point to be reminded that it is John Knox himself who is author of the tender scene – concludes:

> Whereat the said John abashed, burst forth in most abundant tears, and withdrew himself to his chamber. His countenance and behaviour, from that day till the day that he was compelled to present himself to the public place of preaching, did sufficiently declare the grief and trouble of his heart; for no man saw any sign of mirth of him, neither yet had he pleasure to accompany any man, many days together.[68]

On the following Sunday Knox preached for the first time 'to express his Mind in the publick Preaching-place'; the locus was St. Andrews parish church pulpit. He took as his text one of his favourite Old Testament books, the book of *Daniel*, and the words of the seventh chapter concerning Daniel's interpretation of his dream: '*And another king shall rise after them, and he shall be unlike unto the first, and he shall subdue three kings, and shall speak words against the Most High, and shall consume the saints of the Most High, and think that he may change times and laws*' ... etc.[69] An abstract of the sermon follows in the *History*. The tenderness of the previous scene where Knox is reduced to tears is now entirely displaced by the fury and passion of the newly consecrated preacher's diatribe. His performance is typical of the modern popular image of his fiery style of preaching. His target was the 'Anti-christ' or 'Whore of Babylon', an unspeakable personage, he explained, that was 'one contrary to Christ, because that he is contrary to him in life, doctrine, laws, and subjects.'

> And then began he [Knox] to decipher [analyse] the lives of divers Popes, and the lives of all the shavelings [tonsured clergy] for the most part; their doctrine and laws he plainly proved to repugn directly to the doctrine and laws of God the Father, and of Christ Jesus his Son.[70]

Unsurprisingly, we learn from the narrative that: 'Of this sermon, which was the first that ever John Knox made in public, were there divers bruits [reports noised abroad].' Some even said that 'Master George Wishart spake never so plainly, and yet he was burnt: even so will he be.'[71] Typically, Knox clearly regards these reports of his first sermon as encouraging and as an indication of its success, measured in terms of the clear general approval with which it had been received.

Sixteen years later, in the early summer of 1563, Knox railed against what he calls in his *History* the 'stinking pride of women'. It was occasioned by speculation about Queen Mary's marriage. Knox preached his sermon in Edinburgh 'before the Parliament dissolved'[72] and 'before the most part of the Nobility.' Characteristically, he ends his sermon in words carefully crafted to shock the entire congregation:

... I hear of the Queen's marriage: Dukes, brethren to Emperors, and Kings,[73] strive all for the best game. But this, my Lords, will I say, ... whensoever the Nobility of Scotland professing the Lord Jesus, consents that an infidel (and all Papists are infidels) shall be head to your Sovereign, ye do so far as in ye lieth to banish Christ Jesus from this Realm; ye bring God's vengeance upon the country, a plague upon yourself, and perchance ye shall do small comfort to your Sovereign.

Even by the standards of that age extreme pulpit censure of this severity was virtually unparalleled and his language shook everyone present to the core. Knox records in the *History*:

These words, and this manner of speaking were judged intolerable. Papists and Protestants were both offended; yea, his most familiars disdained him for that speaking. Placeboes [yes-men] and flatterers posted to the Court to give advertisement that Knox had spoken against the Queen's marriage.[74]

This time, however, it is not John Knox who uncontrollably bursts into tears. Knox's words provoke the Queen herself, 'in a vehement fume', to 'cry out that never Prince was handled as she was'. Even though she had heard of Knox's sermon only second-hand from her courtiers – the 'placeboes' and 'flatterers' who hastened to inform her – her 'chamber-boy' had still to move quickly to 'get napkins to hold her eyes dry for the tears; and the howling, besides womanly weeping, stayed her speech.'

Easily the most celebrated sermon Knox preached, however, was delivered '*in the Publique audience of the Church of Edenbrough* [St. Giles'], *within the Realme of Scotland, upon Sonday, the.* [sic] *19. of August. 1565. For the which the said Iohn Knoxe was inhibite preaching for a season.*' It was preached in the presence of the king-consort, Henry Stewart, Lord Darnley, whose marriage to Queen Mary had been consecrated, according to the rites of the Catholic sacrament, in the chapel at Holyrood just three weeks before. This is the only sermon Knox ever edited expressly for publication. The title page shows it was printed in 1566, but the place of publication is not given (though according to the British Library ESTC it is almost certainly London); it also includes a prominent scriptural epigraph (not to be confused with the choice of text, which is from *Isaiah*), the reference given as '*1 Timoth. 4.*':

¶ The time is come that men can not abyde the Sermon of veritie nor holsome doctrine.[75]

Below the motto Knox has added these words:

To this is adioyned an exhortation unto all the faythful within the sayde Realme, for the reliefe of suche as faythfully travayle in the preaching of Gods worde. Written by the same Iohn Knoxe, at the commaundement of the ministerie aforesaid.

If the source of the scriptural translation used by Knox in the epigraph on the title page cannot be identified – it is neither by Wyclif from the Vulgate, nor from Tyndale's English rendering of Erasmus's Latin translation in the former's 'diglot' of 1538, nor even, as we might most credibly have expected, from Hall's Genevan English Bible of 1560 – one can safely conclude that not only is the message contained in the epigraph dazzlingly clear, but that Knox has used his own rendering to get it across in the most potent way he knows.[76] The sermon of verity, he claims, while often uncomfortable for the listening congregation, cannot be denied. If a modern reader finds much of the language blunt in the extreme, and almost offensively brutal, what must Darnley – a strangely unattractive figure who yet seemed capable of spellbinding Mary, one of the most beguilingly romantic figures in our national history – have thought of Knox's words as he squirmed on his lonely elevated throne in St. Giles' on that fateful day?

> O if Kings and Princes shuld consider what accompt shall be craued of them, as well of their ignoraunce and misknoweledge [sic] of Gods will, as for the neglecting of their office. ...
>
> ... Wouldst thou O Scotland have a King to raigne over thee in justice, equitie, and mercy? Subject thou thy selfe to the Lorde thy God, obey his commaundements, and magnifie thou that word that calleth unto thee. This is the way, walke into it, and if thou wilt not, flatter not thy self, the same justice remaineth this day in God to punishe thee Scotlande, and thee Edenborough in especiall, that before punished the lande of Iuda, and the citie of Ierusalem. Euerie realme or nation (sayth the Prophet Ieremy) that likewise offendeth, shall be likewise punished.
>
> ... And [referring to the Book of Daniel, chapter 3] when the king after, puffed up in pride by the counsell of his wicked nobilitie, would make an Image, before the which he would that al tongues and nations subject to him should make adoration, ... Oh if the eies of worldly Princes shoulde be opened, that they might see with what humour and lyquor [Darnley was known to be a heavy drinker] their soules are fed, while that their whole delight consisteth in pryde, ambition, and lustes of the stinking flesh. [77]

In the event, Knox was let off surprisingly lightly. In the language of the printed sermon's title page, he was 'inhibite preaching for a season.' Even in the spirit of the times it was an astonishingly mild sentence. [78]

'Liberty of the pulpit' in eighteenth-century Scotland

Like the earlier 'Paisley case' – to which, in legal history, it has a claim to be related, and as understood to be so related by those counsel who participated in both actions – the Court of Session process *Scotlands v The Rev. James Thomson* (1775-76) is of special importance in the context of pulpit censure. Since the background to the Dunfermline case is described in some detail by Boswell in his *Life of Samuel Johnson* and also elaborated on in his private journal, it is infinitely better known than its Paisley counterpart to which in law it is closely related (and not merely chronologically): *John Snodgrass and Others v The Rev. John Witherspoon* (1762-1776). Further, the Dunfermline process earns several pages in Morison's *Decisions of the Court of Session*, whereas there is no mention there (or in any of the other similar digests and indices of Court of Session decisions of the period) of the much longer-running Paisley case. But there are other factors that in aggregate make the Dunfermline case unique and (at least in this author's judgement) point to its special importance as far as cases of pulpit censure of individuals are concerned. These factors can be briefly stated as follows: first, the seriousness of the charge against the minister, Thomson, in the Court of Session; and equally, the seriousness of the charge made by the minister in his sermon, and subsequently, against the three named members of the

Scotland family. And that is not all. One could add to the already potent brew the irony that – in stark contrast with the case of John Witherspoon of Paisley – here there is no printed text of the minister's sermon worthy of the name. All that we have to go on are selected fragments of the minister's sermon cited by successive counsel for both sides in their various Court submissions, printed or in manuscript. We could call it a *'virtual'* sermon.

Finally, there is the episode of James Boswell's utter confidence, as he relates the story to Johnson, that such was the seeming impregnability of the minister's defence – i.e. *liberty of the pulpit* – Thomson would get off, if not scot free, relatively unscathed. But Boswell was wrong and David Rae and Henry Dundas, counsel for the pursuers, were right. Having effortlessly cleared the first hurdle (Lord Gardenstone's first interlocutor), the minister failed at the second (Rae's reclaiming *Petition*) and eventually quit the field altogether before, half-heartedly, attempting one last effort, his brave but ultimately futile appeal to the House of Lords. As we shall see when it is discussed in chapter 8, the Dunfermline case signals the end of an era. From that time on *liberty of the pulpit,* at least in its legal cognizance, is a lost cause.

Arguably, an even more significant lost cause dating from roughly the start of the closing decade of the eighteenth-century in Scotland was that of the established Church itself. Distinguished Enlightenment scholars such as Sher and Broadie have, either directly or by implication, characterised those whom they describe as the Moderate *literati* as preaching '*polite*' sermons, in contrast with others of different outlook (chiefly orthodox – that is, Popular party – and secessionist ministers who are often labelled 'unenlightened', 'enthusiastic' or even 'fanatical'), who rarely flinched from preaching overtly '*political*' sermons. Hugh Blair is often cited as a case in point. His collected *Sermons* only very occasionally stray into political territory and, where they do, Blair, seeming to acknowledge the danger he may be at risk of exposing himself to, quickly moves on, having made his point with tantalising brevity.[79]

In the case of Alexander Carlyle, on the other hand, it is quite the reverse. Carlyle cannot approach Blair in terms of intellect or subtlety but he was nevertheless a formidable pulpit orator. In his little-known fast-day 'jeremiad' sermon of February 1794, *National Depravity The cause of national calamities*, Carlyle preaches one of the few surviving published sermons by a Moderate minister attacking by name both the Friends of the People and the British Convention. Sher in particular makes the telling point that ministers such as Blair, Home and Carlyle – and for that matter, Adam Ferguson, himself a former parish minister – were typical of their caste in aligning their personal politics with that of the 'conservative' or 'constitutional' Whigs. That is to say, these men, and others like them fitting the definition 'Moderate literati', 'scorned almost every variety of radicalism and reform'. But the price they paid for that stance was ultimately 'calamitous', to borrow Carlyle's own word. Meikle, Harris and others[80] have correctly sourced sentiments such as Carlyle's as confirmation of the creeping popular disenchantment with 'priestcraft', and with the established Kirk generally, that set in from around the publication of Paine's *Rights of Man II* (1792) and the start of the war with France (1793). From their pulpits and elsewhere, in their deportment and attitudinising, too many Moderate-minded ministers refused to acknowledge or deign to seek to understand the legitimate grievances of that new phenomenon that baffled and confused them – the *people*. Carlyle's Inveresk, in other words, bore little relation to Paisley, Kirkintilloch or Dundee, to name but three of the acknowledged hotspots of popular radicalism in that last decade.

To conclude this brief survey of political preaching and pulpit censure by extending my hypothesis to the present age, the *right* of Christian clergy (though no longer their *duty*) to use their pulpits as a means of criticising society and human behaviour in the widest sense continues to be urged and defended even as I write. Ministers of religion still, it seems, feel a need to seek to defend their position whenever they stray into what, for some of their opponents, is frequently still viewed as forbidden territory. Thus, as I write this introduction, the newspapers are full of the stir that has been caused through the directness of the respective Easter messages preached at Canterbury and Rome by the heads of the Anglican and Roman Catholic faiths respectively, each venturing to touch on the threat they perceive not just to their own churches, but to Christians everywhere, posed by extreme Islamic fundamentalism. If that isn't political preaching, we might ask, what *is*? Further, the Archbishop of Canterbury has dared to question the paradoxical need, as he sees it, for a 'rich' country like Britain to feel compelled to resort to the voluntary provision of food banks to feed our poor; in the same way, equally, the reforming Pope Francis has not shied away from confronting head-on the apparently besetting problem of wayward priests and bishops in his own church. It would seem that the original concept of the chair of verity has still a lot of life left in it.

Postscript

Pulpit censure and the crime of fornication in Robert Burns's day

Apologies are due to enthusiasts of the life and works of Robert Burns for failing to make anything in this study of the extent to which the bard was himself often at odds with, as well as the primary target of stern pulpit censure and condemnation from the chair of verity. I freely acknowledge that the much argued-over stool of repentance is hardly mentioned here. My excuse is that I have been unable to find any surviving published sermons dealing specifically with sexual mores and the crime of fornication in particular. For such matters one needs to consult church records, especially Kirk Session and Presbytery minutes. Even so, it is readily acknowledged that no offence caused more upset, and certainly none occupied more time on the part of Kirk Sessions (the 'Poacher-Courts') struggling to cope with the plethora of such cases, virtually throughout the whole of the eighteenth century and well beyond. Records of Session meetings in this period are dominated by sexual offences: adultery, the fathering of illegitimate children, infanticide, rape, incest and procurement of abortions being by far the most common.[81]

Many of us are familiar with accounts of Burns's many personal forays into this dark world and the Kirk's handling of them. The modern tendency, it must be said, has been to make light of that side of the poet's life, preferring to forgive his appetites and escapades on the grounds of his assured poetic genius, but also because he himself made light of it in a number of his most entertaining poems. Robert Crawford describes the occasion when Burns made a Tarbolton girl, Elizabeth Paton, pregnant with his first child in 1784.

After his family debated what action young Robert should take – his mother wanted him to marry Elizabeth – he decided to obey the summons of the girl's Kirk Session to return to Tarbolton, to the Paton family's home parish, where the Session ordered him to submit to public penance for the crime of fornication. Crawford notes:

> Usually this meant appearing in church three successive Sundays, occupying the notorious seat of repentance, the 'cutty [low] stool'. Male fornicators had to attend along with their female accomplices to be upbraided by the minister. Burns did as he was told. He did not, however, marry Elizabeth Paton.[82]

But was the stool of repentance all it seemed? Was it, in fact, a *stool* at all in Burns's day? The museum at Alloway, it is true, exhibits just such a stool, though that particular specimen looks more of a milkmaid's stool than anything else; and in any event, if Robert Crawford is right, the whole point of punishment by public penance was that the unfortunate pair should appear together in church as complicit partners. It is certain that stools of the Alloway kind existed in numerous churches for use in discipline cases, but it remains unclear that this was what Burns had in mind respecting his own all too frequent personal experience of that particular kind of church discipline.

A helpful clue to the more probable reality behind the popular myth of the cutty stool exists in Dr James Adair's account of the tour he made of Stirlingshire in the company of Burns in October 1787. Adair records:

> At Dunfermline we visited the ruined abbey, and the abbey church, now consecrated to Presbyterian worship. Here I mounted the cutty stool, or stool of repentance, assuming the character of a penitent for fornication; while Burns from the pulpit addressed to me a ludicrous reproof and exhortation, parodied from that which had been delivered to himself in Ayrshire, where he had, as he assured me, once been one of the seven who counted the *seat of shame* together.[83]

The image presented here of multiple penitents – together with the specific use of the word 'mounted' in Adair's account – is surely significant and accords more or less precisely with the scene in David Allan's famous painting, 'The Black Stool', painted around 1790. [see cover illustration] Here Allan graphically depicts the convicted male fornicator standing on a gallery structure, at eye level with the minister who is haranguing him from the pulpit directly opposite, while the shamed female accomplice sits in the foreground on the low, or 'cutty', stool. The elders, here acting as moral police (who probably 'delated' news of the crime to the minister and/or the Session), are grouped in their chairs below the pulpit, and the beadle (or church officer) is in the act of persuading a large and uncooperative dog to exit the church.

In the light of a universally recognised need to revise the *First* and *Second Books of Discipline*, an Act approving the Church of Scotland's *Form of Process* was passed by the General Assembly in April 1707.[84] The *Form of Process* made specific provision for the crime of fornication which, as Clark observes, because of its inherent rigidity, was 'to some extent its own undoing.' The new law also resulted in Kirk elders becoming a 'moral police' on whom Sessions and ministers relied for 'delating' offences to them. In the end, 'the sin that alone came to be disciplined in the eighteenth century was any breach of the Seventh Commandment.' Not just that. Clark again:

> If there was a child in the case, the proof of guilt had not to be sought for, and so Church records since the eighteenth century began to contain practically only cases of sexual immorality. These are not the only sins of church members, we may be sure, but which of the other deadly sins are so undeniable? [85]

1

Patronage and secession

[Boswell] I introduced a question which has been much agitated in the Church of Scotland, whether the claim of lay-patrons to present ministers to parishes be well founded; and supposing it to be well founded, whether it ought to be exercised without the concurrence of the people? ...
[Johnson] But why should we suppose that the parish will make a wiser choice than the patron? ...
[Boswell] Though I present to my readers Dr. Johnson's masterly thoughts on this subject, I think it proper to declare, that notwithstanding I am myself a lay patron, I do not entirely subscribe to his opinion.
James Boswell, *The Life of Samuel Johnson* (1791), Penguin Classics, ed. David Womersley (2008), 389-92.[1]

Key authors and sermons

Reverend Ebenezer Erskine (1680-1754), minister of Portmoak, near Kinross, from 1703 to 1731; of the third charge of the Rood Kirk (Holy Rood), Stirling from 1731 until suspended, with three other ministers, by the Commission of Assembly in August 1733, as a result of the synodical sermon noted below. All four were subsequently deposed and in December 1733 founded the 'Associate Presbytery', later known to historians as the 'Original Secession'.

The Stone rejected by the Builders, exalted as the Head-Stone of the Corner. A Sermon preach'd at the Opening of the Synod of Perth and Stirling, at Perth, October 10. 1732. To which is subjoin'd a Sermon preach'd June 4th 1732, on the Sabbath Evening after the Sacrament, from Isa. 1x.6. – The Government shall be upon his Shoulder. Both by Mr. Ebenezer Erskine, Minister of the Gospel at Stirling.
Edinburgh: for David Duncan, 1732.

Reverend George Logan (1678-1755), minister of Trinity Church. Edinburgh.
A Sermon preached at the Opening of the General Assembly of the Church of Scotland, in the High-Church of Edinburgh, on the 14th of May 1741; before His Majesty's High-Commissioner: By Mr. George Logan, one of the ministers of Edinburgh, and Moderator to the former Assembly.
Edinburgh: R. Fleming and A. Allison ... M,DCC, XLI [1741]

Reverend John Erskine (1721-1803), minister of Old Greyfriars Church, Edinburgh.[2]
The Qualifications Necessary for Teachers of Christianity, preached before the Synod of Glasgow and Ayr at Glasgow, October 2. 1750.

THE
SIGNS of the TIMES
CONSIDER'D:

OR,

The high PROBABILITY, that the present APPEARANCES in *New-England,* and the West of *Scotland,* are a PRELUDE of the Glorious Things promised to the CHURCH in the latter Ages.

Mat. xvi. 3. *O ye Hypocrites, ye can discern the Face of the Sky, but can ye not discern the Signs of the Times?*

Luke xxi. 31. *So likewise ye, when ye see these Things come to pass, know ye that the Kingdom of God is nigh at Hand.*

John i. 46. *And Nathanael said unto him, Can there any good Thing come out of Nazareth? Philip saith unto him, Come and see.*

EDINBURGH,
Printed by T. LUMISDEN and J. ROBERTSON; and sold by JOHN TRAILL Bookseller in the *Parliament-closs.* MD.CC.XLII.

Title page of John Erskine's first published pamphlet while a young minister in Kirkintilloch (1742).

Glasgow: Robert Urie, 1750. [A second edition was printed in London in 1751 and sold by Kincaid and Donaldson in Edinburgh, and Daniel Baxter in Glasgow. The sermon is also included in the collection entitled *Doctrinal and Occasional Sermons*, Edinburgh, n.d. (1800?) - as is the following title.]

Ministers of the Gospel Cautioned against Giving Offence. A sermon by John Erskine, M.A. One of the Ministers of Edinburgh.

Edinburgh: Sands, Murray, and Cochran. For William Miller. MDCCLXIV. [1764]

Archibald Bruce (*bap*. 1748, *d*. 1816), Antiburgher minister at Whitburn, his only charge.

Corruptions in the church to be eradicated. A sermon preached at the opening of the Associate Synod. At Edinburgh, 1778. By A. Bruce, Minister in Whitburn.

[(Whitburn or) Edinburgh (ESTC)] [n.d. - ESTC states that the paper in the NLS copy bears a watermark date of 1797.]

Reverend William Peebles (1753-1826), minister of Newton-Upon-Ayr.

The Great Things which the Lord hath done for this nation, illustrated and improved; in Two Sermons preached on the 5th of November, 1788, the day appointed by the General Assembly of the Church of Scotland, for a National Thanksgiving, in Commemoration of the Revolution, 1688. To which is subjoined an Ode to Liberty. By The Rev. William Peebles, Minister at Newton upon Ayr.

Kilmarnock: J. Wilson. M,DCC,LXXXVIII. [1788]

Reverend William McGill (1732-1807), Second Charge minister of Ayr.

The Benefits of the Revolution. A Sermon, preached at Ayr, on the 5th of November, 1788, by William McGill, D. D. To which are added, Remarks on a sermon, preached on the same day, at Newton upon Ayr; very necessary for all the Readers of said Sermon.

Kilmarnock: J. Wilson. M,DCC,LXXXIX. [1789]

In Scotland, in the eighteenth century generally, but more especially throughout the age of the Enlightenment, there were several identifiably different manifestations of patronage. Emerson has long properly claimed the centre stage when it comes to revealing the mechanics of how academic patronage operated in the five Scottish universities,[3] while historians including Sunter[4] have shed new light on how patronage worked within government and the political world in Scotland at the time. Patronage also permeated numerous other strata of Scottish society, including commerce, the arts and even aspects of the law, although there was nothing specifically Scottish about that. What, of course, concerns us here is exclusively church patronage in Scotland. Ecclesiastical patronage is a forbiddingly large topic but it is integral to an understanding of the Scottish Enlightenment, even though its importance and its influence, though all-pervasive, is sometimes overlooked (or at least underestimated), and, too, it must be said, often misunderstood.

It is not always appreciated, for example, that church patronage was rooted in the law of statute. Effectively that meant that the powers of the Church itself to change it were not within its own grasp, but subject (after 1712) to the ultimate jurisdiction of the British parliament. That basic fact helps to explain why throughout the eighteenth century many of the most notable pamphlets on the subject of patronage in Scotland were the work of lawyers. It also partly explains why it appears that few sermons dealing with the patronage problem were published by ministers of either faction, the Moderates having been for the most part relaxed about the whole issue (except where it touched on Church polity and governance), while the Popular party had other, greater priorities to contend with. Moreover, it cannot be overlooked that ministers were reluctant, one suspects, openly to oppose patronage so long as their patrons were, practically, supplying their stipend and other emoluments. It was a case of refraining from biting the hand that fed them.

Reference might also usefully be made to (a) Chapter 5 where further information is provided on pulpit allusions to patronage and seceders in the context of the 'Kilwinning heresy', and (b) the 'Patronage timeline' at Appendix A.

The evolution of parties in the Church of Scotland

In *Church and University in the Scottish Enlightenment* (1985) Richard B. Sher credits John Witherspoon's *Ecclesiastical Characteristics* (1753) as 'probably responsible for bringing the term 'Moderate' into general use as a party label.'[5] More recently, in *The Moral Culture of the Scottish Enlightenment* (2014) Thomas Ahnert follows Sher in similarly ascribing to Witherspoon the distinction of having been 'probably' the first to have applied the term to a 'distinct group within the Presbyterian Kirk'; Ahnert further expresses the view (correctly) that it was first used by Witherspoon 'to refer to the group's perceived laxity with regard to the doctrinal standards of the Westminster Confession.'[6] All the evidence points, however, to the term having been in use much earlier than 1753; and, moreover, to its earliest employment in the context of the specific issue of patronage.

In one of the earliest accounts of patronage by one of its most influential legally qualified commentators, if not *the* earliest – *The Present State of the Church of Scotland. With respect to patronages; and the Bill now depending before the Parliament* (London, 1736) – William Grant, at that time the Church's procurator, later the judge Lord Prestongrange and Lord Advocate, explains 'the present Parties in the Church of Scotland':

> The Ministers are not all of one Stamp: there are not a few very ingenious learned and wise Men among the Clergy: These along with some of the more moderate Clergy, though not distinguished for Literature, really make a Majority of the Ministers. This makes up what for distinction sake we may call the moderate Party. There is another pretty large Party, men of small Literature, or Acquaintance with Mankind, exceedingly zealous about some small matters, tenacious of what they call Orthodox, and equally tenacious of every little Usage which obtained among the Presbyterians during their Persecutions as if it were of most express divine Institution: these, though not the Majority of the Clergy, yet being backed by a Majority of Elders, have these two last Years carried all Matters in the Assembly; we call these the warm Party.[7]

Extensively throughout Grant's pamphlet, having defined the two parties,[8] 'moderate' and 'warm' or 'orthodox', the author proceeds to use these terms to indicate how each party approached aspects of the issue of patronage at the most important of its recent critical periods, for example:

Mobs frequently arose about these Inductions, and an universal Dissatisfaction among the People. These Proceedings roused the warm Party, and many of the moderate. [9]...

The moderate Party of the Clergy through despair of Success were not keen for application to Parliament; they distrusted the Prudence of those who should be employed.[10] ...

All the Moderate Clergy [N.B. caps. are here used for the first time] in *Scotland*, and three fourths of the warm Brethren earnestly desired the passing of the Bill, and would have embraced it with all Joy and Thankfulness to God, the King, and his Ministers of State. The Body of the Gentry were of the same Dispositions. The political Members of the Assembly were the only Men who desired that it might be defeated.[11] ...

Altho' the Moderate Ministers and Gentry, and not a few of the Nobility were dissatisfied with some steps taken in this affair by the warm Party in the late Assemblies, and were diffident of their Prudence in the manner of Application, yet they earnestly desire the Success of the Bill. The warm Men having the leading in all Church-Assemblies, the wiser Men know not how in a Body to apply for it without appearance of Tumult, Clamour or counteracting the National Assembly [12].

Grant's pamphlet conclusively shows that the two factions originated out of a specific need: to facilitate the adoption of a particular stance or stances in the General Assembly in the face of a perceived common threat to church autonomy, in this instance the removal of the church's sovereign power to appoint ministers to parishes without outside interference. It is true, of course, that Grant is careful to distinguish fundamental doctrinal issues separating the factions, but from his comments it seems not in doubt that the parties were originally created not out of ethereal, but from much more practical, down-to-earth concerns.

'Spiritual Vassalage': perceptions of church patronage in Scotland

Two fundamentally important features of ecclesiastical patronage are often glossed over by historians. First, as originally conceived in the sixteenth century, the patrons who were entrusted (usually by the Crown, or deputed by the Crown to a proxy, or else simply conveyed by outright grant) with the right of exercising it, [13] normally performed the honour – for so it was perceived[14] – in a spirit of benevolence, and, in the overwhelming majority of cases, as generally welcomed by the people who were at the receiving end, so to speak, of the patrons' presentations. Secondly, and more obviously, when considered alongside the exercise of patronage *outside* the religious context, the definition of church patronage, together with its powers, rights and limitations, became enshrined in the civil law of the state, after the canon law ceased to have effect in Scotland at the Reformation (having then, of course, been supplanted by the judicatures of the reformed Church). That latter complication, or safeguard, call it what you will, meant that changing the procedure of how patronage worked in practice was ultimately always to be subject to primary legislation, arguably in itself an impediment in favour of inertia and the retention of the *status quo*. Finally, there was another almost wholly pernicious factor that cannot be ignored: an imponderable of potential gravity in the form of the Union of 1707, the consequences of which the Kirk, as events turned out, had been right to fear.

As it evolved within the Church of Scotland in the eighteenth century, patronage was therefore regarded as much as a legal issue as a spiritual one. In the eyes of lawyers, it was uncompromisingly a matter of the law. It is no accident that a plethora of lawyers chose to apply their minds to patronage and to publish their thoughts on the subject. These ranged from Francis Cullen, Lord Grant, at the beginning of the century, to William Grant of Prestongrange, John MacLaurin (later Lord Dreghorn), Andrew Crosbie, both Dalrymples, James Boswell, Henry Erskine and Archibald Fletcher, at various times throughout it. By contrast, most ministers chose to avoid the subject in their published sermons for the reason that in the case of the Moderate party they had other priorities, and in the case of the Popular party they, too, had other fish to fry. Both sides shared a common outlook on the issue: on the one hand, they would not encourage the parish to have aspirations towards greater involvement in the choice of their ministers, and on the other, concerning the patrons themselves, they had little desire, it seems, to bite the hands that fed them.

Though one of the most compelling Scottish jurists of his generation, Andrew McDouall (or McDougall), Lord Bankton (1685-1760)[15] – to cite his modern 'editor', W. M. Gordon – was nonetheless 'not a man of great professional distinction'.[16] McDouall discourses at length on the subject of ecclesiastical patronage in *An Institute of the Laws of Scotland in Civil Rights*, a work first published in 1751 and dedicated to one of the two greatest patrons Scotland would experience in the eighteenth century, the third Duke of Argyll.[17] As a work of reference Bankton's *Institute* – or simply 'Bankton' – remains important and has stood the test of time over several generations, having been reprinted (by the Stair Society) as recently as 1993. That Bankton remained both useful and accessible for so long as a standard work of reference was partly because his 'system' was designed to augment Stair and Mackenzie before him, but also on account of the author's decision to offer comparisons between the law of Scotland and that of England in respect of 'divers titles':

> I have subjoined at the end of each title of the first three books, and in divers titles of the fourth, a kind of parallel between our laws and those of England, in relation to the subject of such title, shewing the conformity or disconformity betwixt the one and the other. The lord Stair had no occasion to observe any thing of this kind, nor was it of great use in his time; but now, since the union of the two kingdoms, there is such intercourse between the subjects of South and North Britain, that it must be of great moment, that the laws of both be generally understood, and their agreement or diversity attended to; so that people, in their mutual correspondence, may regulate themselves accordingly; and the respective laws and usages may likewise receive some light from the comparison.[18]

In Bankton's second volume (no longer anonymous like the first, but now attributed to 'Andrew McDouall, *Esq; Advocate.*') he devotes the whole of Title VIII to 'Ecclesiastical Benefices, Patronages, Tithes, Stipends, and other matters relating thereto', of which 'Section V' is the most relevant to this study. Bankton considers the law on patronage that obtained both prior to, and after, 'the British statute' of 1690, by which legislation the 'antient right' of patrons to settle ministers on a parish were restored. We should note in particular what he has to say regarding the roles of 'heritors' [landed proprietors possessing hereditary rights], elders and, perhaps especially, of 'the people' (i.e. the parish congregation) in ministerial settlements. His words need to be cited *in extenso*:

> Notwithstanding that, in strictness of law, the church-judicatories are bound to make settlements of ministers in churches, upon the presentations of patrons, tho' without the concurrence of heritors and elders, or consent of the people; yet, because such settlements are seldom comfortable, and tend not to the success of the gospel in parishes so planted, they for most part do not make settlements in that way, but require the consent of a sufficient number of the heritors and elders, by way of call or concurrence, and likewise the approbation of the people, if it can be had; ... At the same time, the opinion the people have conceived, of a right they pretend to have in the choice of their minister, creates great disturbance to the church-judicatories, and occasions long vacancies, and puts the patron, and others concerned, to no small expence, before a settlement can be compassed; all which would be prevented if such notion were eradicated out of their minds, but which will not be easily done, as it has been allowed to take root.[19]

Bankton is here contrasting the *de jure* with the *de facto* situation prevailing in his day in relation to ministerial presentation. He is quite clear in his own mind where things stood in the matter. The assumed 'right' of the 'people' to have a voice in settlements had no foundation in law; it followed that congregations should be disabused of any view that they possessed such a right in the first place. Above all, he is satisfied that the existing situation could not continue, he strongly implies, on account of the 'great disturbance' often created for all concerned by unpopular and/or disputed settlements. Bankton, we should note, was writing in 1752, a year of great significance in the history of the patronage debate.

It is not hard to see where the people's belief that they had an important voice in settlements, and had a right to articulate it, sprang from; whether that belief was confused, feigned or simply deluded, or a mixture of all three, is beside the point. In the chronicles of the early reformed Scottish church both the *First* and the *Second Book of Discipline* had unambiguously conferred on 'the people' their democratic right to participate in the election of 'their' minister:

> "The admission of the ministers to their office must consist in the consent of the people and church, whereto they shall be appointed, and approbation of the learned ministers appointed for their examination. We judge it expedient that the admission of ministers be in open audience," ...
>
> "Other ceremonie than the publick approbation of the people, and declaration of the chiefe minister, that the person there presented is appointed to serve that church, we cannot approve." [*First Booke of Discipline,* (1560), iv.1§ first 'head of doctrine', 4, 3] [20]

> "Election is the chusing out of a person or persons maist abile to the office that vaikes, be the judgment of the elderschip and consent of the congregation, to whom the person or persons beis appointed. In this ordinar election it is to be eschewit, that na person be intrusit to ony of the offices of the kirk, contrar to the will of the congregation to whom they are appointed, or with out the vote of the elderschip." [*Second Booke of Discipline,* (1578), 3.§iv] [21]

The first mention of the role of patronage in the Acts of [the General] Assembly is found in 1565. In the words of an anonymous nineteenth-century historian of patronage, 'the leaders of the Assembly of those days did not always express that horror of patronage, even in the hands of a Roman Catholic Queen, which is now contended for.'[22] He was writing in 1833, a decade prior to the 'Great Disruption'.

In the tangled and often bloody history of church-state relations in seventeenth-century Scotland these lofty principles were all but lost sight of until the Revolution settlement of 1690 when a reluctant William III agreed, as part of the act restoring Presbyterianism, to the abolition of patronage, even though the right of congregations to call ministers was still limited to the nominees of heritors and elders. Lynch, who seems to understand these matters better than some, insists that the view that the Kirk was thereby liberated from state control is 'a caricature of an ambiguous relationship which hovered between a practical Erastianism and a principled stance on a modified two-kingdom doctrine'.[23]

Just over twenty years later, however, the opponents of patronage in the Scottish church were dealt a body blow, widely perceived as an assault on the church's liberty that took 130 years to remedy. In 1712 in the reign of Queen Anne, a month after the passing of the Toleration Act (allowing freedom of worship to Episcopalians willing to pray for the ruler), the Kirk, virtually without any meaningful prior consultation, was forced to swallow a bitter pill in the form of the Patronage Act, which, on the face of things, appeared to reverse the abolition of patronage conceded in 1690. According to Lynch, this was 'in a sense the root cause of the series of splits and secessions which affected the Church of Scotland over the next 130 years', while he also points out that, in practice, the 1712 Act affected heritors (who in 1690 had been reserved an important role in local leadership in concert with kirk sessions) almost as much as sessions and congregations:

> The issue provoked by the 1712 Act was not a starkly simple one of the rights of the 'people' against those of patrons for only the radicals in the Church favoured anything like congregational democracy; it was rather about the breadth of the landed interest which might be expected to work hand in hand with lay elders of kirk sessions and ministers whose power lay in the presbyteries. For most, the issue was not outright principle but working practice.[24]

One of the most outspoken opponents of the Patronage Act was Sir David Dalrymple, fifth son of James Dalrymple, Viscount Stair, the greatest of all the Scots jurists. Dalrymple was uniquely placed to serve as a critic of the proposed legislation; he had, after all, not only represented Culross in the Scottish Parliament from 1698 to 1707, but had served as a commissioner when the arrangements for what would become the Treaty of Union were under discussion. Dalrymple was elected to the first British Parliament in February 1707 and represented the Haddington burghs from 1708 until his death in 1721. In 1712, after the Bill entitled *An Act to restore the Patrons to their ancient Rights of presenting Ministers to the Churches vacant in that part of Great Britain called Scotland*[25] had been passed – but (from the internal evidence) probably before it went under the seal – Dalrymple caused to be published anonymously in London a pamphlet of twenty pages stating the grounds of his objections. His *Account of Lay-Patronages in Scotland* is a masterly précis of the historical background to the issue but it is much more: in particular, Dalrymple notes that by means of an earlier Act of 1707 'made and expressly declar'd to be, a fundamental and

Essential Condition of the Act of Union', the practice of simoniacal contracts –'which have ever been the abhorrence of all Christian Churches, and none more than the Church of England' – was effectively ended.[26] Accordingly, argues Dalrymple, it is 'hoped' that

> since the Church of *England* complains of Lay Patronage as a Grievance, the Legislature will not again put our Necks under that Yoke, which neither we nor our Fathers were able to bear, especially, since Providence has deliver'd us from it, and that we are as much secur'd against it as our own particular Laws founded upon the Claim of Right, and the Treaty of Union can secure us.[27]

In the event, Dalrymple's worst fears were realized: Scottish church 'necks' were indeed once again brought under the 'yoke' of lay patronage. What Dalrymple feared beyond everything else was that in re-introducing patronage Scotland would be brought, by English initiatives, under a 'Spiritual Vassalage', which, he claimed, 'is the most insupportable of all others'.

Disputed settlements: the deposition of Thomas Gillespie and its consequences

One of the inevitable consequences of the restoration of patronage was the opportunity it gave (and not simply in theory) for parties to dispute presentations. Burleigh has estimated that between 1740 and 1750 there were 'more than fifty' disputed settlements in which presbyteries simply refused to act on grounds of conscience.[28] Acknowledging the problem, Bankton first observes that

> well-disposed patrons do not insist to have a minister thrust in upon a people, which is frequently of bad consequence.[29]

But, he insists, that does not mean that the people ought to be handed the right of a 'popular election', which 'might give occasion to tumults and undue practices'. To avoid any possibility of that happening (or of the people wrongly assuming that they possessed any rights of that nature), the General Assembly had passed legislation in 1732, and amended two years later, giving presbyteries powers in settling ministers in the event of contested presentations. The manner in which they chose to exercise those powers is convoluted and need not concern us.[30] The point is that Bankton, having considered the law in relation to patrons' rights in the case of settlements going against their preferments, concludes that the ultimate authority in such circumstances lies with the Court of Session who

> have a power to cognosce and determine upon the legality of admission of ministers, with respect to their claim to the benefice or stipend, that being a civil right.[31]

That the Church of Scotland in the eighteenth century was beset by disputed settlements is a serious understatement. One has only to read through the proceedings and acts of successive General Assemblies to realize just how many were effectively hijacked by a plethora of (often tedious and prolonged) such cases. Morren covers the point in his 'Preface' to the first volume of his *Annals of the General Assembly* (covering the fourteen-year period 1752 to 1766):

It is true, that in giving effect to the law of Patronage, the practice of the Assembly continued to be in accordance with the precedent set in the memorable case of Inverkeithing, in 1752. Disputed settlements, though less frequent than in the former period, occurred from year to year. Sometimes the differences were adjusted by an amicable arrangement among the parties. [examples are given by Morren]. But, on the other hand, in every case upon record in which the patron or presentee urged the matter to a decision, the Assembly uniformly determined it in their favour.[32]

In other words, Morren suggests, protest was all very well but the possibility of a disputed presentation ultimately going against the original wishes of the patron was remote in the extreme.[33]

One minister of the Popular party had seen the truth of all this with great clarity. A full decade after the publication of his anonymous satire on Moderates and Moderatism, *Ecclesiastical Characteristics* (1753), John Witherspoon, laying aside his serio-comic mode but still writing anonymously, had felt it necessary to offer the public a sober explanation of the reason behind his decision to go into print in the way he had done a decade before. In *A Serious Apology for the Ecclesiastical Characteristics. By the real Author of that Performance* (1763) Witherspoon dedicates his new work 'To the Nobility and Gentry of Scotland, particularly such of them as are Elders of the Church, and frequently Members of the General Assembly.' This time, Witherspoon is not in the business of satirical censure – and we would be wasting our time hunting for a recondite message, mocking the dedicatees, embedded in his prelim. Instead, Witherspoon genuinely praises them for their role, acting as they do, we might say, as a necessary buffer between ministers and the higher courts of the Church in circumstances where, he implies, the wishes of the congregation were the very last thing to be taken into account. And to illustrate his point, he instances a 'very recent' case (reported to the Assembly of 1762) in which it was 'owing to the Honourable members' that 'a sanction was not given to a resolution, of inflicting censures upon ministers, merely for preaching to their own people at their desire'.[34]

That is by no means the sum total of what Witherspoon has to say on the specific issue of patronage in the *Serious Apology*. Early in the pamphlet he recalls that his satire of 1753 had caused an enormous stir at the time:

> The rage and fury of many ministers in Scotland when this pamphlet was first published, is known almost to all its readers. The most opprobrious names were bestowed upon the concealed author, and the most dreadful threatenings uttered, in case they should be so fortunate as discover and convict him. One gentleman in particular, [he means himself] who fell under the imputation of being concerned in it, has ever since been the object of their detestation and resentment; although I think it remains yet very uncertain, what hand he had, or whether he had any hand at all, in its composition'.[35]

And he reflects on the motives that had inspired him to write the piece in the first place. 'What first induced me to write,' had been

> a deep concern for the declining interest of religion in the church of Scotland, mixed with some indignation at what appeared to me a strange abuse of church-authority in the years 1751 and 1752*.[36]

His starred footnote explains precisely which particular cases he had in mind:

*This refers to the rebuking and deposing ministers who did not think themselves at liberty to join in the ordination of a pastor without a people. The first was done in the case of Mr Adam and the presbytery of Linlithgow, who declined being present at the settlement of Torphichen; the second, in the case of Mr Gillespie, in the settlement of Inverkeithing.[37]

The Torphichen (1748-51) and Inverkeithing (1749-53) controversies are monuments to the complex history of church patronage in Scotland. The former case elided into the latter in successive Assemblies and, together, they can be regarded as two sides of the same coin. The cases are often cited in accounts of the religious dimension of the Scottish Enlightenment and are often credited with having been the midwife at the birth of the Moderate and orthodox factions in the Church of Scotland.[38] Torphichen, but more especially Inverkeithing, stand out like beacons in the history of the Church precisely because they mark the decisive point at which the new Moderate party – the group of 'several young members' as they were described,[39] including William Robertson, John Home, Alexander Carlyle and their associates – by their well-drilled tactics (for which Robertson is rightly given the lion's share of credit), out-gunned the orthodox opposition in the Assembly in the guise of the Popular party. Witherspoon, himself by that time an undisputed leader of the 'warm' or orthodox faction, called the young men 'the present rising generation'.[40] Morren notes at the beginning of his report of the proceedings of the 1752 General Assembly:

This meeting was rendered memorable in the annals of the Church, by the two parties (who began to be distinguished by the names of *moderate* and *popular*) coming into more direct and violent collision than ever, in reference to the question – "How far are the members of inferior judicatories bound to give effect to the sentences of superior courts, in opposition to the dictates of their own private judgment and conscience?"[41]

But why did these controversies provoke Witherspoon, or so he tells us, into using them as part justification for the writing of *Ecclesiastical Characteristics*? The 'old' answer was that these two presentation disputes marked the extent to which the Church of Scotland had by that time (1748-53) separated into rival camps, Moderate and orthodox, pointing to the fact that *Ecclesiastical Characteristics*, on its author's own admission, was nothing short of an open declaration of war by the Popular party on Moderates and Moderatism. But, as pointed out earlier in this chapter (pages 29-30), the origin of the parties is considerably older than Witherspoon's notorious satire. In a little-known pamphlet he had published anonymously in Glasgow in 1766 William Thom, a friend and Popular party associate of Witherspoon, notes the longstanding existence of the two main parties within the Kirk at the time he writes and sees a distinct parallel in the seventeenth century Kirk from the time of Cromwell:

The church of Scotland, and of course, the General Assembly, hath, so far as I know, always consisted of two parties, called the STRICT and the MODERATE, and, indeed, it can hardly be expected, that so great a number of men, educated as they are, should see things in the very same point of view. These two parties seem to think differently from one another in matters of doctrine; and they certainly differ very much about several points of discipline, and of church government. If one is acquainted with the ideas and views of the public resolutioners and protesters in the time of Cromwell's usurpation, he will be able to form a tolerably just character of the two parties, which have subsisted all along, and which subsists at present in the church of Scotland: they seem respectively to inherit the temper and opinions of these two parties of ancient Presbyterians. The *strict* party do very much resemble the protesters, and the *moderate* the resolutioners.[42]

The most credible explanation, therefore, behind Witherspoon's resolve to lampoon Moderatism by writing and publishing *Characteristics* is to be found in the astonishing story of the two disputed presentations, and especially, in the resolve of the new group of young Moderates – the 'little band of earnest men'[43] – who used the cases as a hook from which to suspend a determined re-commitment to the upholding of church polity and governance. The supreme irony lies in the apparent apathy on the part of these young men towards the issue of patronage *simpliciter*, the future safeguarding of which drew forth from them an almost wholly agnostic response. When read with care we find, for example, that the paper they gave in to the Assembly of 1752, the celebrated *Reasons of Dissent*, authored wholly or principally by William Robertson, has little or nothing to do with patronage *per se* – the term is not mentioned once in the entire document – but everything to do with the upholding of church authority, governance and corporate responsibility. It was not yet time for Moderates like Robertson to dare to claim openly that patronage was 'good in itself' in helping to improve the quality of the Scottish clergy.[44]

The Popular party authors of their *Answers to the Reasons of Dissent* were not fooled by the arguments put forward by the *'Dissenters'* (the *double entendre* is probably deliberate), finding 'a paper wholly made up, either of loose and unguarded propositions; or of such general principles as nobody denies, quite misapplied in the present case.' Moreover, for their part, the evangelical ministers constituting the Popular party could not be said to have ever been universally enthusiastic in their desire to have the law of patronage removed from the statute book, if by doing so it meant concentrating the power of choosing parish ministers in the hands of the elders and the 'people', thus eliminating the involvement of patrons and heritors. Nevertheless, unlike its Moderate counterpart, the *Answers* is, at least in part, about patronage and specifically cites the 1736 Act of Assembly, insisting on the need to preserve 'harmony and unanimity' in congregations in circumstances where a minister is 'planted' on a vacant parish. That view of things has tended to be neglected by historians who have, entirely reasonably, expressed greater interest in the extent to which the twin 'manifestos' represent an outbreak of war between the two factions, and how these documents may have been characteristic of 'Enlightenment' attributes – or not.

It is certainly true that the presentation disputes of Torphichen and Inverkeithing – especially the latter, with its scapegoating injustice – sparked off one of the most intense rows in the Church of Scotland in the eighteenth century, a row that at its height provoked the criticism that, whatever mattered most in the established church, the *people*, as it seemed to many of those critics, mattered least of all. In that regard, Thom's pamphlet invites attention to a report by the 'Committee on Schism' (November 1765), set up at the previous Assembly, which stated:

... as the *abuse of the right of patronage* has been one chief occasion of the progress of Secession, it is ... overtured, that the General Assembly would be pleased to consider what methods may be employed to remedy so great an evil ... .[45]

A glance at the timeline in *Appendix A* will show that (acknowledging Sher and Murdoch) the 'periodic crises' characterizing the patronage debate in Scotland in the eighteenth century may be said to have consisted of four distinct phases as follows:

1 The period of the 'Original Secession', 1732-33;

2 The Torphichen and Inverkeithing disputes, culminating in the deposition of Thomas Gillespie, minister of Carnock, in 1752;

3 The three-fold 'continuous crisis' of the 1760s, embracing the contested right of town councils in Glasgow and Edinburgh to act as patrons in their own right (1762-64), the damaging Schism Overture of 1765-66, and the anti-patronage campaign of 1768-69;

4 The later *anti*- and *pro*-patronage skirmishes of 1782-85.[46]

To suit his purpose, McIntosh, the historian of the Popular party, adopts a slightly different historiography, according to which the Torphichen case 'marks the start of the *first phase* of the eighteenth-century patronage dispute, the phase which stressed liberty of conscience'.[47]

In 1748 Lord Torphichen had exercised his right as patron by presenting James Watson to the vacancy at Torphichen in the Presbytery of Linlithgow. Objections to Watson's presentation founded on the assertion that he could not be heard in church, but, much more seriously, on the ground that those opposing him 'never could submit to his ministry, in that he had accepted of a presentation without the consent and concurrence of almost the whole parish.' That recalls Bankton's point, as earlier noted, that successful presentations depend on the three-fold 'approbation' of the heritors, the elders and the 'people'. In the absence of approbation being forthcoming on the part of just one of these three elements such settlements, Bankton maintained, are 'seldom comfortable', since according to church law (he cites Acts of Assembly of 1732, 1734 and 1736)[48] the presbytery then had the right to settle a charge. Morren notes that the Torphichen case dragged on over three successive Assemblies, from 1749 until its culmination in 1751, when a long speech was made by (or so Morren speculates) the minister of Falkirk, John Adams ('a leading man on what began to be called the *popular* side'). Adams (if it was he) argued why, despite clear injunctions from the Synod and the Assembly that the Presbytery should proceed with Watson's admission, he and others of the same view did not feel obliged to attend or participate on the grounds that to do so would infringe his (and their) freedom of conscience.[49]

Subtly, Adams (again assuming it was he) pointed out in the course of his address that at the time of the ('Original') Secession the seceders were unable to justify their actions on account of the established church having sought to muzzle them, and because 'the Church did things which they could not approve of, and therefore they would not hold communion with her.' He concluded his speech as follows, with a thinly disguised threat:

> In a word, if uniform obedience to authority in all possible cases shall come to be insisted upon as a term of communion amongst us, in order to distress either presbyteries or

particular members who have not freedom to act in some circumstances; and that too when the nature of the thing and former practice point out methods of effectually executing final sentences which are not attended with those inconveniences; we could make no hesitation in our choice, betwixt peaceable retiring, if the Church-judicatures judged it proper to dismiss us, and acting a part in consequence of measures which, in our humble opinion, must not only prove hurtful, but ruining to our most valuable interests.[50]

Adams' speech provoked mild uproar which, euphemistically, Morren equates to 'long reasoning in the Assembly'. Was the offending Presbytery to be *censured* or not for its recalcitrance in face of a refusal to proceed to admit the minister and thus secure the settlement of the parish? Was it at least to be *rebuked*? Eventually, but only after successive votes on different motions had taken place, it was agreed 'by a very great majority' to proceed to rebuke the Presbytery 'for their disobedience.' But the highlight of the proceedings was about to emerge into the open. On 18 May a brief but well-crafted paper entitled '*Reasons of Dissent*' ('dissent', that is, from an earlier motion to censure the Presbytery) was handed in to the Assembly bearing the signatures of twenty-three ministers, headed by Principal William Wishart of the University of Edinburgh. Contrary to the wishes of its subscribers the Assembly refused to have the paper read out but merely agreed to receive it to lie on the table '*in retentis*'. Important though it was, the real significance of Wishart's paper on the Torphichen incident was that it anticipated an infinitely more ground-breaking document of the same name at the General Assembly of the following year when the debate on the much more disturbing Inverkeithing affair was in process of being wound up. In the meantime, however, through the mechanism of an *ad hoc* device known as a 'riding committee', poor Mr. Watson was finally settled on the parish of Torphichen without the concurrence of the Presbytery, thus demonstrating to the letter the accuracy of Lord Bankton's view that contested settlements were 'seldom comfortable.'

The origin of the so-called Inverkeithing affair also lay in a disputed presentation. But any similarity between the two cases ends there. However acrimoniously, Torphichen was eventually settled and the patron's man formally admitted as minister, though admittedly, for some presbyters, only through gritted teeth. In the case of Inverkeithing, the settlement was also ultimately forced through top-down, though this time with comprehensively greater all-round ill-will, to the extent that the repercussions would be engraved into the corporate consciousness of the church for generations. The minister of Broughton in the Presbytery of Biggar, Andrew Richardson, had been presented to the parish of Inverkeithing by Captain Philip Anstruther, whose family had secured the rights of patronage in 1705, within the living memory of older inhabitants of the parish. The previous two incumbents had each survived for ten years or less as minister at Inverkeithing but *their* predecessor had been 'called' way back in 1692, according to the old way of 'heritors, magistrates, and masters of families showing their free assent thereto with uplifted hands.'[51]

At a meeting of the Assembly Commission in March 1751 it had been agreed that an *ad hoc* committee should address a particularly thorny matter:

"That many dangers may arise to the interest of religion and our happy constitution, by unqualified patrons disponing their right of patronage for a single voice, or during the life of the disponer only, to persons in whom they can confide, and who will present none but such as are recommended by the nonjuring patron; – that by this practice an opportunity may be given of manifest collusion, to the encouraging of persons disaffected to his Majesty's person and government and our happy constitution, and to the disturbance of the peace of the Church and the quiet of the nation; and that, therefore, humble application should be made by the General Assembly to the Legislature, that an effectual remedy may be applied for preventing such evils."[52]

The committee reported to the Commission in April. Rarely had the General Assembly acknowledged such a need for haste. The Reverend Robert Paton,[53] Moderator in 1750 and one of three commissioners who had 'gone to London' to meet with government ministers ostensibly on a totally different mission – to discuss a scheme aimed at a much-needed augmentation of stipends – reported that they had identified an altogether graver issue concerning the possibility of tighter controls on Kirk independence being introduced by parliament. Paton and the others counselled a need for vigilance, a view endorsed by the Commission. More specifically, Paton and his team recognized that it would be necessary to take steps to 'guard against any clause by which the law of patronage may be extended, or more strictly enforced.' At the ensuing May Assembly the fears of those attending were allayed to some extent by the reading of a letter signed by all three Commissioners and the church's procurator (the 'other' David Dalrymple, the future Lord Westhall), concluding that with regard to the perceived threat to apply patronage 'more strictly', there was good reason to believe that 'no such design is formed by those chiefly concerned in the administration.'[54] Notwithstanding these words of comfort, it was against a background of some considerable anxiety for the future safeguarding of the church's constitution – clearly an issue of enormous importance – that the unwelcome news of a serious deterioration in the Inverkeithing saga was received.

The process of Richardson's 'transportation' from Broughton to Inverkeithing had gone through the necessary channels at the end of May 1751 without incident. In June the promoters of Richardson's settlement had appeared before the Presbytery of Dunfermline and requested a date be intimated for his admission. Next month the Presbytery, after conducting a series of interviews with elders and prominent members of the congregation (including members of the town council of Dunfermline), conceded defeat, concluding that

> their admitting Mr. Richardson as minister of Inverkeithing, in the present circumstances of that parish, would be of harmful consequence to the interests of religion within their bounds and that the matter is attended with such difficulties as they cannot get over.[55]

It was *impasse*. It was now for the Synod of Fife to step in to try to resolve the matter. The Synod declared 'by a large majority' they had no confidence in the Presbytery's actions – for refusing, that is, to obey the orders of the Commission of Assembly to proceed to admit Richardson – and the Synod demanded that the Presbytery of Dunfermline comply. A new date, in January 1752, was proposed, this time by the Assembly Commission itself, meeting in November. If the Presbytery *still* stalled, such behaviour, the Commission ruled, would attract a 'very high censure in case of their disobedience.' At the meeting of the Presbytery on 18 December the patron's legal agent appeared in person and called for the Presbytery to comply with the Commission's injunction, an extremely rare occurrence. *Still* the Presbytery prevaricated, and the revised deadline for Richardson's admission passed. After a further meeting of the Presbytery in Edinburgh in March, when it was apparent there was still no movement from their position of intransigence, the Commission of Assembly again met and this time received a petition from the patron and others representing Richardson's supporters, formally complaining that the Presbytery had not carried out the Commission's November instructions and, accordingly, craving that the Presbytery should be censured.

What followed was literally unprecedented. The Commission, probably exceeding its powers, though understandably provoked in the extreme by the persistent failure of the Presbytery to obey its decisions, voted, *first*, not to refer the matter to the Assembly itself — on the limp pretext that to do so would be 'inconsistent' with its unanimous view expressed earlier in the day's proceedings that they did indeed possess the power 'to carry the sentence for Mr. Richardson's settlement into execution'; and, *secondly*, and incomprehensibly, <u>not</u> to censure the Presbytery for its conduct in the affair.

When the full Assembly met on 14 May, in his opening address the High Commissioner, the 7th Earl of Leven,[56] did not disappoint his expectant audience who, to speculate, would almost certainly have thought it likely that he could not possibly pass over the settlement crisis without comment. At the same time, they had no way of anticipating the patently sincere passion with which he gave vent to his frustrations. There had never been an opening address quite like it:

> I know it is unnecessary for me to admonish gentlemen of so much learning, wisdom, and experience, that peace, unanimity, and truth, are the great objects at which you ought to aim. One thing, however, as a well-wisher to the government and good order of this Church, I cannot pass over in silence. Allow me therefore to hope, that as it is our happiness to have regular meetings of our national Assembly, countenanced by our gracious sovereign, you will be careful to support her dignity and authority, and not destroy with your own hands our most valuable constitution, secured by law, so dear to your forefathers, so excellent in itself, and which your enemies have so often in vain attempted to wrest from you. The main intention of your meeting is frustrated, if your judgments and decisions are not held to be final; if inferior courts continue to assume that liberty they have taken upon themselves, in too many instances, of disputing and disobeying the decisions of their superiors. It is now more than high time to think of putting a stop to this growing evil; otherwise such anarchy and confusion will be introduced into the Church, as will inevitably not only break us in pieces amongst ourselves, but make us likewise the scorn and derision of our enemies; for, believe me, subordination is the link of society, without which there can be no order in government. [57]

Lord Leven's words confirm that he at least feared the outcome, and sensed that the affair could have serious longer-term consequences for the Kirk. But we should not be surprised at Leven's obvious sense of exasperation. Thirty years before, as plain Alexander Leslie, a judge of the Court of Session, he had married Mary Erskine, daughter of Colonel John Erskine of Carnock. Colonel Erskine, the High Commissioner's father-in-law, was patron of the parish of Carnock in the Presbytery of Dunfermline when he had presented Thomas Gillespie as the new minister of Carnock in 1741. Gillespie, whose own admission had not been without incident,[58] was one of a group of six ministers in the presbytery who had deliberately and consistently absented themselves on various successive dates prescribed for Richardson's admission, including the latest date (21 May) fixed by the Assembly itself. That date too, the Assembly was informed to its consternation, had also proved abortive: the required quorum of five ministers had not been achieved, only three ministers having attended. Instead, to rub salt into the wound, the Assembly received a representation signed by six ministers out of a total of ten in membership of the Presbytery (including Gillespie), explaining that they could not be willing participants in Richardson's admission to the parish of Inverkeithing; or, as they put it, 'in carrying a settlement into execution',

> where, in our apprehension, there was by no means such a concurrence of persons residing in the parish as might give sufficient weight and influence for promoting the great ends of the ministry. The Assembly know well ... that the law of patronage has been considered as no small grievance to this Church, not to say as inconsistent with our Union settlement; and we find it declared, Act 25th of May, 1736, that it is, and has been, since the Reformation, the principle of this Church, that no minister shall be intruded into any parish contrary to the will of the congregation; and, therefore, it is seriously recommended by the said Act to all judicatories of this Church to have a due regard to the said principle.[59]

The Moderator, Patrick Cuming, for many years the Kirk's 'fixer', 'earnestly recommended' that the six 'consider seriously the situation they were now in' and each, 'one by one', was further given the opportunity 'of saving themselves from the displeasure of the Church.' With all six having now left the chamber, and having read again the paper given in and subscribed by them, the Assembly 'by a considerable majority' voted in favour of a '*Depose*' verdict, and further resolved that *one of the six* be deposed. The ministers from the Presbytery of Dunfermline were then re-admitted to the chamber and informed of the Assembly's resolution.

On the following day, 23 May, after Gillespie had read an ill-judged personal representation, a vote was taken on which of the six should be deposed, and, as the Act states, 'the roll being called and votes marked, it was carried, Mr Thomas Gillespie.' None of the other ministers was even censured, on the ground of the Assembly 'being desirous to mix mercy and lenity with their judgment'; and also on account of the fact that by Gillespie's deposition the Assembly 'not only have asserted the authority of this Supreme Court, but have inflicted upon him a censure adequate to repeated acts of disobedience adhered to tenaciously when at the bar.' The Act went on to fix the date of Richardson's admission as 'on or before' 18 June; any minister who did not attend would be suspended 'from the exercise of their offices in all Presbyteries, Synods, and General Assemblies' (excepting their own Sessions).[60]

Thus was perpetrated possibly the most unjust travesty on the part of any court of the Church of Scotland in the eighteenth century. When Patrick Cuming addressed the Assembly in his closing speech he called it the case which had 'engaged the attention of the whole Church, *viz.* the disobedience of the Presbytery of Dunfermline to the orders of the General Assembly.' 'Something', Cuming insisted, 'had to be done to maintain the authority of the Church':

> We are ministers of the Gospel of Christ, – we are also ministers of a Church established by law, but a subordination of judicatories as established by law. If this is not preserved, we give up our constitution, and the legal advantages of it – we, ourselves, abandon that right we have by the articles of the Union. Far am I from thinking that every difference in judgment destroys that subordination; but what signify acts if they are not executed, and how can there be any government, if there is no last resource, and what must follow, but a dissolution of this frame of government, which will make it necessary that another be established, for neither can we ourselves endure anarchy, nor will the civil government suffer it to continue long.[61]

To paraphrase Cuming's words crudely, we have averted an unprecedented crisis in the manner in which we govern ourselves; had we not acted as we did we would have run the risk of the destruction of our entire constitution, leaving the church wide open to future control by the state. Robert Paton and his *ad hoc* committee of 1751 could not have put it better. But Cuming was defending the indefensible.

Poor Gillespie never set foot again in his church at Carnock after the sentence of deposition was passed on him. For a time he conducted services in the open air, before a meeting-house was opened in Dunfermline where he and his supporters could worship. In October 1761 Gillespie and 'the two other ministers called Thomas' – Thomas Boston the younger, minister at Jedburgh and Thomas Colier of Colinsburgh, Fife – founded the Presbytery of Relief ('for the relief of Christians oppressed in their church privileges'),[62] with an elder from each of their Kirk Sessions. They were joined four years later by James Baine whom Gillespie appointed minister of the new Relief congregation in Edinburgh. Baine had been Witherspoon's colleague (though never his supporter) in Paisley where, prior to his desertion in 1766, he had occupied the pulpit of the High Church as its first minister. Much later, in 1770, Baine published *The Case of the Reverend Thomas Gillespie reviewed*. The sub-title, 'In a Letter to the Reverend Dr W—R.', is explained by the fact that Baine appears to blame William Robertson for failing to use his undoubted influence to promote the case for Gillespie's reponement, a move which failed and was (in Carlyle's words) 'never repeated'.

Pulpit ideas of patronage

1 Ebenezer Erskine: an Original Seceder's view of patronage

Without doubt it was on account of patronage that the 'original secession' was enforced in 1733, to the acute discomfiture of the Church of Scotland.[63] Following the literal walk-out of Ebenezer Erskine and three others from the established Church – and especially in the wake of their subsequent deposition by the General Assembly in 1740 – seceding churches and congregations expanded rapidly as their popular appeal grew in both urban and rural locations, even though there is no means of calibrating the claim of several beleaguered Kirk ministers that 'many' later returned to the fold.[64]

The original seceders were without doubt the most vocal and unambiguous in their dismissal of patronage as an act of blasphemy and evil, a view put across in no uncertain terms by Ebenezer Erskine in two sermons published together in a single pamphlet, *The Government upon Christ's Shoulder*, preached at Stirling on 4 June 1732 and *The Stone rejected by the Builders, exalted as the Head-Stone of the Corner*, which he preached at Perth to the Synod of Perth and Stirling on 10 October, as its newly elected Moderator.

It was his October sermon that provoked complaints to the Synod which, on a tiny majority, resolved to rebuke Erskine. With others, he appealed to the 1733 General Assembly against the decision. The Assembly, however, confirmed the Synod resolution and admonished Erskine. In due process, the Commission of Assembly moved to a 'higher censure', but only by the casting vote of the Moderator. The outcome of this draconian measure was effectively to release Erskine, with three other supporting ministers, from their charges, all four of which were then declared vacant. The four ministers protested and, at the same time, an additional protest was given in by Gabriel Wilson, the minister of Maxton, and six others. In December 1733 the 'Associate Presbytery' was proclaimed and early in the following year there was published in its name the document that became its manifesto, *A Testimony to the Doctrine, Worship, Government and Discipline of the Church of Scotland*, updated in 1736 as the *Act, Declaration and Testimony*.

It is not difficult to grasp why members of the Synod were shocked by Erskine's words on patronage. But first he clarifies what is meant by a minister's 'Call':

> God's Call consists, in his qualifying a man for the work, and inspiring him with a holy zeal and desire, to employ these qualifications for the glory of God and the good of his church. [65]

And who are the proper agents of the 'Call'?

> The Call of the Church lies in the free choice and election of the Christian people. The promise of conduct and counsel in the choice of men that are to build the church is not made to patrons, heritors, or any other particular set of men, but to the church, the body of Christ, to whom apostles, prophets, evangelists, pastors and teachers are given. ... And shall we suppose that ever God granted to any set of men, patrons, heritors, elders, or whatever they be, a power to impose servants on his family, without their consent, being the freest society in the world? [66]

Erskine then resorts to recent history to prove his point. The Toleration Act passed by the government of Queen Anne led to 'an almost boundless toleration of all errors in doctrine and corruptions in worship'. At the same time, Christ's authority 'was invaded by the act restoring patronages, whereby power is given to a malignant lord or laird to present a man, to take the charge of precious souls, who has perhaps no more concern about their salvation than the great *Turk*.'

He reserves his fiercest comments, however, for an act of Assembly passed in the same year as his sermons (1732) which, despite a flagrant violation of the customary procedures in the face of sustained opposition from the lower courts of the church, was allowed safe passage to the dismay of Erskine and his supporters: [67]

And is it not matter of lamentation to see some of the judicatories of this church, whose province it is to contend for the sovereignty of Christ and the rights of his subjects, falling in with patrons and heritors of the nation, in opposition to the known rights of the Christian people, to elect and choose their own pastors? How are the rights of the Lord's people invaded and trod upon by violent settlements, up and down the land? ... A cry and complaint came in before the bar of the last assembly for relief, and redress of these and many other grievances, both from ministers and people; but instead of a due regard had thereto, an act is past confining the power of election unto heritors and elders, whereby a new wound is given to the prerogative of Christ, and the privileges of his subjects. ... I am firmly persuaded, that if a timely remedy be not provided, this act will very soon terminate in the overthrow of the church of *Scotland*, and of a faithful ministry therein, in regard, that the power of electing ministers, is thereby principally lodged in the hands of a set of men, who are generally disaffected to the power of godliness, to the doctrine, discipline, worship and government of this church, as well as to the government of our gracious sovereign King *George,* and the protestant succession in his family.[68]

The Assembly subsequently took the unusual step of publishing its reasons for deciding in favour of these 'highest censures' and at the same time used the opportunity of detailing those parts of Erskine's sermon to which they had taken particular exception.

2 George Logan: an early Moderate voice on patronage and secession [69]

Throughout the eighteenth century and later it was traditional that each General Assembly was inaugurated by a speech of the High Commissioner and a sermon preached by the Moderator of the preceding year. In 1741 it fell to George Logan, since 1732 minister of Trinity parish in Edinburgh, to preach that opening sermon which, in view of the dramatic proceedings of 1740 (the deposition of the Erskines and six others), the well-known scholarly abilities of the preacher and, last but not least, his staunch Whig-Presbyterian sympathies, would in all probability have been awaited with eager anticipation. In that regard Logan did not disappoint his distinguished congregation. A prolific author and pamphleteer, he had published anonymously several pamphlets specifically on the patronage issue, including *A Modest and Humble Inquiry concerning the Right and Power of Electing and Calling Ministers to Vacant Churches* (1732),[70] with two sequels, and *An Overture for a Right Constitution of the General Assembly* (1736).

Predictably dedicated to the High Commissioner (the Earl of Leven) Logan's text was from the first *Epistle of John* iv:1: '*Beloved, believe not every Spirit, but try the Spirits, whether they are of God; because many false Prophets have gone out into the World.* 'In the matter of religion', he says, 'we are not to rely on the sole testimony, and the bare word of any man, or any Society of Men', the allusion to the seceders' *Act and Testimony* being obvious. He refers to 'some who highly value themselves for being free-thinkers', among them Epicurus and 'Mr Hobbs'.

> A freedom of thinking, rightly stated, belongs to every man: and no power upon Earth can call him to account for his opinions, provided he keeps them to himself; but I cannot think, for any thing that have seen advanced yet by these gentlemen, that they should have an unbounded Liberty of venting them, or that there should be an unrestrained Liberty of the Press, to spread blasphemous Doctrines, destructive of all Religion ... .[71]

It is not until much later in his sermon, however, that Logan deals specifically with the problem of schism. He recalls the words of the first *Epistle of John*, this time from chapter 2, verse 19: *'Many false Prophets are gone out in to the world'*, and interprets the passage to refer to a 'schism, and unwarrantable separation from the [early] church'. This brings him to the same issue in the setting of the contemporary Church of Scotland:

> This is the situation, with respect to our Church: some had deserted her Communion on frivolous pretences, and associated themselves into a *Junto* of their own; these persons, in their publick Discourses, have falsely aspersed the Judicatures, and Ministers of the Church, and are so bold as to libel our Rulers in the State; and because of these things, and their manifold irregular practices, the General Assembly, after using all methods for reclaiming them, without any success, did depose them.[72]

But, he goes on, it is worse than that. Comparing the activities of the seceders with the missionary ways of the 'Church of Rome' when they sent 'emissaries and trafficking priests to Protestant countries to seduce the people', so, now

> We have a set of itinerant and wandering unauthorized Preachers among us, who go out into the World, intruding into peaceable Parishes, far and near, to withdraw people from the Communion of this Church, and join theirs, by declaring for their *Act* and *Testimony*, which is a *Farrago* of falsehoods and misrepresentations.[73]

Logan later admits that the established Church has to learn lessons from the pain of the secession. In particular, the 'administration and management' of the Church is gradually enfeebling it, such that the manner in which the law of patronage works in practice is in need of reform:

> We meet in General Assemblies, we make Acts, and pass Sentences, but due care is not taken to put them in execution: Pray, what does a power of legislation signify and avail, if there is no executive power: without this, Government cannot be kept up, but confusion will be introduced, and disobedience to the Church will be encouraged: some inferior judicatures will not put in execution the commands of the superior, nay, of the supreme court of the church: And in the settling of parishes, tho' candidates for the ministry are persons every way well-qualified; yet if they shall declare their willingness to accept of a presentation, the mere Will of the People, without assigning any reason for their opposition, is regarded; and the Authority of a National Assembly, the last resort, is despised, and the subordination of judicatures is overturn'd. In civil courts this can never be done, unless the officers, who are recusants, resign and give up their offices.[74]

George Logan's description of the mess the Church had got itself into over patronage is surely one of the most eloquent statements of the problem in any sermon on the subject:

> All things in religion are not of equal importance; but the bigots lay great stress upon little things and disputable points that are very remote from the foundation, and of no consequence to the good of souls: And yet our keenest and most fierce contests are about minute things; these hot and warm controversies are like the flinging of stones into smooth waters, which form great circles; they produce hatred, envy, anger, malice and revenge ... Our debates and strifes about triffles, and about things that cannot make us

better Christians here, nor promote our happiness hereafter, expose us to the contempt and scoffs of the atheist, the sceptick and profane.[75]

Was this to be the lasting impression of a church under siege? Was Logan's version the authentic story of the Kirk in the eighteenth century? Or, was it more of a caricature of the true situation? It should be remembered that the man who preached the censure had himself been Moderator, *primus inter pares*, in the Assembly of 1740, the Assembly that will always bear the stigma of having finally deposed its own ministers for venturing to go their own way.

Logan concludes his sermon with an attack on what he terms 'the *Spirit of Popularity*'. The message that comes across is once more one of concern about the potential capacity of the lower classes to make trouble for the established church, rather than one founded on simply attitudinising their role. But, first, he clarifies what he does not intend by 'a publick spirit':

> When I recommend a publick spirit, I am not for private persons going beyond the sphere of their proper station ... Some mechanicks and tradesmen, and others of the meanest stations, as herds and servants, who are of low knowledge, and have no authority, are become very pragmatical and assuming [*Note by RLC:* He means they have opinions to express as members of congregations and do so.], and instead of submitting to their teachers in the church, and their rulers in the State, presume to dictate and prescribe rules for church-management and State policy.[76]

The cultivation by ministers of popularity – a practice, he implies, openly indulged in by seceding ministers – is to be deplored:

> Popularity in a minister, as it signifies the teaching of the people in a plain stile, and an easy method, adapted to their capacities, and in a serious and moving manner, is highly commendable; But the affectation of the applause of the vulgar, by humouring them in their *Nostrums*, in their singular and wild fancies, should be avoided by us, as a thing very unbecoming and vastly below us ... If we humour them to gain a following after ourselves, to the prejudice of the ministerial labours of our brethren, we act a very unbrotherly part; since we should strengthen one another's hands in the work of the ministry. Some that have acted a part this way, to have a following, if they go not all the lengths that the people would have them to go, are in danger of losing them; and there are many instances of this among us, and many ministers now see their folly, when they cannot help it; now they are as little in the esteem of the crowd as ever they were admitted by them. ... If we are guided and steered by the unconstant and giddy multitude, we shall never be able to keep a good conscience or act an upright part ... .[77]

Last of all, Logan insists we all need to be fully aware of what this secession has really been about and what it has meant to the Church of Scotland. The main point, he concludes, is that it is *not all bad* –

> By Schism I do not mean a simple Secession, and a quiet withdrawing from a church, without making any head against her; but positively, I understand such a withdrawing and separating from a church, as to make up an opposite body, and set up a church against a church, and *Altar against Altar*, when in this church from which the separation is made,

there is no heresy in doctrine, no idolatry or superstition in worship, and no spiritual tyranny in government and discipline; from a church with which Christ Jesus, the Head, hath Communion, where the Word of Salvation is truly held forth.[78]

There is, in other words, a *way back*.

3 John Erskine: patronage according to an 'enlightened evangelical'

Few Scottish ministers had a more intuitive personal insight into the way patronage actually played out in real situations than the Reverend Dr John Erskine, minister of Old Greyfriars, Edinburgh, from 1767 until his death in 1803. Erskine was one of the best-loved figures in the church in his day and, as the 'enlightened evangelical',[79] could be said to have been untroubled by factional boundaries, without ever denying their existence. For five years Erskine had been minister of Culross in Fife until his translation to New Greyfriars in 1758. Culross is six miles from the estates and parishes of Carnock and Torryburn, which, in turn, are less than three miles from each other. All three parishes were located in the Presbytery of Dunfermline. In 1700, at a judicial sale, Erskine's grandfather, Colonel John Erskine, had purchased most of the estates belonging to the Earls of Kincardine, including the lands of Carnock. On the death of Colonel Erskine in 1743 his eldest surviving son, known as John Erskine 'of Carnock', later advocate and professor of the law of Scotland in the University of Edinburgh, inherited the lands of Carnock and Culross. His only son by his first marriage was John Erskine who, on the professor's death in 1768, succeeded to his father's estates. Thus, it came about that Dr Erskine, Kirk minister, himself became patron of these two parishes – and would have been patron of a third, Culross (his own former charge), if it had not been that his father's Will had conveyed it (with the parishes of Port of Menteith, Kippen and Tulliallan) to John's half-brother, James.

While still a young ordinand in his first charge at Kirkintilloch, a few miles north-east of Glasgow, John Erskine had opposed the deposition of Thomas Gillespie, an action which, with his lawyer's eye,[80] he would always regard as manifestly unjust. In a synodical sermon entitled *The Qualifications Necessary for Teachers of Christianity* (1750), preached in Glasgow on 2 October that year, Erskine has this to say on the responsibilities of a patron:

> Patrons ... are bound to pay a sacred regard to the trust vested in them; and if they exercise their legal right, should first carefully consider what are the qualifications of the person they present to a benefice; otherwise the souls, that may be lost by a bad nomination, will be required at their hands, by him who made and purchased these souls, and in whose sight they are of inestimable value.[81]

He had delivered the sermon just as the Inverkeithing affair was getting off the ground, following the death of the incumbent in the previous year and the subsequent presentation of Andrew Richardson in May 1750.

Years later, on 8 November 1763, Erskine had preached another synodical sermon, this time in Edinburgh, to which he gave the title *Ministers of the Gospel Cautioned against Giving Offence* (published in 1764). This time he is considerably more discursive in his thoughts on patronage and the pitfalls awaiting the injudicious patron:

> There is one thing more in our ordinations, which, I think, merits our serious attention; and that is, the solemnly giving to one, in the name of Jesus, the charge of a congregation unwilling to submit to him, and among whom there is no probability of his usefulness.[82]

There can be little doubt that Erskine has the fiasco of Inverkeithing in mind when he continues:

> If an inoffensive ministry is thus important, how careful should patrons be to present, and parishes still enjoying the important privilege of election, to call none to the pastoral office, who may be in danger of giving offence by their weak abilities, unsound principles, or dissolute lives! – And how foolish and criminal a part do candidates act, who hastily rush into the sacred function, ere they have laid in the necessary furniture for discharging it honourably! Is there not cause to fear, that not their character only, but religion in general, may suffer for the reproach of their youth?[83]

In 1771, while his memory of the Assembly the year before was still fresh, Erskine had contributed a preface to a short treatise by Gillespie published in Edinburgh for William Gray entitled *An Essay on the continuance of immediate revelations of facts and future events in the Christian church*. Erskine was interested in what today we might term the *paranormal* in a religious context, and he takes the opportunity to chide all those who had 'aspersed' Gillespie, those 'ill-natured whisperers and backbiters, petulant declaimers, and dastardly mean-spirited anonymous scribblers'.

John Erskine's seeming fixation with the career of Thomas Gillespie was not, therefore, confined to Gillespie's deposition, although there is no doubt that the Inverkeithing affair continued to affect him for the rest of his life. Gillespie died in January 1774. In August of that same year Erskine contributed a long preface to *A Treatise on Temptation*, an obscure unfinished tract by Gillespie not previously published. Erskine's preface is in part a condensed biography of Gillespie. But the real reason Erskine piloted the work through the press was almost certainly that its content strongly appealed personally to him; perhaps especially 'Section V' which deals with 'Temptations suited to different relations' and, more narrowly, §14, entitled *'Those concerned in chusing a minister'*. Gillespie writes in terms he of all people must have felt more acutely than most: first, on the way it is done in the established Kirk –

> [Church of Scotland] When patrons, heritors, town-counsellors, tutors or curators of minors, factors, presbyteries, or other persons whose station or office afford them weight or influence in the matter of settlement of ministers, are disposed to thrust in a man upon an unwilling and reclaiming congregation in legal establishments [the Kirk]; and Satan knows, for different reasons, such settlements will lamentably obstruct edification, hurt the interest of the gospel, and mar its success; he [Satan] endeavours to make the people drop or forbear just and regular, and necessary, as well as incumbent, opposition to the measure, by fearing them with the apprehension of the resentment of them upon whom they depend ... and by engaging proper hands, by promises, threats, and ouvert acts, that sensibly affect, to endeavour to make them give way.[84]

Then, in possibly the best statement we have of the way in which some patrons resorted to sharp practice in order to continue to control settlements in secessionist congregations, Gillespie declares:

[Secessionist congregations] In congregations voluntarily associated, and who dissent from establishments, the inveterate enemy of an evangelical ministry attempts to keep out one who is the choice of the better part of the society on scriptural grounds, and to bring in one over their belly, who should pretend to feed their souls with the enticing words of man's wisdom ... by causing them who are the especial supports of the congregation, in respect of contributing for the minister's subsistence, the keeping up of the meeting-place, and other incident and necessary charges, strenuously to oppose the serious man, to exert themselves to the utmost in behalf of the polite unevangelical preacher [a Moderate], and to threaten, if they are not complied with in the matter, they will withdraw their subscription, and prevail with their friends to do the same.[85]

4 Archibald Bruce: patronage according to an Antiburgher

Probably the most reliable source of information on dissenting attitudes towards the law of patronage in the later eighteenth century, Archibald Bruce's voice is both an original and important one. In 1778 – the precise date is not known – Bruce delivered a sermon at the opening of the Associate [Antiburgher] Synod at Edinburgh which, judging from the poor quality of typesetting, was almost certainly printed on the press he had personally acquired and set up in Whitburn.[86] The sermon is entitled *Corruptions in the Church to be Eradicated*. It is a long 'literary' sermon and was either preached over more than one service and/or the oral text was subsequently edited and much expanded for the press. Among the various corrupting evils Bruce enumerates have combined to 'encroach' upon the 'rights and liberties of the Presbyterian church', patronage is one of the most significant. Patronage, he maintains, 'has been productive of such hurtful effects', and 'may be considered as a branch or off-shoot ... springing out of ... the root of Erastianism'. As currently practised, patronage makes 'worldly power, wealth or influence, a reason for proportional pre-eminence and lordly authority over an ecclesiastical or spiritual society, to the exclusion of the free power and elective rights belonging to the members of it.' But, Bruce argues, patronage is even worse than that:

> As it is itself an abuse, so it has a direct tendency to introduce and promote other abuses. This mode of planting churches, has turned out to be a principal mean of laying them waste; of which the state of the national church of Scotland, for near a century past, is a striking proof; as this, along with the spreading of corrupt doctrine, and ecclesiastical tyranny, in conjunction with which it has made its progress, has driven the great body of serious people from her communion, and dispersed the most populous congregations in every place.[87]

Bruce has one formidable weapon in his arsenal for effectively arguing the case against the established Kirk, the same weapon that, many years before, John Witherspoon had deployed to devastating effect against the Moderates in *Ecclesiastical Characteristics*: an inventive sense of satirical humour. In two spoof assaults on the Church of Scotland he ridicules patrons and the law of patronage. First, in *The Kirkiad; or, Golden Age of the Church of Scotland* (1774) – cleverly modelled on Pope's *Dunciad*, a favourite template at that time for anyone indulging in lampoonery[88] — Bruce mocks a system that has excluded the people from the process of choosing a minister as their pastor:

> Who asks a howling grumbling pack,
> What master they'll be pleased to take?
> Who asks the simple, bleating sheep,
> What herdsman must them tend and keep?
> O who will say, 'tis reasonable,
> That the dumb tenants of the stable
> Must jointly give the man a *call*
> Who rubs them down and fills their stall? [89]

In *The Catechism Modernized and Adapted to the Meridian of Patronage and Late Improvements* (1791) Bruce entertainingly satirizes not just fawning ministers more anxious to court the attention of their patrons than of the deserving poor in their parishes, but patrons themselves whose primary concern is too often to 'secure a presentee in the full possession of his parish, the stipend, and all pertinents thereof, except the affections and the cumber of the people, according to the urgent injunctions and rules of the General Assembly'. In Bruce's imaginary catechism — like all catechisms required to be learned by heart — a question and answer session is mandatory:

Q. What doth the tenth commandment forbid?
A. All imprudent expressions of dissatisfaction with the restraints of the ministerial character and hardships of the ministerial office; despising or depreciating the Patron's gift; fretting at the opposition, contempt, or desertion of the parishioners, while the teinds and kirk-walls remain; too clamorous complaints of the dilapidated condition of manse or kirk; or immoderate and too expensive estimates for repairs, which may provoke, not only the beggarly people, but the wealthy heritors, if not also the patron.[90]

Bruce reserves his most stinging words for a system that condones ultimate sanctions on the people imposed on the authority of the patron alone. Then he goes on to give examples of the kind of punishments that match up to the consequences of incurring 'the Patron's wrath'

Q. Are mere laymen able, in the present state of the church of Scotland, to bear, without violation, the patronage laws, and the Patron's commandments, and, to conform themselves entirely to them in their full extent and perfection?
A. No mere layman if he be of the vulgar sort, is able, since the introduction of the modern church politics, and the exalting clerical power, fully to digest, or perfectly obey, the whole of these laws as they now stand, and are presently executed, but doth daily violate and execrate them in thought, word and deed.

Q. What doth every offence of this sort, (the sin of sins) deserve?
A. The Patron's wrath, and most emphatic curse and imprecations, — the infliction of civil and ecclesiastical pains, — the loss of farms, lawsuits, double taxes, fines, imprisonment, transportation on board the navy, or to Botany-bay, — judicial rebukes, suspensions,

deprivations (if in office) ab officio & beneficio, excommunications; yea, were these offenders to receive their due, they deserve to be hanged in this world, and damned in that which is to come.[91]

5 William Peebles and William McGill: antagonists in harmony over patronage

It is not their fault that these two ministers, William Peebles, *Auld Licht* minister at Newton-upon-Ayr for an incredible 46 years, and the more celebrated William McGill, *New Licht* minister of the second charge of Ayr parish (for a mere 39 years), are best remembered today as real-life characters, partnered together antithetically in three well-known poems of Robert Burns: *The Twa Herds*, *The Holy Fair* and *The Kirk's Alarm*.[92] We know from these poems and from other sources that Burns respected McGill but never missed an opportunity of ridiculing Peebles, whose lack of 'common sense' irked him.[93] Yet each minister had a part to play, albeit a minor role, in the context of pulpit censure of church patronage in late eighteenth-century Ayrshire. Despite their different affiliations and theologies, their views seem to have coincided in their professed scepticism towards the view that the settlement of ministers by the will of the parish would represent any improvement on existing procedures enforced by the law of patronage.

The Peebles-McGill spat of 1788 is in some ways a re-run of the much earlier slanging match between two other Ayrshire ministers, John Adam of Kilbride and Alexander Fergusson of Kilwinning, the so-called 'Kilwinning heresy', discussed in chapter 5. These two disputes mirror each other remarkably closely, the later controversy opening up most of the same old wounds that Adam and Fergusson had inflicted on each another more than twenty years before. These issues, of course, embraced not just patronage, but also, at least as seriously, the secession controversy, ministerial subscription to the Confession of Faith, and key doctrinal concerns including the doctrine of Christ's 'substitution' or atonement.

All three of the sermons noted here were preached to mark the centenary of the Glorious Revolution and were delivered on the same day, 5 November 1788, the day set aside by the General Assembly that year 'as a day of solemn thanksgiving to Almighty God, for the enjoyment of those inestimable blessings for a century past, and of earnest supplication for their continuance to the latest generations'. None has anything particularly new to say on the subject of patronage. All three sermons, indeed, are egregiously undistinguished. The two sermons by Peebles, for example – 'not intended for publication', but (or so he tells us in the prefatory 'Advertisement'), having been 'solicited by many' to publish them, he has 'reluctantly yielded to their solicitations' to do so – are, it must be said, entirely worthy of the author of *An Ode to Liberty*, a piece of doggerel Peebles includes to bulk up his pamphlet, ironically printed and published by John Wilson of Kilmarnock, the man who had brought out the Kilmarnock Edition of Burns's poems to unprecedented acclaim just three years before. This is the poem Burns mercilessly mocks in *The Kirk's Alarm*, containing the notorious footnote by Burns himself.[94] On patronage, 'shaul' ['shallow'] Peebles has this to say:

> ... this mode of settling ministers is in direct opposition to the word of God, to the Revolution settlement, to the articles of Union, and to our civil and religious liberties. This is acknowledged to be a grievance by almost every description of men in this kingdom, who unite in expressing an earnest desire that some redress was obtained.*[95]

Peebles' starred reference is an injunction to the reader to consult *Tracts on Patronage*, 'published by the late Mr. Randall of Stirling', whose 'treatise on patronage throws more light on that subject than any that has yet been published.'[96] This is difficult to substantiate since Randall's book is in the main an anthology of writings on the subject by prominent persons who had published their views on patronage, including Francis Hutcheson, Sir David Dalrymple and Philip Doddridge. It is probable, on the other hand, that the longest piece in the anthology by far is by Randall himself, *A candid inquiry into the constitution of the church of Scotland*. So what would Peebles propose to replace the patronage system to settle vacant charges? He seems positively luke-warm on the merits of 'popular election', as practised outside the established Church:

> Some *professed friends* of this church [he probably means the Relief Church] have declared for *popular* election – a mode of settlement which does not meet the views and sentiments of the most judicious: others, with a greater degree of reason, have contended for the restoration of the act 1690, as that to which we have a constitutional right.[97]

In the 'Advertisement' prefacing his sermon, William McGill similarly justifies his decision to publish his sermon. In his case, he did so solely 'that the Public may judge whether one can be a loyal subject, and a true member of this church, whose religious sentiments differ widely' from those of his colleague and rival. James Wodrow, the minister of Stevenston in Ayrshire, wrote (on 8 March 1789) to Samuel Kenrick that McGill's riposte had astonished him: it was a 'mixture of mildness and keenness which cuts like a razor ... I had no conception that the Dr had such talents for controversy'.[98]

Predictably, McGill shares his distaste for popular involvement in the presentation of ministers to a vacant charge, but goes much further than Peebles. He contends that 'our religious liberty is often abused by unjustifiable schisms and separations, as well as by the petulance of faction; and yet God forbid it should be abridged on account of these abuses.' In a footnote he takes Peebles to task for implying that Moderates holding sway (with whom, of course, he himself identifies) did not pursue vigorously enough the repeal of the law on patronage which had been interpreted as 'a warrantable ground of separation from the church.' Turning to the specific role of 'the people' in ministerial settlements McGill states:

> There is no instance wherein mobs are more likely to arise in our country, than on account of religion; and yet there is no instance in which they can appear with a worse grace, since being the subversion of all civil order, they must be still more incompatible with religion. They frequently rise in opposition to the settlement of ministers, who come in by presentations, as if the law of patronage were the most intolerable grievance, and might justly be opposed by every means possible, right or wrong. Yet it is a well known fact, that the law of patronage was in force at the period we commemorate, as it had been in former times; and it was not mentioned among the grievances of the nation, at a time when men of ability were appointed to state those grievances at full length.[99]

The sermon in which these words appear was published in the year of the outbreak of the French Revolution. Effectively McGill is warning that to entrust patronage to the will of the people is to endanger popular liberty.

McGill attaches an 'Appendix' to his pamphlet which, at thirty pages, dwarfs his sermon of a mere nineteen pages. The appendix is a wearisome catalogue of hits on Peebles' sermon point-by-point, with much the greater effort on his part concentrated on a rejection of the Newton-upon-Ayr minister's condemnation of the modern practice of qualifying (or even excluding) parts of ministerial subscription to the Westminster Confession of Faith – the issue that had, of course, led to the so-called 'Kilwinning heresy' in a previous generation. The dispute between the pair now turns highly personal. Referring to himself as 'a minister of the gospel, of the same communion', and 'of longer standing in the church' and 'a near neighbour', McGill attacks Peebles for his aspersions on Moderatism, describing his language as an 'insult offered to the whole moderate part of the church of Scotland, which, blessed be God, has generally been the majority, at least in public decisions, for many years past.'

In the second of his commemoration day sermons Peebles extends his criticism of *New Licht* theology and, in the process, reveals himself as an enthusiastic disciple of Dr Thomas Walker, hardline Popular party minister at Dundonald for 48 years until his death in 1780 (and John Witherspoon's uncle). Citing Walker's *Vindication* (1774),[100] Peebles launches a fierce assault on modernist tendencies, some of which, he is in little doubt, are clearly heretical. Without naming names, he is referring in the main to McGill's provocative *A Practical Essay on the Death of Jesus Christ* (1786), with its patently Socinian treatment of key areas of Presbyterian doctrine, including most notably the doctrine of 'Christ's *substitution*' – the doctrine of the atonement, that maintains that Christ died as a 'substitute' for mankind.[101] McGill's views on the subject would prove just one of the bases upon which he would be accused (and, in the event, absolved) of heresy.[102] Of course, Peebles would have been well aware of parallel attacks on McGill from secessionist ministers – naming the culprits for all the world to take note – most notably John Jamieson in *Socinianism Unmasked* (1787/1790)[103] and James Moir in *A distinct and impartial account* (1790). Far from moribund, the patronage problem was about to enter a new phase.

John Witherspoon, painted in the year of his death, 1794, by Rembrandt Peale, after Charles Willson Peale, National Portrait Gallery, Smithsonian Institution, Washington, DC.

2

Profaneness

There is no nation of which history hath preserved us any account, but, in their proverbial sayings, which are the product of time, we find a warning against the infection of corrupt society.
Reverend John Witherspoon, Seasonable Advice to Young Persons (1762), WJW, 2, 488.

It is hoped, there are few or no clergymen in the Church of Scotland who could be capable of such a behaviour as the defender has been convicted of towards these unfortunate gentlemen, the petitioners.
Charles Hay (later Lord Newton) advocate, printed Petition of John Snodgrass Sheriff-clerk of Paisley [five further names follow], dated 25 November 1775, 14.

Key author and sermon

Reverend Dr John Witherspoon (1723-94), minister of Beith, (1745-57); the Laigh Church, Paisley (1757-68); President of the College of New Jersey (1768-94); 'signer' of the Declaration of American Independence (1776)

Seasonable Advice to Young Persons: a Sermon on Psalm i. I. Preached in the Laigh Church of Paisley, On Sabbath, Feb. 21st, 1762. To which is prefixed, An Authentic Narrative of the disorderly and riotous Meeting, on the Night before the Celebration of the Lord's Supper in that Place, which gave occasion to the Discourse.
Glasgow: Robert Urie, MDCCLXII [1762]

Among his other talents as writer and satirist,[1] John Witherspoon, an undisputed leader of the Popular party in the Church of Scotland from the date of publication of Ecclesiastical Characteristics *(1753)* until his departure for America *(1768)*, was one of the most powerful preachers of his generation. In the fledgling United States he proceeded to add substantially to his reputation in that particular regard with his great Princeton discourses, especially the sermon he preached on the eve of the birth of the nation, 'The Dominion of Providence over the Passions of Men' *(1776)*.

The sermon forming the core of this chapter is not, however, remembered for any intrinsic merit but for its key importance within the literature of pulpit censure. Witherspoon used his sermon as a means of publicising a scandal that had recently taken place within his parish, involving seven men of repute in the town and which, according to his judgment, seriously offended against the church's laws on 'profaneness'. What drove the minister to publish it was the opportunity to add a preface to the published version, naming the names and occupations of those he accused, thereby bringing the scandal at the core of the dispute into the public domain. He had not bargained, however, for the men he accused seeking recompense at law through a civil action against him in the Court of Session. Unfortunately for him, his pursuers were led by a clever lawyer – a 'writer' in Paisley – by name of John Snodgrass. The legal process, which the minister lost, would drag on for fourteen years, long after Witherspoon had settled with his family into a new life and career in Princeton, New Jersey. His unfortunate experience at the bar of the supreme civil court, together with the aggressive hostility he had encountered from the preponderance of Moderate clergy in his own Presbytery, probably influenced his decision to leave Scotland for good.

The crime of 'profaneness'

Before describing the specific circumstances that gave rise to John Witherspoon's sermon, provoking astonishing consequences, it is important to consider the legal status of the crime of 'profaneness' as understood in Witherspoon's day. First, however, it should be noted that Witherspoon throughout his sermon is at pains to express what *technically* he is accusing his offenders of having perpetrated, and, equally, it is clear, by exclusion, what they are not held to have done. It was never in the minister's mind to accuse them of the statutory crime of blasphemy. Although 'blasphemy' and 'profaneness' are often bracketed together by the old Scottish jurists the terms Witherspoon uses to describe their offence range from substantives like 'profanity', 'depravity', 'evil', 'vice', proof of 'enmity to God', and such like, to 'treating things sacred with scorn', 'scoffing at sacred things' and 'profane scorn'. Those he alleged were responsible for the crime of which they are accused he calls 'profane scorners', 'profligates' and, on occasion, simply 'sinners'. Elsewhere[2] I have pointed out that the crime, therefore, that Witherspoon is accusing the men of having committed – 'profaneness' or 'profanity' – is not to be confused with the altogether more serious crime of blasphemy as clarified in an Act of Parliament of 1661, the punishment for which in the later seventeenth-century was death.[3]

Doubtless Witherspoon would also have had in mind that as recently as 1753 the Commission of the General Assembly in an 'Act and Warning against Profaneness and Immorality' had taken action to ensure that ministers and elders 'take heed to themselves' in order that they might 'restrain' and 'suppress', in the face of the 'declining state of religion within this Church and land', the 'horrid profanation of the Lord's Day' by 'unnecessary visits and travelling, frequenting taverns, idleness, or people's attending chiefly to their worldly affairs'. The Act further 'earnestly recommended'

> to all judges and magistrates, in this weighty matter to act as the minister of God, by being a terror to such evil-doers; and strictly enjoin Presbyteries within this Church to exert the powers with which they are invested, and to apply to those in civil authority for correcting such gross enormities: and they particularly expect from the elders of this Church, – those in a special manner of distinction and authority, – that they will employ the whole weight of their interest and example, for restraining and suppressing such scandalous licentiousness, profanity, and impiety.[4]

At the same time, it was never Witherspoon's design to pursue in a civil court the men he considered guilty of profanity, or even, it seems, to have them reported to the magistrate. Hume records just one such action of profanation of the sabbath brought against an individual 'within the present century' (he was writing in 1797).[5] Apart from the cost and other difficulties associated with such an extreme ploy, he was a minister of the gospel and, as such, it was his first duty to see that they were reported to and dealt with by the customary judicatures of the church: that meant, first and foremost, the kirk session, (where he almost certainly expected the incident to be settled once and for all) but if for any reason that faltered, at the hands of the higher court, the Presbytery of Paisley. As his authority for following the course of action he took, Witherspoon invoked the Form of Process of 1707, or, to give it its proper title, the *Act approving a Form of Process in the Judicatures of the Church with relation to Scandals and Censures*,[6] a 'blanket' act of the General Assembly of that year confirming and subsuming cognate legislation of 1694 [13 Act] and 1697 [11 Act]. As we shall see, however, it took an expert in church law, the advocate Andrew Crosbie, and attorney for the Snodgrass faction – Crosbie had frequently attended Assembly sittings as a lay commissioner – to point out that the Form of Process counselled both ministers and ecclesiastical 'judicatories' to have recourse to 'private admonition [rather] than by public process' in treating such offences.

By contrast, the only other case examined in this study involving a minister against whom an action was begun in the Court of Session instigated by men he had accused from his pulpit of a punishable civil crime – the 'Dunfermline case' (see chapter 3) – ended with the minister losing the action, then determinedly embarking on an appeal to the House of Lords. On further reflection, and after obtaining *via* his lawyers informal advice from the Lord Chancellor, Edward Thurlow, the minister was persuaded (probably on grounds of cost) to drop his appeal.

The sermon *Seasonable Advice to Young Persons* [7]

The first the Laigh Church congregation got to hear of a 'late riotous meeting' having occurred in their parish in downtown Paisley was when their minister climbed into his pulpit on Sunday February 21, 1762, two full weeks after the event that had moved him to compose his sermon that morning. His text gave no clue of the extraordinary circumstances that lay behind it: it was from the first verse of Psalm I – *'Blessed is the man that walketh not in the counsel of the ungodly, nor standeth in the way of sinners, nor sitteth in the seat of the scornful.'* Witherspoon's sermon began conventionally enough. Its general theme, befitting the religious culture of an orthodox Evangelical, was mortal sin, sin which 'bears so much sway in human characters and action' and has remained essentially unchanged from Biblical times to the present age.

Witherspoon begins by lecturing the congregation on the text,[8] declaring that there is a 'three-fold gradation' within the concept of sin, illustrating the idea as it relates to the author of the Psalms, whether he was David, Ezra or 'some other after the captivity.' He then leads his congregation through each of these stages: *first of all*, there is the *'infectious nature of sin'*. –

> There is no nation of which history hath preserved us any account, but, in their proverbial sayings, which are the product of time, we find a warning against the infection of corrupt society.

He illustrates his point by reference to a number of metaphors affecting sin and the young: *first*, all by nature are 'prone to sin'. Just as the husbandman finds it difficult to restrain weeds, but if he applies himself with 'encouragement and cultivation', what 'an enormous product' he can expect, so, if parents neglect to 'restrain the irregularities of their children,' 'what wickedness may they not arrive at, if they are delivered over to schools of profanity'.

Secondly, young persons are 'ignorant and unsuspicious'; they are 'strangers to the world'. Sin is often clothed 'in a decent garb' and, as a result, young persons unsuspectingly fall prey to 'sensuality and intemperance'. They may not appreciate it at the time, but too often in the eyes and ears of the young

> Sensuality and intemperance is social affection, and good fellowship: filthy obscene conversation is but harmless mirth and freedom: anger and resentment are but honour, resolution, and dignity of mind. In short, the whole tenor and strain of fashionable conversation is often little else than a strong illusion put upon the mind, to pervert the dictates of reason, and evade the reproofs of conscience.[9]

Thirdly, the preacher turns to the 'baiting', as he puts it, of vice with pleasure, 'of which young persons are peculiarly sensible'. 'One of the first and most important lessons, which parents and guardians must teach them, is moderation and restraint'. 'Associating with the profane' can breed 'indulgence', and 'inspire them with an abhorrence of confinement and rule'. He says he is not persuaded by the argument that a parental regime based on 'rigour' often leads to 'the most vicious and abandoned course of life'. He prefers to believe that 'the children of pious parents, who are betrayed into vicious courses, are almost always such as have been most early removed from their immediate inspection'.

Fourthly, Witherspoon briefly introduces a new theme and gives notice of his intention to develop it more fully later in the sermon: the 'danger of corrupt society to young persons' occurring on account of 'their being exposed to ridicule and scorn', which is 'of all other trials hardest for them to bear.' After sin's *'infectious nature'* there is next to be reckoned with its *'hardening nature'*. Having introduced scriptural references to illustrate what Witherspoon calls the 'insensible progress' of sin, he turns to the 'strength and power of inveterate habit':

> It is easy to see every day, the violent attachment men have to employments and pleasures, however trifling in themselves, to which they have been long accustomed. But it is greatest of all in sinful habits, because in them the force of custom is added to the original strength of natural corruption.[10]

The preacher develops his argument by observing the extent to which 'habit and example together operate to the improvement and perfection of guilt, in large and populous cities.' Here, with Glasgow and Edinburgh in mind – Witherspoon was a regular and frequent visitor to both cities – he is doubtless recollecting from his own personal experience scenes he would often have witnessed, describing what he saw as representative of 'a degree of wickedness of every sort, as it is mortifying to think that human nature should be capable of'. He singles out the moral plight of the individual visiting these places from time to time from the surrounding countryside and falls an easy prey to the vice and depravity on offer. It is one of the most stirring passages of his sermon:

> And what pity is it, that there should be found some, who, during their occasional residence in places of great resort, lay down their innocence, instead of their rusticity; and bring home no other accomplishment but an insolence and boldness of countenance, in the commission of sin? That instructed in the principles, as well as habituated to the practice of impiety, they are not content with doing evil, but discover an incredible industry and assiduity in deceiving and seducing others?[11]

And, in what would become a favourite theme of his (at least, in the course of his Scottish career), Witherspoon cannot resist introducing at this point an attack on the malign influence of exposure on the part of the young to 'drinking in the poison of infidel writings':[12]

> And shall I not add, what pity is it, that some, instead of improving and adorning their minds by application to study, or storing them with useful knowledge, do more than lose their time, by drinking in the poison of infidel writings? Instead of fitting themselves to discharge the duties of public or private life, with propriety and dignity, they only acquire the unhappy talent of setting their minds at ease in the commission of sin, and make large additions to their own natural depravity of heart.[13]

Almost thirteen years later these two quotations from his sermon were judged memorable enough to be cited *verbatim* against the Paisley minister in the Court of Session by prosecuting counsel (Charles Hay, later Lord Newton), in his printed *Petition* on behalf of Witherspoon's pursuers dated 25 November 1775.[14] His defence counsel, on the other hand (David Dalrymple, later Lord Westhall), would have none of it, asserting that in uttering those words the preacher 'had nothing personal in view'.[15]

Witherspoon defines the pinnacle of his three gradations of sin as 'of the most criminal and the most pernicious character, *viz.* That of the scornful who are bold enough to treat things serious and scared, with derision.' It is now crystal-clear what Witherspoon is really about in this sermon. He is preparing his listeners for the shock of realisation that something serious has occurred within their own parish; that what took place a fortnight previously – and may even have involved some of their own number, certain to have involved persons from widely respected families in the community – was hardly something trifling, but one of the gravest offences it is possible to commit in the sight of God.

He maintains that 'one of the first principles of all religion is reverence for the Deity, and for every thing that hath a visible relation to him.' And he proceeds to castigate those who, as 'scoffers' and 'scorners', ridicule religion:

> There is a remarkable difference between sins of this kind, and many other sins which are, notwithstanding, very heinous and aggravated in the sight of God. Into many other sins of a very gross nature, a man may be hurried by the violence of passion, or betrayed by the suddenness of temptation; but, if I mistake not, scorn of things sacred must always be a deliberate crime: the sin cannot be committed without a good deal of composure and presence of mind: reason is not over-borne, as in other cases, by appetite; but reason

itself (if the perverted gift of God in such persons may be called so) is principal in the guilt. A scorner is never tempted, properly speaking, but by these acts and exercises of religion, which should excite the veneration of all, and do excite the veneration of many, not excepting some of the most profligate.[16]

Perversely, these 'profane persons' actually find pleasure in their 'impiety'. Not just that, however, they deliberately set out to ensnare and corrupt others who unwisely associate with them; especially they prey upon the young and take advantage everywhere of 'human infirmity':

> It will not be improper here to observe, that one great reason why scorn and ridicule is so hurtful to religion, is, that it attacks things sacred through the medium of human weakness. True piety and virtue is in itself so venerable an object, that it is not possible to render it ridiculous, but by misrepresentation: however, as it is always, in this world, attended with human infirmity, this affords a handle to profane persons to load it with reproach.[17]

How, then should one deal with a sin of this magnitude – the sin of *profaneness*? 'I do not mean by this', says Witherspoon

> to plead for approbation, or even indulgence, to any indecency, by which folly or vanity may abuse or disgrace the worship of God: far from it. I think every thing of that kind ought to be reproved with severity, and opposed with resolution: but I contend, that it is infinitely more proper to treat it with abhorrence and detestation, than with scorn. ... There are many whose visible weakness is to be lamented; and perhaps, there is no human character at all so perfectly decent in every respect, but, by imitation, and a little aggravation, it may be rendered ridiculous.[18]

Witherspoon, he explains, is now able to 'make some improvement' of what he has said up to this point in his sermon. 'Making improvement' is the usual formula for introducing the 'application' of his message in the time-honoured tradition of the Church of Scotland of his day. The minister's 'improvement' is the profitable application of his message to real life, and the congregation of the Laigh Church would have been bracing themselves for this final section of the discourse, some of them doubtless in great trepidation of what he would say. It is a moment of high drama and as such is virtually unique in sermons of the period. He begins:

> ... I think I can discover in the aspect of the audience, that you already suppose I have been led to the choice of this subject, by the late atrocious and flagrant offence, committed in the near neighbourhood of where I now stand; and which has affected every thinking and well-disposed person in the place, with a mixture of indignation and concern.[19]

It is his duty as a minister of the gospel to speak out in condemnation of what has happened. 'Fidelity to my charge' requires it, he says. While he has 'generally avoided bringing in particular accidents that have fallen out in the place', this is different, since

> there are some things so flagrant and atrocious in their nature, so dangerous and hurtful in their effects, that bare silence concerning them would carry in it an imputation of unfaithfulness, or partiality in a minister of Christ.[20]

As if to anticipate the publication of his sermon, or at least at this stage its wider circulation – 'the scandal seems loudly to call for some public notice of it, so it is impossible to make the persons more known than they are already by their own folly' – Witherspoon defends that possibility on the grounds it might have the effect of making the culprits more ashamed and thus, 'it would be an unspeakable benefit both to the public and themselves'.

Nearing the end of his sermon he addresses some words of 'advice and direction' to three discrete groups. *First*, 'to those who are young ... in that lovely, precious, dangerous season of life'. It is easily the most memorable part of the whole sermon, with Witherspoon's prose almost reminding one of Shakespeare having Prince Hal lectured on the perils of Falstaffian high jinks:

> Let me beseech you, first of all, to learn this important lesson, to distrust yourselves: be sensible of your inexperience, and be persuaded of your danger from the admonitions of others. The greatest evidence you can give of real knowledge is to be sensible of your ignorance; and of true wisdom to be willing to learn: ... Above all things shun, as the pestilence, the society of profane scorners. ... [21]
>
> ... Do not look only on those libertines who are in the beginning or middle of their course, whose spirits are lively, and their vigour yet unimpaired; look on the few older practitioners. These were the good fellows and social spirits of a former period; their companions were cut off in the middle of their days, and they remain as beacons for your instruction and warning. Do you see them sullen in their deportment, mean in their attire, and despised by the world itself; their faces bloated with intemperance, and their miserable offspring pale with hunger, or crippled by neglect? These are the terrible fruits of midnight rioting. They were once as merry in their cups, as ready with their jests, and as great despisers of Sabbaths and sermons, of whining and praying, as any of their more sprightly successors, who are in the high road to the same despicable end.[22]

Secondly, addressing himself to parents, he tells them:

> Let it therefore be your care, to preserve your children, as much as possible, from the company and conversation of profane persons, especially those who are tainted with infidelity: and who, as its natural consequence, treat the exercises of piety with contempt and scorn.[23]

Finally, Witherspoon addresses 'a few words to professing Christians in general'. Here he tries to distinguish between the common sins of 'theft and dishonesty' and 'impiety' and claims that different standards apply in human society:

> Were any person known to be guilty of theft and dishonesty, or any fault that is odious and disgraceful in the world, every one would reckon his intimate companions almost, if not to the same degree, abandoned as himself. The same thing will certainly hold as to profanity or licentiousness; though indeed it carries in it a melancholy proof, that sins against piety or purity are far from being held in the same abhorrence, as what endangers our substance or temporal interest.[24]

The sermon closes on a desperately bleak but unusually personal note, with Witherspoon expressing anguish at what he perceives to be a seriously deteriorating moral and religious situation that has developed of late in the town of Paisley – and even in the microcosm that is his own Laigh Kirk parish and congregation – affecting, in particular, the younger generation. This loss of reverence for Christ's kingdom has led to 'the introduction of a worldly spirit by the rising generation', and he implores the men and women sitting in front of him that morning to take steps to rectify the problem before things get any worse. It is pulpit censure in the fullest sense, especially of course the final paragraph which, again, without, tantalisingly, any further detail being supplied by the minister, ensures that the congregation will leave the church with the censure ringing loudly in their ears. There is something almost medieval about the language of Witherspoon's final message to his flock: that they should pray that God would 'snatch' those guilty of the (still indeterminate) profanity 'as brands from the burning':

> Growing in numbers, and growing, I hope, in wealth, as the effect of your own and your fathers industry, you are in danger of the introduction of a worldly spirit by the rising generation. This every good man ought, with the utmost prudence and resolution, to oppose; particularly by doing all in his power to preserve the honour and respect due to true religion, and treating with contempt every open enemy to that important interest. ....[25]
>
> The late riotous meeting was without doubt the most audacious thing of the kind that ever was attempted in this place; and therefore calls for an open and vigorous testimony against it, by every person in his sphere. ... Nothing serves to harden sinners more, than when no notice is taken of their crimes; and they find themselves just as generally, and as well received, as if they had done no evil. On the other hand, when they perceive the deep concern of others on their account, it is an excellent mean of bringing them to serious reflection, and inducing them to tremble at themselves. Wherefore, my beloved hearers let me beseech you to preserve your horror of sin, notwithstanding the boldness of sinners. Do every thing in your power to reclaim the offenders. Be earnest in your supplications to almighty God, that he would snatch them as brands from the burning, and raise them up as trophies of his victorious grace.[26]

The Snodgrass affair(s)

So, what was the underlying cause of Witherspoon's incaution and hot-headedness that lay behind his preaching of the sermon *Seasonable Advice to Young Persons*? All the facts behind the minister's anger are revealed in the 'Authentic Narrative' he included in the printed version of the sermon which Robert Urie of Glasgow published in late May of the same year.[27] The story as told by Witherspoon in his preface runs as follows. On Saturday 6 February 1762 – the evening before the holiest of only two Sabbaths in the year when the Sacrament of the Lord's Supper was celebrated in Paisley by all the churches there[28] – 'some young men' who, according to the preface to the printed version of his sermon, 'it is generally believed had all been at church',[29] proceeded to dine thereafter in a hostelry identified as 'James Chambers' room'. After dinner there, one of the men, Robert Hunter, 'who never was a communicant', produced a communion token. When asked where he had got it, he 'said he got it from Judas Iscariot', and, as reported by one of the company later in giving evidence, 'offered to play odds or evens with him which of them should use it'.

The revellers – by this time seven in all – were then invited 'to a glass' by one of their number, William Wilson, in his room, 'which', Witherspoon adds, 'he chose that night to take possession of; and indeed to give it a very dreadful consecration.' From that point things began seriously to get out of hand. 'In the interval of their meeting' Hunter sent the communion token 'to a young woman in the place' – a thinly veiled euphemism for a known prostitute – 'inclosed in a letter.' The preface continues:

> What were the contents of the letter cannot be known. Common fame said it was inviting her to their sacrament: he himself [Hunter] pretended it was very innocent, but took care, as soon as the rumour broke up, to get the letter and burn it. The reader will immediately reflect what could be the intention, and what might have been the effects of this conduct: it was easy in this way to send the most notorious profligate to the table of the Lord, to the unspeakable scandal of the congregation, as well as mischief to his own soul.[30]

It is at this point in the preface that Witherspoon first identifies the whole company of scandalous revellers by name and occupation. They are:

> ... the said Robert Hunter, and William Wilson manufacturers in Paisley, John Snodgrass writer there,[31] William M'crotchet [aka in the Court of Session records of the case 'M'Croachit' or 'M'Crocket'] ensign or sergeant in the army,[32] James and David Chalmers,[33] and Robert Cross junior, merchants in Paisley.

As to what they were actually engaged in, Witherspoon asserts:

> By their own confessions, and the deposition of several witnesses, they employed a good part of the time in mock-preaching, and that not merely imitating the tones or gestures of ministers in indifferent words, but the only expressions that were distinguished by the witnesses who heard them on the street, were the words of scripture. Two witnesses depone, that to the best of their judgment they heard them praying in mockery; and when asked if they were sure it was praying and not preaching, persisted in affirming it was praying. By their own confessions, and the depositions of witnesses, they were guilty of profane swearing.[34]

But what Witherspoon found most shocking was that not only had the revellers indulged in profane swearing, and 'praying in mockery', but some had gone so far as to use the actual words of the minister when performing the Sacrament of the Lord's Supper – that is, of the 'institution', as he puts it:

> The noise of their meeting was such as alarmed the whole neighbourhood: but what is most tremendous of all, by the declaration of Robert Hunter, one of themselves, William M'crotchet, used some of the words of the institution. The same thing is declared by William Wilson, of John Snodgrass; and upon the strictest re-examination [by the Kirk Session] he persisted in declaring that he was certain it was done in the company, and he thought it was by that person.

Be in no doubt about it, Witherspoon cautions his readers, this was gross profanity:

> When these facts are laid together ... is it possible in words to paint the atrociousness of their crime? ... The very choice of such a night [the evening prior to the celebration of the Sacrament] for such a merry meeting, and the disturbance given to the place almost to

the hour of midnight, though there had been no more in it, were surely highly indecent. But when we add to this the loud profanation of the Almighty's name, and spending the most part, if not the whole of the time, in mocking the exercises of piety, how deep and aggravated is the guilt! Above all, when it is considered that this seems to have been without bounds, not sparing even the most solemn and sacred rite of our holy religion! [35]

He reserves to the last his bitter condemnation of the role in the affair of the lawyer, John Snodgrass, whom Witherspoon clearly adjudges the ringleader. Snodgrass would prove Witherspoon's nemesis over the entire duration of the civil case in the Court of Session. It was on Snodgrass's account that the minister unhappily resorted to (on the most generous construction) underhand tactics in attempting to have him proved guilty in the church courts in a later case in 1764 founded on the lawyer's alleged adultery, *in flagrante*, involving a known prostitute; this case (to which I give the description 'Snodgrass 2' in *LWJW*)[36] proved utterly humiliating to Witherspoon. It failed to convince the overwhelmingly Moderate Presbytery of Paisley, and Snodgrass himself, owing in great measure to his own considerable forensic abilities, got off Scot-free. By that time, of course, the civil case in the Court of Session had been running for almost two years.

The distinguished legal historian John Finlay has revealed a further dark side to Snodgrass much later in his career. Even before the dust had finally settled on the Witherspoon case, it seems that Snodgrass had moved to Greenock 'in the 1770s' where he worked as 'clerk, procurator, and sheriff-substitute,' until the 'murmurings of the people' had become so clamant that he had been forced to quit as substitute. In *The Petition and complaint of James Kibble and others*, dated 20 November 1782, the nature of his alleged offences is fully disclosed:

> Mr Snodgrass has carried on the business of a procurator in this court for six years past to a very considerable extent; and there is reason to believe it has been the more extensive, from an idea which had been industriously sent over the county, that the clerk can do more for his clients than any other procurator.[37]

Finlay shows that the outcome of the case was that Snodgrass and his deputes were prohibited, so long as they remained in office, from acting as procurators in any action before the local sheriff court, but notes also that he remained in office and 'continued to dispute his guilt'. It certainly seems that John Snodgrass, as an experienced lawyer himself, lived on the very edge of the law for much of his adult life. He died in 1785.

Kirk Session, Presbytery and General Assembly

Unfortunately the original Paisley Town Kirk Session records of the period are lost, though the printed Court of Session submissions contain sufficient extracts from them to allow the historian the possibility of a more than adequate reconstruction of the Session's handling of the case. It seems likely that details of the *fama clamosa* would originally have been 'delated', either directly to the Session by an elder of the Laigh Church in whose parish it occurred, or, alternatively, to the minister who would then have reported what happened to the Session, together with his own observations. The *Town* Kirk Session – as distinct from the *Abbey Parish* Kirk Session – embraced the ministers and elders of two churches, the Laigh (Witherspoon's) and the High (then occupied by the Reverend James Baine, who had 'preached in' Witherspoon to his charge in 1757 when he had been translated from Beith to Paisley).[38]

The Kirk Session failed to reach a unanimous verdict on the issue of the guilt of the seven accused. Meeting first on 15 February – that is, just over a week *after* the incident had taken place, and almost a week *before* the preaching of the sermon later entitled *Seasonable Advice* – the Session proceeded to conduct interrogations of each of the accused. Most were heard on 17 February with the exception of John Snodgrass who was examined on Monday 22 February, the day after Witherspoon had preached his sermon. A key witness was William Wilson and, as things turned out, *key* for the reason that his evidence was seen in Witherspoon's eyes at least as proof of Snodgrass's leading role in the scandal.

Wilson confirmed that 'a company of young men' had been in his room on Saturday 6 February and had stayed there 'till about a quarter after ten at night.' When asked a question regarding the alleged abuse of the sacrament, Wilson declared:

> "That John Snodgrass made a motion with his hand, and used the words, Take, eat; and he also remembers some words of a psalm were used by him; to the best of his remembrance, the words were *Enter his gates and courts with praise.*"[39]

As if that were not enough, Wilson said he saw Robert Hunter with a token and heard him say 'he got it from Judas Iscariot'. Worse still, Wilson then said

> "That some of the company brought in some gingerbread into his room, and divided it amongst themselves. And being interrogate, declares, That he cannot remember whether John Snodgrass had any of that gingerbread in his hands, or not, when he used the above words; and *that the words were used with some kind air or tone as of a minister* ... .[40]

Wilson's performance before the Session had seriously run the risk of letting the whole side down. But at least to some extent he had salved his own conscience, and the Session heard him declare that he was 'very sorry for the sin he had committed and the offence and trouble he had given to his neighbours.'

When, a few days later, it was John Snodgrass's turn to appear before the Session, things could not have been more different. Where Wilson had been contrite, Snodgrass was defiantly impenitent. At the bar of the Session Snodgrass denied everything of which he was accused. The substance of his evidence before the Session is given in some detail many years later by Witherspoon's counsel in the civil process, David Dalrymple,[41] and it is clear that Dalrymple had the text of the Session minute to hand when he composed the minister's *Answers*. Among his many denials Snodgrass declared

> That he himself neither cursed nor swore that night, nor did he mimick any person whatever. ... That the sacrament of the Lord's supper was not so much mentioned by any person present, while he was there. ... That he saw no person present, either have in their hands, or speak of tokens that night. Being interrogate, whether he himself, or any other present, to the best of his remembrance, used the words of the institution of the sacrament, or any part of them? Denied that he did, or any thing like it. *Being interrogate, whether he heard the name of God taken in vain, or any other form of swearing in that company? Declared, He thought it an improper question, and refused to answer it.* ... He left that company

when they dismissed altogether, which, to the best of his remembrance, was about a quarter after ten of the clock, or betwixt ten and eleven; he is sure it was before eleven: ... That after, he went to Alexander Robertson's, and supped, and was at his own house, either five minutes before, or five minutes after twelve of the clock.[42]

Finally, not content with Wilson's evidence, Snodgrass insisted that his friend be re-examined by the Session 'in his own presence'. Having been recalled, Wilson modified his previous evidence to the extent that he now thought it certain that the words *'Take, eat'* etc. *"were used in the company; and he thought it was by John Snodgrass"* but "would not swear it, only that he thinks it was him."

We learn from the subsequent Court of Session printed case papers that, using Dalrymple's words, the Session's verdict displayed 'no mark of innocence'. What had resulted from the oral examination of witnesses was a decision by the Session to set up a committee. Again piecing together fragments of Session records cited by both defence and prosecuting counsel in the Court process, it becomes clear that the committee (of which Witherspoon himself was a member) was seriously perplexed by the lack of any unanimity among the witnesses in relation to not only what had transpired, but regarding the distribution and attribution of guilt among the seven accused. Indeed, the committee observed that 'there is a considerable contradiction in their own declarations, one to another, and very little reason to believe they are either sincere or full.'[43] It is left to the advocate Andrew Crosbie[44] to quote the full text of the verdict of the Session in the light of the committee's findings. Crosbie, for the pursuers in the civil action – unlike Dalrymple for the by now increasingly frustrated minister – clearly found great satisfaction in doing so, largely, one suspects, on account of the total disarray among members of the Session that is plain for all to see:

> The session, having compared the several parts of the report, do approve of the same; and it being proposed by some, that the whole matter, as it stands, should be preferred [sic] to the presbytery; and others being of opinion that it is incumbent on the session themselves to pass some censure upon so heinous an offence, that they should take the advice of the presbytery what should be further done to those who are most guilty, the same was put to the vote: the last motion was agreed to. Wherefore, the session taking into consideration, that every one of the persons who were present, and continued to give countenance to so atrocious a riot, were highly criminal, did resolve, that the whole be appointed to be publicly rebuked before the congregation, and laid under censure; and appointed accordingly, and further resolve to take the advice of the presbytery, what other censure shall be inflicted on those who are chiefly guilty.[45]

The words of the Session interlocutor are far from constituting an appeal to the Presbytery. Instead, and extraordinarily, the Session assume guilt on the part of the accused and, in deciding to 'take the advice' of the Presbytery, they effectively invite the more senior court to cap their own rebuke with an appropriate *further* punishment in the case of those 'who are most guilty.' But what the Session did not bargain for – and what Charles Hay,[46] counsel for Witherspoon's pursuers in the Court case, found equally 'extraordinary' – was that John Snodgrass unhesitatingly resolved himself to lodge a personal appeal with the Presbytery. If it was the last thing Witherspoon would have wished for, it was equally a devious move on Snodgrass's part.

As Ian Clark has shown,[47] in Witherspoon's day the composition of the Presbytery of Paisley was predominantly Moderate in its theology and outlook. For the evangelical author of *Ecclesiastical Characteristics* – though originally published anonymously, its authorship was not in doubt when Witherspoon came to Paisley from Beith in 1757 – the Presbytery offered little chance of any sympathy or support for his cause against Snodgrass. In 1762 a total of eighteen parishes belonged to the Presbytery of Paisley. Clark samples Moderate affiliations in the years 1755, 1780 and 1805, all randomly chosen dates, and in 1755, the year closest to 1762, there were seventeen parishes in the Presbytery. In 1755 Clark is able to identify seven Moderates and one member of the Popular party, with the affiliations of the rest uncertain. In my book I have identified seven known Moderates who became involved in the Snodgrass case at the level of the Presbytery; to these should be added the name of James Baine of the High Church in Paisley, Witherspoon's own colleague on the Town Kirk Session, whose diffident propensity for sitting on the fence throughout the process has already been commented on.

The Presbytery minutes record that at their meeting of 17 March John Snodgrass appeared before them not only on his own behalf, but also for the others who were appealing 'against a sentance of the Town Kirk Session of Paisley' whose extract proceedings were produced. Witherspoon appeared for the Session, together with three named elders. The grounds for the appeal having been heard *viva voce*, the Presbytery agreed to refer the 'whole affair' to a committee of four ministers; it emerges that all four were Moderates, led by the Moderator of Presbytery, the minister of Kilbarchan, the controversial John Warner, whose nickname, ominously, was 'the Abbot'.[48] It was at this stage in the proceedings that Witherspoon lost all patience with the Presbytery. Frustrated beyond measure, he made an astonishing threat that, if it turned out that the Presbytery failed to uphold the sentence of the Kirk Session – in Charles Hay's combative words, to 'give him what further satisfaction he wished' –

> he would print the sermon he had preached, prefix the pursuers names thereto, and either bring them to the penitence, and submission which he thought proper, or brand them with infamy and disgrace through all the British dominions.[49]

While doubtless understandable in the circumstances, and conceived out of anger on grasping the Presbytery's unsubtle attempt to throw their full weight against him, Witherspoon's language was intemperate and would be used to his disadvantage years later in the Court action. Hay again:

> The presbytery ... were not in an humour either to be over-awed by the defender's [Witherspoon's] threats, or inflamed by his unjust representations.[50]

On 28 April, with only eleven ministers members present and one lay elder, the Presbytery received the report of its gang of four. The whole tenor of the report is mild and concessionary as far as the appellants were concerned:

> Upon the whole, the Presbytery, after mature deliberation, considering all the circumstances of the affair complexly, found and hereby do find, the conduct of the appellants highly blameable and offensive; and, therefore, ordains their Moderator to rebuke them solemnly at the bar of the Presbytery, with Certification, the process to be issued in this manner.

The appellants 'declared their acquiescence in the sentence'. By contrast, a furious Witherspoon 'in his own name, and in the name of the Session of Paisley, protested and [proleptically] appealed to the ensuing General Assembly', promising to 'lodge his reasons of appeal in due time'. On 18 May the Presbytery resolved to lodge its own appeal to the Assembly 'in case it appears there is any thing contained in that narrative' [the published sermon], that could be construed as 'injurious to the conduct of the Presbytery'.

Minutes of successive Presbytery meetings clearly show that Witherspoon's colleagues were fast losing patience with him. His reckless language, it seemed, was in real danger of bringing the Presbytery of Paisley into disrepute. From Witherspoon's point of view the last straw was when an 'overture' submitted by a Presbytery committee was put into terms uncompromisingly hostile to him:

> They judge it seasonable and incumbent upon them to declare That a minister publishing vending and dispersing thro the World an account of such matters of Scandal as are the subject of Church process & with a particular account of the names and designations of the persons who may have, or are alleged to have been concerned in them, is in the Judgement of the Presbytery at any rate, but more especially when this is done while Church processes relating thereto are in dependence and the matters remain sub Judice, a practice in many respects highly irregular and injurious, contrary to the uniform and established method of procedure in this Church in all such cases; grossly abusive of the great ends of Church discipline and which, were it generally to obtain, would be productive of such mischief in the world as would soon bring all Ecclesiastical processes in matters of Scandal under the utmost degree of contempt and abhorrence, and ... the threatening mischief upon or uttering injurious aspersions of any kind against persons under process ... is a measure highly unsuitable to the Ministerial Character and breathes more of the spirit of private resentment than the meekness that is in Christ Jesus and which must also have a tendency to harden offences in vice, rather than to reclaim them from the error of their ways.[51]

That minute is a record of the Presbytery's meeting of 7 July, well after the close of the Assembly of that year.

From the point of view of all three interested parties – John Witherspoon, the Snodgrass faction and the Presbytery of Paisley – the 1762 General Assembly proved something of a damp squib. For one thing, Witherspoon, it is clear, had second thoughts about proceeding with his appeal. On mature reflection, circumstances probably conspired to make him withdraw his appeal.[52] In the interval between the preaching of *Seasonable Advice* and the start of the Assembly (20 May), he had received a call to be minister at Dundee, which had been universally opposed not just by the Town Kirk Session, but also by the magistrates, town council and 'incorporations of Paisley'. To speculate, Witherspoon must have taken heart from this welcome show of support within his adopted locale.[53] Having withdrawn his appeal, the 'transportation' to Dundee was refused. As I have shown elsewhere, the motives behind Witherspoon's decision are unclear. The Court of Session narrative of events ranged from totally exonerating the minister (Dalrymple), to blaming him for manipulating the timing of the Assembly meeting to coincide with the publication of the sermon (Hay) and, in the case of his most aggressive critic (Crosbie), to finding him guilty of a cynical disregard for the Presbytery case in particular, in the words of his accuser declaring that the Dundee call had 'nothing at all to do with that matter, which issued entirely upon its own merits.'[54] As for the impact of Witherspoon's behaviour on the pursuers, Crosbie is just as unremitting in his scorn:

> The consequence to them ... was very serious; he [Witherspoon] never communicated to them his intention to drop this appeal, so that they incurred all the expence preparatory to a hearing; and, indeed, pretty nearly the same expence as if the appeal had actually been heard; so that Mr. Wotherspoon had a full opportunity of gratifying his rancour to the utmost against them, by means of that appeal equally, as if the appeal had been discussed.[55]

Certainly Snodgrass derived no benefit whatsoever from the appeal. Instead, he and his fellow pursuers were faced with a large bill to meet the not inconsiderable on-costs of their wasted sojourn in Edinburgh for the duration of the Assembly.

Court of Session process: 1762 to 1776

It is a far from easy task to condense the unusual complexities of a legal process lasting more than fourteen years into a few pages and I have concluded it would be unwise to try to do so here. The best that can be done, it is suggested, is to highlight the main issues that came before the Court and try to relate them back to the central theme of this present study: the extent, that is, to which Witherspoon was culpable, or not at all, in taking the line he did in the injudicious pulpit censure that sparked off the whole sorry business. Additionally, since the issue is of unusual historical importance, I append a brief postscript to this chapter in which I re-affirm my contention that the débâcle influenced Witherspoon's decision finally to accept the call of America, bearing in mind, of course, that he went there in 1768, and that the Court process was not finally determined until February-March 1776.

The Court of Session process *Snodgrass and Others v The Reverend John Witherspoon* turned very largely on this central conundrum: was John Witherspoon correct to enforce his perceived ministerial right and duty to 'prosecute' those he believed responsible for having committed the 'atrocious and flagrant offence' with which he had charged them; *or* had he prostituted both his office *and* the notional role of the so-called *chair of verity* in pursuing men who were, it was argued, deserving more of reclamation as sinners against God, rather than having their names 'branded' for all time, near and far.

When David Rae's *Representation*[56] on behalf of the pursuers was received by the Court in February 1763 he was careful to distinguished between the oral sermon – which he admitted contained 'a great deal of sound doctrine' – and the published version. The latter, he said, had exposed his clients 'as persons of abandoned Characters and as guilty of Crimes from which they stand acquitted from the competent Court that Sermon must fall under'. Rae also stigmatized Paisley as 'a Town of Great Trade but where at the same time the Principles of the people are such as give their Ministers very great influence over them And Consequently where any person happening to fall under their displeasure must be attended with very disagreeable consequences.' This last charge is repeated more or less *verbatim* by a young Henry Dundas,[57] acting for the Snodgrass faction, in his much later (printed) *Answers* of 23 February 1768. In response to Rae, James Montgomery[58] for Witherspoon, retorts in his *Answers* that

> ... if he [the 'Defender', Witherspoon] can satisfy the Lord Ordinary of what is most certainly the truth that the preaching the Sermon complained of did proceed from a just sense of his duty and that the publication of the Sermon with the preface or writing complained of did arise from the necessity of self Defence in order to remove from severe reflections that had been thrown out against his Conduct in a publick assembly, he is persuaded his Lordship will not think him blamefull or censurable for what he has done.[59]

Moreover, at this early stage in the proceedings, there is a marked conciliatory, even gentlemanly air evident in Witherspoon's counsel's response to the charge laid against him. Montgomery again:

> If he [Witherspoon] has gone too far in either the Expression or Sentiment he is extremely Sorry for it, and in excuse can only say that he meant no more than an admonition to the pursuers, and to form a Discourse that might be of advantage to his Hearers in general.

This is not the place to re-examine the circumstances behind the grotesque prolongation of the Court process, except to comment that the Snodgrass faction seemed motivated throughout by an extraordinary determination – probably fuelled by the substantial financial resources available to most of the pursuers involved – to see the whole business through to the bitter end, almost whatever the cost.[60] Nor is it appropriate to spend time on the complications posed by the events of a separate, unrelated (and quite possibly manufactured) set of circumstances that came before the Town Kirk Session and Presbytery of Paisley in 1764, and which, to distinguish it from the on-going legal process in the midst of which it became almost inextricably tangled, I have given the appellation *'Snodgrass 2'*.[61] Depending on one's point of view, and, above all, on whose word one holds credence, *either* Snodgrass naively played into Witherspoon's hands by consorting *in flagrante* with a known prostitute, *or* (as is more likely) Witherspoon succumbed to his own bad conscience in seeking to incriminate Snodgrass by fair means or, for that matter, foul.

From the evidence of his implied instructions to counsel as reflected in the relevant printed submissions (especially George Wallace's *Petition* of 16 February 1768) there seems little doubt that with the passage of time Witherspoon trimmed his previously uncompromising position and softened his stance. As we have seen, this was already evident back in 1763 in the conciliatory tone of Montgomery's *Answers* of that year. Why did Witherspoon further modify his attitude towards his pursuers so markedly? It may, of course, be down to a simple fit of conscience, a dawning realisation that he had allowed his heart to rule his head, a sense that he had gone too far, that there was something after all in the opposition of all those shrill voices raised against him. The odds are, however, that this departure from his old implacable stance was due much more to two factors: first, that he sensed (and his agent and counsel doubtless advised) that things were not going well for him. Despite James Montgomery's initial view that the action 'is not competent in this Court' and that Witherspoon's actions 'did not proceed from any enmity to the pursuers, but from the Defender's Sense of his duty as a Minister of the Gospel' – the bedrock of Witherspoon's own personal defence throughout the long years of the process – Lord Coalston's first interlocutor of 1764 had gone against him, finding him 'liable in damages and expences', and, in respect of the latter, allowing the pursuers to give in an accompt thereof.' With that judgment both sides 'acquiesced', and that might have been the end of the matter.

The second factor, however, that forced a clearly unwilling Witherspoon to get as near an apology as his counsel (Wallace) could exert out of him was the need to persuade Snodgrass and his fellow pursuers to adopt a sufficiently lenient attitude to his cause to enable him to leave the country for America, which he planned to do as soon as reasonably possible after his return from London and Rotterdam in the early summer of 1768. The problem was that Witherspoon needed cash from the sale of a property he owned in Paisley – 'a small house, which is very inconsiderable in point of value, but is the only heritable property he has' – but to prevent this sale, and accordingly stall his departure, the pursuers had resorted to the device known in Scots law as an 'inhibition on the dependence'. With delicious irony (but probably no coincidence) the warrant of inhibition was served on the minister on '30th of January last, in the evening, being the very Saturday immediately before the Sunday appointed for the celebration of the sacrament of the Lord's supper at Paisley.' That would have been precisely the 6th anniversary of the mock sacrament held by the Snodgrass faction. Dundas's *Answers* to Witherspoon's *Petition* grants 'the desire of this petition' but only after the minister had agreed to a bond of caution naming three of his friends who were prepared to act as guarantors in the event of the final decree going against him. On 18 May he, his wife and five children sailed for America.

At that juncture the process 'fell asleep' and was 'wakened' two years later only for it to fall asleep once more,[62] as it did similarly on two subsequent occasions, in 1772 and 1774, when Lord Coalston, in a further interlocutor, required Witherspoon to provide answers to the pursuers' 'condescendence' of damages[63] and 'objections to the account of expences given in by John Snodgrass' of 'about twelve years ago'. David Dalrymple supplied these *Answers*, and Charles Hay the *Replys* [sic] to the *Answers*, dealing in the main with the minutiae of the damages and expences issue that was taking so interminably long to bring to conclusion.[64]

Meantime, the game of legal ping-pong continued relentlessly, albeit episodically, to focus on the principle of the minister's sheltering behind the *chair of verity*, with the liberty of the pulpit his first defence, *versus* his opponents' claim that he had breached all the rules of acceptable public conduct in defaming the good name of those he had named and accused in *that sermon*. As far back as 1764, for example, Francis Garden (later Lord Gardenstone)[65] had entertainingly likened Witherspoon's 'errant pride, resentment and vindictive spirit' to the hypocritical zeal of Molière's *Tartuffe* which, Garden maintained, 'distinguished so sensibly & feelingly the Characters of true and false zeal'.[66]

The same theme of excessive zeal, coupled with Witherspoon's supposed hypocrisy, continued into the three long (printed) Court submissions of 1775-76, as did, likewise, protestations of Witherspoon's 'pure' motives, consistent with his strict adherence to the rules of church discipline as laid down by the Kirk's judicatures. Thus, Hay in his *Petition* of 25 November 1775:

In this country, by the moderation and good behaviour of the clergymen, they have acquired the general esteem and good-will of the laity; their character and office are both held sacred; and, as their profession is very different from that of spreading injurious calumnies against their neighbours, so their practice is in general believed to correspond with it; whence the pulpit has been emphatically termed the *Chair of Verity*. It is hoped, there are few or no clergymen in the Church of Scotland who could be capable of such a behaviour as the defender has been convicted of towards these unfortunate gentlemen, the petitioners. But that is no reason why he should be exempted from punishment; on the contrary, the virtues of others render his faults the less excusable, as he cannot pretend to be led astray by the example of other clergymen of his persuasion, or by ignorance of what was his duty.[67]

From the clever artifice of Francis Garden's *Tartuffe* allusion, to the more mundane yet no less wounding short discourse on zeal in its theological connotations, we learn a good deal about the 'technical' sense of the term. Hay again:

Zeal is, no doubt, sometimes very rash and warm in its pursuits, and hurries men into foolish and headstrong measures; but then, like every other violent passion, it is but short in its duration: It may, in an unguarded moment, run men into violent excesses, which they instantly execute, and as quickly repent of; but it will not have the effect of prompting a man, after having time coolly to deliberate with himself, to commit an action which may prove, and in this case actually has proved, the ruin of some unfortunate gentlemen. The preparing a publication for the press is not done in a moment; a man has time to revolve in his own mind the consequences with which it may be attended to himself, and to other people, before he can effect his intention. If, therefore, he continues, after cool reflection, to persist in his first resolution, it must be attributed to another motive than zeal, which, the more violent it is, is always of the shorter duration.[68]

In other words, says Hay, whatever else it was, this was *not* the action of a zealot. Zeal implies rashness and impetuosity; rather, what Witherspoon did was the outcome of 'cool reflection'.

By contrast, in his *Replies* of 11 January 1776 – the last of the five printed Court submissions spanning the eight-year period from 1768 – Andrew Crosbie, at a stroke, sweeps away any vestigial credulity attaching to Hay's claim that the minister's vindictive actions of 1762 could be the result of 'another motive than zeal'. Crosbie aggressively compares Witherspoon's vindictiveness to the mosaic law, the *lex talionis* – 'an eye for an eye', etc. – notwithstanding that even *that* primitive and uncompromising law was sanctioned by God:

[Witherspoon] followed out his malevolent intentions, though the consequences to them [the pursuers] might be forfeiture, ruin, and bankruptcy: had he reflected then on the old maxim, *Quod tibi fieri non vis alteri ne feceris*, and shaped his conduct accordingly, there would have been no occasion for the present process, nor would he have any damages or expences to pay: but he neglected that golden rule, and he ought now to reflect, that though the consequences should be even such as he points out, yet even the law of God promulgated to Moses, gave a sanction to the *poena talionis*.[69]

At long last, in February and March 1776 Lord Auchinleck made determination of the process. Damages totalling £150 sterling were awarded against Witherspoon and he was also found liable to the payment of expenses which in the second (and final) decree were modified to £20 sterling, to which was added the expense associated with the preparation of the Extract Decreet. By that time, of course, Witherspoon had been in America for almost eight years and was set to become an increasingly influential figure in the activities of the Continental Congress and several of its committees. It is highly doubtful if, at all, the outcome of the case gave him many restless nights – though, to his considerable credit, I have shown that the main object of Witherspoon's return to Scotland in 1784 was not to raise funds for the College of New Jersey (which he palpably failed to do), but to repay his debts and discharge the loans he had received on account of the Court process.

A biographer of Witherspoon's most famous student, James Madison, has described this one-time Paisley minister as 'an incredible and perhaps somewhat overlooked figure in the growth of America.'[70] It is hardly an extravagant claim. At the same time, however, to Jeffry Morrison and, one suspects, to numerous other students of his American career, John Witherspoon stubbornly remains the 'forgotten Founder'.

The Snodgrass affair considered as a factor in Witherspoon's decision to quit Scotland for America

One of the more intriguing questions to be addressed in the aftermath of the Court case is the extent to which, if at all, it affected Witherspoon's decision finally, after a period of initial dithering, to accept the call of New Jersey. Successive Witherspoon biographers, if they deal with the Snodgrass affair at all,[71] have for the most part dismissed any claim that it might have had a bearing on that decision. But their view has been reached in the almost total absence of any understanding of the events described above or even of the background to the preaching and publication of Witherspoon's sermon and its dire consequences. My study, *The Lost World of John Witherspoon*, was undertaken in response to a frustrated desire to remove the vagueness and half-truths associated with the legal case down the years. Most certainly, the book was not written with any pre-emptive motive of changing conventional opinion on – to steal a title from one of those earlier biographers – Witherspoon's 'coming to America'.

Having completed my research into the legal and church records lying at the heart of the case, however, it struck me as not just worthwhile, but non-optional to attempt what I call a 'concluding essay' in which, among other considerations, I re-examine the traditional view of the great man's 'coming to America' and also put forward a personal interpretation of that event in the light of my findings. So, what is that traditional view?

There are three essential sources that are required reading before embarking on a study of Witherspoon's Scottish ministry and career. In chronological order of publication (though not necessarily of date of origin) these are:

1   Varnum Lansing Collins, *President Witherspoon* (2 vols., 1925)
2   Lyman H. Butterfield, *John Witherspoon Comes to America* (1953)
3   Ashbel Green, *The Life of the Revd John Witherspoon D.D., LL.D.* (ed. Henry Lyttleton Savage, 1973) [Green's Ms. was written in 1835-40.]

Butterfield's volume was a by-product of the author's research undertaken for his collected edition of the letters of Benjamin Rush.[72] It brings together for the first time the correspondence of Rush (a Princetonian, at that time a medical student at Edinburgh) and Witherspoon in the two-year period between the Paisley minister's receiving the invitation of the governors of the College of New Jersey to be their sixth President, and his departure for America on 18 May 1768. Without minimising Butterfield's achievement in any way – his book is a milestone in Witherspoon historiography – it offers no insight into the issue confronting us here. There is no mention whatsoever of *Seasonable Advice,* John Snodgrass or of Witherspoon's entanglement in the protracted Court process. Further, since Butterfield makes no reference to either of them, we must assume that he had no knowledge of the existence of two annotated pocketbooks, for the years 1763 and 1768, then lost but thankfully now restored to their proper home in the Firestone Library of Princeton University, both containing notes by Witherspoon referencing the Snodgrass process.[73]

Collins' still much-respected but ultimately flawed[74] two-volume biography of Witherspoon came out as long ago as 1925, though the exhaustive research leading up to its publication was begun much farther back. As early as 1904 Collins came to Scotland and visited General Register House, Edinburgh, where he succeeded in accessing some of the papers relating to the Court process. It is impossible to pinpoint exactly what he saw there but it seems most likely that he inspected only the volume containing the Extract Decreet and left it at that.[75] In the first volume of his massive work Collins briefly discusses President James McCosh's claim that it was his entanglement in the Snodgrass process that influenced Witherspoon in his decision to leave Scotland – 'his enemies were making Scotland "too hot" for him', McCosh maintains – but concludes that 'Dr McCosh's statement is merely a paraphrase of earlier and mistaken writers.'[76] But a little learning is a dangerous thing, and in Collins' case he has surely committed *the* cardinal sin in historical scholarship – *viz.* to base an important claim on the sketchiest of evidence. Like Butterfield, Collins had never seen Witherspoon's two annotated pocketbooks, but was, of course, aware that Green had seen them and found extracts from one of them highly relevant to the Snodgrass affair.

Ironically, it is (by far) the earliest of our three sources that is easily the most germane to the issue. Witherspoon's student, Ashbel Green (1762–1848), president of the College of New Jersey from 1812 to 1822, introduces his extensive remarks on the Snodgrass episode in his memoir with the comment:

> Of the occurrence here contemplated, the present Biographer never heard a word from Dr. Witherspoon himself, nor from his amanuensis.[77]

Green explains that he had first learned of the legal prosecution relating to the sermon *Seasonable Advice* from Thomas Crichton's *Memoir of the Life and Writings of John Witherspoon,* first published in 1829 in the *Edinburgh Christian Instructor*[78]. Crichton, who had been baptised by Witherspoon in the Laigh Church in 1761, provided a tantalisingly sparse outline of the facts leading up to the Court action, yet sufficient to stimulate Green to take action to learn more. Using Dr. Greville Ewing, a Congregationalist minister in

James Boswell of Auchinleck by Sir Joshua Reynolds, 1785. National Galleries of Scotland (in the public domain).

Glasgow, as his intermediary, Crichton was able to confirm that at least one of a 'variety of rumours' reported to Green was correct; that David Dale, a wealthy Glasgow merchant who, according to Crichton, 'when a young man, sat in the Low Church in Paisley during the most active period of the Drs. Ministry', had helped the minister discharge his debts arising out of the 'pecuniary difficulties' consequent upon the legal action. [79]

Ashbel Green, who was, of course, closer to his mentor than any other biographer, is finally convinced, on the basis of the information he received from Ewing and, *via* Ewing, Crichton,[80] that, while there can be 'no foundation' for regarding the Court action as Witherspoon's 'principal motive in leaving his native country', the 'hostility which his writings and measures had excited against him' did constitute a factor in his abandonment of Scotland for America; and he concludes:

> His principal inducement to accept the presidency of the college of New Jersey, as he plainly intimates in his first lecture on Divinity, was the hope of extending his usefulness, by promoting science and especially by training youth for the gospel ministry. With this as his chief motive, he might regard it as a favourable circumstance, *and even as a subordinate inducement,* that by leaving Scotland he would be compleatly removed beyond the reach of the persecutions which fidelity in his sacred vocation had there brought upon him: *and the present writer has little doubt that such in reality were the facts of the case.* [italics added] [81]

Green's view on the issue accurately represents my own position.

3

Bribery and corruption

Perhaps you will say, What business has all this to do with the pulpit, as your paper had with the Caledonian Mercury; and those that sin before all, ought to be rebuked before all, that others may hear and fear, and do no more so wickedly.

Reverend James Thomson (1775).

Key author

Reverend James Thomson (1699–1790), first charge minister of Dunfermline Abbey church from 1743 until his death.

[*Note* Uniquely in this study, no published text exists for either of the two sermons discussed here. They were preached by Thomson in the Abbey church in Dunfermline on Sunday, 16 October 1774 and Sunday, 30 October. All that has survived are fragments of the second sermon as taken down and later recalled, in (i) the Court Summons served on the minister, dated 9 December 1775; (ii) the *Caledonian Mercury* for 2 November 1774; and (by various counsel) in (iii) printed papers relating to the Court of Session action for defamation and damages – *John, Robert, and David Scotlands* [sic] *v The Rev. Mr. James Thomson, Minister of Dunfermline* (1775-76). The scriptural texts chosen by Thomson for his sermons were, respectively (16 October), *Romans*, 8, 32: *'He that spared not his own Son, but delivered him up for us all, how shall he not with him also freely give us all things?'*; and (30 October), *Ephesians*, 4, 25: *'Wherefore putting away lying, speak every man truth with his neighbour: for we are members one of another.'*]

The chronology of the Court process is set out in the *Postscript* to this chapter. *Appendix B* provides information on anecdotage of historic cases cited by prosecuting counsel in the Court process as legal 'precedents' designed to show that the minister's actions were actionable and *ultra vires*.

Taken together, the 'Paisley case' as discussed in chapter 2 and the 'Dunfermline case' discussed here are the two pre-eminent examples of pulpit censure recorded in Scotland in the eighteenth century where the victims of the censure, in each case, resorted to pursuing the ministers concerned in Court of Session actions for defamation and damages. Yet the similarities of these cases are far outweighed by their differences. It is not difficult to pinpoint why that is so. To begin with, though both ministers' sermons landed them in scalding hot water at the hands of the men they accused, the earlier and infinitely more protracted Paisley case founded on the preacher, John Witherspoon, coolly resorting to the published form of his sermon as the vehicle for naming his accused (in the preface to his pamphlet), whereas of course the action against Thomson derived from words spoken from the pulpit. Further, while the Witherspoon case had exhausted the established hierarchical Church judicatures when the minister had sought to employ the full force of ecclesiastical discipline against John Snodgrass and the others he accused of profaning the sacrament of the Lord's supper, his Dunfermline counterpart a few years later had no thought of resorting to such mechanisms. Indeed, the presbytery concerned (Dunfermline) was criticised by two ministers from a neighbouring presbytery (Kinross) for its apparent apathy over the affair in a petition and complaint they laid unsuccessfully before the General Assembly of 1776. [1]

The minister's angry outburst in the course of the first of the two Dunfermline sermons was almost certainly unpremeditated. [2] All that changed, of course, two weeks later when he delivered a second sermon, this time with a text from scripture clearly announcing his intention of using his pulpit to bring down the wrath of God on the hapless election agent, Robert Scotland, together with his brother and his father who, he claimed, were also implicated in the alleged crime.

Despite these important differences, there is no denying that both cases highlight the tensions that were building up at this time between an already creaking Kirk discipline regime and the preparedness of individuals who felt they had been badly let down by the same obsolescent regime to proceed to seek recompense via the only course open to them – the law of the land.

James Thomson's sermons of 16 and 30 October 1774

It was a thoroughly sober James Boswell[3] who, in the company of Colonel Archibald Campbell and his election agent, John Moir WS, attended both morning and afternoon services at the Abbey church in Dunfermline on the Sunday prior to the 1774 general election for the Stirling Burghs constituency. Their motivation in doing so was simple if cynical: 'that we might appear decently at church'.[4] In the morning they listened to 'a most curious sermon'[5] from the old minister, the Reverend James Thomson, and Boswell notes that 'a very genuine account' of the sermon was given in *The Caledonian Mercury* [for 2 November 1774]. At that time Boswell had no idea that he would become both personally (as the appointed delegate for Culross, one of the five burghs in the constituency) *and* professionally involved in an important legal action against Thomson in the Court of Session.

If Boswell was aware of Thomson's outburst in the same pulpit two weeks before, on Sunday 16 October, he does not say so. Then, it seems, the minister had 'made a digression' to the effect that, having congratulated Colonel Archibald Campbell 'and his friends' on their electoral success (at the burgh elections), he told them:

> That they had reason to be thankful they had escaped the snares laid for them by that person, who had betrayed the trust reposed in him, and who was eating his bread, and wearing his apparel, yet had lifted up his heel against him. ... ['He then proceeded to observe'] That this person had much better have stuck by his first party, as he had

brought disgrace upon himself and his family, that would redound against him and his generations to come. ['And, after making these and other such observations, he concluded his discourse with the following passage of scripture:'] "He that getteth riches, and not by justice, is as a partridge that sitteth upon eggs, and hatcheth them not, and his latter end shall be as a fool."[6]

On that occasion, while Robert Scotland, the target of the minister's censure, was absent, Thomson pointed from his pulpit directly at 'his seat' and, in doing so, 'turned the eyes of the whole congregation' on 'poor Mrs Scotland' (Robert's wife), with the result that 'no person in the church entertained a doubt that Mr Thomson alluded to him.'[7]

The earlier of Thomson's two sermons had given rise to two important developments, both conspicuously entering the public domain. First, in its issue of 22 October the *Caledonian Mercury* published the following letter from Robert Scotland:

To the Printer of the Caledonian Mercury

SIR,
In your paper of the 19th current, I observe the following paragraph. [paragraph quoted in the paper of 19 October]
As I was one of the agents in Dunfermline for Colonel Archibald Campbell, who served his interest in that borough, with the assistance of other friends and relations, with invariable fidelity and integrity, from Lammas 1773, to the close of the Michaelmas elections 1774, in vindication of their and my character, I look upon myself as called upon to assure the public, that neither I, nor none for me, to my knowledge, have ever received sum or sums of money, fee, gift, or reward, nor promise of money or good deed, in any shape whatever, from the Baronet hinted at, nor from any of his connections, friends, agents, or servants, nor from any person whatever on his or their account; and that every publication, report, or insinuation to the contrary, by whomsoever related, whether from the pulpit, by a blustering blunderbuss of an old military chaplain,[8] a 'peep sma',[9] or all other such like busy bodies, is false and slanderous, and most ungratefully injurious to the good name and reputation of me and my friends; and I challenge all mankind to adduce any evidence to the contrary, or to prove a single instance of my having, during the above period, ever canvassed with, suggested to, or solicited any person, or persons, to any other interest but that of Colonel Campbell's; and as the only mean to expiscate [fish out] the truth, I have given the necessary orders for a prosecution against the first author of this infamous aspersion.
Your giving this a place in your next paper, will be doing a piece of justice to the much-injured character of
your, &c.
Dunfermline, Oct. 21. 1774 ROBERT SCOTLAND

Two days later, the *Mercury* printed a spoof 'card', the publication of which would result in the newspaper being at the receiving end of an action in the Court of Session initiated by the Scotlands. The notice read as follows:

The Pillory presents its most respectful compliments to *Robert Scotland*, and begs leave to assure him, that in due season he shall be honoured with a comfortable armed chair and collar, in consideration of his faithful services to Colonel Masterton. The circumstances of six hundred guineas to himself, a kirk at Edinburgh for his brother, being scarcely a sufficient recompense for his taking in his grey-headed father to break his faith with Colonel Campbell, and for his attempt to seduce different gentlemen at Dunfermline from the interest of that gentleman, previous to the election of Magistrates, encourages the Pillory to assure him, that his chair shall be dignified with the most elevated station, on his taking a seat, and that every other embellishment becoming his distinguished character will be punctually attended to on the day of exhibition.

The *Edinburgh Advertiser* copied the same 'card' and in due course its publisher, too, was summonsed for his pains.

From the *Mercury* of 2 November and David Rae's much later reclaiming *Petition* of 14 July 1775[10] we are able to reconstruct the 'political part' of Thomson's second and much more vicious sermon of 30 October, as communicated to the editor of the paper by a correspondent who 'though he cannot vouch for the identical words, he is persuaded is the purport of what was delivered.' This time, it seems clear, the old minister's sermon and the text accompanying it were carefully rehearsed:

> Having thus explained to you, my Brethren, the different kinds of *lying*, by which we may hurt either our neighbour or sin against our [own] souls, will any man pretend to tell me, after being informed by three incontestable evidences, that *that* man [*pointing to a certain person in the congregation*] did not *lie*, who will pretend to maintain, that he had not engaged to support Col. Campbell's interest, when he was voted into the Council by the friends of C.C. alone and had not a single vote from the other party? I am convinced that these gentlemen had more wisdom and judgment, than to bring in any man into the Council of Dunfermline, unless they had got the most convincing promises that he would stand by him, and the interest of C.C., yet notwithstanding he did not so much as give them one vote. [Omitted by Rae – *Here Mr J. S. rose up and told him he was telling gross lies and falsehoods.*]
>
> There is another species of *lying*, with a view to hurt and defame the name and characters of our neighbours; as for one to say, "such and such a person has got money from C.C. to induce them to support his interest, and that his *brother* has their receipts for the same;" yet that very man, upon being examined anent such defamatory assertions, to deny the having said such things [Omitted by Rae – *Here Mr D. S. rose up and told him, that he was uttering great lies.*]
>
> And you, Robert Scotland, who have wrote a paper which appeared in the Caledonian Mercury, giving me the epithet of an *old military Chaplain*; this is a name I glory in, having lived fourteen years in the army where I was always happy, and well satisfied with my situation. You also term me a *blustering blunderbuss*, which I refuse, and will refer to the whole congregation, if that cap does not more properly fit [Rae, 'suit'] your head than mine.
>
> I have, however, stronger things to say than that. Will any man pretend to maintain but that you *lie*, by saying that you were a faithful and diligent agent for C.C. ; when the contrary can be proven by the evidence of three indisputable witnesses? If you had been a faithful agent for C.C. why were you so often in the camp of the enemy? A man in the army, if he were found in the camp of the enemy, would be shot the next day. Had you acted justly

and honestly, and had occasion to be with the enemy of C.C. upon [Rae adds 'necessary'] business, you ought to have taken one along with you, to prevent suspicion, and to show that you were not doing any thing to hurt C.C.'s interest.

Further, when C. Masterton came to town to entertain his friends, why were you [Rae adds 'so'] anxious to dine with him, after it had been resolved among the friends of C.C. that none of them should dine with Colonel M? and why did you write that day to C.C. that he need not come to town until the evening? By all which his friends thought the cause in great danger of being hurt, had not his coming happily prevented you. [Omitted by Rae – *While Mr T. was delivering this part of his sermon, R.S. arose several times, and told Mr T. that what he was saying was gross lies and false calumnies; very unbecoming to be spoke from the chair of verity.*] If you acted as a *faithful* agent to C.C. why did you insist on having every thing carried to your mind, and endeavour to get some of C.C.'s friends turned out and those who were his opposites, (I will not say his enemies) kept in, and by insisting to bring in those who were either doubtful or in the opposite interest? It is not the duty of an agent to insist in having every thing carried his own way. No doubt but it may frequently be his duty to remonstrate, and lay matters properly before his employer; but he ought to leave it entirely to his constituent's prudence to chuse what he thinks best. –

***** [Omitted by Rae. Presumably to denote a missing section.]

And if the friends of C.C. had not got convincing proofs of your designs to betray their cause, they would not have shut you out from their deliberations, when matters came to a crisis, and it was become necessary to have plans formed for conducting the common cause.

[Rae adds here in italics: *I therefore think, it is plain, that no person is safe to do any business with you, nor your friends.*] Perhaps you will say, What business has all this to do with the *pulpit*, [Rae interposes a question mark and adds: 'But I think it has as much to do with the pulpit,'] as your paper [i.e. letter] had with the *Caledonian Mercury*; and those that *sin before all*, ought to be *rebuked before all*, that others may hear and fear, and do no more so *wickedly*. Wherefore, refrain from *lying* &c.

And the *Mercury* concludes its report as follows:

Immediately after this extraordinary sermon was concluded, and before prayer was begun, Mr R. S. rose up and, with an audible voice, told the minister, that it would be but fair he should inform the congregation what bribe he [Thomson] had got from C.C. in order to induce him to utter and propagate such false and injurious calumnies from the pulpit.

Small wonder that when the case came on in the Court of Session a few months later the same newspaper reported that it was 'impossible for us to do justice to the learning and ingenuity of the counsel on both sides, who, during a pleading of above three hours, afforded the highest entertainment to the most crowded auditory we ever remember to have seen.'[11]

Corruption in burgh and parliamentary elections – the 'Nabob of the North'

To grasp fully the issues at stake in the Court process we need to consider the historical and political background to the Dunfermline case. For an extreme example of how corruption could be said to have permeated political life in the later eighteenth century (and how there seemed no limits to what it could achieve), we need only consider the career of Sir Lawrence Dundas of Kerse, Stirling, and Aske, near Richmond, Yorkshire.[12] Having as a young man left his father's drapery shop in the Luckenbooths of Edinburgh, this Dundas (only distantly related to the prosperous legal dynasty, the Dundases of Arniston), modestly started business life as an entrepreneurial wine merchant before seizing the opportunities he had shrewdly identified as existing in army supplies and field procurement. Lawrence Dundas's subsequent career almost defies belief. A combination of plum appointments and notoriously shady dealings, aided by well-placed bribes, rapidly advanced Dundas up the ladder of success, hugely enriching him in the process.[13]

Dundas's phenomenal and steady climb to riches, power and status initially derived from his winning of contracts for supplying Cumberland's army during the rebellion of 1745, and his securing, successively, the offices of commissary for bread and forage in Scotland (1746-8), commissary in Flanders (1747-9), keeper of stores in Scotland (1748-57), of magazines of forage (1757-8), commissary of bread for foreign troops in Germany (1759) and contractor for horses and wagons for the Hanoverian troops (1760-1). These offices, and to be fair, the immense energy and hard work that necessarily accompanied them, made Dundas the Croesus of his time. Much later, in 1776, when moves to unseat Dundas as the member for Edinburgh were at their height, a succession of pamphlets lampooning his career appeared in the capital. One of them recalls his commercial successes in Germany:

> LAURENTIUS
> I have been charg'd with crimes and misdemeanours —
> ... Gibing with satire my identity:
> "'Twas but the other day this same Laurentius
> "Vended broad raiment in the Luckenbooths;"
> As if it were a crime, kind citizens;
> As if our town had dwindled to decay,
> Nor need a merchant representative.
> Next comes the mighty crime of opulence —
> And the past earnings of the German war,
> In questionable hand-bills to defame me.
> Was it a sin of mighty magnitude
> (Others refusing the advent'rous risk)
> To pledge my fortune for the army's service?
> Then was Laurentius, good, easy man,
> Deem'd madman, idiot, folly's eldest son!
> Now prosp'rous gentleman, then rich purveyor!
> Conqueror of Edinburgh in Germany.[14]

A key figure in Dundas's rise, actively helping him secure at least some of these offices, was Lieutenant Colonel James Masterton, then serving as deputy adjutant-general in the European theatre of war.[15] Masterton had come to prominence as *aide-de-camp* to Cumberland during the '45 rebellion and that position served 'to recommend his close friend for army contracts'.[16] Crucially, Masterton and another mutual friend, James Edgar,[17] had, it seems, the ear of a future prime minister, Lord Shelburne, to whom they had successfully recommended Dundas while all four were together in Germany.[18] Additionally, it did Dundas no harm that Abraham Hume, formerly commissary for the exchange of prisoners, had been appointed commissary general of provisions, stores and forage in 1745 and was known to Dundas, possibly, claims Bannerman (who has made himself an expert in this aspect of Dundas's career), through their mutual interest in foreign mercantile activities.[19]

In 1747 Dundas was returned as the member for Linlithgow Burghs but only after systematically bribing the delegates of the burghs of Linlithgow and Selkirk. The opposition candidate and previous member, James Carmichael (son of the Earl of Hyndford), successfully petitioned against Dundas's election on the ground that the council of Selkirk had refused to take the oath against bribery when electing their representative. Dundas was unseated, having been found guilty of electoral corruption. It marked the beginning of a lifetime of shady deals and electoral malpractice. In 1762, his wealth by now estimated by some at 'between £600,000 and £800,000',[20] Dundas, nothing daunted, secured not only a parliamentary seat (for Newcastle-under-Lyme) but also a baronetcy, in each case through the personal intervention of Shelburne. It was Shelburne, too, in a letter to Henry Fox, Lord Holland, who first described Dundas as 'the Nabob of the North', informing Fox that he had been asked by Dundas to 'get him made a Bart.' Shelburne duly obliged.[21] Nearly ten years later, the newly formed North administration conceded Dundas's request for elevation to the rank of Privy Counsellor. In the same year (1770), the king, for a second time, refused to entertain Dundas's further soliciting for a peerage.[22]

Meantime, Dundas's parliamentary career was navigating stormy waters. He had been elected member for the Edinburgh constituency, unopposed, in 1768 but six years later the trade corporations in the capital, disappointed in their expectations that Dundas might use his influence to advance their cause, withdrew their support and refused to endorse the invitation of the town council that he continue to represent the city in the Commons. Alternative aspiring candidates seized their opportunity and put themselves forward, one (David Loch, a 'trading burgess of small fortune') promising to hold himself aloof from an age he characterised by 'bribery, perjury, and venality', the other (Captain James-Francis Erskine of Forrest)[23] volunteering to rescue Edinburgh 'from the ignominy of being dictated to by the agents of Sir Lawrence Dundas.'[24]

When the town council met on election day, 13 October 1774, for the purpose of electing the member for Edinburgh three deacons formally objected to Dundas being described as a 'proper person' and protested that he was 'disqualified' on the grounds of 'having been guilty of bribery and corruption'. To prove their point, a letter written by Dundas from his Arlington Street (London) home, dated 2 May 1774, to 'one of his political agents, relating to the boroughs of Dunfermline, Inverkeithing, &c.' was produced. Assuming the latter was genuine, the evidence it disclosed, as printed in full in the *Scots Magazine*,[25] was damning. But, incredibly, its impact – while it 'embarrassed the electors, and protracted the business' – failed utterly to have the effect the whistle-blower, Captain Erskine, intended when he leaked its contents. Instead, it had the opposite effect. Dundas secured re-election by a large majority, it having been observed that 'supposing the writing produced to be authentic, it amounted to only an *attempt* [italics added] to bribe, which cannot [be held] subject to penalties and disabilities, unless the attempt be carried into execution'. It was a veritable travesty.

Mischievously, the report of the Edinburgh election fiasco in the *Scots Magazine* continues by citing, without comment, a minute of Dunfermline council dated the same election day, 13 October 1774, recording as follows:

> This being the day fixed for electing a delegate of this borough, the council, by appointment, assembled by eleven forenoon; when the friends of Col. Masterton and Col. Campbell being promiscuously met in council, the former made choice of Provost John Wilson as delegate for this borough against the general election, and the latter made choice of Mr John Maclaurin Advocate. Prior to calling the votes, the oaths against bribery and corruption were put to the members of council separately; and particularly, the oath being put to James Kinloch, deacon of the butchers, upon being asked upon oath, If he had received any sum or sums of money, gratuity, or reward? he answered negatively; but, upon recollection, said, That his wife had received from the hands of Capt. James-Francis Erskine two five-pound notes, which he was then ignorant of; but although he was now informed of it, it should have no influence upon him in this day's election.

On Tuesday 18 October, five days after the election in which he had triumphed, Dundas arrived at Edinburgh and was feted like an eastern potentate. *The Scots Magazine* dryly reported that

> Next day he waited of the magistrates in the council-chamber, and was received as the city-member. He was then entertained by them in a tavern, at the city's expense.

And the *Magazine* goes on to strike the final note of despair:

> A correspondent observes, that as bribery and corruption, and undue influence in various shapes, prevails so generally at our elections, it were to be wished, that our Scottish patriots, instead of wasting their strength in empty and unavailing words, would form themselves into a society, for prosecuting all such delinquents, without favour or friendship.[26]

It would, however, be a totally different story at the next general election. After 1774, opposition to Dundas intensified and there were attempts to overthrow him led by his increasingly powerful namesake and distant relative, Henry Dundas, then Lord Advocate, and the Duke of Buccleuch, who were both now actively aligned in their objectives with the trade corporations of Edinburgh. The anonymous author(s?) of two pamphlets published in Edinburgh in 1777 at the height of the campaign in the capital to unseat Lawrence Dundas describes not only James Masterton's key role in Dundas's early career in its formative stages, but also the extent to which Masterton was abandoned by the tycoon when the two fell out in 1774 on Masterton's defeat by Archibald Campbell in the election for the Stirling Burghs constituency:

> His [Masterton's] good sense first suggested the scheme by which the whole of an immense fortune was acquired. His advice if it had been followed would have saved the half of it. [27]
> ... You have play'd too deep, my dear Baronet, and you had better cut out in time, to save the remains of your money and your credit, now that the run is against you. It is true, that Campbell, who took one set of your burghs from you, is pining in a Yankee jail;[28] and God knows where Masterton is, (though I hope in a very good place, as he was charitable to the poor, and kind to his relations.) It was a great shame to you, by the by, Laurie, and it is a sin that will go very hard with you, if you don't repent, to drop poor Masterton in his latter days, who was a very honest fellow, who had served you so faithfully, and was the best friend you ever had; but the gout, and opposition, and their sins, are apt to make greater men than you fretful and peevish. [29]

It took Lawrence Dundas's unforeseen death in September 1781 to relinquish once and for all his stranglehold over the process of selection of the Edinburgh member. A much-relieved Henry Dundas wrote to John Robinson, Lord North's shrewd political manager for England:

> ... the party by which he [the member] is chosen and which in truth is the party left by Sir Lawrence Dundas must be broke, and the town of Edinburgh brought under some respectable patronage on which Government can rely, for they must not be permitted to govern the town by a knot of themselves without the interposition of some such patron ... for if they do, the first good opportunity that offers some able individual who leads the rest will sell them to any rich man like Sir Lawrence.[30]

The incident referred to in the second of the extracts cited is, of course, the same as lay behind the explosive contents of the leaked letter published in the *Scots Magazine* in October 1774, complete with its reference to a member of the Scotland family being hired to help carry out Dundas's dirty work. Was the letter genuine, or was it a forgery carefully fabricated to shock his supporters and boost the electoral chances of his enemies? It's an open question. The letter had by no means been forgotten in the interval since its first public disclosure. It is, indeed, the circumstances surrounding it, and the 'violent and costly contest' for the Stirling Burghs that inform it, that provide the essential background to the remarkable story of the so called 'Dunfermline case'.

While it would going too far to describe Colonel James Masterton, the member for Stirling Burghs since the general election of 1768, as Sir Lawrence Dundas's stooge, he was certainly his proxy. Dundas, we are told, 'became dominant in the constituency' which became renowned for all the wrong reasons, as 'one of the most venal in Scotland'.[31] The next general election, however, stood matters on their head when Dundas's opponents were able this time to produce an impressive rival candidate in an effort to destroy once and for all his malign influence in the notorious constituency. Masterton had been returned unopposed in 1768, but in 1774, aware that those opposed to him had produced a popular and charismatic figure in Colonel Archibald Campbell,[32] Dundas decided at the eleventh hour to drop his old friend and colleague in favour of

Sir Alexander Gilmour who, according to the *Scots Magazine*, 'was not known to be a candidate till he was voted for'. The official date of the election was 1 November but the results were set to be declared on the previous day. James Boswell, a friend of Campbell, attended the declaration in Dunfermline in his role as the delegate for Culross (one of the constituency's five eligible burghs) and was elated when his man was announced as the new member.[33]

Boswell first records his awareness of unlawful goings-on in the preliminaries leading up to the Dunfermline declaration – and, in particular, of Dundas's sinister involvement in them – in his private journal for 17 October 1774, just a fortnight before the scheduled date of the election. He notes that William Fergusson, 'a schoolmaster', called on him that day after breakfast at his home in Edinburgh and displayed a 'confused appearance of secrecy' before seeking his advice as a lawyer on what should be done with a bond Fergusson had in his possession granted by one of the candidates to a local deacon[34] (Thomas Gibson of Inverkeithing). The bond, later identified as a forgery, was, Boswell guessed, in Masterton's name and Fergusson maintained that he had been offered £500 by Sir Lawrence Dundas to '*give it back*'. Boswell immediately smelled a rat, correctly divining that Fergusson was 'a rogue, and wanted to discover the bond to Colonel Campbell to get money for it': that is, to get *more* money for it from Colonel Campbell, as evidence of bribery, than had allegedly been offered to him by Dundas.[35]

The incident marked the opening shot of an election campaign which has few rivals in terms of the grotesque extent to which it was dominated by overt corruption and skulduggery. Boswell's part in the subsequent Court of Session action that sprang from the election is of particular interest for a number of reasons: *first*, of course, his own personal involvement in the early stages of the election process as delegate for Culross, and his intimate connections with some of the major protagonists; *second*, his professional engagement in the Court action as junior counsel on the side of the defender, James Thomson; and, *thirdly*, his narrating of the case to Samuel Johnson which, as he describes it in his *Life*, led to Johnson's indignation at the verdict, provoking him to compose his 'Oral Essay on Pulpit Censure' in May 1776.

Scotlands v The Reverend James Thomson (1775-76)

The circumstances leading to the minister of Dunfermline making his outburst in church in the course of a digression from his sermon of Sunday 16 October 1774 are *prima facie* convoluted in the extreme; but they unravel readily enough when patiently explained by David Rae (later Lord Eskgrove) in the printed reclaiming *Petition of John, Robert, and David Scotlands* [sic] to the Lords of Council and Session dated July 14 1775. Rae begins by examining the career to date of Robert Scotland who, he states, 'long settled as a merchant in Dunfermline', had a 'considerable interest in managing the business of the burgh and its different corporations'. Captain James-Francis Erskine, Rae continues, had devised plans for 'shaking Sir Lawrence [Dundas's] interests' which included putting forward Colonel Archibald Campbell in opposition to James Masterton 'as a candidate for the Dunfermline district of burghs', a process that began at the Michaelmas election in 1773, a necessary precursor to the general election to be held in the following year. Meantime, what had begun as a mild dispute had arisen between Erskine and Robert Scotland over the selection of the provost of Dunfermline; but the row had intensified after Robert's father, John Scotland, had been elected a councillor and was known to have voted in favour of a candidate for the provostship disagreeable to Erskine who interpreted the father's actions as 'proof that Robert had betrayed his trust and deserted them' [Campbell's party]. Rae observes that 'in fact nothing had happened but what he had all along given reason to expect.'

Although by that time, states Rae, Campbell's position in the town and constituency was secure, Erskine had 'conceived a resentment' against Robert Scotland which developed into a relationship 'as violent as it was ill-founded'. The issue turned ugly when, 'on the very eve of election day' [Rae, confusingly, means the Michaelmas council elections held on or around 29 September, at which 'a majority of [Campbell's] friends were introduced into the council] a mob gathered outside Scotland's shop-door and Erskine himself 'in a loud voice, openly proclaimed that he, Robert Scotland, had been a traitor to Colonel Campbell; warning all his friends no longer to confide in, or to have any connection with him.' From that moment on, Rae asserts, the view was circulated that Robert Scotland 'had been bribed to betray Colonel Campbell's interest'. That view, Rae went on, was soon after 'greatly strengthened' by the conduct of the Reverend James Thomson, 'one of the ministers of Dunfermline'.

The rubric in Morison's summary of the case (in his monumental *Decisions of the Court of Session*) neatly encapsulates the argument deployed by both sides in their tactics, for and against the defender – 'Limits of liberty of the pulpit, with regard to censure.' [36] In his *Life of Samuel Johnson*, Boswell, *qua* advocate (and not this time wearing his hat as the delegate for Culross), confirms that 'The *Liberty of the Pulpit* was our great ground of defence' and he adds: 'but we argued also on the provocation of the previous attack, and on the instant retaliation.'[37] The Court Summons of 9 December 1774 fastens on the same point of law but, as one would expect, entirely negatively, from the point of view of the Scotlands who clearly deny that the pulpit affords any such immunity from prosecution:

> He, the said Mr James Thomson, from that Chair which ought to be ever devoted to the noblest purposes of truth and Piety converting it into a vehicle of private rancour and animosity did publickly, wantonly and maliciously defame and Calumniate the Characters of the Pursuers by accusing them openly in the face of the Congregation, of the most deliberate lyes, breach of faith, Bribery and Corruption naming some of the Pursuers … , and pointing out the others in such manner that all present understood whom he meant.[38]

The 'Chair' referred to in the Summons is, of course, the 'chair of verity', a phrase that recurs in the printed Court submissions, with its perceived undertones of controversy relating to the Dunfermline minister's assumed right to use his pulpit as a vehicle to censure the targets of his allegations.

At precisely this time (early 1775), though not himself professionally involved, Boswell was similarly concerned with upholding the rights of individuals in seeking immunity (or at least *protection*) under the law, in relation to two other important 'liberties' – *liberty of the press* and, not least, *liberty of the bar*. As far as the former is concerned, though not personally employed in the case – his colleague Robert Macqueen (later Lord Braxfield) had accepted the brief – Boswell could not ignore the progress and outcome of two parallel suits initiated by the Scotlands against the *Caledonian Mercury* and the *Edinburgh Advertiser* arising from the insertion of the 'Pillory' spoof card they had unwittingly fallen for in the last week of October 1774. Both actions were later abandoned. In his *Memorial* of 15 February 1775, a key (and to this day still unpublished) document in the *Scotlands v Thomson* process, Boswell describes the action as 'a kind of a Cerberean Summons, there being three pursuers insisting for three separate Claims of Damages for alledged separate injuries'.

The issue of the *liberty of the bar* was, in Boswell's eyes, potentially an altogether more serious matter. On Friday 23 December he was 'late' in the Court of Session awaiting the judgment in the intriguing *Shaw v Bean* process which had stirred up the entire Scottish legal fraternity in the light of the crucial principles clearly at stake. In its issue for 26 December the *Caledonian Mercury* reported that George Bean, a writer in Inverness,[39] had alleged before the Sheriff of the burgh that Angus Shaw, merchant in Inverness, was a 'fraudulent bankrupt'. Shaw retaliated by bringing an action for defamation and damages before the Court. After considering 'several hundreds of pages in print', 'mutual memorials upon the proof', and a pleading which lasted all of ten days, the Court threw out the action, finding the pursuer's claim 'groundless, vexatious and oppressive'. On learning the determination, Boswell mused:

> While the lords were giving their opinions, and a crowd attended with much curiosity, I was wondering if all the particulars of this cause and its determination were predetermined. My brother lawyer, Mr. Grant of Corrimony,[40] sat by me, and I observed to him that it was in vain to argue to the Lords when they were met to decide a cause, for then their opinions were fixed. The bench then was set sail and would pursue its course. While the pleading lasts, the bench is like a ship in the harbour. You may direct it or have a chance to direct it. But when the Lords are met to decide, you may as well call to a ship fairly sailed to return.[41]

Boswell's sole surviving contribution to the *Scotlands v Thomson* process is his unpublished thirty-page *Memorial for the Reverend Mr James Thomson* of 15 February 1775.[42] It is true that almost exactly one year later, his name appears on the last page of the written version of Ilay Campbell's sixty-four page *Petition of The Reverend Mr. James Thomson* of 24 January 1776,[43] but not too much can be made of that, since it probably indicates that Boswell devilled for Campbell throughout the process, and probably assisted with the preparation of Campbell's petition. In this case, Boswell himself explains (*Memorial* f. 2) that the outcome of the 'very full hearing of Counsel on both sides' (on 2 February 1775) resulted in the Lord Ordinary, Lord Gardenstone, two days later ordering memorials to be given in to the Court, of which Boswell's represents the case for the defender.

In his memorial Boswell argues that in 'this enlightened and liberal age' the 'various kinds of Liberty are gradually receiving judicial establishment': these are *liberty of the press, liberty of the bar, and liberty of the pulpit*. Of the first, he has little to say: 'Of the Liberty of the Press, many noble instances have occurred while at the same time its licentiousness has been most properly checked'. As for the 'Liberty of the Bar', it was 'lately very fully considered in the cause Angus Schaw [sic] against George Bean from Inverness, and much instruction was derived from the opinions of your Lo'ps/ at giving Judgment'. What remains to be discussed is 'a Subject very extensive and very important' – the 'Liberty of the Pulpit'. To a modern reader Boswell struggles hard to plead the role of the sermon in Christian worship:

> That a Preacher should inculcate the duties of Morality, and check vice of every kind will not be denied by any rational Man, for if he does not do so, his sermons are no better than empty Sound, or at best a mere amusement of the fancy whether their Stile be gay vivacity or gloomy mysticism, for to some minds there is an amusement in sadness. A Clergyman, like a Physician must proceed according to the circumstances of those under his care. If Gentle admonitions are not effectual, he must not stop short, but must try what can be done by the severity of reproof. If general reprehension is found ineffectual, he must administrate particular rebuke to notorious individuals.[44]

Boswell's tactics for the greater part of the rest of his *Memorial* are transparently obvious. He proceeds – entertainingly but, it has to be said, to modern tastes, laboriously and unsubtly – to lecture the Court on numerous precedents which, in his opinion, reinforce his central premise that the old minister was not only justified in his pulpit rebuke but was by no means the first of his calling to resort to such measures. An enumeration of all these supposed precedents is given in *Appendix B* to this study. By far the most successful and entertaining anecdotes – for that is essentially all they are – are those that resonate directly with Boswell's own real experience: *viz.* (i) the James Baine sermon directed against 'some men in high office who had encouraged the performance of a Ludicrous Play' (Samuel Foote's comedy, *The Minor*); (ii) the amusing anecdote concerning Hugh Blair and Blair's unsuspecting *gaffe* over his choice of text for a sermon he preached 'on the Sunday after the news of the reversal of the great Douglas cause arrived at Edinburgh' ; and, (iii) perhaps above all, the wonderful irony latent in the joke he makes (most probably) about his own father, Lord Auchinleck, a senior judge of the Court of Session, when, more than a little tipsy, he came to church in the afternoon to hear a sermon preached against intemperance on the text *'They that be drunken are drunken in the night.'*[45]

It would be wrong, however, to write off Boswell's *Memorial* as mere theatre. It has its special insights as well as not a few moments of *gravitas*. Perhaps the most impressive and certainly the most original section of the *Memorial* is when Boswell cites as his authority the great seventeenth-century English judge and politician, Sir Robert Atkyns (*aka* Atkins), who had left his mark on the drafting of the Bill of Rights, thereby encapsulating his views on law and government.[46] In his magisterial *Parliamentary and Political Tracts*, a work first posthumously published in London in 1734 – though Boswell uses the second edition of 1741 – Atkyns writes:

> Brook brought an action against Sir H. M. for saying of the Plantiff [sic] Brook, that he had committed felony:
> Sir H. M. pleaded specially to the action That he was a Counsellor at Law, and was retained against the Plaintiff Brook; and at the Trial in giving evidence to the jury, he did indeed speak those words, but averr'd that they were pertinent to the matter, & were part of his

instruction. It was resolved upon a Demurrer,⁴⁷ That the plea was good, the words being pertinent, tho' they were false, and there is a further reason given by the Court in that Case *viz*. The words appear not to be spoken out of malice. And no actions of this sort, nor will any indictment of this nature lie, unless there be malice in the defendant. And where there is any justifiable occasion of speaking words that a man in discharge of his function or calling is led by the subject matter of discourse, *as a Preacher or Pleader* [italics added], or the like, to speak words, in such case, it shall be presumed they were not spoken out of malice. ⁴⁸

It was an ingenious and resourceful demonstration of advocacy at the highest level. In his private journal for the same date Boswell records that he 'Finished Mr. Thomson's memorial before five in the afternoon', then went to see a performance of *The Beggar's Opera*. At the first hearing of the three conjoint actions in the Court a couple of weeks before, he had noted down that not only he had 'pleaded Thomson's cause really as well as I could wish to plead', but that afterwards David Rae, Robert Macqueen and even Lord Gardenstone (Francis Garden) himself, the presiding judge in the process, had been heard to praise his performance. Boswell was in splendid form and the case, he sensed, had brought out the best in him.

Boswell had every reason to feel pleased with himself when just over a month after he gave in his memorial, Lord Gardenstone pronounced his interlocutor of 28 February finding the process against James Thomson 'improper and groundless' and 'assoilzied' (absolved) the old minister. At the same time, Gardenstone decerned that, 'if the pursuers are dissatisfied' with his opinion, 'they may apply directly to the Inner House'.⁴⁹ Effectively, it was a pyrrhic victory that satisfied no one. The minister would doubtless have rejoiced at the words of the interlocutor but he must also have trembled at the inevitable continuation of the action on appeal by his determined pursuers. There was additionally, of course, the small matter of cost, but (unlike the Witherspoon case examined in chapter 2) we have nothing to go on so far as that aspect of the minister's problems is concerned. A few months later (14 July) the case sprang into life once more with Rae's reclaiming *Petition* and the successive trio of printed documents thereafter.

The characteristic legal ping-pong of accusation and counter-accusation (already seen in the 'Paisley case') represented in these four submissions⁵⁰ need not detain us here, except to highlight where their content attaches real importance to the central issue of this study – the issue of pulpit censure and Thomson's assumed belief in that *locus*, together of course with his status as a minister of the gospel, granting him immunity from prosecution at the hands of the law. In chronological order, the following extracts are of particular importance. The references by David Rae and Henry Dundas to the relevance of the *Snodgrass v. Witherspoon* process to the present action are of extraordinary interest:

From David Rae's reclaiming *Petition of John, Robert, and David Scotlands, Merchants in Dunfermline* of 14 July 1775, 9-10 (of 23 pp.)

The pulpit has been well termed the chair of verity, and certainly nothing should be delivered from it, but what is consistent with the great objects to which the use of it is appropriated. Nothing could be more derogatory to the honour of the church and its members, and more destructive of the peace of society, than the [sic] suffering the pulpit to become a vehicle for propagation of private scandal and defamation, or to be made an engine for gratifying private revenge or resentment. The case, too, of a person who has been abused or defamed from the pulpit, is one of the hardest that can well occur. The influence which every minister has, or ought to have, over the minds and opinions of his hearers, the faith due to any thing asserted by him, especially in such a place, and the number of people present on such an occasion, all concur to add an infinite weight to any accusation or aspersion delivered from the pulpit.

The publication of a libel in any other manner, cannot be attended with half the prejudice to the injured party, and a wrong of this kind, is still more inexcusable, that sermons are generally reduced into writing before they are delivered, and nothing is presumed to be spoke, or ought to be spoke from the pulpit, but what has been previously weighed, and deliberately considered by the preacher.

It is impossible, therefore to maintain, that a civil action for damages, does not lie at the suit of the party against a minister who preaches a defamatory sermon against him. Such a sermon is a libel in the proper sense of the word; and it is published, as already said, in a manner much more destructive and pernicious, than any other mode that can well be devised. It is true, that ecclesiastical courts may, and ought to take notice of such abuses, but then, they can only inflict a censure on the delinquent, and cannot award damage or reparation to the party injured. A remedy, therefore, of the latter kind must be competent; and it can be no where sued for with such propriety, as before your Lordships. ... The occasions given for complaints of this kind, have happily indeed been rare both here and in England, but some have occurred. *A minister of Paisley, was some years ago prosecuted before this Court, for a sermon he had preached, thought to reflect upon some of his parishioners, and it was not then pleaded for him, that a sermon, if injurious, was not actionable, but the defence was laid upon a better ground.* [51] [italics added]

From Andrew Crosbie's *Answers for the Reverend Mr James Thomson* of 14 October 1775, 6 (of 14 pp.)

[Note: *It is surely deliciously ironic that Boswell's roguish but brilliant friend and colleague, Crosbie, who as we saw in chapter 2 was especially aggressive towards John Witherspoon as counsel for his pursuers, now radically argues from the very opposite point of view in defending Thomson; that is, his defence is grounded in a minister's right and duty to hold forth and speak out on perceived wrongs in the community under his charge. That is, however, the way of advocates.*]

Indeed, rebuke and reprehension, not only in private, but in a public manner, when it could not otherwise be attended with effect, hath always been held to be a part of the pastoral duty in this country. In this sense, hath been taken that text of Scripture, I Thessal. v. 14. "Now we exhort you, brethren, warn them that are unruly." And the second Book of Discipline, Chap. IV. in describing the duty of a pastor, or minister, says, "He ought also to watch over the manners of his flock, that the better he may apply the doctrine to them, in reprehending the dissolute persons, and exhorting the Godly in the fear of the Lord." The respondent will be far from disputing, that this, as all others, even the very best institutions, [sic] is capable of abuse, and when it appears to be grossly abused, it may be an object of punishment, but, he does humbly conceive, that this is a question of very nice discussion, and incapable of being determined by any general rule; and that your Lordships, and every other court of justice, will be extremely careful to determine all questions of that sort, in such way as may be consistent with the idea of a minister, continuing to exercise his pastoral duty in its fullest extent.

From Ilay Campbell's *Petition of The Reverend Mr James Thomson* of 18 January 1776, 14-15, 17-18 (of 25 pp.)

[Note: *In their interlocutor of 20 December* [52] *1775 the Lords of Council and Session had found 'in respect of the improper conduct of the defender Mr James Thomson, unsuitable to the character of a minister of the Gospel, contrary to the decency, dignity and purity of the pulpit, and highly injurious to the pursuers' and found him 'liable to the pursuers in damages and expences, of which [they] ordain a condescendence and accompt to be given in, and, in this case, refuse to allow a proof of the alleged veritas convitii.'*
Boswell writes in his journal that this verdict, 'by a great majority', was 'very unexpected to me, and I was a good deal hurt by it, having taken a fixed interest in the question, I suppose from its being connected with Colonel Campbell's success, and believing that Thomson thought himself right.' He also noted that the Court were 'very severe' on the minister.] [53]

… the petitioner does sincerely and solemnly declare, that in the course of the sermon preached on the 16th October he had no particular eye towards Robert Scotland; though he is sorry to say, there were several persons in the congregation, who had too much reason to apply to themselves the general censures which he then uttered. If the pursuers do still aver, That any thing was said or done at that time, which can be interpreted to the disadvantage of the petitioner in the present question, as a personal attack against Robert Scotland, attended with circumstances of impropriety, and sufficient to justify the after proceedings of Mr Scotland, your petitioner knows no way in which the matter can be cleared up but by a proof, for he does firmly adhere to the account he has already given of that affair, and does boldly maintain, that he neither said nor did any thing in the least degree beyond the bounds of the most perfect rectitude as a minister of the Gospel, and this he will maintain in every court to which he may be called, whether civil, criminal, or ecclesiastical.

… the question is whether the present action is well founded against him, and whether the said Robert Scotland, and his father and brother, as persons unjustly attacked, defamed and injured, are entitled to recover damages from the petitioner, attended with the severe stigmatizing expressions of criminal charge and conviction against him, which the interlocutor of the Court [for 20 December] presently bears. This is an important question for the petitioner; it is important to the law, to the police, and to the rights, civil and religious, of the subjects of this country, and it is a question, in the consideration of which your Lordships will, *in hoc statu*, take the facts, not as averred by the pursuers, but as set forth by the defender; as it is to be hoped that no instance has ever happened in this country, of a defender in any Court, having been condemned upon facts alleged against him, and denied by him, without evidence being adduced.[54]

If a minister of the Gospel, whose character ought to be unimpeached, and who ought to possess the affections and good opinion of those under his care, finds himself publicly calumniated and abused by a man of doubtful or perhaps bad character, whom he is bound to advise, to admonish, and to rebuke, as one of his parishioners. — If in such circumstances he should happen to go too far in the mode or extent of the correction. — If he should place him on the stool of repentance, and in the warmth of his zeal, reprove him with more severity than the nature of the case requires, the petitioner begs leave to ask, what are the legal consequences? The honest clergyman may be wrong, but is the other party right? [italics added]

From Henry Dundas's *Answers for John, Robert, and David Scotlands, Merchants in Dunfermline* of 4 July 1776, 10, 19-20 (of 31 pp.)[55]

The clergy of this country have been long respectable from the gravity and the purity of their conduct, and their pulpits have been used by them under such impressions as were suitable to the expectations of their hearers, who looked for nothing from thence but found instruction and dispassionate admonitions. *But least of all did any body ever expect to see the pulpit converted into a vehicle of political ribaldry and party scolding. The transactions which give rise to the present process, are, it is believed, the first, and, it is hoped, will be the last, modern example of such a proceeding.* [italics added]

... The respondents do not dispute, that, about the time of the Reformation, very great liberties were used from the pulpit by the zealous and violent men of those times; and, perhaps, we, their descendants, have the less the reason to regret that unbounded zeal and violence, because, in all probability, the important business in which they were engaged could not have been accomplished without exceeding the ordinary bounds of moderation. But it will not be pretended, that there is any thing in the ideas or manners of the present time which calls for such inordinate zeal, and it is a certain truth, that the refinement of modern manners will not bear such practices.

... In certain offences, the law and practice of the church allows congregational rebukes, but this is only done after conviction, either by trial or confession, and it would be intolerable if every clergyman should conceive himself at liberty, without trying, examination, or conviction, nay without even private rebuke or communication, to lay hold of any individual of his parish, to hold him forth as a criminal, and ruin his credit and good name among his neighbours.

Such a doctrine tends to vest the clergy with a right of calumniating or abusing individuals from the pulpit, without control. The occasions given for complaints of this kind have, happily indeed, been rare, both here and in England, but some have occurred. *A minister of Paisley was, some years ago, prosecuted before this court, for a sermon he had preached, thought to reflect upon some of his parishioners, and it was not then pleaded for him, that a sermon, if injurious, was not actionable.* [italics added][56]

[Note: Dundas's Answers ends with further information concerning Captain James-Francis Erskine[57] against whom, it seems, Robert Scotland was also proposing to raise an action in the Court of Session. We learn from Dundas that this Scotland 'meant seriously to have insisted in that process ... for reparation against Captain Erskine; but 'before it could be called', Gardenstone's interlocutor of 28 February 1775 had acquitted Thomson, 'and the respondent was discouraged from going forward with it, with so unfavourable an interlocutor against him in a similar cause.' Significantly, Dundas goes on to add that Robert Scotland 'was likewise discouraged with the expence of this litigation, which turned out much greater than he expected'. In any event, states Dundas, 'though he had succeeded in getting damages and expences determined to him, he did not know how he could recover them, as Captain Erskine, before the process could be called, had left this country, with an intention, as was reported, of going to the East-Indies; and accordingly, he has never been in the country since.'][58]

Court of Session Decreet of 8 August 1776 [59]

Unfortunately the normally reliable editors of Boswell's private journal for 1774-76 (Ryskamp and Pottle) get it seriously wrong in concluding that the process begun on 4 February 1775 was finally determined in the Court of Session by interlocutor of 19 [20] December of the same year, thus reversing Lord Gardenstone's interlocutor of 28 February by the terms of which he had 'assoilzied' [acquitted] James Thomson and ordered the Scotlands to pay the audited costs of the action.[60] Concentrating exclusively on Boswell's own contribution to the defence of the minister, they appear oblivious of the four crucial *printed* submissions set out in extract immediately above, dating from 14 July 1775 (Rae) to 4 July 1776 (Dundas). They also seem unaware of the comprehensive (though, admittedly, severely indigestible) 223 page-long Extract Decreet containing the full and formal account of the entire extracted legal process. (see Bibliography).

Had the editors seen those documents they would immediately have spotted their *gaffe*; that, far from the process being finally settled in the week before Christmas 1775, in fact it continued to be argued over for a further seven months, during which time a series of Representations, Petitions and Answers were given in to the Court. On 8 August 1776, and only after several interlocutors beyond the end of 1775, the Decreet records that their Lordships 'adhered to their former interlocutor reclaimed against, and refused the Petition' and 'modified' expenses to £52 10s but, more important, decerned that Robert Scotland was entitled 'only to five pounds sterling of damages', but found John and David Scotland 'entitled jointly to the sum of twenty five pounds sterling'. The Decreet of 8 August 1776 repeated the wording of the interlocutor of 20 December 1775 describing James Thomson's 'improper conduct' as 'unsuitable to the Character of a Minister of the Gospel & contrary to the decency, dignity and purity of the pulpit', words that account for Boswell having described the Court's treatment of the old minister as 'very severe'.

James Thomson's appeal to the House of Lords

There can be little doubt that Thomson felt massively let down by the Court's verdict, to the extent that he decided to press ahead with an appeal to the House of Lords. His appeal was read before the Lords on 18 November and the Scotlands were ordered to lodge Answers in writing on or before 16 December.[61] In the journal of the House of Lords for 20 November 1775 it is recorded that John Spottiswoode, a solicitor who handled Court of Session business in London (and whom Ilay Campbell identifies as the acknowledged 'solicitor of our Court' [in London] in the final decade of the eighteenth-century),[62] was 'permitted to enter into a recognizance for [effectively to act on behalf of] the Appellant, as desired', he 'living in Scotland'. On 2 December the journal records that 'this day was brought in' the 'Answer of John Scotland and others' to Thomson's appeal. There are no further references to the appeal beyond that date. One must assume that principally on ground of cost Thomson was persuaded to abandon his appeal. In Boswell's *Life of Samuel Johnson* he makes clear that Thomson's withdrawal of his appeal was grounded on advice given his counsel by the English Attorney-General, later Lord Chancellor, Edward Thurlow.

Further, as Ryskamp and Pottle would have us believe, Samuel Johnson 'wrote' [sic] his 'oral essay' on pulpit censure 'for Mr. Thomson', the clear implication being that he did so to aid the minister in his House of Lords appeal.[63] But there is not a shred of evidence that that was the case. It is more likely that Johnson was simply indulging in an intellectual exercise, for the purpose of demonstrating his conviction that the Scottish judges had got it wrong. Interestingly, in his opinion Thurlow himself doubted the legitimacy of the verdict:

> It is impossible to approve the style of that sermon. But the *complaint* was not less ungracious from that man [Robert Scotland], who had behaved so ill by his original libel, and at the time, when he received the reproach he complains of. In the last article, all the plaintiffs are equally concerned. It struck me also with some wonder, that the Judges should think so much fervour apposite to the occasion of reproving the defendant for a little excess.[64]

Samuel Johnson's 'oral essay' on pulpit censure [65]

Boswell relates the facts of the case to Dr. Johnson in May 1776 – the date given in the rubric to the *Life* – which, assuming its accuracy, was at least two clear months before the process was determined, and even substantially before Lord Advocate Henry Dundas's *Answers* to Thomson's *Petition*. More especially, Johnson would have heard the facts of the case many months before Thomson's appeal was lodged in the House of Lords. All of that notwithstanding, Johnson's reaction to the outcome of the Court process as narrated to him by Boswell is hugely significant, not just to the present chapter but to the thrust of this whole study. Johnson's *Oral Essay on Pulpit Censure* is a monument to the right of a minister to use the vehicle of his pulpit to exercise his duty to impart the lesson of right standards of ethical (in this case, Christian) behaviour. Boswell records in his *Life* that in May 1776 Johnson, then aged 67, dictated to him over two sessions an 'oral essay' on 'censure pronounced from the pulpit'. In a footnote Boswell characteristically uses the incident to record his unwavering admiration of Johnson's 'extraordinary powers of composition' and he notes that 'there are in the whole only seven corrections, or rather variations, and those not considerable'. The whole performance, in Boswell's judgment – the lion-hunter *par excellence* typically asserts – demonstrated 'at once the vigorous and accurate emanations' of the great man's mind.

Johnson begins his 'oral essay' by tracing the origin of pulpit censure back to the 'primitive church' when 'religion was yet pure from secular advantages' [and] 'the punishment of sinners was publick censure, and open penance' :

> penalties inflicted merely by ecclesiastical authority, at a time while the Church had yet no help from the civil power; while the hand of the magistrate lifted only the rod of persecution; and when governours were ready to afford a refuge to all those who fled from clerical authority.

He goes on to claim that 'after three hundred years of struggle and distress' magistrates began to cooperate with priests and 'clerical sentences were made efficacious by secular force.' In these circumstances

When religion obtained the support of law, if admonitions and censures had no effect, they were seconded by the magistrates with coercion and punishment.

Johnson attributes to this evolution of a developing partnership between ecclesiastical and secular authorities the 'practice of auricular confession':

> Those who dreaded the blast of publick reprehension, were willing to submit themselves to the priest, by a private accusation of themselves; and to obtain a reconciliation with the Church by a kind of clandestine absolution and invisible penance; conditions with which the priest would in times of ignorance and corruption easily comply, as they increased his influence, by adding the knowledge of secret sins to that of notorious offences, and enlarged his authority, by making him the sole arbiter of the terms of reconcilement.

But, argues Johnson, all of this changed at a stroke with the Reformation. 'From this bondage the Reformation set us free' and the minister no longer has the power to 'torture us by interrogatories, or put himself in possession of our secrets and our lives'. And yet, Johnson confidently states, the important thing is that though 'we have thus controlled [a minister's] usurpations', 'his just and original power remains unimpaired':

> He may still see, though he may not pry: he may yet hear, though he may not question. And that knowledge which his eyes and ears force upon him it is still his duty to use, for the benefit of his flock. ... A minister who has in his congregation a man of open and scandalous wickedness, may warn his parishioners to shun his conversation. To warn them is not only lawful, but not to warn them would be criminal.

A minister's duty, Johnson continues, to warn his flock – and, just as important, the *means* of his doing so – is not just confined to word of mouth. Indeed, he says, there is much to be said for public utterance before the whole congregation, which may be 'deeper' and thus 'more effectual':

> ... if he may warn each man singly, what shall forbid him to warn them altogether? Of that which is to be made known to all, how is there any difference whether it be communicated to each singly, or to all together? What is known to all, must necessarily be publick. Whether it shall be publick at once, or publick by degrees, is the only question. And of a sudden and solemn publication the impression is deeper, and the warning more effectual.

Johnson concedes, however, that there are dangers in this practice:

> It may easily be urged, if a minister be thus left at liberty to delate [= accuse] sinners from the pulpit, and to publish at will the crimes of a parishioner, he may often blast the innocent, and distress the timorous. He may be suspicious, and condemn without evidence; he may be rash, and judge without examination; he may be severe, and treat slight offences with too much harshness; he may be malignant and partial, and gratify his private interest or resentment under the shelter of his pastoral character

And he concludes:

> ... if possibility of evil be to exclude good, no good can ever be done. If nothing is to be attempted in which there is danger, we must all sink into hopeless inactivity. The evils that may be feared from this practice arise not from any defect in the institution, but from the

infirmities of human inactivity. Power, in whatever hands it is placed, will be sometimes improperly exerted; yet courts of law must judge, though they will sometimes judge amiss. A father must instruct his children, though he himself may often want instruction. A minister must censure sinners, though his censure may be sometimes erroneous by want of judgement, and sometimes unjust by want of honesty.

Johnson's oral essay ends with his applying his hypothesis to the practical implications of the Dunfermline case. As Boswell explains in the *Life*, before he had noted down Johnson's dictated essay news came that the case had gone against the minister, despite his defence having been grounded on the principle of the '*Liberty of the Pulpit*'.

Even by his own formidable standards of intellectuality Samuel Johnson's analysis of the evolution of public censure in an ecclesiastical context is, as Boswell has carefully observed, a remarkable *tour de force*. The man they called the *'Great Cham'* is surely on the mark when he contrasts the old Catholic tradition of private confession to the priest *in camera* with the implied Reformed (Calvinist) preference for public penance. Even so, by the same token, Johnson, we might think, is on shakier ground when he robustly declares his preference for the latter. His argument today seems to a modern reader extraordinarily unconvincing when he claims that the more public the censure, the better for all concerned – specifically, in the case before him, the better for the target of the Scottish minister's rebuke. Unsurprisingly, Johnson makes no stipulated allowance for – and would presumably give no quarter on – the modern idea of an alleged 'victim's' right of reply, least of all the assumed innocence of the accused until proved guilty in Court – according, of course, one is bound to add, to accepted modern concepts of natural justice.

Colonel Campbell and his Trustees v Robert Scotland (1778) [66]

The consequences of Thomson's pulpit censure, and the story of bribery and corruption in Dunfermline do not, however, end with the minister's abandonment of his putative appeal to the House of Lords, nor with Johnson's oral essay inspired by the case. There was a final twist that few could have foreseen. In November 1778 Colonel Archibald Campbell and his Trustees (who managed his affairs on account of Campbell's absence 'abroad', while he was being held as a P.O.W. by the Americans) raised an action 'of count and reckoning'[67] in the Court of Session against Robert Scotland. The Court was informed that in 1775, Scotland, a 'shop-keeper' in Dunfermline, had been employed as Campbell's agent for managing his political interests in the burgh. For 'his trouble' in that connection, it was agreed that money paid in instalments, representing a 'large gratuity' amounting in aggregate to the sum of £3,000, should be handed over to Scotland. Morison records that 'no receipt or voucher was given by him for any part of this money.' Further:

> It was afterwards suspected by Colonel Campbell and his friends, that Scotland had betrayed his interest in the burgh, and favoured the other party. ... Scotland was required by them [Campbell's named trustees] to show his accounts for the money he had received; and upon his declining to comply, the trustees brought an action of count and reckoning against him, in their own name, and that of their constituent, and insisted that he should, in the first place, be ordained to produce his accompts.

With, one suspects, his back well and truly to the wall, Scotland acknowledged having received the money, but pleaded in his defence that 'it must be taken subject to the intrinsic qualities [68] under which he makes it, *viz.* that he got the money for the purpose of employing it in bribery', and 'actually employed it to that purpose.' His defence continued:

> The trust committed to the defender was therefore of an illicit nature [*pactum illicitum*], and all action on it is denied by law.

To this defence the pursuers denied that Colonel Campbell had entered into any illicit compact with Scotland: that rather

> ... the money was put into his [Scotland's] hands for the purpose of giving entertainments to the people; but that he had received no instructions from the defender to employ it in bribery. The pursuer is charged with a crime, and he must be presumed innocent till his guilt be shown. The defender's averment fixes only his own turpitude; but he must establish by proof the unlawful concert he alleges, otherwise his defence, which rests on the hypothesis, that an unlawful agreement had taken place, falls to the ground.

In his judgment, however, Lord Braxfield observed, that if the pursuers had been able to produce 'any voucher of this money being in the hands of Scotland', the defender's claim that a *turpe pactum* [shameful contract] had been entered into would have been insufficient to 'screen' him from accounting. Since, however, 'the receipt of the money' rested 'on the acknowledgment of the defender', he felt able to sustain Scotland's defence and he was thus 'assoilzied' [cleared of blame].[69] One feels for the old minister in the light of Braxfield's determination. From the Reverend James Thomson's point of view the case was a pyrrhic victory: on the one hand, there was no question that he could continue to justify his extraordinary behaviour in his pulpit on account of Robert Scotland's clear acknowledgment before a judge of the Court of Session that he had indeed received a large sum of money which, he further admitted, he had used to distribute bribes. The supreme irony, however, lay in the fact that Scotland had won his case by the clever stratagem of counter-accusing his pursuers that, despite strong denials on their part, it was Colonel Campbell and his supporters who had instigated the bribery, and that he was merely the instrument of their corruptibility and, therefore, had been found 'not liable to account.'

Postscript

Chronology of the Court action against the Reverend James Thomson

[*Note* The identity of the counsel participating in the action – or, more strictly, *actions* since the Scotlands also sued the *Caledonian Mercury* and *Edinburgh Advertiser* newspapers for their part in the alleged libel [70] – shows that the process involved some of the greatest names of the age in Scottish advocacy: *for the pursuers*, Alexander Lockhart (later Lord Covington) (Dean of the Faculty), David Rae (later Lord Eskgrove), and Bannatyne William Macleod (later Lord Bannatyne); and *for the defenders* (the two newspapers and Thomson), Robert Macqueen (later Lord Braxfield), John MacLaurin (later Lord Dreghorn), Ilay Campbell (later Sir Ilay Campbell of Succoth), Andrew Crosbie and James Boswell. This chronology summarises the nature and timeline of the documentation relating to the action, printed and in manuscript, throughout its eighteen-month passage through the Court of Session, and concludes with the related process of 1778 initiated by Colonel Archibald Campbell and his Trustees against Robert Scotland.]

1774

16 October

The Reverend James Thomson preaches the first of his two sermons allegedly attacking Robert Scotland, who, though he is absent from church, is presumably informed by his wife, who is present in the congregation, and others there of the minister's intentions, 'that the pursuer, Robert Scotland, was the man he meant … by looking towards his seat during that part of the discourse, and even pointing directly to it, which turned the eyes of the whole congregation on poor Mrs Scotland, the wife of Robert, he himself being then from home; and no person in the church entertained a doubt that Mr Thomson alluded to him.' [Rae, *Petition*, 4]

19 October

Paragraph in the *Caledonian Mercury* claiming 'We can assure the public, that the letter of a certain Baronet [reproduced in the *Scots Magazine* XXXVI, Oct. 1774, 556] would not have been produced against him, if there had not been the most positive evidence of his having bribed a Dunfermline agent to betray his trust.'

22 October

A letter by Robert Scotland 'To the Printer of the Caledonian Mercury' is published in the newspaper of this date, asserting that the accusations against him are 'false and slanderous', and at the same time attacking Thomson as a 'blustering blunderbuss of an old military chaplain'.

30 October

Thomson preaches his second sermon, this time avowedly with the intention of attacking Robert Scotland, his father John and brother David, using a text from *Ephesians* to reinforce his oral assault on all three. Both Colonel Campbell, victorious in the general election, and James Boswell (in his capacity as the delegate for Culross) are seated in the congregation and hear the sermon at first hand.

9 December

Summons served on Thomson in the name of John Scotland, Robert Scotland and David Scotland, all merchants in Dunfermline, to 'Compear before the Lords of our Council and Session' to answer a claim for damages amounting to £1,000 Sterling and of £300 Sterling 'as the expense of process'.

1775

4 February

The process is called in the Court of Session in the form of two actions of defamation, one at the instance of Robert Scotland against the publisher of *The Caledonian Mercury*, the second in the name of Robert Scotland, his father John and brother David against the Reverend James Thomson. Though undated, Bannatyne Macleod's MS *Memorial* for the Scotlands certainly belongs to early February (as does James Boswell's), even though the NRS record has it as 1776.

15 February

James Boswell's MS *Memorial* for Thomson.

28 February

Lord Gardenstone's interlocutor finds the process against Thomson 'improper and groundless' and 'assoilzies' him, but allows the pursuers, if dissatisfied with his judgment, to apply directly to the Inner House.

14 July

David Rae's printed reclaiming *Petition* on behalf of the pursuers, the three Scotlands.

14 October

Andrew Crosbie's printed *Answers* on behalf of the defender, Thomson.

20 December

Court of Session interlocutor signed by Boswell's father Lord Auchinleck reversing, by a majority, Lord Gardenstone's decision of 28 February 1775. Boswell describes the judgment in his private journal as 'very severe' on the minister.

1776

18 January

Islay Campbell's printed *Petition* on behalf of Thomson.

4 July

Henry Dundas's printed *Answers* for the Scotlands.

8 August

Decreet of the Court of Session confirming their interlocutor of 20 December and awarding damages and expenses to the Scotlands.

18 November

Petition and Appeal of James Thomson read and received in the House of Lords.

20 November

House of Lords agree that the law agent John Spottiswoode 'may be permitted to enter into a Recognizance' for the appellant, Thomson, 'he living in Scotland'.

2 December

'Answer' of John Scotland and others 'brought in' by the House of Lords. Thomson's Appeal subsequently abandoned.

1778

28 November

Action for 'count and reckoning' brought by Colonel Campbell and his Trustees against Robert Scotland in the Court of Session determined by Lord Braxfield in favour of John Scotland.

Chalk on paper drawing of Allan Ramsay (1684-1758), poet and playwright, sketched by his son and namesake (1713-84) in 1729 when the artist was just 15 years old. Reproduced by kind permission of the National Galleries of Scotland.

4

The Stage

I preach'd on the Subject, because I thought it seasonable to offer some Correction in Righteousness, to the overgrown Levity of the Age; and chiefly for the same Reason I now make, what I said then, still more publick.
Reverend George Anderson, 'V.D.M.' ['Minister of the Word of God'] (1676/7-1756), from the sermon noted below preached in the 'Trone [sic] Church of Edinburgh' on an unspecified date in 1733.

The Reverend author of Douglas was a worthy member of this society;[1] *and his tragedy, long before it appeared in public was, by this society, extolled with all the noise of declamation; and the little merit it has, exaggerated with all the amplifications of bombast.*
John MacLaurin (later Lord Dreghorn) (1734-96), *Apology for The Writers against the Tragedy of Douglas. With some remarks on that Play.* (1757), 5.

Key author and sermon

Reverend George Anderson (1676/7-1756), 'a preacher, who had formerly been an army-chaplain, and, in his latter years became chaplain to Watson's Hospital, Edinburgh.'[2]

The Use and Abuse of Diversions. A Sermon on Luke xix. 13. With an Appendix, shewing that the Stage in particular is an Unchristian Diversion ... .
Edinburgh: printed by R. Fleming and Company, and sold at Mr. James M'Euen's Shop, MDCCXXXIII [1733][3]

From John Anderson,[4] *preaching in its second decade, to Hugh Blair preaching in its last, the pulpit in eighteenth-century Scotland was the source of literally hundreds of sermons deploring the decline and retreat of 'real' religion, and, in the opinion of the preachers, consequentially an alarming rise in the country as a whole of baseness, profanity and apathy – the stock substantives used being 'infidelity' and 'immorality'.*[5] *Today we would use the term 'decadence' to connote the cynosure of their concern, but the word in more common use at the time was 'diversity'; modern usage might indicate 'amusement' or even 'recreation'. We consider here the specific 'diversity' of the theatre and the stage, focusing, first, on the Reverend George Anderson's diatribe of 1733 against the Edinburgh stage, followed by the later controversy surrounding John Home's tragedy, 'Douglas', and the pamphlet war that trailed in the wake of the play's first performance in the Canongate playhouse, Edinburgh, in December 1756.*

The big Assembly debates of the two preceding years were, of course, on the entirely different issue of heresy and the extent to which the writings of 'Sopho' (Henry Home, Lord Kames) and David Hume were held to have flown in the face of Christian doctrine and belief. It was the same George Anderson who helped pave the way for those debates in 1753.[6] *Yet, the heresy issue can be regarded as generically related to the stage controversy which inevitably saw both factions of the church take up their customary positions, though this time, in the case of the latter, in not so conventionally straightforward a way. The stir created by the issue of the stage and its allegedly devastating impact on morality was not so much delineated by the usual lining up on opposite sides, as it were, of the floor of the Assembly, but was fought out at the level of presbyteries almost regardless of faction. Though perhaps hard to believe, Moderate and Popular party ministers were not always at one another's throats over the problem. John Witherspoon's discourse on the stage, for example, (as McIntosh has remarked) can be interpreted as a refreshingly 'liberal' approach, characterising, he believes, the 'flexibility' of the Popular position and the extent to which its supporters were prepared to go to 'accommodate participation in secular activities.'*[7] *Nevertheless, there are comic, even farcical overtones lying not far below the surface here, graphically illustrative of the dilemma confronting certain individual ministers – notably Alexander Carlyle – torn as they were between their Presbyterian calling and a genuine cultural fascination with contemporary theatrical performance.*

The Kirk, the stage and moral corruption

In his *History of Edinburgh* (1779)[8] the advocate Hugo Arnot provides an account of the 'amusements and public diversions' of the city from earliest times. In his description of the pressures facing the early development of Edinburgh's long (and to this day pre-eminent) love-affair with theatre and the stage, Arnot an Episcopalian, feels compelled to narrate the story of the Church of Scotland's major involvement – not to its credit he would firmly have us believe – in that important area of cultural recreation and 'public diversions'. He writes:

> The presbyterian clergy were possessed with the most illiberal and violent animosity against the stage. The writings of their most popular divines, represented the playhouse as the actual temple of the Devil, where he frequently appeared clothed in a corporeal substance, and possessed the spectators, whom he held as his worshippers.[9]

In a footnote Arnot reveals the source of his claim; he had sourced it from the 'Address to the reader, and postscript to Durham on the ten commandments.' He proceeds to describe the Kirk's active concern to 'attack the stage with more effect', culminating in the Presbytery of Edinburgh's private prosecution in the Court of Session in 1739 whereby, using the provisions of the Walpole administration's Licensing Act of two years before, they sought to pursue groups of strolling players visiting the city, seeking damages from them and restricting their future activities. Capitalising on the requirement for theatres and playhouses to apply to local magistrates for operating licences, the Presbytery won its action against the actors and, Arnot the lawyer informs us, 'warrants being issued for apprehending them, they fled from justice.' What was the significance of Arnot's footnote reference to 'Durham and the ten commandments'?

One of the most extreme yet most enduring statements of orthodox Calvinist concern at what was seen as an alarming growth in contemporary societal moral decadence is James Durham's *The Law Unsealed, or a Practical Exposition of the Ten Commandments*;[10] or, to give it the shorthand name by which it became commonly known throughout the whole of the eighteenth century, 'Durham's *Ten Commandments*'. First published in London in 1675 it went through two separate editions each in Edinburgh and Glasgow over the following two years and was still in demand both north and south of the border in the first decade of the nineteenth century. Durham was a St. Andrews graduate who had distinguished himself as a captain in the Civil War before graduating in divinity at Glasgow. He was licensed as a minister by the Presbytery of Irvine in 1647, admitted minister of Glasgow Blackfriars in the same year and was appointed King's Chaplain in 1650. In 1651 Durham was translated to St. Mungo's High Church of Glasgow (the Cathedral), with specific charge of the west quarter of the city. Hew Scott notes that in 1652 Durham tried unsuccessfully to bring about a reconciliation of the two contending parties ('protesters' and 'resolutioners') in the Church of Scotland.[11]

In his *History* Arnot cites both the address 'To the Christian Reader' and the 'Postscript' (immediately following it) from Durham's book as evidence of the extent to which, even in its author's day, 'the presbyterian clergy were possessed with the most illiberal and violent animosity against the stage.' Both preliminary pieces are not the work of Durham himself but were probably written by an unidentified admirer (or admirers) of his, almost certainly a fellow minister or ministers. From the wording of his footnote, Arnot seems unaware that the preliminary material he cites was not by Durham. In citing both preliminary materials from Durham's book Arnot must have had in mind passages like the following; after condemning men's and women's 'over-costly, curious, vain, and conceity [sic] dressing and decking of the body', 'high extravagances of this age', 'drinking and pledging healths', 'tippling and four-horsing', 'carding and dicing', 'singing and playing of light and wanton songs', 'prophane and promiscuous dancing', the anonymous author turns his attention to the *most* outrageous and unchristian activity of all, the writing, attending and performing of stage-plays –

> ... spectators of prophane interludes and stage-plays, which ... offend against many branches of the seventh command[ment],[12] together, in the abuse of apparel, tongue, eyes, countenance, gestures, and most all parts of the body; therefore (saith the great man)[13] they that go to see such sights and hear such words (what would he have said of the penners or composers of such plays and actors in them?) whom the ancient church appointed to be excommunicated, and on several of both which remarkable judgments have lighted ... . [There follow several examples of actors, theatre-lovers and others suffering 'a fearful end' on account of indulging their 'prophane' appetites.][14]

Durham's orotund 'postscript' (dated July 20 1675) continues in the same tedious vein, concluding with a nodding acknowledgment to the fiercest of all English opponents of the stage, William Prynne:

> What useth now to be said in apology for, and defence of stage-plays, and for reforming of them, yet so as to retain them still, was long since objected by the witty and voluptuous

Pagans, and solidly answered, and strongly confuted by the fathers; as it hath been by several modern writers ... notably by Mr. Pryn (to whose indefatigable diligence in collecting, and great judgment of disposing of many of the particulars, here discoursed, I profess myself much beholden.)[15]

In eighteenth-century Scotland the Popular party's dismissal of stage-plays as a toxic source of moral corruption was entirely predictable. Their condemnation of this worthless, harmful and *satanic* 'diversity' ought to be read as an interpretation of the stage both as metaphor for, and dire warning of man's descent into degradation and mortal sin, and, moreover, *from which there is no retreat*. Such a view, however, is merely symptomatic of the much wider malaise the church corporate had begun to discern and confront in society at large. It was consonant with fears expressed from many pulpits – both Moderate and Popular party – that, if not halted in their tracks, things could only go from bad to worse and the church in Scotland would suffer incalculably, possibly irremediably.[16] Fears of that nature were identified as springing from a number of causes, but predominantly from aspects of 'modernity' – including emboldened popular aspirations as evinced in *more* work, *more* money (producing a love of 'luxury'), and, concomitantly, *less* squalor; that is, in the eyes of the potential beneficiaries, a fuller and better life. All such aspirations, on the other hand, presented real challenges to worship and belief. John Witherspoon echoes those fears when in 1762 he preaches on the theme of the citizenry of Paisley, not the least his own congregation, facing present and future dangers resulting from their increasing inculcation of a 'worldly spirit':

> I have, on several occasions, observed that the present period or state of things, in this place and congregation, demands the greatest concern for the public interest of religion. Growing in numbers, and growing, I hope, in wealth, as the effect of your own and your fathers industry, you are in danger of the introduction of a worldly spirit by the rising generation.[17]

Just three years before, Witherspoon's ally in the Popular party, Robert Walker of the High Church in Edinburgh, was discoursing on much the same theme. Celebrating the *annus mirabilis* that was 1759, and having thanked God for the welcome news of military success combined with the future prospect of national 'prosperity', Walker gives warning that, even so, we could all be deluding ourselves:

> Great indeed is our national felicity; but equally great is our danger of abusing it. ... is it not possible that the fruits of that success with which God hath been pleased to favour us, may, by a like abuse, be perverted into weapons of rebellion against himself? – Luxury is the common attendant upon affluence: ... in consequence of which ... the sensualist ... at length sets himself in opposition to God, and his ways; reproaches with the names of *ostentation* or *hypocrisy*, all serious religion and godliness in others; turns away his eyes from the light that reproves him, and even doth what he can to extinguish it altogether.[18]

In 1763 another of Witherspoon's friends in the Popular party, John Erskine, preached a sermon before the Synod of Lothian and Tweeddale in which he acknowledges the dangers of ministers 'giving offence' in the face of changing times. The dangers of them doing so extended, he maintains, to how they went about their preaching. 'The matter of his sermons', Erskine insisted, could 'give offence' if a minister's 'ideas of the great truths of Christianity are superficial, confused, and indistinct.' He goes on:

> Let the writings of philosophers, of historians, and of politicians, be their study whose business it is to unfold the secrets of nature, to transmit to posterity the memorable deeds of heroes, or to give counsel to their Sovereign in matters of state. These branches of knowledge are at best ornamental, not essential to a teacher of Christianity. He may innocently, nay, usefully, amuse himself with them; but he cannot, without sacrilege, devote to them the greatest part of his time.[19]

Erskine is, of course, referring to the practice of Moderate ministers adopting the winning ways of the *literati* in 'mixing' religion with morality and moral culture and the extent to which, in the eyes of some, these concerns were becoming virtually inseparable, if not indistinguishable. The impact of their doing so had serious repercussions that were not always understood. Just a year before, for example, Witherspoon had put it as follows:

> The corruption of a church always implies a light sense of the evil of sin; and therefore, however plainly I may make it appear, that such and such facts are done, it will be hard to convince many that they are wrong, at least in any great degree. Many a clergyman will not yield the one half of those things to be sins that were admitted to be so a century ago; nor do they see the one half of the evil of sin, either in clergy or laity, that was once taken for granted.[20]

The growing popularity of theatre-going was just one such example of what seemed to some an alarming descent into dangerous trifling with – to quote Witherspoon again – a '*worldly spirit*'. In the eyes of Popular party ministers at least, society was fast degenerating into an age of 'diversities', the most glaring and the most sinful of which was the addictive appeal of the stage. John Witherspoon was one of the first to identify his Moderate colleagues in the church as potentially among the worst offenders when it came to succumbing to the beguiling temptations the stage had to offer.

Allan Ramsay and the Edinburgh theatre

A rare edition of *Macbeth: a tragedy; as it is now acted at the New Theatre of Edinburgh*[21] bears the imprint 'Printed by T. and W. Ruddimans for Allan Ramsay, and sold at his Shop, 1731.' The reference to Ramsay is indicative of his key role in the promotion and encouragement of the theatre in Edinburgh, a career that extended over more than two decades in the first half of the eighteenth century. But precisely *where* and *what* was the 'New Theatre' in the year 1731? Though inconclusive, it seems most likely that the locus of the performance of the 'Scottish play' must have been Taylor's Hall,[22] in the Cowgate, referred to frequently in newspapers of the period as the site of theatrical activity though never identified as the 'New Theatre' beyond the single exception of the *Macbeth* title. It is, of course, possible, though on the whole unlikely, that the date in the imprint is an error.

In 1733 the *Caledonian Mercury* carries frequent notices of performances in the city by a touring group calling itself the 'Edinburgh Company of Players'; among the plays put on that year were *The Beggars' Opera*, and 'several of Shakespear's plays', including

Othello, Hamlet, Henry IV, The Humours of Falstaff and *King Lear and his three daughters*.[23] On 26 December, now calling itself the 'Edinburgh Company of Comedians', the group performed *The Tempest; or Inchanted Island,* 'with all the musick, sinkings, risings, new scenes, and other decorations proper for the performance'. Other plays performed that year included Marlowe's *Tamerlane*. It was also in 1733 that the Reverend George Anderson preached his sermon in the Tron Church of Edinburgh condemning the stage as an unlawful and unchristian 'diversity'.

Despite the *Macbeth* conundrum, however, James Dibdin (who seems unaware of the title) notes that the first theatre to open its doors to the public in Edinburgh was a playhouse in Carrubber's Close [24] – 'the first regular theatrical establishment ever erected in Scotland.'[25] It was the brainchild of the poet, circulating library proprietor, bookseller and former barber, Allan Ramsay. The *Mercury* records that it was due to open on 6 November 1736, but it seems there was a delay and the curtain was not raised until two days later. The newspaper also notes that *The Recruiting Officer* and *The Virgin Unmask'd* were on the same bill.[26] In the *Mercury* of 15 November it is reported:

> EDINBURGH, Nov. 15.
> On Monday last the New Theatre in Carrubber's Close was opened (which is thought by all Judges to be as complete, and finished with as good a Taste as any one of its Size in the three Kingdoms) when the following Prologue was spoken by Mr. Bridges.[27]

> "Long has it been the Bus'ness of the Stage
> To mend our Manners, and reform the Age.
> This Task the muse by Nature was assign'd,
> Ere Christian Light shone in upon the Mind;
> Ev'n since those glorious Truths to Men appear'd,
> Her moral Precepts still have been rever'd,
> And where the sacred Monitors have fail'd.
> Just Satyre from the Stage hath oft prevail'd.
> Tho' some sour Criticks full of Phlegm and Spleen
> Condemn her Use as hellish and obscene;
> And from their gloomy thoughts and want of Sense,
> Think what diverts the Mind gives Heav'n Offence. ..."

Ramsay himself, of course, wrote for the theatre. His 'Scots pastoral comedy', *The Gentle Shepherd,* first published in 1725, but not put on as a stage production until 1729 – when it was acted by the boys of Haddington Grammar School, for whom it may also have been specifically written[28] – was the nearest the normally douce Edinburgh public could claim as an overnight sensation, though the piece only really took off, we are told, after 'all the Sangs' were added. In its 'full' version as a 'ballad-opera', popular demand for the work both as a stage musical *and* a printed text was virtually insatiable. In Glasgow alone the Foulis brothers (later Andrew Foulis *solo*) dashed off edition after edition between 1743 and 1796. It's not difficult to see why *The Gentle Shepherd* became so popular. The use by Ramsay of the Scots vernacular somehow intrigued the audience, in much the same way as it had appealed (but conspicuously less so) to a reading public; this was partly, of course, due to the fact that it all *seemed* new (which to an extent it was), but more on account of its undeniable suitability to the ribald earthiness and sheer bawdy humour of the work, a generation before Robert Fergusson and Robert Burns employed the same use of vernacular for much the same dramatic purpose and were similarly lionised for their notable success in having done so.[29]

That Ramsay loved the theatre and the stage is beyond doubt. In an early poem that first appears in Ruddiman's 1728 edition of his *Poems Volume II*[30] – 'The Address of the Muse, to the Right Honourable George Drummond Esq; Lord Provost; and Council of Edinburgh'[31] – Ramsay writes these lines, pleading that the Council will sanction a theatre which, should it do so, he believes has the potential to 'smile down the follies of the age … and cultivate the growing man'. Perhaps in the light of the impending success of the *Gentle Shepherd*, while a shade disingenuously, and, in a nod to the prim and morally squeamish, he anticipates opposition and seeks to quell it before it can gather a head of steam:

> O! may we hope to see a stage,
> Fill'd with the best of such as can
> Smile down the follies of the age,
> Correct dull pride and party rage,
> And cultivate the growing man;
> And shew the virgin every proper grace,
> That makes her mind as comely as her face.
>
> Nor will the most devout oppose,
> When with a strict judicious care,
> The scenes most virtuous shall be chose,
> That numerous are, forbidding those
> That shock the modest, good and fair.
> The best of things may often be abus'd;
> That argues not, when right, to be refus'd.

As things turned out, Ramsay's fears were all too prescient. His enterprise would be extraordinarily short-lived – to be precise, barely seven months. The 'New Theatre' in Carrubber's Close had opened its doors on 8 November 1736 and on 24 June 1737 Walpole's government succeeded in passing the Licensing Act regulating theatres and stage performances throughout Britain.[32] In practice, it was little short of full-blown censorship with formidable new powers of control vested in Scotland; and as one would expect, executed by the Court of Session and/or the High Court of Justiciary as appropriate. Historians are agreed that the *raison d'être* for the Act's introduction was the daringly outrageous political satire evident in Fielding's play, *Pasquin*,[33] with its attack on Walpole himself. Unsurprisingly, the play was viewed in government circles as positively the last straw. The Act became the vehicle by means of which government was able to control the world of the stage with its alleged potential, real and assumed, for moral grossness on the one hand and seditious political comment on the other. In the end Walpole got his way by using the contrived stratagem of a *virtual* controversial play, the rumoured, fabulously shocking *The Golden Rump*: possibly again the work of Fielding – though no one can be sure, since it was never published nor performed. Some historians have even concluded that, if it *did* exist, the work may have been secretly commissioned by Walpole himself.[34]

According to Dibdin, Ramsay 'lost heavily by his speculation' due to the enforcement of the Act. In the *Gentleman's Magazine* for August 1737 there appeared among the 'poetical essays' *The Address of Allan Ramsay* 'to the Honourable Duncan Forbes of Culloden, Lord President of the Session, and all other Judges, who are careful of the Honour of the Government, and the Property of the Subject.' Ramsay proceeds to 'lay his case' before these men, stressing the proper moral purpose of the stage through the medium of harmless entertainment:

> Last year, my lords, nae farrer gane,
> A costly wark was undertane
> By me, wha had not the least dread
> An act wad knock it on the Head:
> A play-house new, at vast expence,
> To be a large, yet bein defence,
> In winter-nights, 'gainst wind and weet,
> To ward frae cauld the lasses sweet;
> While they with bonny smiles attended,
> To have their little failures mended;
> Where satire, striving still to free them,
> Here, under rules of right decorum,
> By placing consequence before 'em,
> I kept our troop, by pith of reason,
> Frae bawdy, atheism, and treason;
> And only preach'd, frae moral fable,
> The best instruction they were able;
> While they, by doctrine linsy woolsy,[35]
> Set off the *Utile* with *Dulce*. ...
> Is there ought better than the stage,
> To mend the follies of the age,
> If manag'd as it ought to be,
> Frae ilka vice and blaidry free?
> Which may be done, with perfect ease,
> And nought be heard that shall displease,
> Or give the least offence or pain,
> If we can hae't restor'd again.

And the piece ends with Ramsay appealing to the Court of Session that the judges might agree that

Our Lads may be allowed to play,
At least till new-house debts be paid off,
The cause that I'm the maist afraid of;
Which laide lyes on my single back,
And I maun pay it ilka plack.

But failing that outcome,

Now, it's but just the legislature
Shou'd either say that I'm a fauter,
Or thole me to employ my bigging,
Or of the burthen ease my rigging,
By ord'ring, frae the publick fund,
A sum to pay for what I'm bound;
Syne, for amends for what I've lost,
Edge me into some canny post,
With the good liking of our king,
And your *Petitioner* shall – sing.[36]

Inevitably, Ramsay's petition fell on deaf ears. In February 1739 the Church of Scotland took the lead in using the powers of the new Act to further their ultimate desire to close down stage productions altogether. The minutes of the Presbytery of Edinburgh for 1738 record that it had been represented that

> a Company of Stage Players have of late sett up in an house within the precincts of the Abby of Holy Rood house [sic] where they act several Plays in open violation of the Laws & in manifest hurt to religion.[37]

Unusually – possibly even uniquely – the Presbytery went on to initiate an action in the Court of Session against the company of players which they won, resulting in a decreet to the effect that eight of the players concerned were each fined £50, and 'failing their paying the same, to be imprisoned for three months'. In the event, however, it is reported to the Presbytery that on a petition having been made to the Edinburgh magistrates to put the Court's decision into effect,

> [a] search has been made, but neither the said offenders or their Effects could be found.[38]

For a time, stage productions contrived to pass the censor by means of an unsubtle device designed to comply on the one hand with norms of decency and decorum, while on the other paying lip service to the new Act's requirements on the licensing of individual plays and the registration of playhouses. The device often took the form of a patron or patroness – the Duke and/or Duchess of Hamilton, for example, were sometimes complicit in such a role – organising birthday parties for one or other of their offspring at which a play or other entertainment was part of the programme. Dibdin notes several such ploys while also observing that there are only infrequent references to the stage in the newspapers from roughly the time of the Act until 1741-2 when performances of Richardson's *Pamela*, Addison's *Cato* and Gay's *Beggar's Opera* were put on by English touring companies as part of a programme of 'vocal and instrumental music', another device blatantly designed to hoodwink the magistrates. As it turned out, however, the authorities were neither willing accomplices nor were they easily fooled. Several prosecutions are recorded including one against an attorney called Marriott who, it seems, had threatened to throw a Court official out of a window when the latter had visited the theatre in order to deliver his warrant.

After the demise of the Taylor's Hall venue in 1744-45 regular performances resumed in the setting of the new Canongate theatre. According to Arnot, even during the rebellion of 1745-46 the Canongate attracted many *aficianados*, including a young Alexander Carlyle whose prior knowledge of the London stage entitled him to make valid comparisons of some of the leading players of the day, concluding that :

> The Theatres were not very attractive this Season, as Garrick was Gone over to Dublin. There still remained however what was enough for a Stranger, Mrs Pritchard, and Mrs Clive, and M$^{c.}$lin, who were all excellent in their way. But I had seen Hughes and Mrs Hamilton in Edin$^{r.}$, and whether or not it might be owing to the Force of First Impressions, I then thought, that they were not surpass'd by those I saw in London.[39]

A decade later Carlyle would himself have a leading role to play in the high drama surrounding the first performance in Edinburgh of the tragedy called *Douglas*, written by his friend and erstwhile fellow student, the Reverend John Home, minister of Athelstaneford in the Presbytery of Haddington since his ordination there in 1746 (and cousin of David Hume).

The Reverend George Anderson and pulpit censure of the stage

In Ramsay's day orthodox Kirk ministers viewed the theatre as little less than a worthless 'diversity' that was sinful, immoral and unchristian. More generally, however, from 1737 on the shrillest criticism was to the effect that the stage was 'unlawful', a term that reflected the statute of that year requiring stage performances to be licensed and individual theatres registered. Leading the way in pulpit censure of the stage was the Reverend George Anderson, an unattached clergyman who had once served as an army chaplain. As we have seen, Allan Ramsay was, of course, well aware of the frequently seamy side of the stage and, while some of his own works are hardly immune from the charge, he did his best to moderate the potential of individual plays for attracting the wrath of the 'high-flyers' in the Kirk who, he rightly sensed, were constantly on the look-out for practical examples that might have strayed beyond the pale of decency and could thus be reported to the municipal authorities. Ramsay's response was to 'smile down', as he put it, 'the follies of the age', and instead 'cultivate the growing man', while making 'her mind' – the mind of 'the virgin', that is – 'as comely as her face'. Anderson, it goes without saying, would have none of this.

It is almost certain that George Anderson never enjoyed a ministerial charge of his own. M. A. Stewart's *DNB* entry records that in 1732 Anderson was shortlisted for the vacant charge of the new North Kirk in Edinburgh, but was pipped to the post by William Hamilton, principal-elect of the university. Prior to that, Anderson's career – in some ways resembling that of James Thomson of Dunfermline in a later generation[40] – had assumed a military bent, having served as an army chaplain, initially with the Scots Greys in Flanders during the War of the Spanish Succession. He was present at Ramillies (1706) and Malplaquet (1709) and must have personally witnessed the battlefield carnage that took its toll of Scottish troops. Details of his life from then until the late 1720s are sketchy but we know that for a year or two he had pastoral oversight of the garrisons at Fort William and Fort Augustus. There, as Stewart notes, though a staunch Calvinist in preaching, he reported in 1729 that his congregation exceeded the capacity of his church, even though the garrisons were 'predominantly Anglican.' In 1741 Anderson was appointed master of George Watson's Hospital, Edinburgh, where he taught religious instruction. He retired from the post in 1752 and 'devoted his final years to writing.'[41]

In 1733 Anderson published a sermon he had delivered from the pulpit of the Tron Church in Edinburgh entitled *The Use and Abuse of Diversions*. The date when the oral sermon was delivered is not given, though at least we have its pulpit locus; its text is from Luke's Gospel, xix, v. 13: *'And he called his ten servants, and delivered them ten pounds, and said unto them, Occupy till I come.'* Anderson's chief concern in the sermon is to highlight the mounting evidence that presented itself of Scots – especially those in 'this city' – to whom 'an idle Life, made up of Pleasure and Diversions' had become irresistible. It is in the literary Appendix to his published sermon that Anderson addresses the particular evils associated with the stage. In a holograph note on the *verso* of the title page of one copy of his sermon Anderson dedicates the piece to 'The Right Honble Lord King &^c. Lord High Chancellor of Great Britain'.[42] This is not simply fawning sycophancy. Anderson was well aware that ultimate control of the theatre lay with the government at Westminster and that if, as he hoped, regulatory machinery were to be introduced to counter the danger of the stage leading people down the slippery slope to moral perdition, the Lord Chancellor was the key officer in whose hands lay the responsibility for drafting appropriate corrective legislation.

But was it realistic or likely that the government would listen to his concerns? In his preliminary address 'To the Reader', Anderson himself admits he is inclined to doubt it: he explains that in the Appendix to his sermon – written by way of a response to the anonymous pamphlet, *Hints in Defence of dramatical Entertainments* [sic] (1728),[43] now known to have been the work of Ramsay[44] – Anderson gives his 'opinion of the stage', setting out his reasons for deeming it 'unchristian'. As for the government's view of things, he writes:

> I do believe that the Government would discourage the Stage, were they of my Opinion in the Matter. They look upon Playhouses with another Eye than I do; and, as I think, they sincerely differ from me, I hope they will believe, that I as sincerely differ from them; and that they will look upon it as lawful, fair and honest, in a Minister of the Gospel, to warn Christians, whenever he himself is convinced of the Unlawfulness of any Practice of theirs, and especially of a particular Diversion, which, without Danger to the State, may well be dispensed with.[45]

The fact that Anderson had preached his sermon from the Tron Church is significant. The minister of the Tron who had loaned his pulpit to Anderson was the Reverend George Wishart who would himself be steeped in controversy three years later (1756) when he took a prominent part in the extensive pamphlet war occasioned by the Porteous murder and the rash attempt of the Walpole administration to require the act – offering a reward of £200 for evidence leading to the conviction of those responsible – to be read in churches. An impressive number of ministers, Wishart just one among many, defiantly resisted the call to read the act from their pulpits.[46] Faced with the public uproar that ensued Walpole felt he had no option but to withdraw the proposed legislation.

At the same time it would be wrong to dismiss Anderson's sermon as yet another example of a run-of-the-mill assault on pleasure-seekers composed from the narrow point of view of an otherwise unremarkable Scottish Calvinist minister. The twenty-one page appendix has its own sub-title: *'The Stage an Unchristian Diversion'*. Taken together, the sermon *cum* appendix are important to scholars for two reasons; *first*, though aimed at the abuse of theatre-patronage more generally, Anderson's primary target is without doubt the contemporary *Edinburgh* theatre; *secondly*, both the sermon and especially its appendix make clear that the whole work is designed as a response to Ramsay's *Some few hints in defence of dramatical entertainments*, published anonymously in 1728. Ramsay had begun *Some few hints* by asserting, in a reference to William Law, the non-juror who was bitterly opposed to the stage:[47]

> Whereas there has of late been a warm Debate, about the Lawfulness of the Stage, it appears a little odd, that no better Champion can be had, against the useful and polite Entertainment, than one, whose Opinions in Ecclesiastical Affairs, are condemned in our Confession of Faith.[48]

Anderson also displays an awareness of Sir Robert Filmer's *A Defence of Plays* (1707), written as a reply to Jeremy Collier's *A defence of the short view of the profaneness and immorality of the English stage* (1699, re-issued 1705), itself a reply to critical writings on the stage by the playwright William Congreve and others. He further cites in support of his case the English political writer and dramatist, James Drake, author of the anonymous *Antient and Modern Stages Survey'd* (1705).[49] It is clear, therefore, that Anderson's attack on the stage is not merely a piece of pulpit rhetoric rooted in the scriptures alone: it is a polished performance and remarkably well-informed on the prolific contemporary literature of the theatre debate, showing an impressive awareness of all the Scottish and English authors who mattered and had written on the stage in an ethical context, including Filmer, Collier, Law, Drake and, of course, the 'City-hinter' himself, Ramsay.

One of Anderson's primary aims in his sermon is to show that all too often men who profess to be knowledgeable about religion put endless qualifications on their belief, such that the 'divine truths' they learn from the Bible have 'no influence' on the way they lead their own private lives:

> Many there are who believe the great Doctrines and consequential Duties of the Gospel; but then they believe with such *Salvo's* [sic] and Exceptions, with such Reserves and Limitations, with such Additions and Interpolations, that those Divine Truths have no influence at all upon their lives. Tho' one would not be apt to think it, there's scarce a wicked Christian in the World, who hath not a particular and private Religion of his own.[50]

He then explains his choice of text: Christ's parable of the talents – though, to be pedantic, in the version of the story in Luke's gospel (as preferred by the preacher) it is more usually known as the 'parable of the *minas*'.[51] Anderson interprets the story to fit his main message, *viz.* that 'non-improvement of Privileges is Ground of Condemnation':

> Our Lord hath commanded us to *occupy till he come*, that is, to trade with, and improve, all his Gifts and Graces, and to use every Opportunity to the best Advantage. But if we hide our Pound in a Napkin, and *stand all the Day idle* ... instead of being harmless and innocent, as we pretend, we are wicked Servants in the Judgment and Account of our great Master.[52]

Long before he is in sight of the 'application' Anderson discloses the whole point of his sermon. It is an extraordinary claim:

> I believe it is open to the Observation of all, that a Spirit of Idleness and Levity prevails exceedingly in this City; and in Proportion to the Number and Riches of the Inhabitants, *more than in any other City in Europe.* [italics added] [53]

He concedes that many will allege that the pursuits he has in mind are 'harmless and innocent Amusements', but he explains that he now proposes to show that 'their idle Conduct is highly criminal and sinful' for two reasons: 'I. Because an idle Life, made up of Pleasures and Diversions ... is Unchristian, and defective of good Works'; and, also, 'II. Because, in itself, it is sinful and unlawful.' On the first of his propositions he claims:

> It is a Mistake to think, that our holy Christian Faith requires nothing of us but what we are bound to by the Law of Nature. ... to imagine that Christianity requires no more at our hands than *Epicurean Philosophy* doth, is to put a great Dishonour upon our holy Religion.[54]

And on the second he further clarifies his meaning as follows:

> Our stated Behaviour must then be such as becometh Penitents. And a Penitent, you know, must not live to please himself, to follow his own Inclinations, to gratify his Senses, to indulge himself in Ease and Idleness. By no means. His Business is serious and grave, his Vocation laborious, and such as requires Diligence, Activity, Patience and Self-denial. ... Shou'd the Inhabitants of a City, besieged by an Enemy, spend their Time in cleaning their Streets and in adorning their Houses, not to say, in Plays and Diversions; for all their Pains, they would act a most foolish Part, while they neglected the Watch and Defence of their Walls.[55]

Anderson then turns to the issue of what Christians term 'Grace'. Only God can bestow grace on men and women and he does so 'in order to serve God and to save our souls.' Anderson has in mind here §XVIII of the *Confession of Faith* – 'Of Assurance of Grace and Salvation' – requiring subscribing ministers and believers to conform to the doctrinal implications of the 'state of grace' as 'an infallible assurance of faith, founded upon the divine truth of the promises of salvation ... whereby we are sealed to the day of redemption.'[56] But failure to live the life of a penitent is a 'contradiction to the precepts of our holy religion.' 'Ye need' he says, 'but open your bibles at a venture to be fully satisfied, that a life spent in pleasures and diversions is irreligious and unchristian.'[57]

Even so, Anderson more than once protests that he wants his comments to be seen as fair in relation to the natural propensity of individuals to seek diversion – almost as if he is anxious to avoid being labelled an extremist and a puritan. But then, just as quickly, he reverts to type:

> I freely grant, that all Kind of Diversions are not discharged and forbidden all Kind of People, nor will I say that all Sorts of Pastimes are in themselves sinful and unlawful. I further own, that at present (Thanks to GOD for it) our Country is not a Land of Mourning. There is no Occasion to banish all Joy and Gladness out of the Land, nor for the Sons and Daughters of our *Zion*, to wear Sackcloth and Ashes, and for every Countenance to put on Sorrow. All which notwithstanding, the Diversions of this Time and Place, are almost all of them Criminal. ...
> Diversions ... are only so far lawful as they unyoke the Mind from Study and Meditation, and the Body from Toil, in order to recruit and refit both for other and fresh Undertakings. This is their End and this only is their Use. [58]

And in the same vein:

> Diversions, then, only for the Sake of Diversions, or for worse, I am sure, no thinking Man will judge Christian and lawful. And whether most of the many Diversions, which now prevail in this City, are either intended or managed, for any better Purpose than to consume and spend the Time, which hangs heavily upon Hand, or to flatter and indulge a Spirit of Levity, I leave to yourselves to judge. And if this is the End and Use, the Measure and Moderation of your Plays and Parties of Pleasure, I am sure it is an inverting the Order of divine Providence, and making what otherwise is lawful to become sinful, and consequently your Sins to become your Pleasure and Diversion. ... Diversions are only good when used merely for the Relaxation of the Mind, and the Refreshment of the Body. ... But Plays of Profession, Diversions of Days and Nights, of every Day and every Night, that take up and consume all the Time, except what is bestowed upon eating and sleeping, and upon some Visits of Vanity, where Diversion too is generally the Subject of Conversation, must be Criminal in the sight of God, who has made us, not for Sports and Plays, but for the Service here, and the Enjoyment of himself hereafter.[59]

Having now arrived at his 'application', Anderson allows that 'if your plays and diversions are such as you may freely and safely forbear altogether, or use with great moderation, there is no hardship put upon you, in persuading you to the other side'; in other words, there is still time to change your ways. But, on the other hand, you are 'but idly employed' if you don't recognise the need to 'make your labour subservient to the great end of your being.' And the nature of that 'great end of your being'? It is nothing less, he contends, than the 'salvation of your souls'. Accordingly – to return to the message of Christ's parable – resist, Anderson pleads, spending your time idly, and hiding your pound 'in a napkin', for

> We have Time enough given us to work out our Salvation, and we want no more to throw away upon idle and wicked purposes.[60]

Anderson's twenty-page 'Appendix', *The Stage an Unchristian Diversion*,[61] is a literary extension of his pulpit sermon, but, as we might expect, with much more in the way of scholarly refutation of present and past authorities who have contributed to the debate on the usefulness and/or moral dangers of the stage; these range from Plutarch (specifically the *Symposiacs* and *De Gloria Atheniensium*) to Filmer and Drake. Plutarch is cited in support of Anderson's contention that 'for two thousand three hundred years … from first to last, there always were, and are some things to be amended and corrected in stage-plays.' Here Anderson shows off the extent of his classical learning. One of his most telling quotes is again from Plutarch in a footnote to the appendix –

> "As for new Comedy, it is such a necessary Ingredient of all great Entertainments, that, so to speak, one may as well make a Feast without Wine as without *Menander*." [62]

Anderson's main target is, however, the anonymous author of *Some few hints* who at least had sought to introduce realism into the debate. To his credit, Ramsay had not denied that some plays were indeed gross:

> That there are some Plays that have a Tendency to Wickedness, are full of Representations that are profane, and Expressions shocking to a modest and Christian Audience, is not denied … .

At the same time Ramsay had patiently explained that we do not think the less of women because it happens that some are cast as whores in some plays, *or*, let it be added, *of clergymen* on account of some of their number appearing in some plays as clowns and buffoons:

> … is Love and tender Sentiments towards the virtuous Fair (the sweetest and best Cement of humane Society) to be reckon'd a Vice, because mercenary, vile Strumpets are Women? Or is the Regard and Veneration that we in Duty ought to pay to a good Clergyman (the most valuable of Characters) to be in the least lessen'd, tho' a loose Fellow should steal himself into Orders, and entertain his Parishioners with Buffoon'ry, prove a Drunkard, Whore-master, and heretical Incendiary; this is no reflection on the *Holy Order*, he is to be thrown out, as every virtuous Government should do profane Plays.[63]

As for the common assumption that somehow 'Players cannot be the best of Men', Ramsay had countered:

> But Plays are lawful, and Actors may be good Men: for Instance, Mr. *Shakspear* and *Betterton* were, and Mr. *Wilks* and Mr. *Mills* are good moral Men and Christians, who devoutly join in all the sacred Institutions. Mr. *Aston* and his Family behave themselves, to my certain Knowledge, with Sobriety, Justice and Discretion, pays his Debts without being dunn'd, is of a charitable Disposition, avoids the intoxicating Bottle, and in every other Light appears what we call an honest Moralist.[64] For his Principles about the more refin'd Distinctions of Religion, I'll not take upon me to condemn or justify, he being of the Church of *England* Communion, a Religion different from mine, who am a Member of the present Establishment of the Church of *Scotland*. [65]

Also in 1733, the same year in which he published his sermon, Anderson felt obliged to bring out a 'vindication' of the Appendix entitled *A Reinforcement of the Reasons proving that the Stage is an Unchristian Diversion*. It was written 'in answer to the remarks of an Anonymous Author.' The pamphlet which caused Anderson to resume his pen – *Some Remarks upon the Rev*d. *Mr. Anderson's Positions concerning the Unlawfulness of Stage-Plays* – is cited by John Witherspoon some years later in his *A Serious Inquiry into the Nature and*

Effects of the Stage [66] where he writes of 'Anderson's *Reinforcement*' or 'Anderson's *Positions*'

By the time of the first General Assembly debate on heretical writings in 1755 Anderson was almost eighty. He died in Edinburgh in December the following year, while the pamphlet war he had begun with *An Estimate of the Profit and Loss of Religion* (1753), attacking the writings of 'Sopho' (Kames) and Hume for their supposed atheism, was still at its height. Anderson's *Estimate*, a treatise of almost 400 pages, is far from an occasional rant against 'infidel writings', but a learned, reasoned and, on occasion, brightly entertaining contribution to the debate. This is what he has to say on what he calls the 'economy' and 'frugality' of the established church, citing as sympathetic back-up for his argument 'one Robert Cragie [sic], Esq; a gentleman learned in the law, and a ruling elder in church-government': [67]

> He that doth not complain of the expences of the prophane playhouse, can never complain of the expences of such sacred and religious assemblies [church services]. ... for time and expence, the established church of *Scotland* is remarkably frugal. Of all holy days in use in other churches, only the first day of the week is retained for public worship, by appointment civil and ecclesiastical: [Craigie had 'lately informed the house of commons that] the Presbyterian government was most agreeable to the nation ... because it is the cheapest.[68]

In the year of his death the prolific Anderson also published a major work refuting the quirky religious views of Henry St. John, Viscount Bolingbroke – his massive *Remonstrance against Lord Viscount Bolingbroke's Philosophical Religion* – as well as a pamphlet, *The Complaint made to the Presbytery of Edinburgh verified*, by means of which he sought presbytery censure of the printer (Robert Fleming) and publishers (Alexander Kincaid and Alexander Donaldson) of Kames's ('Sopho's') *Essays on the Principles of Morality and Natural Religion* (1751).[69]

Douglas, a tragedy (1756) – a 'poppy that would fain pass as a rose'

On 9 June 1757 John Wesley was in Berwick-on-Tweed and records in his journal:

Douglas, the play which has made so much noise, was put into my hands. I was astonished to find, it is one of the finest tragedies I ever read. What pity, that a few lines were not kept out; and that it was ever acted at Edinburgh.[70]

Wesley clearly enjoyed reading the play as a work of literature. But anticipating Goethe and Charles Lamb he had (for entirely different reasons) serious reservations about *Douglas* as a stage performance and, above all, about it having been performed in, of all places, Edinburgh, the spiritual home of the Church of Scotland.

One of the very first commentators on the literary *and* dramatic worth of the Reverend John Home's[71] tragedy, *Douglas* – first performed in the Canongate Theatre on 14 December 1756 [72] – was his cousin, David Hume. Several years before, in his *Enquiry concerning the Principles of Morals* (1751), Hume, clearly familiar with the experience himself, had used the image of a man entering a theatre, observing 'the actors to be animated by the appearance of a full audience', as a metaphor for his hypothesis '*Why* Utility *pleases.*' –

A man, who enters the theatre, is immediately struck with the view of so great a multitude, participating of one common amusement; and experiences, from their very aspect, a superior sensibility or disposition of being affected with every sentiment, which he shares with his fellow creatures.
He observes the actors to be animated by the appearance of a full audience; and rais'd to a degree of enthusiasm, which they cannot command in any solitary or calm moment.
Every movement of the theatre, by a skilful poet, is communicated, as it were by magic, to the spectators, who weep, tremble, resent, rejoice and are enflam'd with all the variety of passions, which actuate the several personages of the drama.[73]

In his dedication prefacing the *Four Dissertations* (1757) Hume addresses his kinsman 'The Reverend Mr Hume, Author of Douglas, a Tragedy' – the spelling of his cousin's surname is mischievously deliberate – and he amiably confides:

I have been seized with a strong desire of renewing these laudable practices of antiquity [i.e. of classical writers using a dedication in order to do honour to the dedicatee 'without degrading the author'], by addressing the following dissertations to you, my good friend: for such I will ever call and esteem you, notwithstanding the opposition, which prevails between us, with regard to many of our speculative tenets. These differences of opinion I have only found to enliven our conversation; while our common passion for science and letters served as a cement to our friendship.

Hume tells the playwright he believes the respect they entertain for each other is mutual despite 'when I imagined that you lay under the influence of prejudice' and, too, when 'you sometimes told me, that you excused my errors, on account of the candor and sincerity, which, you thought, accompanied them.' Hume goes on to admit to his reverend cousin that he has an ambition 'to be the first who shall in public express his admiration, of your noble tragedy of Douglas; one of the most interesting and pathetic pieces, that was ever exhibited on any theatre.' And he goes on in the same uncharacteristically extravagant vein:

Should I give it the preference to the *Merope* of *Maffei*, and to that of *Voltaire*, which it resembles in its subject; should I affirm, that it contained more fire and spirit than the former, more tenderness and simplicity than the latter; I might be accused of partiality: And how could I entirely acquit myself, after the professions of friendship, which I have made you? But the unfeigned tears which flowed from every eye, in the numerous representations which were made of it on this theatre; the unparalleled command, which you appeared to have over every affection of the human breast: these are incontestible proofs, that you possess the true theatric genius of *Shakespear* and *Otway*, refined from the unhappy barbarism of the one, and licentiousness of the other.[74]

It was not long before Hume began to be ridiculed for having been so lavish in his praise of the play and its author, and, specifically, for the extravagant language he had used in his dedicatory preface. The assault on him was spearheaded by John MacLaurin (the future judge, Lord Dreghorn), eldest son of Colin MacLaurin, professor of mathematics at the University of Edinburgh. Young MacLaurin was responsible for not less than three (possibly four) anonymous pamphlets, all published in 1757, on the subject of Home's play.[75] Two of MacLaurin's pamphlets are in the style of farcical theatrical performances

– an 'opera' and a 'tragedy' – while the third is an altogether more sober assessment of the literary merits of *Douglas* (if, that is, MacLaurin implies, there be any):

The Philosopher's Opera
MacLaurin supplies a preliminary address 'To the Reader' in which he writes:

> If Scotch clergymen may, with impunity, not only write plays, but go to see them acted here, and absent themselves for months together from their parishes, in order to solicit their representation at London, the religion and manners of this country are entirely changed. If Shakespeare and Otway [in a direct reference to David Hume's comments in the *Four Dissertations* dedication] are to be cried down, and the author of *Douglas* set up in their stead, the taste of this country is at an end.

The cast of the farce that follows includes 'Mrs. Sarah Presbytery, relict of John Calvin', 'Mr. Genius' [John Home], 'Mr Moral Sense' [David Hume] – and 'Satan' who has the following lines: 'There are to be nine clergymen in the playhouse to-night. Curiosity to see people of their character in such a place, would of itself secure the poet of a good third night; but my emissaries have taken care that he shall have a full house every night his play is acted.'

The Deposition, or Fatal Miscarriage: a tragedy
In this spoof tragedy MacLaurin further ratchets up the scorn and derision he feels towards the real merits of *Douglas* as he perceives them, and this time reserves his greatest condemnation for what he sees as the hypocrisy of the Kirk. The name he gives his piece is a reference to the deposition of Thomas Gillespie, minister of Carnock in the Presbytery of Dunfermline at the time of the notorious 'Inverkeithing case' of 1752.[76]

Apology for The Writers against the Tragedy of Douglas. With some remarks on that Play.
This pamphlet by MacLaurin is particularly important in the light of its reference to the institution of a group calling itself a *'select society'*, 'which usurps a kind of aristocratical government over all men and matters of learning.' Unsubtly, MacLaurin has a go here at the Select Society of Edinburgh, the 'brainchild' of the painter Allan Ramsay (eldest son of the poet),[77] either because he fancied becoming a member himself, or, more realistically, because (as in the case of most clubs) as an onlooker and bystander he had reservations about the claims of others to aspire to membership. David Hume, of course, was one of its founders, and MacLaurin again cannot resist poking fun at the great man: '... *Shakespear* of late is so much decried, that a noted historian, the *Coryphaeus*[78] of this society, when disapproving of a wretched sentiment, adds, "What could *Shakespear* have said worse?"' MacLaurin assigns his quote to Hume's *History of Great Britain* 'vol. I in a note'. And he continues: 'The Reverend author of *Douglas* was a worthy member of this society; and his tragedy, long before it appeared in public, was, by this society, extolled with all the amplifications of bombast.' He concludes his *exposé* of the many flaws in *Douglas* – comparing Home adversely to Shakespeare (e.g. '*Glenalvon* is a very bad imitation of *Iago*.') – by dismissing the whole work contemptuously:

Upon the whole, we were so far from attempting *To crush down to the ground a lovely plant*, that we have only endeavoured to trample on a poppy, which would fain pass for a rose.[79]

At the other extreme, there are the excited words of '*Crito*' in his letter to the *Caledonian Mercury* of Saturday 18 December, just four days after the play's first night. *Crito* writes:

> If the merit of a work could be ascertained by the general approbation it receives during its representation, and the ardour with which all ranks crowd to the Theatre, or the irresistible power it has of drawing tears from every spectator, we might safely pronounce the tragedy of DOUGLAS to be one of the most perfect works of genius any age has produced.

One staunchly unrepentant enthusiast for the play, and for the stage in general for that matter, was John Home's good friend and erstwhile fellow student at Edinburgh, the Reverend Alexander ('Jupiter') Carlyle of Inveresk. A member of the inner circle of Edinburgh *literati* and elite Moderates that also included William Robertson, Hugh Blair and Home himself, Carlyle paid a heavy price for his over-enthusiastic support for the tragedy.[80] In his autobiography Carlyle tells the full story of how he came to write and publish (of course anonymously) 'half a sheet' he entitled *A Full and True History of the Bloody Tragedy of Douglas, As it is now to be seen acting at the Theatre in the Canongate*. He explains that he had dashed it off as an eye-catching puff for the play on learning from the actor-manager of the Canongate, West Digges, that unless 'some contrivance was fallen upon to make the Lower Orders of Tradesmen and apprentices come to the Playhouse', *Douglas* would need to close. This must have occurred in mid-December 1756 although the ESTC dates the handbill to 1757. Early in 1757 Carlyle merely succeeds in pouring petrol on the flames when he published, again anonymously, his *Argument To prove that the Tragedy of Douglas Ought to be Publickly burnt by the Hands of the Hangman*. The piece is a clever satire on the controversy that nevertheless must have scandalized many who read it, with lines like the following, embracing obvious references to his recently departed Reverend brother, George Anderson, as well as to the works of other giants of the Popular party, such as John Erskine and Alexander Webster:

> Had this youth of genius [John Home] followed the true theological track, and devoted himself to smoking tobacco, to drinking of ale, and the study of controversy, which has been so beneficial to the Christian church, he might have made his name immortal, by some valuable treatise, like the late account of *the present state of* Judas Iscariot;[81] or, *the candid and impartial estimate of the profit and loss of religion*.[82] Had he employed himself in the study of city politics, and human nature, he would certainly have become a master in experimental preaching, and one day might have produc'd some such searching piece of eloquence, as, the *rise and fall of* Haman;[83] or, the other characteristical discourse of an eminent author.[84]

Carlyle's naivety and lack of judgment were not easily forgiven by many of his ministerial peers, especially since in the first place, as he himself put it, the 'High Flying Set' [the Popular party] 'thought it a Sin for a Clergyman to write any Play, Let it be ever so Moral in its Tendency'. In consequence Carlyle was initially pursued by his own

Presbytery of Dalkeith, then (admittedly half-heartedly) by the Synod of Lothian and Tweeddale, and had finally to suffer the ignominy of making an unreserved apology for his indiscretions before being formally rebuked at the bar of the 1757 General Assembly. Even so, it was held necessary by the Assembly to conduct a vote on his case; he undoubtedly derived comfort from learning that it was only after full debate that it was resolved that, while the Synod's judgment was confirmed, no further proceedings would be taken against him. In his *Autobiography* [85] Carlyle makes clear that, despite his apology, he privately remained unrepentant for his actions:

> I took a firm Resolution not to Submit to what I saw the Presbytery Intended, but to Stand my Ground, on a firm Opinion that my Offence was not a foundation for a Libel, but if any thing at all a mere Impropriety, or Offence against Decorum, which ought to be Done at Privy Censures, by an admonition. This Ground I took and never Departed from it.[86]

In Carlyle's defence it must be said that it was not just the orthodox arm of the Church of Scotland that, predictably, deserted him in his hour of need. He himself devotes a long footnote in his autobiography to explaining that detestation of the stage also spilled over to embrace, and was much in evidence at the very pinnacle of the Scottish justice system. While Andrew Fletcher, Lord Milton, had been won over to *Douglas* and on its author's behalf had actively canvassed the Duke of Argyll's support for the performance going ahead in Edinburgh, by contrast Lord Arniston (Robert Dundas 'the Younger'), appointed Lord Advocate in 1754, consistently made no secret of his detestation of the stage. Arniston had taken out his spite against Dr Robert Wallace and even his advocate son, George, on learning that Wallace senior sympathised with Carlyle's plight. According to Carlyle, young Wallace, having been 'under the Protection of the Family of Arniston', was subsequently 'totally neglected'.[87]

On 5 January 1757 – less than a month since the first performance of *Douglas* – the Presbytery of Edinburgh issued an updated version of a document, similarly titled, which they had originally published thirty years previously:

ADMONITION and EXHORTATION

By the
Reverend Presbytery of *EDINBURGH*
To all within their Bounds.

The Presbytery taking into serious Consideration, the declining state of Religion, the open Profanation of the Lord's Day, the Contempt of public Worship, the growing Luxury and Levity of the present Age; in which so many seem Lovers of Pleasure, more than Lovers of God: And being particularly affected with the UNPRECEDENTED COUNTENANCE given of late to the Playhouse in this Place, when the State of the Nation, and the Circumstances of the Poor, make such hurtful Entertainments still more pernicious; judged it their indispensable Duty to express, in the most open and solemn manner, the deep Concern they feel on this Occasion.[88]

The broadsheet was essentially a re-working of the Presbytery statement of 30 November 1727, but conceived under entirely different circumstances. Whereas the much earlier *Admonition and Exhortation* had been devised to thwart the performance of a play 'fill'd with horrid *Swearing, Obscenity,* and Expressions of a *double Meaning,* tending directly to corrupt the Minds of the Spectators', [89] the update of early 1757 was specifically targeted at the masterwork of one of their own number in the Kirk, the serving minister of Athelstaneford parish[90] in the Presbytery of Haddington – though without once mentioning his play by name. Of course, the *general* purpose of both documents was the same: to draw the attention of the public to the evils associated with the performance of stage plays and theatre-going. For the historian, the language employed is such that, even if disaggregated from the original, one is hard put to identify which document it is taken from, *e.g.*

Presbytery of Edinburgh *Admonition and Exhortation*: 1727 version

The Presbytery ... do therefore, in the fear of the Lord, warn, exhort and obtest all within their bounds, as the regard the glory of God, the honour and interest of our holy religion, and theSalvation of their own souls, and of the souls of such as are dearest to them; that they seriously lay to heart the spirit and genius of our holy religion, and endeavour in their stations to promote, by their example and influence, the faith and practice of it; and for that end to discourage these *Stage-Plays*, to abstain from attending upon them themselves, and restrain such as depend upon them, or are under their influence from doing so.

Presbytery of Edinburgh *Admonition and Exhortation*: 1757 version

... On these accounts, and for many other obvious and weighty considerations, the Presbytery, warmed with just concern for the good of souls, do, in the fear of God, warn, exhort, and obtest, all within their bounds, as they regard the glory of God, the credit of our holy religion, and their own welfare, to and all the ordinances of divine institution; and by discouraging, in their respective spheres, the illegal and dangerous entertainments of the stage.[91]

Adam Ferguson and John Witherspoon join the debate

If a note penned to the title of a library copy of the pamphlet written by Adam Ferguson as his contribution to the *Douglas* debate is correct, then we can assume that Ferguson published his piece, *The Morality of Stage-Plays Seriously Considered*, in February 1757, barely a week or two after the Presbytery decree was read from pulpits.[92] He is particularly hard on the Presbytery's action, and, as a former student of divinity, ordained minister and army chaplain himself,[93] he shows an awareness of *both* the 1727 *and* 1757 statements. First, Ferguson deals with the earlier version –

We hear indeed of certain Proceedings of the Presbytery of *Edinburgh* about thirty years ago, when they published an admonition to discourage the Stage. We would willingly believe, for the honour of the dead, that they took this step in opposition to some faulty and immoral Plays which were then acted, and that they would have been loth to discourage performances of a better tendency, which might promise a reformation of such abuses.[94]

He then turns to the latest version just announced and, once again, disseminated from pulpits throughout the Edinburgh churches:

> A body of men respectable for their learning and gravity, who constitute a judicature in this city, have, without any exception, declared their disapprobation of the Theatre in general; and, to show that no exception could be admitted, have taken the alarm, just when the Tragedy, which I have had occasion to mention [*Douglas*], was introduced. ... Men of learning need not be told, that part of every liberal education consists, in learning to distinguish between Theatrical performances which are faulty, and those which have a moral and a good tendency; they know that a good Tragedy has been in all ages esteemed amongst the chief productions of human ability; that the authors of such works become more renowned with posterity than the princes and monarchs of the earth.[95]

At the same time, of course, aside from their antipathy towards the theatre and stageplays generally, Kirk judicatures were faced with a serious dilemma in approaching the issue of *Douglas*: the tragedy had, after all, been written by one of their number, while still an ordained serving minister — though Home would resign his charge later in 1757. Adam Ferguson, who had himself ceased to be an ordained minister only a couple of years or so previously, refuses to duck the issue though it is not, he explains, the highest concern on his agenda:

> It is needless to mention the names of clergymen of unquestioned reputation in the Christian church who have written plays for the stage; or to mention how frequent it is to consider a right taste and judgment in such performances, as an accomplishment necessary to every man of letters, whether clergyman or layman. Such authorities can be but of little avail after we have had the subject itself before us, and an opportunity of judging for ourselves.[96]

As one might expect from one of the greatest names among the Edinburgh *literati*, Ferguson — who, one suspects, relishes his role as an insider with intimate knowledge of not just the Kirk's disciplinary regimen, but of its strengths and weaknesses as well — adopts what can only be described as a common-sense approach to the issue. He effectively decides to play the Presbytery at their own game:

> This respectable body of men have passed a severe sentence against one of their number, for being present at this representation we are speaking of. This likewise seems to proceed from some powerful motive not sufficiently known: for they were not led to this act of severity, in execution of any law or statute of this Church. It must have been one of those extraordinary cases where a discretionary power is necessary. ... It is happy for us, that the law of our Church has expressly forbid the exercise of any such arbitrary and dangerous power.[97]

The 'severe sentence' to which Ferguson refers was the censure of suspension passed by the Presbytery of Edinburgh on 12 January 1757 on one of their number, the minister of Liberton, Thomas Whyte, who, when charged of having attended the playhouse to see *Douglas*, admitted the charge but pleaded in mitigation that he had gone there only once and *'endeavoured to conceal himself in a corner'* lest his presence gave offence — a scene, it could be said, straight out of modern West End farce. Not content with that sentence, the Presbytery had also written round certain other presbyteries — those of Haddington, Ayr, Earlston, Chirnside, Duns(e) and Dalkeith (the last-named Alexander Carlyle's presbytery) – informing them that while ministers 'in our bounds' have done everything 'in their power and their sphere to put a stop to entertainments so hurtful and illegal', 'our endeavours for suppressing them have been much interrupted, and in some measure defeated by [left blank for name(s) to be inserted] of your members] [further blank], minister at [blank], who, we are creditably informed, [was] present in the playhouse at the head of the Canongate, within the bounds of our Presbytery, while a tragedy called *Douglas* was acted.' The missive concludes:

> As this conduct is extremely offensive, we are persuaded your Reverend Presbytery will take this matter into their consideration, and follow out such measures as to them shall seem meet, for discountenancing such unwarrantable conduct, for vindicating the credit and promoting the usefulness of the holy ministry, and supporting the interests of religion.[98]

Not every presbytery felt comfortable with the Edinburgh letter. The Presbytery of Haddington (to which John Home's parish of Athelstaneford belonged) demurred, postponing any judgment in the matter, and, eventually, referring it upwards to the Synod. In classic Kirk style, on further reflection by the Synod and the Presbytery it seems that the whole affair simply withered on the vine. The Presbytery of Duns decided it was necessary to make reply to their brethren in the Presbytery of Edinburgh, politely reminding them of the doubtful practice they had resorted to in sending their missive round arbitrarily selected addressees in the first place:

> Presbyteries know best the characters of their own members, the state of religion, and the temper of the people within their bounds. They can best judge, whether, in any particular instance, the censures of the Church might not, instead of extinguishing a scandal, contribute to increase it.[99]

The Haddington decision proved a particularly troublesome flea in the ear of the Presbytery of Edinburgh.

In the meantime, John Witherspoon of Beith, soon to be minister of the Laigh Church in Paisley,[100] already known to most insiders as the author of *Ecclesiastical Characteristics*, added his voice to the debate. The internal evidence of his text confirms that Witherspoon became aware of Ferguson's (anonymous) pamphlet only when his own was almost complete.[101] In a rare lapse, Ahnert has Ferguson *replying* to Witherspoon's *Serious Inquiry into the Nature and Effects of the Stage*.[102] It was, of course, more a case of the other way round, even though Witherspoon had not set out to reply to anyone in particular. He quotes at some length from Ferguson's piece, names it in the text and also cites it in a footnote.

Ahnert, nevertheless, is certainly right in pointing out (as does McIntosh before him) that, perhaps surprisingly, the importance of both works lies in the extent to which their authors can (and do) seem able – almost one might say in a liberal kind of way – to agree on *some* points of principle, much more than highlighting the fundamental differences that separate them. In that regard, at least, one can agree with both Ahnert and McIntosh when they affirm it is often too easy to focus on the differences separating the orthodox and heterodox parties in the eighteenth-century Church of Scotland and ignore those features of commonality that allow at least a measure of shared outlook. For McIntosh in particular the significance of the *Douglas* controversy is 'not that it represented another instance of the Popular-Moderate split', but that the stage was still held in contempt by many ministers, regardless of affiliation, and as a gross and 'sinful' arena on account of the fact that 'for social as well as religious reasons, theatre-going raised inconsistencies with their professions of faith and with their duties both as ministers and as Christians.'[103]

But that is not to say that the views of Ferguson and Witherspoon at all coincide in regard to the 'usefulness' of the stage. Ferguson concedes that plays exist that have a potentially corrupting tendency. At the same time, he is vigorous in pointing out that by the same token *some* plays, of which *Douglas* is possibly one, have the capacity to offer 'a just moral and true representation of nature' which 'will carry the preference with every audience from more splendid and showy performances.' Accordingly, he maintains,

> When we see an audience therefore in tears [a clear reference to the first night of *Douglas*] for an object of compassion, when we find them affected with the generous sentiments which come from a virtuous character, deeply engaged in wishes for the success of the good, and for the disappointment of the wicked, it would scarcely occur that such an audience could be better employed in an hour of leisure.[104] ...
> ... I ... cannot imagine, that objections which ly against bad Plays only are now all the objections they have to plead against a good one, which may be considered as an attempt to make the Stage truly useful and instructive.[105]

But the comments of the anonymous author of *The Morality of Stage-Plays* to which Witherspoon takes special exception are when he (Ferguson) writes on the commercial and industrial 'improvements' that Edinburgh has enjoyed since the time of the opening of the Canongate playhouse barely ten years before:

> We may venture to ask, whether knowledge, whether industry or commerce have declined in this city [Witherspoon adds 'Edinburgh'] since the Play-house was first opened here. It will be owned that they have rather increased.[106]

Witherspoon's response must surely count among the rhetorical pearls of his Scottish career:

> It is, doubtless, an easy thing at present, to acquire a superficial knowledge, from Magazines, Reviews, Dictionaries, and other helps to the slothful student. He is now able, at a very small expence, to join the beau and the scholar, and triumphs in the taste of this enlightened age, of which he hath the comfort to reflect, that he himself makes a part. But, for our mortification, let us recollect, that, as several writers have observed, human things never continue long at a stand. There is commonly a revolution of knowledge and learning, as of riches and power. For as states grow up from poverty to industry, wealth, and power, so, from these they proceed to luxury, and vice, and by them are brought back to poverty and subjection. In the same manner, with respect to learning, men rise from ignorance to application, from application to knowledge, this ripens into taste and judgment, then, from a desire of distinguishing themselves, they superadd affected ornaments, become more fanciful than solid, their taste corrupts with their manners, and they fall back into the gulph of ignorance. The several steps of these gradations commonly correspond; and

if we desire to know of what period in each, we of this nation are at present, it is probable, we are in the age of luxury as to the first, and, in the eve at least, of a false and frothy taste as to learning, and may therefore fear, that as a late very elegant writer [107] expresses it, We shall relapse fast into Barbarism. [108]

With his response to Ferguson's claim that the stage is useful and instructive, Witherspoon, it can be argued, elevates the entire debate into the stratosphere, far above the pros and cons of a controversial play that just happened to have been the work of a Kirk minister. To be fair to Ferguson, he too, of course, is just as concerned in the task of contriving an image of the loftier purpose of dramatic art and its 'uses', as he sees them, to enlightened societies, including, and possibly in particular, those residing within the city of Edinburgh. Had he still been alive, poor George Anderson, one senses, would have been dissatisfied with the views of both men on the issue; but, then, he was of a different, generally *un*enlightened cast.

Ironically, the final verdict on Home's tragedy must be that David Hume was, of course, ultimately proved wrong: that *Douglas*, whether viewed as a work of literature *and/or* as a stage play, was never likely to stand the test of time. Modern readers know it is absurd to claim that Home even comes close to rivalling Shakespeare – or even perhaps, for that matter, the now largely forgotten Thomas Otway. But there was one enduring factor about *Douglas* that sets it apart and renders it important in any study of the literature of the Scottish Enlightenment. The play was the undoubted catalyst that hastened the end of the church's condemnation of the so-called evils of the stage. It was the tragedy of *Douglas* that would prove the nail in the coffin of orthodox conviction that the playhouse was the locus and source of near-satanic immorality. It was Home's play that made it possible for an enlightened view to be taken in future of theatrical production; a view that could regard the theatre as a useful, decorous and enjoyable 'diversity.' For Hugo Arnot, the Church of Scotland's display of 'fanaticism', allied to its manifest 'hypocrisy', made it inevitable that the public would regard their approach to theatre as 'illiberal' and 'oppressive', paving the way towards a final closing of the book on 'the prejudices which had hitherto subsisted against the stage.'

5

'Heresy'

... Are they not justly chargeable with doing their business privily, who disseminate as far as they can in private conversation, what they dare not vent from the pulpit; their opposition to the truth, in the chair of verity, consisting chiefly in omitting to assert it, and sometimes artful insinuations against it? Indeed this clandestine way of importing, or rather smuggling, among us opinions in religion, so different from the doctrine of the church, is almost a convincing demonstration of their falsehood.
    Anon. From *The Grounds of the Process set on foot by the Synod of Glasgow and Ayr against Mr Alexander Ferguson, Minister at Kilwinning; As the same is represented in a Series of Letters, published in the Scots Magazine, on both Sides of the Question.* 'Introduction', 1. Glasgow: Printed in the Year, MDCCLXIX. [1769]

I well knew that there are many of our party who never think themselves suitably employed unless they have a heresy-process before them. I knew from the instance of Mr Ferguson himself, who is now found to have been all the while innocent, that these brethren, in cases of this nature, never examine farther into the grounds of such a process than to see if it be barely possible to make a process. In the interval of peace which the termination of this process has afforded them, I am sensible that they are already beginning to grow impatient, and to look about them for new employment.
    Anon. [The Reverend William Thom], *A Vindication of Doctor Tail, from the Charge of Heresy* (Glasgow, 1770), xv.

Key authors and sermons

Reverend John Anderson (1671-1721), minister of Dumbarton, later of the North-West Church, Glasgow (the 'Ramshorn').

A Sermon Preach'd in the Church of Air. At the opening of the Synod. On Tuesday the First of April 1712. By John Anderson Minister of the Gospel in Dumbarton. Published at the desire of the Synod of Glasgow and Air.
  Glasgow: printed by Hugh Brown [1712?]

Reverend John Adam (1720-92), minister of West Kilbride (1751-69), Greenock Middle Parish (1769-92).

How a Minister should approve himself unto God. A sermon, preached at the opening of the Synod, in the High Church of Glasgow, on Tuesday April 9. 1765.
  Glasgow: printed for John Gilmour, ... MDCCLXV. [1765]

Several monumental cases of heresy exercised the General Assembly in the earlier eighteenth century, some involving ministers or former ministers – John Simson (twice: in 1714-17 and in 1726-29), Archibald Campbell (1736) and William Leechman (1743) – though undoubtedly the best known are the Assembly assaults of 1755 on the 'heretical' writings of David Hume and 'Sopho' (Lord Kames), and the following year on Hume's alone. Decades later, there was the case of William McGill (1786). Although Adam's synodical sermon gave vent to the row known as the 'Kilwinning heresy', the term as applied to this case is something of a misnomer, the debate it inspired having (initially at anyrate) little to do with the notion of 'heresy' in the conventional doctrinal sense; hence the title of this chapter being apostrophized. In reality, the protracted battle of words consequent on Adam's sermon began as little more than a heated ministerial dispute but then, when it broadened out, it attracted contributions from leading exponents of both church factions.

As it continued to intensify, the Kilwinning controversy extended into a number of issues: first, the interpretation of church discipline in both its senses; that is, in relation to 'rule' (or 'regimen'), in the sense of 'governance' or 'polity', and, further, the use and application by ministers and kirk sessions of discipline meted out to individuals according to procedures expressly designed for use by church judicatures. The primary cause of the issue that came to dominate the debate, however, lay in Alexander Fergusson's provocative comments in the 'Scots Magazine' on how a minister should regard the matter of subscription to the Confession of Faith on his admission and ordination, and his own controversially liberal attitude to the matter. In essence, the Kilwinning affair is of almost unlikely importance in helping to define and expose the essential differences in both theological outlook and moral culture between the Moderate and Popular factions in the Church of Scotland at this time in the age of the Enlightenment.

Some of the issues highlighted in this chapter – ministerial subscription, matters affecting orthodox and heterodox doctrine (including the role of 'reason' within the debate), discipline and morality (and, of course, the persistently vexatious question of patronage) were all treated satirically by John Witherspoon in his 'Ecclesiastical Characteristics' (1753); later, also in the same vein (though much less known), by William Thom, orthodox minister of Govan, who chose to enter the Kilwinning debate on the side of Alexander Fergusson. Thom's intervention in the affair is here examined for the first time.

John Adam's debt to John Anderson and John Witherspoon

John Adam *secundus* had ministered to his father's charge of Kilbride parish church since his ordination in 1751, first as his assistant and then as his successor the year before his father's death in 1763. Six years later Adam was translated to the Middle Parish of Greenock where he remained until his death in 1792.[1] We know from John Witherspoon's annotated pocketbook (almanac) of 1763, now at Princeton University, that there existed at that time what could be termed a south Ayrshire *coterie* of ministers of shared Evangelical theology who in that year (and possibly on a regular annual basis) exchanged pulpits in the month of July.[2] As the former minister of Beith[3] (only a few miles inland from the Firth of Clyde coast), Witherspoon was regarded as part of that arrangement and one can easily imagine that, for his part, he, with his wife (a countrywoman from Beith) and their five children, would have relished a summer weekend spent at the seaside, away from the urban sprawl of his busy charge in Paisley. The group of four consisted of Witherspoon (Laigh Church, Presbytery of Paisley), Adam (Kilbride, Presbytery of Irvine) Thomas Walker (Dundonald, Presbytery of Ayr – and Witherspoon's uncle)[4] – and Robert Dow (Saltcoats, Presbytery of Irvine). All four were bound together by much more than a mutual liking for summer seascapes, salt water and sand. The four were united not just by their calling, but by their enthusiastic devotion to the orthodox theology and doctrine espoused by the Popular party of the Church of Scotland. For a considerable period before his call to America in 1766 and his departure from Scotland two years later Witherspoon was acknowledged as one of the leaders of that faction within the Kirk.

Apart from John Adam's professed indebtedness to the synodical sermon preached by the Reverend John Anderson more than fifty years before, it is likely that in the preparation of his own synodical effort of 1765 Adam also had much in mind his friend John Witherspoon's by then legendary satirical mockery of Moderates and Moderatism, *Ecclesiastical Characteristics* (Glasgow, 1753). A sixth edition of Witherspoon's popular classic, scorned by the Moderates, had come out in London in the year of Adam's sermon.[5] In his most celebrated work – arguably one of the greatest literary monuments of the religious enlightenment in Scotland, though, of course, *anti*-Moderate to the core – Witherspoon artfully (and in the self-acknowledged style of Swift and, more especially, Defoe) attacks the habit of Enlightenment writers of attributing to 'reason' a convenient panacea for the sacred truths behind revealed religion. In that regard, of course, when he thinks of 'reason', and the enlightened idea of logical, rational argument endeavouring to provide neat answers to the mysteries of Christian revelation, Witherspoon has especially in mind the works of Kames ('Sopho') and Hume. In his neglected long 'Dedication' prefacing *Ecclesiastical Characteristics* – a work that uses the classic trope of satire saying the opposite of what the author supposedly intends – Witherspoon explains that his decision to dedicate his book 'to a dead man' [Francis Hutcheson who died in 1743] is 'either almost or altogether unprecedented'. Yet, he says, he is 'not much concerned, though this method of proceeding should be thought bold or new',[6] since 'this is the character which the incomparable Mr. – [Home, i.e. Lord Kames] gives of his own essays upon the principles of morality and natural religion.' At least to his own satisfaction, Witherspoon devastates the philosophical conclusions of two of the greatest pillars of the Scottish Enlightenment.

By contrast, in the case of his more assured literary debt to Swift and Defoe we may be certain that Witherspoon *does* mean what he says. Thus, in his own Dedication he begins by noting the dedication of Swift's *Tale of a Tub* 'to Prince Posterity', then (without naming the author this time) comments on Defoe's now largely forgotten long satirical poem in twelve books, the *Jure Divino* (1706):

> I have also seen a satirical poem, called Jure Divino, dedicated with great solemnity to Prince (or rather I believe to King) Reason.

Witherspoon daringly concludes his Dedication with a satirical account of Hutcheson's continuing but by then, of course, posthumous influence on 'moderation':

... If, therefore, one of these authors might dedicate a book to a faculty of the human mind and the other to an abstract idea, I hope it is no great presumption in me to dedicate mine to you [Hutcheson], though "in statue mortuorum", especially as there is not a living man who hath so good a claim to the compliment of a treatise upon my subject. ...

It is probable you have not been accustomed, these two or three years past, to hear your own praises celebrated; and therefore I shall no farther launch out into them than to say that there is not one branch of the character recommended in the following pages in which you were not eminent and that there never was one stone by you left unturned for promoting the good cause, – That you may still sit upon the throne and, by your powerful, though invisible influence, make the interest of moderation prevail is the ardent wish and the pious prayer of [Your most obedient and admiring Servant] [7]

John Adam chose as the text for his synodical sermon Paul's second epistle to *Timothy*, verse 15: *Study to show thyself approved to God*. While the same text is recurrent in John Anderson's sermon of more than fifty years before, also preached before the Synod of Glasgow and Ayr, Anderson's principal text – on the same general theme of ministerial duty – is from *Acts* 20, verse 28: *Take heed therefore unto yourselves, and to all the flock, over which the Holy Ghost hath made you overseers, to feed the church of God, which he hath purchased with his own blood.* The message of both sermons is generally, however, the same. And it is at once evident that Adam finds much in Anderson to inspire his own message.

'Reason' v divine revelation

Adam sees, for example, in the language of his long-dead mentor, the quirky minister of Dumbarton, much of what reminds him in his own time of virtually the same societal concerns. He also recognises some of the most important characteristics distinguishing the 'moderate' man from the man who can recognise 'divine revelation' when he meets it, even though, to state the obvious, Anderson in a technical (though not necessarily in an epistemological) sense substantially ante-dates the inception of 'Moderatism', as it came to be known.[8] First, Adam:

[*Adam*] There are, it is to be feared, [those] who are much wanting in this candid and impartial enquiry into divine revelation, who yet make high pretensions to it; nay, would be thought the most, if not the only honest enquirers after truth; ... They have fixed their principles, not on scripture, but on what they think the light of reason; and what they do not see in the light, they are determined not to believe. They come to the scriptures, not to submit their principles to be directed by revelation, but (as if their judgment was unerring) to employ all their genius and criticism to bring down the scriptures to their principles ... .[9]

Then he quotes from 'Mr Anderson' on the same message. True to his injunction 'that Preaching is to be managed in a Simple Unaffected Stile of *Language*', Anderson observes:

[*Anderson*] "... in divine matters our own reasonings [Anderson – 'Arguings and Ratiocinations'] are never to be trusted, except when they are directed and regulated by [Adam – 'divine' added] revelation: for [Anderson – 'And tho'] there are many things to be believed by us, perfectly incomprehensible by that measure of reason [Anderson – 'it'] which God hath vouchsafed to us, or to any meer creature." [10]

Elsewhere in his long sermon Anderson covers much the same subject in a memorable use of language reminiscent of John Knox at his best. He even at times comes close to anticipating the fusion of *doctrine* and *works* which Ahnert and others have identified as hallmarks of *heterodox* ministers in the heyday of the religious enlightenment:

> [*Anderson*] Others again, who have a tincture of *Antinomianism*, are apt to call the insisting on such Subjects *Moral Preaching*; but the Truth is, such Persons seem not to know what either Religion or Morality means. 'Tis true if Ministers urge these Duties merely upon moral Arguments, upon such only as Natural Reason suggests, and which are to be met within the Writings of the Heathen Philosophers, without insisting likewise of the Authority and example of Christ, and such other Topicks as are peculiar to the Gospel; they can neither be justifyed nor excused. But otherwise, Moral Duties are not only a Part of Religion, but a most substantial Part too, the Neglect of which causes the Gospel to be evil spoken of. The practical Part of *Instituted* Religion is superstructed upon *Natural* Religion.[11]

Adam, that is, has effectively hijacked parts of a sermon written many years before in order to expose the unfortunate contemporary consequences arising from the Church of Scotland's factional orthodox/heterodox split. The major point Adam strives to make is this: how ill it sits with a minister's calling for him to dare to contrive to make worldly sense of the mysteries of the scriptures; to employ the power of 'reason' alone to seek to explicate the inexplicable by attributing such mysteries to other than 'divine revelation'. But where Anderson has arrived at his conclusion through a doggedly implicit reliance on his own Knoxian brand of Calvinist *doctrine*, Adam, by contrast, has in mind the heterodox mentality and way of life of some of his Moderate fellow-ministers, with their predilection for 'charity' and a high regard for what they perceived as 'moderation' allied to 'enlightened' values in religion. This concern with attributing to 'reason' the way of the Moderates in generally seeking a rational explanation of divine revelation is rightly seen by Ahnert, Kidd and others as not incompatible with the views of some later *orthodox* writers who arrived at remarkably similar conclusions.[12] As Anderson ingeniously and wittily puts it in his master-work, *A Defence of the Church-Government, Faith, Worship & Spirit of the Presbyterians* (Glasgow, 1714):[13]

> [*Anderson*] ... generally the Objections against the *Presbyterian* doctrine arise from pretended *Reason*: Whereas the Objections against the *Arminian* Doctrine are founded, not only upon plain *Reason*, but express Declarations of *Scripture*: And where these are, and the Contest is 'twixt seeming *Reason* and the clear *Revelation* of God; it seems but good Manners to yield to God.

Patronage

On one level Anderson's 1712 sermon can be read as a classic Scottish Calvinist manifesto, anticipating the dire threat perceived to the survival of religion posed by the growth and spread of what would be termed (in a future Enlightenment setting) 'moderate' ideas. Adam seems to have grasped this and proceeds to highlight three areas of particular concern, acknowledging as appropriate his debt to Anderson. His greatest debt to the quirky charismatic minister of Dumbarton undoubtedly concerns the key issue of patronage. And here we need to keep in the forefront of our minds the date of Anderson's political sermon: it was preached on 1 April 1712. Precisely one month later, on 1 May that year, the Patronage Act came into force, restoring the law governing patronage within the Church of Scotland. Anderson observes:

> [*Anderson*] ... there is a great deal of Truth in that common Saying, *Vox Populi est Vox Dei* ['The Voice of the People is the Voice of God']: So that, when a serious Intelligent People Center upon one to be their Minister, it may, without any Force, be construed to be the motion of the Holy Ghost.
>
> Now, this, I think, without further adoe, sufficiently overturns the Doctrine of PATRONAGE: For how a Minister can be said to be *made an Overseer by the Holy Ghost*, who enters to that Charge, upon the *Presentation* of One, who possibly may be a Drunkard, a Whoremonger, a common Swearer, a Papist in his Heart, and that, not only without the Consent, but against the Will of the People, is beyond all natural Comprehension and Common Sense: Yea and I add further, is without the least Vestige of the like Practice in Antiquity for many hundreds of Years from Christ downward. And, now that this Church is as yet free of that Thraldom, as every good Christian will pray She may be so kept; so I am confident, none will seek the Reintroducing it, who have any Sense of Religion, and don't [Adam, 'do not'] design the pest'ring Her with a Ministry, which few Wise or Good Men will think worth the owning. [Here Adam introduces a †] [14]

Adam, citing liberally from this passage, adds a revealing footnote to his written text; as we shall see, his fears would turn out to be remarkably prescient:

> [*Adam*] † This gentleman's [Anderson's] sentiments in this matter will, no doubt, by many who are bigottedly [sic] fond of patronage, be sneered at, as quite antiquated and out of date. But they come nearer the opinion of some, who have keenly supported it, (viewing it no doubt to be their duty) than they may imagine. A minister of this number, and my particular acquaintance, who, a very few years ago, made a considerable figure in this church, and had the honour to preside in the General Assembly,[15] said very seriously to myself, that he was persuaded patronage would be the ruin of the church of Scotland. But, added he, It is the law – But I would ask, have we contribute[d] nothing to bind this hard law upon ourselves and the people? [16]

Discipline

Another key issue linking the two sermons is that of church discipline. It is important to grasp that the Westminster Confession of Faith (1647, and as ratified by Act of Parliament of 1690) – to which all ministers were required to subscribe on their ordination – specifically dealt with the grave issue of ministerial duty in exercising and upholding 'church censures'. This requirement stated that 'church censures were necessary for the reclaiming and gaining of offending brethren' and prescribed various gradations of punishment such as 'admonition, suspension from the sacrament of the Lord's Supper for a season, and ... excommunication from the church, according to the nature of the crime, and demerit of the person.' [17]

Early in his sermon Adam addresses the need for ministers 'as we would approve ourselves unto God' acting within the moral compass of their lives as 'a check on others, if in our presence they should do or say what is foolish or indecent, sinful or prophane.' We should, he insists, 'rebuke with all authority, but at the same time with prudence and good temper', and he goes on:

> [Adam] Sure, if the Jews were commanded by any means *to rebuke their brother* when he sinned, and, if all Christians are called to exhort one another daily, the ministers of religion ought to be exemplary in the practice of this duty. And, as we shall hereby approve ourselves to God, and to every man of right discernment, so, oftener perhaps than we think, even to these we are afraid to irritate by practising our duty. By an unchristian cowardice or sinful complaisance, a minister often becomes the object even of their contempt, whom he seeks thus to please.[18]

For his part, Anderson had asserted he was in no doubt that 'the Key of *DISCIPLINE* is committed to the Presbyters equally with the Key of *DOCTRINE* : Nor is it in the Power of any Government to deprive them thereof.' Later in the sermon he, too, expatiates on the duty of ministers to 'rebuke' and 'reprove' sin:

> [Anderson] We displease People if we do Reprove Sin; but we displease GOD if we do not. What Proportion is there 'twixt these two Arguments? We are oblig'd to suffer Martyrdom, if call'd thereto, for the Sake of a *Truth*: And shall we not venture the Anger of Men for the Sake of *Duty*? Duty is as Considerable as Truth; and Vice as hurtfull to the Soul as Error. Wherefore, a Minister must resolve to be Couragious for the LORD, and Tax People's Vices with the same Freedom they commit them. ... *With all Doctrine* ... a Minister ought to apply himself to the Understanding and Conscience of the Sinner; and Convince him of the Evil, Folly, and Danger of the Sin for which he Reproves him. *With all Long-Suffering* ... he ought to Treat the Sinner with a due Gentleness, endeavouring to *Restore such a one in the Spirit of Meekness.*
>
> Now when a Reproof is managed by these Rules, one must be of more than a Brutal Rudeness, if he be irritated thereby. But, if he be, as indeed there are some Sinners, not only Impudent and Obstinate, but Blust'ring too; 'tis Necessary to rub his Sores with Salt and Vinegar, that he feel 'em smart. If this Course don't reclaim *Him*, it will at least scare *Others.*[19]

Like Anderson, Adam seems to regard discipline and doctrine as inseparable and powerfully argues that ministers who are lax in exercising discipline are somehow failing to implement their scriptural, ordained duty. It is with that statement, and other similar ones to follow, that he unwittingly ensures the wrath to come at the hands of his putative Moderate-minded, though sternly unforgiving critics. Though not of his making, Adam's words would shortly provoke and set in motion a public scandal destined to become a major talking-point in polite Edinburgh circles thanks to its exposure in the columns of the *Scots Magazine*. The incident would come to be known as the 'Kilwinning heresy', after the location of his most outspoken critic's parish. But the issues that most concerned the sternest of Adam's critics, including the minister of Kilwinning himself, were not so much 'heretical' in the strict sense as issues that were rooted in the church's own polity and procedures. In the main, such issues tended to relate to ministerial practice and procedure as they had evolved since the not so distant days of the National Covenant:

[*Adam*] *First*, In the faithful exercise of discipline in the church. This is an ordinance of Christ, intended for the sinner's reformation, as well as preaching: nor are we to imagine ourselves at liberty to exercise it or not, as we please. And is it not to be regretted, that the reins of discipline are so much slackened in this church, once famous for the strict exercise of it; and to whom is this owing, but to ourselves? …

If some, in the pride of their hearts, contemn and refuse subjection to the discipline of the church, evidently appointed by Scripture, are we therefore to drop the exercise of it; and if they, by their obstinacy, shall lay us under the disagreeable necessity of denying them, in a continued way, the distinguishing privileges of Christians, let them blame their own pride and folly, and not pour out false and ill-natured reflections upon the ministers of religion for doing their duty.[20]

Ministerial subscription to the Confession of Faith

Such remarks lead Adam briefly to consider a different but key issue in his sermon – 'another material instance, in which we are called to approve ourselves to God' – the 'licensing and ordaining of such men for the work of the ministry, as we have reason to hope shall be pastors according to God's own heart.' Adam poses the question: 'Can we be too cautious in this matter, when we consider the great importance of the thing'? ; 'How nearly the glory of God, the honour of his church, the credit of religion, and the good of immortal souls are concerned here.' He does not, however, specifically mention the Confession of Faith. It might be thought deeply ironic that whereas Adam's comments fall far short of anything more than a passing reference to the issue, this above all others is, as we shall see, the very issue that would come to dominate the prolonged and bitter debate which his sermon provoked.

Anderson is silent on that issue (at least in his sermon of 1712),[21] but Adam's friend and orthodox champion, John Witherspoon, has a good deal to say about it (of course, in satirical mode) in *Ecclesiastical Characteristics*:

> It is a necessary part of the character of a moderate man never to speak of the Confession of Faith but with a sneer, to give sly hints that he does not thoroughly believe it, and to make the word orthodoxy a term of contempt and reproach.
>
> The Confession of Faith, which we are now laid under a disagreeable necessity to subscribe, was framed in times of hot religious zeal; and therefore it can hardly be supposed to contain anything agreeable to our sentiments in these cool and refreshing days of moderation. So true is this, that I do not remember to have heard any moderate man speak well of it, or recommend it, in a sermon, or private discourse, in my time.[22]

Witherspoon is, of course, referring to the Westminster Confession of Faith as originally approved for use in the Church of Scotland in 1647, following its adoption at the Westminster Assembly of Divines, and as subsequently ratified by Acts of Parliament in 1649 and, especially, 1690. The General Assembly overture of October 1690 had judged it necessary

> that all probationers licensed to preach, all intrants into the ministry, and all other ministers and elders received into communion with us, in church government, be obliged to subscribe their approbation of the Confession of Faith … and that this be

recommended to the diligence of the several Presbyteries, and they [be] appointed to record their diligence thereanent in their respective registers.[23]

Burleigh notes that in ratifying the 1690 Act for its own use the Kirk had declared the Confession of Faith to be 'the public and avowed confession of this Church' and, in so doing, held it to be 'the perfect compend of Scripture doctrine, and therefore the perfect norm for the correct interpretation of scripture, which the church must uphold at all costs.' But then he adds, that the Confession 'answered the questions that were being urgently debated when it was composed, perhaps too conclusively and comprehensively, leaving little room for diversities of theological opinion'.[24]

In the first of two important essays on the Kilwinning episode Colin Kidd has convincingly demonstrated the 'surprising' absence of *anti*-subscription – writings, that is, opposing the requirement for ministers to subscribe to the Westminster Confession of Faith as the confession of their own personal faith on admission and ordination – in eighteenth-century Scotland, and he relates such 'reticence' in these doctrinal matters to a more general apathy regarding theology as a whole; 'surprising', given, that is, the prolific 'articulacy' of men like Adam Ferguson, Hugh Blair and William Robertson.[25] McIntosh agrees, noting 'little Moderate interest in doctrine [or] apologetics'.[26] Sher (cited by Kidd) makes the same point, but a little more forcefully: 'None of the Moderates [*i.e.* in Robertson's circle, which ... clearly excluded men like Alexander Fergusson] had any scruples about subscribing to ... the Westminster Confession of Faith, and none of them ever overtly denied its fundamental tenets.' Kidd allows, however, that the issue came spectacularly into the public domain not long after the publication of Adam's sermon and would persist for several years thereafter.[27] Certainly, we can be confident that the author of the letter that sparked off the 'Kilwinning heresy' would have disdained any such reticence.

'A.B.'s letter to John Adam: the *Scots Magazine* correspondence

One would be hard put to recall a doctrinal dispute to rival in its intensity the so-called 'Kilwinning heresy' – in terms, that is, of the astonishing long-running bitterness and ill-feeling it engendered between ministers of the two rival factions in the Church of Scotland, orthodox and heterodox. Incredibly, this notorious affair was occasioned by a generally unremarkable published sermon by an adherent of the Popular party, the hapless minister of West Kilbride, John Adam. It is probably not overstepping the mark to claim that it is virtually impossible to identify *any* case that comes close to matching it, if, that is, our criteria were to include full public exposure in a periodical publication widely available throughout urban polite society in the heyday of the Scottish Enlightenment.[28] The tangled history of what only became public knowledge after two years had passed since the preaching of Adam's sermon of April 1765 serves to explain the background to the affair's importance and widespread notoriety.[29]

In their issue for April 1767 the publishers of the *Scots Magazine* informed their readers that they had been offered for publication a copy letter signed 'A.B.'. The letter, they explained, was of a 'personal' nature and 'animadverts on a pamphlet which must be unknown to most of our readers'. This can only be the printed version of Adam's sermon. It had at first been resolved not to publish A.B.'s letter on the ground it was 'written in a strain too like most of our polemical controversies'. On further reflection, however, the *Magazine* proprietors announced it would publish sample extracts to gauge whether or not 'the public' desired the entire letter to appear. From responses received, it emerged that the consensus was that the letter *should* be published in the full magazine (not simply on the blue paper cover) and the publishers duly obliged in their April issue, printing immediately before A.B.'s letter a list of 22 persons, with their occupations, who had indicated their support for the letter's inclusion.[30] In the same issue the publishers prefaced A.B.'s letter by a short letter from the minister of the new Relief congregation in Edinburgh, the Reverend James Baine – a recent fugitive from the Kirk whose case had rocked the General Assembly the year before – opposing the inclusion of A.B.'s letter.[31] Baine, now ministering to his Relief flock in Edinburgh, writes:

> The truth is, the performance itself is so loose, inconsequential, and heavily told, as to derive little credit to your collection, or entertainment to the readers of it. But who is safe, if an anonymous correspondent may by your Magazine publish personal invective, and retail all the private ill-natured stories which he has gathered from the weak, or designing, while the slanderer himself [John Adam] sculks in the dark? Proclaim immunity to this, and what becomes of the peace of society, and the honour of families?[32]

But Baine's pleas were to no avail. A.B.'s letter was released into the public domain and it was not long before his true identity came out: he was none other than one of Adam's ministerial colleagues in the Presbytery of Irvine, old Alexander Fergusson [*aka* Ferguson], minister of the neighbouring parish of Kilwinning since 1721, and a man who, as the *Magazine* itself observed without elaboration, was found to be no stranger to controversy. Morren records that in 1744 the May Commission of the General Assembly received a report of two libels preferred against Fergusson by one James Leitch, both of which his accuser failed to prove and were eventually dismissed. Leitch, a 'wright', was then in turn accused by the Presbytery of Irvine of having slandered Fergusson and, after intensive investigation, he was 'placed under the lesser excommunication, a sentence which the Synod affirmed.' The substance of Leitch's complaints is not disclosed by Morren [33] and the case has not been researched until now. *Appendix D* in this study reveals for the first time the unusual charges against Ferguson as documented in the records of the Presbytery of Irvine: they had arisen from a routine meeting of heritors, elders and 'heads of families' convened by the Presbytery in Fergusson's church in Kilwinning on 28 April 1742.[34] No case more fully exposes the extent to which ministers in rural parishes were used to having their way with errant members of their congregations who dared to contest their sovereignty. More important, in the eyes of his friends and foes alike it could not now be denied that Fergusson had had 'previous'.

Fergusson's reputation for obstinacy and speaking his mind did not stop with the Leitch affair. In 1759 he had provoked a minor pamphlet war with the publication of *A Warning relating to the Present Schism in the Church of Scotland* (1759) and *A Second Warning* [1761].[35] Both writings stirred up hostility towards the expanding secessionist churches in Ayrshire as well as more generally. Fergusson claimed that the secession came about as a result of a mischievous interpretation of scripture and false doctrine. In another of his pamphlets on the same issue, *A Display of the Act and Testimony* (1761), he expressed the view that the seceders' betrayal of Presbyterianism was not confined to theology and doctrine but extended into the wider issue of 'disaffection of the civil government, avowed in the Testimony and conduct of the schismatic brethren.' Quoting from their *Act, Declaration and Testimony* (1737) Fergusson seeks to prove that seceders' leaders had claimed that the Union of 1707 had not only been positively harmful to seceders' interests, but was 'contrary to, and condemned by the Word of God':

> [Original Secession: *Act, Declaration and Testimony*]
> Whereupon the said *Union* is become one of our *publick National sins*; and from this Time, instead of making Progress in Reformation-work, we have been declining and backsliding every Day, and have fallen under the Weight of such Grievances as shake the Foundation of our Presbyterian church Government and Discipline.[36]

> [Alexander Fergusson: *A Display of the Act and Testimony*]
> They rail at the Union, and call it 'a public national sin'. ... Though every reader of the least knowledge may see, that in all these texts, God is threatening the Jews for confederating with idolaters, and not trusting in himself. And though it is certain, that the Union is, next to the gospel, and the reformation from Popery, the greatest blessing that ever Scotland met with. It has put an end to the hereditary hatred, which long prevailed between the two kingdoms, to their great hurt: and secured the peace and prosperity of both; against the pernicious influence of France in Scotland. And the restless plots of a Jacobite and Popish party in it, and in England. It has introduced arts, agriculture and commerce: whereby Scotland has been raised from poverty, to wealth. The church has got a better human security, than it ever had, for the continuance of its present establishment. It has civilized the barbarous parts of Scotland, by making them more accessible; and by introducing knowledge, industry, and justice, instead of ignorance, idleness, and oppression of all kinds, which formerly prevailed therein. Instead of that slavery we were under, by the feudal powers, and the hereditary jurisdictions; and a Scotch Privy Council, which tyrannized over the whole nation. It has put us, as to liberty, on the same footing with England: a nation of all others the most famous, for its struggles, and success in the defence of it. Ought they then to be looked upon, as well affected to our constitution, who dare thus avow their enmity to the Union.[37]

Conveniently, all the tangled and convoluted facts of the Kilwinning affair are set forth in meticulous, if tedious detail in an anonymous pamphlet published in Glasgow in 1769 entitled *The Grounds of the Process set on foot by the Synod of Glasgow and Ayr, against Mr Alexander Ferguson,* [sic] *Minister at Kilwinning; as the same is represented in a series of letters, published in the Scots Magazine, on both sides of the Question*. The last six words in the title, however, are disingenuous in the extreme. The authorship of the *Grounds of the Process* has never been identified but it is clear from the five-page 'Introduction to the Affair relative to Mr. Ferguson' (expressed in the first person throughout) that the writer is solidly on the side of the Popular party – unequivocally, that is, on John Adam's side – seeing great harm being done to the future of the church, and even to religion in Scotland, so long as the ill-feeling the case has engendered continues to aggravate those holding religion to be the ultimate binding force in society:

> If it were only open and avowed enemies with whom we had to do, the danger would not be so formidable: but the case is far otherwise, when the opposition arises from the principal members of the church, who not only *profess* our religion, but have *engaged* themselves, by the strictest ties, to support and maintain it. The disease is at the heart, and actually prying upon our vitals ... .[38]

And what, in the anonymous author's view, constitutes the issue at the heart of John Adam's sermon that provoked the dispute in the first place? For him, it is the continuing vexation aroused by Fergusson's apathetic view of the role of the Confession of Faith in ministerial ordination:

> Do not those men *creep in unawares*, who, at their entrance, not only conceal their *heretical* sentiments, which, if they take for truth, they surely cannot pretend to be *valiant for the truth upon the earth*; [39] but, with the most cowardly and hypocritical dissimulation, subscribe their *assent* to the doctrine established in the church, as a confession of their faith, through the grace of God, to assert, maintain, and defend it to the outmost of their power? And are they not justly chargeable with doing their business *privily*, who disseminate as far as they can in private conversation, what they dare not vent from the pulpit; their opposition to the truth, in the **chair of verity** [bold italics added], consisting chiefly in *omitting* to assert it, and sometimes artful insinuations against it? Indeed this clandestine way of importing, or rather smuggling, among us opinions in religion, so different from the doctrine of the church, is almost a convincing demonstration of their falsehood.[40]

In the closing section of his introduction the author of the *Grounds of the Process* sarcastically insists that, were things not to be put right 'in this matter' in the highest courts of the church, we are 'upon the eve of so important a revolution in religion', and

> it is hard to say what the consequences may soon be; or what will be the situation of such ministers as believe what they profess, and teach what they promise to do. The very principle of self-preservation, and the opposition that must arise to the maintainers of the prevailing party [the Moderates], from all who are sincere in their engagements, may lead at length much farther, that they themselves have yet any conception of: in so much, that were they now to be told, what some of us may live to see, they might be ready to say with Hazael; *What! is thy servant a dog that he should do such* [a great] *thing*.[41]

Despite the numerous contrary voices for and against its content at the time it was first published in the *Scots Magazine*, there can be no be denying that Fergusson's letter is a masterpiece of compression. Early in the letter he confides that he would have supplied his opinion of Adam's synodical sermon 'sooner' had it not been for 'my wife's indisposition, and my own frequent ailments.'[42] That off his chest, the old minister comes to his first point; on the doctrine of *original sin* – delineating one of the traditional and most trenchant lines of doctrinal demarcation between the Moderate side and the 'high' party – he lectures Adam in his typically bare, succinct prose:

> No sentiment can be more unworthy of God, than to think that he creates intelligent creatures sinners. He makes us upright, and *we make ourselves sinners*.[43] [italics added]

To a man like Adam, a man who was said to have regarded John Witherspoon as his 'leader', such a statement would have been shocking.[44]

Fergusson moves on to the issue of subscription and here he is as bold and direct as he is contemptuous of Adam's brief but uncompromising remarks on the subject:

> I have been told you said you would pronounce them villains who had signed the Confession of Faith, and did not believe every proposition in it to be truth, and adhere to it as such. This is a censure unworthy of a Christian, and far more unworthy of a teacher of Christianity. I fancy you learned it from your leader*;[45] who has in a printed sermon asserted, that we are not to think charitably of such as have opinions or principles different from ours. The apostle Paul, who was a better divine than either of you, teaches a quite contrary doctrine, Rom. xiv. It plainly appears from your censure, you would deprive us of our natural right of private judgment, and the invaluable privilege of inquiring after truth, and of improving in the knowledge of it. ... I aver, that no man ought to sign his assent and adherence to any human composure, but in so far as it is agreeable to the scriptures; which are the only rule of faith and manners; and not the opinions of men, let them be ever so learned, pious, and upright.

And he would have the last word on the subject in the 'Appendix' to his letter:

> No human government has a right to impose a subscription, in matters of faith and morals, to a composition of fallible men, but in so far as it is agreeable to the scripture[s]. ... Such an imposition is inconsistent with, and destructive of, the natural right of mankind to private judgment, freedom of inquiry after truth, and improvement in the knowledge of it. ... As the scriptures are the only rule and standard of faith and morals, no human composure ought to be put on an equal footing with them; and no man who acts with conscience will sign the Confession of faith, or should be thought to sign it, but in so far as it is agreeable to the scriptures, though he do not at signing express that qualification.[46]

Having chided Adam with the jibe that his sermon was privately published rather than 'at the desire of the Synod', Fergusson accuses him of falling into the trap that, he says, ensnares many ministers; that is, of hypocritically preaching one thing and practising another. He is particularly severe on Adam's alleged misinterpretation of the meaning of charity:

> Instead of gospel truths, you deliver uncharitable censures, and unjust calumnies, (with an air of assurance and omniscience, as if you knew men's hearts) against all in general who differ from you about the meaning of the scriptures, in some points of divinity. Did you think that preaching things so contrary to charity and truth, was the way to show yourself approved unto God? If you did, your zeal for systematic, but unscriptural doctrines, must have blinded your charity and your understanding: for you have not been aware, that these censures and calumnies might, with equal assurance, and on much better grounds, be retorted on yourself. If you did, your zeal for systematic, but unscriptural doctrines must have blinded your charity and your understanding ... .[47]

Fergusson then turns to the vexatious topic of the deployment of reason and rational argument to interpret 'the meaning of the scriptures':

> ... you [he refers to page 16 of Adam's sermon] justly grant that we are to use our reason in searching into the meaning of the scriptures; yet you argue against and decry reason. I

wish you had told your brethren what you meant by *reason* [italicised only in the *SM* and GOP versions]; whether the intellectual faculty, or the use of it, or evident propositions naturally revealed; for the word *reason* [do.] is used in all these senses; and we are to admit nothing that is contrary to common sense and understanding: for the scriptures can be no rule of faith and manners to us, if the understanding God has given us is not to be a rule of judging their meaning.[48]

Next, Fergusson tackles the prickly issue of *discipline* in the Church. In his sermon (pp.30-31) John Adam had particularly irritated Fergusson by impressing on his congregation that 'the reins of discipline are so much slackened in this church, once famous for the exercise of it'. This part of Fergusson's letter is worth quoting in full since it has largely been overlooked (and perhaps overshadowed by the subscription issue). To introduce the subject Fergusson cites what Adam has to say about 'a new kind of discipline'[49] – that is, the increasing practice on the part of kirk sessions and ministers of 'converting the censure appointed by the scriptures, and the laws of the church, into a little money for the use of the poor'.[50] Citing scriptural precedent for legitimate use of monetary fines, Fergusson continues:

> I aver, that though a public rebuke before the congregation prevailed for some centuries in the primitive church, to vindicate the Christians from the aspersions of the Pagans, who called their meetings nurseries of lewdness and vice, it was not intended to be a perpetual rule in the Christian church, when Christians and Pagans were not living in a mixed society; and when by daily experience, that utensil, the Repentance stool, is found to be a cause of many gross crimes. And though it is converted into a piece of money for the poor, all that is of importance in discipline is still kept up; viz. confession of sin, profession of repentance, rebuke, which, though privately transacted before the Kirk Session, are not the less acceptable to God. For these reasons, and that we might act like honest men, without partiality to people of station, who will not submit to a congregational appearance; I heartily wish it was abolished. That period of our church which you say was once famous for the strict exercise of discipline, was the most culpable since the Reformation. For they carried discipline higher than the scriptures authorised them, even to persecution; which made many hypocrites.[51]

Fergusson's letter was composed in 1766, a year in which John Witherspoon was continuing to defend what would prove a grotesquely protracted action for defamation and damages in the Court of Session, and just a couple of years before he left it all behind and sailed for a new life in America. Further, it cannot be overlooked that earlier in his letter Fergusson had made scathing reference to Witherspoon as 'your [*i.e.* Adam's] leader'. The old Moderate minister mercilessly goes on to deliver the *coup de grâce*, and, cleverly, he does so in satirical language of which, one is tempted to add, Witherspoon himself might even have approved:

> You say, the excuses for dropping of discipline, in this, and other instances, are by no means good; which is but a begging of the question. I wish you would publish a confutation of what I have here offered, in your inaugural sermon at your translation to Paisley, or the Relief-kirk at Glasgow; one of which I am told you expect, and are preparing for it ... .[52]

Fergusson's references to Paisley and the Glasgow Relief congregation need explanation. First, in coded language he is here poking fun at Adam, knowing full well that, on the one hand, Witherspoon (who, conjecturally, would have been the talk of the Synod at this time) was fighting a fraught action in the Court of Session that had been set in motion by an ill-judged published sermon, and, on the other, he demonstrates his awareness that Adam and Witherspoon were not just close colleagues but personal friends into the bargain. To continue to speculate, Adam may well have winced when he read these comments, viewing them as egregiously below the belt. On safer ground, it seems more than likely that Fergusson, with his proven antipathy towards seceders and secessionism in general,[53] would have despised the expanding and popular Relief movement, a branch of secessionism that had opened its doors in Glasgow in 1761, followed by James Baine's appointment to the new Edinburgh Relief congregation five years later. (Baine, we should not overlook, was formerly minister of the High Church in Paisley and a constant thorn in Witherspoon's flesh.) By that time, moreover, Kilwinning itself had earned a reputation as a particularly flourishing centre of Antiburgher worship over several years.[54]

Fergusson reserves to the last his rebuttal of Adam's views on patronage. It will be recalled that in his printed sermon Adam had added a footnote in which he declared that a minister of his acquaintance, and a recent Moderator of the General Assembly (the likely candidate is William Leechman), had confided in him that patronage would be 'the ruin of the church of Scotland', but had added, 'It is the law.' The old Kilwinning minister angrily responds to this anecdote:

> Your only argument against it [patronage] is a scrap of a sermon condemning it, and a little chit-chat between you and another minister, (who always acted in support of patronage in his own and other men's settlements and transportations, but, like a politician as he was, wanted to soothe you by pretending to be of your opinion) that patronage would be the ruin of the church of Scotland. You ought to have shown what you meant by the church, and how patronage would be the ruin of it. The word Church is used to signify the house where the people meet to worship God; the clergy; and the Christian people. I defy you to show that in any one of these senses patronage is or will be the ruin of the church: for the Kirks are all kept in repair; the benefices are not lessened; and the rights of the Christian people are not incroached on. You should have been ashamed of such a silly proof of patronage being the ruin of the church. But indeed you had no better arguments: for there is no place in all the scriptures that gives the people a right to chuse their ministers. And it would have been as absurd to give them such a right, as to give school-boys a right to chuse their teachers.[55]

Ironically, Fergusson employs much the same kind of language to express similar sentiments on the issue of patronage to those Witherspoon himself had resorted to in his address in the course of the patronage debate in the General Assembly of 1760. Just three years after he himself had been a victim of the system on his call to Paisley from Beith, Witherspoon told the Assembly, in a debate on the disputed Kilconquhar settlement, that he could not support a system that empowered 'any Christian, as such', with a 'right to call a minister on an establishment.'[56] For his part, Fergusson gets highly personal on the subject, meanly comparing his own settlement in the distant past – when, it seems, he had received a 'unanimous call' without presentation – with Adam's more protracted settlement at Kilbride, which had finally been achieved only through (or so Fergusson alleges) pressure having been brought to bear on the patron, the young and inexperienced Earl of Eglinton. And, warming to his theme, Fergusson sweepingly condemns as worthless *all* sermons that are consciously designed to appeal to the known prejudices and predilections of 'the people':

> If the church suffer, it is entirely owing to such as you; who, from an affectation of popularity, blow from the pulpit the trumpet against patronage, and thereby incense the populace against both the church and the state, to the great dispeace of the country, and hurt of religion, without any just ground. For patronage with us, as it is limited, can have no bad effect of itself on the practice of religion. ... Popularity acquired by sermons calculated to inflame the populace, is built on a sandy foundation, despised by men of sense and integrity, and not worth the esteem of any wise men.[57]

A.B.'s letter concludes with an 'Appendix' in which he stubbornly returns to the theme of subscription, insisting that

> It is not to be imagined, that the parliament [of] 1690, when it enacted the subscription of the Confession, meant it as an uniformity in principle; a thing impossible; for men's minds are differently formed, and till God frame them all alike, they must view things differently: so they could only mean it as a test of conformity to the Presbyterian establishment.[58]

Reactions to Fergusson's letter and the heresy case

It was inevitable that A.B.'s letter would provoke a variety of response, and doubtless the magazine publishers had bargained for that outcome, while not perhaps foreseeing the volume or longevity of the debate that continued to chunter on in the wake of their decision to publish. After the April 1767 issue, containing the full text of A.B.'s letter (besides the letter from James Baine opposing its publication), the May number prints a letter from 'F.' who (clearly not himself a clergyman) makes a refreshingly original point: referring to the issue of subscription – and allowing that, if A.B. is right, then the public has a right to know when ministers are sincere to their calling or not – 'F.' writes:

> The ministers of this church have, of a while, boasted of their subservience to the interests of government and loyalty: but what sort of instruction and example do some of them now give their fellow-subjects? Such clergymen as taste somewhat of the royal beneficence will, I dare say, think themselves particularly called to give some testimony effectually on this subject.[59]

In the July number a *'well-wisher to the Church of Scotland'*, writing from Aberdeen, focuses on the subscription issue and takes A.B. to task for having himself once subscribed to the Confession of Faith while secretly qualifying the terms upon which he had subscribed. *That*, the 'well-wisher' insists, is comparable to someone signing 'the decrees of the Council of Trent, or the different points of the Mahometan Koran; as little needed a Papist or Mahometan have any scruple to sign the Confession of Faith.'[60] In October the inevitable occurred: a letter appeared from 'S.D.' ('student of divinity'?) *defending*

A.B. and *censuring* 'Mr. F.' It is a clever letter. Instead of censuring A.B. for his approval of a minister's 'right' to qualify the terms of his subscription, 'S.D.' protests that he should be praised for his honesty in openly declaring the nature of that qualification.[61] As 'S.D.' points out to the magazine proprietors in a note prefacing his letter we now have the ridiculous situation of 'letters sent you upon letters on letters'!

In the October number there is a lengthy contribution signed '*Philanthropos*' [lover of mankind] under the running-title, 'Charity in judging of subscription recommended'.[62] Citing yet another sermon preached at the opening of the Synod of Glasgow and Ayr, this time by the Reverend James Morison (who had succeeded Witherspoon as minister of the Laigh Church in Paisley), 'Philanthropos' seeks the middle way, *viz*. a compromise that would 'require the enemies of truth to speak out all their objections, and to deter no man'. His solution?

> … let honest men join together, in … lessening the evil to the utmost of their power: let all who subscribe and teach, be understood, unless the contrary can be clearly proved, to do so in such a manner as to save their consciences; and let the judgment of conscience be left to him whose alone right it is.[63]

To leave matters to individual conscience, however, was never going to satisfy the orthodox diehards. And so it proved. In the *Scots Magazine* of January 1768 a new correspondent enters the lists. At the end of his massive twelve-page epistle – more a mini-treatise than a letter – he signs himself '*Philalethes*', [lover of truth].[64] In keeping with his choice of pseudonym it is 'Philalethes' who first reveals the identity of A.B. First, he comments that the seceders had 'always alleged, as a chief ground of their secession, our departure from the doctrine of the church of Scotland.' But, he goes on, such an allegation 'has always been denied on our part, and treated as a calumny.' And as just one example among many of what were called *testimonies* – a technical term first used in the Reformation to mean an open declaration of doctrine, but in post-1733 Scotland characterising any statement specifically representing an affirmation of secessionist doctrine – 'Philalethes' names one person in support of his assertion, 'namely, that of Mr Alexander Ferguson [sic] minister of Kilwinning.'[65] It was no more than a crude device to expose A.B.'s real identity:

> If Mr Ferguson be the author of this letter signed A.B. will he, or any of his adherents, now pretend to wipe off the aspersions by the same argument.[66]

Nonetheless, 'Philalethes' makes a good point. Fergusson's (now egregiously rare)[67] pamphlet of 1761 – published in Glasgow 'for Mr Robert Wodrow' [68] – is, in part, in contradiction of what he had to say in his copy letter to John Adam of October 1766 – at least, so far as the issue of subscription to the Confession of Faith is concerned. 'Philalethes' mercilessly casts Fergusson's own words back in his teeth:

> "It is false and calumnious to the highest pitch, 'That the church is corrupt in doctrine, discipline, worship, and government.' [a quotation from the *Act, Declaration and Testimony* which, in his 'Advertisement', Fergusson says he is using for that purpose] As to doctrine, if the Confession of faith is sound, she cannot be corrupt in it; for all who are admitted members in it, are obliged, by acts of parliament and assembly, to sign it; and they do sign

it; and, further, are taken engaged to adhere to the doctrine contained in it: *and none are allowed to vent doctrines contrary thereunto, without being censured when proven guilty*." [italics are by 'Philalethes'] [69]

'Philalethes' not only exposes Fergusson's hypocrisy in his Adam letter, but sees in the old Kilwinning minister, a Moderate and a high Tory, an extreme example of the scepticism of the age manifesting itself even among the ranks of ordained ministers of religion:

> Scepticism, or doubting about the truths of religion, seems to be the prevailing disposition of the present age, especially among those who (very inconsistently) boast of the superior light whereby they think it is distinguished; as if the fewer important truths there be that are known and believed, and the lower the degree of men's persuasion of them, so much the more extensive were the bounds of their knowledge.[70]

All this is seriously ironic given that the theme of Fergusson's pamphlet, identified by 'Philalethes' as the source of the very inconsistency and hypocrisy he is anxious to expose, is the extent to which, in Fergusson's estimation, the original seceders – and, he argues, their successors – have *themselves* betrayed the doctrine and discipline (the latter in its broadest sense) of the established Church of Scotland. Having made his point, 'Philalethes' moves on to an equally grave issue. He now directs his fire on matters affecting the current unsatisfactory approach to church discipline; what 'Mr Ferguson and his adherents in the Synod' insisted on, namely that 'a prosecution upon a *fama clamosa* [a matter of public scandal] was an unjustifiable part of our constitution', and that 'not the least notice of it ought to be taken in the way of discipline, unless a private prosecutor gives in a libel.' According to 'Philalethes', however, 'the exercise of discipline is the *only cure*' [italics added].

Soon 'Philalethes' was unmasked as the Reverend Thomas Walker, minister of Dundonald in the Presbytery of Ayr, just a few miles from West Kilbride and Kilwinning, the respective parishes of John Adam and Alexander Fergusson. Walker was, of course, John Witherspoon's uncle. Both men, it seemed, uncle and nephew, had a similar outlook on church discipline and the need to preserve the Kirk's, or at least the Popular party's, uncompromising determination to uphold discipline in the fullest sense of the term. The future of the Kirk, they insisted, depended on it. But, as we saw in chapter 2, Witherspoon would pay a heavy price for his unswerving resolve to pursue the men he incautiously named within the public arena of his published sermon of censure. Whether or not we agree with the view that the Court of Session action brought against him – not finally determined until 1776 – lay (even in part) behind his decision to quit Scotland for a new life as college President in New Jersey, there is not a shred of evidence to support any thought that Witherspoon himself, in the course of the last years of his Scottish career, or subsequently, suffered any remorse of conscience for having acted misguidedly in the so-called Snodgrass affair.

With the publication of the letter from 'Philalethes' the correspondence arising from John Adam's sermon ceased and the *Scots Magazine* wound down its interest in the episode. But that was by no means the end of the matter. Just a year later a pamphlet entitled *The Grounds of the Process* came out in Glasgow, the idea of a resourceful but unknown printer who reckoned on a ready market for an anthology of all of the relevant materials relating to the Kilwinning affair – with the glaring exception, that is, of the sermon that had initiated the debate in the first place. Flushed by the success of his apparent demolition of Fergusson's letter (and, in particular, his overt exposure of A.B.'s hypocrisy), Thomas Walker decided to resume his fierce anti-Moderate stance in his little-known polemic, *An Alarm to the Church of Scotland* (1771). This work, usurping the same title of an anonymously authored pamphlet of 1728 condemning the alleged heresy of Professor John Simson, was nothing less than a wholesale assault on Moderatism and all it stood for. Walker accused the 'prevailing party' of 'a worldly spirit' and took particular exception to the General Assembly having elected as their Moderator for 1770 'a noted champion for the stage', meaning, of course, the arch-Moderate, Alexander Carlyle. It is Thomas Walker's father, the minister of Temple, to whom Carlyle refers when he describes 'Walker' as 'a rank enthusiast, with nothing but heat without light.' Was the son a chip of the old block? It certainly looks like it.

Alexander Fergusson died in February 1770. From around the time of his unmasking by Walker until a few months before his death he had been subjected to the full rigour of the Kirk in its increasingly dubious guise as both inquisitor *and* ecclesiastical judicature, a role that he himself had questioned and found wanting in his (*i.e.* A.B.'s) response to Adam's sermon. Furthermore, an embarrassing libel on a charge of heresy was preferred against him by 'an obscure, illiterate man', one James McConnell, a former soldier turned town drummer of Beith, John Witherspoon's old parish before his translation to Paisley in 1757, a libel which stretched the credulity of both the predominantly Moderate Presbytery of Irvine and the predominantly Popular Synod of Glasgow and Ayr.[71] McConnell must have known Witherspoon in the old days, for in a pamphlet he had patched together two years after Fergusson's death representing his version of events, he discloses that he had written twice to his former minister, now of course resident in America, asking for his opinion on the 'heresy'. Unsurprisingly, there is no record of any reply to McConnell from New Jersey.[72] Kidd has implied that McConnell's pamphlet may have been produced by a 'ghost-writer', and he is probably right.[73]

After an astonishingly convoluted game of legal ping-pong – of which, it seems, the Kirk was then too frequently culpable – judgment in the Kilwinning affair was finally reached late in 1769 by the Presbytery of Irvine to the effect that 'it never was [Fergusson's] intention, in anything he had published, to deny the scripture doctrine of the satisfaction of Christ, *or encourage disingenuity in subscription.*' [italics added] The Presbytery unanimously 'dismissed the whole affair, judging this issue of it to be most for edification.'[74] It is worth adding that at one stage in the process, when the Synod unwisely took matters into their own hands (away, that is, from the clutches of its opponents in the Presbytery of Irvine), entrusting the resolution of the affair to a committee of no less than twenty ministers and five or six elders, Fergusson instructed his agent to deliver into their hands a strongly worded letter of protest. In what may have been the last letter he ever wrote the ailing old minister, quoting the *Form of Process* (the Kirk's rulebook in discipline procedures), contested the legality of the action, and at the same time told his peers that he did not recognise the authority of the church court trying him. John Graham later commented that 'this letter was certainly very strong'.

Shortly before Fergusson's death, and again almost immediately after it, his cause attracted a powerful though unlikely ally. In successive pamphlets published anonymously, William Thom, the idiosyncratic and iconoclastic Popular party minister of Govan and erstwhile friend and associate of John Witherspoon, – and constant thorn in the flesh of the principal and most of the senate of the University of Glasgow – wickedly satirised the insensitive and uncharitable approach which, he believed, the Synod had brought to the matter.[75] The earlier of Thom's pamphlets is cast in the form of a spoof funeral sermon preached by Dr. Robert Traill – Thom calls him 'Dr Tail' – professor of divinity at Glasgow and, it seems, the leading proponent of the case for further investigation by the Synod; the 'deceased', according to Thom, represented by the Synodical Committee which had sat in the Laigh Kirk in Glasgow to hear the facts of the Ferguson case. (It was eventually wound up without reaching any meaningful conclusion). The slightly later pamphlet brazenly incorporates Thom's sketch of 'Doctor Tail's Faithometer', with the observation that such a device might hang in 'every parish-church in this kingdom' and that on it 'should be marked the degree of credence professed by the present incumbent; which mark should be confirmed, or altered, at every successive ordination.' [See illustration and Postscript to this chapter, page 152]

A second, much less entertaining yet infinitely more sober assessment of Alexander Fergusson's stance came less than a year after his death with the publication by Cadell in London and Balfour in Edinburgh of a remarkable 'tract', *The Religious Establishment in Scotland examined upon Protestant principles*. Its authorship was unknown and for some time the work was erroneously attributed (*e.g.* by Hew Scott) to the minister of Portpatrick, John Mackenzie. In a later edition of the *Fasti*, however, Scott correctly re-assigns it to the pen of John Graham, minister of Dunlop in the Presbytery of Irvine, later (from 1779) of Kirkinner in the Presbytery of Wigtown.[76] Scott describes Graham as 'a learned divine, and an authority on Church law.'[77] In the 'Advertisement' prefacing the book Graham refers to the 'late heresy process' involving Fergusson, making the point that his own thoughts on it could not be published while the process, current 'at a time when the rage of religious animosity was at its greatest height'. Graham allows that heresy 'properly speaking' is a 'departure from any part of our established, religious Constitution'. He implies that the Fergusson case – he means the treatment of Fergusson by Presbytery and Synod subsequent to the publication of his copy letter to Adam – does not readily fit into the standard definition of heresy: hence the apostrophized title of this chapter.

Graham is an unrepentant apologist for Fergusson and, of course, fully shares his liberal Moderate principles. His book is undeniably an original and still remarkably readable account of a Kirk partly in chaos, but also partly in search of a more *enlightened* approach to doctrine and procedure. On the lessons to be learned from the Kilwinning affair Graham reveals that shortly before his death Fergusson had had the opportunity to read the draft unpublished text of *Religious Establishment*. And Graham comments on Fergusson's death-bed defiance:

> He was pleased to approve it. It met the sense of his own noble spirit; and, with his dying breath, he demanded that it should be published. You may regard it as coming from *him*. He has left it as a legacy to the orthodox.[78]

In relation to the specific issue of subscription, Graham, as one might expect, champions (in Kidd's words) a 'more relaxed approach' to the issue, arguing that if the reasoning he has employed 'be just', then surely the sensible way out is for any minister who subscribes to the Confession of Faith to do so, while feeling 'at full liberty' to 'change his mind, upon conviction, and even publish this change to the world, without being under any obligation, from his subscription, to leave the church.' Further, according to Graham's plan no church judicatory would be 'under any obligation, from that subscription, to inflict any censure.'[79]

Predictably, however, Graham's *apologia* merely had the effect of infuriating the orthodox opposition, the so-called 'high party'. His book had not only savaged 'the preconceived opinions of the people',[80] but was especially hostile to 'Philalethes' and his like. In 1774 the opposition – in the guise of 'Philalethes', himself, now, of course, unmasked as the Reverend Thomas Walker – struck back. A veritable compendium of every orthodox principle 'for preserving Purity of Doctrine' (from its sub-title), Walker's *A Vindication of the Discipline and Constitution of the Church of Scotland* was published by his nephew's (John Witherspoon's) favourite Edinburgh publisher, William Gray. The title-page identifies its author, now 70 years old, as not just the 'minister of Dundonald', but as 'author of the letters upon that subject in the Scots Magazine, signed Philalethes'. The *Vindication* may have been conceived in the nature of a reply to the *Religious Establishment* – Walker says he is 'utterly ignorant of the author of the book which I have answered' – but it is much more than that. A big book (almost 450 pages), one senses this is Walker's life-work. As in the case of a much earlier publication of his – *The Terms of Ministerial and Christian Communion imposed on the Church of Scotland by a Prevailing Party in the General Assembly* – Walker's *Vindication* is turgid, dense and prolix. Nevertheless, both works, separated by over twenty years, are in their own way monuments of extreme, decidedly unenlightened orthodox moral culture and belief and, as such, deserve to be better known. This is, for example, what Walker has to say on patronage:

> I cannot help ... observing to you upon this Occasion [it is written in the form of a dialogue], that I take it to be one of the bad Consequences (perhaps among other good ones) of our having so many Lawyers in the General Assembly, that the Settlement of our Vacancies is so much considered in the Court in the View of private Rights of particular Persons. Many Gentlemen who have a seat in that House are so much accustomed to other Courts, where the Matters litigated come under no other View, that 'tis little wonder, all Things considered, if they look upon the planting of a vacant Parish in no other Light, but as the Disposal of so much temporal Property as the Emoluments of the Office amount to.[81]

Even so, the *Vindication* is at times a dark book with a pointedly grim message. Here is what Walker has to say about the unknown author of the book to which he has chosen to make reply:

> I wish I could not add, that it affords sufficient evidence of the surprising progress that infidelity has already made among us. – I say, *infidelity*; nor do I think I have gone too far. – I will not say, that our author knows himself to be an infidel; neither can I say the contrary. This, however, I may venture to say without any fear of contradiction, that the profession

he makes of Christianity, and the regard he professes for the Bible as the standard of religion, is no sufficient evidence of his being a real believer.[82]

In relation to the subscription issue Walker is equally forthright and, once again, totally uncompromising:

> If there are any honest men, who might be useful preachers of Christ, that have different apprehensions of some of the *minutiae* of our religion, men who are firm believers of all the most important articles of our common Christianity, while, at the same time, they have a scruple about adopting some expressions used in the Confession of Faith, and even doubt the truth of some less important determinations therein, ... there is none who would be better pleased than I would be, to see the difficulties of such men removed, if this could be done without involving it in the total ruin of the Christian religion.[83]

These exchanges did not end with Walker having the last word. Just a year after the publication of the *Vindication* Graham hit back with a pamphlet Cadell brought out for him in London entitled *Subscription to Human Articles of Faith*, specifically designed, of course, as a more economic riposte to the Dundonald minister's massive work. It was largely a re-working of his earlier thoughts on the subject.

There thus came to an end one of the bitterest factional feuds in the eighteenth-century church in Scotland. It had arisen, innocently enough to begin with, as the result of a largely undistinguished sermon preached by a largely undistinguished minister. It dramatically entered the public domain by virtue of a contentious letter which the *Scots Magazine* had at first refused to print – and eventually changed its view only when prodded to do so. The dispute was concluded after a formal charge of heresy was endlessly and shambolically tossed to and fro, from Presbytery to Synod and back again, before finally being thrown out. No one emerges from the dispute with his credit enhanced or head held high. No one was rash enough to claim the victor's spoils. At the same time, however, there must surely be little argument with the verdict that the ultimate loser was the church itself. By their actions and behaviour towards each other, neither faction would ever, of course, concede that, essentially, that was the conclusive outcome.

In the more recent of his two stimulating essays on the Kilwinning affair Professor Kidd suggests that the episode ought to be viewed as evidence of 'a major gulf' existing in that particular locale of the west of Scotland 'between liberal proponents of the need to adjust doctrine in the light of changed circumstances and a decidedly conservative, albeit clever and sophisticated, counter-Enlightenment.' If that argument holds water, he argues, such a conclusion 'sits awkwardly' with the conventional picture of a 'broad-based' Church of Scotland embracing, to some extent, alliances of Moderates and Evangelicals.[84] It is certainly true that before the century closed there would be further evidence of similar infighting involving doctrine and varieties of doctrinal interpretation; the McGill heresy case noted in chapter 1 is the outstanding example and, of course, it too involved an Ayrshire minister. Nevertheless, on the evidence of the preaching ministry, and more particularly in the case of the sermons noted in this study, weighty matters of doctrine were set to take a back seat where ministerial disputes were concerned, even in a rural, or at least non-metropolitan context. In the latter decades of the century where ministers fell out with one another and presbyteries grew restive – as, for example, in the extreme case of William Dunn discussed in chapter 6, involving other ministers including William Moodie and James Lapslie – it had nothing to do with doctrine and everything to do with the prevailing socio-economic and political state of the nation. Concomitant with the age of improvement and popular enlightenment it seemed that the church corporately had at last ventured tacitly to acknowledge, albeit painfully slowly at times, that on the one hand the ideals associated with Moderatism were no longer relevant to an industrialising Scotland, while on the other, rigid orthodoxy wedded to authoritarian pulpit censure were now totally at odds with the heady spirit of reform. In the final analysis, one might be forgiven for asking the question: was Alexander Fergusson born too soon?

Postscript

'Doctor Tail's [i.e. William Thom's] Faithometer'
— extracted from *A Vindication of Doctor Tail, from the Charge of Heresy* (1770), 83-4.

DOCTOR TAIL'S FAITHOMETER.

Mr. Believing

That the whole is a Joke,

The Confession

The Scriptures

Entitles the Believer to

A professorship in Divinity, and a lead in the Church.

A benefice in the Church of Scotland.

Heaven

'Explanation':

a Great reservoir of credence.
b Faith – answering to the *mercury* in the natural barometer.
c The present mean altitude of faith in this nation.
d The lowest degree of belief.
e Degrees of faith above the Confession, – each degree, by the proposed scheme, to rise in value above another in the proportion of *L*. 10 Sterling, and to qualify the possessor accordingly.
f The top *open*, – to signify that this sort of mercury may rise *in infinitum*, the element which acts upon it being capable of all degrees of *grossness*.
g Clouds.

'Observations':

1*st*, In this scale there are three *capital* degrees of *belief*, – and *these* are removed from one another by intervals whose proportions have been calculated with mathematical exactness.

2*dly*, The interval between the first and second is an exceeding great one; that between the second and third is remarkably small – as the mathematical reader will of himself very readily perceive.

3*dly*, The present mean altitude of faith in this nation, though it still stands considerably above the scriptures, yet reaches not near to the Confession. It is, indeed, much nearer the former than the latter. The element which acts upon it has not for some time been so *gross* in *general* as were to be wished.

4*thly*, This scale, as will be evident to the learned, is constructed upon a plan entirely *new* – being adjusted by the rules of the *ancient* geometry †.

5*thly*, Were it once established in this nation, the Confession and Formula would both be superfluous, and I should very readily give my vote for abolishing them.

6*thly*, All that it wants, therefore, to render it *a perfect* and *permanent faith-measurer*, is the sanction of *parliament*.

7*thly*, To obtain *this*, it is hoped both parties will concur – as it is calculated so as to answer the *present* views * of *both*. The heterodox faction will have the pleasure of seeing what they have so long wished for, the Confession *invalidated*; and to the orthodox I need not recommend it.

8*thly*, It would be proper, I mean in case the legislature should agree to it, that every parish-church in this kingdom be furnished with one of them; on which should be marked the degree of credence professed by the present incumbent; which mark should be confirmed, or altered, at every successive ordination. The proper place for fixing it in, would, in my opinion, be directly below the nail on which the minister hangs his hat when he ascends into the pulpit. In this position it would always be *concealed* when he stood *upright*, and, consequently, during the whole time the preaching continued it would be impossible for the congregation to know what faith he was of.

9*thly, and lastly*, – It would also be convenient that an exclusive patent should be made out, vesting the sole property of them in *me*, and giving me full and conclusive powers to make, vend, distribute, and supply the nation with good and sufficient *Faithometers*.

† Is not the Doctor intituled to a premium from the Society of Arts for this invention?
* This seems to be the Doctor's last effort to reconcile the parties.

Thomas Hardie (sic) (John Kay)

6

Reform

The people have ever been, in some degree, sensible of their rights, and have felt their wrongs. Impelled by these sentiments, they have never ceased to claim the former, and to seek redress of the latter. ...
A minister of the gospel turned courtier, is always an absurd, often a very corrupt character, and hostile to improvement.
                    Reverend William Dunn: his synodical sermon of 1792, 13, 26.

Key authors and sermons

Reverend William Dunn (*aka* Dun) (1745-98), minister of Kirkintilloch.[1]

A Sermon, preached at the opening of the Synod of Glasgow and Air, at Glasgow, 9. October, 1792. From Rev. xxi. 5. And he that sat upon the throne said, Behold, I make all things new, And he said unto me, Write: for these words are true and faithful. By The Rev. William Dunn, A. M. Minister of Kirkintilloch.
Glasgow: Brash & Reid, 1792.

Reverend Thomas Hardy (1747-98), minister of New North Parish, or 'Haddo's Hole' (West St. Giles Church), Edinburgh.

Fidelity to the British Constitution, The Duty and Interest of the People. A Sermon, preached in the New North Church, Edinburgh, On Thursday, February 27. 1794, being the day appointed by His Majesty for a General Fast. By Thomas Hardy, D.D. One of the ministers of the City, and Professor of Ecclesiastical History in the University of Edinburgh. Published at the request of the Managers of the Charity Workhouse, for the Benefit of the Charity.
Edinburgh: David Willison. M.DCC.XCIV. (1794)

The short-lived radical reform movement in Scotland in the early 1790s, and the Edinburgh sedition trials of 1793-1794, justifiably continue to occupy the scholarly attentions of modern historians. One compelling aspect of the period is, of course, the extent to which early radicalism is associated with the concomitant growth of industrialisation, urban sprawl and popular self-enlightenment.

That religion should have played an important part in the radicalism of the period should come as no surprise. Ministers played out their adopted postures on both sides of an increasingly fraught and divided society. The Church of Scotland, corporately and individually, opted on the whole to play the loyalist card, while, individually, a few Popular party adherents – but, more prominently, ministers of seceding churches – saw it as their duty (and opportunity) to lead and try to comprehend the contemporary mood of 'the people', often publicly and defiantly aligning themselves with the issues espoused by the campaigners for reform.

Though to date largely ignored by both popular and academic historians, the Reverend William Dunn's synodical sermon of October 1792 sheds useful further light on the background to Thomas Muir's trial for sedition in the High Court of Justiciary, Edinburgh in August 1793. Dunn's sermon also helps to reveal the extent to which the Dundas regime was prepared to go to subvert individual Kirk ministers as part of their efforts to stabilise the country. It is the only example known of a serving parish minister having been convicted of a criminal offence and sentenced to a custodial term of imprisonment.

The Kirk and 'the people'

There are valid alternative ways of interpreting the role of the Church of Scotland in terms of its relationship to government and the establishment throughout the 1790s – a period characterised by Harris as *relative* stability in Britain; though stable only, it must be qualified, if Scotland's position in that regard is favourably compared with the turmoil then prevailing in Ireland and parts of England.[2] The usual view is that whereas the Moderate party in the Kirk found it easy to cooperate with government – and with Henry Dundas in particular – members of the Popular party were much less coy in seeking to introduce secular politics into debates at the highest level of the General Assembly and, thereby, it is argued, contrived to stir things up according to their agenda of siding with 'the people', however open to interpretation the term may be. On the whole, Ian Clark takes a benevolent view of the Moderate line:

> The Moderate principle of 'cooperation' took the form of consultation with the representatives of the government of the day, but this was designed to promote the harmony which they conceived to be proper, rather than to subjugate the Church to secular policy.[3]

Clark is careful to point out, however, that 'the crisis and the fear of upheaval produced a remarkable degree of unanimity between the two parties' and he (perhaps a shade lamely) cites in support of his contention a report in 1792 of a future Moderator, James Finlayson,[4] to the Lord Advocate, Robert Dundas, to the effect that he had found only one minister in the Synod of Lothian and Tweeddale who had shown any sympathy with 'the licentious spirit of the times.'[5] Fry, too, adopts a similar view to Clark, pointing out that in respect of Popular party ministers ' there was very little support among them for political radicalism.'[6]

The countervailing view to Clark's runs roughly as follows: that, far from primly standing aside from the movement for popular reform – preferring not to rock the government boat – the Kirk *ex suo officio* displayed a corporate disregard for the reform movement which Moderate ministers like Hugh Blair, Alexander Carlyle and William Moodie described as 'licentious', 'dangerous' and as the inevitable outcome of misguided leaders led astray by 'the unruly violence of a turbulent multitude'. In 1793, for example, the first year of the war with France, the Moderator of the General Assembly's 'dutiful Address to His Majesty' 'on the subject of the present War', while admitting that 'some of the People under our care were deluded by the dangerous Principles which were industriously propagated', goes on to assure the monarch that

> we have employed all our influence in counteracting the tendency of the Seditious Writings which were assiduously circulated, and in warning the People committed to our care against the busy efforts of designing or deluded men.[7]

Even that iconic figure of the later Scottish Enlightenment, Thomas Reid, himself once a Kirk minister, in the year that saw in Edinburgh the ghastly public hanging, beheading and dismemberment of Robert Watt for high treason (and just two years before Reid's death), discoursed on the 'danger of political innovation', believing that

> If we see, or think we see, imperfections in the constitution, or in the government, we ought to consider, that there never was a perfect human government on earth; we ought to view such defects, not with a censorious and malignant eye, but with that candour and indulgence with which we perceive the defects of our dearest friends. It is only atrocious conduct that can dissolve the sacred tie.[8]

Kidd sees the issue rather differently and altogether more subtly, tracing the Kirk's overwhelmingly loyalist position in the 1790s to its having 'long been in thrall to an Anglo-British interpretation of history, a spell which events during the [period] did nothing to break.' In such circumstances the Kirk 'retreated into a loyalist sycophancy.'[9] Bluntly, and to paraphrase, the Kirk was alarmingly out of touch with, and distanced itself ever farther from the whole of God's people. It explains why both Henry Meikle and Bob Harris, writing nearly one hundred years apart, thought it central to their theme to seek to weigh in the balance the role of the Church of Scotland in the 'first' radical period, at its zenith in the middle years of the final decade of the century. Meikle and Harris both conclusively find that the Church's adopted position over the period was, in that regard, seriously wanting. In essence, each believes that the Kirk lost its way and came close to deserting 'the people'. They might have added, however, that partly in consequence, and partly in any event, 'the people', for the most part, had lost confidence in the Kirk.

Historians like Devine, McFarland and Dickinson, on the other hand, rightly caution against exaggerating the depth and scale of popular support for the Scottish reform movement in the 1790s. Even so, there can be little argument but that, especially after the outbreak of war with France early in January 1793, the temperature of Scottish political activity rose significantly as things turned steadily nastier, and 'real' radicalism – admittedly never more than patchily in discernible enclaves throughout Scotland – began to take hold. What set out in the beginning as a movement for burgh reform was arguably *always* set to be a patchy kind of business. Geography, the nature of industrial enterprise and local tradition[10] were key determinants of the presence and extent of Scottish radical activity. Harris, in particular, puts his finger on one of the central issues:

> Edinburgh's leadership of the radical campaign in 1792-4 was to prove a major source of weakness to radicalism nationally, reflecting the local importance of the luxury economy,

the extent to which its key institutions were dominated by the Dundas interest, and the conservatism of its elites and ministers.[11]

The two most formidable of these 'elites' were, of course, the twin pillars of Scots religion and Scots law, both with their headquarters in the capital city. In retrospect, it could be said that partiality and blind allegiance to government policy too often seemed the way of both the pulpit and the bench.

Furth of Edinburgh, and not for the first or last time, it was a different picture. In the century to come – above all in the first decades leading up to the 'Radical War' of 1819- 20 – it would be to the west of Scotland that the centre of gravity of radical politics would gradually shift, where it would remain during the industrial era.[12] But in the closing decades of the eighteenth century industry generically, the nature of specific industries in a given locality, seemed to go hand in glove with the quantum of radical sentiment found there. One of the most reliable examples of the association of 'advanced' political thinking and radical activity with particular industrial economies is the proven link between what we would now term early socialism (specifically the rise of 'combinations', or, *ur* trade unionism) and the localised presence of handloom weaving, textile production and cloth manufacture. Paisley, then the third largest conurbation in Scotland, with its traditionally strong radical associations, alongside its reputation for popular self-enlightenment,[13] is an important case in point, although there were other radical hotspots, including much smaller centres of population in the west, of which Kirkintilloch is one of the most impressive examples. For the historian what is particularly intriguing is the fact that the entire parish of Cadder, in which Kirkintilloch was then sited, had an enviable notoriety for 'hot' religious politics extending back to the anti-Catholic troubles of the mid 1780s.

Within a few years, what had begun as a seemingly innocuous, often naïve aspiration for burgh reform dramatically changed course. Government ministers and their supporters began to display tell-tale signs of, if not near-panic, then certainly of genuine anxiety – often in proportion to the increased presence throughout reform 'hotspots' of Reevesian placemen on the one hand, and the intensification of contrived (frequently subsidised) loyalist propagandist pamphleteering on the other. Equally, the extent of their personal commitment to, and wholehearted involvement in the cause of reform on the part of able, well-read men like the advocate, Thomas Muir, and the English Unitarian minister with his base in Dundee, Thomas Fyshe Palmer, could no longer, it was concluded, be ignored by the authorities. Secessionist ministers, in particular, seemed to have sensed a particularly strong commitment to the cause of reform, including such as Neil Douglas, James McEwan, James Donaldson, James Ellis (*aka* Alice),[14] Patrick Hutchison and Archibald Bruce, the first three of whom attended as delegates to the second and/or third General (i.e. British) Conventions of the Scottish Friends of the People. Kidd describes Bruce as a man who 'remained thirled to an older age of arid and prolix Calvinist scholasticism'. Despite that bleak picture of him, we cannot ignore that Bruce had an unexpectedly rich and inventive comic side which occasionally rose to the surface in clever satires like *The Kirkiad: or, Golden Age of the Church of Scotland* (1774).

With his Popular party sympathies to the fore, the Reverend William Dunn, in his article on Kirkintilloch for Sir John Sinclair's ['Old'] *Statistical Account* of 1791, praised seceding ministers and their congregations for the good effects they produced upon the members of the established Church of Scotland:

> The existence of Seceders, and of seceding meeting houses, has perhaps no bad effect upon the manners and sentiments of the people, either here, or any where else throughout the kingdom. They are in some degree spies and checks upon the members of the established church; and the discourses of their clergy are often adapted, with singular felicity, to the capacity and the prejudices of the least enlightened classes in the community.[15]

To an alarming degree in the eyes of those most publicly committed to reform, these were highly charged, potentially desperate times. Among all classes of society there was a palpable tension as the fear of invasion from Europe became more widespread. Threats generated by anxieties of that kind were soon reflected from the pulpit in numerous sermons of the period. Once himself parish minister at Kirkintilloch for nearly nine years,[16] John Erskine of Old Greyfriars, for example – a champion of the Popular party and one of its acknowledged leaders – preached a sermon 'before the magistrates of Edinburgh' on 2 September 1792. Suppressing normally conventional misgivings about political preaching in general, Erskine freely admitted that the 'reflexions' he spoke of were suggested by the 'confusions in Paris, 10th August that year.'[17] Uncompromisingly he sees nothing but unmitigated evil in the news from France:

> When anarchy succeeds order and government, every son of folly and pride accounts himself to rule. Every one is exposed to the baneful effects of these absurd claims.[18]

True to their Calvinist roots, Kirk pulpits could once more, for a time at least, be depended upon as a barometer of the mood of the people. William Dunn, orthodox minister of Kirkintilloch, was not only set to play a not inconsiderable personal role in these troubled times, but his well-chosen remarks in his *OSA* article on the salutary qualities of seceding ministers and congregations accurately anticipate their important, occasionally central role in the impending reformist struggle. Assuredly Dunn would not have shared Erskine's strictures on 'these absurd claims' of the French people, even though expressed by an acknowledged champion of the Popular party.

Inevitably within the ranks of ministers of the established Kirk there were sharp differences of view on the state of the nation. Never far from the surface at the best as at the worst of times, politics in the pulpit infiltrated many sermons of the period. John Erskine, we have noted, broke his own golden rule to exclude politics from the pulpit. Even that paragon of correct form and procedure, the archetypal Moderate Hugh Blair, friend of Henry Dundas, felt compelled to add his voice. Normally the mildest of men, and commanding wide respect throughout Britain and America for the good sense and religiosity of his published sermons,[19] Blair's innate sense of order and propriety could not overcome his support for the policies of an embattled government. For Blair, however, as for most Moderates, a cerebral and restrained approach to pulpit censure marked the limit of his concern.[20] That was never going to be the case with William Dunn.

William Dunn's synodical sermon of 9 October 1792

Modern Kirkintilloch is a town of around 20,000 persons, no more than eight miles or so to the north-east of Glasgow city centre, and just over two miles from neighbouring Milton (formerly 'Mill-town') of Campsie. In the late eighteenth century it was a relatively minor but not insignificant centre of handloom weaving. According to one contemporary account, the Kirkintilloch weaver

> could ask from eighteen to twenty shillings a week, and that, working ten hours a day, with now and then a holiday for digging in his garden, rambling in the country, or some merry-making; and the old race of weavers were the best educated, most reading, and most respectable of all the operatives of the north.[21]

William Dunn's *OSA* contribution for 1791 puts the population of Kirkintilloch parish for that year at 2,639. Of that number, he states, 1,536 'reside in the town', 'among whom are 185 weavers and 11 stocking makers'. This should be compared with the town and parish of Paisley where, in the same year, the *OSA* contributor (the Reverend Robert Boog of the Abbey Church) found that with a combined population of just under 20,000 – then one of the fastest-growing industrial conurbations in all of Scotland (Smout's 'extreme case') – there were employed 'in the various weaving branches' a total of 2,500 looms in the town itself, with a further 1,100 looms in the 'suburbs', a statistic that did not include the 'country part' of the parish, with many other looms operating 'in the villages of Nielstoun [Neilston], Bar-head [Barrhead], Beith, Dalry, Kilwinning, &c. &c.'

Both Dunn (in his Kirkintilloch entry), and Boog (writing of Paisley) concur in warning of the dangers to the health and morality of people employed in these industries of what today we would term environmental factors, allied to appalling working conditions forced upon operatives, especially young children. Dunn writes:

> The poor of this parish are not numerous. The weekly collections at the church-doors have hitherto been found more than sufficient for their support. ... But, it is to be feared, that if a greater proportion of the inhabitants shall be induced to apply themselves to manufactures, one disadvantage which must necessarily arise from this increase of industry, is such a change in the manners of the lower classes, as may reduce them much oftener to a state of helpless poverty.[22]

Such concerns notwithstanding, in some measure at least Dunn remains generally optimistic for the future:

> ... the population, wealth, and industry of this parish, can hardly fail to increase considerably, even before the close of the present century.[23]

At the same time he fears the 'corruption of Morals likely to attend the increase of Industry' in his parish:

> One unhappy circumstance, that may attend the increase of industry, and the introduction of new manufactures among us, is too important to be overlooked: Children becoming sooner able to subsist by the profits of their own labour, will, of consequence, sooner disregard the authority of their parents, acquire earlier habits of expence; and, being exposed to the infection of vice and dissipation, before the powers of their minds are

in any degree matured, or their characters formed, – will be much more worthless in manhood, and more helpless in old age. It would be a happy circumstance, therefore, if politicians could contrive some means, to preserve the virtue and morals of the people, while they are endeavouring to increase their numbers, to enliven their industry, and to augment their wealth. [24]

Writing of Paisley[25] – an important centre of weaving, cotton thread spinning and cloth manufacture dwarfing anything Kirkintilloch had to offer – Boog similarly uses the pages of his *OSA* contribution to 'preach' a near identical message to Dunn's:

> It is painful to think, that a manufacture which gives employment to so many hands, and which may be a source of great wealth to individuals, may be productive of very unhappy effects upon both the health and morals of the children employed in it. This there is some reason to apprehend. ... Tempted by the wages, parents send their children to this employment at a very early age, when they have got little or no education; and the close confinement deprives them of the opportunity of acquiring more. Ignorance, disease and mortality, are but too likely to prove the effects of this manufacture, if carried on by unfeeling and selfish men.[26]

More than most, William Dunn would have known and understood the national need for something like Sinclair's *Statistical Account*. Born a farmer's son, at the age of 15 he had fulfilled the requirements for his MA at the University of Glasgow and was licensed to preach by the Presbytery of Kintyre two years later. In 1774, on the death of the incumbent minister, Dunn was presented to the vacant charge of Kirkintilloch by the tenth Lord (Charles) Elphinstone and his wife, Clementina, daughter of the Earl of Wigtown. By one of those strange quirks of history, the Elphinstones' son-in-law was William Adam, then MP for the pocket borough of Gatton in Surrey who would marry Eleonora Elphinstone in 1777.[27] It was Adam, both a qualified advocate at the Scottish bar and an English barrister, who, as MP for Ross-shire, initiated three debates in the House of Commons in 1793–1794, calling not only for the convicted Scottish radicals Muir and Palmer to be granted right of appeal to the House of Lords, but for a full-scale inquiry into the Scottish criminal law. Neither motion succeeded. [28]

Less than a year after William Dunn compiled his *OSA* article for Sinclair, he was invited to preach the customary 'synodical' sermon at the opening of the Synod of Glasgow and Ayr, meeting in Glasgow on 9 October 1792. A few weeks later the sermon was published by Brash and Reid who advertised it in the Glasgow press alongside '*Burke on the French Revolution*', '*M'Intosh's [sic] Vindication*'[29] and Mary Wollstonecraft's '*The Rights of Woman Vindicated.*' The extravagant wording of the advert was clearly designed to sell the sermon and, for that reason, it is unlikely that Dunn himself had any hand in it; indeed, in the light of future events, the advert's implications must, one speculates, have troubled him considerably –

> This day is published, price Six pence
> Containing, amidst a good deal of very uncommon matter, what the Author deems, the
> GENUINE PRINCIPLES OF A FREE GOVERNMENT

ADVERTISEMENT

It is now offered to the Public, and dedicated to THE FRIENDS OF THE CONSTITUTION IN CHURCH AND STATE, AND OF THE PEOPLE: that such as have thought proper to approve of it, may be more satisfied, that their approbation was not altogether misapplied; and that those of different principles may be convinced, that their censures of it were not well founded. [30]

In their issue for 6 November the *Glasgow Courier* published a long public notice intimating the formation of a new constitutional society in William Dunn's own parish. The notice is headed 'Kirkintilloch, 3^d. Nov. 1792':

A number of the inhabitants of this Town and Parish previously acquainted with the sentiments of each other, resolved to form a Society. Having met this evening, for this purpose, in William Wallace's tavern, they instituted themselves into a Society under the name of THE ASSOCIATED FRIENDS OF THE CONSTITUTION AND OF THE PEOPLE

The Society elected
Mr. HENRY FREELAND, President,
Mr. ROBERT WADDELL, Vice President,
Mr. JAMES BAIRD, Secretary

The Society afterwards unanimously

Resolved ...
That the publick and private account of the *Reverend William Dunn*, their parish minister, has long raised him high in the affections of his people, and, particularly, that by his noble, manly, and eloquent vindication of the cause of Reform and of Freedom, in his Sermon at the opening of the last Provincial Synod of Glasgow and Ayr, he deserves well of his country. ...
Resolved ...
That the thanks of this Society are due to Mr. Muir, younger of Huntershill, for his unremitting exertion in the cause of freedom and of humanity.

Just a week or two prior to the formation of the Kirkintilloch Society, the *Glasgow Courier* (20 October) had published a report headed 'Reform', supplying details of a much more populous meeting in Glasgow of a burgeoning constitutional society. This was clearly an organisation that would have engaged the attention of the authorities, not just on account of the considerable numbers said to have taken part, but because of the active role played in its proceedings by its vice-president, an energetic young advocate, Thomas Muir of Huntershill. The *Courier* account is notable for its emphasis on the orderliness and 'most perfect decorum' of the event and, in particular, of Muir's own carefully crafted, non-inflammatory speech, which he delivered with 'much propriety'. One section of the report in particular (in added italics below) is also remarkable if ranged alongside the verbal assault on Muir by the Crown prosecution in the course of his trial in the High Court less than two years later. Here at least, as portrayed by the clearly sympathetic *Courier*, Muir comes across as anything but a firebrand or rabble-rouser:

The Associated Friends of the Constitution and of the People (Col. Dalrymple in the chair) held their third meeting at the Star Inn [Glasgow], on Wednesday last, at which about four hundred persons were assembled; of whom one hundred and twenty-one were new members. Several other Societies presented themselves and were affiliated; after which, suitable addresses were made to them by Mr. Muir, the Vice-president. The whole business was conducted with the most perfect decorum and unanimity; and the meeting concluded with an address from Mr. Muir, in which he, with much propriety and eloquence, pointed out the nature and patriotic views of the institution, with the benefits which may be expected to result from this and other associations on the same principles. *He also strongly recommended and enforced to the members the necessity of order and moderation in their behaviour, and warmly exhorted the affiliated Societies not to admit any person as a member, unless recommended by one or more of their committee.* [italics added]

Loud and universal applause proceeding from the heart afforded the most convincing proofs of the favourable reception of this address, and of its effect on the auditors.

The die was cast. Muir and Dunn, in the most public and visible way possible – in the columns of a city newspaper of repute – were now partnered together in the cause of 'reform' and 'freedom'. This was dangerous terminology that, as we shall see (though in totally different ways and degrees) would seal their common fate: criminal prosecution at the hands of His Majesty's Advocate and the High Court of Justiciary. From this time on, in the eyes of government both were marked men. In the case of Dunn, it would simply prove too much to bear. His published sermon would have dire consequences he could never have foreseen.

There was certainly no doubting William Dunn was an enthusiastic supporter of political reform. His sermon has no title, but the words of scripture on which it is based would have fooled no one: they were from *Revelation*, xxi, verse 5:

And he that sat upon the throne said, Behold, I make all things new, and he said unto me, Write: for these words are true and faithful.

In the preface Dunn informs his audience that though his sermon was 'originally spoken from Notes', he is 'certain, that, as it now stands, it is very little different from what it then was'. That is, he assures his readers, he has not added to, or removed anything from what he said in the pulpit that autumn day in Glasgow. We might be forgiven for taking that with a large pinch of salt. In the commentary that follows it will emerge that Dunn does not always conform to his protestations of editorial integrity.

Dunn begins his sermon by contrasting the permanent presence of God – the '*punctum stans*'[31] – with the three 'relations' or 'modes' which man necessarily experiences; the past, the present and the future. When God speaks of his 'acting on human things in that mode of time which is compatible with his own perfection', he is maintaining in human beings 'a principle of innovation', and thus never ceases to 'make all things new' in the sense intended in his text. He illustrates his thesis by reference to 'these three things, the Arts, Government, and Religion.' Of the Arts he distinguishes between 'the fine or liberal' – the 'offspring of genius' where 'men are born, not made, poets, painters, musicians' etc. – and the 'useful or mechanical arts' which, Dunn explains, 'are the offspring, not of genius, but of [self] interest.' Where the useful arts are concerned, men acquire knowledge 'with a pace continually accelerated, and which is at this day, and in this very country, more rapid than ever it was in any other age or nation.' In agriculture, industry and navigation, to take but three –

> Is it requisite to remark, that these began in a state of the greatest rudeness, have ... been gradually improving, and will ... continue to improve? [32]

Dunn turns to the second of his chosen areas of interest to illustrate God's direction of this 'principle of innovation' – 'Government'. First, he deals with the 'civil constitution':

> ... however wisely it may be framed, and however well its rules may be adapted to the situation, and calculated for the welfare of those, who have placed themselves under it, till some hand be provided, which will give execution to the whole, it is but a dead letter, a mere speculation, altogether inefficient and unproductive. [33]

And he invents a phrase to describe these men – 'public functionaries.' 'Patriarchs, Princes, Archons, Consuls, Kings, or Emperors, it makes no difference':

> The nature of the thing is not altered. They are created, payed and honoured by the community, depend upon it, and are its servants: ... To the community at large, they are accountable for their conduct in the discharge of the trust thus committed to them. Intitled, while they act properly, to honour and reward; but liable to be censured, cashiered, or otherways punished, for extravagance, wilful mismanagement, or betraying their trust. [34] ...
>
> ... Of the now existing governments of Europe, of all these at least, of the more extensive states, and where monarchy has been admitted, it is to be remarked, that none of them can trace up their pedigree to an origin so respectable as that which reason would point out to this most important of human sciences. On the contrary, it was the violence and iniquity of conquest that gave them birth. Their younger years were nursed by the exertions of mere power, often of tyranny, and now in their age, the most part of them are extremely unwilling to be separated from the evils that have long been inherent in them. [35]

Concomitant with the rise to power of despotic forms of rule in Europe is, Dunn argues, the rise in popular discontent leading to claims of 'rights' and redress of 'wrongs':

> Meanwhile, the people have ever been, in some degree, sensible of their rights, and have felt their wrongs. Impelled by these sentiments, they have never ceased to claim the former, and to seek redress of the latter. Their efforts have, on some occasions, been perhaps improper. They have often proved ineffectual. In every country of modern Europe, however, they have made some, and in a few they have made great progress in regaining, from the retentive grasp of usurpation, what it had very unjustly seized. [36]

If the language sounds familiar to a modern reader, one wonders what it would all have conveyed to Dunn's synodical congregation, comprising roughly equal numbers of Popular and Moderate party ministers and their similarly affiliated lay elders in the autumn of 1792? [37] This was, after all, the year that saw not only the publication (under bizarre circumstances) of the second part of Tom Paine's *Rights of Man* – the 'brightest and most powerful political skyrocket in English history' [38] – but also Paine's trial and conviction in London *in absentia* for having written and published such an 'atrocious' seditious libel. It was also the year in which, with the active support of government, John Reeves and John Bowles first co-organised and initiated the loyalist counter-attack on Paine and his followers leading to the period often described as 'Pitt's Terror.' The loyalist fight-back extended to Scotland where several pamphlets condemning Paine and adherents appeared in notable reformist strongholds in the west such as Glasgow and Paisley.[39]

The next section of Dunn's sermon, by all the acknowledged criteria as then defined,[40] is technically seditious:

> At this day, these efforts [see previous quote] are great above any thing known in former times. The acquisitions are proportionably [sic] great. And it is surely the fervent prayer of every one, who wishes well to our common nature, and who takes an interest in the felicity of mankind, that these exertions may never abate, and that these acquisitions may never be checked, till a system of general liberty, and equal laws, vouched by reason, and cherished by religion, be established in every nation of Christendom: whence may the same blessings be speedily diffused throughout the world! Thus shall government be at last placed on its proper basis: a situation from which it has too long been far removed!
> It is, however, an undoubted, though a provoking truth, that the people have never hitherto been able to gain any thing to the side of public liberty, without recourse being had to open force, or to threatenings of it. Even Britain, that favourite country, that nurse of freemen, that land in which public liberty set up her ancient, and, as we hope, her permanent rest, exhibits, throughout the whole of her history, striking proofs of this melancholy remark.[41]

Ironically, by far the weakest and least original part of the sermon is Dunn's exposition of the third 'mode' of man's experiences in his passage through life – 'religion':

> The visible church hath ever since [the beginning of the Christian era] been extending her limits. The progress still continues, and will not reach its utmost limit, till the consummation of all things; when knowledge, piety and beneficence, those celestial strangers who have ever accompanied the steps of true religion, shall, following their divine Leader, conduct an innumerable host of choicer spirits up to that throne of mercy whence they originally descended.[42]

Dunn concludes this part of his sermon by returning to his central 'principle' of God's 'progressive' plan for the Arts, Government and Religion. But, Dunn asks, 'Hath this principle met with no opposition?' 'Hath improvement had no obstacles to encounter?'

> Have the vices and follies of men raised no barriers in the way of their own felicity? Just the contrary. Here, as in every thing else, men have been true to the erroneous maxims of their own deceived hearts. In every one of the instances we have mentioned, strong opposition has been made to the principle we have been illustrating.[43]

In the Arts, Luddism has striven 'by the outrages of mobs and riots, to prevent the introduction of new machinery, or improvements on the old':

> But when the period arrives, and arrive it will, in spite of all the opposition of the narrow and the mercenary, these once necessary, but now superannuated aids of infant arts and

civilization, shall be swept aside amongst the lumber of past time; the way will then be open, and the course of improvement in useful arts free, and therefore rapid.[44]

The following section of Dunn's sermon deserves to be included as a key text in any anthology of the radical Scottish Enlightenment. When we analyse them, his words amount to a rousing popular rallying-cry, nothing less than a vision of a kind of *ur* socialist utopia – or, at the very least, a faltering *apologia* for one. It is worth quoting in its entirety.

> [Note: Dunn's rhetorical technique, as my added italics indicate, relies on making a statement and then either qualifying or partially withdrawing it, possibly in order that government agents (the 'public functionaries' of the sermon), on the constant look-out for seditious material, might not have cause to report anything incriminating to Sheriffs, who by that time had been instructed to forward their concerns to the Lord Advocate's office in Edinburgh, either direct or via the local sheriff-substitute.]

> In Government, the bulk of the people, whose estate consists chiefly in their capacity of bodily labour, in their skill, and in their dexterity and address in the execution of manual operations; who thus carry the most valuable part of what is theirs about with them, and who, therefore, would risk but little, were even the most dangerous crisis of the resisted spirit of improvement to occur, are generally zealous friends of political reformation. Amongst them, public liberty has, in every nation, spent her infant years. By their rude hand, her tender age has been nursed, and, in the undisguised simplicity of their hearts, they openly profess their attachment to her. Impose they cannot, but mistaken they may be. And *hence the necessary weight of government may, by them, be sometimes regarded as a grievance; salutary regulations they may sometimes, by misapprehension, consider as capricious restraint: the idle, and, in some respects, hardly innocent parade of a court, they regard, often with justice, as the cause of their own poverty; and seeing a great deal of what they have earned with the sweat of their brow, spent by public ministers, on what to them seems, and inmost cases needless, they submit with reluctance to pay the many and great taxes which are now levied, and which the profusion of modern politics has, in every nation, made indispensably requisite to supply, what are, with no great degree of correctness, called, the necessary demands of the state.* [italics added] Hence their natural feelings, prompted by such circumstances, make them, on all occasions, strenuous advocates for what they take to be the doctrine of our text.[45]

At this point, Dunn is on the verge of being carried away by his own passion. His language is a long way off mimicking the rhetoric of Tom Paine, but his own distinctive voice nonetheless displays an impressive blend of directness and authenticity:

> In opposition to this tendency of the people, a formidable and determined band appears. The whole body of public functionaries, with all their dependents, to the remotest degree of the gradually diminishing scale of court attraction, arrange themselves on this side. They enjoy the power, the profits, and the honours of the situation things are presently in. They have, therefore, an immediate interest in wishing and endeavouring to retain them in that situation. The united influence of these selfish considerations, which cannot but prove, in the mind of the most part, too hard for the cool and liberal dictates of reason and humanity, prompt them to resist every alteration. Improvement itself they view with a jealous eye, and reformation they brand with the odious name of sedition.
> *In the middle space, between these parties, men of property, great landholders more especially, have*

their station. Being on the one side connected with the people, they feel something of the same passions, and enter into the same views with them. Being by their rank, their education, their habits of living, and hopes of rising into the higher spheres of political honour and emolument, allied on the other side to the crown, they are inclined to adopt the maxims, and to favour the measures, of the established system. [do.]

Thus occupying an important place in society, the balance between the people and the court is naturally lodged with them. And into whatever scale they throw their weight, it must necessarily preponderate. When embracing an enlightened and liberal policy, they resist the demands of the people, only when those demands are wrong, public peace and prosperity is the consequence. But when they unfortunately act in a different manner, public disorders must ensue. The arm of power is improperly elevated; iniquity is established by a law; the limits of a legal constitution are obliterated. Unconscious of it, *they forge chains by which even their own posterity are fettered to the yoke of tyrants.* [do.][46]

Dunn's attempt to define just who he means by 'the people', in the context of the reform movement [47] he espouses, broadly resonates with the view of William Skirving, who acted as secretary to all three national conventions of the Friends of the People:

The Friends of the People... generally-speaking, are not men of respectability in the sense of the epithet which the weakness and prejudice of the human mind has appropriated to it. The greater number of them belong to the lower classes of citizens who have hitherto been non-entities in the political state.[48]

Again, however, Dunn just manages to step back from the brink. Only the Sovereign himself has the wisdom and authority to 'moderate the impetuosity of the people' on the one hand, and, on the other, to control the intrigues of the 'court' (the 'public functionaries'):

To this rank it belongs to moderate the impetuosity of the people, and to control the intrigues of the court. Happy Britain! thy efforts for reformation can never be disappointed. Thy throne is filled by a gracious Prince. Thy landed interest is generous and of enlarged views. The opposition of mean spirited and selfish men must utterly fail.[49]

Dunn now approaches the climax of his sermon. He returns to the role of religion in the strained and tense political environment he has been at pains to delineate, and is in no doubt it is a *special* role:

... it is, perhaps, the distance at which the religious establishment of Scotland is placed from politics; its total want of the honours of rank in the state, and the very scanty manner in which it is endowed, (a circumstance, the inconveniency of which we all personally feel, but of which the public reaps the advantage,) that makes those who are members of it, more useful public instructors, and, at the same time, preserves the institution itself from so great a perversion. Competency gives firmness of mind, and befriends honesty in public teachers of religion; opulence is the parent of negligence, and tempts to frequent the haunts of politics. *And a minister of the gospel turned courtier, is always an absurd, often a very corrupt character, and hostile to improvement.*[50] [italics added]

... It surely becomes you, Brethren, to give efficacy to the principle of the text, and to support a progressive improvement, by every means in your power. This your character requires: – this your country expects; – and this your duty to God and man makes your indispensible obligation.[51]

The sermon ends limply on a cautious note, and, it has to be said, on a slightly vague and tentative one. It seems possible that Dunn – conceivably on the verge of near-panic, and now well aware of the considerable risk the plainly seditious content of his sermon carries – may have 'doctored' this section at the eleventh hour prior to publication, in order to mitigate the Paineite echoes of the printed version:

> ... be stedfast, be vigilant, be active. Enemies to riot and sedition, unintimidated by difficulties, and incapable of forgetting your birth-right as Britons, love your God, honour your King, venerate the constitution, maintain the laws of your country. Inherited from your ancestors, they are yours; perfect what they have so happily begun, add what is wanting, regenerate what is decayed, correct what is amiss. Contribute your part to make all Europe sensible, that the profligate opinion is no longer to be received, That the people are made *for* the prince, and not the prince *by* and *for* the people, that nations are no longer to be sacrificed to the vanity of princes, and to the rapacity of these about them.[52]

But massaging the text of his copy for the printer was not enough. The predictable loyalist riposte was not long in coming. Using the same Glasgow publishers as had Dunn for *his* sermon 'lately published', William Moodie, minister of St. Andrew's Church in the New Town of Edinburgh, and a future Moderator of the General Assembly,[53] retorted anonymously in a pamphlet entitled *Political Preaching: or the Meditations of a Well-Meaning Man*, which he signed off as 'Adam Whyte':

> Political sermons are attended with many bad effects. They lead almost unavoidably to the perversion of the sacred scriptures; they degrade the dignity of religion, by connecting it with the faction of the day, and turn the attention of the people, from subjects which might improve their hearts, to subjects which can serve only to inflame their passions. ... We have seen in France that politics have banished every form of religion, and that the *frantic songs* of what is termed Liberty, have been substituted for the *Praises of God*. God forbid! That this should ever be the case in our land. The inhabitants of Great Britain have hitherto been distinguished among the nations, as a religious people. I trust that this will ever be their character. Their little libraries are filled, as yet, with books of piety and devotion, with the writings of Watts and Henry, and other worthy men. But, I confess, I have been alarmed, of late, to see some of them purchasing with such avidity, the political pamphlets which are circulated, I think, with too much zeal; and I was shocked the other day, when one of my neighbours informed me, that he had sold that valuable treatise "The Life of God in the Soul of Man",[54] in order to purchase the works of Paine. What shall the end of these things be?[55]

A few months later a considerably more distinguished Edinburgh minister than Moodie, the Reverend Professor Thomas Hardy, in his Moderatorial year of office, published a highly political sermon he entitled *Fidelity to the British Constitution*. It is remarkable for its strictures on democracy. Hardy's reflections on the subject show total opposition to the reformist views of such as William Dunn, and are worth quoting on account of their wider importance in the context of this study as a whole:

A Democracy, or a government of the Many, possesses, as its advantages, an universal and perpetual attention to civil liberty, and a jealous inspection of the public administration, which renders its officers cautious in the discharge of their trust. Its disadvantages are, that it is unsteady in its measures, subjected to all the fluctuations of public opinion; that personal safety depends upon the popularity of the day; that the most violent and unprincipled demagogues often take the lead in the State; that justice is borne down by tumult; that the best and most enlightened citizens are exposed to the most imminent peril; and that it can only be tolerable either in a small State, or among a people so perfectly virtuous in their own principles, individually and universally, as exceeds by much the standard of any nation within the experience of history.[56]

These were not simply the words of the minister of West St. Giles, or even of the Moderator of the General Assembly of the Church of Scotland; they were the words of the professor of ecclesiastical history in the University of Edinburgh. Above all else, they were the words of the author of *The Patriot* (1793), one of the best-selling loyalist works of the period in which Hardy condemns utterly and absolutely the republican revolutionary sentiments of Thomas Paine and, on that account alone, earned himself a handsome government pension.[57] Meikle suggests Hardy 'wrote it to order' and all the evidence suggests he is right. As we shall see, Hardy was not the first Kirk minister to be rewarded for his anti-reform activities. Robert Dundas was certainly full of praise for the popularity of *The Patriot* thus far in Scotland and looked forward to its equal appeal south of the border. Dundas writes to his kinsman the Home Secretary:

> I hope Hardy's *Patriot* meets with the same approbation in London that it universally does here. Moodie's *Political Preaching* in answer to Dunn at Kirkintilloch has had the most beneficial effects.[58]

The case against William Dunn

If the established Church in Scotland represented a formidable obstacle to the achievement of even a modicum of political reform in the late eighteenth century – Kidd has called it 'a willing bastion of loyalism'[59] – we need to address the possibility that, collectively, the Scottish courts and judges represented an even more important barrier: the 'community of the College of Justice', as it came to be called. At this remove of time, it is something of a shock to the system to discover a wall of such implacable established opposition to the case for reform erected against the people who had set out their stall through the medium of their societies and conventions. It is much too simplistic to claim that this was no more than the aggregate outcome of the 'Dundas despotism'. Borrowing the term from Henry Cockburn, Fry acknowledges that in a curious way it was rather the very *independence* of Scots law that was held by some of the leaders of the reform movement in Scotland to have been one of its worst features; that is, that the judges sitting in Edinburgh felt independent, confident, bold and assertive in their judgments and consequently took upon themselves 'with a degree of audacity which can hardly be made credible to a stranger to make … little laws (acts of parliament as they call them) materially affecting the liberty of the subject.'[60] But if the Scottish legal system was *not* 'inherently repressive or inhuman', as Fry claims, there is equally no denying that at times it certainly *seemed* to be heading in that general direction.

Lord Cockburn concludes his chapter on the trial of Thomas Muir with a quote from Samuel Romilly (a champion of English criminal law reform) who had attended at least some of the Muir trial sessions in Parliament Hall, where the High Court sat at the time. In a letter to Jeremy Bentham from Edinburgh dated 2 September 1793 – just two days after the verdict – Romilly writes

> I am passing my time here very pleasantly; principally, however, in a society which you would not at all relish – lawyers. Indeed, I doubt whether this would be a very safe country, just at this moment, for you to be found in; for I heard the judges of the Justiciary Court, the other day, declare, with great solemnity, upon the trial of Mr. Muir, that to say the courts of justice needed reform was seditious, highly criminal, and betrayed a most hostile disposition towards the Constitution, of which the courts of justice form a most important part.[61]

Cockburn famously describes Thomas Muir's trial for sedition in the High Court of Justiciary in Edinburgh on 30-31 August 1793 as 'one of the cases, the memory whereof never perisheth. History cannot let its injustice alone.' The sheer drama of it all has excited high passion as much as the infamy of its verdict – and of the way in which generally the trial was conducted – infuriates normally mild-mannered individuals. In short, the trial is seen as a travesty and a disgrace and is often said to have left an ineradicable stain on Scotland's reputation for the maintenance and protection of justice and human rights. Our concern, however, is for the part played in it by two ministers of the established Church of Scotland: one a champion, the other an enemy of the people.

Writing only three years after Muir's trial David Hume's nephew and namesake, (Baron) David Hume, advocate, jurist, and professor of the law of Scotland in the University of Edinburgh, attempts his own definition of sedition and, in the process, refers to the recent trials in the High Court. 'Sedition', Hume begins, 'is a crime at Common Law'. It 'reaches all those practices, whether by deed, word, or writing, or of whatsoever kind, which are suited and intended to disturb the tranquillity of the State'.[62] Hume iterates the succession of Scottish sedition cases which in chronological order range from the case of 'three young men', Morton, Anderson and Craig (8 January 1793), the Thomas Muir case (31 August 1793), and the case of Thomas Fyshe Palmer (13 September 1793), to those of Skirving, Margarot and Gerrald (respectively 7 January, 14 January and 14 March 1794), and he observes that new legislation had to be passed in England to enable judges there to 'inflict the same punishments that are competent in Scotland', since the powers of the common law as exercised in England 'were found to be unequal'. Statute *Geo. III. c.7* was passed in Parliament and Hume notes that in consequence 'the growing audacity of the licentious in this quarter of the kingdom, had in a great measure been repressed.'[63] Hume finds that those guilty of 'practices which amount to [acts of] sedition' must include

> him who in a pamphlet, sermon, or other public and advised discourse, shall exhort dissenters to refuse payment of taxes till repeal of the Test Act; or shall question the lawfulness of septennial Parliaments, and advise the people to meet at the end of three

years, and choose another Parliament for themselves; *or who shall devise a new form of league, association, or convention for the people, whereby to constrain and overawe the Legislature into compliance with their desires, upon any point which is popular at the time.* [italics added] [64]

In the months leading up to Muir's trial as a result of the preaching and publication of his sermon Dunn had become a marked man in the eyes of government. His case was not helped by his friendship with Muir. Moreover, both their names had been partnered together in the unfortunate *Courier* advert on behalf of the Society at Kirkintilloch. Early in January 1794 matters came to a head when the Sheriff of Dumbarton, acting on information he had received (possibly from the Reverend James Lapslie or another paid informer) conducted a 'precognition'[65] in Dunn's parish. The government 'raid' – for that is what it was – was probably the result of a tip-off from a paid spy who had succeeded in infiltrating the local reform society. This man may have been Lapslie, the minister of Campsie (a neighbouring parish to Kirkintilloch) – a known informer and government agent – but we cannot be sure. More important, it remains uncertain if Dunn himself was the main or secondary target; or, on the other hand, was simply unlucky, as a known associate of the government's number one target, Thomas Muir, to have allowed himself to become involved.

In accordance with normal Court practice the Lord Advocate's *Petition and Complaint* of 25 February 1793 [66] was deliberately tentative. Dunn was formally served that the Court would consider if a case had been made for him to defend. On the face of things, however, although his published sermon would scarcely have aided his cause, it seems, at least on first examination, that the sermon was not the main problem. Specifically, the 'Complaint' set out in the *Petition* – it has not the weight or status of a full-blown indictment [67] – held that Dunn, knowing 'that the Sheriff was in the town of Kirkintilloch, and taking a precognition', had concealed and then burned three leaves of a book containing minutes of 'a Society for Reform' in the village of Kirkintilloch. The *Petition and Complaint* also refers to Dunn having 'emitted and signed a Declaration, the particulars of which the Complainer does not think it proper at present to state to the Court.' As we shall see, it was left to Dunn himself (*via* an agent) to print a copy of the Declaration in the form of an Appendix to his *Answers*.

In an Appendix to the minister's *Answers* of 6 March[68] we learn the whole story behind the Lord Advocate's decision to take action against Dunn and, more to the point, the role of Dunn's sermon as a key element in the charge. In the main body of his *Answers* Dunn not only protests that he had never at any time been a member of the Society, 'nor ever attended a single meeting, nor did he ever see their book till that occasion.' Further, not only had Robert Dundas's *Petition* alleged that the Kirkintilloch Society 'had been guilty of certain seditious proceedings', but that its minutes 'did contain certain treasonable matter and correspondence.' Much of the Lord Advocate's writ is based on a mix of unproven assertion and speculation; for example –

> What these three leaves contained, is in the present question immaterial. If the Complainer's [the Lord Advocate's] information is well-founded, they contained matter of a highly seditious, perhaps treasonable, nature. But whether they did so or not, a fact which it will not be easy for the Complainer now to ascertain, it is impossible for your

Lordships to hesitate in being of opinion, that the conduct of this gentleman has been extremely unwarrantable and illegal.

The substance of the charge is grounded on the removal of the three leaves. The Appendix to the *Answers* prepared by Dunn's agent (and probably close friend), Alexander Grant WS [69] – containing a copy of the Declaration signed by Dunn and the Sheriff-depute of Dumbartonshire, Sir James Colquhoun of Luss, dated 4 January 1793 – makes clear the potentially disastrous connection of the *sermon* with the minister's removal and destruction of the offending three leaves:

> That thereupon the declarant looked into said books [of 'the Reform Society of Kirkintilloch'], and seeing, that in the three last written leaves of said book, the declarant had received *a vote of thanks* from the Society,[70] and that *his name was mentioned* on all these three leaves, he proposed to the members present to tear out these leaves; and he accordingly did so, and has since destroyed them. ...
>
> That the vote of thanks, above referred to, was *on account of a sermon* which the declarant delivered and published; and the said vote of thanks was communicated to the declarant by three members of the Society, namely Robert Waddel, and two others, whose names the declarant does not recollect.

Destroying the pages was held to be 'extremely unwarrantable and illegal.' Part of the hidden agenda of incrimination (which the Court chose at this stage not to reveal) was that the pages made clear reference to Dunn's sermon which had been preached before one of the most senior bodies of the Church of Scotland – the Synod of Glasgow and Ayr.

Dunn's *Answers* amount to a clumsy albeit qualified admission of guilt. The document begins with the respondent admitting that, while he 'does not exculpate himself' he is 'sensible that he acted precipitately'. He 'would be extremely sorry to lengthen the proceedings in a case which has given him the utmost pain' and he pleads that the leaves torn out contained 'nothing but the admissions of members, and adjournments of meetings, with resolutions previously published and circulated in the newspapers, and the appointment of a delegate to their convention at Edinburgh.' As for the sermon he had delivered before the Synod of Glasgow and Ayr, if any doubts persisted as to his client's loyalty, these would be removed, *first*, by reference to that part of it relating to the 'character of our Prince, who delights to be the father of his people, the equitable temper of our legislators, the light and humanity of the age'; and, *secondly*, to the part concerning the progressive nature of the British constitution:

> ... when we take a view of government in the wide survey of all nations, ancient and modern, or in the narrower one of modern Europe, or in the still more limited one of modern Britain, we can, on the whole, notwithstanding manifold irregularities and interruptions, trace the steps of a progressive improvement.

It is a wholly contrite response from a clearly penitent minister. Not a word here about the people as 'zealous friends of political reformation'.

Dunn's plea meant, of course, that no trial by jury was now necessary. The High Court on 11 March 1793 – the Lord Justice Clerk, Lord Braxfield, with Lords Henderland, Eskgrove, Dunsinnan and Abercromby [71] – found Dunn guilty of 'a high misdemeanour and offence in the suppression of evidence' and, therefore the said Lords decern and adjudge the said Mr. William Dunn to be carried from the bar to the Tolbooth of Edinburgh therein to be detained for the space of three months from this date, and upon elapsing of the said period of imprisonment Grant warrant to and ordain the Magistrates of Edinburgh and keepers of their Tolbooth to set him at liberty. [72]

Braxfield (signing as Robert Macqueen) endorsed the verdict and Dunn was committed to the Tolbooth. A custodial sentence was a shocking outcome for a minister of religion – and, not least, for his faithful parishioners – to have to bear. Yet, we are entitled to conclude that by the yardstick of other verdicts imposed on defendants of admittedly much more serious charges in Scottish 'reform' cases of the period, Dunn was let off realtively lightly. Whatever else it was, Dunn's offence was finally acknowledged not to have conformed to the prevailing contemporary construction of sedition *per se* – even though the Lord Advocate's indictment had given notice that it *could* have been found to so conform. In the last analysis, nevertheless, we cannot ignore Lord Henderland's observation at the determination of another case,[73] when considering the punishment that was 'appropriate', imprisonment in 'the jail of Edinburgh' was

> to make them [Morton, Anderson and Craig] denizens as it were of that unhallowed place, which is the sink of corruption, – where everything that is vicious, base and criminal, are huddled together, – where, if they preserve their health, they cannot for a long tract of time escape the contagion of vice and more sordid criminality ... .[74]

Faced with that kind of punishment many would have left the Tolbooth angry and defiant. It seems more likely, however, that William Dunn came out a broken man.

In the same year as William Dunn's release from prison Brash and Reid published an anonymous pamphlet now known to have been written by Dunn under the title *An Address by a Scotsman, to his Countrymen and Fellow Citizens, respecting the situation of public affairs, the reform, and the war impending from France.*[75] The language of the pamphlet is tediously loyalist in the extreme and its sentiments a world away from those of Dunn's sermon of the year before. The content and tone, indeed, are now *so* different that it must be considered likely that Dunn agreed to write the piece under pressure from the authorities – the very *'public functionaries'* to whom he had taken such exception in his synodical sermon. Where before there was reasoned scepticism, we now find unmitigated patriotic zeal to an almost embarrassing degree. If not a loaded pistol having been put to his head, then at the least we can be pretty certain that Dunn was now writing to order, and quite possibly under threat of even more severe further charges being brought against him if he failed to toe the government line:

> If a view of what you deemed necessary reform sometime ago, gained perhaps a little too much on [in] the minds of some of you; come now with me, my Fellow Citizens, for the reassuring of your breast, and the satisfaction of your countrymen, fix and avow an unalterable determination, that, forgetting every other object, you will exert your utmost to support the executive government, and strengthen the hands of administration; till the unprovoked hostilities, so rudely threatened, are repressed; and the nation is placed in a situation of safety and repose.[76]

Dunn's spectacular climb-down and his painful expression of remorse are a far cry from the acclaim accorded his synodical sermon in the report of the inaugural meeting of the Kirkintilloch Society of the Friends of the People of 3 November, when it was described as 'a noble, manly, and eloquent vindication of the cause of Reform and of Freedom.' Yet Dunn had still one enormous hurdle to clear before he could be said to have completed the dual process of self-redemption and freedom from harassment at the hands of the authorities: the trial of his one-time friend and fellow seeker after constitutional reform, Thomas Muir of Huntershill to which he had been cited both by the Crown and Muir himself. Where Dunn, however, was a minnow in the eyes of government Muir was a veritable leviathan.

Dunn's role in the trial of Thomas Muir

Thomas Muir's trial on a charge of sedition came on at the High Court of Justiciary in Parliament Hall, Edinburgh 'a few minutes after 10 o'clock in the morning' of Friday, 30 August 1793. It did not have an auspicious start. Muir was reprimanded in his absence for keeping the Court waiting. His agent said 'he would appear in a few minutes', and he 'presently came into Court', whereupon the indictment was read out. The first day's proceedings were not concluded until half past one on Saturday morning at which time, it was announced, the Court would adjourn until '12 o'clock of that day', when it was expected the verdict would be delivered, and 'the [15 man] jury were immediately enclosed.' [77]

The twenty page indictment of Muir as read out to the Court concludes with a list of forty witnesses cited by the Crown prosecution, led by the Lord Advocate himself, to appear on its behalf, together with (as was the practice) a separate list of forty-five names comprising the 'Assize', or members of the jury. The fifteen jurymen as finally selected were all members of the Edinburgh Goldsmiths' Hall Association, the leading anti-radical (loyalist) organisation in Scotland at the time; its secretary for a time was William Creech, the publisher and bookseller, who would himself later serve on the jury at the trial for sedition of Joseph Gerrald in March of the following year. According to standard practice, the original list of forty-five was whittled down to fifteen selected jurors, of whom Gilbert Innes of Stow[78] and John Balfour the younger of Pilrig[79] were designated 'Chancellor' and 'Clerk' respectively; accordingly it is their names that subscribe the formal written verdict. The composition of the assize is also significant. Heading the long list are five baronets, including Sir John Clerk of 'Pennycuick' [sic], Sir William Dick of Prestonfield, Sir John Inglis of Cramond and Sir Archibald Hope of Craighall. There follow no less than twenty names of landowners with their estates all in the city or environs of the capital. Thereafter, the Assize is completed with the names of ordinary token mortals including merchants (7), bankers (4), booksellers (3), a hatter, a perfumer, a hosier, a portioner,[80] an upholsterer, and a slater – all 'in Edinburgh.'

As in the case of members of the assize, the names and occupations of the forty witnesses named by the Lord Advocate are significant. The first group of twenty consists entirely of known associates of Muir to the north of Glasgow, more specifically in the villages of Campsie, Lennoxtown and Kirkintilloch (14 individuals, including 'The Rev. Mr William Dunn minister of Kirkintilloch'), together with a smaller group (6) from the city of Glasgow including a maidservant, a barber, two booksellers/stationers

(James Brash and William Reid), and two manufacturers. After two further Church of Scotland witnesses – the first an elder of 'Calder' [Cadder] parish church, the second 'The Reverend Mr James Lapslie minister of Campsie' – the Crown list continues by citing three men of known reformist sympathies including Muir's friend and fellow advocate John Morthland, Colonel William Dalrymple of Fordell, and William Skirving 'of Strathruddie, residing in Edinburgh'. Completing the Lord Advocate's list is a group of senior legal magistrates (5), a student of medicine, officials from the city or county of Edinburgh (3), with, last of all, a justice of the peace from the county of Wigtown. By no means all of these witnesses were called to give evidence.

Muir's list of witnesses 'in exculpation', totalling no less than fifty-five names, includes three also cited by the Lord Advocate; apart from Dunn and Skirving, Muir cites Dalrymple of Fordell.[81] In the event, however, Dunn was not called in the strict sense of the term. The trial took a sensational turn when a Crown witness, William Muir, a weaver in Kirkintilloch,[82] refused point-blank to swear the oath on the grounds of his membership of a religious sect known as 'the mountain', or Cameronians,[83] whose scruples, like those of Antiburghers, would not permit them to swear oaths even on the Bible. The man would not budge even when the judges warned him that they would have no option but to commit him to 'perpetual' imprisonment which, they affirmed, was defined as limitless and 'eternal'. At this point, Thomas Muir stated that he not only believed the man to be 'good and conscientious', but was prepared to forego the requirement that his evidence be given on oath and would 'admit every word which he utters, although not upon oath, to be as true as if it were.' After conferring, the judges were at one in maintaining that the law concerning oaths could not be dispensed with and the hapless William Muir was then committed to prison, the Court having declared 'they knew no mode by which, by the law of Scotland, he could be liberated.'

In due time Dundas informed the Court that he had been advised that William Muir was a parishioner of the Reverend Mr. Dunn, 'minister of Kirkintilloch, one of the witnesses inclosed against the panel.'[84] He went on: that, 'if Mr. Dunn was allowed to converse with him he might remove his error, and preserve him from suffering the dreadful punishment due to his obstinacy', and he proposed that the Court allow Dunn 'to converse with William Muir for the purpose.' At this point Thomas Muir, opposing Lord Advocate Dundas's motion, nonetheless reiterated his preparedness to admit the declaration of William Muir against him to be 'true, although not accompanied by an oath.' It was a noble gesture. For the sole purpose of sparing the weaver's ghastly punishment, Thomas Muir 'would surrender the right which the law gave him' (i.e. of denying the truthfulness of the witness's evidence on the grounds that it was given unaccompanied by an oath). At the same time, however, Muir objected to 'conversation' between Dunn and the witness; and he explained:

> ... not that he suspected anything improper to take place in that conversation, but that this was a great and important cause; a trial that might create precedents dangerous to those who might come after. By the law of Scotland all witnesses must be examined apart from each other. The law is jealous of their conversation: The law dreads their collusion, in framing together a consistent story. If, in this case, you allow Mr. Dunn and the witness,

of both of whom I have no suspicion, to converse together, you cannot refuse it to others. It will be sufficient for two witnesses, who may have an interest in a trial, to play the same concerted game, in order to tell the same concerted story with more accuracy and with greater safety.

In response, Dundas said that he would not call William Dunn. The Court directed that Dunn's conversation with William Muir should proceed 'in the presence of an officer of the court, or of some person on the part of Mr. [Thomas] Muir.' Dunn informed the Court that he 'could not promise to remove the man's scruples, but that he would endeavour to do so.' He was then sent to converse with the witness 'in the robing room in presence of one of the macers,[85] but was ordered to confine himself solely to the removing of his scruples, and not to say anything on the subject of the trial.' A little later William Muir, at the direction of the accused *qua* advocate, was brought back to the bar and this time consented to swear on oath. In the event, his evidence proved unhelpful from the accused's point of view. The Kirkintilloch weaver told the Court that 'a copy of Paine's works was taken out of the great-coat pocket of Mr. Muir', and that he did not remember 'what was said about the book: that he is not sure that Mr. Muir spoke about the will of the people being the sovereign will but that it was said that Paine said so'.

William Muir went on to depone that he had acquired eleven copies of *The Patriot* [86] and a copy of the *Political Progress* from Thomas Muir in his father's house. The former serial publication had been specifically named in Muir's indictment as a seditious publication. James Thomson Callender's *The Political Progress of Britain* was not so named but its publication in the previous year by the Edinburgh bookmen, James Robertson and Walter Berry, was the main ground in their indictment, together with Callender's, on a charge of 'wickedly and feloniously printing, or causing to be printed any seditious writing or pamphlet', of which *genre* the *Political Progress* was held to be a prime example.[87] The weaver completed his evidence by – again somewhat lamely from Thomas Muir's point of view – responding that

> he does not remember to have heard him [the accused] speak against government; that Mr. Muir did not advise unconstitutional measures, that he heard him speak about the government; that he heard him tell how Old Sarum was represented.[88]

James Lapslie: minister of Campsie and government informer

As soon as the public prosecutor adduced the minister of Campsie as a witness, Muir retorted: 'Let the witness be removed, I have many objections to state against him.' He went on:

> I have said that I have many objections to state, both to the admissibility and credibility of this witness. My delicacy, with regard to that man, will at present permit me to adduce the least weighty only; for I mean to prove the most important, in a different shape, when he and I shall exchange places at this bar. I know not what title this reverend gentleman has to act for the Crown; but this I offer to prove, that he assisted the messengers of the law in exploring and citing witnesses against me; that he attended the sheriffs in their different visits to the parishes of Campsie and Kirkintilloch; that, previously to the precognition,[89]

he conversed with the witnesses of the Crown; that he attended their precognition, put questions to them, and took down notes; nay more, that, without being cited by the prosecutor, he offered himself ultroneously [90] against me, and insisted that his declaration should be taken in the unusual form, with his oath attending it, to attest its truth.[91]

Muir's forceful objection, deploying an impressive mix of legal terminology, proved irresistible to the Court. The Lord Advocate reluctantly conceded that he had no option but to crave the authority of the Court to examine further Muir's serious contention, bearing on the witness's credibility and containing 'a question of importance', *viz.* that Lapslie was 'an agent of the cause'. His request was readily agreed by the other judges. Shortly afterwards Robert Dundas 'gave up Mr. Lapslie's evidence', whereupon it was conceded by the Crown that 'there no longer remained any necessity to examine more witnesses with regard to the conduct of that gentleman.' It was probably Muir's greatest success in the course of the entire trial.

In his otherwise strikingly racy account of the trial Armstrong – who, disappointingly, fails to mention anything of William Dunn's part in it – notes a few lines of anonymous doggerel that the *Edinburgh Gazetteer* published in its issue of 10 September 1793, just days after the verdict:

> *My Name's Jamie Lapslie, pray mind what I say,*
> *In the clachan*[92] *each Sunday I preach and I pray.*
> *Ye men of my parish I pray you take heed,*
> *While I give you a sketch of my orthodox creed,*
> *With my black coat and my cravat so white.*[93]

James Lapslie, a Glasgow graduate, was licensed by the Presbytery of Glasgow in March 1780 and was then appointed tutor and travelling companion to young Sir James [Grant-] Suttie of Prestongrange,[94] in whose company he toured Europe for more than three years. John Cameron states that it was at this early stage in his life that he became 'an extreme' or '*ultra* Tory'. While Lapslie was in Europe he had learned of the vacancy created in the parish of Campsie, his own birthplace, by the death of the incumbent, William Bell, who had served as minister there for over 35 years. The patronage of the charge was vested in the Crown, which according to Cameron, had in the past the effect of stifling any local potential opposition to any nominee unlikely to appeal to the congregation. Cameron feels sure that, aware of this, Lapslie had taken the precaution of 'arranging' his presentation by asking the influential Suttie family to contrive it through their government friends; incredibly this was effected within a mere seven weeks of Bell's death.[95]

Maybe so, but Ronald Sunter tells a different story. According to Sunter's research almost all of the Campsie heritors (the men in whose hands the inherited power of nomination was vested) were 'united with the body of inhabitants' in favour of a man called Burns to be their minister, and they requested Sir Thomas Dundas, then the county MP, to obtain a presentation in Burns's favour. Because, however, of a change of practice at that time allowing the Treasury to have a voice in presentations where the patron was the Crown, Lord North, no less, stepped in and decided on the evidence of the Registers of Exchequer – from which it appeared 'that the owners of much of the greater part of the property in the district interest themselves for Mr. Lapslie' – to back Lapslie who secured the presentation, despite the fact that 'two of Lapslie's supporters were not members of the Church of Scotland.'[96]

In these circumstances, it was inevitable that vehement opposition to Lapslie's presentation would follow. Cameron states that this took the form of a widespread declaration of preference for Bell's assistant, James Crawford. In any event, a deputation from the Campsie Kirk Session proceeded in person to the Glasgow Presbytery to make them aware of their strenuous opposition to the heritors' choice of minister but, as Cameron tells the story, it was all in vain: in his words, an unsympathetic Presbytery drove the protestors 'out of the church of their fathers by their [the Presbytery's] fatuous policy and arrogant dictation'. Just eleven months after Lapslie's induction the Presbytery of Relief formally agreed to take the protestors 'under their inspection and give them what supply of sermon they can afford.' When, accordingly, Lapslie took up office as minister of Campsie he found he had no kirk session, 'all the elders having withdrawn before his ordination.' He had no option but to go cap in hand to the Presbytery who empowered the ministers of neighbouring churches to act along with him in identifying and electing a new session. For Lapslie it was a grossly inauspicious start to his ministry. But much worse was to come.

Thomas Muir would, of course, have been well aware of all of this. As an advocate he would also have committed to memory the terms of his own indictment naming Lapslie as Crown witness number 22.[97] It is unlikely, however, that Muir could have anticipated the venom behind Lapslie's hatred of reform and all it stood for. In his contribution to Sinclair's [Old] *Statistical Account of Scotland* published less than two years after the trial,[98] and obviously still nursing the wounds of the unwelcome public scrutiny it had brought him, Lapslie feels it necessary to use the *OSA* as a vehicle by means of which he could proclaim his scorn for any measure of reform and, equally, his condemnation of those members of his own parish who had been brazen enough to declare their support for it.

First, Lapslie sets out his stall on the issue of church discipline where, predictably, he openly declares his support for the principle of 'public penance' in the case of fornicators, on the grounds that 'the shame of doing penance operates to deter others'. In that regard, he asserts, public penance 'is to be considered as answering the ends of edification.' And he affirms it is his clear view that his belief in the deterrent value of penance may also have important lessons 'in a political light':

> I am inclined to believe, that it would be much more the interest of the community, in a political light, that the laws of discipline should be more rigidly adhered to; for if once the vulgar of any country, consider incontinency as a venial fault, they are almost ready for the commission of any crime … .

Warming to his theme, Lapslie launches an astonishing assault on the people of his own parish of Campsie:

> Although this parish has been always conspicuous for its attachment to its sovereign; whether of the Stewart family, as in the last century, or of the Hanoverian family, as in the present century … I cannot help taking notice … of a remarkable fact relative to the conduct of some of the inhabitants of this district, which one would almost say contradicts

the opinion of their loyalty. In the midst of the most profound peace, and, I may say, of the most unparalleled prosperity; all at once, as it were by inchantment, the operative part of this community conceived themselves to be groaning under the most abject slavery. They immediately associated themselves under the appellation of the Friends of the People: The first society was constituted at the Milton of Campsie, I think, upon Thursday the 8th of November 1792; the second was constituted at New Birbiston of Campsie, the Saturday thereafter:[99] Two other societies were attempted to be formed in other parts of the parish: I believe, however, they did not succeed: The two former met often, kept books, subscribed small sums of money for purchasing political pamphlets, and sent delegates to the different Conventions met at Edinburgh.

Who were these men calling themselves the 'Friends of the People'?

They were chiefly formed from amongst the journeymen and apprentices at the different print-fields, and a few operative weavers in the village of New Birbiston, mostly lads from 17 years of age to 30: There might be amongst them a few half educated people, whose vanity consisted in raising the astonishment of their more ignorant companions, by a detail of political grievances, which had never entered into the hearts of the other to conceive; various causes co-operated to render Campsie a proper hot-bed for such folly.

Lapslie then lists what, in his view, were the main elements that came together to cause his parish of Campsie to be regarded as 'a proper hot-bed for such folly' and as 'friendly to these Jacobin societies'. These were, he maintains:

In the *first* place, a considerable degree of licentiousness had begun to prevail in this district, owing to high wages; and as the influx of such wealth had been rather sudden, due subordination of rank was almost totally forgotten.

In the *second* place, a Relief meeting, about 10 years ago, being erected in this parish, which had drawn off a considerable number of people from the Establishment [i.e. the parish Church of Scotland, of which Lapslie was minister], and rendered them in some measure, hostile to the powers that be; and I am doubtful but the spirit of innovation was encouraged in a certain degree, by their public teachers, with a view to increase the adherents to their own tabernacle.

In the *third* place, Mr Muir, advocate, the unfortunate gentleman who was tried for sedition, having some connexions, and being well acquainted in the place, was naturally induced to try the power of his eloquence upon the inhabitants; and he succeeded.

If to these causes we add the particular circumstance of the character of young people at the different printfields; men, who have abundance of time in the evenings to cabal together; men, too, from their profession, rather given to wandering, and fond of novelty, and somewhat naturally addicted to form associations against their master's authority; we will not be surprised that Campsie should be so often mentioned as friendly to these Jacobin societies.

He concludes his astonishing *OSA* digression with what he intends as a reassuring claim that, for all the negativities shown by the people of Campsie, 'the farmers and the inhabitants in general' were 'remarkable for their loyalty and attachment to Government: indeed the loyalists very early formed themselves into constitutional societies, for the defence of Government, and published resolutions. Notwithstanding all the bustle which was occasioned by their folly, the different Jacobin societies in this parish altogether never contained above sixty persons.

Whether or not Lapslie is right to go on to claim that what he calls the 'subordination of rank' may help to account for new ideas in the nation of liberty and democracy is obviously open to question. John Millar would not have agreed though he, too, wrote at length on the same general issue. But what surely is of greatest interest in Lapslie's catalogue of influences on the growth of the reform movement in the parish of Campsie – and by implication throughout the industrialising townships of suburban west central Scotland at the time – is his conviction that an important factor must be the arrival there, and the subsequent flourishing of a seceding Relief congregation and the extent to which it took hold, within a remarkably short period of time, among those whose natural affiliation had previously been to the established Kirk. This is a revealing statement, even when Lapslie's fundamental antipathy towards the Relief congregation (deriving, that is, from the personal misfortune he claims he had suffered at their hands in his early ministry at Campsie) is stripped out of his strictures. At the least, his comments might be said to sit comfortably enough alongside similar assertions by modern historians of the period concerning the impact of the plurality of secessionist churches on contemporary attitudes to reform on the part of established Kirk ministers.[100]

Paradoxically, William Dunn and James Lapslie were unsuspecting victims of the same euphoria which moved ordinary people to demand a fairer life for themselves and their families amid what some of them at least clearly grasped was the dawning of an age of improvement. But whereas Dunn engenders our sympathy, we are left only with scorn for the villain Lapslie. One is a figure of pathos and disillusionment; the other, an ogre bent on self-gain and mischief-making. Both stand on the margins of this dismal episode in Scottish church, legal and social history. While we remember the human tragedy of Muir and the rest of the Scottish 'martyrs', few spare a thought for these two ministers of the gospel who, in opposing ways entirely, made costly errors with which they had to live for the remainder of their lives.

In the same year as the Muir trial, Lapslie was appointed chaplain to the Blue Gown Beggars with an honorarium of £50 a year;[101] for this he was required to preach a sermon annually in Stirling. Meikle, who memorably describes him as 'the worst specimen of his class', tells us that he 'continued to pester the Lord Advocate, Robert Dundas, for even greater recognition of his services'.[102] After Thomas Hardy, Lapslie was the second Kirk minister to be handsomely rewarded by government for services rendered relating in both cases (though in markedly different circumstances) to their vigorous opposition to reform and their robust defence of the status quo.[103]

William Dunn died on 3 November 1798 aged fifty-three. Almost before Dunn had drawn his last breath the influential minister of the Wynd Church in Glasgow, Dr William Porteous, once the darling of the Popular party, dashed off a note to Lord Elphinstone, patron for the now vacant charge of Kirkintilloch, which he copied to Robert Dundas, Lord Advocate. Porteous's relief at the opportunity the vacancy presented of securing a reliable successor to what he clearly regarded had been a troubled and troublesome ministry, is palpable, as is his implied insistence on the need for haste:

> My Lord
> Mr Dun at Kirkintilloch died this day at at [sic] one o clock – with the utmost earnestness I beg you to procure a determined but prudent man to that parish – I write the same request to the Lord Advocate and
> I have the honour to be
> My Lord
>
> your faithfull ser vt
>
> William Porteous
> Glas^w 3 Nov^r. – 98 [104]

It seems that the patron complied with Porteous's request. Whether he was influenced by Dundas or not is unknown. The Reverend James Jack was presented to his Kirkintilloch congregation on 16 April in the following year.[105] Since virtually nothing is known about Jack's subsequent ministry we can safely assume that he was the 'determined but prudent' man sought and identified by Elphinstone, Porteous, the Presbytery of Glasgow, and, not least, by the government in Scotland.

Postscript

From Alexander Rodger's *Poems and Songs humorous, serious, and satirical*, ed. Robert Ford, 178. (Paisley, 1897)

'There's pensioner Jamie, corruption's chief tool,
Whose tears flow as freely as whisky at Yule,
With his black coat, and gravat sae white;
So keenly he feels for the suffering poor,
That he'd willingly do what he did for Tom Muir,
To get them sent aff to a far better state,
By hanging or starving them out o' the gate,
With his black coat, and gravat sae white.'

Hugh Blair by Sir Henry Raeburn (detail). Reproduced by kind permission of the Minister of the Canongate Kirk, Edinburgh, the Reverend Neil Gardner.

7

Patriotism

We live in a land of pure religion, of liberty, and laws, and under a just and mild government.
Reverend Dr Hugh Blair (1793), 'On the Love of our Country', 'Sermon VI', in
Sermons, v. V, 1801, 138.

I declare myself, (said he), Moderator, to be a Revolution Whig; and, consequently, to have the greatest respect for the people. ... In this sense, Sir, of unconquerable firmness and irresistible force, the vox populi is the vox Dei. But, though they cannot be corrupted or overawed, yet, alas! Sir, they can be sadly misled!
Reverend Dr Alexander Carlyle (1794): cited in 'Assembly-speeches on Popery',
General Assembly of 1779, as reported in the *Scots Magazine*, 41, June 1779, 313.

Key authors and texts

Reverend Dr Hugh Blair (1718-1800), second-charge minister of the High (or New) Kirk, St. Giles's Church, Edinburgh.[1]

On the Love of our Country, 'Sermon VI' in *Sermons by Hugh Blair, D.D. F.R.S.Ed. One of the Ministers of the High Church, and Professor of Rhetoric and Belles Lettres in the University of Edinburgh. In five volumes.* V., 114-139.
('Preached 18th April 1793, on the day of a National Fast appointed by Government, on occasion of the War with the French Republic.')
London : printed by A. Strahan, Printers-Street; for T. Cadell jun. and W. Davies, in the Strand; and W. Creech, Edinburgh. MDCCCI [1801]

Reverend Dr Alexander Carlyle (1722-1805), minister of Inveresk.[2]

A Sermon on the death of Sir David Dalrymple, Bar.^{t.} Lord Hailes; from Eccles.VII. 3. Preached in the Church of Inveresk, on Sunday the 9th Day of December, 1792. By Alex.^r Carlyle, D.D.F.R.S.E. Chaplain to His Majesty, & Minister of that parish. With an address to the Congregation suited to the circumstances of the times.
Edinburgh: printed for John Balfour. M DCC XCII [1792]

National Depravity The Cause of National Calamities, a Sermon, from Jeremiah vi. 8. Preached in the church of Inveresk, on Thursday Feb. 25. 1794; Being the day appointed by his Majesty for a General Fast. By Alex. Carlyle, D.D. F.R.S. Edin. Minister of the Parish, And one of his Majesty's Chaplains.

Edinburgh : published by John Ogle, bookseller Parliamentary-Close, for the benefit of the poor of the parish of Inveresk. M.DCC.XCIV. [1794]

The Love of Our Country, Explained and Enforced in a Sermon from Psalm CXXXVII, 5. 6. Preached in St. Andrews Church Edinburgh, March 19 and in Dalkeith Church, April 2. 1797. By Alex. Carlyle, D.D. F.R.S. Edin. Minister of Inveresk, and one of His Majesty's Chaplains.

Edinburgh: printed for William Creech. M,DCC,XCVII. [1797]

Both Hugh Blair's sermon and the second of Alexander Carlyle's three sermons listed above were preached on a national fast-day, within less than a year of each other. Blair seldom strays into overt politics from his pulpit, preferring (in Broadie's words) to concentrate on 'the godly life ... spelled out in terms of the stoic virtues of self-discipline and of patience in adversity.'[3] *Here, however, because of the gravity of the situation – the war with France had not long begun, fear of invasion was on many minds and lips, and the whiff of sedition was in the air – he regards it as his duty to speak out. It remains conceivable that, as in the case of Thomas Hardy's polemic, 'The Patriot' (1793), Blair's sermon was delivered 'to order'. Unlike Carlyle's 'National Depravity', however, Blair's sermon was never published as a stand-alone piece, but only included in the final (fifth) volume of his hugely popular collection of sermons and, therefore, not released into the public domain until the year after his death. In common with the views and the 'modus vivendi' of his friends and associates among the Moderate literati in the capital city, Blair 'saw a close link between rhetorical improvement and the polite society, and between sensibility and good taste and moral excellence.'*[4] *As a preacher, Blair in his day stood head and shoulders above all of his ministerial contemporaries throughout the church in Scotland; further, he emerges as 'by far the most successful sermon-writer in eighteenth-century Scotland.'*[5] *Even so, it is argued here that 'On the love of our Country' is in some ways one of Blair's least inspiring compositions and that it must be concluded that political preaching was not his stock in trade.*

It is surprising that the three sermons by Carlyle considered in this chapter – two of which are overtly political, while the third (as its title-page makes clear) includes a generous measure of political content – are among the least known of his published works. The last to be published, 'The Love of our Country', is an extremely rare title, only one copy known to exist anywhere in Britain. All three sermons display Carlyle's innate conservatism, as well as his unwavering loyalty to the Crown and the Pitt/Dundas administration, the latter throughout its period of ascendancy and dominance in Scotland. In the more spacious context of the Scottish Enlightenment in general Carlyle is not remembered for any particularly lasting contribution he made to the literature of the period, but much more for his ubiquitous presence at many of the great moments in his own lifetime and, above all, for his intimacy with numerous giants of the age, in the persona of their generally reliable observer and memorialist. Carlyle lived a long life and his memoir (not published until 1860 under the title he gave it, 'Anecdotes and Characters of the Times') is not simply his personal monument, but an incomparable record of the golden age of Enlightenment culture in Edinburgh at a time when it was one of the greatest centres of literature, science and learning in the whole of Europe, comfortably rivalling London, Paris and St. Petersburg in that regard.

Bibliographical note

The phrase 'love of our country' used by Blair and Carlyle in the titles of their sermons of 1793 and 1797 respectively is borrowed in each case from Richard Price's starry-eyed sermon on aspects of the French Revolution, *A Discourse on the Love of Our Country* (1789). The English dissenting minister's sermon was preached to the 'Society for Commemorating the Revolution in Great Britain' in the Old Jewry Meeting House, London, on 4 November 1789. In his published pamphlet Price had included a watered-down version of a passage in his oral sermon attacking Charles James Fox, who, though not named, is clearly the principal target behind his much-disputed claim that Parliament was disgraced by 'licentiousness' and personal immorality. Edmund Burke was enraged by Price's comments and his own – as originally conceived – brief work on the French Revolution, then nearing completion, was given the title *Reflections on the Revolution in France, and on certain Proceedings of the Revolution Society of the 4th of November, 1789, concerning the affairs of France*. The sub-title is significant. What began as a 'pamphlet reply' to Price's discourse, in the words of Burke's modern biographer Lock, 'soon outgrew its original purpose in subject as well as scale, eventually embodying his most considered and profound thoughts about politics.'[6] Burke's great assault on the Revolution with its militantly secular, republican aspirations, did not appear until 1 November 1790. It was Burke's *Reflections* that, in turn, inspired the first part of Thomas Paine's *Rights of Man* (16 March 1791), a work that would become almost as sacred as the Bible itself in the eyes of extreme radical reformers in Britain. Even though Richard Price had died in April 1791, it is estimated that 'nearly a third' of Burke's *Reflections*[7] was written in the form of a riposte to Price's final work, *A Discourse on the Love of Our Country*.

Religious doctrine and social stability

Having identified an important 'paradox' relating to the practical applications of Moderate ideology in the eighteenth-century Scottish church, Sher explains that the paradox he has in mind

> ... involves the tension between the Moderates' exceptionally liberal views on such matters as intellectual freedom, religious tolerance, and the need for politeness, learning, and enlightenment, and their staunchly conservative stance on most questions of social, political, and ecclesiastical law and order.[8]

That, in turn, begs the question: how is it possible to reconcile such liberal Enlightenment values upheld by the Moderate literati of Edinburgh with their avowed distaste for radicalism and reform, palpably felt and openly expressed by several leading Moderate ministers, particularly in the closing decade of the eighteenth-century when Moderatism was beginning to show clear signs of having passed its zenith? Or, to put it more bluntly: how did it come about that the years of reform reveal an established church increasingly out of touch with, and ever more distant from the 'people'? In that regard, Sher rightly takes issue with Chitnis who had misleadingly described the proponents of Moderatism as 'enlightened radicals.'[9]

Conversely, the historian of the Popular party, McIntosh, examining the same issue in terms of the prevailing consensus of the orthodox faction, succeeds in identifying a discernible connection between belief, religious conviction and contemporary social order:

> There was ... a clear conviction that there was a significant, even a crucial, connection between faith and social stability. Decline of faith led to the collapse of society. Infidelity was to be feared not just on religious grounds, but also on social ones.

But he adds:

> ... Strikingly absent, however, was any stress on the social implications of Calvinist doctrines of original sin, total depravity, or consideration of the question of free will.[10]

McIntosh, that is, finds scant evidence[11] to support any threat to the old doctrines of Calvinism attributable to contemporary changes in social stability, while at the same time recognising that there was a clear connection between loss of faith and societal breakdown. Yet in one case, at least, belief in original sin, for example, was alive and well considerably later than McIntosh would have us believe.

While it is the tendency of some modern historians to seek to minimise doctrinal differences between the two factions, and to identify the 'political' (and, thus, strictly non-doctrinal) issue of patronage as the most credible dividing line between them, caution is necessary. [See the 'Endnote' to this study for conclusions on this issue.] One of the major stumbling blocks, for example, is the extent to which literal orthodox belief in the doctrine of original sin – often conjoined with the related doctrine of Christ's atonement in response to the incubus of human depravity – simply refused to wither away and die; indeed, it was still being urged on congregations by a few orthodox ministers right up to the end of the century and, spasmodically, even later. In an ordination sermon preached in Paisley Abbey Church in 1758 John Witherspoon, in his 'Charge' to the young minister, Archibald Davidson (a future principal of the University of Glasgow), told him to take heed of the common complaint that 'from many pulpits they [*i.e.* 'serious persons' in congregations] hear little or nothing of the doctrine of the grace of God; that the grand and leading truths of the gospel are either flatly contradicted or kept entirely out of view, and something else substituted in their place.' Witherspoon further explains:

> If, therefore, there be any one among us, who does not preach the doctrine of original sin, of Christ's imputed righteousness, justification by free grace, the necessity of regeneration, and the operations of the Spirit, he is guilty of perjury of the worst kind, for which I know no excuse. Such a person is not only chargeable with departing from the faith, but with an absolute prostitution of conscience, and a whole life of hypocrisy and deceit.[12]

One of the most striking illustrations of continuing adherence to the doctrine of original sin is found eighteen years later, in revolutionary America in 1776, the year of the Declaration of Independence. In the printed version of the most celebrated sermon he ever preached, *The Dominion of Providence over the Passions of Men*, delivered at Princeton on the eve of the Declaration (to which document he himself would subscribe as the only churchman to do so), Witherspoon takes serious issue with Thomas Paine over Paine's dismissive words on original sin in his iconic pamphlet, *Common Sense*.[13]

Pitching up in New Jersey in 1768, Witherspoon had softened his once uncompromising view on the 'poison of infidel writings', and now felt able to recommend Hume and Kames to his students. Despite this apparent *volte-face* on the part of the author of *Ecclesiastical Characteristics*, his American sermons show that he remained stubbornly committed to his old Calvinist convictions and, more specifically, was unremitting in his continuing faith in the eternal truths of 'natural' religion and original sin. For Witherspoon, the doctrine of *'regeneration'* was just as valid in a sinful United States as ever it had been in a morally corrupt west of Scotland. The gospel message he chose for several of his sermons, both in Scotland and America, held true regardless of when or where they were preached: *Except a man be born again, he cannot see the kingdom of God.*[14] In the view of Calvinist Evangelicals like Witherspoon, there was simply no easy option: re-birth was the *sole* key to man's regeneration. It followed, that in the absence of personal commitment to re-birth, access to the kingdom of God was denied, even if one lived one's life in a spirit of dedicated Christian *caritas* and a commitment to good works. In the absence of professed re-birth, Witherspoon (and others sharing his theology) argued that consequently men could not pass through the heavenly threshold.

Intriguingly, much later in the century, another Paisley orthodox hardliner, John Snodgrass of the Middle Church, preaching to a meeting of the SSPCK in Edinburgh in May 1794 – only a few months before Witherspoon's death at his home in Tusculum, New Jersey – identifies the debasement of the doctrine of original sin as one of the prime causes of a disturbing escalation of human depravity manifest in society at large:[15]

> With respect to the doctrine of original sin, perhaps it is not sufficiently considered, that to deny that mankind are in a guilty and ruined state, is to subvert the very design of the gospel; as it makes Christ to come upon a mistaken and useless errand, namely, to save a world which was not lost: and to admit this general guilt and ruin, is in effect to acknowledge the very doctrine which is now in question.[16]

It is important to note that this John Snodgrass is often confused with Witherspoon's nemesis, a writer in Paisley of the same name (they may have been related), who, with others, brought a successful action for defamation and damages against the Laigh Church minister in the Court of Session. The Court process lasted fourteen years from 1762, and according to his student and amanuensis, Ashbel Green – expressing a view this author shares[17]– played a part in his final acceptance of the call from New Jersey. The Reverend Dr John Snodgrass was a true disciple of Witherspoon and shared the Scottish 'signer's' Calvinist orthodoxy.[18] As if to recognise their common beliefs, Snodgrass was admitted an honorary doctor of divinity of the College of New Jersey in 1793.

The particular ogre targeted in Snodgrass's sermon was an English dissenter of a previous generation, John Taylor, whose *The Scripture-Doctrine of Original Sin* (1740) had been expressly written in order to pour cold water on the doctrine. Taylor's book had subsequently provoked the inevitable counterblast from John Wesley. But the link between theological doctrine and social stability – Leibniz coined the word 'theodicy' for it – has subtler implications. Colin Kidd, whose views on ministerial subscription were considered in chapter 5 ('Heresy'), has more recently (2015) developed an original hypothesis in which, while admitting that, as he puts it, there were 'flashes of reaction', nonetheless 'Scotland lacked a vigorous and sustained Counter-Enlightenment':

Opposition to the Enlightenment within Scotland was spasmodic and disjointed. ... the enemies of heterodoxy did not amount to a coherent anti-Enlightenment movement. ... the voices of opposition to the Enlightenment were muted, or confined to the margins of Scottish life.[19]

While recognising the long-running sore of patronage as a case apart – boiling up from time to time and causing resentment between the rival factions in the Kirk – Kidd is able to conclude that 'the axis of division in church politics ... was largely a matter of church government, not a more fundamental fault line predicated upon matters of doctrine and belief.'[20] Yet he goes on to disprove any *universal* application of that judgment, preferring to focus on the 'micro-climate' represented by mid- and late eighteenth-century Ayrshire and Renfrewshire.

Kidd's primary exemplar representing Renfrewshire in his hypothesis is, as one might have predicted, none other than John Witherspoon, minister at Beith, Ayrshire (1745-57), then Paisley, Renfrewshire (1757-68), whom he describes as a 'needling presence' in the region, and *Ecclesiastical Characteristics* (1753) as 'his most notorious work'. To illustrate his argument in respect of Ayrshire, Kidd chooses to examine (i) aspects of the Fergusson affair (the 'Kilwinning heresy' of chapter 5) – including, most notably, the role in it of Thomas Walker, the hardline Calvinist minister of Dundonald (and Witherspoon's uncle) – (ii) John Goldie, author of the work that became known as 'Goudie's Bible' (1779), and, most revealingly of all, (iii) the notorious William McGill heresy case when charges of Socinianism were levelled at the Ayr minister, though, as Kidd points out, the case equally had serious relevance to the patronage issue. Kidd's original and inventive essay casts a final backward glance at Paisley, citing in the process the eccentric doggerelist, James Maxwell, 'S.D.P'.,[21] a fierce loyalist and opponent of the 'satanic' verse of Robert Burns, and of the heretical ministers of Ayrshire into the bargain. On the evidence he presents, drawn from eighteenth-century Ayrshire and Renfrewshire, Kidd concludes that, in that region of Scotland at least, there existed 'an enduring hostility to the Enlightenment which persisted throughout the second half of the century', leading him to claim that 'it is possible to trace clear continuities in the rhetoric of this regional counter-Enlightenment.'[22]

It is difficult to find fault with Kidd's analysis, except that it is capable of enlargement. It is valid, for example, to extend his argument, especially in the context of Renfrewshire. Specifically, on the issue of links between religious belief and social stability it is worthwhile to consider a further argument for which no originality is claimed here. It goes something like this: the continuum of old-style Calvinist pulpit rhetoric and zealous religious orthodoxy readily discernible in certain of Paisley's pulpits virtually up to the end of the eighteenth-century – let us use Kidd's own phrase the presence of '*anti*-Enlightenment' – is consistent, to a remarkable degree, with Paisley's co-terminous and well-documented involvement in substantial, at times extreme radical activity. It should be recalled, after all, that, as well as the fiercely loyal Maxwell, Paisley was also once home over the same period to the radical poets Alexander Wilson (probable author of the *Paisley Declaration of Rights*, a key Crown production in the trial of Thomas Muir in August 1793), and Wilson's bosom friend, the 'extreme radical', James Kennedy, a man constantly on the run from the authorities, and erstwhile accomplice of the London radical bookseller and publisher, Daniel Isaac Eaton.[23] In their verse, both Wilson and Kennedy not only lionised Paine but were openly contemptuous of 'priest-craft',[24] and both 'fugitated' from Scotland at around the same time, ending up in permanent exile in the United States.

Sher's paradox regarding Moderatism and Enlightenment values and, equally, McIntosh's corollary concerning the Popular party – both formulated in relation to the issue of contemporary social order and stability – appear even more insightful when an important additional factor is taken into account. According to Clark's calculations, the creeping ascendancy of Popular party settlements – resulting in orthodox ministers eventually outnumbering Moderates in membership of the Presbytery of Paisley – is not in doubt.[25] Above all, the spectacular commensurate growth of seceding congregations in Paisley over roughly the same period paints the same picture. Even in Witherspoon's day Paisley basked in its reputation as a stronghold of expansionist secessionist (Antiburgher) enthusiasm.[26] The hoary Antiburgher minister, James Ellis (or Alice), was not just a good friend of Witherspoon's but, astonishingly, survived long enough to have almost certainly been one of Paisley's representatives at the first General (*i.e.* British) Convention of the Friends of the People in Edinburgh in December 1792.[27] Moreover, the minister to the thriving Castle Street Relief congregation in Paisley, Patrick Hutchison, caused an outcry when in January 1796 he was accused by six members of his congregation of 'mixing in his discourses political things'.[28] *Pace* Colin Kidd, we can take a last look at James Maxwell, who, on this occasion, is blaming the seceding churches for failing to present – in the sense of standing shoulder to shoulder with members of the established Kirk – a united front in the face of so much evil stalking the country:

> O then let ev'ry party now unite,
> Against the common foe let all now fight.
> Stand to your arms, ye diff'rent parties all,
> And for the help of Heav'n united call.
> Ye ancient Mountaineers,[29] whate'er you do,
> Ye Burghers, and ye Antiburghers too;
> And ye who have been forc'd by wrong, thro' grief,
> To join a party to obtain Relief,
> With all the faithful of the Church, unite,
> And for the cause of truth with courage fight.[30]

Hugh Blair: a reluctant political preacher

It is not difficult to account for Hugh Blair's collected sermons becoming bestsellers for decades in both Britain and America. The prose is elegant but never flowery in a Johnsonian way, and the message always direct, coherent and, above all, readily intelligible even to a reader unacquainted with theological doctrine. Blair himself was very clear on the requirements for a successful preacher:

> Usefulness and true eloquence always go together; and no man can long be reputed a good Preacher who is not acknowledged to be an useful one. ... it is a very false notion to imagine, that they always preach the most profoundly, or go the deepest into a subject,

who dwell on it the longest. ... Sometimes it is the taste of poetical preaching, sometimes of philosophical, that has the fashion on its side; at one time it must be all pathetic, at another time all argumentative ... Each of these modes, in the extreme is very faulty ... and this will never give its sanction to any strain of preaching, but what is founded on human nature, connected with usefulness, adapted to the proper idea of a sermon, as a serious persuasive Oration, delivered to a multitude, in order to make them better men. Let a Preacher form himself upon this standard, and keep it close in his eye, and he will be in a much surer road to reputation, and success at last, than by a servile compliance with any popular taste, or transient humour of his Hearers.[31]

In the same piece, 'Lecture XXIX' on 'Eloquence of the Pulpit' in the *Lectures on Rhetoric and Belles Lettres* (1783) — Sher calls the work 'the bible of Moderate pulpit oratory' — Blair is virtually silent on the issue of the subject-matter of sermons. His greatest concern is with *'eloquence'* appropriate to the pulpit, just as he was concerned in the previous two lectures with, respectively, the 'eloquence of popular assemblies' and the 'eloquence of the bar'. But even his silence on the issue is significant, since, while he seems to rule nothing in, he also appears relaxed about ruling nothing out, always provided, is the clear implication, the soundness of the theology is never in doubt:

To give rules for the choice of subjects for Sermons, belongs to the theological more than to the rhetorical chair; only in general, they should be such as appear to the Preacher to be the most useful, and the best accommodated to the circumstances of his Audience.[32]

In any sense of the term it is impossible to regard Hugh Blair as a political preacher. At the same time, it may come as a surprise that John Erskine, his Evangelical contemporary (and good friend) was, when it suited him, an outspoken political preacher. And yet, Blair is rarely coy in addressing the problems of the 'real' world outside his pulpit. Many of his sermons show real concern for the misery and hardship of others, often brought on, he extrapolates, by the hard-heartedness of the ruling class. [See Endnote for a different view of this aspect of Blair's preaching.] In one of his most famous sermons, 'On Gentleness', he touches in rapid succession on the controversial topics of slavery and its abolition; equality between the sexes; marriage; war; despotism; and the inhumane punishment of offenders:

Wherever Christianity prevails, it has discouraged, and in some degree, abolished slavery. It has rescued human nature from that ignominious yoke, under which, in former ages, the one half of mankind groaned. It has introduced more equality between the two sexes, and rendered the conjugal union more rational and happy. It has abated the ferociousness of war. It has mitigated the rigour of despotism, mitigated the cruelty of punishment; in a word, has reduced mankind from their ancient barbarity, into a more humane and gentle state.[33]

Of course, this is all very far from definitive pulpit censure, from which, one senses, Blair (and Erskine too for that matter) would have instinctively recoiled. Nevertheless, he constantly emphasises his conviction that Christianity is much more than doctrine or mere passive belief in scripture:

Christian faith is not a system of speculative truths. It is not a lesson of moral instruction only. ... it is calculated to elevate the mind, to purify the affections, and by the assistance of devotion, to confirm and encourage virtue.[34]

In the same mode, there is the stunning elaboration of perceived Enlightenment values in the sermon 'On Sensibility'. No one could possibly term it political preaching, but at the same time the words ring true as an optimistic account of how the social history of an urban society (such as Edinburgh) was, at least in Blair's judgment, utterly transformed by the humane and ennobling spirit of the age:

> In modern times, the chief improvement of which we have to boast is a sense of humanity. This, notwithstanding the selfishness that still prevails, is the favourite and distinguishing virtue of the age. On general manners, and on several departments of society, it has had considerable influence. It has abated the spirit of persecution; it has even tempered the horrors of war; and man is now more ashamed, than he was in former ages, of acting as a savage to man. Hence, sensibility is become so reputable a quality, that the appearance of it is frequently assumed when the reality is wanting. Softness of manners must not be mistaken for true sensibility. Sensibility tends to produce gentleness of behaviour; and when such behaviour flows from native affection, it is valuable and amiable. But the exterior manner alone may be learned in the school of the world; and often, too often, is found to cover much unfeeling hardness of heart.[35]

And in one of the most stirring of all his sermons, 'On the Disorders of the Passions'[36] – it is not going too far to regard it as one of the most powerful and moving sermons preached in Scotland in the eighteenth century – Blair is inspired by the Old Testament book of *Esther*, and in particular by the story of King Ahasuerus (the historical Persian tyrant, Xerxes, son of Darius) and his prime minister, Haman, the evil courtly official who spectacularly fell from power and paid the ultimate price for wrongly imagining he had the king's full authority for acting without his express consent. Here Blair conveys the moral lesson to be learned from the old Bible story:

> The story of Haman only shows us, what human nature has too generally appeared to be in every age. Hence, when we read the history of nations, what do we read but the history of the follies and crimes of men? We may dignify those recorded transactions, by calling them the intrigues of statesmen, and the exploits of conquerors; but they are in truth, no other than the efforts of discontent to escape from its misery, and the struggles of contending passions among unhappy men.[37]

And he concludes his sermon:

> Haman was not delivered up all at once to the madness of revenge. His passions rose with the rising tide of prosperity; and pride completed what prosperity began. What was originally no more than displeasure at Mordecai's disrespect, increased with every invitation he received to the banquet of the Queen; till it impelled him to devise the slaughter of a whole [Jewish] nation, and ended in a degree of rage which confounded his reason, and hurried him to ruin. In this manner, every criminal passion, in its progress, swells and blackens; and what was at first a small cloud, such as the prophet's servant saw, *no bigger than a man's hand rising from the sea*,[38] is soon found to carry the tempest in its womb.[39]

Blair would have been fully aware of the political undertones implicit in his choice of scripture. Since Tudor times the biblical story of Queen Esther, King Ahasuerus, Mordecai and Haman had been used by preachers as a kind of ready-made notice-board on which they could pin the transparent allegory of over-exuberant political power resulting in the downfall of courtiers/ministers who imagined they could do as they please and get away with it. It was the same passage from *Esther* that had prompted John Skip in the Chapel Royal in April 1536, in the presence of Queen Ann (Boleyn), to raise the issue of the undue influence exercised over the king by his cunning adviser, Thomas Cromwell. And in 1740, and again in June 1746, it was the story of the downfall of Haman, the 'prime minister' – who, the king commanded, should 'set his seat above all the princes that were with him' – that inspired Alexander Webster, the minister of the Tolbooth, to harangue against, first, Sir Robert Walpole; and to employ the same story in a new sermon six years later to connote the deliverance of the entire British nation from the Jacobite rebels under the arch-villain, this time in the person of Charles Edward Stewart. Intriguingly, long after Webster's death, his sermon of 1740 was re-issued in 1797 with a new preface that left little room for doubt that it had been hi-jacked for the blatant purpose of stirring up opposition to Henry Dundas, Pitt's right-hand man and uncrowned king of Scotland. The message is just as crystal-clear as before, though the target this time is a totally different one:

> It is the undoubted right and the duty of every British subject, to watch over the administration of Government. Instead of being an improper interference in any one, it is only an exercise of natural and acknowledged civil right to animadvert on the conduct of those who have the management of public affairs, and even to petition the Throne for their removal from such high stations. If ever the period arrive, when this principle shall be generally called in question, and the People deterred from acting on it by the charges of sedition and anarchy, it will be an inauspicious aera for British liberty.[40]

Blair would have known and understood all this – including the Webster sermons – even though it is not his purpose to traipse down the allegorical path of the biblical story, as Webster and others before him had done. The purpose behind Blair's re-telling of the downfall of Haman is generally to remove the drapes from the wilful capriciousness of human politics, even though it remains his primary aim to disclose the simple morality of the tale. The point is that it is just not Blair's way to conceal within it any reference, coded or not, to the prevailing 'real' world of contemporary affairs.

Uniquely in the entire collection of ninety sermons spread over the five volumes of his collected pulpit works, there is a superscription to the printed sermon 'On the Love of our Country' – included as 'Sermon VI' in the posthumously published fifth volume of Blair's *Sermons* of 1801 – indicating its date and provenance: '*Preached 18th April, 1793, on the day of a National Fast appointed by Government, on occasion of the War with the French Republic.*' When it is considered there was an interval of no less than eight years between its preaching and its publication in the posthumous fifth and final volume, it seems unlikely that Blair had ever countenanced publishing it independently in pamphlet format, even though at that time in Scotland politically charged sermons, for and against political reform, were flowing thick and fast from printers in Edinburgh and Glasgow. A possible further factor operating against its prior publication as a stand-alone pamphlet is its comparative brevity.

'On the Love of our Country' is far from being the greatest of Blair's pulpit works, but to the student of his life and works it must rank as one of his most interesting for several reasons. First, it is quite untypical of the style of sermon we have come to associate with Blair. It is, of course, impossible to judge whether or not Blair may have been in the habit of delivering political discourses from time to time. We do have it, however, on the evidence of one not uncritical member of his congregation, James Boswell, that he had worked himself into a rage against Blair for a fast-day prayer the minister had put up against the American cause late in 1776, the consequence of which was that Boswell started to 'shun' the New Kirk whenever he learned that it was Blair's turn to preach there.[41]

Then again, the sermon is one of his shortest on record. Matheson has calculated that the average extent of Blair's published sermons was 'about thirty [octavo] pages, although they could exceptionally extend to fifty-six.'[42] 'On the Love of our Country' occupies just over twenty-five pages. Above all, and perversely, the sermon stands out from the rest on account of the fact there are, one would have to say, more than a few uncharacteristic banalities in Blair's prose that might be thought unworthy of the man who has been called 'by far the most successful sermon-writer in eighteenth-century Scotland.'[43] One is tempted to speculate if it is conceivable that Blair was actively encouraged by some of his friends in high authority to publish the piece but only authorised its publication at the end of his life, and then, against his better judgment. Was it, dare one ask, *preached* 'to order', as Thomas Hardy's influential *The Patriot* was *written* 'to order'?[44]

The sermon opens with Blair citing the commonplace truism that we take the best things in life for granted. This 'unhappy weakness' is evident not just in 'the light of the sun' and 'the beauties of nature', but in other 'blessings' we enjoy: among them, 'health, peace, religion, and liberty.' But it's not just a question of our taking such blessings for granted –

> Nay, is it not much to be lamented that there should have sprung up among us an unaccountable spirit of discontent and disaffection, feeding itself with ideal grievances and visionary projects of reformation, till it has gone nigh to light up the torch of sedition.[45]

Before considering the 'grounds on which love for our country tests' together with the 'duties to which this affection naturally gives rise', Blair suggests we should first take notice of 'the speculations of some pretended philosophers, who represent the love of our country as hardly entitled to any place among the virtues.' These men, who affect to consider love of our country as 'a mere prejudice of education', conclude that we ought 'to view ourselves as citizens of the world, and extend our benevolence, equally, to all nations and all mankind.' 'Nothing,' pleads Blair, 'can be more empty and futile than such reasonings', adding:

> He who contends that he is not bound to have any more concern for the interests of Great Britain, than for those of France, or any other country, ought to hold, on the same grounds, that he is under no obligation to consult the welfare of his children and family, his brothers and friends, more than that of the most distant stranger ...'.[46]

For Blair, 'such reasonings' must be dismissed as 'false philosophy'. His rejection of Enlightenment claims that *'citoyens'* really meant 'citizens of the world' (in the full technical sense understood by Diderot and other *philosophes*) is important. Blair's identification and apparent subsequent rejection of the Enlightenment doctrine of cosmopolitanism as one of the great revolutionary axioms, and thus to be opposed at all costs, is the most engaging (and, equally, the most surprising) section in the entire sermon. Blair would certainly have recognised the technical, epistemological significance of the phrase 'citizens of the world'. He would have understood it, first, in the ancient classical sense (and, there, not just as a variety of Stoic cosmopolitanism first coined by Diogenes the Cynic), but much more recognisably and immediately in its Enlightenment applications. Thus, as Pagden reminds us, in 1768 Diderot had written sycophantically to Blair's great friend, David Hume, that 'you belong to all nations ... I flatter myself that I am, like you, a citizen of that great city, *the world*.'[47] Blair would undoubtedly have recognised that the cosmopolitanism of the *philosophes* had its roots in what Montesquieu had called 'the Stoic sect'.[48] But it cannot be overlooked that Blair's sermon was delivered in April 1793, just a few months before the trial of Thomas Muir, whose 'radical cosmopolitanism' has been explained (and championed) by some modern scholars.[49] The real point is, of course, that, as the sermon shows, the mere mention of the phrase 'citizen of the world', with its clear overtones of Jacobin dogma, was anathema to Moderate literati like Hugh Blair.

Blair then proceeds to consider 'our native country' from three different points of view: first, as the 'seat of private enjoyment and happiness'; secondly, as the 'seat of true religion'; and last, as the 'seat of laws, liberty, and good government.' With regard to the first of these, we discover the earliest long example of the several banalities exposed in the sermon:

> When we name our own country, we name the spot of the earth within which all that is most dear to us lies. To be long absent from it, is a circumstance of distress; but to be excluded from the hope of ever returning to it, sinks the spirits of the worthy and the brave into extreme depression. Its very dust appears to them to be precious. *etc., etc.*[50]

As we are entitled to expect and could have predicted, Blair is more assured when he deals with the second of his three chosen topics concerning the advantages conferred on all our country's citizens; this time, 'our country' viewed as the 'seat of true religion':

> Religion has among us neither been the engine of ecclesiastical tyranny, nor the instrument of princely despotism. It has maintained a proper alliance with the regular government of the state, and the order of public tranquillity.[51] The church that has been established by law, in the two separate divisions of the island, is suited to the genius and dispositions of the people in each. While to the established church is given that protection and support from government, which both the interests of religion and the welfare of the state render proper and due; yet no rigid conformity to it is exacted. All persecution for conscience sake, is unknown. They who, in their modes of thinking, or in their religious forms differ from the established church, are at full liberty, without reproach, to worship God, according to their own opinions and the rites of their fathers, as long as they infringe not the public tranquillity, nor disturb the state.[52]

He goes on to state what was in his lifetime technically true in relation to Britain's traditional enjoyment of religious *tolerance*. English dissenters, Scottish secessionsists, and nonconformists of every hue were free under the law to practise their varieties of Christian belief. The modern reader will, of course, note that he excludes gross religious *inequalities* in his time, conventionally commenting that 'our countrymen' were 'freed from the dominion of Popish superstition and darkness which so long overspread the earth'. He declares that 'here (he means in Scotland) they worship God according to their own opinions and the rites of their fathers', adding knowingly 'as long as they infringe not the public tranquillity, nor disturb the state.'[53]

In the most stirring part of his sermon Blair says we would be mad to give all this up in exchange for what now prevails in revolutionary France. His rhetoric here, it might be said, comes close to resembling that of Burke himself in his pomp:

> Can there be any among us so infatuated as to wish to exchange it [our established religion] for that new form of things which has produced such fatal effects on a neighbouring land? Were it ever to be introduced among us, it is not the return of antient superstition, it is not the bondage of the church of Rome we would have to dread; evils great in themselves, but small in comparison of what such a revolution would produce. As soon as under the guise of philosophy, and with the pretence of unlimited toleration, the established forms of religion were demolished in France, the flood-gates were opened to pour a torrent of avowed infidelity, atheism, and all the grossest immoralities, over that devoted country. We have beheld the throne and the altar overthrown together; and nothing but a wretched ruin left, where once a stately fabric stood. We have seen the venerable ministers of religion, stripped of their subsistence, torn from their churches, driven from their homes, and forced to wander as exiles, and beg their bread in a foreign land. ... Such have been the blessed fruits of that new order of things which boasted of being [able] to restore happiness to all the nations. Such are the consequences we have to expect among ourselves, if ever the like dangerous opinions shall prevail in Britain.[54]

This brings him to the third and final advantage of 'our country'. 'We love our country', he insists, 'as the seat of liberty and laws; a mild and happy government.' But, Blair concedes, this 'opens a much wider field of discourse than the bounds of a sermon admit.' First, he admits that 'a perfect government is a mere chimera.' Nevertheless, it is his view that

> In its present state, it may justly be accounted to ... have approached nearer to the perfection of social order, than any other government, antient or modern. ... It [the 'British constitution'] stands among the nations of the earth, like an antient oak in the wood, which, after having overcome many a blast, overtops the other trees of the forest, and commands respect and veneration. All foreigners look to it with wonder, and with envy, as the happiest system that ever was devised for uniting dignity in the magistrate and liberty in the subject, with protection and security to all.[55]

Clearly, either Blair had not read (which is unlikely), or simply wished to ignore Richard Price's discourse bearing the same name as that of his sermon. Had he expressed familiarity with the work, he might have taken note of Price's diametrically contrary view:

> It is proper to observe that, even in this sense of our country [he could have inserted inverted commas here to stress his true meaning], that love of it which is our duty, does not imply any conviction of the superior value of it to other countries, or any particular preference of its laws and constitution of government.[56]

And, naturally, not a word here about Thomas Paine's devastating critique of the British constitution and 'system' of government in his officially seditious *Rights of Man* – available for covert sale in all the radical booksellers the length and breadth of the country and, despite the ban on its sale and distribution, still the talk of the cities and the towns, the law courts, churches, the marketplace and the taverns.[57]

Conventionally, the sermon launches into a fawning eulogy of loyalist sentiment and adoration of the British constitution and the monarch:

> Justly may we challenge those who attempt to criticise it [the British constitution], to produce, from the annals of history, any example of such a multitude of men as the British subjects, held together in the bonds of civil society, under so few restraints, and with such full enjoyment of freedom as we possess: blessed too for a whole century past with a succession of princes, who made the laws of the land the rule of their government; blessed now with a Sovereign at the head of the empire, to whom faction itself cannot impute, throughout his long reign, any acts of tyranny, cruelty, or oppression; whose personal virtues and whole domestic conduct hold forth to the nation such a high example of piety, decency, and good order, as, if generally followed, would render all his subjects happy.[58]

Blair's encomium of George III delivered from his pulpit in April 1793 has to be set alongside Paine's comments in *Rights of Man* of almost exactly two years before:

> As to who is King in England or elsewhere, or whether there is any King at all, or whether the people choose a Cherokee chief, or a Hessian Hussar for a King, it is not a matter that I trouble myself about – be that to themselves; but with respect to the doctrine, so far as it relates to the Rights of Men and Nations, it is as abominable as anything ever uttered in the most enslaved country under heaven.[59]

Next, it is the turn of republics and republicans to earn Blair's scorn. 'There are', he states, 'no advantages claimed by a republic, but what under the British constitution are enjoyed to the full.' Further, 'no odious distinctions take place between the nobility and the people' and

> no severe exclusive privileges are possessed by the former to the prejudice of the latter; but merit in every rank has the freest scope, and examples abound of persons rising by their talents from ordinary rank and humble birth to high distinction in the state.[60]

On a comparison of 'oligarchies' and 'democracies', Blair states:

> It has ever been, and never can be, any other, than a perpetual contest between oligarchy and democracy; between the rich and the poor; between a few popular leaders who aspire to the chief influence, and the unruly violence of a turbulent multitude. ... while public agitations allow a few individuals to be uncommonly distinguished, the general condition of the people remains calamitous and wretched.[61]

He compares the condition of people labouring under 'despotic governments' with those 'under a multitude of popular governors'; he is in no doubt that the second mode leaves 'the people' worse off since 'by republican tyranny the humble and obscure are liable to be as much harassed and vexed as the great and wealthy.' One has only to look at what has happened in France in the recent past for evidence of 'all the evils against which men, joined in society, ought to stand on their guard.' –

He will behold the republican halls hung round with monuments of proscriptions, massacres, imprisonments, requisitions, domiciliary searches, and such other trophies of the glorious victory of republicanism over monarchical power.[62]

The final section of Blair's sermon is packed with a succession of clichés that would not be out of place in a modern government-sponsored election broadcast:

The full opportunity that is given for the voice of the people being at all times heard, the freedom of discussion on all political matters that is allowed both in discourse and writing, is a sufficient guard against all approaches to unwarrantable stretches of power in the ruler, and to unlimited submission in the subject.[63]

This 'high advantage' of the 'liberty of the press and the freedom of political discussion' combine to act as a 'censorial check on all who are in power.' The sermon, there can no longer be any doubt, is nothing less than a utopian picture of an earthly paradise where 'every heart and hand' is united 'in the common cause.' Blair, one is tempted to interject, has not heard of – or, again more likely, chooses to ignore Thomas Erskine's Crown and Anchor speech, subsequently published as his *Address to the Public*, of January in the same year as the sermon was preached. On that historic occasion, Erskine had declared:

... if every writing is to be prosecuted which they may not have the sense to understand, or the virtue to practise; if no man is to write but upon *their* principles, nor can read with safety except what *they* have written, lest he should accidentally talk of what he has to read; – No man will venture either to write or to speak upon the topics of government or its administration – a freedom which ever has been acknowledged by our greatest statesmen and lawyers to be the principal safeguard of that constitution which liberty of thought originally created, and which a Free Press for its circulation gradually brought to maturity.[64]

In sharp contrast Blair's sermon limply concludes with one final crowning banality:

We live in a land of pure religion, of liberty, and laws, and under a just and mild government.[65]

Only a few months later, Thomas Muir, advocate, would be sentenced to fourteen years' transportation in the first of the infamous Scottish sedition trials; and in little over a year Robert Watt would be hanged, beheaded, drawn and quartered in the Tolbooth, having been found guilty of high treason. Blair's portrayal in his sermon of contemporary British society, at ease with itself, of a sunny, contented Britain basking in fair laws, freedom of speech and of the press, and of a citizenry never having had it so good under a constitution second to none in the entire world, marks a veritable watershed in the popular credulity of the *Chair of Verity*. But even worse was to come for the Kirk, ultimately stretching things to breaking point and, in the process, exposing the divide between fiction and reality even more trenchantly.

Alexander Carlyle's brand of Moderate conservatism

Taken together, the three political sermons of Alexander Carlyle discussed here offer the most coherent picture possible of Carlyle's personal political affiliations. Just as important, they represent perhaps the best examples we have of 'pure' political preaching in an age when the established church in Scotland increasingly had its back to the wall. At the same time, it cannot be overlooked that, whatever we may think of them today, Carlyle's loyalist sermons – though without doubt distinguished representatives of their genre – are three among many.

To begin to unravel the political rationale as well as the religious conviction that inspired all three sermons, we could do worse by noting carefully the scriptural text underpinning each of them. Preached over a five-year period between 1792 and 1797, Carlyle's political sermons derive their scriptural inspiration exclusively from books of the Old Testament; chronologically, from *Ecclesiastes* (1792), *Jeremiah* (1794), and *Psalms* (1797). Of itself, that is unremarkable since, perhaps a shade ironically, both Moderate and Popular party ministers were attracted to accounts of Old Testament prophets, finding them generally sympathetic to the message they desired to convey, and discovering an attractive earthiness in the allegorical potential many ministers of the period commonly associated with the *OT*. Where, for example, a man like John Witherspoon employed the *Psalms* to urge a message of restraint on the emergent American nation on the eve of her independence, we find Carlyle, the very epitome of Moderatism, employing the same book to preach a sermon of 'self-reproach' that conveniently also satisfies his secondary purpose – that is, to chastise and scold his audience.

The term 'depravity', used to describe the human condition in the title of the 1794 fast-day sermon, is, again, perhaps not one we would normally associate with a man like 'Jupiter' Carlyle. In the heyday of the Scottish brand of eighteenth-century evangelicalism 'depravity' is often bracketed together with the doctrine of original sin to indicate the extent to which man in his fallen state is capable of redemption *only* if he is prepared to acknowledge his sin, confess Christ as his saviour and be 'born again'. But the Moderates followed a different course. As Ahnert succinctly puts it:

> The eighteenth-century Moderates who had articulated a "religion of morality" were doing so because of their theological views about the conditions of salvation. They were trying to steer a middle course between the extremes of an overemphasis on doctrinal orthodoxy on the one hand, and religious enthusiasm on the other, which was characterised by a belief in sudden, dramatic conversions, of a type associated with the revivalist movements that emerged in the eighteenth century. [66]

In *National Depravity* (1794), the earlier of the two wholly political sermons examined here, Carlyle loyally defends the *status quo* he neatly defines as society, king and state. He consciously manipulates the old application of the term 'depravity' to fit its perceived modern connotation as he chooses to portray it; that is, that the only hope of forgiveness for headstrong and wayward reformers is for them to acknowledge the error of their ways and speedily return to an affirmation of patriotic love of country. In a way, it is a new slant on the idea of re-birth, this time shorn of all doctrinal connotations. Carlyle is much more down to earth. In the term '*National Depravity*' he diagnoses the cause of '*National Calamities*' and concludes:

> ... sin is the cause of all national evils, and if persisted in by any people, will provoke the Almighty *to cause his soul depart from them.*

This is hardly the language we might expect of a Moderate minister. But it soon becomes clear what Carlyle's true purpose is when we recall his text – *Jeremiah* 6. 8: *Be thou instructed, O Jerusalem, lest my soul depart from thee: lest I make thee desolate, a land not inhabited.* He explains its relevance to present circumstances in prosaic cadences that the modern reader may find almost Churchillian: the *kingdom* will become *desolate*, and the *land not inhabited* in consequence of unrepentant man [*i.e.* mankind] persisting in sin. He then plunges into an examination of the great divide that he sees threatening our national stability and harmony, striking at the very heart of contemporary British/Scottish social stability:

> On hearing these words [*Be thou instructed,* etc.] as a ground of meditation on a day of fasting, of contrition and repentance, to avert national calamities, I doubt not but every one of us, as usual, will endeavour to throw the blame from himself, and fix it on his neighbour. The poor will accuse, in their hearts, the rich and the great, for their pride, and luxury, and inhumanity; and the rich and great will, in like manner, accuse the poor, for their faithlessness, their ingratitude, and their double dealings. They who govern, will accuse those who are governed, of disaffection, wantonness, and sedition; and the governed will accuse their governors, of corruption, and venality, and the abuse of their power. But we must not forget, my brethren, that although the immediate causes of the downfall of states may be ascribed to the iniquities of particular orders of men, yet it is the accumulated guilt of a whole nation, collected often for many years, that forms the procuring cause, in the counsels of the Almighty, of the dreadful calamities that befall nations.[67]

Unlike Hugh Blair, however, Carlyle is evidently thoroughly at home in the genre; almost as if political preaching is his specialist trade. Where, as we have seen, Blair seems ill at ease in the guise of government man haranguing the populace (and, as preacher, extolling the constitution and those who defend and maintain it), Carlyle has utterly no qualms in discharging his set task. He positively *revels* in the role:

> General corruption of manners at first unhinges all government, for it makes men weary of the controul of laws. As the private vices of the individual make him daily trample on the laws of God and man, they make him spurn at the regulations of political order, and ready to rebel against them, when his interest or pleasure shall seem to make it necessary for him. Universal depravity leads to irreligion, *for men love darkness better than light, when their deeds are evil;* [68] and when God is no longer acknowledged among any people, it is time *that his soul should depart from them*. This is the greatest provocation they can give the Almighty. ... And when a due respect to religion no more pervades and conducts the counsels of any nation, you may be certain that they are in the high road to perdition. They have lost their light, and must wander in darkness.[69]

This prompts Carlyle to embark on his 'application', beginning with the general observation that the consequence of loving darkness rather than the light is nothing less than 'an end of order and good government'; for, he maintains, men will not long remain where neither person nor property are secure; and, on the contrary, it is a certain proof, that the government is not radically wrong when the country is populous, and when the inhabitants are industrious and prosperous; for the end of government is the happiness of the people.[70]

Specifically he tackles the sensitive issue of the late American *débacle*, a war 'which we carried on against our revolted colonies with so much inauspicious conduct, and so many adverse events':

> You may all remember how much humbled and dismayed we receded from this contest. Our strength was wasted, our funds exhausted, and even our credit at the lowest ebb. Our commerce, it was supposed, had received a deadly blow. The most fatal presages were entertained in the hour of our shame and disgrace; and few they were, indeed very few, who still had hopes that Britain might again rear her head among the nations.[71]

But, 'soon', God was pleased to 'revive our drooping spirits, and to give us rulers and counsellors who gained the confidence of the nation.' Before long, he exclaims, 'Our stock and industry opened for itself new channels', and 'our commercial spirit was restored in all its energy'; 'our fears of being undone, by the loss of our colonies, were soon dissipated.' Carlyle indulges in a history lesson, tracking the recovery of the country economically and militarily since 1783 to the French Revolution – the threat that that momentous event posed to our own country – and, of course, the war into which the country has been forced to commit itself:

> The minds of the lower orders, had been prepared by repeated factious appeals from the decrees of the Legislature, to their better judgment. Seditious writings were thrown in among them. Daily papers of the most pestilent nature augmented the shame. Foreign correspondence encouraged the levelling spirit. They became ripe for revolt. They believed the false professions of the devouring monster, which, under pretence of fraternising the world, meant to give law to all nations. They were ready to rise around the mock Tree of Liberty, though planted by a foreign hand. ...
> ... Hence the arrogance of the new usurping Republic. Britain united is a match for all the world, but divided by faction, may become a prey to every invader. Hence their attempt on a neighbouring Protestant ally, that they might direct her naval power against us; and hence their declaration of war, without any just pretence, though we, forgetful of their treacherous interposition in our dispute with our colonies, were far from intermeddling in their internal divisions. ... We must confess that our lofty thoughts have been thrown down, and that our dream of uninterrupted prosperity is at an end. We are most unexpectedly engaged in a war with the most powerful nation in the world, the termination and consequences of which it is impossible to foresee. Our best hopes of being soon relieved from it are, under God, derived from that spirit of dissension and anarchy that prevails among them, and their total renunciation of those religious and moral principles which bind men together, and their actual commission of every dreadful crime, *that can provoke the almighty, and make his soul depart from them.*[72]

Carlyle insists it is 'our sins are the cause; nothing else can interrupt the course of divine favour.' If we succeed in eradicating sin, the country can enjoy stability once more.

He proceeds to enumerate the 'many national dangers we have escaped and the many blessings we enjoy'. In words that distinctly recall Blair's sermon *On the Love of our Country*, these include 'that admirable constitution of government ... by means of which we enjoy freedom and security, both personal and political, beyond any nation under heaven.' But, Carlyle laments, 'with such peculiar blessings' how did we show our gratitude? Did we indulge in 'wise improvement', as might have been expected of us? Not a bit of it:

> ... alas! We have not only misemployed our talents, but have provoked God by committing many heinous sins. ... Our national prosperity has swelled us with arrogance and pride. We have made our wealth subservient to luxury and dissolute manners. Our liberty has degenerated into the most ungovernable licentiousness, and that government of laws in which we gloried with so much justice, we have to the utmost of our power subverted, by our contempt of all the restraints of law.[73]

If we discount William Thom's American sermons, uniquely in an eighteenth-century Scottish sermon Carlyle turns the spotlight on taxes, and prices and wages. In doing so he displays a surprisingly accomplished knowledge of contemporary government policy, as well as demonstrating an understanding of the basics of input/output economics:

> ... with respect to taxes, which no doubt have been increased, by means of the wars in which we were engaged, with the almost unanimous consent, however, of the nation, yet the most prudent care has been taken, that they shall as little as possible affect the labouring poor; for it has been demonstrated, that a person in that condition, if he lives with becoming frugality, has not to pay in taxes for all he purchases during a whole year, above the value of the wages of five days labour.[74]

And, with reference to wages, Carlyle adds a personal touch from the pulpit which must have struck a chord among members of his congregation:

> It is true, that the price of some of the necessaries of life is raised; but that rise, it must be observed, bears but a very small proportion to the rise of the wages of labour. Whilst some of the most common articles of living are not at all raised, and some only by a third or a fourth, you must admit, that the wages of labour in every instance has been doubled, which has mended your situation much more than could have been imagined by any one who had not been a witness (as I have been), how your fathers and grandfathers lived before you.[75]

Having praised the 'nobility' for their outstanding qualities (as had Hugh Blair in his fast-day sermon of the year before) – their characters would 'stand a comparison with those of any other order of men in the kingdom' – Carlyle directs his fire on 'the enemies of our happiness', those who 'prepare your minds for the total overthrow of subordination, the subversion of property, and the introduction of universal anarchy.' These people, he insists, 'have not even spared our most gracious King, the pattern of every private virtue, whose reign is the acknowledged model of mild and legal government.' Another 'sin' has got abroad and, 'if carried to excess, must produce the greatest national calamities', *viz.* a 'spirit of faction and party.' 'When this party spirit becomes factious',

> it sets no bounds to its opposition, let the measures be ever so necessary, then it encourages *disaffection and sedition*, which are most likely to end in *revolt and rebellion*.[76]

Instability, that is, is the price we all have to pay for the sins of others. *National Depravity* was delivered in February 1794. On the same fast day as Carlyle preached his sermon, Robert Walker, Moderate minister of the Canongate church in Edinburgh, thinks fit to begin his sermon with a *verbatim* quote from William Pitt's rousing speech at the opening of Parliament on 21 January, less than a month before:

> We are called, in the present age, to behold the moral and political phenomena of a mighty and civilized people, formed into an artificial horde of banditti, throwing off all the restraints which have influenced men in social life, displaying a savage valour, directed by a sanguinary spirit, forming rapine and destruction into a system, and perverting, to their detestable purposes, all the talents and ingenuity which they derived from their advanced stage of civilization, all the refinements of art, all the discoveries of science. [77]

The year 1794 witnessed a redoubling of government efforts in Scotland to eradicate sedition and discord. The Scottish trials for sedition continued unabated in the High Court of Justiciary in Edinburgh. The year opened with William Skirving – Cockburn calls him 'a Scotchman, educated originally for the Secession Church, but afterwards a farmer; a person of good character' – receiving the same extreme sentence as had Thomas Muir the year before: fourteen years' transportation to Botany Bay. A week after the Skirving verdict, Maurice Margarot, who had been re-arrested in Paisley after a huge radical demonstration there in which the poet Alexander Wilson had enthusiastically participated, suffered the same fate. Just a couple of weeks before Carlyle preached his sermon denouncing radicalism from his pulpit in Inveresk, Alexander Scott, the proprietor of the *Edinburgh Gazetteer* – one of the papers Carlyle would have had in mind when he dismissed such organs as 'of the most pestilent nature' – failed to appear at his trial, was thus deemed to have 'fugitated' and was summarily declared an outlaw. Over four days in March that same year the case of Joseph Gerrald came on at the High Court. Of the trial of Gerrald, 'an Englishman, a gentleman, and a scholar', Lord Cockburn commented:

> None of these cases made such an impression at the time, or has sunk so deeply into the heart of posterity, as Gerrald's – not however so much from his superior innocence, as from his character and heroism. [78]

Gerrald, too, would be sentenced to transportation for fourteen years, but died not long after reaching New South Wales.

Carlyle's brand of pulpit censure and the Friends of the People

On the surface of things, it may seem strange that Carlyle's sermon *National Depravity* has been overlooked in by far the majority of standard works concerned with radical activities in Scotland in the closing decade of the eighteenth century. That that is the case may result from a wider issue, more to do with the strange reluctance on the part of most historians of the period (with the honourable exception of Emma Vincent Macleod)[79] to harness the political sermon to help unravel the predominant spirit of the age. A particularly compelling illustration of this odd omission is to be found in all three of Carlyle's political sermons of 1792-1797, and it comes into sharpest focus if we concentrate on his comments, liberally scattered among all three, condemning the aims and activities of the Friends of the People – for they are his main targets.

In his contribution to Sinclair's *Statistical Account of Scotland* for the parish of Inveresk (written in 1793-4 and published in 1795), Carlyle had given clear notice of where his loyalties stood – and it is abundantly clear they do not lie with 'the *people*'. Of his own flock he writes:

> They are in general contented and unambitious, and would always be so, did not their constant intercourse with the capital, which is of so much advantage to them in other respects, expose them to the false arts of indefatigable seducers, who, under pretence of *Reform*, wish to *subvert* the present happy government, and introduce democratical anarchy in its stead.[80]

Carlyle's *OSA* contribution is merely a foretaste of what lay in store from the main avenue of denunciation open to him – his pulpit. No political preacher of the 1790s comes anywhere near him in the sheer merciless ferocity of his pulpit censure of popular radicalism. The unrelenting denial and condemnation of the movement for reform seems to rouse his passion like a red rag to a bull. Ironically, *National Depravity* was preached less than a year after the calamitous second British Convention of the Friends of the People (30 April to 3 May 1793), but also in the year that, as most historians of the period agree, marked the beginning of the end of radical extremism in Scotland for a generation and more. Carlyle, of course, was not to know this and towards the end of his sermon launches a broadside against his chosen targets calling them 'the determined Band of dark Conspirators', and the 'deluded party among the commons' who

> first appeared by expressing their harmless wish for a Reform, which they did not understand, and then, under the specious name of the *Friends of the People*, to attract the multitude; and lastly, when they became more daring, after the French had declared war, and promised them assistance, when they assumed the proud *Title of the British Convention*, with the avowed purpose of forming a league among the people, for overturning the constitution, and introducing such a republican anarchy as that of France. The civil magistrate at last took the alarm, and with that justice which the danger called for, and the laws authorised, have inflicted deserved punishment on some of the ring-leaders.[81]

Having urged support for the war 'with unanimity and vigour' he cannot resist a final swipe against '*this insolent Convention*', who mean 'to overturn every government, not to give laws to the whole world.'

It was the same theme he had visited a couple of years earlier, but on that occasion in wholly unexpected circumstances. Towards the end of 1792 – a year throughout which the government was under pressure to adopt draconian measures against not only a rising tide of popular dissent and disturbance, but a worsening of the threat from France – Carlyle had preached a memorial *Sermon on the Death of Sir David Dalrymple, Bar^t.*, the prominent Scottish judge and historian (and his personal friend), Lord Hailes.[82] The published version includes an 'Address to the congregation suited to the circumstances of the times.' With due deference to the departed Dalrymple, the 'Address' is easily the most eye-catching part of the literary sermon. Carlyle milks the situation occasioned by Dalrymple's death for all it's worth in order to get across the universal message he wishes to convey: 'We have good reason', he says, 'in our degenerate days, deeply to regret the loss of one person of marked and pre-eminent virtue.' He goes on to praise his late friend as advocate, judge, scholar, researcher and historian of Scotland.[83] And he concludes:

> There is another part of his character which I must present to your view, because it has respect to the times, and because I know that you had a reverence for his worth, and a just regard for his opinions. Ill indeed can the times bear the loss of such an affectionate patriot, and able guardian of the laws of his country. ... Gracious Heaven! Why hast thou at this critical hour, deprived us of so able and zealous a friend to our assaulted constitution?[84]

'In the midst of this happy period of our history', Carlyle continues, 'which for a century past has been such as cannot be paralleled in any country under the sun' – when, in other words, Britain and Britons never had it so good – the 'enemy of human happiness' interfered 'to mar so promising a harvest':

> Some evil spirits, taking advantage of the late occurrences in a neighbouring country, have endeavoured of late, by sophistry and false arguments, by misrepresentation and lies, by raising fears and hopes that are equally groundless: By traducing all the superior orders of men, by every bold and insidious art, that malice could invent, and scurrilous tongues and pens express, to subvert the minds of a peaceful and happy people, and to persuade them, that they now are and have long been under a sad delusion: that their condition is totally the reverse of what they have experienced it to be; that they have no constitution of government, that they enjoy no liberty; that their equal laws are oppressive and unjust; that though the poor man enjoys the fruits of his labour undisturbed as he ought to do, yet the rich [man] has no right to what has been acquired by labour of his forefathers; and that even our mild and virtuous king, who holds his throne no less by the love and affection of his subjects, than by the law of the land, is an Usurper and a Tyrant.[85]

'And what is the purpose and design of all this false representation?' Carlyle asks. He supplies the answer in terms that would not have disgraced a colonialist like Rhodes in a future age:

> It is not, as they give out, merely to correct abuses in government, or to amend any defects that may be in the constitution, No, no. These objects require no such violent means for their accomplishment. These are subjects of a parliamentary reform, whenever they are of moment enough to deserve its attention, and lead to no opportunity of mischief. No, no, their design is, though concealed from the simple and the weak among them, yet avowed by the master spirits, to excite the minds of the people to commotion, to tumult, to revolt and rebellion, that they may lay in ruins the goodly fabric of this government, the work of ages, the envy of all the nations of the world, which so happily unites the possession of all the rights of men, with national prosperity; and by means of which at this hour, over all the world, a citizen of Britain wherever he comes, is treated with distinguished respect, as a being of a superior order.[86]

The sermon ends with Carlyle issuing a stark warning 'to take heed and beware! To beware of those lying spirits who would seduce you to your ruin.' And, he asks: 'Who are they? And what are their means for accomplishing their boasted designs?' –

> It would be improper, from this place [the pulpit], to give them the harshest epithets they deserve; but surely they are not the most enlightened and wise, the most liberal and disinterested, the most sober and industrious members of society.[87]

A sentence of epic proportion brings Carlyle's tirade to a grandstand finish:

> And what are their means for accomplishing their designs? They have none, but either a foreign force, which would at once turn the rage of every Briton against them, or following the example so lately set before them by that very foreign enemy on whose aid they can rely, to raise an ignorant, an unruly and desperate mob, which all great cities can furnish, who, having nothing to lose, delight in scenes of riot and confusion; and with them, as with an engine that has no will or direction of its own, to perpetrate their wicked purposes, and through rapine, havock and blood, to overturn religion, law, and the ancient constitution, that, under pretence of a free democracy, they may acquire dominion and wealth to themselves.[88]

In the third and last of his overtly political sermons, *The Love of Our Country Explained and Enforced* (1797), Carlyle again confronts the threats he perceives to national stability. Interestingly, he dedicates the published version to 'Her Grace, Elizabeth, Duchess of Buccleuch, at whose desire it is published'. In the minutes of the first General Convention of Societies of the Friends of the People for 13 December 1792 a delegate ('Mr Drummond') had informed the Convention that

> one of the most amiable female characters in the whole aristocracy of Scotland, *viz.* the Duchess of Buccleuch, had the other week discharged her haberdasher, paid him his account, and informed him that he would get no more of her employment because he had joined an association of the Friends of the People.[89]

The Duchess's husband, the third Duke of Buccleuch,[90] was a close friend of Henry Dundas and an enthusiastic supporter of the Pitt regime. Buccleuch would turn out to be a key player in advising both Dundas and Pitt in the creation of a Scottish militia in the same year as Carlyle's sermon.

Once more Carlyle takes his text from the Old Testament, this time the famous words of the AV from *Psalm CXXXVII*, 5. 6: *If I forget thee, O! Jerusalem, let my right hand forget its cunning. If I do not remember thee, let my tongue cleave to the roof of my mouth; if I prefer not Jerusalem to my chief joy.* The reason behind the choice of text is explained:

> Happy had it been for them if the same passionate love for their country had, in due time, made them listen to the voice of the prophets, who had so long called them to repentance, or had inspired them with zeal and courage, in defence of that constitution in church and state, the overthrow of which they now so pathetically deplore.[91]

The contemporary application of the passage is obvious:

> That we may not be reduced to the same wretched condition, the being obliged to lament the evils which by wise and manly conduct we might have prevented; that we may not fall into the deepest misery of the human mind, self-reproach and despair, is the object of this discourse.[92]

For Carlyle it is the same unvarying message that he grinds out:

> In what region of the world are the multitude of men, or have they ever been, so much the care and object of the state? Or have they ever enjoyed such an equal share of advantages,

in whatever can attract human wishes? In religion and liberty, in property and personal security, in all the enjoyments of life, in an open road to power and pre-eminence, by superior talents and virtues? In what portion of the habitable globe, or in what period of time, shall you find the annals of any country so little loaded with oppression, or stained with blood, as the history of Great Britain, since the Glorious Revolution.[93]

'Who then', he asks, 'is there among you who does not prize this happy government?': 'That the British isles may continue to be *a praise in the whole earth*, the wonder and envy of all nations!' –

> There are some ... it must be confessed, who deny that there is any such thing as public affection: and there are, no doubt, appearances which would lead us sometimes to suspect, that this antiquated virtue is now altogether lost and buried under selfishness an avarice.[94]

Carlyle calls the ring-leaders 'seducers of the multitude'.

More forcefully than in either of the other political sermons already considered here, he pleads that the public might allow ministers their trust and confidence to permit them to conduct the war for the purpose of securing a happy outcome:

> I ask no more than you readily bestow on every man, who is supposed to understand his own business better than you. I ask only of you that degree of confidence in the king's ministers, which you daily grant to the physician or the lawyer whom you employ. Be assured of it, that it is not their interest to protract a calamitous war. On the contrary, there is no safety, much less honour, for them, if they miscarry in the great object of war, which is an honourable peace. For if it is not honourable, it can neither be safe nor lasting.[95]

Carlyle attacks the pacifists and traitors in our midst who would end the war no matter the cost:

> Let me therefore pray you to beware of those who are clamorous for peace at any rate, and on any conditions. Who are they do you think, who are loudest in this cry? Are they not those who first pretended to be friends of the people; and who, being discovered in their traitorous designs, changed their plan into opposition to the war at its commencement, that their intrigues might have their full scope? Are they not the seditious, who, after sowing the seeds of French principles, intended to overturn the government, and introduce revolutionary anarchy among you?[96]

The sermon he entitles *The Love of Our Country* ends on a dramatic note. It is March 1797 and Carlyle, who expertly knows how to second-guess his congregation's thoughts and feelings, rises to the occasion:

> This great nation [France], for so many reasons our unrelenting foe, is openly preparing for an invasion of these realms; and recent events have demonstrated, that it is possible fort them to effectuate their purpose. They have already made an attempt on our sister kingdom, but were happily dispersed by the same storm that kept our fleets in port. With the malice of infernal friends, they effected a landing on a part of the coast of Britain, with no other design, it would seem, than to infect us with the contagion of their flagitious crimes. These facts demonstrate, that they may evade the vigilance of our navy, and make good a landing. For this event it is that we ought to be prepared.[97]

Postscript

1. From Alexander Wilson's poem, 'Address to the Synod of Glasgow and Ayr' (1792)[98]

>   The power of clergy, wylie tykes,
>   Is unco fast declining;
>   And courtiers' craft, like snaw aff dykes,
>   Melts when the sun is shining;
>   And Monarchy, wi' cruel paw,
>   Her dying pains is gnawing;
>   While Democracy, trig and braw,
>   Is through a' Europe crawing
>   Fu' crouse this day.

2. From James Kennedy's poem, 'Treason, or not Treason. Dedicated to The Majesty of the People' (1795)[99]

>   George Guelph the Third, to you I call!
>   Slight not advice in season:
>   Remember Charley Stuart's Fall —
>   Kings *can* commit High Treason!
>   And trust me George a sim'lar fate
>   Will on a sim'lar conduct wait;
>   Bold British hearts you can't retain
>   By muzzles, or oppression's chain.
>
>   See, George, in terrible array,
>   A country's wrongs assemble!
>   Let Courtiers who on Monarchs prey,
>   With guileful lips, dissemble;
>   While I, who live by honest toil,
>   Nor dread your frown, nor court your smile,
>   *Perhaps* more anxious for your weal,
>   Ring in your ears A WARNING PEAL.
>
>   List to a suff'ring People's cries —
>   Resign the sword of terror:
>   Spurn *evil Counsellors, Crimps*,[100] and *Spies*,
>   Who lead you into error.
>   Not all the *sycophants* at Court
>   Can guard the land, the State support!
>   The People *can*, and *they alone* —
>   *Their favour* lost, *your pow'r* is gone.

Alexander 'Jupiter' Carlyle in old age, by Archibald Skirving.

8

America

It is indeed very likely that some of you will blame me, because I have told you the truth. You will cry out, that I have departed from the usual track of sermons; that I should have preached on faith and repentance; that I have not a thorough understanding of my subject; that I meddle with things that are above me; and that I am not a friend to my country. And was I to publish this sermon, those who feel themselves pinched by its doctrine may hire some abject and prostitute scribbler to varnish over their oppression with specious colours.

Reverend William Thom: *The Task-Masters* [aka *Seasonable Advice to the Landholders and Farmers in Scotland* (1770) (see below), also in Thom's *Works* (1799), 227.]

I am not fond of National Animositys but I feel and indulge the Indignation of the present Case with much Satisfaction. Every well meaning Clergyman ought to stuff his Sermon with it on the approaching Fast Day. And to tell the Americans in Particular how they were spared by Providence while their wishes were in appearance sincere for the Redress of Grievances, but how they and their mighty Friends have been scourged since they rejected the Redress of Grievances to become Traytors to their King and their Fellow Citizens and the Instruments in the Hands of Inveterate Ennemys [sic] *for the Destruction of Both.*

Letter of Adam Ferguson to William Eden (later 1st Baron Auckland), 2 January 1780, on the failure of the Carlisle Peace Commission, of which Eden was a member and Ferguson, though not a member, its secretary.[1]

Key authors and sermons

Reverend Dr John Witherspoon (1723-94), President, College of New Jersey (formerly minister of the Laigh Church, Paisley); signer of the Declaration of American Independence and of the Articles of Confederation.

The Dominion of Providence over the Passions of Men. A Sermon preached at Princeton, on the 17th of May, 1776. Being the General Fast appointed by the Congress through the United Colonies. To which is added, An Address to the Natives of Scotland residing in America. By John Witherspoon, D.D. President of the College of New-Jersey.

Philadelphia: Robert Aitken, printer and bookseller, M.DCC.LXXVI. [1776] [*WJW*, 3, 17-46]

Reverend William Thom (1710-90), minister of Govan.

Seasonable Advice to the Landholders and Farmers in Scotland. A sermon, on Exod. iii. 7, 8. ... By a minister of the Gospel.
Edinburgh: printed by J. Robertson ... 1770.

The Revolt of the Ten Tribes. A Sermon, preached in the Church of Govan, on the Forenoon of the Public Fast, December 12th, 1776. By the Reverend William Thom, A.M. Minister of Govan.
Glasgow: Robert Chapman and Alexander Duncan, M.DCC.LXXVIII. [1778]

Achan's Trespass in the Accursed Thing considered. A Sermon, preached in the Church of Govan, on the Public Fast. February 26th, 1778. By the Reverend William Thom, A.M. Minister of Govan.
Glasgow: James Duncan, M.DCC.LXXVIII. [1778] [reprinted, Edinburgh, 1779]

From whence come Wars? An Enquiry into the Origin, with a View of the Progress and Effects, of War. A Sermon, preached in the Church of Govan, on the Public Fast, February 9th, 1779. By the Reverend William Thom, A.M. Minister of Govan.
Glasgow: Robert Chapman and Alexander Duncan, M.DCC.LXXXII. [1782]

Reverend Dr George Campbell (1719-96), principal of Marischal College, Aberdeen.

The Nature, Extent, and Importance, of the Duty of Allegiance: a Sermon, preached at Aberdeen, December 12, 1776, being the Fast Day appointed by the King, on account of the Rebellion in America. The Second Edition, with Notes and Illustrations. By George Campbell, D.D. Principal of Marischal College.
Aberdeen: J. Chalmers and C°. MDCCLXXVIII. [1778] [first ed. published in Aberdeen, without apparatus, in 1777]

Reverend Dr Alexander Carlyle (1722-1805), minister of Inveresk.

The Justice and Necessity of the War with our American Colonies Examined. A Sermon, Preached at Inveresk, December 12. 1776, being the Fast-Day appointed by the King, on Account of The American Rebellion. By Alexander Carlyle, D.D. Minister of Inveresk, and Almoner to his Majesty.
Edinburgh: J. Murray, London, and J. Dickson, Edinburgh. M,DCC,LXXVII. [1777]

The two great revolutions of the eighteenth century may legitimately be regarded as on the one hand the seminal manifestation of the age of the Enlightenment, and on the other as its inevitable consequence. Both events presaged cataclysmic change, change that would spare no one. Republics replaced monarchies, colonies gave way to independent autonomous legislatures, the ancient idea of democracy began to be dusted down and re-conceived as something consonant with 'modern' (i.e. more appropriate) interpretations of government and governance — and a new word, the 'people', *entered the vocabulary as a powerful force to be reckoned with, yet still far from being unchallenged. Into this cauldron of new politics there was hurled the catalyst of unbelief, disbelief and scepticism that, to a degree, substituted Reason for God.*

But, in the end, it was religion that arguably suffered the most prodigious shock to its foundations with the progress and ultimate resolution of the American, and even much more fundamentally and more violently, the French revolution. The terms of the constitution of the United States ensured that there would be no official religion of the state and, of course, the National Assembly in Paris would entirely sweep religion away for a generation or more in France, leaving its practitioners wide open to persecution and, on occasion, brutal death. If, in an admittedly tenuous way, the war in America was intellectually a war of religion, or more precisely, a war of Presbyterianism versus Episcopacy, it certainly didn't seem like that to the majority of the combatants.

As these sermons show, the American war of independence, one of the deadliest and most enduring to be fought by Britain in the eighteenth century, provoked a divided reaction from the Church of Scotland and from individual ministers. There was never any chance that it would be otherwise, since the nature of the American crisis was bound from the start to elicit strong differences of view throughout the regions of Britain. Pulpits in Scottish towns and cities echoed with diverse political opinions in a way that has rarely been experienced before or since. Easily the greatest sermon preached in the course of the protracted war was, however, preached in America by a Scottish evangelical minister who in a former career had been an acknowledged leader of the Kirk's Popular party.

Finally, it is worth observing that when the quirky and disputatious Professor John Anderson of the University of Glasgow in a long rambling letter of 26 August 1793 petitioned George Washington to show him favour, he begins by establishing his credentials, indicating that he is 'personally known' to 'The Revd Doctor Wotherspoon [sic], to Doctor [Charles] Nisbet, and to a great variety of persons from this Country, now settled in America'.[2] That Anderson is indulging in blatant name-dropping is obvious, but that he chooses to name two ministers of the Church of Scotland who emigrated to America is surely something to ponder. Anderson ends his letter by prophesying that the 'madness of Britain and France' shown in the 'ruinous war' between them will only have the effect of increasing the 'power and wealth' of the United States 'by the emigration of multitudes of our best and most useful people'.

Scots loyalists and American patriots

What is now fashionably termed 'transatlantic studies' has over the past two decades or so become all the rage among historians. Many books and articles have been written under this general head and numerous biographies of some of the major figures of interest in both a Scottish and an American context have been, and continue to be published in Britain and the United States. This is to be welcomed in the light of the historic bond existing between the two nations that goes back to the years substantially before the revolutionary war when numerous Scots families began to make the long haul to the British colonies across the Atlantic ocean – or at least to make sojourning visits in an effort to get the feel for life there, in all its aspects, before deciding whether or not to commit themselves to more permanent arrangements. In the early days this was sometimes an imposed, but more usually it was a case of self-imposed exile, a process that gathered momentum for different reasons throughout the remaining years of the eighteenth century, and well into the nineteenth and twentieth centuries, then petering out only in the late 1950s, to be replaced by the much more selective 'brain drain', to an extent still with us – and perhaps set, as this is written (2017), to enter a new phase. It would be wrong, however, to conclude that Scots in America have always enjoyed the most amicable of relations with the indigenous residents.

Andrew Hook was one of the first transatlantic scholars to analyse the extent to which contemporary unpopularity of the *'Scotch'* became widespread in the course of the revolutionary period in America. In his influential *Scotland and America* (2nd. edition, 2008) Hook traces throughout the period of the war a steady deterioration in the status, standing and reputation of Scots immigrants, such that 'far from being the original opponents of the oppressive policy of the British government, the proclaimers and the successful defenders of American liberty, the framers of the Constitution, and the most powerful influence for everything good in the American way of life, [the Scots] were certainly the most unpopular national group in the colonies.'[3] One of the most extreme examples of that distrust of Scots and Scottishness was a statute passed by the Georgia Assembly in August 1782, declaring that 'the People of Scotland have in General Manifested a decided inimicality to the Civil Liberties of America and have contributed Principally to promote and Continue a Ruinous War, for the Purpose of Subjugating this and another Confederated State.'[4] Further, legend has it that it was only owing to the intervention of John Witherspoon and a lawyer from Fife, James Wilson, both 'signers', that the final version of what would become the Declaration of Independence would drop Thomas Jefferson's notorious reference in his original draft to 'Scotch and other foreign mercenaries who were being sent by the British government to invade and destroy us'.[5]

Deserved or not, the unfortunate image problem that would cling to Scottish settlers in revolutionary America was not going to be easily dispelled. It was certainly an issue that engaged John Witherspoon's attention eight years after he himself had responded to the call of America. In the greatest sermon of his life, *The Dominion of Providence over the Passions of Men,* delivered at Princeton on 17 May 1776 – a fast-day declared by Congress to be observed throughout the 'United Colonies' (as the putative nation was known until changed by Congress to the 'United States' on 9 September) – Witherspoon curtly abandons any reservations he might previously have entertained regarding the introduction of politics from the pulpit.[6] In Paisley, ten years before he sailed for America, he had condemned the practice: in 1758 he had taught his Laigh Church congregation that 'ministers take care to avoid officiously inter-meddling in civil matters'.[7] Now, in a different setting in an altogether different world, where his American *persona* had evolved into part-time minister, part-time journalist, part-time higher education administrator and not so part-time politician, any such quibbles were laid aside. Yet Witherspoon cannot easily forget those far-off days and he quotes from a sermon he had preached in Paisley, also in 1758, which puts him in mind of the present circumstances; that it was persecution for their faith that had driven the Puritan brethren from England to seek refuge in America. 'Was not' he asks, 'the accuser of the brethren, who stirs up their enemies, thus taken in his own craftiness, and his kingdom shaken by the very means which he employed to establish it?'[8] It is a delicious irony Witherspoon, *qua* American patriot, savours to the full.

In August 1774 Witherspoon had written an essay, *Thoughts on American Liberty*, in which he submitted a number of proposals for the consideration of the meeting of the First Continental Congress to be held in Philadelphia in the following month. These included a recommendation to Congress 'To profess ... our loyalty to the King, and our backwardness to break our connection with Great Britain, if we are not forced by their unjust impositions.' He provides a clear foretaste of what might come to be expected of him in affirming the colonists' rights:

> The Congress is, properly speaking, the representative of the great body of the people of North America. ... There is not the least reason as yet, to think that either the king, the parliament, or even the people of Great-Britain, have been able to enter into the great principles of universal liberty, or are willing to hear the discussion of the point of right, without prejudice. ... To declare, not only that we esteem the claim of the British parliament to be illegal and unconstitutional, but that we are firmly determined never to submit to it, and do deliberately prefer war with all its horrors, and even extermination itself to slavery, rivetted on us and our posterity.[9]

Witherspoon's biographer, V. L. Collins, believes this essay – his 'first known writing on the American controversy' – 'marks the completion' of his 'transformation into an American'.[10] Maybe so, but there is also a strong case for arguing that it represents only the beginning of the transformation process that was completed with the *Dominion of Providence* sermon.

The text chosen by Witherspoon for his sermon was from *Psalms* 76, 10: '*Surely the Wrath of Man shall praise thee; the remainder of Wrath shalt thou restrain*'. He had, he explains, chosen this theme since he believed it suited his purpose for this great 'national' occasion; that purpose being to declare that God's power is absolute and that man's 'disorderly passions' are ultimately under the control of divine providence. Divine providence extends to things of 'great moment', as well as to other lesser things including 'things seemingly most hurtful and destructive', and he then offers examples from history by way of illustration of how providence has intervened, referring to the Reformation, the Spanish Armada and, in the light of what is to come, most significantly of all the fact that both John Hampden and Oliver Cromwell 'had actually taken their passage in a ship for New England when by an arbitrary order of council they were compelled to remain at home'.[11] Depending on your point of view it was providence at work – or a quirk of fate.

The second section of his sermon is of greater interest to the historian. Here, Witherspoon applies the general principles he has developed earlier to 'our present situation', so as to 'illustrate and improve' his text, and 'to apply it more particularly to the present state of the American colonies and the plague of war'. First, he reports on the progress of the war in language that would not be out of place in the contemporary Philadelphia newspapers and magazines he was now getting used to:

> It would be a criminal inattention not to observe the singular interposition of Providence hitherto, in behalf of the American colonies. ... Some important victories in the south have been gained with so little loss, that enemies will probably think it has been

dissembled; as many, even of ourselves thought, till time rendered it undeniable. But these were comparatively of small moment. The signal advantage we have gained by the evacuation of Boston, and the shameful flight of the army and navy of Britain, was brought about without the loss of a man.[12]

He then reverts to the more conventional language of the jeremiad, citing the stirring words from the Old Testament story of David and Goliath – the allegory is obvious – in support of his firm conviction in the power of God, the Lord of Hosts, 'great in might and strong in battle'. At this stage in his sermon he seems to relax, and the language he now employs is rhetorically different, less stilted and more conversational than before. Here we can almost picture the preacher leaning over the pulpit, bible in hand, Billy Graham style, looking the congregation straight in the eye:

> You are all my witnesses, that this is the first time of my introducing any political subject into the pulpit. At this season, however, it is not only lawful but necessary, and I willingly embrace the opportunity of declaring my opinion without any hesitation, that the cause in which America is now in arms, is the cause of justice, of liberty, and of human nature.[13]

Dare one say it: though delivered from the pulpit, it is almost the rhetoric of *Common Sense*, the self-same direct style of near-conversational prose that Tom Paine had used to such great effect in the very pamphlet, a section of which Witherspoon takes great exception to in a footnote to the published version of his sermon.[14] What he calls the 'true and proper hinge' of the war with Britain is his insistence that no one would voluntarily give up 'his estate, person, and family to the disposal of his neighbour', even though he was able to choose the best master, so that 'for these colonies to depend wholly upon the legislature of Great Britain, would be like many other oppressive connections, injury to the master, and ruin to the slave.' Ironically, the behaviour of the British government has only made us *more* united and our 'public spirit' is so strong among us, that 'we have much more reason to be thankful for its vigour and prevalence, than to wonder at the few appearances of dishonesty or disaffection.' But, he continues, it is vital we remain united and you should be cautioned 'against the usual causes of division'; and he supplies examples of what might arise in that regard. 'Firmness and patience' will be needed, and he cites the Old Testament once more, this time from the book of the prophet *Samuel*: '*Be of good courage, and let us behave ourselves valiantly for our people and for the cities of our God, and let the Lord do that which is good in his sight*'.

Signalling he is nearing the climax of his sermon, Witherspoon invokes three broad principles, constituting 'exhortations to duty'; these principles relate religion to the great cause in which all are engaged – first professing 'he is the best friend to American liberty, who is most sincere and active in promoting true and undefiled religion' and that 'whoever is an avowed enemy to God, I scruple not to call him an enemy to his country'. This first principle includes 'the concern which every good man ought to take in the national character and manners, and the means which he ought to use for promoting public virtue; and bearing down impiety and vice'. In view of their special responsibilities, some have an unusual duty to conform to these needs, including 'magistrates, ministers, parents, heads of families, and those whom age has rendered venerable'. The second 'exhortation to duty' he directs to 'all who are not called to go into the field to apply themselves with the utmost diligence to works of industry'. Thirdly, and finally, Witherspoon recalls an exhortation from his Scottish past: 'In the last place, suffer me to recommend to you frugality in your families and every other article of expence.'

Witherspoon's message is now crystal-clear. Even the cherished goal of American liberty cannot be held to be somehow 'exchangeable' with the Christian regeneration of our American souls; the fulfilment of one is ultimately dependent on the spiritual sacrifice of the other. Indeed, the two concepts are not just inter-dependent but virtually synonymous. As an agent of God's ministry of reconciliation, it falls to him to deliver the Christian Evangelical message of salvation. It is precisely the same message with which he had charged young Mr Davidson in Paisley Abbey all those years ago,[15] in several of his other Scottish sermons, and, of course, in the *Practical Treatise on Regeneration* (1764): Christ's injunction as related in John's gospel – '*Except a man be born again, he cannot see the kingdom of God.*[16] This time, however, the 'charge' is not addressed to an individual, or even to the assembled Princeton congregation at large, but to the entire emergent nation, the 'confederacy of the colonies', which now, as a committed and involved American himself, he addresses jointly and severally. His sermon concludes with these words of benediction:

> God grant that in America true religion and civil liberty may be inseparable, and that the unjust attempts to destroy the one, may in the issue tend to the support and establishment of both.[17]

Yet John Witherspoon, too, would bear witness to conventional hostility towards Scots in America. Perhaps unsurprisingly, his American 'conversion' failed to engender universal approval. Writing in his diary in July 1777, Ezra Stiles of Yale[18], a Congregationalist, took serious issue with Witherspoon's attempts to link American strivings for liberty with aspects of Scottish history. Gideon Mailer notes : 'For Stiles the responsibility for the bloody battle that America fought with Britain lay with nationalistic Scots such as Witherspoon.' In reality, Stiles maintained, it was *'Scotchmen'* in America who had 'used the ensuing turmoil to facilitate their rise to prominence and then worked to reconcile America's independence with specific interests in Scotland.' It was *'Scotchmen'* in the British government who had provoked the war in the first instance. According to Stiles:

> The Dr [Witherspoon] is a politician. We may use him as far as he is for America—but scorn to be awed by him into an ignominious Silence on the subject of Scots Perfidy & tyranny & Enmity to America.[19]

Back in Britain, too, Witherspoon's seemingly traitorous conduct towards his homeland by no means went unnoticed.[20]

Stiles, of course, is here referring to comments by Witherspoon in his *Address to the Natives of Scotland residing in America*. Until 1788, when they were first published in London as separate pamphlets, *Dominion of Providence* was customarily bound in with an Appendix, the *Address*.[21] For all the undoubted distinction of the famous jeremiad, the accompanying *Address* merits consideration on its own account, if only because it reinforces and confirms the unfortunate image then attaching in at least some colonies to

Americans of Scottish provenance. Witherspoon explains:

> It has given me no little uneasiness, to hear the word SCOTCH used as a term of reproach in the American controversy; which could only be on the supposition, that strangers of that country are more universally opposed to the liberties of America, than those who were born in South-Britain or Ireland. I am sensible that this has been done, in some newspapers and contemptible anonymous publications, in a manner that was neither warranted by truth, nor directed by prudence. There are many natives of Scotland in this country, whose opposition to the unjust claims of Great Britain has been as early and uniform, founded upon as rational and liberal principles, and therefore, likely to be as lasting, as that of any set of men whatever.[22]

As for Great Britain itself, he continues, time has shown that it is 'very disputable' if there is 'any such ground for the distinction between *Scotch* and *English* in this subject at all.' He does not propose, he says, to say much on the subject, supposing some of the assertions to be true for some colonies, but *if* they were to some extent true, what, he wonders, caused the outrage. The first and 'radical cause' was, he believed, the baleful influence of John Wilkes and his supporters evinced in 'many writings and news-paper dissertations' and in 'one or two colonies', in some of their 'most respectable meetings', that 'manifested their attachment to him [Wilkes], and seemed to consider him as their friend and patron.' And in that regard, he singles out the notorious 'number XLV' [April 1763] of Wilkes' broadsheet, the *North Briton* – at least the first two numbers of which were reprinted in New York in 1769 six years after the date of their original publication in London – as 'the most offensive number of a worthless paper'.[23]

If the main purpose behind Witherspoon's *Address* is to seek to justify the 'necessity' of American independence and to paint a picture of America that will entice Scots residents to dispel any thoughts of returning to Scotland, his subsidiary aim is to try to convince his fellow Scots-Americans of the injustice, as he sees it, of the increasingly strident claim that they were somehow disloyal to the American cause. Another motive for publishing the pamphlet is to show that American anti-Scottish sentiment, where he acknowledges it exists, was 'closely related to identical English feelings'.[24] That latter point was not to excuse Scots loyalism, but to seek to explain it by setting it in its proper, that is, a fairer context.

Despite Witherspoon's protestations, however, there is little doubt that loyalism among Scots in the American colonies was far from uncommon.[25] As Devine has put it: 'The fact that Witherspoon from Paisley was one of the most eloquent speakers favouring American resistance to imperial authority, or that John Paul Jones from Kirkcudbright became America's first naval war hero, did not weigh much in the overall balance.' And he cites a modern analyst of loyalist claims on the British government after the war showing that Scots claimants accounted for almost 37 per cent of all those made by persons born outside America, 'a much higher proportion than the Scottish-born share of the colonial population.'[26] More anecdotally, it remains true that even some of the several individuals who came over with Witherspoon – notably Hugh Simm, a Paisley weaver, whose letters to his brother back home form an impressive body of evidence tending to the same conclusion – remained loyalist to the end, Simm himself returning to Scotland in his later years where he was rewarded with a government pension.[27]

The Scottish Enlightenment and the American crisis

In his *Life of Samuel Johnson* James Boswell records a meeting of unusual interest that took place in May 1776 over dinner in the elegant London home of the Dilly brothers, Edward and Charles, literally above their bookshop at The Poultry, near the Mansion House. The Dillys' bookselling business enjoyed a flourishing export trade with numerous proprietors in Philadelphia, Boston and New York, including with the émigré Scots bookmen, Robert Bell and Robert Aitken.[28] Charles, the younger brother, made a short visit to America in 1764 in the course of which he visited Philadelphia. The Dilly brothers were wholeheartedly on the American side during the war, though their motives for being so were probably not entirely ideological. The Dillys' dinner guests that evening, apart from Johnson and Boswell, included one Arthur Lee; it happened that also in the company was none other than the charismatic John Wilkes, an ardent but reckless supporter of the American cause. Lee, writes Boswell, was 'not only a *patriot*, but an *American*': he was, he says, 'an old companion of mine when he studied physick at Edinburgh'.[29]

In reality, Arthur Lee, an old Etonian, was an American spy who used his position as London agent for Massachusetts to act as a conduit for the relaying of sensitive information to the Committee of Secret Correspondence of the Continental Congress.[30] In that guise he corresponded with other American spies there, including with the notorious Charles-Guillaume-Frédéric Dumas, a confidante of Benjamin Franklin's from their days in the Netherlands. With Franklin and Silas Deane, Lee would later go to France to negotiate a treaty and solicit aid for the 'glorious cause'.[31] Boswell notes that when Wilkes was identified in the company on that summer evening in London, Lee 'had some difficulty to restrain himself', and from that point on Johnson and Wilkes took turns in making jokes at Boswell's expense, mainly about the Scots and Scotland. Both men would have appreciated the irony of the occasion from Lee's point of view since the creator of the *North Briton* had inspired and fomented contemporary unpopularity of Scotsmen and all things Scottish, not just in England, but also in America – as John Witherspoon was, of course, endeavouring to downplay in *An Address to the Natives of Scotland*.

In the longer term, however, this anti-Scottish prejudice would prove no laughing matter. A few months after his dinner date, Lee wrote a secret letter to Dumas enclosing 'several pamphlets … on the American question'. One of these is *'Rights of Great Britain &c.'* which, Lee informs Dumas, is 'full of the grossest falsehoods', including a list of 'bounties' granted on American produce which the pamphlet credits to the generosity of the British Parliament. Lee, however, astutely seeing through the ploy, correctly divines that 'those bounties were given for their [Britain's] own interests only.' In support of that contention, Lee cites 'Dr. Smith, a Scotchman, and an enemy to American rights', who, 'in his late laboured and long-expected book on the Wealth of Nations' made it plain that 'Whatever expense Great Britain has hitherto laid out in maintaining this dependency, has really been laid out in order to support their monopoly.' And he further cites Smith's book on the same bounties issue:

> Speaking of the debt occurred last war, he [Smith] says: "This whole expense is in reality a bounty, which has been given in order to support a monopoly. The pretended purpose of

it was to encourage the manufactures, and to increase the commerce of *Great Britain*."[32] The operation of this monopoly against the Colony, he states thus: "The monopoly of the Colony trade, therefore, like all the other mean and malignant expedients of the mercantile system, depresses the industry of all other countries, but *chiefly that of the Colonies*."[33]

*

When you write to the Congress it would be well, I think, to mention that as all the evils have been produced by *Scotch* counsel, and those people prosecute the business with more rancour and enmity, a distinction ought to be made between the treatment of them and other people, when made prisoners.[34]

Arthur Lee's letter is, of course, using as his source and authority the newly-published *Wealth of Nations* to prove a point: that in reality the Americans have been duped and deceived by the statistics presented in pamphlets such as the anonymous and semi-official *Rights of Great Britain Asserted* (in reality the work of James Macpherson of Ossian fame), which purports to show how generous the mother-country has been to her colonies, when, as Lee finds Smith has proved, they indicate nothing of the sort. Smith's cerebral, unprejudiced analysis of mercantile policy in relation to the British colonies shows that the use of so-called 'bounties' is actually to the advantage of Britain's own manufacturing industries and operates *against*, not *in* the interest of the colonies.

Setting aside its sinister reference to how Scots prisoners might be singled out for especially harsh treatment after capture, Lee's important letter, with its reference to the frankness of Smith's unbiased critique of just one aspect of British mercantile policy towards her colonies in America, conveniently prompts a necessarily brief consideration of how three of the greatest names in the Scottish Enlightenment – Smith, Hume and Ferguson – regarded the American question. First, however, to understand the basis of Smith's approach to the underlying problem of America we need to examine how his views were at odds with those of his old mentor at Glasgow, Francis Hutcheson.

An Ulsterman resident in Scotland, Hutcheson used his personal experience of Britain's treatment of the less fortunate areas of the British isles to inform many of the principles enunciated in his *System*, including the concept of the state of nature, as propounded by Locke, and the central notion of a 'mutual agreement or contract between the governors thus constituted and the people, the former obliging themselves to a faithful administration of the powers vested in them for the common interest, and the later [sic] obliging themselves to obedience'.[35] Above all, Hutcheson's political philosophy, in Fate Norton's words, 'provided a foundation for revolution and independence'[36] in the specific circumstances of a colony in relation to its mother-country; such that if 'anything oppressive' were attempted by the mother-country towards that colony, 'and the colony be able to subsist as a sovereign state by itself ... the colony is not bound to remain subject any longer: 'tis enough that it remain a friendly state'.[37]

The extent to which Thomas Jefferson may have been influenced by prescient remarks of Hutcheson like these in drafting the early versions of the Declaration has doubtless been exaggerated (certainly by Wills among others). In the last analysis, any debt Jefferson owed Hutcheson can only be speculated upon. What is not in doubt, on the other hand, is that the Reverend Francis Alison – another Ulsterman, a Glasgow graduate, 'Old Light' Presbyterian and unwavering disciple of Hutcheson – disseminated his mentor's thoughts in the philosophy classes he conducted, first, at his classical school at New London, Chester County, Pennsylvania, then at the College and Academy of Philadelphia (the forerunner of the University of Pennsylvania), where Alison would serve as vice-provost under Provost William Smith. Smith was an Aberdeen graduate with distinctly episcopal aspirations, and ultimately Benjamin Franklin's *bête noir*.[38] On the basis of such evidence Fate Norton arrived at a remarkable conclusion: to conceive of the influence of Hutcheson's thought, as disseminated by Francis Alison, as nothing less than a contributory *cause* of the war of independence.[39]

For Adam Smith, of course, what was of greatest interest were the economic aspects of the American dispute as they affected Britain's colonial policy as a whole. In the *Wealth of Nations* he devotes a good deal of space to America. Hugh Blair famously complained that *too much* space, virtually a monograph, had been allocated to the problem and to the options that lay open to the British government in tackling it:

> You enter into a description about the measures we ought at present to take with respect to America, giving them a representation etc. which I wish had been omitted, because it is too much like a publication for the present moment. In subsequent editions when public measures come to be settled, these pages will fall to be omitted or altered.[40]

Smith argued that there was 'not the least probability that the British constitution would be hurt by the union of Great Britain with her colonies':

> That constitution, on the contrary, would be completed by it, and seems to be imperfect without it. The assembly which deliberates and decides concerning the affairs of every part of empire, in order to be properly informed, ought certainly to have representatives from every part of it.[41]

His hypothesis of appropriate colonial rule envisaged a union of the kind that might eventually lead to the 'produce of America' exceeding that accumulated by British taxation, so that 'the seat of the empire would then naturally remove itself to that part of the empire which contributed most to the general defence and support of the whole.'[42] Smith's remarks had behind them much more than the immediacy of the American crisis. Despite the year of publication of *Wealth of Nations* coinciding with the Declaration of Independence, Smith was addressing his thoughts beyond the immediate concerns of the on-going war and, even, of the American crisis in its entirety. As Skinner points out, in articulating them he was really addressing a *British* problem. Smith's great work of genius is not, even in part, about the American revolution at all. In *Wealth of Nations* Smith argues the need for a different revolution: effectively, one can argue, a new kind of British revolution that would embrace rejection of the colonial system *in toto*, dismissing it as a 'project altogether unfit for a nation of shopkeepers; but extremely fit for a nation whose government is influenced by shopkeepers'.[43]

Hume, too, had been deeply sceptical of Britain's position in the American crisis. But, as ever, Hume the moral and political philosopher should not be confused with Hume the historian. As early as 1741, when aged 30 he had published the essay *Of the First Principles of Government*, Hume had considered the 'surprising' fact of 'the easiness with which the many are governed by the few', and confronted the issue of how that had come about. The usual reply to that question, he had concluded, was two-fold, *viz.* (i) 'interest', by which he means the general advantage in having a particular kind of government in place, and (ii) 'right' – especially 'right to Power and right to Property'. In the same essay he dismisses as 'dangerous novelties' a form of democratic government that, conceding the popular vote, 'would soon reduce it to a pure republic; and, perhaps, to a republic of no inconvenient form':

> For though the people, collected in a body like the Roman tribes, be quite unfit for government, yet when dispersed in small bodies, they are more susceptible both of reason and order; the force of popular currents and tides is, in a great measure, broken; and the public interest may be pursued with some method and constancy.[44]

But, he concludes, that last hypothesis is unlikely to become a reality. His words explain something of Hume's transatlantic appeal, since in the same essay he refers to a 'noted author' who 'has made property the foundation of all government'; this is probably James Harrington, the author of *The Commonwealth of Oceana* (1656), who argued that balance of power was ultimately dependent on balance of property. And, of course, it was Harrington who is regarded by Pocock and some other modern American political historians as 'the main figure in the Anglo-American version of the republican tradition' – though Hume finds Harrington 'carrying the matter too far'.[45]

For Hume the historian, the American question was simply incapable of resolution to the satisfaction of the British government. In February 1766 he writes a long letter to the Earl of Hertford expressing his optimism that the repeal of the Stamp Act, already carried in the House of Commons by a large majority, will similarly go through the House of Peers.[46] On 8 May – the Stamp Act was repealed on 20 March – he informs Hertford that he has had access to the terms of an 'Express from New York to the board of Trade, which is kept secret and contains the most interesting Articles of Intelligence':

> I was told, that the general Assembly of the Provinces ... voted that the Parliament of England had no Right to impose on them any Taxes whatsoever; that they had no Right to make any Laws for them where they found their advantage; that they were determin'd to maintain these Principles to the last Drop of their Blood; and that the whole Militia and Arms be carefully inspected, in order to maintain the Colonies in a State of Defence against all Invaders.[47]

And Hume adds: 'It does not seem probable that the Repeal of the Stamp Act will suffice.' Becoming ever more cynical regarding the American question with the passage of time, and by then beginning to be weighed down by what would prove his terminal illness, Hume writes his best-known letter on the subject to his London publisher, William Strahan, on 26 October 1775:

> We hear that some of the Ministers have propos'd in Council, that both Fleet and Army be withdrawn from America, and these Colonists be left entirely to themselves. I wish I had been a Member of His Majesty's Cabinet Council, that I might have seconded this Opinion. ... Arbitrary Power can extend its oppressive Arm to the Antipodes; but a

limited Government can never long be upheld at a distance, even where no Disgusts have interven'd: Much less, where such violent Animosities have taken place. ... Let us, therefore, lay aside all Anger; shake hands, and part Friends. Or if we retain any anger, let it only be against ourselves for our past Folly; and against that wicked Madman, Pitt; who has reduced us to our present Condition.[48]

But Strahan would have none of this, and speedily replied to Hume on 30 October to the effect that he differed *'toto caelo'* from him on the subject of America, expressing the conventional wisdom that he was 'for keeping them [the colonists] subordinate to the British Legislature, and their Trade in a reasonable Degree, subservient to the Interest of the Mother Country'.[49] On 13 November, refusing to let go, Hume replies to Strahan saying he could not agree with him 'in your hopes of subduing, and what is more difficult, of governing America'. In 'eight or nine years' France could not subdue and govern the small island of Corsica, 'which is within a day's sailing'; and he adds –

> But the worst Effect of the Loss of America, will not be the Detriment to our Manufactures, which will be a mere trifle, or to our Navigation, which will not be considerable; but to the Credit and Reputation of Government, which has already but too little Authority. You will probably see a Scene of Anarchy and Confusion open'd at home, the best Consequence of which is a settled Plan of arbitrary Power; the worst, total Ruin and Destruction.[50]

As an afterword, it cannot be ignored that alone among the great names of the Scottish Enlightenment, Adam Ferguson, consistently a government supporter, actually got to go to America. From June to November 1778 Ferguson was in America as secretary of a small team put together by Lord North and led by the fifth Earl of Carlisle with the aim of negotiating with the Continental Congress a cessation of hostilities. In principle, the Carlisle Peace Commission was authorised to grant concessions to the Americans that might in theory end the war. Before the commissioners were even in sight of America, however, Washington had been instructed by Congress not to grant them safe passage, let alone begin to discuss with them terms that inevitably excluded any possibility of outright American independence. It was a foregone conclusion that the peace commission would fail – and fail it did.

William Thom: advocate of emigration to America

Alexander Carlyle and William Thom were contemporaries at the University of Glasgow where they attended classes taught by Francis Hutcheson and his disciple, William Leechman. Carlyle describes Thom at that time as 'a Learn'd Man of a very particular tho' an Ingenious turn of Mind', who 'had Great Sway among us.' On the basis of that remark, and also because his presentation to Govan by the University of Glasgow (the patrons of Govan parish) had originally been opposed by the Presbytery, Landsman has been led to conclude that Thom had started out on his ministry as a Moderate, only later espousing the Popular party.[51] For two reasons, however, it seems unlikely that that was the case: first, although young Carlyle and his coterie were perhaps in awe of the much older Thom's *savoir faire*, it does not follow that they also aped his theological stance. More seriously, Landsman errs over the circumstances of Thom's presentation. It was not the 'parishioners', but the Presbytery who had opposed Thom's call. The General Assembly of 1747, having heard an appeal by the patrons against refusal on the part of the Presbytery of Glasgow to sustain the University's presentation of Thom as minister of Govan, 'reversed' the sentence and directed the Presbytery to proceed with the settlement 'according to the rules of the church'. In a footnote to his report of the case Morren makes it clear that the charge of Govan lay vacant for two years longer than it should have done on account of the patrons having originally offered a leet of two 'young men', 'after having indulged the parish with a hearing of four'. The settlement at Govan was not resolved until the meeting of the Assembly Commission in November, followed by a special meeting of the Synod in December at which a recalcitrant Presbytery was finally brought to heel and Thom's presentation allowed to proceed.[52]

On an unknown date in 1770 Thom preached a sermon before 'a congregation of farmers', which he later published in Edinburgh under the title *Seasonable Advice to the Landholders and Farmers in Scotland*. Or did he? Unusually, we are not told where the sermon was preached or the circumstances that led to its preaching. The sermon was included in Thom's collected *Works* (1799), published almost a decade after his death, but this time under the more arresting title, *The Task-Masters*, a term borrowed from scripture. Even by the standards of the time it is an extraordinarily long sermon, occupying eighty-two pages, which raises the possibility that the original pulpit version (assuming there *was* one) was preached over more than one service[53] and/or subsequently expanded into a literary text for publication purposes. Another possibility is that the wily Thom merely employed the device of a 'sermon' to get a number of important points across concerning a particular bee in his bonnet, in this instance the straitened circumstances of Scottish farmers and the related need, as he perceived it, to get them to consider an admittedly drastic solution to all their problems, *viz.* quitting Scotland altogether and emigrating to America. If so, it would not be the only time Thom had resorted to the device of a mock-sermon: he had done it the year before in *The Happiness of Dead Clergymen, provided they die in the Lord*, a spoof-sermon in the guise of a no-holds-barred satire on the disputatious professor of divinity at the University of Glasgow, Robert Traill.[54] Further, *Seasonable Advice* would by no means be the only time Thom would encourage emigration from Scotland to America, a topic on which, as we shall see, he shows a remarkable degree of informed knowledge.

The text from *Exodus* informing *Seasonable Advice*, aka *The Task-Masters*, is the famous passage in which God speaks to Moses, telling him that he has seen the 'affliction' of his people in Egypt and has heard 'their cry by reason of their taskmasters' and knows their sorrows. He will 'deliver them out of the hand of the Egyptians' and bring them out of that land, 'unto a land flowing with milk and honey'. In Thom's allegorical sermon the people of God are the oppressed farmers and the oppressive 'taskmasters' are no longer the Egyptians, but the 'pitying oppressors', the land-owners of Scotland whose 'exorbitant rents' have for years past compounded the 'misery' of those working the land in difficult conditions – and for meagre reward. Thom develops the old Bible story of making bricks without straw; its modern analogy is obvious, he says:

The question to the Israelites was, "Wherefore have ye not fulfilled your task, both yesterday and this day?" The question to our farmers is, Wherefore have ye not paid your Martinmas and your Whitsunday terms rent? When the Israelites could not furnish the tale of the bricks, they were beaten: Our farmers, when they cannot pay, if they be not beaten in a literal sense, are imprisoned and beaten with hunger; any thing they have is barbarously taken from them, and they are turned out and left to the mercy of the wide world.[55]

Displaying an impressive knowledge of contemporary rural economy and land management – as he does also in the unsigned *Letter of Advice to the Farmers, Land-Labourers, and Country Tradesmen* (1771) – Thom prompts his flock to recall that in the Bible story, at the end of the seven years of famine, 'when the whole land had become the property of Pharaoh', Joseph had decreed that 'the king should have the fifth part'. He compares the position of the exiled Israelites with the contemporary predicament of farmers in Scotland where, in calculating rents, account has to be taken of 'various circumstances', including quality of the land, and the degree of 'skill, toil and industry' on the part of the farmer, *etc*. And he concludes:

If we may judge by this rule, which appears to be equitable, it is undeniable, that, in many parts of Scotland, too high a rent is exacted, and that many industrious farmers are oppressed: By their utmost labour and industry they cannot live, though their industry entitles them not only to an insured livelihood, but to a certain profit over and above. This oppression was begun long ago, it hath been growing for a course of years; and is at this day risen to a very great height.[56]

But not all landholders are so unscrupulous. There exist men 'of prudence and humanity who suffer their tenants to live in tolerable ease'; but the number of such men is 'yearly decreasing'. Too often, landholders are 'incited by the workings of avarice' and employ managers whose sole aim is to fix 'the highest value on an estate that is to be sold, or a farm that is to be let', and their efforts are applauded 'for their good management'. Thom then goes into 'a few particulars' and in the process displays an insightful grasp of the facts. And it is at this point in the sermon that one becomes aware of the possibility that this is not really a sermon at all, but more a kind of manual of good practice. The slightly later *Letter of Advice* is couched in precisely the same didactic language. Thus, he adversely contrasts the contemporary situation in Scotland with conditions in England, and concludes that 'over all England', whereas the rent of cornfields 'is not more than two-ninths of their produce' – the rent of good fields in Norfolk, for example, is typically 10s. an acre – rents 'here' [in Scotland] of 40s., 30s., or 'even 20s. an acre' represent 'too high a rent for ordinary land'. More generally, the high rate of land here occasions 'a sort of hostility between the rich and the poor'. Moral degeneracy results; and worse, the 'common people become stupid and unconcerned about religion and their mortal souls'.

Amid such wretchedness, it is no wonder, says Thom, that tenants dread the approach of their masters. 'If any man in rich equipage and dress is seen near their houses', they immediately think 'it must be their landlord, and are at once thrown into a dreadful alarm'.[57] In the case of a normal relationship of servant to master, 'the poor would rejoice to see them, and think themselves honoured to meet and converse with them.'

'Time', Thom continues, 'would fail me to mention all the deplorable effects of the high rate of land.' But there are some unsuspecting repercussions he is bound to cite:

> These I have taken notice of relate to the farmers who are oppressed; but its effects are grievous and distressing to others also, and destructive to the public. When a large territory is thrown waste, the poor people who are driven away become a burden on some neighbouring district or parish; or they resort to cities, which is the cause that such swarms of beggars are to be seen on the streets and in the neighbourhood of great towns.[58]

That is worse than most people imagine, since 'in this nation we have no poors [sic] rates'; in consequence

> the landed gentlemen, and whoever is rich, have almost to a man deserted the church, where contributions are made for the poor; by which means the farmers and tradesmen have got the burden of supporting the poor; and as the number of them, by the means of high rents, hath multiplied so fast, to support them is a very grievous burden indeed.[59]

It is the duty of an afflicted people to 'cry unto God'. Prayer is the duty of men 'at all times', but especially 'in a time of distress'. 'Affliction', he insists, 'should bring men to God'. But when, he continues, you cry to God on behalf of yourselves, 'you ought also to pray for those who by rigorous demands are the cause of the hardships you suffer'. But God has 'promised deliverance to his people, and by an outstretched arm he made his promise good.' Still, 'relief' is at hand in your own situation, he tells his congregation. He is not now speaking of miracles, and in any event 'prophecy hath ceased': but do not despair he tells them:

> ... humanly speaking, you have just now a surer prospect of effectual and speedy relief than the Israelites had when Moses called upon them to leave Egypt: The relief I mean is in the wide and pleasant fields of America, lately added and secured to the dominions of our mild and gracious sovereign. And dare any man say that such a large accession of territory to the empire of Britain hath not been purposely provided by divine providence to afford a comfortable habitation to those who are so ill used and so much borne down in this country? It was when the Israelites were compelled to make brick without straw, that the cup of the Amorites began to be full: It was when the rate of land in this country was rising so high that laborious farmers could not live by it, that the God of war and peace provided abundance of room for them in a different part of the world.[60]

'Emigrations' are, on occasion, not only 'necessary'; there are precedents for their occurrence –

> Such emigrations or removals of a whole people from one land to another have nothing disagreeable in them; they were frequent in former ages, and not long ago we have instances of them. When a country is overstocked with inhabitants, so that the land is unable to maintain them, it becomes necessary for them to seek out new dwellings: when a people are under tyranny and religious persecution, it is natural for them to fly away to another land. To this cause the most industrious and flourishing of the British colonies owed its origin and increase ... .[61]

Thom expands on his reasons for recommending America as the answer to the farmers' plight. He enumerates a list of seven advantages that must motivate Scots farmers to wish to go to America to settle: some of these are particularly noteworthy, including [5], a short essay on the merits of 'English laws' [sic] which Thom praises as 'the perfection of human reason', and [6] where he anticipates Adam Smith's celebrated prophecy in the *Wealth of Nations* that it is only a matter of time before America 'will become the seat of the British government':

> 1. The lands in North America, of which I speak, are parts of the British empire, and the inhabitants are the subjects of our illustrious sovereign King George. ... to go from this [country] to America is as safe in the eye of the law, as it is to leave one parish to go and dwell in another. When you have gone there, you are Britons as much as you are at present ... .
> 2. The land which God in his providence hath provided for you is fertile; it is a good land. ...
> 3. The continent of North America, now the property of Great Britain, is large. ... Was it only some narrow province, though ever so good, the thought of going to it would yield little comfort to so great numbers as are here oppressed, because it could bring relief but to a few: But as it is fruitful, it is also large, and almost unbounded, extending from the British settlements on the sea-coast (which reach along the shore 2000 miles), west-ward to these immense rivers Mississippi and Saint Laurence; a country large in a literal sense, fifty or an hundred times as large which is spoken of in the text; a country which is able to accommodate twenty times as many people as are at this day in Scotland. ...
> 4. The land in view is cheap and almost without taxations. ... You can hardly conceive how great a proportion of the fruit of your labour every one of you pays yearly by the impositions that are laid on houses, windows, soap, salt, drink, candles, shoes, and every thing you need. The other thing is, the maintenance of the numerous poor, many of whom have been reduced to beggary by the rapacity of the landholders; and the burden of supporting them falls, as I have shown, upon the farmers and tradesmen. But from both these grievances the inhabitants of America are almost totally exempted.
> 5. North America is a land of civil and religious liberty. ... If despotic power prevailed in America, poor would be the encouragement derived from its mild climate, its rich pastures, and its fruitful plains: but in North America, liberty in the largest sense is established according to the generous principles of the law of England: The lives and property of even the poorest men are there secure. ...
> 6. You may esteem America to be the more desirable a retreat from your oppression, because, in all probability, it will in a course of years become the seat of the British government. ... Politicians have laid it down as a certain maxim, that whatever European kingdom hath the property and possession of North America, it must also, by its trade and the strength of its navy, have the empire of the sea, and bear the chief sway in Europe: And I think it is not much less evident, that when a small and a large country, supposed to be but equally good, are under the dominion of the same sovereign, the greater, when once it comes to be sufficiently peopled, must become the residence of the court, and the seat of the civil administration.[62] ...
> 7. That this land, so good and so large, may be reached in a very short time. ... As it requires but a few days to sail from our shore to that of North America,[63] so there is nothing that hinders you to embark for that country.[64]

In one section in particular of what he rightly calls 'this unusual sermon', Thom displays an astonishingly detailed knowledge of the topography and agriculture of the American colonies. How did he acquire this level of information? We can be certain that Thom himself never ventured across the Atlantic, yet he reveals an extensive virtual familiarity with the terrain and the local circumstances relating to Scots already settled there:

> There are indeed large tracks of ground belonging to our king in the far northern parts of America, concerning which this cannot altogether be confirmed; I mean Newfoundland, and some parts of Nova Scotia: but the land I speak of, and which is ready to receive you, is on the back of the flourishing and extensive colony of Virginia, and along the banks of the Ohio. There may be places where one might be safe enough from oppression, and which may be tolerably fertile too; but by the want of water, or the unwholesomeness of the climate, (such as was that of Darien) it is not desirable to live in them. But in this good land, though still in its natural state, the soil is fertile; the climate is mild; the air serene; the heat not sultry in summer, nor the cold excessive in winter; the prospect of the hills delightful; and the valleys plentifully watered with crystal streams descended from the upper grounds.[65]

Almost certainly such facts as detailed as these were communicated to Thom by Scots-Americans, people of his acquaintance – among them, most probably, representatives of families in his own parish and congregation who had emigrated to America and were able by dint of their own experience to send back to Glasgow practical and useful knowledge to potential emigrants *via* their former parish minister. For his part, Thom was clearly only too pleased to pass on the information in readily available format such as his published sermon. Barbara De Wolfe proves the point: in *Discoveries of America* she reprints the entire contents of a now scarce pamphlet published by John Bryce of Glasgow in 1774 entitled *News from America. Letter 1. From Alexander Thomson, late Tenant at Corkerhill in the Parish of Paisley,*[66] *now Proprietor of a considerable Estate in Pensilvania. To A Gentleman near Glasgow.* De Wolfe reveals that Thomson's correspondent was none other than 'William Thom, minister of Govan.'[67] Her source is the 'James Whitelaw Papers' held by the Vermont Historical Society at Montpelier, Vermont.[68]

Thom was not alone among church ministers in willingly performing this service for potential emigrants to America. We know from John Witherspoon's annotated pocketbook for 1768 now in the Firestone Library at Princeton[69] – it was, of course, the year of his emigration to America – that numerous members of his own congregation, as well as other Paisley citizens, beat a path to his manse door in advance of his departure to ask him to seek out what prospects might exist for them or family members in 'the Jerseys' or elsewhere in the American colonies. Thus: 'James Robertson weaver desires to be informed if there be any Encouragement for him to remove his family there consisting of a Wife 4 Daughters & a son the Eldest 13 next 11'. In the event, several individuals from Paisley (including, most notably, the self-taught and highly articulate weaver, Hugh Simm)[70] accompanied the Witherspoons on the voyage.[71] And, of course, Witherspoon continued to provide information to potential Scots emigrants long after he had himself settled into life in Princeton and become an American.[72] Similarly, John Erskine made himself something of an authority on America, though in his case his enthusiasm for the colonies – which, as we shall see, took the specialized form of extolling the American brand of evangelical preaching and theology – did not stop at encouragement of emigration, but would involve him in political controversy as an unbridled supporter of the American cause in and even before the revolutionary war.[73]

Thom's trilogy of American war sermons

The key to an understanding of Thom's mindset and idiosyncratic brand of orthodox evangelical preaching is his restless, *unorthodox* interpretation of his ministerial calling. Though by no means uniquely for a member of the Popular party, Thom is a political preacher *par excellence*. Some of his sermons read at times like news bulletins, sometimes like gazetteers. We have already noted that he was particularly well versed in agricultural issues, often of a highly technical nature, and is happy to pass on *via* the pulpit opportunities for Scots emigrants to America. Thom's directness and fearlessness, combined with an assured mastery of the facts behind the situation he is discussing, underpins every message to his flock. And he offers much more from his pulpit than mere words of comfort. When he addresses a congregation of farmers he not only sympathises with them in these hard, cheerless times, but didactically he instructs them how, in his judgment, they might best set about ameliorating their condition. There is little hidden, obscurantist philosophy in Thom's preaching, and little 'wild' enthusiasm either. But that does not at all mean there is an absence of intellectuality; indeed, there are occasional flashes of great insight as, for example, when he discourses *en passant* on the doctrine of passive obedience, or the Hutcheson-refined theory of the divisibility of rights into 'perfect' and 'imperfect' rights, and how these may relate to the current political situation. In the last analysis, however, Thom is a difficult man to categorise. Simplistically, Thom is Thom; he is a veritable one-off. Carlyle was on the mark: Thom *was* a quarrelsome eccentric, but with an 'ingenious turn of mind'.

One contemporary of Thom's who shared some of his less endearing traits was Professor John Anderson, professor of natural philosophy at the University of Glasgow. There is evidence that Anderson admired and may even have been complicit in Thom's several efforts to reform aspects of the academic and administrative organization at Glasgow. Just as Anderson was notoriously unpopular with many of his professorial colleagues and, above all, with the principal, William Leechman (who never found a way of controlling his litigious ploys), so there is evidence that Thom 'seized every opportunity to blacken the name of his alma mater and its officers'.[74] That jibe, of course, is superbly ironic given the background to the university's role as patron in Thom's presentation to the parish of Govan. But the intellectual and theological ties between Thom and Anderson should come as no surprise. John Anderson's father – and, more particularly, his grandfather, the quixotic Reverend John Anderson, latterly of the Ramshorn Church in Glasgow, formerly of Dumbarton[75] – were old-school Calvinists. Professor Anderson shared the theology of his forebears while, at the same time, sharing with Thom a joint radical conviction that the kind of education taught at Glasgow – and by extension at the other Scottish universities as well – was outmoded and increasingly inappropriate to the needs of a country bent on economic and industrial growth. Both men preferred to think of educational priorities in terms of the *'useful'* arts and sciences, an approach also favoured in the writings of the Marischal College academics, David Fordyce and George Turnbull. Thom certainly approved of the dissenting academies that had sprung up in England modelled on the original Doddridge academy in Northampton, and, of late, beginning to be replicated in a few centres in Scotland. But there was another vitally important, though less obvious link between these two eccentrics; a common interest in America, a belief in its future and a common disapproval of Britain's increasingly questionable colonial objectives in the revolutionary war.[76]

The most comprehensive study to date of Thom's American war sermons is Donovan's essay in *The Glasgow Enlightenment* (1995).[77] The focus of Donovan's interest is in identifying 'evangelical civic humanism' in the sermons, but he also makes a number of important, more general points: *first*, that, in addition to exhibiting a 'religious seriousness', the sermons 'display other traits of Popular party homiletics', and, in his view, are 'cautious and conciliatory politically, despite their outspoken language'; *secondly*, Thom's 'aversion to philosophy', leading him in this trilogy of war sermons to avoid comment on the ideology behind the colonial protest. Above all, Donovan perceptively notes Thom's ultimate trust in the competence of the 'people' to end the injustices of the American war. All three sermons, delivered at intervals over a period of three years, during which the outcome of the war from a British perspective became progressively more uncertain, might perhaps be expected to betray a similar gradation of despair on the part of Thom – as far, that is, as the prospect of any vestige of justification for the British cause is concerned. But that is not the case and, indeed, at times, Thom seems anxious to avoid any exposure to any accusations of partisanship.

One word strangely absent in Donovan's critique, however, is 'allegory'. The earliest of the American war sermons is pure allegory; indeed, it is deliberate that the words 'America' and 'American' do not once occur in the first sermon of the trilogy, *The Revolt of the Ten Tribes* (1776). Instead, we have surprisingly tentative and frequently opposing views; thus

> ... though subjects may judge they are aggrieved by some particular laws, and feel themselves overburdened by a heavy yoke, yet, in all ordinary cases, it is their duty to yield obedience to the lawful magistrate.[78]

But then, recalling Whiggite loathing of English Tory churchmen of the late seventeenth and early eighteenth century preaching the doctrine of non-resistance and passive obedience, Thom swiftly qualifies his words:

> I dare not say, that resistance is in all possible cases criminal. This doctrine, absurd and slavish as it is, hath sometimes been fashionable in this country. It is not yet a hundred years since passive-obedience and non-resistance was, from many pulpits in Britain, weekly obtruded upon the early credulity of an injured and abused people; and, amidst the wonderful changes that happen daily, it may soon usurp the pulpit again, and become as fashionable as ever.[79] ... However, government is the ordinance of God; and anarchy, rebellion, or civil war in a country, are any of them so dreadful, that subjects ought to suffer much before they begin to think of resisting established authority. They ought,

dutifully, and earnestly, and repeatedly, to petition the throne for redress; they ought to wait long and patiently for that relief which they wish for. And unless their yoke, like that of the Israelites, be altogether intolerable, and unless they be almost sure of bettering their condition by resistance, they ought not to resist at all.[80]

Unless 'their' (the American colonists') 'yoke' is 'intolerable, says Thom, 'they ought not to resist at all'. John Witherspoon, once a staunch ally of William Thom, has a completely different take on the issue of non-resistance, advising his students at Princeton at around the same time Thom preached his sermon:

> The once famous controversy on passive obedience and non-resistance seems now in our country [he means of course America] to be pretty much over; what the advocates for submission used to say was that to teach the lawfulness of resisting a government in any instance and to make the rebel the judge is subversive of all order and must subject a state to perpetual sedition. To which I answer, to refuse this inherent right in every man is to establish injustice and tyranny and leave every good subject without help, as a tame prey to the ambition and rapacity of others. No doubt men may abuse the privilege, yet this does not make it void. Besides it is not till a whole people rise that resistance has any effect, and it is not easy to suppose that a whole people would rise against their governors, unless when they have really received very great provocation.[81]

For a number of reasons *The Revolt of the Ten Tribes* is the least satisfactory of Thom's trilogy of American war sermons; resorting to the device of scriptural allegory is his way of opting out of apportioning blame to either side. The 'Israelites' are the American colonists, it is obvious, but, preached in December of the year of American independence, Thom's sermon deliberately omits any narrow association of the word *'revolt'* in his title with the independence question, or even with the broader issue of the currently escalating war, still with no end in sight. Not that anyone would have been in any doubt as to his true meaning, or where his true sympathies lay:

> ... when, like the Israelites, a people have been long overburdened with a grievous yoke, and see coming upon them all at once an additional burden, which would crush them to the ground, and render life itself insupportable, they may sometimes be exasperated and provoked to act as that people did; and if there be unanimity among many tribes or provinces, who have separate interests, and were many of them formerly jealous of one another, this seems to be a decisive proof, that the provocation given them hath been extremely great.[82]

The second sermon of the trilogy, *Achan's Trespass*, is, by contrast, considerably more successful, partly because its preaching is more powerful and much less equivocal in its unambiguous condemnation of the British cause. At the same time, scriptural allegory abounds here as it did in the first sermon of the trilogy – the *'accursed thing'* of the title is the *'public monies'* committed by Britain in furtherance of the war in America, and 'Achan', the villain of the bible story, is either Lord North or, conceivably, Great Britain personified (or both). This time, however, the allegorical content is of secondary importance to Thom's full-blooded censure of the British conduct of 'this lasting American war', 'this expensive, tiresome, and inglorious war', 'this irksome and ruinous

American war', 'this tedious war', as he mercilessly piles on the blame. He takes special exception to those apologists for the war who point to the fact that it can be paid for out of additional taxation. Just as Achan had stolen the 'shekels of silver and the golden wedge', so our government has 'misapplied' the additional revenue it has raised from taxation on 'foreign, or in unnecessary wars, or in providing places, or pensions, or bribes, for any of the legislative body'. 'To misapply the revenue impoverishes the nation', 'disappoints the people of their just expectations' and 'brings disgrace upon the kingdom'.

In one of the most rousing passages in the sermon, Thom characteristically contrasts the treatment of the rich with the treatment of the poor. Here, interestingly, he anticipates the third sermon in his putative trilogy by citing a verse, not just from the New Testament but from the same book he will use there, the *Epistle of James*:

> "Do not rich men oppress you?"[83] was a question put above seventeen hundred years ago by a man inspired; and the same question would be answered in the same manner it was then, were it put in the age we live in.[84]

Even Achan's high birth and rank, not to mention his great wealth, could save him from his terrible fate – 'a public trial, and as public a punishment'. Now, in our own age, he says, 'matters go quite differently': if 'a British Achan is half-detected' his friends will rally round him 'and plead strongly in his behalf',

> But if a poor cottager groaning under heavy taxes, and dreadfully oppressed by a screwed rent; or if a work-man, living under the dreadful expectation of new corn-bills steals a beggarly sheep to keep in the lives of his starving family; then, then the spirit of our judges and lawyers, like the spirit of a pack of dogs when a timid hare is started, is all up at once; the law is armed with rigour against this poor thief; the edge of it is sharpened, is levelled against the neck of this friendless, this contemptible offender. But I like not to say more about the different manner in which great and poor offenders are treated; it is certainly shameful, and deeply to be lamented.[85]

Without mentioning him by name, Thom paraphrases the famous words of Chatham in the House of Lords debate of May 30 1777 on his prophecy that for Britain to conquer 'English America' was 'an impossibility':

> We have heard that a great statesman, who, it is said, was no ways hasty to spill the blood of our inveterate enemies on the plains of Minden, but was well enough disposed to pursue coercive and sanguinary measures against our revolted brethren in America, did not long ago declare in parliament, that he at length saw that Great Britain could not conquer America; and that if she could, that conquest would not be for the interest of Britain.[86] It is evident, that if America is conquered at all, it must be done either by persuasion or by force, or by a mixture of both: By persuasion, by mild and equitable measures, such as might have been espoused at first, I hope a reconcilement may still take place; or, if the Americans are first overawed by the British armies and fleets, and then allured by gentle offers, they may be, I am sure they ought to be, reconciled to the parent-country. To conquer in either of these ways would, I think, be for the present interest of Britain. But if by conquest the noble lord meant mere force, I am not sure but we shall be obliged to accede to his opinion. Mere force may imply a complete extermination; and how this could tend to the interest of Britain, I cannot for my life perceive.[87]

COMMON SENSE:

ADDRESSED TO THE

INHABITANTS OF AMERICA,

ON THE FOLLOWING

INTERESTING SUBJECTS:

I. Of the Origin and Design of Government in general; with concise Remarks on the English Constitution.
II. Of Monarchy and Hereditary Succession.
III. Thoughts on the present State of American Affairs.
IV. Of the present ability of America; with some miscellaneous Reflections.

A NEW EDITION; with several Additions in the Body of the Work.

To which is added, an APPENDIX: together with an ADDRESS to the People called QUAKERS.

Man knows no Master save creating HEAVEN,
Or those whom Choice and common Good ordain.
THOMSON.

PHILADELPHIA, Printed:
[To promote the traitorous purposes therein set forth.]

EDINBURGH, re-printed:
[To shew the real spirit and views of the Colonies, or rather of their leaders in rebellion; which cannot fail to rouse the indignation of every Briton, without leaving them from henceforth a single advocate, who is not utterly lost to *loyalty*, to *patriotism*, and to COMMON SENSE.

Sold by CHARLES ELLIOT, Edinburgh; and WILLIAM ANDERSON, Stirling.

M.DCC.LXXVI.

Title page of Charles Elliot's Edinburgh edition of Thomas Paine's *Common Sense* (1776).

The third and final sermon of the trilogy, *From Whence Come Wars*, is by far the most complex of the set. Here, Thom keeps up the same onslaught on ministers of the crown directing the war begun in *Achan's Trespass*, but daringly now goes much farther, specifying their 'covetous and bungling' ineptitude as one reason for its longevity. Significantly, Thom's choice of scriptural text, alone among the three, is from the New Testament, from the fourth chapter of the *Epistle of James*, the first three verses beginning: *'From whence come wars and fightings among you? Come they not hence, even of your lusts that war in your members?'* [88] The scope for allegory is now virtually non-existent. This is no blood-curdling tale of the Israelites in Egypt, nor of Achan's treasure guaranteeing his destruction. Instead, we have St. James the Evangelist preaching the Christian message of repentance and regeneration. *'Submit yourselves therefore to God'* — plucked from the same chapter a few verses later — is the key message now. Thom, the preacher, has cast himself as minister of the gospel of reconciliation, and in that guise addresses these words of James to *both* sides in the conflict:

> One year of this tiresome war, a second, a third, a fourth, hath gone over our heads, and another year of it is begun. 'The harvest is past, the summer is ended, and we are not saved.'[89] May not this be a presumption that Heaven is displeased with our aim, and by repeatedly counter-working our efforts, intimates to us that abundance of blood is shed already. – I sincerely wish, that the fomenters of this war, on both sides of the Atlantic, may be of this mind.[90]

Even more candidly he pleads:

> I honestly declare, that though, as I think, these Colonists were treated with too much harshness formerly, it is my opinion, they would now act the wise part, would they frankly submit to the terms that have been offered them by the parliament of Britain. ... Ah! Is there not some patriot, or some illustrious band of patriots, who shall try, and try with success, to renew this kindred connection? who shall wisely, and for the relief and happiness of the two contending parties, bring about this so much desired reconcilement and peace?[91]

In the most stirring part of the sermon, using flowery yet curiously prophetic language while maintaining his new-found even-handedness, Thom prays for the intervention of 'a man' who has the means and the ability to bring peace and reconciliation to both sides in the conflict, someone

> who shall bid the Americans disband their armies, bid them subdue and cultivate their unimproved, but naturally fertile and widely extended territories, ... who shall teach them the arts of peace, to promote population, and, by establishing equal laws, and a generous system of liberty, to render their country an asylum to the many thousands who are, alas! at this day, borne down and impolitically oppressed in Europe; and who shall, at the same time, call home the British armies and fleets to protect this fair, this exhausted, and ill-defended island against the unprovoked attempts of France, and even to strike, in self-defence, a merited blow against that menacing and faithless power. Who doth not pray, that Heaven may, as formerly, raise up such a patriot? Who doth not wish to see so happy a turn of our affairs?[92]

Donovan says he detects in Thom an 'aversion to philosophy, which marks his attacks on higher education', leading him 'to shun philosophizing in his works, all of which aim at a practical moral result'.[93] Perhaps so; but in *From Whence Come Wars*, focusing more on the evil of war between nations, and even within society more generally, William Thom must be given credit for adopting what can only be termed a philosophical view of war. In so doing, he succeeds in elevating himself (*qua* preacher) and his sermon on to a higher plateau. Employing the Aristotelian formula refined by his old mentor at Glasgow, Francis Hutcheson, he distinguishes between the concept of imperfect and perfect rights – or, as we might say, between conventional fixed notions of an *unjust* and a *just* war:

> There are indeed certain claims, called imperfect rights, which, though they be violated, yet the injured party cannot by any law compel the fulfillment of them by force. ... but it is quite otherwise with respect to the rights which are called perfect; the right which a man hath to his property, to his life, to defend the life of a parent, to protect his innocent family, to defend the honour of a sister, or a daughter, or a wife. Whensoever any one offers to injure him in any of these particulars, he hath right to repel the injury by force; and if the injury be already done, he hath right to compel the injurious party to make complete reparation, or to make him suffer a condign punishment for his crime.[94]

Thom was not the only Popular party minister to apply the theory of perfect and imperfect rights to the American crisis. In his *Lectures on Moral Philosophy* ('Lecture VIII') John Witherspoon teaches his students at Princeton about the division of 'rights' into those that are 'natural' and those that are 'acquired', and that rights may be 'considered as perfect and imperfect'. Further, he notes:

> Rights are alienable and unalienable. The first we may, according to justice and prudence, surrender or give up by our own act; the others we may not. A man may give away his own goods, lands, money. There are several things which he cannot give away, as a right over his own knowledge, thoughts, etc. Others, which he ought not, as a right to judge for himself in all matters of religion, his right to self-preservation, provision, etc. Some say that liberty is unalienable and that those who have even given it away may lawfully resume it.[95]

Witherspoon follows Hugo Grotius, Samuel Pufendorf and Jean-Jacques Burlamaqui in assigning to perfect rights 'all the duties of justice'. All three authorities are specifically recommended to his students in the *Recapitulation* to the *Lectures on Moral Philosophy* where he prescribes 'some of the chief writers upon government and politics'.[96]

Almost as an afterthought, Thom ends *From Whence Come Wars* by discoursing on 'another sort of war', which he defines as 'wrangling about abstruse points and metaphysical opinions'. From the earliest days of Christianity, he tells his flock, 'metaphysical disputes' within the church 'have often led to persecution, to war, and to bloodshed.' He is referring to 'a war of narrow-minded theologians'. And 'like other wars', it 'springs from the lusts of men', and 'not from the calm love of truth'. Alternatively, such wars may derive from 'the lust of covetousness and ambition', and he elaborates on what he means:

> Some person is like to be preferred to a lucrative and honourable place; his character must be blown; a report must be circulated that he is deeply tinctured with heterodox

principles; a process of heresy must be raised against him, that so he may be rejected, and that his accuser, or some one of his accuser's friends, may step into the place. But to investigate the origin, to mark the progress, to show the folly, the wickedness, and the dreadful effects of this theological war, would require a long discourse.[97]

Thom's curious digression on the potentially evil aspects of church patronage – possibly autobiographical in origin, since he himself had to undergo some of the worst features of a disputed settlement – introduced at the close of his sermon, is obviously inappropriate and to some extent mars the whole performance if considered from a rhetorical point of view. For all that, Thom's achievement is undiminished, ensuring that his American war sermons are to be ranked among the most important, if atypical, examples of political preaching of the period.

Fast day responses to the events of 1776

In the fateful year 1776 Charles Elliot, a well-known and successful bookseller in Edinburgh,[98] with his opposite number and accomplice in Stirling, the 'notorious' William Anderson,[99] published an edition of Thomas Paine's runaway bestseller, the pamphlet *Common Sense: addressed to the Inhabitants of America*. The first edition of Paine's egregiously successful title was published by the émigré Scot from Glasgow, Robert Bell of Philadelphia, early in January that year but Bell and Paine fell out shortly after its publication when the rights to future editions were assigned by an angry Paine (in much too loose terms that he would subsequently regret) to Bell's rivals, W. and T. Bradford. The row between the hot-headed Englishman and the mercurial Scot was intense and merely ensured that during the rest of the year in Philadelphia alone seven different editions of the pamphlet were issued,[100] with unauthorized editions also appearing over the next few months in New York, Salem, Newport, Hartford, Lancaster, Newburyport, Norwich, Albany and Providence. Meantime, pirated editions were published in London (eight alone in 1776), Dublin, Newcastle and Edinburgh, to say nothing of incomplete versions or long extracts (in English or in translation) appearing in Rotterdam, Warsaw, Copenhagen and St. Petersburg.

The title page of Elliot's Edinburgh edition of Paine's pamphlet [see illustration] is of unusual interest. It is described as 'A NEW EDITION; with several Additions in the Body of the Work. To which is added, an APPENDIX : together with an Address to the People called QUAKERS.' Gimbel has unravelled the extremely complex publishing history of *Common Sense* and from his comments it is possible to establish that like all of John Almon's eight London editions published in 1776, the Elliot Edinburgh edition of the same year 'has hiatuses, although not as many' as in Almon's; by 'hiatuses' Gimbel means omissions of the original text 'where passages occurred casting reflection upon the Crown and government'.[101] We might say that the text has been censured by an anxious publisher. But Elliot goes much further by exercising a high degree of partiality in the design and content of his title page, immediately making clear where his position stood in relation to the American question, and, above all, why he had resorted to publishing Paine's explosive pamphlet in the first place:

To shew the real spirit and views of the Colonies, or rather of their leaders in rebellion; which cannot fail to rouse the indignation of every Briton, without leaving them from henceforth a single advocate, who is not utterly lost to *loyalty*, to *patriotism*, and to Common Sense.

It was also in 1776 – on 24 November to be precise – that James Boswell notes in his private journal that he was 'at the New Church in the forenoon' and there he had been 'edified by Dr. Erskine'. This was in stark contrast with his entry for the preceding Sunday, 17 November, when, after attending the morning service in the Tolbooth Church (where he had heard Dr Webster [102] 'with much satisfaction'), he had gone in the afternoon to the New Church where he had expected to hear 'Mr Walker'[103] preach, but was disappointed that the preacher turned out to be 'Mr Johnston at Leith'.[104] Boswell explains why he had foregone the High Kirk, where he often worshipped: he had 'shunned Dr Blair ... as he prayed against the Americans.'[105] As things turned out, however, it was a bad choice since Johnston 'prayed more violently than Blair.' Earlier in the same month (1 November), Boswell had recalled sitting in Alexander Donaldson's 'back shop' (in Edinburgh High Street) 'and heard much in favour of the Americans.'[106] He returns to the subject of America in his private journal entry for 12 December, 'the fast appointed by the king to pray for success to his arms against the Americans.' Boswell goes on caustically: 'I paid no regard to it, but studied a confused cause and dictated part of a paper upon it.' Later in the afternoon he went to have tea with, and to play cards at the home of his close friend and fellow advocate, The Hon Alexander Gordon (later the judge, Lord Rockville), and he notes, 'Maclaurin was there', [107] thereby guaranteeing, one might think, a lively conversation. Boswell continues:

> I maintained that it was shocking in a nation to pray to GOD for success in destroying another nation; and that it was equally allowable for an individual to pray for destruction to his enemy, like the old Laird of Gilmillscroft, who prayed in his family worship: "Pour down, O Lord, of thy choicest curses on Hugh, Earl of Loudoun, and Mr James Boswell of Auchinleck, Advocate." Maclaurin agreed with me.[108]

Boswell's unfavourable comparison of Hugh Blair with John Erskine was clearly based on their respective, and very different positions regarding the American question and the continuing war.

When Boswell went to the New Church on 24 November to hear Erskine, and was 'edified' by his special brand of orthodox preaching, the odds are that the distinguished Old Greyfriars minister had brought something of the American war into his sermon and/or his prayers that morning and uttered sentiments that had been sufficiently non-sycophantic to the government cause for these to resonate with the young advocate. In 1776 Erskine had had reprinted in Edinburgh his 'discourse' entitled *Shall I go to war with my American brethren?* The pamphlet had originally been published anonymously in London in 1769. The new Edinburgh edition, however, was not merely a reprint with, this time, the author's name identified on the title page: in a brand new preface Erskine said that the date of the first edition had prevented him 'urging in it' the 'case of Governor Melvin', [the case] 'of Mr Mortimer' and 'of the Quebec Act', 'among other appearances of the encouragement of Popery', the latter topic in many ways the author's major concern in his pamphlet (and on that account considered in chapter 9). Erskine's new preface is important not just for the vigour of its condemnation of *all* war but, of course, for clarifying his own position in relation to the apparently endless American war:

> Anonymous writers have aspersed me as an enemy to my King and country, because I cannot approve certain measures of administration. No attack could have been more wanton, injurious, and unprovoked. *My sermons have never hinted at these measures.* [italics added] Had I been satisfied that they were just and expedient, my prayers for peace would not have been altered or suppressed.

Erskine admits that while it is true he was ultra careful to offend no one from his pulpit, or causing anyone hearing him to accuse him of partiality, he does own up to having been rather less cautious in his letters abroad:

> I have given my opinion to the few in America, to whom I could write with freedom, that the colonies waging war with Britain, would probably issue, first in their ruin, and then in ours. If this was exciting them to take up arms, then, and not otherwise, I plead guilty.[109]

Two further pamphlets by Erskine on the situation in America (both published anonymously) came out in Edinburgh in 1776.[110] Even so, his strict decision to avoid casting aspersions *in his sermons* on the British government's colonial strategy in America is significant and probably explains the reasoning behind his resorting to the 'discourse' format, *i.e.* partly to clear his conscience, but also to allow himself freer rein to his views on the controversy than he would have considered proper if articulated from the pulpit.

Predictably, the numerous fast day sermons preached throughout the latter years of the American war by Moderate ministers are all cut from the same cloth. The minister of North Leith, for example, David Johnston – the man who had dismayed Boswell with his prayers that he considered even more 'violent' than Hugh Blair's – preached in February 1779 on 'the most probable means of obtaining a … Divine Interposition in the present conjuncture of public affairs'.[111] A more extreme example is Alexander Gerard's fast day sermon of the year before, *Liberty the Cloke of Maliciousness* (1778). But it is the fast day sermons that were published in the year that had seen the Americans declare their independence from the mother-country that are of greatest interest. On 12 December 1776 – on the same day as Thom's *The Revolt of the Ten Tribes* was preached in Govan – George Campbell preached in Aberdeen a rousing sermon on the *Nature, Extent, and Importance of the Duty of Allegiance* (1777, second ed., 1778), the content and orientation of which are evident from the title.[112] One of the main planks of Campbell's strategy is to take issue with sentiments such as those expressed by Richard Price in *Additional Observations on the Nature and Value of Civil Liberty, and the War with America* (1777), which the Welsh nonconformist had written as a sequel to his *Observations on the Nature of Civil Liberty* (1776), both unreservedly in defence of the American patriots.[113] Without identifying his source, Campbell cites part of Price's famous assertion on war in general in the section of *Observations* he entitles 'Of the State of the Nation and the War with America':

POPERY *another Gospel:*

OR,

A Demonstration that the **Romish Religion** is not the Gospel that CHRIST hath left his Church, but what **Antichrist** hath since devised, to the Destruction of Christianity and the Souls of Men.

IN

Six SERMONS

From *Gal.* i. 8.

Preached in Time of the Rebellion, *Anno* 1745,

AND

Published to give Warning to all PROTESTANTS through *Britain* and *Ireland* of the damnable Errors and Cruelty of **Popery**, and of the dreadful Danger and Tendency of the present **Insurrection** in its favours.

WITH

A PREFACE, relating to the Justice of the REVOLUTION-PRINCIPLES and present Establishment, and the Unreasonableness of *Jacobitism* and *Disloyalty*.

By Mr. JOHN WILLISON, Minister of the Gospel in *Dundee*.

EDINBURGH,
Printed by THOMAS LUMISDEN and JOHN ROBERTSON, and sold at their Printing-house in the *Fish-market*. 1746.

Title page of John Willison's *Popery another Gospel* (1746)

War is a dreadful evil; and those who involve a people in it *needlessly*, will find they have much to answer for. Nothing can ever justify it, but the necessity of it [to secure some *essential* interest against unjust attacks. But, it seems, there is no interest to be secured by the present war.][114]

Alexander Carlyle's *The Justice and Necessity of the War with our American Colonies Examined* (1777), also preached on the December 1776 fast day, similarly takes Price to task for his efforts 'to decry the present government of Britain, and to present us with an idea of something infinitely more perfect, which we are soon to see established in America, and ... hope may likewise take place at home.' Carlyle preached it in his pulpit in Inveresk, a few miles from Edinburgh, and, significantly, the title should be seen as a defiant reply to the rhetorical question posed in Erskine's discourse, *Shall I go to war?*, reprinted in Edinburgh earlier in the same year. Not only that. The text chosen by Carlyle for his sermon is precisely the same as used by Erskine: *Shall I yet again go out to battle against the children of Benjamin my brother, or shall I cease?* (*Judges*, 20: v. 28). Carlyle's choice of text was scarcely adventitious. He cites three authorities in support of his argument that the colonists are misguided and that in consequence it is morally defensible for Britain to have taken steps to oppose them: John Roebuck's *An Enquiry, whether the Guilt of the Present Civil War* [sic] *in America, ought to be imputed to Great Britain or America* (1776), the anonymous pamphlet *The Rights of Great Britain Asserted against the Claims of America* (1776) (written by James Macpherson, probably 'to order') and George Campbell's fast day sermon on *Allegiance* (1777, 1778).

As in the case of Carlyle's later sermons preached in the 1790s during the war with France discussed in chapter 7, his point of view at this stage in the sermon is unambiguously to side with British government policy, right or wrong. In that regard, of course, he is merely toeing the Moderate party line, the same line already followed by Campbell, to whose *Allegiance* sermon Carlyle obediently defers.[115] A striking example of his characteristically conservative approach to the American crisis is when he poses the question: 'Were we Americans', [would we not] 'think and act as they do'? To which he supplies the answer: 'I have often heard it rashly answered in the affirmative', but explains that by 'rashly' he means that 'a wise and good man would deliberate maturely before he would agree to a change that ... might introduce the most uncertain effects, perhaps slavery and the worst of all governments.'[116]

The second part of Carlyle's sermon is more of a breast-beating jeremiad in the course of which he berates 'ourselves' and the moral condition of the country: 'Infidelity and irreligion, neglect of God and of his worship, and the most licentious morals, as they are intimately connected together, so have they generally preceded the declension and fall of states'. These are, he claims, the *'signs of the times'*. A 'torrent of corruption' has overwhelmed the nation and 'may be the cause' why God 'should now visit us with sore calamities'. Yet in the most innovative section of his sermon Carlyle is unsparing in his criticism of aspects of the handling of the American crisis on the part of the British authorities, while at the same time taking pains to qualify with precision exactly what he means:

'... that weakness of government, which has been of late so much felt and complained of, and which no capacity seems hitherto able to repair. I mean the machine of government itself, (not the administration of it), which has lost much of the spring and energy it had in former times; witness the infamous abuse that has been suffered, the dangerous tumults that have passed unpunished, and the relaxation of the executive power, even in respect of crimes against itself. In vain has opposition, with her warning voice, and faction, with her clamorous tongue, ascribed this imbecility to the hands who direct the machine; for the chiefs of every party in the state have directed, in their turns, with no better success.[117]

He then develops what would become a favourite theme of his in some of his most politically charged sermons of the next few years: abuses of the 'liberty of the press' – responsible for a 'torrent of calumny and reproach, which, for some time past, has poured itself upon the public ear'. He is particularly severe on 'publications that have proceeded from men of gravity, of professedly good intentions, and of no mean talents*'. And his asterisked footnote reads: '*See the works of the Reverend Dr Price and others.'

Carlyle's loyalist and patriotic preaching concludes nonetheless on a note of severe censure of the actions of British troops – 'deeds have been committed in another quarter of the globe, by natives of these islands, that will make the odious names of Cortes and Pizarro be forgotten, and stain the British annals to the latest posterity' – balanced by warm praise of 'the alacrity and courage of our soldiers in the cause of their country', and an encomium of 'our King', whose character, like the sun, shines the brighter for the spots with which faction and rebellion, for a while, have endeavoured to obscure it.' And the final message to the congregation of Inveresk on that December day in the year that saw America declare its independence? Archly, Carlyle resorts to the opening words of the Declaration itself:

Since, then, my brethren, to yield to the claims of America would be inexpedient and dishonourable; since the war is just and necessary, let us prosecute it with vigour, with chearfulness and perseverance, till the rebellious children of our brother Benjamin find, that the same ardent national spirit that could cherish, can also correct; and that the same powerful arm that stretched across the Atlantic to save, is not now so weak but it can punish. Thus shall we do all in our power to preserve to posterity a government, the most favourable to human nature that ever existed, and to prolong the period of light, and liberty, and happiness among mankind.[118]

John Erskine (John Kay).

9

Popery

[Rubric – '16. The disability of papists.'] Religion likewise makes a difference as to persons capacity of civil rights; and thus papists, and they who marry papists, are declared incapable to inherit, possess or enjoy the imperial crown of Great Britain, by the treaty of union, and statutes therein referred to. Again, if any person professing the protestant religion shall apostatize from the same, by professing the popish religion, he shall from thenceforth forfeit to his next protestant heir at law his whole heritable estate, as if he was naturally dead. And further, professed papists are under a disability to purchase heritable subjects, or to succeed to their predecessors therein, as is observed in their proper places; and as to the clergy, popish priests, Jesuits, and trafficking papists are, by express statutes, liable to banishment, under certification that if they return they are to be subjected to the pains of death, and a premium is due to those that can discover and seize any of them, so as they shall be convicted.
Anonymous [Andrew McDouall, Lord Bankton (1685-1760)], *An Institute of the Laws of Scotland in Civil Rights*, v. I, M.DCC.LI. (Edinburgh, 1751), Bk. I, Tit. II, §16, 49.[1]

Key authors and sermons

Reverend John Willison (1680-1750), minister of the South Church, Dundee.

Popery another Gospel: or, A Demonstration that the Romish Religion is not the Gospel that Christ hath left his Church, but what Anti-Christ hath since devised, to the Destruction of Christianity and the Souls of Men. In Six Sermons from Gal. i.8 Preached in the Time of the Rebellion, Anno 1745. ... By Mr. John Willison Minister of the Gospel in Dundee.
Edinburgh, Printed by Thomas Lumisden and John Robertson ... 1746.[2]

Reverend Dr William Wishart (1691/2-1753), minister of the Tron Church (second charge), Edinburgh and principal of the University of Edinburgh.

Publick Virtue recommended. A Sermon preach'd in the High-Church of Edinburgh, On Thursday, May 8th, 1746. At the Opening of the General Assembly of the Church of Scotland. By William Wishart D.D. Principal of the College of Edinburgh.
Edinburgh: Printed by R. Fleming: For A. Kincaid, MDCCXLVI. [1746]

Reverend Dr Hugh Blair (1718-1800), minister of the Canongate (second charge), Edinburgh.[3]

The Wrath of Man praising God. A Sermon preached in the High Church of Edinburgh, May 18th, 1746. Before His Grace the Lord High Commissioner to the General Assembly of the Church of Scotland. By Hugh Blair, A.M. One of the Ministers of Canongate. Published by Desire of the Lord High Commissioner.
Edinburgh, Printed by R. Fleming: For A. Kincaid, M.DCC.XLVI. [1746]

Reverend Dr John Erskine (1721-1803), minister of Old Greyfriars, Edinburgh.[4]

Prayer for those in civil and military offices recommended, from a view of the influence of Providence on their characters, conduct, and success: a Sermon. Preached before the election of the Magistrates of Edinburgh, Oct. 5. 1779, And published at the request of the Magistrates and Town-Council. By John Erskine, D.D. One of the Ministers of Edinburgh.
Edinburgh: Printed for W. Gray, Front of the Exchange. MDCCLXXIX. [1779]

Reverend Dr James Fordyce (1720-96), minister at Brechin, then Alloa, before his admission as minister of the dissenting Presbyterian congregation in Monkwell Street, London.

The Delusive and Persecuting Spirit of Popery: A Sermon, preached in Monkwell-street, on the 10th of February last, Being the Day appointed for a General Fast: By James Fordyce, D.D.
London: T. Cadell, MDCCLXXIX [1779][5]

Reverend Dr Patrick Grant (1706-87), minister of Urray in the Presbytery of Dingwall; Moderator of the General Assembly, 1778-79.

The Spirit of Moderation in Religion Recommended. A Sermon, Preached on the 20th of May 1779, In the High Church of Edinburgh, Before His Majesty's High Commissioner, At the opening of the General Assembly of the Church of Scotland. By Patrick Grant, D.D.
Edinburgh: Balfour & Smellie. M,DCC,LXXIX. [1779]

Anti-Roman Catholic sentiment in Scotland is discoverable throughout the eighteenth century in numerous published sermons by ministers of the Church of Scotland; just one extreme example is 'A Sermon against the Idolatrous Worship of the Church of Rome' preached in Glasgow in November 1725 by William McCulloch, and published in the following year. McCulloch is the man who, with the great Methodist preacher, George Whitefield, rallied thousands to hear their 'enthusiastic' brand of preaching in the course of the 'Cambuslang Wark' of 1742. Another extreme example of anti-popery pulpit rhetoric is Daniel Macarthur's 'The Church of Rome, the Mother of Abominations' *(1778), preached in the Black-Friars Church* [the College church] *in Glasgow in November 1778.*[6] *Described as a 'Preacher of the Gospel', MacArthur was not, however, a minister of the Kirk; not without significance the title page warrants that the piece is published 'at the earnest desire of many of the hearers'.*

The sermons discussed here are representative of each of the three main periods in eighteenth-century Scotland when the barometer of anti-'popery' sentiment rose highest on the scale of what *today would be regarded as intolerable (and illegal) religious bigotry and prejudice. These high watermarks, when sermons and/or 'discourses' with substantial popery content were commonplace, are exposed in (a) the common threat to the British throne and constitution, and to the national Reformed churches posed by the rebellions of 1715 and (especially) 1745; (b) before and in the course of the American revolutionary war, from c. 1776 to c. 1780; and, above all, (c) in the anti-popery crisis in Scotland of 1778-79, brought on by an ultimately futile attempt on the part of the Lord Advocate, Henry Dundas, to introduce a Scottish version of the English Catholic Relief bill (The Papists Act, 1778). For all that, David Walker is probably right when he comments that, except for the period before and immediately after the Jacobite rebellion, 'the anti-Catholic laws do not seem to have been very rigorously enforced'.*[7]

The Church of Scotland's perceived role in the identification and persecution of Catholics

The epigraph from Bankton's *Institute* prefacing this chapter encapsulates the law of the land in relation to Roman Catholics in eighteenth-century Scotland and conveniently summarises the extent to which Catholics were statutorily deprived of all rights affecting inheritance and the purchase of heritable land and property, not of course to mention their *de facto* exclusion from freedom of worship. Bankton's ruling also embraces forfeiture of estates in the event that a man 'apostatized' from Protestantism in favour of the Catholic faith. Even more draconian in its application, scope and intent, 'popish priests', 'Jesuits'[8] and 'trafficking papists' were liable to banishment, with the death penalty the ultimate price for illegal return in the event of conviction. As late as 1803, whereas the provisions of the English Catholic Relief Act had been extended to Scotland a decade before,[9] it became transparently clear that by no means did that legislation confer on Catholics anything like full parity under the law with Protestants, Episcopalians or even dissenters. In an important test case of that year the Court of Session 'unanimously' declared for the pursuer in an action brought against a Catholic freeholder, finding him on grounds of his religion not entitled for inclusion on the roll of electors, 'though admitted by the freeholders'; the man complained of having been unable/unwilling to swear the formula prescribed by the Act of 1707 (that part of the Treaty of Union expressly preventing Catholics 'possessed of sufficient property' from voting at elections).[10] Full Catholic emancipation in Scotland was not entered upon the statute book until 1829 when the Catholic Emancipation Act finally liberated Catholics throughout Britain, conferring on them equal rights under the law to those professing other faiths.[11]

The important question is this: why was 'popery' not just vilified in Scotland in the eighteenth century, but aggressively condemned by the majority of social groups and organisations within the establishment, and, pre-eminently, by the established church? At the same time, of course, it is necessary to take account of the varying degrees of enthusiasm towards the issue on the part of individual Kirk ministers, depending on their allegiance to either the Moderate or Popular faction. Part of the answer to the question lies in the extent to which Roman Catholicism was identified in Protestant Scotland with sustained attempts by a foreign power or powers – in these specific instances France and, of course, the Pope in Rome – to subvert the throne and government of Britain in the rebellions of 1715 and 1745, tainted as they were by the Stuart cause and its traditionally strong links with (those relatively scant) Jacobite elements among the ranks of certain of the Scottish nobility and some Highland clans.

Late in the century the jurist, (Baron) David Hume, discourses in his *Commentaries* (1797) on how it has come about that even after the strictly limited form of Catholic relief conceded in 1793, important statutory disqualifications remain in force:

> The reason why the members of the Roman Catholic Church continue to be excepted from our common rule of toleration, does not lie so much in any peculiar aversion to the articles of their spiritual creed; as in certain principles of theirs, which are attended with a plain danger to our civil state and constitution of government. Such in particular it is, that Popery implies the acknowledgement of a foreign power as supereminent to the Sovereignty of these realms; and this a power, which in its very nature is at perpetual war with our Sovereign, and with our whole frame and political order of things. From this peculiarity of the doctrines of Popery, which makes them matters of the most temporal consequence, not of conscience and speculation only, comes the regular severity with which Papists are chastised by our laws, and distinguished from all other non-conformists.[12]

As we shall see later in this chapter, however, Hume's explanation was not, at least for many decades, the corporate view of the Church of Scotland; nor was it the view of numerous individual ministers who strove in their sermons, pamphlets and bulkier treatises to expose the gross theological 'errors' they discerned in 'popery' – and who consequently saw it as their bounden duty to take appropriate measures to stamp it out wherever it was discovered to rear its head, seducing the people, as they had been led to believe, to subscribe to its 'errors' and false teachings.

How did the Kirk mobilise its resources in going about its task to combat the perceived evils of popery? There were three main agencies that combined to assist the Church of Scotland in its anti-popery programme throughout most of the eighteenth century:

- The Royal Bounty;
- The Society in Scotland for the Propagation of Christian Knowledge (SSPCK);
- *ad hoc* initiatives, including 'collections' – *e.g.* the 'Breslaw Collection' of 1750.

Of these, by far the most far-reaching in its implications was the Royal Bounty. It was at the General Assembly of 1725 that intimation was made in the King's Address that George I had instructed the Lord High Commissioner for that year, the Earl of Loudoun, to communicate details of an annual Bounty of £1000 for the purpose of employing the money to help 'put some Stop to the spreading of Ignorance and Prophaneness on the one Hand, and the Trafficking of Popish Priests and Emissaries on the other, in the Highlands and Islands, of which frequent Representations have been laid before Us from several preceeding Assemblies and their Commissions.' The Bounty was maintained each year until the end of the century and beyond into the reign of George IV when it was increased to £2000. In the 1737 all-Scotland document, 'A State of Popery', the application and purpose of the Bounty are defined as 'to bestow yearly £1000 Sterling to be given to Itinerant preachers & Catechists to go into those parts where popery abounds, and be assisting to the Ministers established therein, to enlighten the people and arm them against the practices of the popish Priests that resort thither'. At regular intervals thereafter we learn that the General Assembly instruct presbyteries to update statistics of Catholic activity within their parishes, though seldom on the huge scale of the 1737 exercise. In their 'Answer' to the 'King's most Gracious Letter' of 16 May 1746, written just a few weeks after the rout of Culloden, the General Assembly refer to the 'pious Donation in order to reform the barbarous Parts of our Country', and wryly observe that 'some have lately made the most unworthy Requital'.[13] The unequivocal message is that rebellious Jacobite clans have ungratefully bitten the very hand that has fed them.

At first, the use and deployment of the Royal Bounty was administered by a fairly large group of ministers and elders, who received annual reports, but from around 1759-60 these arrangements were changed in favour of a less clumsy, purportedly more effective mechanism which conferred powers on the Church Procurator to make recommendations from time to time on how the money should be spent. Notwithstanding these changes it was still open for presbyteries and synods to submit proposals; thus, in 1762 the Assembly considered a petition and representation of the Presbytery of Strathbogie who complained that 'there was a great number of Papists and other disaffected people within their bounds', yet, they went on, 'the committee for managing the royal bounty has withdrawn the itinerancy, not only from the Enzie, but also from Ruthven [discrete parishes within the Presbytery]; and praying that both these itinerancies might be restored.' We learn, however, that 'the desire of the petitions was refused.' [14]

For historians, one of the more interesting elements in the administration of the Royal Bounty lies in the requirement of the Commission of Assembly that it receive, at indeterminate intervals, extensive reports from presbyteries and/or synods covering, often in considerable detail, the 'State of Popery' then prevailing throughout the whole of Scotland, not just in the Highland regions to which the Bounty was originally targeted.[15] These reports were expected to include a detailed census of known Catholics in the parishes concerned, desirably by identifying each recusant by name. One of the most comprehensive of these inventories was compiled and submitted in 1737 and has been assiduously researched by the French historian, Professor Clotilde Prunier.[16] Others who ante-date Prunier in beginning to mine these mostly unpublished church materials include (in chronological order) Wilby,[17] Donovan,[18] Johnson[19], and Szechi.[20] Their individual and cumulative efforts helped restore a long-needed historiographical balance to the controversy by shedding important new light on the anti-popery issue within and outside the Kirk, focusing not only on how the national church mustered its resources to combat the perceived threat from popery, but also for the first time taking account of contemporary Catholic accounts of their necessarily covert mission in Scotland.[21]

The 1737 document is of special importance on account of the fact it literally covers the whole of Scotland and is not confined to Catholic hotspots in the Highlands and Islands. To the modern eye, the entire document is a chilling dossier/census *cum* record of espionage activities on the grand scale. Thus, here is the report from the Synod of Lothian and Tweed[d]ale:

> There is 7 presbytries here, and 123 Ministerial Charges therein but few profest papists having their Constant Residence in any of them, Except one Mr Alexander Limner in New Kirk parish of Edinburgh his Wife & two Children But diverse papists resort frequently

thither. In Cannongate Lady Jean Keith & diverse others to the Number of 13. In South Leith, Thomas Morgan. In the presbytrie of peebles, The Earl of Traquairs family, Lady children & servants consisting of 19 in all, also Mr Thomas Sinclair with his spouse & daughter in the parish of Stobo.[22]

The agency devised by the Kirk to manage on the ground its anti-popery strategy was the Society in Scotland for the Propagation of Christian Knowledge (SSPCK). Founded in 1709 on the model of the English SPCK the Scottish Society derived funding from special collections and (usually anonymous) benefactors, later (from 1760) supplemented where necessary by *ad hoc* grants out of the Royal Bounty. The SSPCK regarded itself as the official missionary arm of the Church of Scotland. In 1741 it is reported that the Society maintained 131 'charity-schools' in the Highlands of Scotland 'at which upwards of 5000 scholars are educated'. In 1747 we learn that the Society had spread its wings across the Atlantic 'in those dark corners of the world' among 'the infidel Indian natives, living on the borders of the provinces of New York, New-Jersey, and Pennsylvania, by means of the missionary ministers employed there'. In 1761 John Hyndman, a minister of the West Kirk in Edinburgh, notes in the published version of his anniversary SSPCK sermon preached that year in the High Kirk, that the 1760 General Assembly had appointed a group of 'some ministers', of whom he was one, 'to visit those places where the itinerants and catechists are employed'. Hyndman reports:

> To the continued endeavours of this society, to the application of his Majesty's pious and princely donation, ... it must chiefly be ascribed (under God) that the clouds of ignorance, superstition, and disloyalty, which so long covered some parts of the highlands, are now breaking and flying away ... .[23]

As late as 1775 the historian-minister of Elgin, the legendary Reverend Lachlan Shaw, could write with the benefit of a long and intellectually active life, that in 1726 he could find 'in all Glengary and Achadrom, which may consist of 800 souls, ... very few Protestants', and that since that time 'they have not become much better; but have diffused their errors into the neighbouring Countries of Abertarf, Glenmoriston, and Strathglass.' Thanks, however, to the efforts of the SSPCK, Shaw notes the 'happy effects' of 'this truely pious Institution are visible in this Province' [Moray]: 'Christian Knowledge is increased, Heathenish customs are abandoned, the number of Papists is diminished, disaffection to the Government is lessened ... '.[24] According to Shaw, at least, the Society was fulfilling its purpose and succeeding in its objects.

Finally, throughout the eighteenth century until approximately its last two decades the General Assembly regularly responded to requests for financial and moral support from beleaguered Protestant churches in Europe and America that had communicated to the Kirk their fear of engulfment by the forces of popery. A typical example is the so-called 'Breslaw Collection' of 1750. Morren records that at the Assembly that year a minister of the Reformed Church of Breslau[25] introduced the issue of the plight of the church in that city which he describes in the following graphic terms:

> A Church! which is surrounded with Popery, and rears up its head as a bulwark against the errors of that idolatrous religion: A Church! which is situated in the capital of an extensive

country, a large trading city; and therefore, by the blessing of God, may be of important service to the truth as it is in Jesus, to give a check to Popery, and to bring many souls out of darkness to the light of the gospel: A Church! which, if once well settled, is likely to be of great use to the neighbouring Protestants in Hungary, Poland, and Bohemia, who are still groaning under the yoke of Popish bondage ... .

In response, the Assembly passed an Act 'appointing a collection to be made for building and endowing a church and school for this suffering community at the doors of all the parish-churches in Scotland'. The collection raised 'upwards of £900', over £160,000 at the time of writing (2017). Similar collections were proposed for the 'reformed congregation at Saarbruck' (1758) and for the 'Belgic Churches' (1759) – 'wherein the interests of the Protestant religion, as well as that of the British nation, were so deeply concerned'.

The man to whom the Assembly for many years delegated responsibility for organising such collections was the Edinburgh 'merchant' and 'banker', William Hogg, senior partner in the firm of William Hogg and Son.[26] In 1753, in response to an appeal from Dr Samuel Chandler, the nonconformist co-pastor of the Old Jewry Chapel in London, the Assembly had agreed to commend to presbyteries the raising of support for protestant emigrants in Pennsylvania, thus extending to North America an existing scheme involving the church in Holland and 'several in Germany'. At the next Assembly Hogg is reported to have remitted to Chandler the proceeds of the Pennsylvania collection, the grand total of £1140 9s 11d, 'the whole amount of the collections he had then received'. For his pains Chandler was awarded an honorary D.D. by Edinburgh (1755) and Aberdeen (1756).[27]

Anti-popery and the device of the re-cycled sermon: Hugh Blair, John Willison and James Fordyce

At its height in the late 1770s the popery controversy highlights the extent to which, almost as never before in Scotland, the printed word was employed in the service of pamphleteers to get their dubious message across to an eager readership, whipping up popular resentment of Roman Catholics and Catholicism. The pamphlet deluge was particularly fierce once it came into the public domain that steps were being taken by Lord Advocate Dundas to introduce a Scottish version of the English Catholic relief bill. In reality, however, considering the numbers of Catholics then resident in Scotland, any threat to the survival of the Reformed church presented by a Scottish bill was virtually non-existent. In his speech to the General Assembly in May 1779 William Robertson estimated that Catholics numbered less than 17,000 out of a total Scottish population of 1,300,000, or 1.3%.[28] All of this is, of course, well known. What is much less known is that, admittedly only in a few extreme cases, some church sermons were not just altered and re-cycled many years after the date of their original delivery and publication – *either* to purge them of their toxic (i.e. popery) content, *or* to re-issue them *more* or *less* in their original state, in both cases in the expectation that their authors (or, if deceased, their enthusiastic followers) continued to believe that the 'message' they contained, whether 'doctored' or left intact, was still held to be relevant. The three sermons examined here represent examples of several different 'treatments' of that *genre*.

After the successive failures of the 'Fifteen' and 'Forty-Five' rebellions it was inevitable that a plethora of printed sermons should flow from Scottish printers as Kirk ministers jostled with one another to discover scriptural (often allegorical) parallels in the successive Jacobite attempts to overthrow the Hanoverian succession and restore a Stuart to the throne; and, of course, in the process, to restore the Catholic faith as the official state religion of Great Britain. One of the more distinguished examples of the *genre* is Hugh Blair's sermon of May 1746 which he was invited to preach in the course of the General Assembly that year before the Lord High Commissioner (the King's representative), the Earl of Leven. Unusually, but understandably in the circumstances then prevailing — the bloody field of Culloden had been fought over barely three weeks before, on 16 April, and, technically at least, the rebellion was still in progress — there was great confusion and uncertainty surrounding the opening of the Assembly. Although Commissioners reported on the due date appointed for the official opening (Friday 9 May), the Lord High Commissioner was absent and, in consequence, the opening was postponed for one week. That meant that, exceptionally, the 1746 Assembly was treated to *two* sermons: the customary sermon preached on what had been intended as opening day by the outgoing Moderator — Principal William Wishart — but with Lord Leven absent from the congregation; and on Sunday 18 May when the preacher was the up and coming minister of the second charge at the Canongate Church, one Hugh Blair, then aged 28. Both men, of course, preached in the High Church of St. Giles, but it was Blair alone to whom fell the honour of preaching before the Lord High Commissioner. In their printed form both sermons were dedicated to Leven in accordance with tradition.

Both Wishart's and Blair's celebratory sermons — for that is their predominant purpose and tone — are generally unremarkable, Blair's betraying some of the signs of relative *juvenilia* and youthful exuberance. And yet, Blair's sermon is important for two reasons. First, in terms of content and even vocabulary it drearily mimics aspects of Wishart's parallel sermon of the previous week. Secondly, and much more significant, Blair's sermon deserves to be remembered in the canon of his works if only on account of his re-cycling of it in later life, when it made its re-appearance carefully purged of all its contemporary politico/historical references. There is, of course, nothing unusual or even exceptional in ministers recycling their sermons; doubtless the habit still chunters on in the modern church. Blair's motive in re-working his old Assembly sermon of 1746, however, was to permit its inclusion in the early collected editions of his *Sermons*. Just why he considered the content of the original version obsolescent and inappropriate for the sophisticated, 'modern' readership of his maturity may be obvious, but his re-working of it is nonetheless important, and has to date been wholly overlooked by scholars.

Both sermons take as their texts verses from the *Psalms*: Wishart's from Psalm 122, 6-9: *Pray for the peace of Jerusalem, they shall prosper that love thee. Peace be within thy walls, and prosperity within thy palaces. For my brethren and companions sakes, I will now say, peace be within thee. Because of the house of the Lord our God, I will seek thy good*; Blair's from Psalm 76, 10: *Surely, the wrath of man shall praise thee: the remainder of wrath shalt thou restrain*. Secondly, the message of each sermon is identical: 'victory', 'peace' and 'deliverance'. Thirdly, both sermons make specific reference to 'popery' — though each on one occasion only — and, interestingly, both Wishart and Blair choose to conjoin the threat of the reintroduction of popery with the notion of consequential 'slavery':

[*Wishart*]

[Of Cumberland] One, whom we may justly look upon as a second *William* the Deliverer of these Lands, from the threatened Danger of Popery and Slavery! [29]

[*Blair*]

Had it not been for the *avow'd* Attempts then made against our Religion and our fundamental rights, *Britain* might have been now under a *Popish* Sovereign: and ... we would have been the Subjects, or rather *Slaves*, of those who arrogantly claim us as their *Property* by *Divine Right*. [30]

Finally, and above all, both sermons contain a warm encomium of the Duke of Cumberland, the third son of George II, and the general to whom the king had entrusted command of the army not just on the bloody field of Culloden but subsequently in the Highlands, his troops mercilessly hunting down the remnants of the survivors until as a fighting force they ceased to exist. To Wishart and Blair, however, the man Scots for generations would revile as 'Butcher' Cumberland is 'the Deliverer of these Lands', 'an illustrious young Hero', 'the Darling of the Nation' (Wishart); and 'an illustrious Deliverer', 'a Blessing to his Country', 'the Hero, Great', 'this chosen Instrument of our Deliverance' (Blair).

The official record of the 1746 Assembly (*Principal Acts*) notes that in addition to the usual 'Answer' to the king's 'most gracious letter' [31] it was resolved exceptionally to send a separate 'Congratulatory Address' to the king 'upon the victory obtained by his Army, under Command of his Royal Highness the Duke of Cumberland over the Rebels in this Country'. Almost as an afterthought, moreover, it was later resolved to send a 'Congratulatory Letter' to Cumberland himself in a communication of 19 May – the date of the Monday session of Assembly after Blair's High Church sermon on the preceding sabbath. The sycophantic language of this latter document mirrors almost precisely that of both sermons: in the eyes of the General Assembly Cumberland is the 'Deliverer of this Church and Nation':

Every loyal Subject, every sincere Lover of the Religion, Laws and Liberty of his Country, is ready to express his just Gratitude to your Royal Highness, by whom these inestimable Blessings are preserved to us: The Church of *Scotland* are under peculiar Obligations to offer their most thankful Acknowledgments to Almighty GOD, who has raised you up to be the brave Defender of your Royal Father's Throne, the happy Restorer of our Peace, and at this Time Guardian of all our sacred and civil Interests. [32]

Though not received until after the Assembly had risen, a reply from Cumberland was forthcoming dated 21 May in which he praises 'the very steady and laudable Conduct of the Clergy of that Church [of Scotland], through the whole Course of this most wicked, unnatural, and unprovoked Rebellion.'

When Hugh Blair chose to include his old pulpit discourse in his collected *Sermons* – the anthology that would earn him the sobriquet of the 'Scottish Tillotson' [33] – the sermon he proceeded to work on became a vastly different version of the original he had delivered at the 1746 Assembly and subsequently published 'by desire of the Lord High Commissioner'. For one thing, and most obviously, the title has changed: no longer *The Wrath of Man praising God*, but now *On the Divine Government of the Passions of Men* [34] (with perhaps a passing nod to the title of John Witherspoon's great Princeton sermon of 1776 that was then still the talk of the town).[35] Also, the 'new' version is much shorter – cut by as much as a fifth. How has Blair managed such economy? He achieves it by a combination of skilful editing and ruthless expurgation of what can only be termed the *political* content of the original. As we saw in chapter 7, Hugh Blair was never happy with political preaching *per se*, and certainly *Divine Government* is anything but a political sermon. His re-cycled version contains no reference whatsoever to 'popery', least of all to the view he had expressed more than thirty years before that, had the authors of the rebellion prevailed, the logical outcome of 'a Popish sovereign' would have been slavery in the sense that all subjects of the crown would thereby have been claimed as 'Property by Divine Right'. At the same time, Blair has erased the entire passage extolling the military virtues of the Duke of Cumberland.

It is unlikely that *Divine Government* was ever preached in a pulpit. Instead, like the majority of Blair's sermons this expurgated version, shorn of its crude sycophantism, is entirely a literary production, a refined and polished rhetorical gem, designed to be read rather than heard. It cannot, however, be overlooked that the year in which Blair's sanitized version of his 1746 original first became available – in 1780 as Sermon XIV in volume 2 of the Strahan/Cadell/Creech edition of the collected *Sermons* – was barely a year after the anti-popery riots that resulted in the destruction of Bishop Hay's house in Edinburgh. The subsequent General Assembly was a cynosure of high passion, the star turn having been William Robertson's last and greatest performance in which he appealed for tolerance and sought (on the whole successfully) to defend his personal role in the dramatic sequence of events.

Blair's re-cycled version of *The Wrath of Man* was by no means a freakish one-off. The sermon that immediately follows *Divine Government*, as Sermon XV in the same volume of the *Sermons* (1780), is also a re-cycled version of a much earlier published sermon. In 1750 Blair had preached, and Robert Fleming had subsequently published, a sermon he entitled *The Importance of Religious Knowledge to the Happiness of Mankind*. He had delivered it in the High Church on 1 January that year before the SSPCK who had arranged for its publication. As was the usual practice with SSPCK 'guest' sermons, the pamphlet incorporates 'a short Account of the Present State of the Society'. Although this time he retains the same title for both versions, the deliberate expunging of references to popery is even more dramatic than in the case of Blair's 1746 General Assembly sermon. The differences between the two versions are striking:

> [1750 version] Further, religious knowledge assists in preparing the Way for all useful and ornamental Improvements in Society. It has, in Fact, been found, that, along with the Increase of *religious* Light, *Learning* has flourished, and useful *Arts* have been cultivated and advanced. The true Knowledge of the Lord promotes a *free* and *manly* Spirit. It teaches Men to think for themselves, to form their Principles upon a fair Inquiry unto the Word

of God; and not to resign their Consciences implicitly to Men. Hence, it is strongly connected with a Detestation of Oppression of every kind; and forms a Taste for *Liberty and Laws.* We see that tyrannical Governments have taken the firmest Root, in Nations blinded by *Mahometan* and *Pagan* Darkness, where the Throne of Violence is *supported* by Ignorance and Error. In the Christian World, as long as *Popish* Superstition reigned undisturbed, *Darkness, Oppression* and *Slavery* were in its Train. For some Centuries, the Cloud sat *thick* and *deep* over all *Europe*, and threatened a Relapse unto ancient Barbarity: Till, at the auspicious Aera of the *Reformation*, together with the true *Knowledge of the Lord, Learning, Liberty* and *Arts*, began to shine forth and resume their Lustre. At this Day, the *Protestant Religion* is, in our own, and some other States, the great Bulwark of *Liberty*.[36] [underlining added]

[1780 version] Religious knowledge forwards all useful and ornamental improvements in society. Experience shews, that, in proportion as it diffuses its light, learning flourishes, and liberal arts are cultivated and advanced. Just conceptions of religion promote a free and manly spirit. They lead men to think for themselves; to form their principles upon fair inquiry, and not to resign their conscience to the dictates of men. Hence they naturally inspire aversion to slavery of every kind; and promote a taste for liberty and laws. Despotic governments have generally taken the firmest root among nations that were blinded by Mahometan or Pagan darkness; where the throne of violence has been supported by ignorance and false religion. In the Christian world, during those centuries in which gross superstition held its reign undisturbed, oppression and slavery were in its train. The cloud of ignorance sat thick and deep over the nations; and the world was threatened with a relapse into ancient barbarity. As soon as the true *knowledge of the Lord* revived, at the auspicious æra of the Reformation, learning, liberty, and arts, began to shine forth with it, and to resume their lustre.[37] [underlining added]

How are we to account for Blair's editorial circumspection – and, in particular, for his eradication of all references to 'popery' evident in the early version of the sermon, along with omission of the cringing Cumberland encomium? In addition, we should note that where Blair mentions 'slavery' in the 1750 version he conventionally relates it to, and associates it with the foreseen consequences of 'popery'. By contrast, in the 1780 version his reference to slavery – though he continues to see it as a consequence of 'gross superstition' – is also clearly now meant in the 'modern' sense of the *traffic* in slaves. To put such revision down to mere tinkering on his part, combined perhaps with a natural desire to improve on performances that somehow betrayed a combination of relative immaturity and naïve patriotism, is unconvincing. Essentially these re-cycled pieces can only be explained as testimony to Blair's enlightened Moderatism. To put a positive gloss on it, the radical changes he insisted on making to these early sermons should be seen as further evidence, if any were needed, of Blair's pre-eminence as one of the greatest figures of the religious enlightenment in Scotland. At the same time, we should acknowledge an alternative view, ascribing the 'improved' versions simply to Blair's desire to put the past behind him.

Although quite different motives from Hugh Blair's lie behind the re-cycling of sermons in two other cases at this period – the later editions appearing often years after their original composition and publication, and in one case even long after the death of the author concerned – these, too, are highly relevant to the popery controversy. An extreme example is a fiercely anti-popery pamphlet entitled *Popery another Gospel* by John Willison, the controversial orthodox minister of the South Church in Dundee. Willison's title had first appeared in Edinburgh in 1746; it contains six sermons, all on the same theme, that he had preached in his pulpit 'in the time of the Rebellion' in 1745. Whatever the merit of their content – often, to modern taste, offensively wearisome[38] – it would seem that Willison's sermons struck exactly the right note among his many loyal supporters who aligned themselves with his extreme anti-Catholic views. John Willison died in 1750.

The historian of the Popular party, McIntosh, describes Willison as 'probably the most commonly read religious writer in eighteenth-century Scotland', as well as 'the earliest and possibly the most fundamental opponent of Moderatism.'[39] Scott comments that Willison 'sympathised with the Seceders, though not to the extent of joining with them'.[40] That might account for the fact that a pirated edition of his *Popery another Gospel* was re-issued in Falkirk in 1779, the year when anti-Catholic feelings ran high, by a local printer, 'Daniel Reid', on the initiative of a secessionist 'preacher',[41] one 'W. Burns'. Burns is described in the imprint as 'the Publisher'. The same man, described this time as 'Preacher of the Gospel', resorted more ambitiously in 1798 to an unauthorised edition of John Gillies' monumental *Memoirs of the life of the Reverend George Whitefield*, originally published in London in 1772 by the Dilly brothers 'and Messieurs Kincaid and Creech, at Edinburgh'; this time the printer in Falkirk is 'T. Johnston'.[42] We know almost nothing of Burns except that from a short preface, 'To the Reader', in the Whitefield reprint, having noted the great Methodist's achievements in itinerant preaching, he tellingly adds: 'For my own part, I account it the happiest circumstance in my lot, when the tender state of my eyes permits me, in my little sphere and measure, to imitate so great an example.' It seems that Burns, inspired by the great Whitefield, may also have been a preacher on the move.

What prompted an obscure secessionist preacher in Falkirk, a parish within the national church's presbytery of Linlithgow, to commission a reprint of Willison's anthology of anti-popery sermons originally published nearly thirty years before? The date of the reprint is, of course, the give-away. Anti-Catholic feelings in the central belt of Scotland were near boiling point in 1779 on account of the rumours surrounding the possible introduction of a Scottish Catholic relief bill. Printers were finding it hard to cope with the succession of pamphlets expressing outrage at the move and stirring up all the old scare-mongering about popery, not this time focusing on the Jacobite threat *per se*, but more on the 'errors' that Roman Catholicism was held to be founded upon, and on its supposed continued hostility towards all Reformed churches. What had now supplanted Jacobitism in pamphlets of the 1740s was the American war and, more especially, the alarming alliances the Americans had entered into with Catholic France and Spain.

It is unnecessary to pick over the actual contents of Willison's six sermons which, in any event, are notably much less appealing to a modern eye than the pamphlet's fascinating bibliography. Lumisden and Robertson's [43] 1746 edition of *Popery another Gospel* bears an unusually wordy and cluttered title page [see illustration on page 237], incorporating no less than three independent sub-titles, *viz*:

Main sub-title 'A Demonstration that the Romish Religion is not the Gospel that Christ hath left his Church, but what Antichrist hath since devised, to the Destruction of Christianity and the Souls of Men.'
1st subsidiary sub-title 'Published to give Warning to all PROTESTANTS through Britain and Ireland of the damnable Errors and Cruelty of POPERY, and of the dreadful Danger and Tendency of the present INSURRECTION in its favours.'
2nd subsidiary sub-title 'With a Preface, relating to the Justice of the Revolution-Principles and present Establishment, and the Unreasonableness of *Jacobitism* and *Disloyalty*.'

All three sub-titles are faithfully reproduced on the title page of the 1779 Falkirk reprint.

A further detail from Willison's original 1746 preface is also worth noting. Having acknowledged that 'the present awful dispensations of God to the land are very humbling', he goes on to introduce a blatant puff for his Edinburgh publishers' latest title: James Burgh's anonymous pamphlet, *Britain's Remembrancer: or, The Danger not over* (1746), which Lumisden and Robertson had recently brought out in a pirated version of Mary Cooper's London original of the same year. Burgh, a Scotsman living in London, had written his pamphlet to warn against the Jacobite menace; he represented the recent rebellion as a portent of serious ills that were bound to engulf the nation if the citizenry failed to mend their ways by giving up their licentious behaviour that was threatening Britain's future prosperity and well-being. Inevitably, Burgh includes the re-introduction of popery as one of the most serious of all the many possible dire consequences just round the corner:

> I mention giving up the Protestant Religion for Pleasure, because nothing in the World is so likely to open a Door to Popery as unbounded Luxury and Voluptuousness; it being a Religion calculated for the Indulgence and Gratification of the Lusts and Appetites of Men.[44]

The third exemplar in this brief checklist of re-cycled sermons with significant popery content – in many ways the most significant of all three – is James Fordyce's 'Sermon on Popery', *The Delusive and Persecuting Spirit of Popery*, preached before the Synod of Perth and Stirling at Perth on 16 October 1754. The Foulis brothers subsequently published the sermon, though only 'The Second Edition' (1758) has survived: there may never have been a first edition, though Gaskell suggests that another Glasgow printer of repute, Robert Urie, may conceivably have been involved.[45] In 1779, an anxious time for Catholics in Britain, Fordyce re-published his old synodical Perth sermon, retaining the same title, but precious little else. This re-worked version – twenty-five years separating it from its original counterpart – was preached by Fordyce in the dissenting Presbyterian church at Monkwell Street, London on the occasion of the General Fast that government had ordered to be held on 10 February that year, that the country might pray for a good outcome in the seemingly endless American war.

Like his equally distinguished older brother David, tragic author of two of the most influential books of the 'Atlantic Enlightenment', *Dialogues Concerning Education* (1745-48) and *The Elements of Moral Philosophy* (1754),[46] the Reverend James Fordyce (1720-96) was a product of Marischal College, Aberdeen. In 1744 Fordyce was the Crown presentee to the second charge at Brechin, but failed to impress both the incumbent minister and the congregation, and eventually was called to Alloa in 1753 where he established a reputation for the excellence of his preaching. In 1760 Fordyce was admitted to the honorary degree of D.D. by the University of Glasgow, the same year in which he made the momentous decision to move to London where he took office initially as assistant to the formidable Samuel Lawrence, minister of the flourishing Protestant dissenting congregation of Monkwell Street. Lawrence died soon after Fordyce's arrival and, having succeeded him, the Scot developed — and doubtless cultivated — a taste for mingling in the society of the great and the good. James Boswell records that it was Fordyce who introduced Hugh Blair to Samuel Johnson on 24 May 1763, the first occasion on which Blair called on Johnson.[47] That the link between Fordyce and Johnson was much stronger than previously supposed is no longer in doubt following the discovery that Johnson is the anonymous author of the preface to Fordyce's anonymous and highly popular *Sermons to Young Women*, published in two volumes by Andrew Millar and Thomas Cadell in 1766. Fordyce and Blair, too, shared a common interest: they both held sacred the primary role of preaching in Christian worship and both published their views on the subject, Blair, of course, within his classic *Lectures on Rhetoric and Belles Lettres* (1783); Fordyce much earlier in his lesser-known though in its day much respected *The Eloquence of the Pulpit* (1752) [48] as well as subsequently in *An Essay on the Action proper for the Pulpit* (1753).

The Monkwell Street connection with Fordyce and popery is important. Fordyce's re-cycled version of his *Spirit of Popery* sermon was preached in his London pulpit almost precisely at the time of the Edinburgh anti-Catholic riots; that places it about eighteen months before the much more serious Gordon riots in London of early June 1780 when more than 200 people were killed by panicky troops and an enormous destruction of property resulted, including the wholesale torching of known Catholic premises in Westminster, the City and Holborn. Recent research into the identity of the 40,000 + signers of the London petition got up by Lord George Gordon, in his role as president of the Protestant Association, has revealed that there were numerous clerical signers, among them John Wesley, as well as many lay members of dissenting churches. The petition also contained a number of signatures to which *'Monkwell Street'* has been added after the names. Was this, one wonders, a reference to Fordyce's dissenting congregation? It certainly looks like it, especially since 'James Lindsay' also signed the PA petition, Lindsay having been Fordyce's assistant and eventual successor at Monkwell Street.[49]

To all intents and purposes, the two versions of Fordyce's *Spirit of Popery* sermon, while retaining the same title and using the same scriptural text for their inspiration — Revelation 18, 23-24: *By thy sorceries were all nations deceived; and in her was found the blood of prophets, and of saints, and of all that were slain upon the earth.* — are different sermons. If this is re-cycling, it is re-cycling on an almost unprecedented scale. At the outset of his London sermon, however, Fordyce disingenuously claims that his new version represents the '*greater part*' of the one he had preached in Scotland all those years before:

> ... I lay before you the greater part of a Sermon on Popery, which I preached five-and-twenty years ago, in the presence and by the appointment of a numerous and respectable body of the Scotch Clergy, with whom I was then nearly connected.

And further, in the prefatory 'Advertisement' he justifies having recourse to a work that remains identified with a past now long behind him. He declares he values the 'approbation' of those in his congregation who heard his sermon preached at Monkwell Street, since it is no more than 'a well-meant attempt, at a crisis when this country seems to be in growing danger from Popery.' The 'encouragement lately given to it [popery] here' – he is, of course, referring to the passing through both Houses of the Catholic Relief Act in England – may, he says, be a blessing in disguise if it serves to 'awaken the vigilance of those Protestants who are still concerned for the interests of truth, of virtue, and of liberty'. And he continues:

> Is there not room to suspect, that amidst the noise and bustle of our political contentions, the Protestant cause is now, with many on both sides, an inferior consideration, if any consideration at all?

It now becomes clear that what has provoked Fordyce to dust down the sermon he preached at Perth a quarter of a century before is not simply his concern that apathy is driving the new political liberalism that tolerates popery; it is also the American war, clearly now entering upon its decisive stage, and especially the despised American-French alliance. He finds bitter irony in the colonists' 'struggle for temporal independence' leading them unwittingly into 'spiritual tyranny'. But Fordyce also reveals an interesting personal idiosyncracy in his attitude to popery, a characteristic that distinguishes him from all the other clergymen of his time who wrote and preached on the subject. In cultivating France as an ally, America, he says, is effectively sleepwalking into 'so close a connexion with a people', who have the means of corrupting her own youth. It is at first glance an extraordinary argument, but entirely in keeping with the man of feeling who was, after all, the author of hugely popular works including *Sermons to Young Women* (1766), *The Character and Conduct of the Female Sex, and the Advantages to be derived by Young Men from the society of Virtuous Women* (1776), and their companion piece, *Addresses to Young Men* (1777). 'If America', he postulates, 'is under no anxiety on these articles, does she fear nothing for her Youth from the contagion of French manners?' –

> Will her Youth be in no danger from familiarity with Coxcombs and Profligates, pouring in upon them from a country which may be considered as the very school of false gallantry, and polite dissimulation, of atheism assuming the name of philosophy, and adultery reduced to a system? Will the vivacity of her Females, in particular, run no risk of being perverted by so many smooth and sprightly seducers?[50]

It is an extraordinarily convoluted argument and a world away from the predictable anti-popery vitriol of Fordyce's Perth prototype. Yet, in a perverse kind of way, it is at the same time a curiously more detached approach to the entire controversy. At least, his London version, amidst the wearisome clichés on the evils of Rome and popery, breaks new ground in sparing a thought or two for a calmer, even more liberal attitude towards the ordinary Catholic whose sole aim is merely to be allowed to worship freely without impediment. To have uttered such thoughts twenty-five years before to his synodical congregation in Perth would, of course, have been unthinkable:

> For my own part, I scruple not to declare, that I have a better opinion of the most implicit believer in Popery, who nevertheless means honestly, lives virtuously – a case neither impossible nor uncommon – I have a much better opinion of this man as to his heart, and

feel much more affection for him in mine, than I am able to entertain for those people who are perpetually haranguing about the beautiful qualities before mentioned, but discover no veneration for their Maker, no attention to his worship, and no regard for morals. ... many Roman Catholics abhor every kind and degree of inhumanity; and many, we doubt not, disapprove of those tenets which they apprehend to be impious or immoral.[51]

It is rather 'the system itself' for which he feels contempt. And yet, in the only reference to the very recent disturbances in Scotland, he can write at the same time:

We thank God for inclining so many of our brethren in Scotland, among persons of the best understanding and greatest humanity, to express a disapprobation of any measure that might expose their part of the kingdom yet more to the inroads and machinations of Popery.[52]

A final thought on Fordyce and his new-for-old sermon; we are left pondering the distinct possibility that at times he finds it difficult to be conventionally critical. As Samuel Johnson had put it in his preface to Fordyce's *Sermons to Young Women*[53] (1766) some years before:

To entertain the imagination chiefly, were a poor, and indeed a vicious aim in a preacher. To engage the heart, with a view to mend it, should be his grand ambition.[54]

Popery and the enigma of Dr John Erskine[55]

No Kirk minister of either faction in the eighteenth century played a more prominent role in the anti-popery crisis of the later 1770s than John Erskine, the orthodox minister of Old Greyfriars, Edinburgh, friend and respected associate of leading Moderates such as William Robertson, Hugh Blair and Alexander Carlyle. Erskine's most recent biographer describes him as an 'Enlightened Evangelical', but at the same time acknowledges that at bottom he remains an eccentric, even an 'enigma'.[56] Yet, recalling Baron Hume's account of why the popery debate was so heated and prolonged throughout the eighteenth century – down-playing, that is, its theological aspects in favour of the primacy of its continuing political threat – Erskine's numerous contributions to that debate lie somewhere else, uncomfortably nearer the centrality of the Kirk's doctrinal objections to the supposed 'errors' of the Catholic faith. As we shall see, Erskine's dedication to the issue would become near-obsessive.

The serious riots that took place in Edinburgh and Glasgow early in 1779 have their origin in the rumours that began in the latter half of the previous year to the effect that the Lord Advocate, Henry Dundas – in what would prove a rare moment of serious misjudgement – was (accurately) reported to be contemplating a Scottish version of the English Catholic relief, or *Papists Act*[57] which had sailed through both houses of Parliament in May 1778. Dundas mistakenly believed that a Scottish bill would similarly fail to excite much in the way of opposition north of the border. The question we have to address is this: is it credible that ministers of the Church of Scotland opposed to Dundas's proposed bill actually helped foment these riots by their preaching and/or publications, stirring up latent anti-Catholic passions? Some contemporaries certainly held that view.

But did 'a Correspondent' have Erskine, among others, in his sights when the *Caledonian Mercury* reported his suggestion 'that several of the clergy seem to have taken an active hand in giving every opposition in their power to the proposed bill'?[58] It does seem likely. In the same vein, it is sometimes overlooked that in the course of his great speech to the 1779 General Assembly in the course of the protracted popery debate of that year, William Robertson – uncharacteristically speaking 'of himself' and of the personal abuse he and his family had undeservedly attracted over his role in the issue of Catholic relief – revealed that he had sought John Erskine's views on the wisdom of government resorting to tampering with the Scottish bill in an effort to mollify the shrill voices of anti-popery. Robertson was forced to concede that the move had been futile. Erskine, Robertson's fellow minister at Old Greyfriars, and a Kirk elder ('Mr John Walker'),[59] thought so too, and had advised Robertson that it was much too late for such a manoeuvre; 'they were persuaded', orated Robertson, that 'nothing would satisfy the people than a resolution to drop the bill altogether'. Clearly, in consulting Erskine and Walker, 'a respectable minister and elder of this church', Robertson had at first believed that they 'deservedly possess much credit with the opposers of the repeal', and that, consequently, his decision to consult them was defensible on the ground that their opinion was likely to be seen as authoritative and binding. In the event Robertson was wrong and Erskine and Walker's opinion turned out to be prophetically correct.

It may be overegging the case to claim that John Erskine's role in the anti-popery crisis in Scotland in 1778-79 was interventionist, as well as decidedly *un*enlightened. Yet, when we consider the plethora of anti-Catholic pamphlets and discourses attributed to Erskine at this time – attributed or not [60] – we must conclude that the jury is still out as to the extent to which his publications actually helped fan the flame of popular resentment. That is not to dispute the probable accuracy behind the legend that at the height of the unrest, when Bishop George Hay's house and adjoining chapel were burned to cinders by the mob, Erskine, it is said, personally appealed to the rioters, successfully urging their dispersal.[61] It is even claimed that William Robertson himself, then sheltering with his family in Edinburgh Castle after receiving death threats,[62] owed the sparing of his own residence to Erskine's personal efforts.

What are the facts? Erskine's apparent obsession with popery goes much further back than 1779. In chapter 8 of this study the two versions of his discourse *Shall I go to War with my American Brethren?* – the anonymous original that came out in London in 1769 and the attributed Edinburgh version of 1776 – are briefly discussed. Although seven years separate these editions of the same publication – the Edinburgh re-issue is noted in the *Scots Magazine* for May 1776 – Erskine retains the same title in the later (now attributed) pamphlet. First, to point out the obvious, in 1769 the title represents a simple interrogatory question, whereas in 1776 the same question has become purely rhetorical; that is, in 1769 Erskine speculates on the consequences of war with America in the light of Grenville's Stamp Act and other British punitive measures, whereas in 1776 not only is the war into its second year, but it has become all too clear that it is a revolutionary war that is being fought and that, for the colonists, independence of the mother country has become the undoubted primary aim.

Secondly, where all Erskine's publications are concerned his sources are always important to him.[63] Specifically, to understand the background to Erskine's views on popery we have to grasp the significance of his debt – expressed in <u>both</u> editions of *Shall I go to War?* – to the controversial English theologian, Francis Blackburne (1705-87). Blackburne, archdeacon of Cleveland, was a brilliant eccentric, attacking leading clerics of his day from Bishop Joseph Butler, whom Blackburne accused of coming close to holding Catholic values, to Bishop William Warburton, whose ideas on what was termed the 'intermediate state' (of the soul *post mortem*) clashed with his own. As a proto-Unitarian, however, Blackburne had consistently displayed a virulent antipathy towards Roman Catholics and the wider issue of Catholic emancipation to which he was implacably opposed. There seems little doubt that it was their aggressive hostility to popery, beyond any other special theological characteristic inherent in them, that attracted Erskine to Blackburne's writings.

In *Shall I go to War?* Erskine warmly endorses Blackburne's long treatise, *Considerations on the Present State of the Controversy between the Protestants and Papists of Great Britain and Ireland*, which Millar and Cadell published in London in 1768. Erskine's language, directly reflecting Blackburne's, is similarly uncompromising. Pronouncing Blackburne's book 'very seasonable and interesting', he writes that the Englishman's views 'partly strengthen' suspicions that 'the hand of Joab was springing a mine, for dividing a kingdom against itself, in order to its destruction'; while, too, Erskine goes on, such views 'partly demonstrate the danger of quarrelling at this time with our sincere friends', the American colonists. On the specific issue of popery Erskine clearly sympathises with the facts as laid bare by 'Mr. Blackburn' [sic]:

> For some years past, Popery has mightily increased in England. Tares have been sowed, and sprung up in abundance, while the watchmen, both in church and state, have slumbered and slept. Jesuits, banished from Popish countries, for their immoral and treasonable opinions and practices, have found in our Protestant island an undisturbed retreat; and the wished-for opportunity of spreading their poisonous tenets, unobserved, or at least not sufficiently checked. It is to be feared, that, when they can venture it with safety, they may again betake themselves to assassinations, massacres, or gun-powder-plots, the arms with which they have formerly fought for the Catholic cause.[64]

As Erskine is fully aware, however, Blackburne has little if anything to say about popery in a Scottish context. Nothing daunted, in little more than an aside Erskine cites the 'reports' of 'Doctors Hyndman, Dick, and Walker' in support of his contention that 'in many places of the Highlands and Islands of Scotland, Popery has also increased'.[65] Now he returns to Blackburne's *Considerations*,[66] specifically this time to state his concern that 'the English Papists are now disposed to acknowledge the suspicions of the late Pretender's birth well founded, and to make a push, was it in their power, for his Sardinian majesty':

> To these circumstances I would add, that genealogical tables of the house of Stuart are said to be handed about among them, in which the house of Hanover are branded as usurpers, the late Pretender and his two sons are altogether omitted, and the house of Savoy is pointed out as entitled by hereditary right to the British crown.[67]

Erskine's new preface to the 1776 re-issue represents his *apologia* for troubling his readers to re-engage with the same important issues he had originally raised seven years before. He now desires to make it clear that his purpose in declaring himself author of the piece is to be seen in the light of his renewed conviction, now stronger than ever, that he was right in his prediction that a war with America would, both politically and doctrinally, turn out to be disastrous for Britain's survival as a bulwark of Protestant constitutionalism on the one hand, *and* as staunch defender of the true Reformed faith on the other. In 1769 he had iterated his 'apprehensions … as to the danger to which a war with her colonies might expose Britain' and, more specifically, had expressed the view that any such dispute was playing into the hands of France and Spain whose designs to invade Britain or Ireland were based on 'the small number of troops left in them', as well as by 'hopes of assistance from Tories and Roman Catholics.' Writing in 1776, these same countries, Erskine insists, 'may have more ground, than government are aware of, for entertaining such hopes.' Finally, he clarifies why he has decided to re-issue his pamphlet, dealing in the process with the criticism his controversialist stance in the matter had inevitably attracted:

> I have given my opinion to the few in America, to whom I could write with freedom, that the colonies waging war with Britain, would probably issue, first in their ruin, and then in ours. If this was exciting them to take up arms, then, and not otherwise, I plead guilty. I now republish what formerly appeared without my name, on the inexpediency of war with America, and of addresses for coercive measures. Painful as it is, and presumptuous as it may seem, to arraign the opinions of wise and worthy friends, I submit to the unwelcome task, that I may be free from the blood that shall be shed on either side, in this unnatural quarrel. I know not what censure I am likely to incur, from many whose characters I esteem, and whose favour I regard. But sense of duty, and the peace of my own mind, constrain me.[68]

As matters turned out, however, Erskine's personal involvement in the popery issue in its darkest hour would only intensify. Fuelled by rumour and counter-rumour, the prospect of Catholic relief in the form of a Scottish bill requiring separate legislation – necessary since the penal acts against Catholics ante-dated the Union – prompted serious anti-popery riots and popular demonstrations in Edinburgh and Glasgow in late January and early February 1779. On 2 February the newly constructed Catholic chapel and associated priests' houses were totally destroyed by the Edinburgh mob; these included the residence of Bishop George Hay, the Catholic vicar-apostolic of the Lowland district of Scotland. The Edinburgh magistrates issued a strikingly tepid Proclamation which, after warning the 'bad and designing men' who had committed these acts that any future trouble would be met with 'vigorous measures', went on to assure the populace at large that 'with regard to the repeal of the penal statutes against Papists, … the Lord Provost is authorised [presumably by Henry Dundas himself] to assure them, that the bill for that purpose is totally laid aside'.[69] Meantime, Hay issued a pastoral letter under the *alias* of the 'Bishop of Daulis' (to which See he had been nominated as far back as 1768) in which he laid the blame for stirring up the people squarely at the door of the press and the pamphleteers:

The minds of the people, especially in Edinburgh, had been so much inflamed by the virulent misrepresentations both of our principles and practice, which in the news-papers and other pamphlets had been published among them, that no submission on our part was capable of pacifying their fury; but they seemed in some degree determined on our destruction.[70]

In May the General Assembly met and inevitably the issue of Catholic relief dominated the agenda. Unusually the May number of the *Scots Magazine* devoted its first seven pages to Assembly business, and in this case exclusively to the 'debate on popery'; not only that, but in the section on 'New Books' it continued to provide a further five and a half pages of extracts from George Campbell's *Address to the People of Scotland, upon the alarms that have been raised in regard to Popery* – on top of the eight pages from Campbell's discourse already published in its April issue. As if that were not enough, readers were treated to a long extract from William Creech's pamphlet, *Protestant Interest Vindicated*, in which the enterprising Edinburgh publisher reproduced various letters to Burke 'and other eminent persons' by 'Valerius Corvinus' (the blind poet, Thomas Blacklock), before the number concluded with six more pages of Assembly business.

It was not until its August number that the *Scots Magazine* published the whole transcript of William Robertson's moving Assembly speech, the speech that marked the apotheosis of his years as leader of the Moderate party. On the popery issue *per se* Robertson is reassuringly, typically insighted, and also true to his enlightened, Moderate guiding principles:

> Though I had observed, with pleasure, the rapid progress of liberal sentiments in this enlightened age; tho' I knew that science and philosophy had diffused the principles of toleration through almost every part of Europe; yet I was so well acquainted with the deep-rooted aversion of Britons to the doctrines and spirit of Popery, that I suspected this motion, for giving relief to Papists, to be premature.[71]

On his personal role in the issue Robertson is unusually confiding: 'When', he tells the Assembly, 'I foresaw bad consequences from persisting in a measure which I had warmly approved, I preferred the public good to my own private sentiment'. Extraordinarily, it was not until its September issue that the *Magazine* concluded its account of the speeches constituting the popery debate at the May assembly.

On 5 October John Erskine delivered an important 'commissioned' sermon entitled *Prayer for those in civil and military offices recommended, from a view of the influence of Providence on their characters, conduct, and success,* subsequently published by William Gray of Edinburgh. Erskine's sermon is effectively the antithesis of Robertson's speech of reconciliation and moderation; almost defiantly, it preaches the message that his audience of town officials and magistrates expected and desired to hear. No wonder it is dedicated to 'the Lord Provost, Bailies and members of the Town-Council' – and no wonder it was 'published at their desire'. In general, to be fair to him, Erskine was almost always scrupulously true in his adherence to his conviction of many years standing that the practice of pulpit censure was to be shunned.[72] But in this sermon he seems to have abandoned (or conveniently forgotten) that scruple. It is one of the most overtly political sermons Erskine would ever preach and publish.

Erskine's text is from the Book of *Joshua*, 1, v. 17: *Only the Lord thy God be with thee, as He was with Moses.* Against all expectations, God has appointed Joshua to lead the people of Israel out of captivity to Canaan, while Moses is denied that honour and 'sentenced to die on the other side [of] Jordan.' The people whom Joshua leads are 'men of a truly excellent and worthy spirit' and they pray to God that he 'would cause a double portion of his spirit to rest on his successor', and prosper him so 'that the beauty and strength of government might not be diminished by the change of the ruler'. Immediately, thereby, Erskine is led to his first 'application':

> Such, my brethren, should be our wishes and prayers at all times for those who rule over us, or who command our fleets and armies, and more especially in such a day of danger and alarm as this.[73]

Erskine proceeds to a general contemplation of the purpose and design of government. 'Without government', he asserts, 'our lives, and estates, and liberties would soon become a prey to the covetous and cruel'. –

> The world would be as the troubled sea, whose waves continually call forth mire and dirt; and the inhabitants of the world, as the fishes of the sea, the greater devouring the lesser. ... It is therefore necessary, from the depravity of mankind,[74] that some should be armed with power and authority for preventing these evils, and for securing the peace and order of society. Laws must be enacted for preserving to men the undisturbed enjoyment of the blessings of nature and providence. Courts must be held for composing differences, determining claims, and redressing injuries. Magistrates must bear the sword, that they may be a terror to evil doers, and a shield and defence to them who are quiet in the land.[75]

Among the 'rights secured to us in these lands by government', Erskine continues, 'one of the most valuable is, the right of worshipping God, according to the dictates of conscience, and the rules of his word.' It is unfortunately true that 'piety, true patriotism, and zeal for the interests of religion are less conspicuous in many who hold civil or military offices, than they have been in some former periods'; but that should only 'encourage us to intercede, that God will have men of all ranks and stations to be saved, and to come to the knowledge of the truth.'

In the same way, Erskine argues, we have to understand and acknowledge that

> It is from divine influence that rulers diligently search what conduct is just and wise; hearken to salutary advice, from whatever quarter it comes; and have clear understandings to discern, and sound judgements to chuse the right path, even in situations the most intricate and perplexed. ... *We should pray, that, in consequence of good dispositions and eminent abilities, rulers may actually adopt the measures which tend to promote the public good.* [italics added] ... [A ruler] must vigorously enforce and execute laws for restraining wrong, and wicked lewdness, and help forward the enacting such new laws as may be needful for doing this effectually.[76]

When, however, we read of Erskine's concern for the adoption of 'measures which tend to promote the public good', we might be forgiven for recalling George Hay's pastoral letter with its words of comfort for his small flock of suffering fellow Catholics; and also William Robertson's insistence that however his critics regarded his actions in the period leading up to the riots, together with the virulent attacks on his personal reputation, his first concern had always been for 'the public good', rather than his own 'private sentiment'.

Nevertheless, rulers and others in authority have to put up with criticism of their actions. 'It is under God', Erskine explains, 'a chief security of our other liberties, that we in these lands enjoy the liberty of canvassing, and even arraigning, the measures of administration.' Using Junius's letters and Wilkes' *North Briton* in a footnote to illustrate his point that 'the best things may be perverted' and that 'this important privilege [the liberty of the press] hath been often abused' – extending on occasion to 'the insolent treatment of our sovereign in some publications' – yet, even so, he pleads, 'when it is exercised by a free and candid discussion of political questions', 'though many may err, useful knowledge will be increased.'

At the core of his sermon Erskine returns to the story of Israel in Egypt and how it came about that 'part of the burden of Egypt' lay in God setting the Egyptians against one another, 'every one against his brother, and every one against his neighbour, city against city, and kingdom against kingdom'. The allegory soon becomes clear:

> If ever a season demanded fervent prayer for our rulers and commanders, surely the present demands it, when we are in danger of being deprived of the inestimable blessings we have enjoyed under the illustrious house of Hanover. For this purpose powerful monarchs are setting themselves, and taking counsel together. Unhappily we were not convinced of their hostile designs, till we had let slip the easiest and surest opportunity for guarding against and disappointing them. ... It was not attended to, that Britain, when opposed by North America, must be less formidable to the house of Bourbon, than she had been when North America fought under her banners. ...This consideration renders it of the last importance, not to Britain only, but to North America, and to every Protestant state in Europe, that the designs of France and Spain should be disappointed.. The conquest of Britain would soon be succeeded by that of North America, and that again by the conquest of Holland, of the Protestant states of Germany, and of the Protestant cantons of Switzerland, if not by enslaving every other state in Europe.[77]

In other words, Erskine envisions a new inter-continental war of religion, with France and Spain joining forces against Britain and the other Protestant states of Europe. The problem is, he foresees, the prospect of apathy at home among those 'who are unconcerned for the fate of their king, their country, and their religion'. Such people, being 'unwilling ... to risk their persons, or even to part with their money', are only motivated by self-interest and greed. Echoing the same sentiments he had already vented in his pamphlet of the year before – *Considerations on the Spirit of Popery*, written to combat '*The intended Bill for the relief of Papists in Scotland*' – Erskine warns:

> Some who are themselves sincere Protestants, and warmly attached to civil liberty, have unwarily damped the zeal of others, by asserting, that the spirit of Popery is now become gentle and tolerant; and that it is not the temper of the present times to persecute for religion.[78]

On the other hand, he continues: '... some who once derided all danger from our Popish foes, are now ready to despair of our effectually resisting their ambitious designs'.

In one of the most memorable and powerful passages of any sermon Erskine preached in his long career, he poses a series of rhetorical questions of his congregation – a congregation that included on the front pews the highest city dignitaries in the persons of the Lord Provost of Edinburgh, Bailies and magistrates :

> Do you prefer the Bible to the Mass-book; a pure and rational devotion to idolatry and superstition; and Protestant teachers, who recommend religion by the soft and gentle methods of argument and persuasion, to Jesuits and Dominicans, whose compassion to souls hath often appeared in treasons and assassinations, persecutions and massacres, and all the horrors of the inquisition? Do you prefer the right of examining doctrines by reason and scripture, to blind submission to a pretended infallible guide; and a religion, that cements the union of princes and people, and enforces the observance of their reciprocal duties, to a religion which absolves subjects from oaths of allegiance to their lawful princes, and obliges princes to destroy subjects whom they have sworn to defend?[79]

The sermon closes on a clearly sycophantic note, with a ringing endorsement of the wisdom and foresight of the Edinburgh magistracy and their judicious continuing practical exercise of their right of patronage:

> Nor let us, in this city, forget what we owe to a series of magistrates, who have watched over our tranquillity, as, on other accounts, so for their regard to merit, to the voice of the public, and to the inclinations of their fellow-citizens, in supplying vacancies in schools, in the university, and in our churches. [80]

Patrick Grant's sermon of moderation and reconciliation

In the course of the General Assembly of 1778 the Lord Advocate, Henry Dundas, 'who was then in the house', was pressed by 'a gentleman' to give the Assembly 'some account' of the Catholic relief bill as it might apply to Scotland, 'as the information hitherto received concerning it was vague and uncertain'. At an earlier Assembly session the same individual had requested that an insertion be made into the draft reply to the king's letter relating to a putative Scottish bill, but, after a 'warm debate', he had agreed to withdraw his request on receiving an assurance that the matter would be returned to in the event that 'the bill should be found to have any tendency to hurt the interest of the Protestant religion'. When that debate eventually took place, with the Lord Advocate in attendance, Dundas himself had been forced to rise and clarify the position. The report in the *Scots Magazine* reads as follows:

> His Lordship then informed the house, that the bill alluded to did not extend to Scotland; but that he did not doubt, in some future session of parliament, a similar bill might be brought in for this country. He further observed, that the bill meant only to repeal a penal law, which had, from the beginning, been considered as so cruel, as seldom to be put into execution.[81]

The report continues: Dundas's brief speech 'did not satisfy the gentlemen who insisted for the motion'. A heated debate ensued on a second motion proposed by John Gillies, the Popular party minister of the College church in Glasgow (the Blackfriars)

– supported by Charles Nisbet of Montrose and a few other like-minded evangelicals – authorising the Commission of Assembly to be 'very watchful' in regard to the introduction of a Scottish bill and for its members to be delegated authority to call an extraordinary meeting to discuss what further action may be necessary if they thought the prevailing circumstances warranted it. In the event, however, Gillies's motion was heavily defeated by the Moderates who (in Sher's words) invoked their 'cherished principle of religious tolerance'.[82] In the chair for that difficult debate was the new moderator, the Reverend Dr Patrick Grant, the only Moderator in the entire eighteenth century who was a serving minister of a Highland parish.[83]

Grant was then, and remains a peripheral, even obscure figure. Just why he was chosen Moderator is something of a mystery. Or is it? In an age when patronage was the assumed order of the day in the majority of senior posts in government, the Courts, the universities, and, above all, of course (by parliamentary statute) in all ministerial Church settlements, the office of moderator was theoretically unlikely to be exempt. Patrick Grant, who received an honorary D.D. from the University of Aberdeen in 1774, was minister of Urray and Tarradale [*aka* Urray and Kilchrist] parish in the Presbytery of Dingwall, within the Synod of Ross. No records have survived to confirm it, but a speculative hypothesis cannot exclude the possibility that Dundas, eager to tie up all the loose ends on a putative Scottish version of the English bill, was looking for a moderator whose tolerance of popery might give hope that he was a 'soft touch' and likely to espouse the government side. But, one hastens to add, historians are not permitted to make assumptions, and no records exist to back up such a theory.[84]

What we do have, on the other hand, is the remarkable sermon that Patrick Grant delivered at the 1779 General Assembly. According to the usual practice, Grant preached it as outgoing Moderator. His sermon is not merely remarkable on account of its content, but also because church historians have conspicuously ignored it. We have a strong clue as to its content from the *double entendre* in the title he gave it when published: *The Spirit of Moderation in Religion Recommended* (1779).[85] Almost everything about the sermon is bold, 'enlightened' in the broadest sense, unconventional and innovative. From Grant's idiosyncratic choice of text – Paul's epistle to *Philemon*, 4. 5, *Let your moderation be known to all men* – to the sermon's relative brevity, and above all, its stark opening words, it is clearly designed to ruffle the feathers of the anti-popery caucus of John Gillies, Charles Nisbet *et al* – and, even perhaps, to turn away the wrath of old Assembly hands like John Erskine:

> Our holy religion is peculiarly recommended to the esteem of mankind by the intrinsic excellence of its precepts, which are obviously framed in the best manner to allay unruly passions, to sweeten the tempers of men, and reform their manners, to promote the peace and welfare of society, to improve, exalt, and perfect human nature; in a few words, to make us happy in ourselves, and in each other, in time and to eternity.[86]

These are hardly profundities, and they would not have taxed the intellectual powers of the fathers and brethren. At the same time, Grant's words offer what may be thought the basic, simple *Christian* message of comfort, 'charity' and reconciliation in a year that had witnessed the desperately ugly side of what counted for 'religious' passion in the streets of Edinburgh and Glasgow. At the outset Grant announces that he intends to use the term *'moderation'* 'particularly with reference to religion'; an apt synonym, he suggests, is *'gentleness'*. Two opposite extremes in that regard are, on the one hand, 'lukewarmness or indifference', and on the other, 'a violent and indifferent zeal.' 'Both', Grant insists, 'are inconsistent with Christian moderation'. Of these, the latter is 'by much the more dangerous of the two': for it is 'all heat without light, and acts precipitantly [sic] without judgment or discretion'. Zeal in that sense, he says, 'is the Torrid Zone in religion; it burns up charity, and destroys the most substantial Christian virtues, mercy, justice, truth.'[87] –

> When this wild and extravagant zeal gets the ascendant, one cannot tell where it will stop. Men have been prompted by it to commit the greatest outrages upon their fellow men, and to exhibit to the world the most atrocious scenes of massacre and blood. ... History, civil and sacred, furnishes numberless instances of the fatal effects of an ill conducted zeal, enough to fill our minds with horror. .[88]

By contrast, a 'right zeal' must be directed towards a 'right end' and pursued by 'right means'. He proceeds to clarify what he means and in doing so, Grant's words, one senses, must have caused some discomfort among many ministers in his congregation that day in the High Kirk, Moderates and Popular party members alike:

> ... with some who would be thought first-rate Christians, if not the only Christians upon earth, this very zeal hath passed for the highest sanctity, and sanctified the grossest immoralities, equivocation, lying, perjury, treachery, oppression, assassination, private murders, public massacres, disturbing the peace of society, unhinging governments, and every other mischief. Zeal is nothing else but a hearty concern for what is right, accompanied with a suitable indignation at what is wrong.[89]

Fearlessly, Grant twists the screw even more tightly, defining 'right zeal' in terms of the unhappy circumstances of the modern church; and, of course, he means the Church of Scotland, deeply divided between the Moderates, with whose side in principle he clearly aligns his own views, and the followers of a perverted religious zeal according to his own preferred definition. It is probably not an exaggeration to suggest that nothing like it had been heard before in a formal moderatorial sermon, with the king's representative, the Lord High Commissioner, present in the congregation:

> ... it is our duty to listen to others who offer us a reason for their persuasion. Thus, to do to all men as we would wish, and might reasonably expect, that they should do to us in similar circumstances. If this be the case, we ought calmly to hear, and as calmly to answer, when the great and fundamental truths of our religion are controverted; much more so in *controversies of smaller moment*. [italics added] Such I venture to call those which have so long agitated and subdivided the members of this church; but mark them who cause divisions, and let us follow after the things which make for peace, and wherewith we may edify one another.
> Christian moderation implies forbearance and charity towards such as may differ from us in sentiments or modes of religion.[90]

It is only at this point in Grant's astonishing sermon, with its plea for enlightened tolerance and 'moderation', that we are at last able to identify the highly specific backdrop against which his preaching should be interpreted; that is, he is directing the full force of his argument against those of his fellow Kirk ministers who continue to condemn popery, and to seek to deny Scottish Catholics the freedom of worship under the law that they desire – legitimate aspirations which Henry Dundas was now forced to deny. It is impossible to read Grant's words without an image forming of a pin being heard to fall in the High Kirk that day. It is pulpit censure in its fullest and most impassioned sense, and the real wonder is that it is preached at the opening of the supreme court of the Church by a minister of that Church, *primus inter pares*, by way of outright condemnation of his peers. He continues:

> A Protestant has no more right to assault the life or property of a Papist, than a Papist has, to assault that of a Protestant. A Christian, merely because he is a Christian, has as little right to invade the life or property of a Jew, a Mahometan, or Pagan, as they have to invade his. No zeal for God or religion can ever atone for the violation of justice or mercy, duties of eternal and indispensible obligations, so that, if we had actually in our power to establish the Christian religion by force of arms, over all the earth, we have no manner of right to do it.[91]

The entire Kirk, Grant continues, must share the blame for the situation now confronting us all, with its warring factions and divisions operating against our own affirmed interests – not to mention the teachings of our founder. And, for the first time in his sermon, Grant indulges in playful irony to make his point:

> When we view the complection of the Christian religion, consider its frame and structure, how admirably well fitted it is to civilize and cement mankind, to calm their minds, to subdue their passions, and to breathe over all a mild, moderate, and peaceable spirit; when, I say, we consider this, we may think it strange, that the votaries of this religion should be so very apt to split into parties and factions, and oppose one another with violence and rage: And still more strange may it be thought, that this very religion, so well calculated for promoting harmony, peace, and good will, among all ranks of men, should itself become the occasion, surely the innocent occasion, of discord and broils, of bloodshed and slaughter; yet the fact is undeniable; for, there never were in this world more violent or more bloody contests than among the professors of Christianity, not only upon a civil but upon a religious account, on account of this very religion which is as inconsistent with such practices as light is with darkness.[92]

Patrick Grant's ground-breaking sermon ends with a recapitulation of his central premise, *viz.* the supreme importance of the principles of moderation governing the opinions and attitudes of ministers of religion towards those in their pastoral care, especially when considering and reflecting on the great issues of the day. Once again – from the point of view of his audience, even more uncomfortably – he rebukes 'some who profess themselves to be of us', on the grounds that their rancour has merely replicated the 'errors and practices' of those whom they themselves regard as the enemies of our Protestant religion:

> The propriety and necessity of instilling these principles into the minds of our people are evident, from the sample of intemperate zeal so lately exhibited amongst us, to the no small disgrace of a good Protestant cause. For shame! that, even in horror or dread of

Popery, some who profess themselves to be of us, should fall into some of its worst errors and practices. [93]

Inevitably, however, Grant's noble words fell on stony ground. A general emancipation of Catholics throughout Britain was almost fifty years distant and, in Scotland, even a watered-down form of relief, comparable to what had been conceded for English Catholics in 1778, would have to wait another decade.

Principal William Robertson by Sir Henry Raeburn, painted in 1792, the year before Robertson's death. Reproduced by kind permission of the University of Edinburgh, in whose Old Senate Room the portrait hangs.

10

Slavery

The same principles, which seem to have determined us to abolish servile tenures, oppressive jurisdictions, and lawless attachments, have induced us totally to abolish the inhuman usage of slavery: for we seem, by degrees, to have become sensible of the inhumanity of it, to have departed from it, and by departing from it, tacitly to have abolished it. So far as I have been able to learn, no vestige of it remains in Scotland.

George Wallace (1730-1805): *A System of the Principles of the Law of Scotland*, v. 1[1] (1760), Bk. III, Tit. II, 'Of Slavery', §§130-1, 89-90.

Key authors and sermons

Reverend Dr William Robertson (1721-93), minister of Gladsmuir in the Presbytery of Haddington (1744-58), of Lady Yester's Chapel, Edinburgh (1758-61), and of Old Greyfriars, Edinburgh, (1761-93); Principal of the University of Edinburgh (1762-92).

The Situation of the World at the Time of Christ's Appearance, and its Connexion with the Success of his Religion, considered. A Sermon preached before the Society in Scotland for propagating Christian Knowledge, At their Anniversary Meeting, In the High Church of Edinburgh, On Monday, January 6. 1755.
Edinburgh: Hamilton, Balfour, and Neill. M,DCC,LV. (1755).[2]

Reverend Dr Thomas Hardy (*aka* Hardie) (1747-98), minister of New North Parish, or 'Haddo's Hole' (West St. Giles' Church)[3], Edinburgh; Regius Professor of Divinity and Ecclesiastical History, University of Edinburgh.

The Progress of the Christian Religion. A Sermon, preached before the Society in Scotland for Propagating Christian Knowledge, at their Anniversary Meeting in the High Church of Edinburgh, Thursday, May 30. 1793. By Thomas Hardy, D.D. One of the ministers of the City, and Regius Professor of Divinity and Ecclesiastical History in the University of Edinburgh.
Edinburgh: John Paterson. MDCCXCIV (1794).

The survival of slavery in its various forms into the age of the Enlightenment, and ultimately the ensuing movement for the abolition of the African slave trade in Britain and her colonial territories overseas, present problems for historians. On the one hand, it is undeniable that the master/servant, liberty/enslavement and equality/inequality antitheses, taken together, not only form one of the most powerful of all Enlightenment ideas — found throughout the works of numerous Scottish and European moral and political philosophers of the period — but in their extended form help partly to 'explain' the American and, more especially, the French revolution. On the other hand, there is no escaping the paradox that two of the greatest names of the Scottish Enlightenment — Adam Smith and Adam Ferguson — seem ill at ease with the concept of universal entitlement to equality and are even ambivalent on the issue of an indiscriminate end to the traditional master-servant relationship.

A further difficulty — and one that will engage us here — is the patchy and luke-warm response to the abolition debate on the part of the Church of Scotland and individual Kirk ministers, rising to the surface at around the same time that popular radicalism was being actively suppressed by a desperate government, and anti-clericalism — or at the least wariness of 'priest-craft' — began to stalk our industrialising towns and cities.[4] It is no comfort to find that the Kirk's ambivalence towards slavery and its abolition was by no means unique among the traditional Christian denominations, Diarmaid MacCulloch for one pointing out that in that regard they were all left far behind by the Quakers who even out-distanced English evangelicals (e.g. Newton, Clarkson and Wilberforce) in their zeal for abolition of the 'wicked trade'.[5]

Enlightenment ideas of liberty, equality and enslavement

These days historians approach the idea of liberty as it was understood in the eighteenth century with an awareness that paradox lies heavy in the air. We now recognise that many of the great parallel themes commonly found in eighteenth-century philosophical and legal 'systems' often collide, one with the other, and were taught by a mix of moral philosophers and jurists, though in different ways and with different emphases. Thus, the multi-nuanced liberty *motif*, and its first cousins — equality, freedom (not always the same thing as liberty), emancipation and its more technical relation, manumission — simply go on recurring throughout many of the works of the great European moral, juridical and political philosophers. Some of these writings influenced actual historical events, among them, most profoundly, the two great revolutions in America and France, but also the movements for British parliamentary reform from the early 1790s, and, co-terminously, the eventual abolition of the African slave trade in Britain and her overseas colonies. One man's moral thoughts on slavery tend to emerge and evolve out of another man's philosophical and/or legal focus on the issues at stake in the master/servant antithesis. That is certainly true of the writings of John Millar, who begins the final section ('Political consequences of Slavery') of the last chapter ('The Authority of a Master over his Servants') of his masterwork (*The Origin of the Distinction of Ranks*)[6] with these words:

> In the history of mankind, there is no revolution of greater importance to the happiness of society than this which we have now had occasion to contemplate. The laws and customs of the modern European nations have carried the advantages of liberty to a height which was never known in any other age or country. In the ancient states, so celebrated upon account of their free government, the bulk of their mechanics and labouring people were denied the common privileges of men, and treated upon the footing of inferior animals.[7]

A recurrent problem, however, is that some of the Enlightenment writers who engaged with the slavery issue were not always so clear or consistent in their views as Millar, or even, it seems, wholly seized by their subject in the first place. When, for example, Montesquieu – according, at least, to one of his contemporaries (Jean de Pechméja, in 1770, in his contribution to the *Histoire Philosophique*, an enormous work usually but mistakenly attributed *in toto* to the Abbé Reynal) – grapples with the issue, he is accused of having condemned slavery 'only tentatively' and of being 'incapable of dealing with the question in a sufficiently earnest manner'.[8] Similarly, Adam Ferguson, a great admirer of Montesquieu and 'deeply influenced' by him, is, one senses, never quite at home with the notion of equality and is content to defend rank and aristocracy on the grounds of his belief in a fore-ordained harmonious order in the human race. Such views on equality were totally at odds with those of Rousseau, d'Holbach and Helvétius. Whether one can agree with Professor Israel in consigning 'the Scots' (he presumably means the major figures of the Scottish Enlightenment) to an 'entirely different' perception of equality is a point to argue.[9]

Much earlier in the century, in 1749 to be precise, Jean Barbeyrac[10] invoked the authority of both Grotius and Pufendorf in finding nothing amiss with the concept of human beings as property and, even more controversially, that children of a slave mother ought to remain in law the property of the master. Though directly opposed to Gershom Carmichael's denunciation of slavery on grounds of both human morality and the rules of natural law, such views were not then universally regarded as morally repugnant in the way we would consider them today. Similarly, a luke-warm, ambivalent and generally sit-on-the-fence outlook on slavery is to be found in the late 1770/early 1780s in the fledgling United States, most notably in the *Lectures on Moral Philosophy* by an ordained Church of Scotland Evangelical minister turned College president. Addressing his students at Princeton, John Witherspoon invokes scriptural authority to justify indecision and uncertainty towards the issue:

> Upon the whole, there are many unlawful ways of making slaves, but also some that are lawful; and the practice seems to be countenanced in the law of Moses, where rules are laid down for their treatment, and an estimation of injuries done to them different from that of free men. I do not think there lies any necessity on those who found men in a state of slavery to make them free to their own ruin.[11]

And Witherspoon, we should note, possessed personal insight into all of this. Many years before, in his parish of Beith, Ayrshire in 1756, he had instructed a 'Negroe boy' – 'James' or 'Jamie', formerly 'Shanker' – prior to baptizing him, and was careful to warn him that the mere act of reception into membership of the church by profession of faith was, he feared, insufficient to justify the boy's claim thereby to be legally free. Subsequent to his baptism, the boy's assumed owner had forcibly removed him to Port Glasgow where he had placed him on a ship bound for Virginia but Jamie had succeeded in escaping to Edinburgh, only to be apprehended (after public advertisement) (see illustration on page 293) and imprisoned in the Tolbooth. The boy had contrived, nonetheless, to proceed with an action in the Court of Session against his alleged master, *Montgomery v Sheddan* [sic], but had died before the case could be determined.[12] Cairns observes that in the printed

Memorials of the process counsel for both sides had taken up the specific issue of scriptural authority, determining, they claimed, on the one hand that 'slavery was inconsistent with Christianity', and, on the other, that 'baptism did not free from slavery'.[13]

Witherspoon's Princeton *Lectures on Moral Philosophy* are riddled with apparent doctrinal inconsistencies. On the one hand, he has no difficulty in recommending to his students what in his previous career as a suburban Kirk minister in the west of Scotland he had termed the 'poison of infidel writings' (the works of Hume and Kames), yet he is able to maintain a continuing belief in the orthodox doctrine of original sin against the withering scepticism of Thomas Paine in the latter's iconic pamphlet *Common Sense*.[14] Witherspoon's reading list – embedded in the famous 'Recapitulation' at the close of his *Lectures* – recommends to his students the works not only of such major figures of the Scottish Enlightenment as 'Hutchinson', Hume, Kames, Ferguson, Reid and Beattie, but also finds room for Grotius, 'Puffendorf', 'Barberac' and, specifically, 'Montesquieu's *Spirit of Laws*'.[15]

For a young Scottish advocate, writing in 1760, Montesquieu could do no wrong. To George Wallace, author of *A System of the Principles of the Law of Scotland*, Montesquieu is simply 'the greatest and the most humane politician of this, or perhaps of any age' who has written on the subject of slavery. In the 'third, fourth and fifth chapters of the fifteenth book of *De l'Esprit des Loix* (1748) Wallace identifies with, and extensively cites from the work that has inspired his own thoughts:

> ... I am ashamed to have bestowed so many words on so plain a theme [slavery]. I would not have done it, had I not found, that some, who pretend to have taken the most extensive views of human affairs, have defended the inhuman system*.[16]

And his long starred footnote begins – 'The question concerning the lawfulness of slavery has been seldom debated in this country.' He proceeds to cite and explain two subsequently much-discussed *causes célèbres* that had come before the Court of Session: *Allan and Mearns v Steen of that Ilk and Burnet of Mountboddo* (1728), and the infinitely better-known (and much more recent) *Shedden v Montgomery* (1757). The former case, Wallace notes, was 'set aside' because 'it was held to be hurtful' to the fishermen who were the subject of the action; the latter, concerning a 'niger boy' who had 'refused to return to his master, because he said he was, like every other British subject, a free man in Britain', had failed to be determined on account of the boy's premature death. Ironically, George Wallace, advocate, would himself (in February 1768) professionally defend John Witherspoon for his behaviour in the protracted Snodgrass affair, the case of 'a minister from Paisley', a Court action that Witherspoon eventually lost and almost certainly contributed to his decision to accept a move to America. The case forms the subject of chapter 2 of this study – 'Profaneness'.[17]

Cairns has noted that: 'Of contemporary Scots doctrinal writers on law, only George Wallace presented an argument against slavery.'[18] Wallace's *System* is of importance to this study for two reasons. *First*, although (as noted on his title page) they represent the views of an 'advocate', his radical comments on slavery, equally, come across as pearls of enlightened moral philosophy; thus, typically the following, anticipating to some extent the opening lines of Rousseau's *Le Contrat Social* (1762), then just two years off:[19]

> I take it to be undeniable, that every man is born equal to every other; for every one, who lays his hand upon his heart, must be conscious, that he cannot help thinking so of himself. Hence Liberty is said to be a *natural* faculty, *naturalis facultas*; and slavery is said not only to owe its original to the arbitrary constitutions of men but to be *contrary to nature*. ... From these principles it follows, that all inequality, all dependence, all servility, all superiority, all subjection, all pre-eminence, which is not *necessary* to the welfare of society, is unnatural; and that, if it could, it ought to be destroyed. Men ought to be reduced to a level as much, that is, they ought to be as free, and as independent of one another, as is consistent with the good of Society.[20]

'Aye', Wallace continues in the nature of a rhetorical flourish, 'but our colonies would be ruined, if slavery was abolished.' His reply? 'Be it so; would it from thence follow, that the bulk of mankind ought to be abused, that our pockets may be filled with money, or our mouths with delicates?' Further rhetorical questions follow in quick succession, to all of which he finds there is just one answer:

> Have not these unhappy men a better right to their liberty and to their happiness, than our American merchants have to the profits, which they make by torturing their kind? Have not these unfortunate Africans, who meet with the same cruel fate, the same right? Are not they men as well as we? And have they not the same sensibility? Let us not, therefore, defend, or support a usage, which is contrary to all the Laws of humanity.[21]

Secondly, and just as extraordinarily, George Wallace's 'On Slavery' (and the colonial slave trade) is totally devoid of any religious, let alone any Christian reference. At one point he writes: 'We ought to form our judgments from the dictates of nature, and from the obvious suggestions of humanity.' His is in all senses of the term what today we might regard as a *humanist* statement. In the eighteenth century, as his 'Introductory Discourse' makes plain, Wallace would have been termed a Deist.[22] Published in 1760, the year of George III's accession – when the General Assembly sought and obtained the new king's oath to 'inviolably maintain and preserve the settlement of the true Protestant religion, with the government, worship, discipline, rights, and privileges of the Church of Scotland' – that may be thought remarkable for an author whose father the Reverend Robert Wallace ('the learned, the ingenious, and the virtuous Author of a *Dissertation on the Numbers of Mankind*') was a distinguished 'early Moderate' minister and has been described as 'a role model for members of the ecclesiastical moderate party of younger men who gained control of church politics in the 1750s under William Robertson's leadership.'[23]

From 1750 to 1793 Montesquieu's *The Spirit of the Laws* was published in Scotland in no less than ten different editions – both in the original French, or, more commonly, in translation – in Edinburgh,[24] Glasgow and Aberdeen, with a further two editions of the companion-work, *Persian Letters* (1721), published in Glasgow in 1751 and 1760. Further, extracts from the enormous work (or, more accurately, works) usually, but misleadingly, credited to the Abbé Raynal *solo* – the *Histoire Philosophique* (1770),[25] and/or its English derivative, the *Philosophical and Political History of the Settlements and Trade of the Europeans* [variant: *of the British Settlements and Trade*] *in the East and West Indies* [variant: *in North America*] – were published in six Scottish editions from 1776 to 1792, the latest two in the full six-volume spread. Such was the appeal and inspiration of writers especially identified with the liberty/enslavement antithesis in the age of the Scottish Enlightenment. As a postscript, it is useful to note that the printed two-page booklist, dated 1797, of the radical Edinburgh bookseller, Alexander Leslie, shows that the works of both Montesquieu and Raynal (as well as titles by Volney, Beccaria, Voltaire and Helvétius) may, we are informed, be had on demand on enquiry to his shop in Nicholson's Street; appropriately the slogan adorning Leslie's list is *'Unite and be Free'*.[26]

That slavery was one of the most ubiquitous topics to feature in the teaching of moral philosophy in four of the five Scottish universities throughout the eighteenth century is not in doubt.[27] How could it be otherwise when both the moral and legal implications of slavery had figured prominently in the works of Hobbes, Locke, and, to an extent, Hooker and Sidney in the previous century? That alone ensured that scholars like Gershom Carmichael and Francis Hutcheson covered slavery within their taught 'systems' for use by their own students. Carmichael, Hutcheson's predecessor in the Glasgow chair of moral philosophy, is especially unequivocal in condemning slavery in his *S. Puffendorfii De Officio et Gentium ... Supplementis & Observationibus* [Supplements and Observations upon the Two Books of Samuel Pufendorf's On the Duty of Man and Citizen according to the Law of Nature composed for the use of students in the Universities] (Edinburgh, second ed., 1724) – an abridged edition, in Latin, of Pufendorf's *De Jure Naturae et Gentium* (1672).[28] In particular, Carmichael contrasts the owning of slaves, 'like cattle' in the classical period, with the practice in his own time:

> I have treated the matter of these last three sections at some length because this usurped right of *owning* slaves like cattle, as it existed among the ancients, is exercised today by men who profess to be Christians, to the great shame of that holy name, with greater tyranny perhaps than it was by the ancient pagans. It is not practiced to be sure *by Christians among themselves* nor do we find it *in most parts of Europe*, but we do find it in other parts of the world. I am deeply convinced that its existence, to use the apt expression of Titius,[29] is *a sure sign of the death of sociability*.[30]

David Hume employs the same extended simile, comparing slaves to cattle, in his essay 'On the Populousness of Ancient Nations':

> At present, all masters discourage the marrying of their male servants, and admit not by any means the marriage of the female, who are then supposed altogether incapacitated for their service. But where the property of the servants is lodged in the master, their marriage forms his riches, and brings him a succession of slaves, that supply the place of those whom age and infirmity have disabled. He encourages, therefore, their propagation as much as that of his cattle, rears the young with the same care, and educates them to some art or calling, which may render them more useful or valuable to him.[31]

Francis Hutcheson is careful to distinguish between the natural rights of masters and servants when he contrasts the right of a master to transfer a slave to another without that slave's consent, yet making clear at the same time

> But no cause whatsoever can degrade a rational creature from the class of men into that of brutes or inanimate things, so as to become [wholly the property of another,] without any rights of his own.[32]

According to Hutcheson, in a famous phrase, the right of 'natural liberty' is 'suggested' by 'our *moral sense*', representing 'our own voluntary actions as the grand dignity and perfection of our nature.' Hutcheson is particularly severe on Aristotle whose doctrine of regarding some men as 'naturally slaves' he finds 'surprising', given that Aristotle was a 'zealous asserter of liberty':

> He lived in that singular century, in which Greece indeed produced more great and ingenious men than perhaps the world ever beheld at once: but had he lived in our times, he would have known, that this beloved country, for sixteen centuries, hath seldom produced any thing eminent in virtue, polity, arts, or arms; while great genii were often arising in the nations he had adjudged to slavery and barbarity.[33]

The Marischal College regent, David Fordyce, who was drowned in September 1751 on the voyage home from Rotterdam to Leith when his ship capsized in a storm, had studied under Hutcheson at Glasgow in the mid 1730s. Fordyce's *Elements of Moral Philosophy* was published posthumously by Dodsley of London in 1754. His modern editor notes that the work 'was introduced into the curriculum of the American universities, where it became a standard text at Harvard University and one of the most widely used texts in American universities in the second half of the eighteenth century.'[34] In chapter IV of the *Elements*, entitled 'Herile and Servile Duty', having cited his mentor, Hutcheson, on 'The Rights of Masters and Servants',[35] Fordyce comments:

> To those, who under Pretext of the Necessities of Commerce, drive the unnatural Trade of bargaining for human Flesh, and consigning their innocent, but unfortunate Fellow-creatures, to eternal Servitude and Misery, we may address the Words of a fine Writer; "Let Avarice defend it as it will, there is an honest Reluctance in Humanity against buying and selling, and regarding those of our own Species as our Wealth and Possessions."[36]

Identifying Fordyce's 'fine Writer' is of considerable interest, obviously in the light of his source's colonial American relevance, but much more so on account of the important slavery reference. Fordyce is quoting from an obscure English cleric, Thomas Rundle (1687/8-1743), who utters the words condemning slavery in a sermon he preached and published while prebendary of Durham in 1734. Just one year later Rundle would be consecrated Bishop of Derry in the Church of Ireland. The context in which Rundle made his comment is of particular interest. He had preached his sermon in St George's Church, Hanover Square, London on 17 February, 'To recommend the charity for establishing the New Colony of Georgia'. The section from which Fordyce has made his extract deserves to be quoted in full:

> The peopling new Colonies with the industrious, who, tho desirous of work, are unemployed, was always esteemed humanity to the necessitous, and new strength to the Parent nation. 'Tis removing out of temptation those who might probably have had no means for a livelihood but rapine, violence and disorder. 'Tis making those useful to the whole, who by idleness might have been debauched, and by want embolden'd to injure, perhaps our selves, or those we love better, our dearest friends and relations. 'Tis cultivating a country by them, whose soil and climate produce the greatest abundance, and yet where the fewest necessaries of life are wanting. No settlement [he means the

colony of Georgia] was ever before established on so humane a plan. Slavery is absolutely proscribed from this Colony; the misfortune, if not the dishonour of other plantations. Let avarice defend it as it will, there is an honest reluctance in humanity against buying and selling and regarding those of our own species as our wealth and possessions. [37]

The extract from Rundle's sermon admired by Fordyce shows the apparent ease with which his own approach to ethical problems shifts from theory to practical real-life applications – in this case the founding and settlement of the new colony of Georgia in 1733 by James Oglethorpe, a highly principled but, as time would tell, totally inflexible British army officer. The tragedy of Georgia was simply that Oglethorpe's idealistic determination to prohibit black slavery in the colony ultimately proved so unpopular among the cotton plantation owners that his successor trustees had to concede defeat and petition Parliament for repeal of the increasingly controversial legislation. The consequences would, of course, be dire as the State of Georgia would tragically experience throughout the course of the American Civil War.

The same problem that Francis Hutcheson had grappled with – interpreting how slavery was regarded and practised in the ancient world, this time articulated from the narrow point of view of its impact on population growth/decline – came to the fore in the well-known 'polite' literary dispute between David Hume and the polymath Church of Scotland minister and 'early Moderate', the Reverend Robert Wallace. Robert Wallace was the father of the advocate, George Wallace, author of the *System of the Principles of the Law of Scotland*, a work that contained, as we have seen, one of the most comprehensive condemnations of slavery to emerge in the age of the Scottish Enlightenment and was much admired by early abolitionists such as the Huguenot Quaker, Benezet.[38]

Hume's essay 'On the Populousness of Ancient Nations', first published in his *Political Discourses* (1752), led to a verbal, but always good-mannered and restrained scholarly disagreement with Wallace *père* concerning the statistics of population of ancient civilizations, and the extent to which slavery in classical times was responsible for the disparity between 'Numbers of Mankind in antient and modern Times'. Robert Wallace's *Dissertation* came out in 1753, though it was based on a much earlier paper of which Hume had certainly been aware, possibly going as far back as 1745 or 1746, originally read by Wallace to the Philosophical Society of Edinburgh, of which he was a founder member.[39] Hume's biographer, Mossner, tells the full story of the controversy, conducted entirely without rancour between two gentlemen, showing that although Wallace's interest substantially ante-dated Hume's, the two men had embarked on their researches independently of each other.[40]

Much of the argument on both sides turns on the arcane evidence of obscure sources. For our purpose the main interest centres on the esoteric references to slavery in the classical age and, more generally, on the insistence of both authors that the argument, to use Mossner's phrase, was 'integral to the Age of Enlightenment', Hume regarding it as 'the most curious & important of all Questions of Erudition.' Hume's firm view was to reject the notion of population decline in the modern era, an argument that had gained the ascendancy until around the middle of the seventeenth century.[41] Wallace refuted that view and disagreed with many of Hume's interpretations of his arcane sources, maintaining his belief in the 'superior Populousness of Antiquity' (the sub-title of his

Dissertation). Both Hume and Wallace expound at length on the situation affecting slavery as practised by the ancient and 'modern' nations, Wallace including an orotund Appendix to his *Dissertation* (containing further 'observations on the same subject', in the course of which, point by point, he seeks to demolish Hume's case). The argument is at times difficult to follow, such is the unintended obscurantism of the sources cited, but it is always evident that Wallace succeeds in steering well clear of any possible accusation of point-scoring against his distinguished adversary:

> [Hume] The remains which are found of domestic slavery, in the American colonies, and among some European nations, would never surely create a desire of rendering it more universal. The little humanity commonly observed in persons accustomed from their infancy, to exercise so great authority over their fellow-creatures, and to trample upon human nature, were sufficient alone to disgust us with that unbounded dominion.[42]
>
> ... 'Tis computed in the *West Indies*, that a stock of slaves grow worse five *per cent*. every year, unless new slaves be bought to recruit them. They are not able to keep up their own number, even in those warm countries, where clothes and provisions are so easily got. How much more must this happen in *European* countries, and in or near great cities? I shall add, that, from the experience of our planters, slavery is as little advantageous to the master as to the slave, wherever hired servants can be procured. A man is obliged to clothe and feed his slave; and he does no more for his servant. The price of the first purchase is, therefore, so much loss to him; not to mention, that the fear of punishment will never draw so much labour from a slave, as the dread of being turned off and not getting another service, will from a freeman.[43]
>
> [Wallace] Modern slavery seems to be on a much worse footing than the antient. In particular, slavery in Turky, Algiers, Tunis, Tripoli, Morocco, and other African countries, is both very severe, and under bad regulations: if we add to this the oppression and bad policy of these governments in other respects, can we be surprised at their want of people? ... To conclude this account of slavery, ... it is referred, if many of the preceeding observations are not confirmed by the practice in our *American* colonies? If the planters are not fonder of purchasing home-bred slaves, though at a dearer price, than of buying directly from *Africa*? ... and finally, if the planters instead of desiring such multitudes of slaves as are poured in upon them from *Africa*, have not been often deliberating about preventing the importation of *African* slaves altogether? According to good information, all these questions will be answered in the affirmative.[44]

Copies of both works were later sent to Montesquieu by the 14th Earl of Morton, in his capacity as a member of the Philosophical Society of Edinburgh, and a false rumour got abroad that he had done so in order that the Frenchman might arbitrate in the dispute. Montesquieu let it be known that he denied that he had ever been invited to act as arbiter, but instead praised the way in which both participants in the 'contest' had behaved 'in such a noble, disinterested manner and so modestly concerning themselves'. But the matter did not end there; other *philosophes* joined in,[45] and it was finally left to Malthus to synthesize the arguments of Hume and Wallace in his *Essay on the Principle of Population* (1798).

If we imagined that Adam Smith was solely interested in the economic implications of slavery, to the exclusion of the great ethical challenges it posed, we would be seriously wrong. It is true that no Scottish Enlightenment figure, engaging on the subject of slavery, has attracted quite so much by way of conflicting scholarly assessment. For Alexander Broadie, for example, there are, quite simply, no doubts: 'Some of Smith's most powerful words deal with this [slavery] issue', and Broadie cites the following in support of that contention:

> There is not a negro from the coast of Africa who does not ... possess a degree of magnanimity which the soul of his sordid master is too often scarce capable of conceiving. Fortune never exerted more cruelly her empire over mankind, than when she subjected those nations of heroes to the refuse of the jails of Europe, to wretches who possess the virtues neither of the country which they come from, nor of those which they go to, and whose levity, brutality, and baseness, so justly expose them to the contempt of the vanquished.[46]

On the basis of this and other evidence, Broadie concludes that Smith's 'abolitionist credentials' are 'impeccable'. Jonathan Israel, on the other hand, still entertains serious doubts which are as 'startling' (his word) as his conclusions in relation to Smith's real feelings on the issue:

> While it may be true that Smith regarded slavery with moral distaste, it is far from evident that his 'abolitionist credentials' were, as has been claimed, 'impeccable'. On the contrary, emancipating enslaved blacks is simply not an issue that figures at all substantially in his perspective. Rather, his perfunctory remarks about the abolitionist movement in Pennsylvania are to a modern reader distinctly startling. 'The late resolution of the Quakers in Pennsylvania to set at liberty all their negro slaves, may satisfy us that their number cannot be very great. Had they made any considerable part of their property, such a resolution could never have been agreed to.' In general, he offers no real moral objection to the continued use of slavery in the sugar and tobacco colonies where at the time their use seemed the only practicable option. His argument against slavery, such as it is, mainly pivots on the economic inefficiency of the institution.[47]

In Israel's judgment Adam Smith has to be seen as 'much more of an apologist for empire, aristocracy, and the *ancien régime* social hierarchy generally than he has often been taken to be.'[48] While Broadie bases his judgment on Smith's early work, *The Theory of Moral Sentiments* (1759), Israel is arguably too severe on Smith whose condemnation of slavery as human trafficking has to be judged on the full extent of his thinking on the subject, especially the many references in the 'second-hand' *Lectures on Jurisprudence* (1762-66). Smith, ever the realist, explains to his students why he is deeply pessimistic about the prospect of abolition ever being achieved:

> Notwithstanding of these superior [of] advantages it is not likely that slavery should be ever abolished, and it was owing to some peculiar circumstances that it has been abolished in the small corner of the world in which it now is. In a democraticall government it is hardly [hardly] possible that it ever should, as the legislators are here persons who are each masters of slaves; they therefore will never incline to part with so valuable a part of their property; and tho as I have here shewn their real interest would lead them to set free their slaves and cultivate their lands by free servants or tenants, yet the love of domination and

authority and the pleasure men take in having every (thing) done by their express orders, rather than to condescend to bargain and treat with those whom they look upon as their inferiors and are inclined to use in a haughty way; this love of domination and tyrannizing, I say, will make it impossible for the slaves in a free country ever to recover their liberty. … In the same manner we see at this time the great stock of a West India planter consists in the slaves he has in his plantation. To abolish slavery therefore would be to deprive the far greater part of the subjects, and the nobles in particular, of the chief and most valuable part of their substance. This they would never submit to, and a general insurrection would ensue. … This institution therefore of slavery, which has taken place in the beginning of every society, has hardly any possibility of being abolished.[49]

Smith's fundamentally pessimistic view of the chances of outright abolition of slavery – not just of a permanent cessation in the trade in slaves – becoming a reality was not shared by his favourite pupil, John Millar. Millar, essentially a 'rights theorist',[50] is rightly perceived as unique among Scottish Enlightenment writers on the subject on the grounds that he did not stop at theorising on slavery, but actively campaigned for its abolition and was optimistic that that aspiration would one day become a reality.[51] Like so many other writers on slavery before him, Millar, too, uses the analogy of cattle to depict slaves viewed merely as calculable items of property. In his case, however, he wryly observes that: 'It is impossible even to multiply cattle beyond a certain extent, without having previously enriched the pastures upon which they are fed.' In a clear reference to the Wallace-Hume exchange, Millar grimly observes: 'Some persons have imagined that slavery is conducive to population, on account of the frugality with which the slaves are usually maintained, and on account of the attention which is given by the master to their multiplication.'

Like David Fordyce before him, John Millar deals with the slavery issue not simply as a hang-over from classical times but as potentially a contemporary international scandal of momentous proportion, that especially (though by no means uniquely) besets Britain and her colonies overseas and which ought sooner rather than later to be confronted head-on with a view to its permanent removal:

Considering the many advantages which a country derives from the freedom of the labouring people, it is to be regretted that any species of slavery should still remain in the dominions of Great Britain, in which liberty is generally so well understood, and so highly valued.[52]

In a famous passage, slavery for Millar, he insists, begins at home. He instances what he clearly regards as appalling working and employment conditions of colliers and salters in Scotland:

From the manner of working the mines, a number of slaves are usually collected together, and may therefore be placed under the command of a single person, who has it in his power to superintend their behaviour, and to punish their negligence.[53]

Millar sees little or no difference between the 'slavery of the colliers' and the 'slavery established in our colonies'; the latter, however, he concedes, is 'attended with difficulties which cannot be so easily removed.'[54] At the same time, he cannot resist remarking on the considerable irony in the line taken by the Americans who, on the one hand, 'talk in a high strain of political liberty', yet 'make no scruple of reducing a great proportion of their fellow-creatures into circumstances by which they are not only deprived of property, but almost of every species of right.' –

> Fortune perhaps never produced a situation more calculated to ridicule a liberal hypothesis, or to show how little the conduct of men is at the bottom directed by any philosophical principles.[55]

In, however, the final edition of *The Origin of the Distinction of Ranks* published in his lifetime (1779), John Millar, jurist, has the last authoritative word, at least for the present. Citing a purported version of the Court of Session judgment in *Knight v Wedderburn* (interlocutor by Lord Swinton, May 1774; Court determination upholding Swinton's interlocutor, January 1778)[56] Millar concludes:

> This last decision ... is the more worthy of attention, as it condemns the slavery of the negroes in explicit terms, and, being the first opinion of that nature delivered by any court in the island, may be accounted an authentic testimony of the liberal sentiments entertained in the latter part of the eighteenth century.[57]

Pulpit censure of slavery: 1. William Robertson (1755)

In the decades when Scottish moral philosophers and jurists were busily discussing the ethical and legal implications of the 'master and servant' relationship we might have expected *prima facie* a parallel interest in slavery to emerge in the Church of Scotland corporately and, if not there, then on the part of individual ministers in the course of their published sermons. Apart from a few distinguished exceptions, we would be disappointed. Perhaps it was, quite simply, not that kind of subject. Burleigh attributes this gradual abandonment of 'preaching to the times', once 'a favourite and characteristic activity of Scottish ministers', to the removal of government to 'far-off Westminster' in 1707.[58] Whatever the reasons, in the century following the Commission of Assembly's Darien letter of 1699 – with its well-tempered advice on how to handle requests for Christian baptism of slaves in the Scots colony of 'Caledonia' [59] – until right up to the 1790s, when a minister refers to 'slavery' or 'enslavement' the odds are he is using the term to connote what would become of the Reformed church if it ever fell prey to 'popery'. Alternatively, and by the same token, where a minister risks introducing the topic into his sermon, he invariably does so to demonstrate the remarkable degree of political and religious liberty his congregation, and all others like it, were enjoying ever since the days of King William and the Glorious Revolution when, he might argue, the forces of anti-Christ were finally routed. At least, to put a narrower construct on it, *orthodox* ministers would have taken that line; Moderates would doubtless have preferred on the whole to let sleeping dogs lie. Of course, to be pedantic, the point needs to be made again and again that we are necessarily referring throughout this study to *published*, consequently literary sermons. For all we know, ministers from time to time protested at the outrage of slavery and the slave trade in the course of their everyday sermons and prayers. In any event, we simply cannot be sure and we would be unwise to make assumptions.

Easily the most distinguished among the small company of ministers who, we can be sure, were decidedly unafraid of introducing the touchy issue of slavery into their sermons is William Robertson. In 1755 when he was only 34 and while serving as minister of Gladsmuir parish church in the Presbytery of Haddington, Robertson had been invited by the SSPCK to preach a sermon to which he gave the name *The Situation of the World at the Time of Christ's Appearance*. As was customary in the case of Society sermons by east of Scotland ministers it was delivered from the pulpit of the High Kirk (St Giles') in Edinburgh. Though perhaps hard to believe, it would be the only sermon Robertson would see through the press in his lifetime. Gladsmuir was Robertson's first charge to which he had been co-presented by the Earl of Hopetoun and the Crown, succeeding his uncle in 1744.[60] He would remain there for the next fourteen years. Later in his career – by that time minister of Old Greyfriars, Moderator of the General Assembly, historian of world standing, and university principal – Robertson was the acknowledged and undisputed leader of the Moderate party in the Kirk. His sermon was reviewed in the short-lived *Edinburgh Review* where it was praised (by the Reverend John Jardine) as 'an excellent discourse' and its author celebrated for his 'genius and skill in composition'.[61] Not only that. As Whyte and others have shown, the advocate Allan Maconochie was just one of several Scottish lawyers whose anti-slavery views were partially conditioned by 'the ideas of Moderate churchmen' and, in Maconochie's case, specifically by William Robertson's 1755 sermon.[62]

Prima facie it seems strange that Robertson's choice of text has largely been passed over by historians. It is from Paul's letter to the *Colossians* 1: 26: *'Even the Mystery, which hath been hid from Ages, and Generations, but now is made manifest to his Saints.'* The verse immediately before the passage chosen by Robertson is also necessary to understand the thrust and orientation of his sermon. Addressing the church at Colossae [aka 'Colosse'] the apostle explains that he has been 'made a minister' in order to fulfil God's word. It is one of the shortest of Paul's letters to the early churches and it is only when we read the last two of the four chapters that it becomes evident just why it was of special appeal to Robertson. *Colossians* 3 embraces one of the most famous and most controversial of the apostle's many injunctions to followers of the early Christian church: (AV)

18 'Wives, submit yourselves unto your own husbands, as it is fit in the Lord.'
19 'Husbands, love your wives, and be not bitter against them.'
20 'Children, obey your parents in all things: for this is well pleasing unto the Lord.'
21 'Fathers, provoke not your children to anger, lest they be discouraged.'
22 'Servants, obey in all things your masters according to the flesh; not with eyeservice, as menpleasers; but in singleness of heart, fearing God.' [*NEB*: 'Slaves, give entire obedience to your earthly masters, not merely with an outward show of service, but with single-mindedness, out of reverence for the Lord.']

And, continuing into *Colossians* chapter four:

1 'Masters, give unto your servants that which is just and equal; knowing that ye also have a Master in heaven.' [*New English Bible*: 'Master, be just and fair to your slaves, knowing that you too have a Master in heaven.']

There can be little doubt that Robertson would have been acutely aware that by using this text in particular he was focusing on the clearest expression by far within the New Testament of the well-trodden theme, common to works of jurisprudence and moral philosophy, of the master/servant antithesis, and its familiar classical roots in Roman law. In his sermon, as part of his desire to ascribe to Christianity values consistent with the progressive spirit of the Enlightenment, Robertson wished to challenge conventional wisdom about how slavery in the ancient world was translated on to the moral and political map of his own time. He had hit upon the perfect scriptural vehicle for doing so: Paul's injunction to the church at Colossae on the need for obedience and the rules in that department to be observed by husbands and wives in regard to one another, children to their parents, and fathers to their children, slaves who should obey their masters with 'single-mindedness', and, equally, masters who are enjoined to be 'just and fair' to their slaves. Further, and not least, Robertson, the consummate churchman *cum* historian, would not have missed the delicious irony arising from scripture that, accompanying the messenger Paul, charged with delivering his letter to the Colossians, is Onesimus, 'one of yourselves'. Though inconclusive, one instinctively feels this is the same Onesimus who turns up in Paul's letter to *Philemon*: if so, he was a runaway slave freed by Philemon and Paul asks a favour of his former master – to take him back 'for good', and 'no longer as a slave' but as a 'dear brother.'[63] Just two years after Robertson preached his sermon in the High Kirk a real-life process involving a runaway slave – *Shedden v Montgomery* – came on before the Court of Session in Edinburgh.

Robertson begins his sermon with an astonishing statement, which, as someone destined to become the outstanding historian of the age, he was unusually qualified to utter: that a knowledge of the 'civil history of mankind' facilitates insight into the 'plan of God's providence' for the world. 'Sacred history' enlightens our discovery of a 'skilful hand' behind the 'revolutions of human affairs' and in that regard at least 'facts', as communicated to us by 'inspired writers', are of no less importance than 'doctrine'. Coming as it does from a minister who would become one of the most influential historians of the eighteenth century this is at once authoritative and arresting. In the context of sacred history Christ's coming confirms 'speculative opinions' by 'real and striking examples'. 'Divine power and wisdom' made possible the sowing and flowering of the early church – 'this feeble plant' – and in time its progress could not be resisted. But, Robertson says, this poses two important questions: 'Why was the gospel of Christ so long concealed from the world? '; equally, 'Why was it published at that time?'

The theme of the sermon and, equally, the formidable challenge Robertson had accepted in addressing it, are now clear. Christ appeared and the mystery of the gospel was made known to man 'at a time when the world stood most in need of such a revelation, and was best prepared for receiving it.' At first, little of all this was understood by men: the 'obscurity of the dawn went before the brightness of the noon-day'. But, in time,

> men came by degrees to understand this progressive plan of Providence, and to conceive how systems temporary and incompleat might serve to introduce that concluding and perfect revelation which would declare the whole council of God to man.[64]

With the 'utmost perspicuity' ancient prophets had foretold the coming of the 'person employed to publish this revelation'. The entire nation of Israel, 'groaning under the Roman yoke' and 'stimulated by the desire of liberty and vengeance', now expected their 'Deliverer'. In due time God sent forth his son, thus fulfilling the prophecies. Jews and Gentiles alike received him eagerly. Had, however, Christ appeared at an earlier period, 'the world would not have been prepared to meet him with the same fondness and zeal.' All of this is a prelude to Robertson declaring his intention to go on to consider the political, moral, religious and domestic state of the world 'about the time of our Saviour's appearance'.

The *political state* of the world was at that time characterised by small, independent nations, leading frequently to 'the most violent convulsions and disorders'. It was a 'turbulent and restless period'. 'Commerce' had not yet facilitated communications between nations, in stark contrast with the present age:

> The world may now be considered as one vast society, closely cemented by mutual wants; each part contributing its share towards the subsistence, the pleasure and improvement of the whole.[65]

In those 'more simple' ages intercourse among nations was 'extremely inconsiderable'. Then the Romans came on the scene, fired with their plan of 'conquering the world', which ultimately they succeeded in achieving. But 'by enslaving the world, they civilized it; and while they oppressed mankind, they united them together.' At the time of Christianity's first appearance it was 'divine wisdom' behind the choice of that 'particular conjuncture' to publish it at that moment. Favoured by the 'union and tranquillity of the Roman empire' Christ's disciples 'executed their commission to great advantage'.

What of the *moral state* of the world at the time of Christ's first appearance? In the absence of 'divine revelation' 'pure and undefiled virtue' could not be found where 'unenlightened reason' produced error, although even in those less favoured ages, 'righteousness had not altogether perished from the earth.' The small, independent states already mentioned 'struggled for liberty and obtained it.' At the same time, the conduct of every citizen was 'subjected to the eye of the magistrate', and the 'smallest crimes could not escape observation'. On such a foundation of public liberty 'antient virtue' rested – something unknown in 'modern times', Robertson claims, when 'the views of legislators are confined to inferior objects'. In the meantime, Roman power continued unabated and it was impossible to 'divert or resist' it. Yet, 'by subduing the world, the Romans lost their own liberty'. The consequence was that 'many vices', 'engendered or nourished by prosperity', placed them under the yoke of the 'vilest race of tyrants that ever afflicted or disgraced human nature'. A time of 'universal corruption' ensued. If Christianity had not appeared to 'check and mitigate' the worst excesses of those depraved times it is 'hard to say how far they might have gone toward extinguishing the name and exercise of virtue among men'.

What of the world with regard to its *religious state*? The national character of the Jews was 'deeply tinctured with superstition'. While the Pharisees 'undermined religion', the Sadducees, 'by denying the immortality of the soul, wounded it in a vital part'. The 'deplorable situation of the heathen world in regard to religion' called for 'an immediate interposal of the divine hand'. But while Roman tyranny controlled to a degree some of the 'poisonous and destructive' qualities of the old religions, superstition continued to make its advances and 'exercised an uncontrouled dominion in every corner of the earth':

> Superstition breaks the spirit, and prepares it for servitude. Tyranny, for this reason, encourages superstition, and employs it as an useful auxiliary to illegal power.[66]

Consequently, it was at this time that 'a good God', pitying his 'deluded creatures', published the Christian revelation.

Thirdly, Robertson considers the world with regard to its *domestic situation*. One clearly senses that he intends this section as the pinnacle of his entire sermon. Recalling the words of Paul's letter to the *Colossians* he confronts his own congregation in the High Kirk, doubtless that day comprising a distinguished gathering of the great and the good in Edinburgh polite society:

> The private and domestic situation of mankind is the chief circumstance, which forms their character, and the great source of their happiness or misery. Any poison in this fountain communicates itself to the manners of men; any bitterness there, infects all the pleasures of life.[67]

Marriage is the key to a stable domestic situation – 'the union betwixt husband and wife'. He proceeds to condemn polygamy on the grounds that it was not only 'contrary to the intention of the Almighty', but also had the effect of banishing from domestic life 'all those enjoyments which sweeten and endear it'. It was a case of 'subjection without love, fidelity, or virtue.'

More seriously

> One half of the human species became the property of the other; and the husband, instead of being the friend and protector of a wife, was no better than the master and tyrant over a slave.[68]

But 'where-ever the Christian religion is established', an end has been put to 'an institution so inconsistent with the felicity of domestic life'. The married state fell into 'disreputation and contempt' and, among the Romans, 'domestic corruption' escalated 'to an incredible height', so that 'perhaps, in the history of mankind, we can find no parallel to the undisguised impurity and licentiousness of that age'. It was in that 'rank soil' that 'every vice, that power nourishes in the great', thrived and 'grew up apace'. But, at last, 'divine wisdom interposed' and just when 'the evil had become intolerable' the 'promulgation of Christianity' delivered an 'effectual and timely remedy'.

The doctrines Christianity taught 'added such dignity and lustre to human nature, as rescued it from the dishonourable servitude into which it was sunk'. By the teachings of Christ 'no human creature can be regarded as altogether insignificant and vile', and 'men approach nearer to that original equality, in which they were at first placed, and are still viewed by their impartial Creator.' –

> No inequality of condition, no superiority in power, no pretext of consent, can justify this ignominious depression of human nature, or confer upon one man the right of dominion over the person of another ... It is not the authority of any detached single precept in the gospel, but the spirit and genius of Christian religion, more powerful than any particular

command, which hath abolished the practice of slavery thro' the world. ... Where-ever such opinions prevail, no human creature can be regarded as altogether insignificant and vile; even the meanest acquire dignity, exterior distinctions disappear, and men approach nearer to that original equality, in which they were at first placed, and are still viewed by their impartial Creator.[69]

... And is no admiration due to the generous spirit of that religion, which restored liberty, not to one nation or society alone, but rescued from the worst servitude, far the greater number of the human race, and acquired for them that happy freedom, which they still enjoy.[70]

[Having cited Isaiah in a conflation of passages from 51:1 and 14:3 relating to the prophet having been sent by God to 'proclaim liberty to the captives' and release from the 'hard bondage wherein thou wast made to serve', Robertson develops his thoughts further on the issue of human slavery, first by means of the following important footnote to the published sermon concerning slavery in the British colonies in America.]

[*Footnote*] The practice[71] of slavery in our *American* colonies, is a specious, not a real objection against the reasoning under this head. The genius and tendency of any religion are known by the operations of its vigorous, not of its declining age: And if avarice hath revived, in a degenerate world, an institution, which Christianity had utterly abolished; this, like many other vices, which prevail among Christians, must be charged upon the corruption of the human heart, not upon that religion, which testifies against it.[72]

The abolition of 'domestic slavery', however, produced a further 'change in the manners of men': captives taken in war were 'in all probability' the 'first persons subjected to perpetual servitude'. This, in turn, produced a demand for slaves and 'every new war' recruited new supplies of slaves, thus accounting for the 'fierce and desperate spirit, with which wars were carried on among antient nations'. But, 'by putting an end to the cruel institution of slavery', Christianity 'extended its mild influences to the practice of war; and that barbarous art, softened by its human spirit, ceased to be so destructive.' This creates an opportunity for Robertson to wax lyrical on the extent to which

It hath become a fashionable topic among political reasoners, to celebrate the mildness and humanity of modern manners, and to prefer the character of present times before the antient.[73]

To what cause should we ascribe 'this important revolution, in the sentiments and dispositions of mankind'?

Not to the influence of better instituted governments; for in legislative wisdom the antients far excelled us: Not to the effects of a better-directed education; that duty, shamefully neglected by us, was among them an object of chief attention: Not to our superior refinements in elegant and polite arts; there we must be content to equal, without pretending to surpass the antients.[74]

The true cause of such progress is the Christian religion – the 'only cause capable to produce so great an effect'. The sermon closes with a ringing endorsement of the continuing relevance and importance of the Christian religion in the modern world. To hear these words from a man who perhaps was more entitled than most to characterise and portray the age of the Scottish Enlightenment, since he helped immeasurably to create it, is a rare privilege.[75] In terms of its language and sentiments, *The Situation of the World* has rightly been praised (by Richard B. Sher) as an emblem of the Scottish Enlightenment on account of the fact it 'reflected the dominant mood of Scotland in the second half of the eighteenth century.'[76] Stewart J. Brown, on the other hand, sees it as 'testimony to Robertson's belief that true Christianity corresponded to the highest moral and cultural ideals of the age in which he lived.'[77] By whatever yardstick one chooses to adopt, Robertson's achievement represents one of the greatest flowerings of Scottish political preaching yet seen and heard in the eighteenth century.

Robertson's sermon is not quite the sole representative of Enlightenment views on slavery to emerge from the pulpit at this time in Scottish religious history. Sporadically and fragmentarily, a few other examples exist, perhaps most notably one by the rhetorician Hugh Blair. If we discount his own SSPCK performance of January 1750 (*The Importance of Religious Knowledge to the Happiness of Mankind*) – in the course of which he adds his pennyworth to support for the Society's anti-popery activities[78] – it is clear that whereas Blair was never entirely comfortable with the idea of political preaching of any kind, he did bring himself in at least one published sermon to touch on slavery in its historical religious context. In the sermon entitled 'On Gentleness', included in the first edition of his collected *Sermons* (volume 1, 1777), he refers to the influence of Christianity in the partial abolition of slavery in the modern era:

> Wherever Christianity prevails, it has discouraged, and, in some degree, abolished slavery. It has recued human nature from that ignominious yoke, under which, in former ages, the one half of mankind groaned.[79]

It must not be overlooked, however, that this was composed several years before the full horrors of the slave trade, with its 'indefensible barbarity', were publicly known in Britain. In 1783 Granville Sharp circulated the court proceedings relating to a slave ship *Zong*, owned by Liverpool merchants, the master of which had taken a decision to throw overboard 133 slaves, rather than have them die on board which would have resulted in the vessel's owners bearing the financial loss.[80] A year later the Reverend James Ramsay, a graduate of King's College, Aberdeen, published two pamphlets[81] attesting to his having personally witnessed conditions aboard a slave ship, as well as to his life as a pastor on the sugar island of St Kitts, complete with graphic details of the brutal punishments regularly meted out to the slaves by their white (often Scots) masters. The efforts of Ramsay and others like him, who were prepared to publish the evidence of their own eyes, eventually bore fruit in sermons by such as Joseph Priestley 'On the subject of the Slave Trade' (1788).[82] Nothing comparable, however, emerged in Scotland at this time.

Pulpit censure of slavery: 2. Thomas Hardy (1794)

It is impossible to dispute Iain Whyte's claim that although in the 1750s Moderate ministers like Robertson and Blair had used the pulpit 'to take issue with slavery', they had done so without alluding to 'the West Indian connection, still less the slave trade itself', and that generally, they had 'painted with a broad brush'.[83] Another effort to condemn the practice of slavery from an Edinburgh pulpit, but this time from a wholly different perspective, refreshingly drawing inspiration this time from the African's point of view, came over forty years after William Robertson's 1755 masterpiece. From the same High Kirk pulpit and under the same auspices (the SSPCK), Thomas Hardy preached a sermon on 30 May 1793, *The Progress of the Christian Religion* (1794). The General Assembly had risen just three days before when Hardy had served as its moderator.

One of the élite among the surviving ranks of Moderate *literati* of the older school, Hardy had earned a deserved reputation as an 'acclaimed preacher'.[84] Unusually, he succeeded in combining the duties of minister of a busy Edinburgh church, West St Giles (or 'Haddo's Hole'),[85] with those of the chair of ecclesiastical history at the University of Edinburgh where, according to Thomas Somerville – Somerville had been offered, but declined the chair on Hardy's death in 1798 – his class was 'one of the best attended' in the whole university.[86] In 1791-92 Hardy had stood shoulder to shoulder with Alexander Carlyle, Somerville and other leading Moderates in expressing their condemnation of the movement for popular reform in Scotland and, in his own case, had been handsomely rewarded for his loyalism by a grateful Henry Dundas who was instrumental in his receiving a government pension for life.[87]

Thomas Hardy's sermon, we should be clear, is strictly not about slavery at all. It is deeply concerned, on the other hand, with the factors that had helped re-establish slavery in the modern era. Shockingly, Hardy's paradoxical message is that one of the most telling of the several factors behind the modern satanic trade in slaves has been the Christian religion, or at least a corrupted version of it; and, he prophesies, it would be Christian principles that would finally eradicate the trade in the western world by finally creating the means of a 'universal religion'. This highly controversial theme is set out in the very first line of the sermon:

> The idea of an Universal Religion is liberal and great.

The nub of the paradox, as his sermon explains, is that whereas only Christianity is capable of bringing that idea into reality, it is the Christian religion that has consistently frustrated all efforts to develop a true universal religion. In that regard, the major stumbling-block has been 'superstition', as practised down the centuries. It does seem likely that in expressing his deep aversion to the corrosive role played by superstition throughout the history of Christianity Hardy is borrowing heavily from Robertson's SPCK sermon of 1755, of which a sixth edition was published by Elphingston Balfour of Edinburgh in 1791.

Hardy uses his sermon to get across his firmly held view that the great error made by Christian 'enthusiasts' is to have assumed that heathen peoples were desperate to be converted by their European 'visitors'; in that regard it is superstition that has perverted and corrupted the thinking down the centuries behind such a false and discredited notion of Christian mission. In some ways, Hardy's sermon of 1794 is the perfect sequel to Robertson's sermon of 1755; for he echoes Robertson's near-identical message in *The Situation of the World* that the greatest impediment to the advance of Christianity everywhere in the world has been superstition:

> Christianity as an institute of the Divine Law speaks home to the natural conscience; it sets at nought the whole artifice of superstition, the folly or the fraud by which the world has been held in bondage.[88]

In his histories, too, as Nicholas Phillipson and others have shown,[89] Robertson had used the example of the *conquistadores* to demonstrate that their enforced methods of conversion had only served 'to impose a faith on the Amerindians which that people were incapable of understanding.' That, Phillipson explains, had led to 'the creation of systems of government based on slavery and superstition rather than on toleration and civil liberty.'[90]

So, too, Hardy is similarly impressed by the example of the native Americans whose extermination is now threatened by the 'European colonists'. Essentially a nomadic people, the Americans were now threatened with extinction partly on the ground that their age-old tradition of wandering, with no idea of a fixed settlement, was somehow deemed compatible with their apparent mental inability to accept Christian doctrine. Deliberately, Hardy strays here into the vexatious topic of race and he touches on the view, only to reject it, that had begun to be prevalent much earlier in the century, *viz.* that native peoples, or 'savages' (for example, black Africans and native Americans) were racially and intellectually inferior to Europeans.[91] In a notorious footnote added to a later edition of his essay, 'Of National Characters', Hume had expressed that same thought in relation to 'negroes' almost forty years before – although, it seems clear, he later had second thoughts about it.[92] The point Hardy seeks to stress is the 'prejudice, which has been often entertained on this subject', to the effect that

> You must first make them men ... You must teach them to live in fixed habitations, to associate in villages, to cultivate the soil, and then you may hope that they will hear and understand when you unfold the sublime principles of the gospel.[93]

That opinion, says Hardy:

> supposes the gospel to be something more intricate than any of Christ seem to imply. It opposes the claim of Christianity to be an universal religion, considering it as adapted to mankind in some situations, but not in all; and it would place a final bar in the way of our hopes of any success to our religion on the side of Tartary and America, where the reluctance of the people to a stationary life is part of the national character. That in the case of the Americans, a change of life to fixed habitations, to agriculture, to civilization and the arts, would be a matter of immense benefit to the people themselves, is undoubted: it is indeed the only expedient which can save the whole old nations of the Continent from that extermination with which they are threatened by the European colonists.[94]

'Shall it be said', Hardy goes on, 'that the Indian wanderer has not a comprehension equal to the admission of the Christian doctrine?' That premise has been offered as the 'current apology for the failure of the missions'. But it is not 'the real truth of the case'. –

> The human mind is not in any country below the reach of discipline and religious instruction. The American Indian, the Pacific Islander, and the African Negro are shrewd men, whose intellectual capacity will not suffer in the comparison with the uneducated classes of people on the Continent of Europe. Indeed, the popular speculation on national diversities of character [see note 92 to this chapter], as fixed appearances in the human species, and the classification of intellects, according either to physical causes or modes of living, is at best but hypothesis; and in the degree to which it has been sometimes carried, is extravagant hypothesis and presumption. The savage people now mentioned possess already the sublime doctrines on which Christianity is reared. They acknowledge the great Spirit, and adore him with humble prostration; and they trust that they shall again meet their friends and companions in the world of spirits. With so much true religion they have almost no superstition; and have little to unlearn, except in some moral habits, which Christianity would correct and reform. What is there then in the state of these people which should wholly obstruct their reception of the truth? [95]

Hardy's comment on race presenting no impediment to Christian conversion shows a clear and consistent interpretation of how the 'Religious Enlightenment', as we might term it, had achieved maturity as articulated in the sermon of a Moderate Church of Scotland minister in the late eighteenth century. Not simply that, and much more significantly, the words were uttered at precisely the time when an increasing clamour for abolition had come hard up against a parallel concern (no matter how radical, localised and patchy) for popular liberty and equality. While it is true – as discussed elsewhere in this study (*e.g.* see chapter 6, 168-169) – that in common with the vast majority of his Moderate party colleagues Hardy could not bring himself to support those liberties in any shape or form, he is nevertheless egregiously ahead of his time in pinpointing the principal faults and flaws in the traditional and much-vaunted approach to Christian mission:

> It is … true, that if the teachers of Christianity … go to the Mississippi, or to the Gambia, with a system of metaphysics in their hands, instead of the rational and attractive theology of the New Testament, they will find that the natives are indeed utterly unprepared to attend to the jargon which is offered to them for religion, and that it is absolutely impossible to make converts to a scheme of hard words, nice distinctions, and the quirks which European divines have been accustomed to employ in their scholastic or synodical litigations. [96]

This is serious religious radicalism. All of this, he explains, was in sharp contrast with the doctrines of the early church when there was consciously 'no invasion on the rights of the people', nor any 'association of the idea of conversion to Christianity with that of subjection to a new sacerdotal authority in all the points of opinion, discipline, and worship.' But corruption had set in during the fourth and fifth centuries and views were then inculcated such that 'superstition is necessary in human life', that 'simple and rational religion cannot attract and fix the bulk of mankind', and that 'the people must in some degree be deceived for their good'.

Hardy cites numerous examples of how, throughout 'the long period in which superstition had fixed its throne on the ruins of Christianity before the Reformation', the success and progress of the reformers was resisted by the 'Pharisees, the Sadduccees, and the Herodians of the age, with the Chief Priests and Scribes' – a clear reference to the reactionary forces of popery and the Counter-Reformation. He concludes this part of his sermon with the blunt statement: '*superstition is useless*' [italics added]. Hardy then focuses his attention in his account of the progress of Christianity on the modern contemporary world, the 'present aspect'. It is here that we begin to wonder if it is credible that Hardy's use of the word 'progress' in its title is at bottom sarcastic. "Is this *progress?*" seems to be the rhetorical question he puts to his congregation. First, learning is 'wholly and exclusively in the possession of the Christian nations'; secondly, although it is fair to claim that Christians are 'improving in the article of forbearance', there is the 'humiliating recollection' of the 'scenes of violence which were exhibited in London and Edinburgh in the year 1780, by persons pretending to support the Protestant interest, even while they were borrowing from Popery its worst attribute, incurring the guilt of persecution, and tarnishing the best honours of the Reformation.'[97]

There follows easily the most arresting part of the whole sermon, where Hardy makes an important and, it must be said, subsequently almost totally ignored contribution to the slavery debate in its Scottish context. Turning to the third of his examples of how Christianity is progressing in the modern world by focusing on the extent to which the 'commerce of the world is in the hands of the Christian nations', he comments:

> The commercial system in modern times has risen to a magnitude which is without precedent in the history of human affairs. It is a new operative power introduced into the scheme of providence, and is obviously capable of producing great effects. ... No people nor tribe are so obscure as not to be in some degree affected by their [Christian missionaries'] operations, or brought within the sphere of their influence. ... The preparations are visibly in forwardness; they are advanced; it requires only that the Christians should do their duty, and the great work will be accomplished.[98]

So, why is 'nothing done'? Attempts, says Hardy, have been 'often made both by Catholics and by Protestants, every one of which has totally failed, and ended in nothing.' 'Why', he asks, 'will not the nations listen?' The answer is that 'God has given reason to them all.' –

> Will the American Indian obey the stranger who bids him give up his simple adoration of the great Spirit, to repeat the words in an unknown tongue before a picture or over a string of beads? – Will the Chinese renounce the institutions of Confucius, to commit his soul and conscience to the custody of an Italian priest and his emissaries, and give up his understanding to be confounded with fictitious duties and fictitious sins? – Will the Hindoo abandon the Divine Being, whom he reveres under the threefold character of the Creator, the Preserver, and the Destroyer, to bow the knee to St Antony, St Francis, and St Dominic; to submit to a fantastic ritual addressed to a whole host of dead men and women of the western nations? The undertakings of these missionaries is desperate in its own nature; it cannot succeed any where.[99]

And, further, although the Protestant churches 'reject the whole apparatus on which the Catholics lay the stress of religion', they, too, 'have totally failed'. The crux of the message, therefore, is this: first, in their treatment of the 'Indian', and of the native American, is there anything for Christians to be proud of? Is any of this _progress_?

> Let the missionary shew with both understanding and fervour, that Christianity teaches men to live soberly in the world; is he likely to be credited, when the Indian can reply, that the men of his nation were temperate until the Christians came to corrupt them; that these strangers have brought among them the means and the habits of intemperance, and are profligate in their manners beyond any example known in savage life. ... Let the missionary also whisper, that Christianity teaches men to live righteously in the world; but where has he the face to say so? Is it to the tribes of America, where the first steps of the Europeans were marked with rapine and bloodshed; where, by a great and regular system of unrighteousness, the natives are yearly robbed of fresh tracts of their land, and are driven from valley to valley, and from river to river: and where the white men in every transaction study to cheat their red brethren, the men of the woods? [100]

Hardy reserves his most withering sarcasm, however, for Christians' treatment of the black African. It is an astonishing and uncannily moving message (though almost certainly wholly the product of his imagination) and deserves to be much better known in the history of Scottish voices against slavery and the slave trade in the eighteenth century:

> Is it in Africa that the missionary would speak of righteousness as the law of the Christians? perhaps the native might reply: "When I was a child, I heard of the Christians, I have known them in riper years, and my opinion of their principles is not likely to alter: for from them my heart received its first wound, and now they have broken it. My father was bringing water to us from the brook when the Christians fell upon him. They sprung from the thicket, like the tiger on his prey; they beat him to the ground with clubs, they chained him down in a canoe, and bore him off into slavery. In my youth they made me drink of affliction, but now in my age its waters have overwhelmed me. I was at a distance from my home, when the Christians and their menhunters but two moons ago made war, as they call it, in our valley: at the dead of night they beset the village, they set fire to the houses, they seized the flying families; and, among the rest, my wife, my only son, and my infant daughter were carried off, and are now on the ocean, fastened to bolts of iron in their ships, never to know rest or peace until the grave shall become their refuge from the Christians. Christians, your ships are red with innocent blood; ye make merchandise of the souls of men; your crimes hold Africa in ruins; the broken families of its natives appeal to God against you; it is you who destroy our morals and our comfort together; it is you who spread treachery, cruelty, despair and heartbreak over a whole continent. Until the Christians abandon this monstrous system of outrage, Africa will never become Christian." [101]

Inevitably, after this, the rest of the sermon, with its tedious repetition of the superstition _motif_, is anti-climax. Of greater interest is a reference to 'one great nation', the 'Hindoos, where 'the leading casts are composed of men of study, and habituated to profound reflection'. Here Hardy's esoteric learning leads him to cite the great English orientalist and authority on modern India, Sir William ('Selim') Jones FRS, an edition of

DE
L'ESPRIT
DES
LOIX.

TOME PREMIER.

.... *prolem sine matre creatam.* Ovid.

NOUVELLE EDITION,

Avec les dernieres CORRECTIONS & ILLUSTRATIONS

De l'AUTEUR.

Title page of 'the Edinburgh Montesquieu' of 1750, v. 1

RUN away from the Subfcriber, living near Beith, Shire of Ayr, ONE NEGROE MAN, aged about 22 Years, five Feet and a half high or thereby. He is a Virginia born Slave, fpeaks pretty good Englifh; he has been five Years in this Country, and has ferved fometime with a Joiner; he has a deep Scare above one of his Eyes, occafioned by a Stroke from a Horfe; he has alfo got with him a Certificate, which calls him James Montgomerie, figned, John Witherfpoone Minifter. Whoever takes up the faid Run-away, and brings him home, or fecures him, and gets Notice to his Mafter, fhall have two Guineas Reward, befides all other Charges paid, by me

ROB. SHEDDEN.

Morrifhill, April 26th 1756.

N. B. The Negroe run away the 21ft inft.

Advertisement from the *Edinburgh Evening Courant* of 4 May 1756 relating to the runaway slave baptized in Beith by John Witherspoon.

whose translation of the *Sacontálá* by Kalidaja (regarded as the greatest poet in classical Sanskrit literature) had first appeared in Calcutta in 1788-89, and would be reprinted in Edinburgh in 1796.[102] Jones, Hardy notes, had advanced the view in *Asiatick Researches* (first published in Calcutta in 1788-89)[103] that there was 'only one mode in which an impression [*i.e.* of Christian mission] may be possible', *viz.* that a book on the essentials of Christianity be prepared, without 'commentary' or 'reflections'. Controversially, Hardy says, Jones had recommended that 'it is necessary that Europeans should take no further charge of it' – that is, of Christian mission – but, rather, 'let it be found as the treasure which has been hid in a field, let it work its way in silence upon the Asiatic mind.' Jones' proposal, says Hardy, 'carries with it the strong characters of genius'.[104] According to his biographer, Jones was delivering Europe-wide an image of Indian culture and mysticism that offered 'a key to *universal religion*'. [italics added] Clearly, when we recall the opening line of his sermon, with its undisguised aspiration for a genuine universal religion, we can be confident that that is the specific appeal that brought the genius of William Jones and his work to Thomas Hardy's notice.

The Kirk joins the abolition debate

At their fifth session on 27 May 1788 the General Assembly considered overtures from the Synods of Lothian and Tweeddale, Merse and Teviotdale, and Angus and Mearns relating to the slave trade. 'After long reasoning', a motion was put forward and seconded, to the effect that the Assembly approved of the 'spirit thereof', which called on them 'as men, as Christians, and as members of this National Church' to 'declare their abhorrence of a traffic so contrary to the rights of mankind, and the feelings of humanity', and to express their 'earnest wish, that the wisdom and mercy of the Legislature may be speedily exerted for the relief of that unhappy portion of their fellow-creatures.' Ironically, it was the year that marked, in celebrations throughout Britain, the centenary of the Glorious Revolution which, to borrow a phrase from the Moderator's special address to the king on the commemoration, had 'delivered us from Popery and arbitrary power', thus fixing 'that constitution of government which is the wonder and envy of the world, not more for civil and political liberty, than for justice and humanity'. The slavery item went unreported in the *Scots* Magazine.

Next year (1789), it is recorded that an 'overture anent the Slave-trade' was 'read and ordered to be on the table'; at a later session we learn that 'the [unnamed] Member who brought in the overture relative to the Slave Trade, withdrew the same, in respect the Assembly had already made a resolution upon that subject, and had not time to enter upon any new proposition.' Three years on (1791), it is now a larger issue, and we sense a rather greater urgency in the air. The Assembly considered further overtures on the slave trade, this time from two of the three Synods that had sought approval for theirs in 1788. Again, the Assembly 'approved of the spirit thereof', and again, 'called upon as men, as Christians, and as members of this National Church', declared their 'abhorrence' *etc., etc.* Significantly, however, a new rider was added to the resolution: 'but they judge it unnecessary at present to proceed farther in this business, trusting that the wisdom and mercy of the Legislature will take such steps as they shall think proper for the relief of that unhappy race of men'. If there were any cynics sitting among the fathers and brethren on that day they might have been forgiven for concluding that this was a step backwards. All that had happened was that the Assembly resolution had simply mirrored the decision of the 'legislature', *i.e.* Parliament. On 20 April 1791 Wilberforce's motion, *viz.* that the House 'bring in a bill to prevent the farther importation of Slaves into the British colonies in the West Indies', was roundly defeated with 88 MPs for and 163 against.

At the 1792 Assembly once more we see the General Assembly tide of opinion on the issue of abolition flowing in roughly the same direction as that of Parliament. On this occasion, however, the outcome was considerably more positive, thanks largely to the intervention in the national debate by Henry Dundas, Pitt's home secretary. On 23 April Dundas, with his usual blend of acumen and nose for compromise, proposed in the Commons that the slave trade be abolished from 1 January 1800. Wilberforce and his supporters would not accept this and made a counter-proposal – that the date be set at 1 January 1795 – but although this was defeated by forty votes they did manage to carry a date of 1 January 1796. In the event, that date would prove both unattainable and unrealistic for a variety of reasons, not the least that the House of Lords was distinctly and overwhelmingly unsympathetic. Nevertheless, in the eyes of the General Assembly, this was viewed as measurable progress.

On 24 May, therefore, the Assembly's 'former resolution' (carried over from the year before) was further considered and this time was substantially strengthened and embellished with such phrases as the Assembly's 'joy in the enlightened views which have been taken of this subject, and in the liberal sentiments concerning it that have been expressed by the Commons of Great Britain, in Parliament assembled'. A motion was then made and agreed to, without a vote, as follows:

> That the Assembly think themselves again called upon to testify their abhorrence of a system of traffic, incompatible with the great principles of morality and religion, and attended with circumstances of injustice and cruelty, shocking to the feelings of virtuous minds: To declare the satisfaction they have received, from the liberal views and sentiments respecting this interesting subject, entertained by people of every rank and denomination, and especially by their representatives in Parliament; and to express their ardent wishes, and earnest prayers, that this iniquitous trade may, by the blessing of divine Providence, upon the deliberations of Parliament, be speedily and completely abolished; that thus the national character may be vindicated from the charge of oppression, the cause of public virtue promoted, and an example of humanity, and enlightened policy, given by Great Britain to the other countries of Europe.[105]

It is against this background of political trimming on the General Assembly's part that probably the best known printed example of preaching on the specific issue of abolition by a Kirk minister at this time ought to be considered. On 15 April 1792 Dr Thomas Somerville, Moderate minister of Kelso in the Presbytery of Jedburgh, preached a *Discourse on Our Obligation to Thanksgiving for the Prospect of the Abolition of the African Slave Trade*. Somerville had taken a leading role in the lengthy and heated Assembly debate of 1779 on the supposed introduction of a Scottish Catholic relief bill when a motion proposed by his presbytery (from which he had personally dissented), opposing the measure, was roundly defeated. In his memoirs Somerville reveals that his anti-slavery sermon became entangled in the parallel crisis relating to popular radicalism and the Scottish sedition trials: the sermon had given 'great offence to some of the gentlemen in the country, who uncharitably imputed it to those spreading seditious principles, which at that time were the occasion of just alarm to all the friends of order and peace.'[106] Somerville's *Discourse* is memorable not so much for its content as for its historical interest in having probably been the sole Scottish example of a sermon that focuses entirely – as its title implies – on the 'prospect' of abolition. Virtually the only other point of interest lies in his reference (in the sermon itself and in a long footnote) to a recently launched scheme to settle free slaves in Sierra Leone, a scheme he praises as evidence of 'a recent example of the beneficial effects of the right of the subject to petition the Legislature for the redress of grievances.'

Of equal interest is a sermon preached by a relation by marriage of Somerville,[107] the Reverend Dr Samuel Charters, whose charge, the parish of Wilton, also lay within the Presbytery of Jedburgh. A student of Adam Smith at Glasgow before moving to Edinburgh, Charters had belonged to a circle that included the well-known pioneer of the Academy movement, Philip Doddridge, whose religious writings had already profoundly influenced the young William Wilberforce. Charters' *Sermon on Alms* was originally preached under SSPCK auspices in the 'Old Church of Edinburgh' (St Giles') in June 1788, but new life was breathed into it through the publication of a third, and much expanded edition in 1795. This new edition contains no less than forty-five pages of added notes designed to update the reader on the latest position regarding the progress of numerous examples of humane good works ('alms') and, specifically in the abolition context, what Wilberforce and his supporters were currently up to. Perhaps understandably, not much scholarly notice has been taken of the content of Charters' sermon but at least the extensive notes [108] are of historical interest if only because they include references to Wilberforce and 'the Thomas Firmin of Glasgow', linking them to the Glasgow abolitionist and philanthropist, David Dale.[109] Other celebrities of the times praised by Charters for their 'alms' include Robert Raikes, Jonas Hanway, John Johnston (a 'writing-master' in Edinburgh credited by Charters for having revived in Scotland 'the art of instructing the deaf and dumb'), and two other local benefactors, Andrew Hunter (the 'Orphan Hospital') and George Drummond ('an Infirmary at Edinburgh'). Along with Wilberforce Charters singles out John Howard, the English penal reformer, for greatest praise.

One comment in particular from Charters' hugely expanded literary sermon seems to encapsulate the dilemma that haunted the anti-slavery movement in the dying years of the eighteenth century in Britain. Charters wrote:

> In reading *the evidence on the Slave Trade*, ... many interesting thoughts arise ... on the dishonours of our native land, and the infamy of Britain among the nations: on the violated law of our Redeemer, and the reproach extending to all who are called by his name; ... on the time foretold in prophecy, when the merchants of the earth, whose minds are *earthy*, *sensual*, *devilish*, shall lament the fall of their traffic in slaves and the souls of men.[110]

Samuel Charters stands virtually alone among Kirk ministers at this time in acknowledging and confronting – through the vehicle of a printed literary sermon – the hugely challenging problem religion faced throughout the slavery debate. Wilberforce and other abolitionists fully acknowledged that conclusion, and, as we have seen, though expressed in different ways, it is essentially the same problem tackled head-on by William Robertson and Thomas Hardy.

Postscript

Extract from [A] *Letter from the Commission of the General Assembly, of the Church of Scotland to the Honourable Council and Inhabitants of the Scots Colony of Caledonia in America. Dated at Glasgow, July 21, 1699.* [111]

Be careful in doing Justice betwixt Masters and Servants: Let their Service be a reasonable Service, and Time allow'd them for their Publick and Privat Worshipping of God, for they are your Brethren: …

If you shall have Servants for Life, or Slaves, of other Nations; (for the *Natives* of *Darien*, we consider as your Confederats and Allies) as we Wish you to be Tender, both of their Souls and Bodies, and to Encourage their Conversion to *Christianity*, by all proper Means; So we do not Urge that their absolute Liberty, and Freedom from their Service, should, as in some other Places, be made the immediat Reward of their Professing to receive the Gospel: For this hath tempted Masters to withhold them from the Means of their Conversion, lest they should be Indammaged by the Lose [Edin. version, 'loss'] of their Service; and hath occasion'd the Slaves to make Counterfeit Professions, to gain their Liberty. But we Recommend a Gentle-Rule, a Mild Treatment, and that full Access and Time be Allow'd for their Christian Instruction, and let such Rules be agreed on, as that these at least of them, who shal, not only Profess the *Christian-Religion*, but have such a Gospel-Adorning Conversation, as may Recommend them to the Consciences of the Godly, as Christians indeed, may have their full Freedom by such Means, and upon such Terms, as may be Safe and Advantagious, both to their Masters and Them. Immortal Souls are of great Value, and the Blessings of These, who are ready to Perish, are not to be Despised.

Endnote

Soon after I had published the pamphlet Common Sense, in America, I saw the exceeding probability that a revolution in the system of government would be followed by a revolution in the system of religion. The adulterous connection of church and state, whenever it has taken place, whether Jewish, Christian or Turkish, has so effectually prohibited by pains and penalties every discussion upon established creeds, and upon first principles of religion, that until the system of government should be changed, those subjects could not be brought fairly and openly before the world; but that whenever this should be done, a revolution in the system of religion would follow. Human inventions and priestcraft would be detected, and man would return to the pure, unmixed and unadulterated belief of one God, and no more.

Thomas Paine (1737-1809): 'The Author's Profession of Faith', from *The Age of Reason. Being an Investigation of true and fabulous theology.* (London, 1794).

By the close of the eighteenth century the chair of verity had ceased to be the surrogate voice of the people. There can be only one explanation why that was so: it was simply that the people had discovered they had a voice of their own. Church attendances in any event had fallen away markedly in Britain, and that included in Presbyterian Scotland. Poets and dreamers like Robert Burns, as well as philosophers including David Hume had, of course, prophesied these things decades before; or at least they had anticipated an awakening of popular enlightenment (though Hume was never sympathetic to popular causes). It is a matter of dispute just how much of this was due to the two great revolutions that had set the western world on fire, but that they were hugely influential in promoting the cause of 'the people' is, of course, not in doubt.

In Scotland the waning of church authority and influence was hastened by two factors: first, the principal court of the Kirk, its General Assembly, struggled to find useful things to talk about. Somehow, and over a remarkably brief period, the Assembly lost its way and increasingly found it lacked the resolve to be (or sound) important. A second and less acknowledged factor was that individual ministers had begun to fall out and dispute among themselves, a sure sign that all was not well either in the sense of their own self-confidence, or in the execution of their perceived corporate mission. It took an outsider, Archibald Bruce, an Antiburgher, to describe, sarcastically, what was going on:

> *O come, thou Genius of the times,*
> *Breathe thro' those Hudibrastic rhymes!*
> *As in the immortal Characteristics*
> *Thou op'd the depths of Church-politics,*
> *And set before our rising youth*
> *The road to benefice and truth.*[1]

Such infighting was by no means confined to the fringes of the Kirk. Even that pillar of the Edinburgh religious establishment, Thomas Hardy, former Moderator, darling of the Pitt regime and government pensioner, refused to maintain his silence. As we saw in the final chapter of this study, Hardy dared to confront the taboo of how one of the Christian church's fundamental doctrines – to go out into the world and win converts among the heathen – was in actual practice discharged. The principle of mission was fundamental to doctrine, especially since Christ himself had first enjoined his followers to be the prime agents of spreading the good news he himself had taught, a cause enthusiastically promoted by the apostle Paul. But, as Hardy pointed out, the church's proselytizing mission had a dark and destructive side, even at times sailing uncomfortably close to waters inhabited by the forces of inhuman evil. That could not be right, he mused.

Though sometimes viewed as just another elitist powerbase, it would nevertheless be seriously wrong to dismiss the Scottish church in its decline in the 1790s as just another *anti*-Enlightenment agency of reaction in the face of all that was inherently promising in a fast-changing world of improvement and new ideas. At the same time, it is legitimate to argue that it is *only* when we concede such a hypothesis that we are best able to view individual churchmen in their true colours. Paradoxically, for example, Alexander Carlyle and John Erskine are often regarded as twin pillars of the Scottish religious Enlightenment, yet one is entitled to question if that is a fair or valid judgment. For all his clowning over his espousal of the stage Carlyle demonstrably helped bring about a modern re-assessment of theatre and the dramatic art as a refined, pleasurable and educational experience. And yet it is inescapable that the same Carlyle emerges from the pages of his literary sermons as an unlikely Enlightened minister, his many undisguised denunciations of the people betraying his immense distaste for the new and increasingly fashionable values of reform and social justice. By the same token, Erskine's entitlement to the description of 'enlightened evangelical' is certainly warranted in some contexts (notably the general warmth of his humanity and his instinctively benevolent attitude to the American cause); yet his obsessively, even aggressively hostile attitude to popery must surely stand in the way of his claim to be so recognised.

More surprisingly, even that archetypal Moderate minister, rhetorician and sermoniser, Hugh Blair, is revealed in his true colours when he preaches on patriotism, as a man essentially aloof from 'the people'. In 1779, for example, an anonymous critic wrote of his first published volume of literary sermons, that whereas it was 'so much admired in the world by men of all sorts', it cannot be denied that it 'contains no gospel for the poor; – no good news to the weary and the heavy-laden; no healing to the broken-hearted.'[2] [See chapter 7 for more on this aspect of Blair's preaching.] In the eyes of far too many, the entire Kirk appeared similarly distant and aloof: just another elitist powerbase perhaps, little different, it seemed, from all the other elitist powerbases of the age, including Parliament itself, central and local government, all branches of the military and, even on occasion it could be said, the courts of law.

Perhaps, therefore, the greatest paradox to emerge from this study of the chair of verity at both chronological extremes, its zenith and its nadir, is that the real and only winners in the story are the oft-despised, much-misunderstood, yet at times curiously *enlightened* ministers of the Popular party. William Thom of Govan, John Erskine of Old Greyfriars – if we disregard his anti-popery performances – John Witherspoon of Paisley and Princeton, and a mere handful of others: is theirs, we might ask, the true and authentic voice of 'the people' in enlightened times? Respected by many, dismissed by others, none of them for sure was ever a candidate for admission to the inner circle of the *literati*, even though they were all staunch critics of aspects of contemporary society as they perceived it. The point is that for all their numerous faults, these men used the chair of verity to educate, communicate and, as they saw it, demonstrate the necessity of the people mending their ways through a process of seeking God; in that regard they were at least rigorously true to their calling. *Except a man be born again*, Witherspoon never tired of preaching to his Scottish and American congregations, *he shall not see God*. In a way, and unlikely though it may at first seem, regeneration and re-birth was the perfect message for an at times puffed-up, self-satisfied enlightened age.

Finally, as the epigraph prefacing this endnote shows, even Tom Paine – that incandescent popular philosopher who contrived to figure in the *dramatis personae* of both great revolutions of the eighteenth century – was (or so he said) prepared to trim his radicalism to conform to natural religion and the centrality of the deistic faith in which he (reluctantly) claims he believed. In a way, it was a message that transcended traditional denominational religious belief. And in a curious way, too, Paine's words define all that was wrong with the long history of factional intrigue and in-fighting that much too often characterises the Church of Scotland in the period. Thom, Witherspoon and Erskine – very different exponents of orthodoxy as they were – all upheld and subscribed to the allegory of regeneration and re-birth, on both personal and more general ethical grounds,[3] in the literal setting of a New World. Only John Witherspoon, we should not overlook, meant it in a non-virtual sense. He alone not simply canvassed and encouraged Scots to sample that experience for themselves, but also felt entitled from his own experience to reassure them that the good life awaiting them there he had already tasted in abundance and found agreeable.

Appendix A

Patronage from 1560 to 1785: a timeline

1560

Papal Jurisdiction Act 1560 ordains that 'the bischope of Rome haif na jurisdictioun nor autoritie within this realme in tymes cuming'. [This Act is still in force in Scotland in 2017.]

First Book of Discipline insists on the 'consent of the people' being necessary in the 'admission of the ministers to their office'. Under the Fourth Head, *Concerning the lawful Election of Ministers*, the power of election is vested in the parishioners.

First General Assembly of the Reformed Church of Scotland (20 December) decrees that the election of ministers should be in the public church 'by the People', and that notice should be given of it on the Sunday preceding.

1565

First mention in the Acts of the General Assembly of the role of patronage in church settlements.

1567

'The courtiers, though unwilling to part with the patronages, agreed, however, that the power of patrons should be restrained.' (Dalrymple, 6).

By the 7th Act of the first Parliament of James VI, accordingly, it was decreed that the examination and admission of Ministers 'be only in the power of the Kirk', and that the patron present 'a qualified person' within six months of the decease of the former incumbent to the Superintendent* or others, otherwise the Kirk 'to have power to dispose of the same to 'a qualified person'. In case of failure by the Superintendent or Commissioner of the Kirk to admit a qualified person presented by the patron, there lay an appeal to the Superintendent 'and Ministers of the Province', and if they refused to admit the qualified person, an appeal was to be made to the General Assembly 'whose determination was to be decisive.'

[*Note:* The 'Superintendent' was 'a minister on a large scale.' The *First Book of Discipline* envisages certain ministers being chosen to superintend provinces or dioceses, 'as the ten great areas were called into which it was proposed to divide the whole country.' (Burleigh, 169-70)].

1578

Second Book of Discipline goes further than the *First Book* in linking to the 'consent of the congregation' the 'judgment of the eldership' in the election, or 'chusing out', of ministers and 'ony of the offices of the kirk'.

1581

Despite these restrictions on patrons, 'benefices were conferred upon unqualified persons, both by the King and other Lay Patrons'. (Dalrymple, 8).

1592

By the 2nd Act of the twelfth Parliament of James VI the right of presentation is devolved to presbyteries in the event that patrons fail to present a qualified person within six months of an incumbent being deprived of his charge (for reasons specified). (Hill, *Appendix*, 111-3).

[*Note:* Andrew Crosbie states that 'The partisans of settlements by presentation hold ... and pretend, that the ecclesiastical judicatories can only reject the presentee in case they find him unqualified. ... this statute is not to be understood in the strict sense the friends of patronage understood; and that no more is meant by these words, than that the presbytery shall not have it in their power to bestow the benefice, or civil right to the stipend, on any other person than the presentee, in case he is a qualified one.' (Crosbie, 14-15).]

1596

Act of the General Assembly concerning 'Corruptions in the office' of minister. What was intended by this Act [and by the Act of 1638] was that the existence and the exercise of the right of patronage was not condemned or complained of, but that it was the *abuse* only of that right by the patron 'forcibly thrusting' presentees 'into the ministry and upon congregations' that the Assembly sought to have outlawed. (*Early History of Church Patronage*, 41).

1606

By the 2nd Act of the eighteenth Parliament of James VI Bishops are established in Scotland and the power of presentation is lodged in the archbishops and bishops, 'but the patrons by their interest in Parliament had the luck to keep their patronages on foot under several restrictions, which did not remove the evil that from the beginning was complained of, *Simony,* which is a direct bargain betwixt the patron and the minister to be presented ...'. (Dalrymple, 9).

1638

General Assembly, meeting at Glasgow, confirms and reinforces the Act of 1596: 'That there be respect had to the congregation, and that no person be intruded in any office of the Kirk contrary to the will of the congregation to which they are appointed.'

1649

'All these restrictions not being found sufficient against the abuses of Lay Patrons, they were totally abolished by Act of Parliament.' (Dalrymple, 10). Patronage is replaced by election by presbyteries and kirk sessions. 'The act of 1649 favoured clergy-dominated presbyteries over local kirk sessions and paid little more than lip-service to the rights of congregations.' (Sher and Murdoch, 204).

1662

Episcopacy and patronages are restored by Acts of Parliament in King Charles II's reign, 'from 1662 and downwards.' (Dalrymple, 10).

1690

By virtue of an Act of the Scottish Parliament c.23 of 19 July, the power of patrons to present ministers to vacant churches 'hath been greatly abused, and is inconvenient to be continued in this realm'. The patrons' power of presentation is thus cancelled. (Dalrymple, 11).

The 'Meeting of Estates turned into a Parliament' (and 'a reluctant' William III) restored Presbyterianism.' (Wodrow, 485).

'The most controversial aspect of the act was the decision to include *all* [italics added] Protestant heritors in that process [*Note by RLC:* Heritors having, that is, been granted a key role in the selection of ministers for vacant churches outside the burghs], thereby giving Episcopalian landowners an active role in the re-established Presbyterian church.' (Sher and Murdoch, 205).

1707

Act of Union includes provision for the security of the Scottish church as an integral part of the settlement. It provides *inter alia* that the 'Act for securing the protestant religion and Presbyterian church government with the establishment in the said act contained' is to be a 'fundamental condition of the Union' and 'to continue in all times coming'.

1712

British parliament passes Church Patronage (Scotland) Act 1711 [sic] restoring lay patronage. The act was 'a direct infraction of the Act of Union'. (Clark, 292). The bill was introduced at short notice on 20 March 1712 and received royal assent on 22 May.

1713

Motion for the repeal of the Act of Union is lost in the House of Lords by a majority of four votes.

1717

Commissioners of the General Assembly visit London for the express purpose of giving in to parliament a representation opposing the 1712 Act of Queen Anne restoring patronage. The paper is read, but never considered.

1719

Church Patronage (Scotland) Act 1718 [sic] is passed. The intention behind it is to put an end to the practice of some abuses relating to patronage, including unscrupulous patrons deliberately appointing ministers known to be hostile to the patronage system, in the expectation they would refuse, thus keeping parishes vacant in some cases for several years, 'during which time the patrons retained possession of the stipend, thereby defrauding the church of its patrimony, and the people of a minister.' (Hetherington, 343).

1732

Act of General Assembly cites the 1690 legislation as the required procedure for the filling of vacant parishes in situations where patrons fail to present a minister within six months.

1733

'Original' secession' from the Church of Scotland; formation of the Associate Presbytery.

1736

Act of General Assembly declares that 'no minister shall be intruded into any parish contrary to the will of the congregation' and 'recommends to all judicatories of this Church to have a due regard to the said principle in planting vacant congregations; and that all Presbyteries be at pains to bring about harmony and unanimity in congregations, and to avoid every thing that may excite or encourage unreasonable exceptions in people against a worthy person that may be proposed to be their minister'. (Burleigh, 281-2).

First occasion on which Assembly directs its Commission to 'make due application to the king and parliament for redress of the grievance of patronage, in case a favourable opportunity for so doing shall occur'. This became an annual injunction until set aside in 1784.

William Grant (later Lord Prestongrange) publishes his *The Present State of the Church of Scotland.With respect to patronages; and the Bill now depending before the Parliament*, containing the earliest known references to, and definitions of the 'Moderate' and 'warm' or 'Orthodox' parties in the Church. [See chapter 1, 'The evolution of parties in the Church of Scotland']

1752

Thomas Gillespie of Carnock is deposed by the General Assembly, in the wake of the Inverkeithing settlement.

1753

Publication in Glasgow of an anonymous satire on Moderates and Moderatism, *Ecclesiastical Characteristics: or, the Arcana of Church Policy*. Author later identified as the minister of Beith, Ayrshire, the Reverend John Witherspoon. The work has much to say on the patronage issue.

1761

Presbytery of Relief is founded by Thomas Gillespie and his followers, who 'resigned their livings in the Church, solely on the ground of the rigorous application of the law of patronage.' The 'more immediate cause' of its formation is found to have been the transportation of the minister of Elie, Dr. John Chalmers, to be minister of Kilconquhar. In his speech opposing the decision of the Assembly Commission to allow the transportation, its supposed right to do so, as well as the Assembly's subsequent upholding of the decision, John Witherspoon, now minister of the Laigh Church in Paisley, declared that 'nobody has a right to call a minister on an establishment excepting those to whom the law has given it.' (Morren, 204).

1765

Committee of Overtures reports to the General Assembly on 'this alarming evil' – the growth and spread of seceding congregations. The Assembly appoints a committee to report on the matter; it does so on 19 November, noting that (a) 'no fewer than 120 meeting-houses are already erected', and (b) expressing the opinion that 'the *abuse of the right of patronage* has been one chief occasion of the progress of Secession'. (Morren, 311).

1766

The schism debate at the General Assembly. On a vote, the Assembly rejects both the committee's overture and its opinion relating to patronage having been a deciding factor in the spread of seceding congregations. In a major speech, 'the eminent doctor' (William Robertson) 'favoured' the Assembly 'with a sketch of the history of patronage in the church of Scotland, with a particular view to shew its happy influence on the characters of ministers.' (*Scots Magazine*, July 1766, v. xxviii, 337-41, account of schism debate by an anonymous reporter).

1768-1770

Campaign in General Assembly initiated by the advocate, Andrew Crosbie, and the Popular party to muster support for an application to parliament calling for repeal of the act of 1712. The move eventually fails and Crosbie's (anonymous) pamphlet on the subject, *Thoughts of a Layman concerning Patronages and Presentations* (1769), attracts not a single response from presbyteries to which, by Assembly resolution, it had been sent for comment. A protest at the Assembly's treatment of the matter is published in the *Scots Magazine*, calling attention to a number of serious repercussions consequent upon the Assembly refusing to pursue the issue, including that their decision 'stifles an inquiry into the opinions of the landed interest of Scotland concerning presentations'. (*Scots Magazine*, May 1769, v. xxxi, 227-8).

1781-1785

A new wave of interest in the democratic right of congregations to have a role in the settlement of their ministers is provoked after (and possibly because of) the retirement in 1781 of William Robertson as unofficial leader of the Moderate party in the General Assembly. A motion at the General Assembly in 1783 to invite synods to report their objections to patronage, intended as part of the preparations necessary to make application to parliament to abolish patronage, is defeated by nine votes. At the 1784 General Assembly the Moderates triumph, gaining a large majority for rejecting calls from two synods (Glasgow and Ayr, and Stirling and Perth) to continue to press for the repeal of the 1712 Act, resolving that such activity is 'inexpedient, ill-founded, and dangerous to the peace and welfare of this Church'. (Meikle, 34-40; *Acts of the General Assembly, 1784*, 819-822). [See also under 1736]

Sources in chronological order as noted above

'Burleigh' – J. H. S. Burleigh, *A Church History of Scotland* (London, 1960).
'Dalrymple' – Sir David Dalrymple, *An Account of Lay-Patronages in Scotland* (London, 1712).
'Hill' – George Hill, *A View of the Constitution of the Church of Scotland* (Third ed., Edinburgh, 1835).
'Crosbie' – Andrew Crosbie, *Thoughts of a Layman concerning Patronages and Presentations* (Edinburgh, 1769).
'A Member of the Faculty of Advocates' – *The Early History of Church Patronage* (Edinburgh, 1833).
'Sher and Murdoch' – Richard Sher and Alexander Murdoch, 'Patronage and Party in the Church of Scotland, 1750-1800', in *Church, Politics and Society,* ed. Norman MacDougall (Edinburgh, 1983).
'Wodrow' – Robert Wodrow, *The History of the Sufferings of the Church of Scotland, from the Restauration* [sic] *to the Revolution* (Edinburgh, 2 v., [1721-]1722).
'Clark' – Sir George Clark, *The Later Stuarts 1660-1714*, Second Edition (Oxford, 1956).
'Hetherington' – W. M. Hetherington, *History of the Church of Scotland* (Edinburgh, 1843).
'Morren' – Nathaniel Morren, *Annals of the General Assembly 1752-1766* (Edinburgh, 1840).
The Scots Magazine, v. xxviii (July 1766); v. xxxi (May 1769).
'Meikle' – Henry Meikle, *Scotland and the French Revolution* (Edinburgh, 1912; reprinted London, 1969).
'Acts of the General Assembly' – British History Online.

Appendix B

Scotlands v The Rev. James Thomson (1775-76) [1]

James Boswell's unpublished 'Memorial'

The Court of Session papers relating to the 'Dunfermline case' (both printed and non-printed) offer unusual insight for anyone wishing to grasp what pulpit censure is all about, how it was interpreted by leading advocates in the course of an important civil process, and, as detailed below here, how so-called 'precedents' were manipulated to their advantage by both defending and prosecuting counsel. In the records of this process — one of the two most important cases of pulpit censure to come before the supreme civil court in Scotland in the latter half of the eighteenth century — successive counsel for the minister's defence, James Boswell,[2] Ilay Campbell and Andrew Crosbie,[3] cite several examples of ministerial censure where, as it seemed to them, a preacher's actions might be excused on the ground of 'liberty of the pulpit' (to use Boswell's phrase). Though we might find them today far-fetched, such stories were clearly thought by lawyers to have a meaningful use in their seeking to justify James Thomson's remarkable outburst in his Dunfermline pulpit. Unfortunately for them, as well as for Thomson, the majority of incidents cited as legal precedents are, to be realistic, not of any legal substance whatsoever but ought rather to be seen (to employ the language of one of the pursuers' counsel, David Rae) as 'entertaining anecdotes' and, consequently, most unlikely to move the judges of the Court of Session to sympathise with the defender.[4] And so it proved. Further, to rub salt into the wound, at one point in the proceedings even Rae joins in the fun and cites a wholly obscure anecdote out of Foxe's Book of Martyrs (which he had culled from Matthew Bacon's 'New Abridgement of the Law'), in an effort to help turn the tables on the minister.

While a modern reader will doubtless find it difficult to believe that the judges hearing the case would have taken such contrived anecdotes with other than a large pinch of salt, perhaps we should not be too eager to focus our minds on the evident difficulty of counsel, on both sides, to identify credible examples of conceivable precedents for Thomson's sermon that might hold up in court; after all, at least some of the so-called precedents described here may well have been suggested to his legal team by the minister himself in the first place. At the same time, it is impossible to dismiss Boswell's comment that Thomson preferred to rest his believed innocence on 'simple and plain' arguments, presumably relating to his status and responsibilities as a minister and to his implied duty to speak out on the important issues he had chosen to censure in the most glaringly public manner open to him.[5]

John Knox

In his *Answers* of 14 October to Rae's *Petition* of 14 July 1775 Andrew Crosbie notes a powerful example of pulpit censure on the part of Scotland's greatest reforming preacher:

> John Knox, though he is not to be commended for his harshness, made his Sovereign, the beautiful Queen Mary, shed tears.[6]

In his long *Memorial* for the pursuers [7] Bannatyne W. Macleod (later Lord Bannatyne) counters with a short history lesson for the benefit of the Lords of Session:

> He [Thomson] has indeed thought proper, in evidence of this right [the 'right of public censure'] to mention examples of very great liberties used in former times by the Scottish clergy. Your Lordship has been reminded of the uncommon freedom with which our great Reformer Knox used to reprimand from the Pulpit persons of the highest rank, and to stigmatize the vices even of his Sovereign herself ... [8]
>
> ... When we find therefore this great Reformer arraigning in the Pulpit and that with indecent liberty, the supposed vices of the greatest persons in the nation, and even of the Sovereign herself, we may justly perhaps excuse him upon his particular situation and the character of his times, but it is a jest to found on his conduct in those particulars, as a justification of similar excesses in the present age, when the Church and State enjoy an equal degree of felicity and the Constitution of both is, in this and all other particulars, settled upon firm and permanent principles.[9]
>
> ...Were our nobility & gentry to plead the consuetude of their ancestors in vindication of such private violence, and plunder [?] on such atrocious offences against the State as then passed unnoticed or escaped an effectual punishment, it is believed your Lordship would pay little regard to the argument, and yet it is precisely the same with what is used by this defender, when he states the freedoms used in the Pulpit by John Knox, the head of an infant Church struggling for the establishment in the midst of this national anarchy in vindication of a minister using improper liberties in the present times. ...[10]

Hugh Latimer [11]

Crosbie's *Answers* cites in defence of the minister, James Thomson, the briefest of references to 'Bishop Latimer' having 'wielded the spiritual sword amongst the courtiers of Edward VI without fear or restraint'.[12] But perhaps Hugh Latimer (1485?-1555), Bishop of Worcester, who has been described as 'of all the [English] reformers, the most persuasive in the pulpit',[13] deserves much more than this. Latimer, a Lutheran convert, early in his career was called before Cardinal Wolsey to explain his doctrine and belief and, having been heard, dismissed with his licence to preach throughout England intact and confirmed. He is remembered today in popular histories of the time as the martyr who, from the stake – to paraphrase John Foxe – exhorted his colleague Nicholas Ridley, the former Bishop of London, to 'play the man' in order that 'we shall this day light such a candle by God's grace in England, as shall never be put out.' Most relevant for our purpose here, Latimer's biography reads almost like the story of pulpit censure writ large.

FRVITFVLL SERMONS:

PREACHED BY

the right Reverend Father, and constant Martyr of Iesus Chrift, Mafter HvGH LATIMER, newly imprinted with others not heretofore fet forth in print, to the edifying of all which will difpofe themfelves *to the reading of the fame.*

¶ Seene and allowed according to the order appointed in the Kings Majefties Injunctions.

Printed at *London* by *Thomas Cotes*, for the Companie of STATIONERS.
1635.

Cum Privilegio.

Title page of Hugh Latimer's *Fruitfull Sermons* (1635), the edition used by Boswell in his *Memorial for the Reverend Mr James Thomson* dated 'February 15th. 1775'.

The NRS bundle of supplementary materials relating to the Dunfermline case includes James Boswell's MS *Memorial* of 15 February 1775; the document remains unpublished. Boswell has more to say on Latimer than any of his legal colleagues, for or against the minister. Naming as his source the 1635 London edition of Latimer's *Fruitfull Sermons*, f. 105, Boswell cheerfully introduces his long quotation as follows:

> And good old Bishop Latimer in what he calls very truely 'a most faithful Sermon preached [in March 1550] before King Edward the 6th. and his most honourable Council in his Court at Westminster.' —
>
> 'We Preachers have come & spoken unto you, we have drawn our swords of Gods word, and striken at the roots of all evil to have them cut downe; and if ye will not amend, what can we do more? And preaching is cause of sedition here in England, much like as Elias was the cause of trouble in Israel, for he was a preacher there , & told the people of all degrees their faults: & so they winced and kicked at him, & accused him to Achab the King, that he was a seditious fellow, & a troublous preacher, & made much uproar in the realm: So the King sent for him, he was brought to Achab the King, who said to him: Art thou he that troubleth all Israel? And Elias answered & said, Nay, thou and thy fathers house are they that trouble all Israel. Elias had preached Gods word, he had plainly told the people of their evil doings, he had shewed them Gods threatnings : In Gods behalf I speak, there is neither king nor Emperour, be they never in so great estate, but they are subject to Gods word, & therefore he was not afraid to say to Achab: it is thou and thy fathers house, that causeth all the trouble in Israel. Was not this presumptuously spoken to a king? Was this not a seditious fellow? Was not this fellows preaching a cause of all the trouble in Israel? Was he not worthy to be cast in *bocardo*[14] or little ease? No, but he had used Gods sword, which is his word, and done nothing else that was evil … .' [15]

But if Boswell's aim was to show that sometimes a preacher had to resort to extreme measures and extreme language to get his point across, he might with advantage have cited Latimer's sermon in an earlier passage than the one he chose. Latimer's theme, after all, is 'covetousness' and was, therefore, highly germane to the circumstances of Thomson's pulpit tirade against the bribery and corruption he had allegedly witnessed for himself and/or heard from others in the course of the burgh elections at Dunfermline:

> Therefore, you Preachers out with your swords and strike at the roots; speak against covetousnesse, and cry out upon it. Stand not ticking and toying at the branches, nor at the boughs (for then there will new boughs and branches spring again of them) but strike at the root, and feare not these [Giants of England, their] great men and men of power, these men that are oppressors of the poor.[16]

Bernard Gilpin [17]

Andrew Crosbie finds something of a parallel in the story of Bernard Gilpin:

> … a remarkable story is told in the life of Bernard Gilpin, a divine of the same reign, who preached before the Bishop of Durham [Richard Barnes, consecrated in 1577], at a time when many abuses were committed in that diocese; and, he plainly told his Lordship, "In the presence of God, his angels and men, I pronounce you to be the author of all these

evils, yea, and in that strict day of the general account, I will be a witness to testify against you, that all these things have come to your knowledge by my means, and all these men shall bear witness thereof, who have heard me speak unto you this day." [18]

Crosbie then quotes from William Gilpin's biography, where the consequences of his ancestor's actions are narrated as follows:

"During that day, nothing else was talked of; every one commended what had been said, but was apprehensive for the speaker. Those about the Bishop, waited in silent expectation, when his resentment would break out. After dinner, Mr Gilpin went up to the Bishop to pay his compliments to him before he went home. Sir, (said the Bishop) I propose to wait upon you home myself. This, he accordingly did, and as soon as Mr Gilpin had carried him into a parlour, the Bishop turned suddenly round, and seizing him eagerly by the hand – Father Gilpin, says he to him, I acknowledge you are fitter to be Bishop of Durham, than I am to be parson of this church of your's. I ask forgiveness of past injuries. – Forgive me father. – I know you have enemies, but while I live Bishop of Durham, be secure, none of them shall cause you any farther trouble."[19]

Patrick Simpson (as related by Gabriel Wilson, quoting John Row)

Patrick Simpson (1556-1618) was minister at Stirling (previously at Cramond) and opposed episcopacy and, specifically, James VI's proposal to re-introduce bishops into the Church of Scotland. John Row (1568/9-1646) was minister of Carnock and author of *The History of the Kirk of Scotland, from the year 1558 to August 1637*, first published in Edinburgh from Row's original manuscript by the Wodrow Society in 1842.[20] Gabriel Wilson (d.1750) was minister of Maxton in the Presbytery of Selkirk. Scott writes of him: 'Next to [Thomas] Boston himself, no man did more to disseminate the doctrines of the *Marrow of Modern Divinity* ... and in 1733 he protested against the sentence passed on the four Seceders.'[21] Wilson later espoused the views of the Glasite church, though the Presbytery took no action to condemn his teaching or doctrine. The passage cited by Crosbie is from a synodical sermon of Wilson that would lead to his being admonished at the 1722 General Assembly for having stated 'three points of doctrine, wherein the Synod represent that he did not satisfy them as to his orthodoxy.'–

In the preface to a sermon by Mr Gabriel Wilson, printed at Edinburgh 1723, the following curious anecdote is mentioned: "Another instance of plain-dealing which was in use among the honest ministers of this church, in days of old, I shall give you from Mr Row's manuscript-history, concerning Mr Patrick Simpson, minister at Stirling, a learned, holy and straight man, of whom some extraordinary things are recorded in the Fulfilling of the Scriptures. Being a man very meek and modest, the court professed a greater respect for him than for any other of the men who bore testimony against their declensions and corruptions. He happening to preach before King James, *anno* 1592, after the vile murder of the Earl of Murray by Huntly, who, to say no worse, was connived at by the king in that affair; when Mr Simpson cam to apply his text, Gen. iv, 9. Where is Abel thy brother? He said to the king publicly, Sir, I assure you, in God's name, the Lord will ask at you, Where is the Earl of Murray your brother? Unto which, the king answered,

Mr Patrick, my chamber-door was never steiket upon you, you might have told me any thing you thought in secret: To which, Mr Simpson replied, Sir, *the scandal is public.* And being sent for to the castle after sermon, he went with his Bible under his arm, saying, That would answer for him." [22]

'A minister of the name of Douglas' in the reign of Charles II

Without identifying his source, Crosbie proceeds to enumerate precedents in an attempt to give 'instances of the bold freedom with which conscientious clergymen have rebuked, what they considered to be wrong, ... in every age'. He scrapes the proverbial barrel when he turns his attentions to a case from the time 'when Charles II was in Scotland'. –

> When Charles II was in Scotland, the General Assembly appointed a minister of the name of Douglas, to rebuke him on account of his amours. Douglas understood that his majesty had been discovered, in some of his hours of dalliance, with the windows open, and he [Douglas], in in a more genteel manner than was usual among the clergy of his country at that time, admonished the king, by telling him, that when he was so engaged again, he should at least be decent enough to shut the window boards. The General Assembly took this lenity very much amiss; and Mr Douglas was reprimanded for having been too gentle.[23]

But there are serious difficulties here. Both the Extract Decreet,[24] as well as Macleod for the pursuers, change the identity of the minister from 'Douglas' to 'Henderson'.[25] It certainly seems to bear out that the tale is indeed no more than an 'entertaining anecdote.'

'Parson Prick' and the Greenwood (or Grimwood) case [26]

The citing of historical anecdotes as supposed legal or quasi-legal precedents was not the exclusive preserve of the defence counsel in the cause. In their printed submissions to the Court of Session for the Scotland family all three prosecuting counsel – Rae, Dundas and Macleod – cite as their source Matthew Bacon's *Abridgement* ('voce *Libel*') for an incredibly obscure 'English case' from the reign of Queen Elizabeth, going all the way back to the earliest versions of John Foxe's *Martyrology* (or to give it its more familiar title, *Book of Martyrs*) – that enormous (in all senses of the word) work, first published in 1563, which continued to be regarded as worthwhile reprinting until early in the nineteenth century.

The basic facts of the case – at least concerning the preaching of the sermon and the presence in the church of the alleged 'martyr', Greenwood *aka* 'Grimwood', in order to hear the parson's words of 'posthumous' censure – though perhaps hard to believe, are historically not in dispute since it involved no less than the chief justice of the Queen's Bench in Elizabeth's reign, Sir Christopher Wray. Despite this, Foxe felt obliged to remove the case from later editions of his book on having realised he was unable to claim it as an authentic case of martyrdom. Intriguingly, almost a couple of centuries before the case was cited in the Court of Session in Edinburgh, it was cited in an English case of slander, *Brooke v Montague*, Sir Edward Coke referring to it when the then Chief Justice of the King's Bench, Sir John Popham, had pronounced Wray's verdict 'good law.'[27]

The passage in Bacon's *New Abridgement* – a third edition 'corrected' had come out in 1768 – quoted by the three prosecuting counsel in the Thomson process runs as follows:

> Here it may be proper to insert the remarkable case of Parson Prick, who in a sermon recited a story out of *Fox's Martyrology*, that one *Greenwood*, being a perjured person, and a great persecutor, had great plagues inflicted on him, and was killed by the Hand of God; whereas in truth he was never so plagued, and was himself present at that sermon; and he thereupon brought his action upon the case, for calling him a perjured person; and the defendant pleaded not guilty; and this matter being disclosed upon the evidence, *Wray* Chief Justice delivered the law to the jury, that it being delivered but as a story, and not with any malice or intention to slander any person, he was not guilty of the words maliciously, and so was found not guilty.[28]

In his seventy-three page *Memorial for John, Robert, and David Scotland Merchants in Dunfermline* [29] Bannatyne Macleod explains that the Elizabethan parson 'neither declines the jurisdiction of the Court, nor disputes that an injury committed in the Pulpit was a just ground for a claim of damages at the instance of the private party, but lays his defence on the particular proofs which shewed that he had no injurious intention.' Macleod concludes, therefore, that the case 'clearly shows' that 'even in that early period, the freedom of the Pulpit was not admitted as an excuse for improper attacks made on the conduct of particular persons, and it is well known to your Lordships that in latter times the Clergy have been always held subject to the civil authority for the abuse of the freedom of speech enjoyed in that place'.[30]

'Dr. [Robert] South' [31]

Having referred to the 'various kinds of Liberty in a civilized society' which were 'gradually receiving judicial establishment' – 'liberty of the Press' and 'liberty of the Bar'[32] – Boswell's *Memorial* of 15 February 1775 turns to the third of these liberties, the 'Liberty of the Pulpit' which, he announces, 'is now to be the subject of discussion, and' he adds, 'it is a subject very extensive and very important.' He comments:

> A Clergyman like a Physician must proceed according to the circumstances of those under his care. If gentle admonitions are not effectual, he must not stop short, but must try what can be done by the severity of reproof. If general reprehension is found ineffectual, he must administrate particular rebuke to notorious individuals.[33]

And he illustrates his point by reference to 'Dr. South':

> Dr. South in a Sermon preached at Lambeth Chapel on the 21 of November 1666[34] from these words "Rebuke with all authority" – says 'This authority is a Spiritual Sword put in the hands of every Church ruler, and it is not put into his hands with an intent that he should keep it there for no other purpose but only for fashion's sake as men used to wear one by their sides.'[35]

Just why Boswell should have gone to a sermon by the relatively obscure English 'trimmer', South, is not, at least on first examination, entirely clear. The answer, however, almost certainly lies in his extensive cultivation of Samuel Johnson's tastes and prejudices.

In the *Life* Boswell puts South's name into the mouth of Johnson on two occasions. In October 1769 while debating the relative merits of the Roman Catholic and Presbyterian religions in the light of his concern that it may not be wise to encourage a Bohemian servant he had just hired to accompany them to Scotland, the servant being a Catholic – Johnson declaring at one point he 'preferred' the 'Popish' to the 'Presbyterian' form of religion – Boswell records that he was advised by Johnson to 'read South's *Sermons on Prayer*.' Almost ten years later, in April 1778, the Scottish tour now a distant memory,[36] Johnson was invited by Boswell on behalf of an acquaintance to express an opinion on 'what were the best English sermons for style.' Having commented on *Atterbury* (Johnson: 'one of the best'), then *Tillotson* (Johnson: 'I should not advise a preacher at this day to imitate Tillotson's style'), he says of South: '*South* is one of the best, if you except his peculiarities, and his violence, and sometimes coarseness of language.' Here, in passing, is one clear example where Boswell *qua* advocate is indebted to Johnson for assistance in storing up received wisdom of practical use to him in his professional career.

The case of the 'ludicrous play' – '*The Minor*'

Continuing his defence of James Thomson's actions in his *Memorial*, Boswell changes tack completely when he turns to the stage for a recent, *local* example of pulpit censure:

> Nay not many years ago, a very respectable clergyman of this City preached a sermon which was well understood to be directed against some men in high office who had encouraged the performance of a Ludicrous Play, which he imagined had a tendency to throw ridicule upon some of the Doctrines of our holy religion and therefore he thought it his duty to take publick notice of what he most seriously disapproved, but it was never once thought that he was liable to an action of damages for this sermon.[37]

The 'very respectable clergyman' was none other than the Reverend James Baine, quondam minister of the High Church in Paisley who had 'preached in' John Witherspoon to his Laigh Church charge in the same west of Scotland manufacturing town in 1757, after Witherspoon had been 'translated' there from his first charge, Beith in Ayrshire. In 1766, disillusioned by the direction he saw the established Kirk moving nationally – and, it should not be under-estimated, probably also on account of his own unfortunate engagement in local church politics, not the least those involving Witherspoon in the long-running 'Paisley case' (see chapter 3) – Baine controversially deserted his Paisley charge and espoused the Presbytery of Relief. He was then offered appointment as minister to the new Relief congregation in Edinburgh. Baine's *The Theatre Licentious and Perverted* (1770, reprinted twice in the same year) is the published version of the sermon to which Boswell, without naming the title or its author, refers in his *Memorial*. The 'men in high office' who had 'encouraged the performance' of the play were, of course, the magistrates of Edinburgh who were responsible for the grant of a licence to the theatre. As we saw in chapter 3, the introduction (albeit anonymously) into the Thomson process of one of the key figures in the grossly protracted (and, in certain respects, parallel) Court case concerning 'a minister of Paisley', is seriously ironic.

The author of the 'ludicrous play' was Samuel Foote (1721-77) and the piece that had alternately wowed and shocked the audience in the new Theatre Royal, Edinburgh on Saturday, 24 November 1770 was a farce called *The Minor*. This was a comedy in three acts that, depending on one's understanding of its thinly veiled comic allusions to George Whitefield and Methodism, had similarly entertained, confused and outraged London audiences some ten years before when it first came on the stage; it was then published in many successive editions for more than a decade afterwards. Boswell, outside the Court of Session and out of his advocate's wig and gown, knew the play well[38], had seen it 'at the little theatre in the Haymarket' in the course of its first run in 1760 and, like everyone else, had himself laughed at the antics of some of the coarse, outrageous characters, especially 'Shift' (played on occasion, we are told, by the author himself), 'Mrs Cole' and 'Sir William Wealthy', characters to whom James Baine took particular exception. Indeed, young Boswell relished *The Minor* so much that his first ever publication as a twenty-year old was a critique of it in which he observed that the comedy

> has not failed to produce a violent concussion of the sides of each spectator, and consequently has met with prodigious applause. At the same time, as it contains a good deal of keen and poignant satire on the great leader of the *Methodists* [George Whitefield], it has very much raised the indignation of that sect, so that the whole fraternity are up in arms against the author … .[39]

Boswell later regretted his early enthusiasm for the play. In a note penned inside a signed copy of *Observations* he writes:

> 'This was an idle performance and written inconsiderately; for I disapprove much of the Minor, as having a profane and illiberal tendency.'[40]

Anticipating his next foray into anecdote for the supposed edification of His Lordships, Boswell then reveals in his *Memorial* why is he doing all this:

> As in the case now mentioned, a Clergyman will often accidentally preach upon a Subject which may be liable to an application which he never intended.[41]

Hugh Blair and the 'Douglas cause'

The next anecdote cited by Boswell in his *Memorial* involves one of the greatest names in preaching in the Scottish Enlightenment period, Dr. Hugh Blair,[42] minister of St. Giles' Church (to be precise, the New Kirk) where Boswell often went to hear Blair preach – as did several of the pillars of the Edinburgh legal profession.[43] While admiring Blair's intellectuality and his just fame as a preacher, Alexander Carlyle, typically caustic in his judgment, sums up Blair's personality as 'mild and elegant' yet without any 'relish' for humour, 'naif' and even 'timid and unambitious'. Yet Blair remains a far more important figure than Carlyle and one of the greatest of the Edinburgh *literati* of the period.

Boswell's 'joke' in his *Memorial* concerns the deadly serious business of the final outcome of the Court action associated with the 'Douglas cause':

> Some wag put into the London newspapers, that on the Sunday after the news of the reversal of the great Douglas cause arrived at Edinburgh,[44] the Rev[d.] Doctor Hugh Blair preached before the Lords of Council & Session from these words 'What pleasure then had you in these things whereof you are now ashamed.'[45] It was literally true that Dr. Blair

did preach upon that Text, and upon that day, but the meaning which was put upon his doing so, was as remote from his thoughts as any thing whatever.[46]

What came to be known as the 'Douglas cause' ranks as the greatest legal dispute involving rival inheritance claims heard in a Scottish court in the entire eighteenth century.[47] The case first came before the Court of Session in December 1762 and almost at the same time an action before the 'Tournelle' – one of four courts responsible to the French *Parlement* – began in Paris. In Scotland the process was determined not until five years later, at which time seven judges 'voted' for one claimant, and the same number for the other, and was finally laid to rest only by the casting 'vote' of the Lord President, Robert Dundas 'the Younger'. Johnson told Boswell that 'a more dubious determination of any question cannot be imagined.'[48] But many more than Dr. Johnson were thoroughly dissatisfied with the outcome. The decision was appealed to the House of Lords who, early in 1769 reversed it. Aspects of the case, in which Boswell was never more than peripherally involved, rumbled on for some time beyond.

The 'joke' Boswell makes in his *Memorial* at the expense of Hugh Blair was by no means the first he had devised around the Douglas cause. In the March issue of the *Scots Magazine* for 1767 he had published anonymously a satirical ballad ridiculing aspects of one of the legal claims in the affair, a poem he then proceeded to have printed:

> You may even make a bonfire of Bankton and Stair [49],
> And betake you to Sherwin, to Cocker and Mair; [50]
> The Roman Twelve Tables[51] exploded shall be,
> The table of *Multiplication*[52] for me. [53]

Boswell knew he was sailing close to the wind despite being warned by one of the judges of the Court of Session, Lord Hailes, to 'put it in the fire' as he would make himself enemies by it. Still, David Hume and Sir Adam Fergusson told him they found it to their liking and, no doubt encouraged by this, Boswell's interest in the Douglas cause was further displayed in no less than four titles he caused to be published in the same year.[54]

Boswell's second joke, this time at the expense of his father

Continuing his *Memorial* for the Dunfermline minister Boswell plunges into his second comic episode with a private family story relating to a little known episode concerning his own father, Sir Alexander Boswell. Boswell's father had been elevated to the bench of the Court of Session in 1754, and one year later to the High Court of Justiciary when he had taken the title Lord Auchinleck. Relations between father and son were often strained, to say the least, but at least here there is no malice or nastiness in the story. Boswell may have refrained from identifying the judge concerned but it is inconceivable that those for whose attention the 'precedent' is intended would have had the slightest difficulty in doing so:

> A very grave and decent Gentleman now one of your Lordships number, when he was Sheriff of the Shire of Wigtoun,[55] and also Provost of the Town of Wigtoun[56] used to have the Magistrates and Council to take a Glass with him on Sunday between Sermons. One day they had sat a little longer than usual tho' by no means drinking to excess, and

the Congregation was kept for some time waiting for them. When they came to Church in the afternoon the Text which the Minister read out was, "They that be drunken are drunken in the night."[57] and he gave a very suitable discourse against intemperance. Some foolish members of Council insisted that the minister meant to attack the Sheriff and his Company, but the Sheriff told them they were very much mistaken, and after the Sermon joked a little with the minister as to what had passed, and the worthy man declared what indeed the Sheriff well believed, That it never entered into his imagination that he was touching any persons in particular.[58]

Appendix C

The Stirling 'black bond' (1772): corruption and Church patronage

In his *Answers* of 9 December 1775 in the action *Snodgrass et al. v The Rev. John Witherspoon* David Dalrymple – comparing the 'plumb-bond' that Snodgrass and the other pursuers had taken out in the Edinburgh Commissary Court in June 1762 with the so-called 'black bond' of Stirling – conceded that the bond taken out by the Paisley men was '*not so bad*' as its infinitely more notorious (and much more recent) Stirling counterpart. A brief note of explanation is necessary, especially since the circumstances surrounding the Stirling bond are clearly relevant to the dire state of politics in the burgh of Stirling at around the same time as James Thomson's sermon, forming the cornerstone of chapter 2.

What became known as the 'black bond' was taken out in 1772 by three Stirling councillors (Henry Jaffray, James Alexander and James Burd) in order to combine their interest in matters relating to local elections with a view to nothing less than securing for the 'bondsmen' the 'total management of the burgh' during their lifetimes. Their more immediate objectives were to 'weaken the interest' of the Dean of Guild at Stirling [Nicol Bryce] 'and his friends from the council altogether' and, even more outrageously, to

> unite and consider together ourselves as one man in managing the elections of the burgh, and to take no step but for the mutual interest and with the concurrence of each other. … That we shall likewise be united in the administration of the affairs of the burgh and of the hospitals; and that each of us shall have an equal share in the disposal of all such offices as are dependent upon the council, and shall bestow them upon our friends; … as it will be in our power, in time coming, at every election of a member of parliament for the district during our lives, to give the vote of the burgh of Stirling to any candidate for the said district, who shall be most acceptable to us; and that we will be intitled at every such election to receive money and rewards suitable to the occasion, and which rewards it is reasonable we should divide equally among us; we do therefore bind and oblige ourselves to make an equal division of all monies so to be received by any of us upon occasion of any election for the district, and of all profits and emoluments arising from offices conferred upon any of us by the member of parliament, or by any person or persons standing candidate to represent us in parliament, during our joint lives.

As if that were not enough, the bond goes on to disclose the means by which the three bondsmen propose to ensure the circumventing of the rules of church patronage to their own advantage, and to the advantage of the 'bulk of the people' (without, however, specifying how that is to be achieved). Nothing like the following is known, or (most likely) has ever been contemplated in the entire history of the operation of the Patronage Act:

In order to render ourselves popular in the burgh, and that our management may be acceptable to the whole inhabitants, we engage, that when a vacancy happens in the change of any of the town's ministers, we shall procure the same to be filled up with an Evangelical minister or preacher, such as shall be most agreeable to the bulk of the people.

Finally, the three men subscribe the bond solemnly engaging 'that all and each of us shall keep this bond an inviolable secret from every other person.'

In November 1773 a petition and complaint was lodged with the Court of Session at the instance of John Paterson, Deacon of the Weavers and others, as constituent members of the Town Council of Stirling that Alexander, Jaffray and Burd had, since 1768, 'managed the elections and affairs of the burgh according to their pleasure'. In their judgment of 1 March 1775 the Court pronounced two interlocutors expressing their 'utmost detestation of the bond and bondsmen', and in the first of these declaring the bond 'illegal, unwarrantable, and *contra bonos mores*' and that it indeed (despite the protestations of the defenders to the contrary) had an undue influence on the burgh elections of 1772 and 1773. The Court accordingly found the outcome of the 1773 election 'null and void' and 'reduced the election of the magistrates and town-council,' also finding the complainers 'entitled to full costs of suit.' Before they could be punished by the Court – they had been summonsed to appear in June for the purpose – the three bondsmen lodged an appeal in the House of Lords where they were represented by Henry Dundas and Alexander Murray, advocates.[1] The Journal of the House of Lords for 8 November 1775 records that in the petition and appeal of James Alexander *et al.* against John Paterson *et al.* the Lords 'affirmed' the Scottish Court's interlocutors of March that year and, in consequence, dismissed the appeal.

Sources

1. Morison, *Decisions of the Court of Session*, (1811), v. xxiii-xxiv, sect. 12, no. 71, 1775, 1 March, 9527-9. 'John Paterson and Others, *against* The Magistrates and Town-Council of Stirling, elected at Michaelmas 1773.'
2. House of Lords Journal v. 34, 8 November 1775 (British History Online).
3. *The Scots Magazine*, xxxvii, March 1775, 163-4; Appendix 1775, 731-2.
4. British Library – 'James Alexander, Esq; provost; James Burd, [and others] … appellants. John Paterson, deacon of the weavers, and deacon conveener [sic] of the seven incorporated trades in the said borough; [and others] … respondents. The appellants case.' [London, 1775] [ESTC T209769]
5. [Do.] – 'The respondents case.' [London, 1775] [ESTC T209770]
6. Ryskamp & Pottle (eds.), *Boswell: The Ominous Years 1774-76*, 70 and note 5, 155-6.
7. Milne (ed.), *Boswell's Edinburgh Journals 1767-1786*, 192. Disappointingly note 32 merely cites *verbatim* the footnote from *The Ominous Years*.

Appendix D

The Reverend Alexander Fergusson and the affair of James Leitch: the *Chair of Verity* challenged (April 1742 to August 1744)

With tantalising brevity Nathaniel Morren[1] reveals that the minister of Kilwinning, the Reverend Alexander Fergusson, was no stranger to controversy at the time he fired the opening shots in the bitter dispute described in chapter 5 of this study – his letter of 1767 to his colleague in the Presbytery of Irvine, the Reverend John Adam, minister of West Kilbride, setting alight the so-called 'Kilwinning heresy'. Research into the original Presbytery records held in the NRS has disclosed the extensive details of the case. It is a story worth probing. According to Morren, almost twenty years before Fergusson's notorious letter to Adam was published in the Scots Magazine *the minister had been forced to defend two libels preferred against him by James Leitch, a 'wright' – a joiner or cartwright – in Kilwinning. The Leitch affair dragged on for over two years. Morren supplies only the thinnest detail, though he is clear on its conclusion: that the minister's accuser failed to prove the substance of his charges to the satisfaction of the Presbytery, the Synod of Glasgow and Ayr, and finally, of the Commission of Assembly which latter body confirmed in May 1744 the Presbytery's deliverance dismissing the case against Fergusson, thus clearing the way for the sentence passed on Leitch by the Presbytery – the 'Lesser Excommunication'[2] – to be put into effect.*

In the light of its broader importance in the history of church discipline in Scotland in the eighteenth century – aside from its relevance to the Kilwinning heresy episode – it is strange that the affair has not previously been fully investigated. For one thing, it represents one of only a handful of cases involving a layman challenging not just the actions and lifestyle of his own parish minister, but his moral character and reputation in the community as well. For another, the case exposes the glaring deficiencies of church law in failing to accord both the pursuer as well as the accused the basic rights of natural justice they might have expected had either party decided to prosecute his action in a civil court. Further, the Leitch affair represents a rare example of a pursuer in a Scottish ecclesiastical court employing professional legal counsel to argue his case. Finally, there are lessons to be learned from the case that are relevant to popular conceptions of the varying degrees of repute attaching to the pulpit as the 'chair of verity' in a parish setting in rural Ayrshire in the 1740s.

Beyond the high seriousness of his dispute with Fergusson there are rich comic strains evident in parts of Leitch's narrative to the Presbytery as he tries in his unaffected way to communicate his complaints about aspects of the minister's highhandedness – none more farcical than in his unintentionally hilarious description of the shooting of a rival's champion cock, reminiscent of the eighteenth-century Scottish rural life paintings made famous by such as David Allan.

Fergusson was aged 53 at the outset of the Leitch episode, and had served as minister at Kilwinning, a rural town in Ayrshire, for twenty-one years. He would remain there for a further twenty-eight years until his death in 1770 aged 81. Hew Scott notes that 'towards the end of his life, being unable through age and illness to perform his duties, he was assisted by five probationers in succession, to whom he gave the whole stipend.'[3] There is no reason to suppose that among his congregation he was not a respected – though, one suspects, not necessarily a much-loved – figure. Indeed, the presbytery records of the case suggest it is likely that Fergusson had an unfortunate reputation for being awkward, domineering, headstrong and downright 'thrawn'. His father had been sheriff-depute of Ayr and he himself had married the eldest daughter of a writer (see note 6 to this Appendix) in Edinburgh. The law was in Fergusson's blood, therefore, and that simple fact becomes clear enough from the obviously accomplished way in which he dealt with the serious charges made against him by the local man and his successive professional advisers.

The first reference to the affair is contained in the minutes of the Presbytery of Irvine concerning a parish visitation to Kilwinning made on 28 April 1742. In accordance with normal custom, the Presbytery had convened the visitation by means of a pulpit intimation requiring heritors, elders and 'heads of families' to forgather in the church on that date for the purpose of declaring their satisfaction, or otherwise, in respect of the 'doctrine, life and pastoral work among them' of their minister. Although visitations of this kind were usually routine meetings they were clearly taken seriously by everyone involved. According to protocol, the minister whose parish was visited was required to remove himself for the main business of the meeting at the end of which all attending were invited, after interrogation by the Moderator, to signify their content with their minister – or not.

The minutes of the Presbytery of Irvine visitation to Kilwinning of 28 April record that, with the minister 'removed', all present were then 'interrogated' and 'made no objection excepting James Leitch, wright, who gave in a paper' dated the same day as the visitation. Alexander Fergusson having been recalled – the visitation had the status of a meeting of Presbytery – Leitch's paper was read out to the assembled company. It consisted of no less than seven heads of complaint against the minister. One can imagine that for Fergusson it must have been an acutely uncomfortable experience. The paper, we learn, 'contained several queries' and, as numbered successively in the minutes these were:

1 On the question 'Whether he visited the parish' it was 'affirmed' by Leitch that Fergusson 'had not visited several Families for several years';
2 'If he visited the sick, because he had been negligent therein … and even did not come when called till after they were dead';
3 'Whether he had any Elders who prayed for the sick as they ought, except Mr Logan';[4]
4 'Whether he had not discharged penny Weddings, and yet tolerated them upon payment of four pounds Scots';[5]
5 'Whether he had left his parish without Sermon and stayed at Ed^r. [Edinburgh] during the Session, and neglected to intimate a Fast appointed by authority';
6 'Whether he had not when newly come home from Ed^r. from a Law plea called a Session on the Sabbath Day and intimate[d] the dispensation of the Lords Supper that very day, and if he did not neglect an essential part of that Sacrament not reading his Warrant';

7 'If he had not called some of his parishioners confounded Villains or damned confounded Villains and Rascals'.

The reading of Leitch's paper concluded, it was noted by the clerk that the Presbytery had observed that 'if Mr Fergusson refused them [denied the implied charges] and any part thereof nae proven, he should be censured.'

Fergusson then took the floor and proceeded to reject all of the accusations except 'both branches' of the sixth which he admitted were 'very true', but added that 'there is no fault in either,

> And if the Last [he means the second] Branch was faulty, *viz.* not reading the words of the Institution, the Complainer himself took no offence at it, for he was a Communicant which shews his integrity.

Respecting the last query, Fergusson answered that 'he does not remember that he ever used such expressions to any man, and desired the presbytery to cause James Leitch name the persons, time and place of such expressions and condescend on [iterate] any other grounds of complaint against him.' When it came for the meeting to call Leitch 'and any person who would adhere to him' to 'condescend' upon their grounds of complaint against the minister 'and offer proof thereof', only one man – a shoemaker in Kilwinning named Thomas Scot – 'declared his adherence to James Leitch & his complaint'.

At the meeting of the Presbytery on 8 June discussion of the case resumed. The record of the meeting makes clear that in the interval Leitch had resorted to professional legal advice and had appointed one 'Robert M^{c}dormitt' [McDermitt?/ McDermott?], 'writer[6] in Ayr his procurator'. By January 1743 we learn that Leitch was now being represented by 'Robert Crawfurd', 'writer in Irvine, as pro$^{tor.}$ [procurator] for him'.[7] Intriguingly, however, it does seem that *both* were advising Leitch at times throughout the process. At the first of numerous Presbytery meetings when the agenda included the Leitch affair his lawyer expressed the view that to 'tie down' his client to prove in his article of complaint that 'Mr Fergusson called *him* [italics added since this is the first time we are told that this allegation is made personal to Leitch] a Damned villain and Rascal within 5 years' was inadmissible, since 'there was no Law for this in criminal cases, and that it should not prejudge them of a proof in that matter.' To this the Presbytery replied that, by the Church's own procedural legal rule-book, the *Form of Process*,[8] 'they were not restricted to this time, and they even doubted if witnesses could be sworn upon words that has passed above three years.'

There follows an interesting precedent cited by the Presbytery, who, one strongly suspects, were put up to it by Fergusson himself: 'And that in the case of Professor Simpson this was not allowed.'[9] The official report of the proceedings records that Fergusson speaks out at this point, and from his words we learn the background to the substance of Leitch's *animus* towards him: 'The whole complaint', he says, 'proceeded from Malice.' The minister alleges that the origin of Leitch's aggressive hostility towards him lies elsewhere:

> There was no *Fama clamosa*[10] nor the least offence taken against him on account of the things laid in the queries till raised by the said James Leitch by any body in the parish, yea

not by Leitch himself who attended his Ministry till he was summoned in December last at the instance of the Kirk Session for the mortcloth[11] to his first wife & her two children which he refused to pay though three years due.

Round one to Fergusson. The Presbytery found Leitch's libel unconvincing and allowed Fergusson and the elders respectively to proceed to prove the pursuers' allegations under certain heads of his complaints [queries 1-3 in his list]. Leitch's procurator protested and intimated that his client would appeal to the Synod of Glasgow and Ayr, an action which, as we shall see, was not an empty threat.

On 30 November 1742 it is reported that Leitch had 'dropped his appeal'. It soon becomes clear, however, that the dispute between the two men was far from over. Leitch gave in a petition to the presbytery in which he detailed the grounds of a fresh row that had broken out between them:

> ... he had dropped his appeal from [sic] the consideration that Mr. Fergusson and he a little before the Sacrament of Kilwinning [the Communion season, when Fergusson's church and other local churches celebrated the Sacrament of the Lord's Supper] were reconciled as appeared from this, that Mr. Fergusson had sent for him to Alexander Cunninghames[12] and forgave him all injuries that he had done him, and drank to him, and that he should took [sic] it for granted that they were reconciled until Mr. Fergusson refused to baptize his child, pretending that he could not do it unless by a sponsor as he had scandalized him & his Session by the aforementioned prosecution, and that he had consulted some of his Brethren [fellow ministers in the Presbytery] who advised him to this.

The petition concludes with Leitch informing the Presbytery that 'he had written to five neighbouring ministers to know if Mr. Fergusson had consulted with them anent baptizing his child, who all refused it.' This ambiguity can probably be interpreted to mean that the five ministers had similarly refused to baptize the child, but it might also be argued that the sense of the minute was that they had denied that Fergusson had ever discussed the issue with them. In other words: *Had there been collusion among them, prompted by Fergusson, or not?*

When it was Fergusson's turn to reply to Leitch's paper he chose to do so orally and at once went on the offensive. He maintained that 'the aforesaid Representation contained a great many untruths'. One of the central points in his defence was that Leitch had informed him (*via* the elder Logan) that he was prepared to abandon the process only if the Presbytery 'would not censure him as a Calumniator'. Further, Fergusson insisted that Leitch had got it all wrong over the issue of consultation with five other ministers on the baptism of the child. All that he, Fergusson, had done was to consult his colleague 'Mr. Dow',[13] and 'he cannot help though Mr. Dow should have forgot it, & the presbytery' he continues, 'may observe how disingenuously James Leitch acts in saying Mr. Dow absolutely denies that he did it, for his letter only bears he did not remember it.' Fergusson's comments on the baptism issue seemed to destroy the credibility of Leitch's case and it is at that point in the record – their having listened to Fergusson's appeal – that we learn the Presbytery's decision:

> The presbytery having read the petition and heard parties, Judge that according to the protestation taken at the Synod, his appeal is fallen down; The reasons he offered for

not insisting in his appeal in due time being insufficient, and that though the presbytery approve of and wish that his Minister and he be in perfect friendship, yet they cannot drop the process unless that he acknowledge a fault in accusing the Ministers [sic] and Elders of Kilwinning before the presbytery & this to be intimated to the Congregation, which if he refuses to do they proceed to take Mr. Fergussons Exculpation, and that if he fail, James Leitch be allowed to prove the facts.

When the Presbytery interlocutor was made known to him Leitch 'positively refused to submit himself to censure' and, accordingly, Fergusson was not allowed to proceed to give in his 'exculpation' to the next meeting, whereupon he named eight witnesses in his defence. On 11 January 1743, however, before Fergusson could reveal the grounds of his exculpation, Leitch, now accompanied by Robert Crawfurd, 'writer in Irvine', told the Presbytery that they desired to give in a new petition. By way of introduction, Leitch's counsel conceded that in his client's previous submission (presumably the work of his former legal adviser, 'McDermitt') the infamous 'queries' were 'too generally & improperly laid for an Accusation and Libel'.

In laborious detail Leitch's new petition lists the names and addresses of the men and women whose families Fergusson allegedly neglected by not visiting them – in several cases, it was made out, for years on end, and even in one case citing a member of his congregation whose home was 'not half a mile from his manse'. In another case, Leitch avers that when the minister found time to visit the family he spent the time with them

> instead of ministerial instructions, enquiring into the state of their souls & their progress in Religion & presiding in prayer, he sometimes or commonly used to ask a few questions about the price of Victual and so went off, and generally makes little or no enquiry what new servants are come to any family, whether they have Certificates of their good behaviour in the parish they came from: These are but specimens of his neglect of this important duty, perhaps but one of a dozen or score that might be given to prevent the great trouble, noise and expence of calling the greatest part of the parish.

The petition continues in similar vein, not just fleshing out the much sketchier and unsubstantiated accusations in the original libel, but now with much more detail added, above all supplying graphic new evidence of the minister's alleged neglect and malpractice extending this time to nine separate charges. Of this new list of charges against Fergusson formulated by Leitch's lawyer, Crawfurd, four stand out in particular, each astonishing if true:

1 Baptisms of 'premature' babies

'I must now beg leave to take notice that Mr. Fergusson has baptized several children of the fathers presenting, born some six, seven, eight, nine or near ten weeks before expiring of nine months after the parents marriage without any enquiry except in one case, where he [indistinct] the midwife that she was to be called, and directed her what answers to give, particularly that the child had no nails; and in some of these cases he so far glories in his overlooking such faults as to tell some of the parents that he owed him a harvest day, and when the midwife appeared before the Session and had answered according to direction; being [?] asked how long she thought the child might be born one month before the time, to which Mr. Fergusson answered gloriously, You have given it one month, we will give it another, and those children being mostly baptized privately to make the matter look the better: It is too much trouble for Mr. Fergusson to lecture upon or explain a portion of the Scripture as the Act of Assembly prescribes.'

2 Refusal to baptize Leitch's child: accusation that Fergusson had abused the 'Chair of Verity'

'The history of another instance [i.e. of how Fergusson was alleged to have been guilty of the 'prophanation and abuse of the Lord's Day'] is this, That after the presbytery had lately given orders to Mr. Fergusson to baptize my youngest child provided the Session had nothing further to lay to my charge than my accusing of my Minister, the Session of Kilwinning or rather their Minister having called me before the Session last Novr. on a Lord's Day Mr. Fergusson was pleased to tell me that the Session rebuked me for not attending the Ordinances and ordained me to attend more punctually for the future, and I answering that I would take no rebuke from him unless the Session voted it, and he having asked their votes, the Session did not vote me to be so rebuked, and yet notwithstanding Mr. Fergusson the next Lord's Day after reading the said Act of Presbytery told the Congregation from the pulpit that the Session had rebuked me for not attending the Ordinances and ordained me to attend more punctually for the future, or words to that purpose, tho thereafter he had assumed [presumed] to rebuke me in the Sessions name without their authority, They afterwards in his own presence voted no rebuke.

If this was not plainly asserting untruth, and from the Chair of Verity too [it] is submitted to the presbytery I have already taken notice in my last petition to the presbytery Mr. Fergusson's disingenuity in the presence of his Brethrens forbidding him to baptize my child, – which is cleared up by their letters contradicting him, to which I refer for shortness sake as to that point.' [bold type added]

3 'A temper very unbecoming the Character of a Gospel minister'

'About or within those three years Mr. Fergusson understanding that a cock of Thomas Scot,[14] in Kilwinning fought his sons cock,[15] he came to Thomas scot and his parent, and desired them to put away said cock, else he would shoot him, which Scot refusing to do, so Mr. Fergusson & his son not only went about the manse and glebe with a gun to shoot said cock, but he also roused one Mories [Morrice?] shoot at said cock not on his ground, and Mories missing him, he roused one Hugh Coller [to?] go with him with a charged gun to shoot cocks and hens that pestered his glebe and missing them, then he came [indistinct] to the side of Thomas Scots Hay yeard, where Mr. Fergusson perusing Thos. Scots cock and two hens which appened to be his Hay^d. lying, ordered Coller to shoot them, which he accordingly did, & some of the fowls not being quite killed, flightered into a yeard which gave the minister the trouble of climbing over a dyke, into a ditch whereof he fell, in quest of the prey, which he finding came to the street of Kilwinning with them & hollowing & sounding aloud his triumph over the dead birds waved them round his head and at length coming to Scots house with them told him his great exploit and offered him his fowls, but he refusing to take them, Mr. Fergusson told him he would give them to the poor, but instead of this gave one of them to a man who had been working to him, and who it is commonly reported received no other reward for his days labour.'

4 Case of 'a Seceder' about to flee the country: compelling a servant to sign an oath

'About April 1739, Mr. Fergusson having called Mary Dickie[16] servant to Mr. Baillie Advocate out of her masters house, and discoursed [discovered?] her in the Green, he ordered her to follow him to a certain house in Kilwinning, where he, she an Officer and others being present, he drew a Representation that John Starrat weaver in Kilwinning had now got all his fathers efforts into his hands, was going to fly the country and defraud all his fathers creditors, whereof she was one, therefore craving a Warrant to apprehend and imprison him till he should find Bail or pay her upon which Representation Mr. Fergusson also wrote out a Judges Deliverance, ordaining her to swear that Starrat was about to fly the country or *in meditatione fuge* [italics added] or words to that purpose; Upon which Mr. Fergusson desired said Mary Dickie to swear that Starrat (who by the by was a Seceder)[17] was going to leave the country and defraud her of her money; but she answering she could not swear that for her conscience would not allow her to do so as she had no such thoughts of him but believed him to be a very honest lad or man, adding God forbid I should swear so for I know nothing of his designing to leave the country. [The minute of Leitch's petition continues the anecdote in similar vein, closing with Fergusson being accused of having manipulated the girl's innate honesty to get her to sign the oath which he himself 'wrote out to this purpose'.] ... she in tears and grief declared It was not her fault, she was ignorant and imposed upon by Mr. Fergusson, who made her do it.'

With the reading of Leitch's second libel at and end, the Presbytery debated their next move and eventually resolved to allow Fergusson to proceed to call witnesses in support of his 'exculpation'. In following that course, they had in mind that 'it was a hardship to delay this affair further, as he [Leitch] might appeal from it without end, whereby Mr. Fergussons character might suffer, and before any thing be done the witnesses might die'. At that, Robert Crawfurd, Leitch's procurator, reportedly said: 'Proceed as far as you please' – and the clerk adds, 'and so both went off.' On hearing seven different witnesses cited by the minister in support of his claim to have visited families and the sick in contradiction of Leitch's charge to the contrary in his first petition, the Presbytery found that Fergusson had fulfilled his duties in that regard but prudently held back announcing their interlocutor 'till the appeal be discussed'.

On 22 February 1743 it is recorded in their minutes that Leitch had given in his 'reasons of appeal' to the Presbytery of Irvine. A committee of three – including, remarkably, Alexander Fergusson himself – was appointed to 'draw up answers to them' and to have these ready to produce at the presbytery's 'meeting at Glasgow' on 6 April.[18] In the light, however, of the Synod having in the interval rejected Leitch's appeal (as reported by 'some of the ministers who attended the Synod'), the Presbytery concluded they could now proceed to announce their verdict on the first libel. Having resolved that 'Mr. Fergusson had fully exculpated himself from all the articles of the said first libel which they by their former judgement on the relevancy had found censurable', they declared Leitch's first libel 'false & groundless':

> And the said James Leitch is to be censured as a Calumniator, but delay to determine what the Censure shall be till they have gone through his second libel, which they now require him to prosecute & give in a list of witnesses to prove it, that the said libel and list may be out into Mr. Fergussons hand to be seen and answered.

Predictably, when the verdict was read to Leitch he protested 'and dictated his protest'. Having learned that he was not entitled to an extract of the reasons of appeal on the grounds that the clerk had 'no orders so to do', Leitch protested 'for cost, skaith and damage & remeid in Law', further insisting that he be allowed a proof 'of all the facts and circumstances of the first libel by way of query & the last [i.e. second] libel before they proceed upon any sentence'.

Amid the tangled sequence of events juggling between Presbytery and Synod and the two separate sets of charges laid against Fergusson by Leitch in both petitions, Fergusson is cleared to proceed to give in written 'Answers' to the second libel at the Presbytery meeting at Irvine on 14 June 1743. His long and detailed paper occupies almost five pages of the record of the meeting, and in it Fergusson does not spare his accuser and 'his associates'. Two main lines of argument emerge from the minister's answers. *First*, he clarifies and amplifies what he meant in his earlier defence by assigning to a mix of 'calumny, falsehood and malice' Leitch's motives in his action against him. Specifically, he returns to the issue of the mortcloth debt. Leitch's malice had sprung from 'being prosecuted for his debts to the Kirk Session' in that regard and the duration of the debt was now 'more than three years'.

But, continues Fergusson, that same malice was not confined to Leitch alone. Malice on the part 'of a few other persons of the same size & temper associate with him' was also evident; and

> among those I have reson to reckon his proctor [sic] Robert Crawfurd, whose wife is in the Fee of a fourth of a Mealling life-rented by her mother,[19] for tho I was his friend and benefactor on all occasions, he has concerned himself in this dirty & malicious affair by not only being the Framer & Writer of this lybel, but threatening me with it before commenced ...

Crawfurd's alleged complicity in the *conspiracy* – for that has to be the implication – to 'frame' Fergusson is obscure, but is somehow bound up with his wife's hereditary entitlement to income from the letting of pasture ('Grass' in the minutes). Intriguingly, Fergusson states that Crawfurd

> told me I might blame myself for what trouble I had met with & would meet with, for, added he, if you had sought the reparation & Grass from the Earl of Eglinton we would have supported you.[20]

Secondly, Fergusson's answers are remarkable for the extent to which his general legal knowledge and, more specifically, knowledge of ecclesiastical evidence and procedure, exposes numerous flaws and defects in Leitch's (and his procurator's) action. Thus, demonstrating his easy familiarity with the *Form of Process* he tackles the issue of a minister of the Kirk having been accused of not performing his sacred duty:

> That this process is commenced contrary to the rules laid down in the Form of Process, which for good reasons requires That none accuse a Minister without first acquainting himself & some neighbouring ministers as in Chap. 7th. pass. 4.10.11. Indeed Leitch may plead ignorance, but the proctor [sic] cannot, and if he had acted an honest part to his client, or not been acted with the like base disposition against me, he would have

directed him to have followed that rule, but its plain he intended that whether there was ground for this process or not the Articles should be published & my character suffers. This disposition further discovers itself in the malicious manner wherein he has conceived this whole lybel and in the false & calumnious way wherein he has resumed some of the Articles of the first lybel already discussed.

Fergusson then directly confronts the case of Mary Dickie – where Leitch had sought to impugn him for having allegedly compelled the girl to attest her oath – and he refers to the implication that he had somehow had it in for Starrat, the alleged would-be fugitive, on the grounds that he was a seceder – an accusation he strenuously denies, while also at pains to point out that seceders ('those people') were still keen to employ the resources of his church and even his own ministerial services:

> Its taken notice of [in Leitch's second libel – case 4 above] that John Starret [sic] was a Seceder, as if I had assisted her [Dickie] out of ill nature against him on that account, but its well known that though I caused Compulsators[21] to be used against those people for the payment of the dues owing to the precentor & Beddle [sic] at Marriages & Baptisms that they not only allow but even desire me to do the duties of a minister in my course of visiting and entertain me in the kind of manner, so little notion have they of my being acted with any spite against him [Starrat].

The Presbytery, doubtless anxious to wind up a long, trying meeting, proceeded to give its decision on how each separate charge in Leitch's second libel should be dealt with, one by one, all nine of them *seriatim*. In the majority of these, they appear content to follow their own tentative conclusion that 'there was not very great ground to regard the 2nd lybel as given in by him', but even so decided that 'James Leitch give in to Mr. Fergusson the list of witnesses to each article separately as to each of the facts mentioned in the lybel ten days before next meeting at which time the Presbytery will appoint a day for examining the witnesses'.

At long last, it seemed things were coming to a head. But at its meeting of 12 July one can almost sense the frustration and irritation in the words of the clerk's report that Leitch had supplied Fergusson with a list of no less than 190 witnesses, together with a 'protest' to the effect that he 'should have the liberty of adding more'! The Presbytery was unimpressed:

> … in regard it is absurd and impossible that 190 witnesses could be witnesses to every part of the lybel, its ridiculous to examine them as required, & [?] it would be needless multiplying of oaths; and besides, as they are not classed on the several heads Mr. Fergusson cannot know on what light to view them …

It was agreed that Leitch should give in his list of witnesses to Fergusson, 'properly classed', ten days before the 10th of August 'at which time the Presbytery are to meet at Kilwinning for examining said witnesses'. When this interlocutor was made known to Leitch, however, he offered another paper '*de novo*' 'which he called a petition'. This unforeseen petition was read and, unsurprisingly, the Presbytery 'found nothing in it to cause them alter their method of procedure'.

Predictably, the meeting of 10 August proved yet another marathon. It began with Fergusson intimating that Leitch had supplied him with a revised list of witnesses, this time 'classed' according to the sequencing of the charges in the second libel as desired by the Presbytery. Then Fergusson entered upon his own protest:

> That tho he has defended himself in the second libel exhibited against him by James Leitch for the honour of the presbytery & the vindication of his own character, it may be without prejudice to him to prosecute the said Leitch before a competent Judge for the calumnies he has therein uttered against him to the great hurt of his Reputation and Ministry.

In revealing his threat to take the matter before a civil court, and so effectively out of the hands of the Presbytery altogether (and to seek damages for Leitch's alleged defamation), Fergusson had clearly scored an enormously important point and a potential match-winner. The minute goes on (and here one senses that these are the minister's own words used by the clerk):

> Mr. Fergusson further protested, that his proponing defences in this process may not be interpreted as acquiescing in or homologation of any sentence the presbytery may come to in this process. In regard the presbytery is not a competent judicatory or judge of what is proper for the reparation of the damage done to his character and ministry, whereupon he takes instruments.

Fergusson's threat notwithstanding, the Presbytery conscientiously went ahead with the hearing of his 'exculpation', including the testimonies of his supporting witnesses. The meeting continued into the afternoon at which point Leitch began supplying proof of his libel. The first witness called was the shoemaker Thomas Scot whose evidence was judged inadmissible on the grounds he and his wife were 'near relations' of the pursuer. Several more witnesses cited by Leitch were also rejected, some on the ground of their partiality to Leitch and known 'hatred' of Fergusson. Significantly, some of Leitch's witnesses could not even bring themselves to corroborate the stories related in his second libel – as, for example, that concerning the triumphalism Leitch affirmed Fergusson had displayed over the incident of the shooting of fowls. Other witnesses were immediately objected to by Fergusson himself, one ('John Miller') on the ground he was a 'scandalous person' and 'in habit and repute a person of a very bad character'. On putting the issue of Miller's reliability to a vote, however, it was agreed to enquire into his character, to which decision McDermitt (now apparently restored as Leitch's procurator) protested. Miller's character was subsequently investigated at the hands of several witnesses and eventually it was resolved to reject him.

On 13 September 1743, with twelve ministers attending[22] including Fergusson himself, the Presbytery of Irvine 'proceeded to consider what issue to bring this process unto',

> And having observed that James Leitch has been guilty of slandering Mr. Fergusson in a scandalous manner by the two libels given in by him; seeing that by all the witnesses examined not one Article is proven against Mr. Fergusson, excepting the neglecting to visit a few families, for which the Moderator is appointed to admonish him in terms of the Interlocutor: And therefore the Presbytery Judge that the said James Leitch be

censured with the sentence of the Lesser Excommunication,[23] that he be appointed to be rebuked before the Congregation of Kilwinning; and that the sentence be intimated whether he appear or not; And because the affair has made a great deal of noise in the neighbourhood, they appoint that a short abstract of this be intimated from all the pulpits in this presbytery, But in regard, that James Leitch had appealed to next Synod at a former meeting, the presbytery supersedes execution till after the next meeting of the Synod. And this is the unanimous judgement of the Presbytery.

There are no further references to the affair in the Presbytery minutes until 12 June 1744 when it is recorded:

There was produced and read an extract from the commission of the last General Assembly, affirming the sentence of the Synod of Glasgow and Ayr – & of the presbytery of Irvine in the process at the instance of James Leitch against Mr. Fergusson. The presbytery therefore resolved to proceed to the execution of the sentence, and accordingly they did & hereby DO appoint that Mr. Fullarton[24] exchange pulpits with Mr. Fergusson upon the third Sabbath of July first to come, and then & there to execute said sentence; and they further appoint that James Leitch compear before the Congregation of Kilwinning said day to be publicly rebuked, and that an extract of this appointment duly attested by the Clerk, be delivered to him by the presbytery's officer.

Even yet the affair was not concluded. On 7 August it is noted that John Fullarton, minister of Dalry, had made it known that it would be 'extremely inconvenient' for him to exchange pulpits with Fergusson on the prescribed day, so that unpleasant duty had fallen instead on John Montgomery, minister of Stewarton.[25] In the event, Leitch failed to appear.

Source
NRS Records (Minutes) of the Presbytery of Irvine, 1742-1744: CH2/197/4-5 (digitised).

Notes

Introduction

1 For the use of the word 'verite' (e, ie) in the time of Knox see the DOST – 'The chayre of veritie, the pulpit.' Knox seems to have been particularly fond of the word.
2 But either John Knox himself, or the printer, gets it wrong, the text reference as cited as epigraph on the title page being '*1. Timoth. 4.*'
3 Overton, *John Wesley* (1891), 87.
4 Ronald Knox, *Enthusiasm*, 423.
5 Wesley, *Journal* ed. Curnock, Part 17, 12 May 1774, v. 6, 19.
6 Ibid.
7 Wesley, *Journal* ed. Curnock, Part 18, 17 June 1779, v. 6, 239-40.
8 *Enthusiasm*, 459.
9 Wesley, *Journal* ed. Curnock, Part 7, 15 August 1747, v. 3, 314.
10 Boswell wrote of the pamphlet: 'Of this performance I avoided to talk with him; for I had now formed a clear and settled opinion, that the people of America were well warranted to resist a claim that their fellow-subjects in the mother-country should have the entire command of their fortunes, by taxing them without their own consent ... I was sorry to see him appear in so unfavourable a light.' (Boswell's *Life of Samuel Johnson*, ed. Womersley, 430).
11 Aberdeen University Press, 2014.
12 *The Oxford Handbook of the British Sermon 1689–1901*, ed. Francis and Gibson, Preface, xiii.
13 Broadie, *The Scottish Enlightenment*, 149-50.
14 'In contradiction to what is commonly assumed, orthodox Calvinist theorists were in fact generally far more confident of the capacity of human reason to arrive at various religious truths, including the existence of an afterlife, without assistance from revelation than the Moderates were.' (Ahnert, *The Moral Culture of the Scottish Enlightenment, 1690-1805*, 94-5.
15 *An enquiry into the causes of the decline of religion. A sermon preached in the High-Church of Glasgow, April 14th 1761*, 30.
16 Ibid., 24.
17 Morren, *Annals of the General Assembly 1752-1766*, 54-61 (1755 Assembly) and 86-98 (1756 Assembly). Morren records: [At the 1756 Assembly it is reported that] 'Some members of Assembly, not satisfied with the general declaration against infidel writings which had been passed the former year ... proposed, in the committee of overtures, that a special censure should be directed against certain infidel writers. The controversy had been carried on since last Assembly; and not long before the present meeting, a pamphlet had appeared, with the title Infidelity a proper object of Censure.'
18 *Infidelity a proper object of censure.* (Glasgow, 1756). Walker was John Witherspoon's uncle, being older brother to the Paisley minister's mother Anne (or Anna). See Crawford, *LWJW*, 148, note 31 for further biographical information on Walker. In the first edition of *Church and University in the Scottish Enlightenment* (1985, p.71) Sher attributes the work to the Reverend

George Anderson but corrects this, 'probably' in Walker's favour, in the re-issued 'Edinburgh Classics Edition' (2016), xxxiv.

19 The result merely encouraged George Anderson – 'a preacher, who had formerly been an army-chaplain, and, in his latter years became chaplain to Watson's Hospital, Edinburgh' – to raise 'a complaint' against the printer [Robert Fleming] and publishers [Alexander Kincaid and Alexander Donaldson] of Kames's *Essays on the Principles of Morality and Natural Religion*. Answers to Anderson were given in to the Presbytery by James Ferguson and John Dalrymple, advocates for the defenders, but Anderson died before he could compose a reply. The Presbytery continued, however, to debate the process and only dismissed the action on consideration of a pamphlet given in by Dalrymple but widely believed to have been largely the work of Hugh Blair – *Objections against the Essays on Morality and Natural Religion Examined*. According to Morren, Blair had also played a key role in the Assembly debate of 1755.

20 'On the Instructions to be Derived from Recalling the Memory of our Fathers', Sermon XVIII, preached in the Tron Church, Edinburgh, on 19 May 1797 in Moodie's posthumously published *Sermons* (Edinburgh, 1813), 304-323. Moodie was minister of St. Andrew's Church in the New Town, Edinburgh. For more on Moodie see chapter 6 'Reform'.

21 *The Fatal Consequences and the General Sources of Anarchy* (Edinburgh, 1793), 10-11. Erskine's preface is important. He explains that he had been forced through ill-health to lay the sermon aside for some time. It had been 'not written' – 'like many I have preached for some years past'. He would not have proceeded to 'compose' or 'preach' it, 'had not the reflexions it contains been suggested to me by the confusions in aris, 10th August that year.' The specific timeline suggests he is referring to the massacre of the Swiss guards, quickly followed by the storming of the Tuileries, the arrest of the king and the royal family, and the appointment of Danton as Minister of Justice. Erskine closes his preface by adverting to the 'melancholy transactions at Paris, 2d and 3d September, on the first of which days I preached the Sermon'. He is now referring to the infamous 'September massacres' when, it is estimated, some 1,200 –1,400 inmates of jails in Paris were slaughtered at the injunction of Marat.

22 *WJW*, 2, 438, sermon dated 7 September 1758, 'The Charge of Sedition and Faction against Good Men.' The sermon was first published by Bryce and Paterson of Glasgow in the same year.

23 Ibid., 471, a fast-day sermon dated 16 February, 1758, 'Prayer for National Prosperity and for the Revival of Religion.' This sermon was first published in the same year in London by Thomas Field.

24 'And Haman said unto king Ahasuerus, There is a certain people scattered abroad and dispersed among the people in all the provinces of thy kingdom; and their laws are diverse from all people; neither keep they the king's laws: therefore it is not for the king's profit to suffer them. /If it please the king, let it be written that they may be destroyed: and I will pay ten thousand talents of silver to the hands of those that have the charge of the business, to bring it into the king's treasuries.' (*Esther,* 3, 8-9).

25 c. 1617-1665. Scott, *Fasti*, New Series, VI, 319.

26 Chadwick, *The Reformation*, 421. The biblical reference to Rab-shakeh, one of Sennacherib's messengers to Hezekiah is *2 Kings*, 18, 17-37, especially verse 36: 'But the people [in response to Rab-shakeh's speech of mockery] held their peace, and answered him not a word: for the king's commandment was, saying, Answer him not.'

27 English text from the Church History Information Centre website www.churchinhistory.org: 'Three Sermons in Defiance of the Nazis' by Bishop Clemens von Galen.

28 Jane Dawson, *John Knox,* 291.

29 1503-1559. Estienne is called 'Robert Stephens' by some eighteenth and nineteenth century English writers. His 1553 edition of Calvin's *Institutio Christianae Religionis* is regarded as a masterpiece of the art of printing.

30 Wilson states that 'the Author has now stood a Pannel [= the accused in a trial] before four Synods, and as many Committees of that Synod [Merse and Teviotdale]' and that finally 'the Commission of the Church … transmitted the whole Process to the next General Assembly.' Cleverly and sarcastically, Wilson explains that the Synod's charge against him consisted of 'Twelve Remarks, Twelve Questions, and Twelve Slanders.' His play on the word 'Twelve' would have instantly gone home among Wilson's readers, since he had been one of the famous group of twelve ministers who had initiated the Marrow controversy and had fired the opening shots in a huge dispute that rocked successive Assemblies from 1720 on and eventually led to the 'great' secession of 1733. *The Trust* was reprinted in Glasgow (1765), Kilmarnock (1781) and Hawick (1785).

31 Act XI of the 1723 Assembly 'anent Mr Gabriel Wilson, Minister at Maxton, his Sermon, preached before the Synod of Merse and Teviotdale' found him guilty of representing 'three points of doctrine' which failed to satisfy the Synod 'as to his orthodoxy': 1st. 'That the moral law to a believer is divested of the curse or threatening of eternal damnation, and hath no other sanction but fatherly chastisement'; 2nd. 'That gospel or saving repentance is not necessary in a sinner, in order to the pardon of his sins in justification.'; and 3rd. 'That assurance, or a man's persuasion, that he shall be saved by Christ, is of the essence of justifying faith.' Wilson was admonished and prohibited from writing, printing or preaching, 'publicly or privately', any 'expression upon these three points of doctrine.'

32 The 'application' in a sermon of the period is the concluding section in which the minister attempts to relate the burden of cited scriptural authority to the particular circumstances of his overall message to the congregation.

33 In Latin in 1536, then revised and expanded in three subsequent editions, 1539 (Latin, but issued by Calvin in a French translation in 1541), 1543 (Latin and French) and 1559 (do.). Of special interest here is the impressive Glasgow quarto edition of Thomas Norton's 1561 translation of the final version of the *Institutes* printed by John Bryce and Archibald M'Lean for Alexander Irvine in 1762. Norton (1530x32-1584), Archbishop Thomas Cranmer's son in law, also translated Alexander Nowell's *Catechismus* (1570) – a key work in the instruction of a protestant clergy and in the promotion of English as the language of the reformed faith. He is, of course, much better known to students of Elizabethan drama as the co-author, with Thomas Sackville, of *The Tragedie of Gorboduc* (1562).]

34 V. H. H. Green, *Renaissance and Reformation*, 175-6.

35 In either 1563 [Oxford *DNB*] or 1565 [*ESTC*] the same London printing shop at the same address, but with the printer named as 'Richard Serll', printed and published Fills's translation from Theodore Beza (aka de Bèze) – Calvin's brilliant successor – of a standard work of Beza's which Fills entitles: A briefe and piththie [sic] summe of the Christian faith made in forme of a confession. In the dedication Fills boasts that he was 'somewhat acquainted' with Beza.

36 The title page runs 'Printed at London by Rouland Hall, dwelling in Gutter Lane, at the sygne of the halfe Egle and the Keye. 1562.' Fills's translation was reprinted in London (Thomas Fawcett for Matthew Wallbanck and Lawrence Chapman) in 1643.

37 *The Lawes and Statutes of Geneva* (1562), 6.

38 Donaldson, *Scottish Church History*, 52. For the best exposition of Scottish church courts before and after the Reformation see Gordon Donaldson, 'The Scottish Church Courts', in the Stair

Society's *Introduction to Scottish Legal History* (1958). The same piece is reprinted as chapter 5 of Donaldson's *Scottish Church History*, (1985), 40-52.

39 For example, as did James Leitch, a wright in Kilwinning, Ayrshire, in 1742 when he lodged an official complaint with the Presbytery of Irvine against the Reverend Alexander Fergusson. See Appendix D.
40 MacCulloch, *Reformation – Europe's House Divided 1490-1700*, 593.
41 Calvin, *Institutes*, trans. Beveridge (2009), IV.12.3-4, 814.
42 Ibid. IV.12.2.
43 Ibid. IV.12.8-10. For the information contained in much of this and the previous paragraph I acknowledge my indebtedness to *The Calvin Handbook*, ed. Herman J. Selderhuis, 11, 'Ethics and Church Discipline', 332-344. The version of the Institutes I have used is Henry Beveridge's translation (Peabody, Mass., 2009).
44 It is important to note that 'discipline' as here intended implies the broader definition of 'rule', 'regimen' or 'system of governance'.
45 See Dawson, *John Knox*, 200, 204, for the authorship by the 'six Johns' (Knox, Willock, Spottiswood, Winram, Douglas and Row) of the *First Book* (1560), which 'specified the process by which discipline should be upheld and adopted, the Reformed "consistory" comprising the minister and elders' [i.e. Kirk Session].
46 But Maxwell observes that the Kirk's active role in the discipline of moral offences, in his own personal experience, 'was by no means abandoned till almost within living memory' and the records of his own parish (Dunbar, East Lothian) 'show that certain sexual lapses in particular were dealt with by the kirk session, privately, until twenty years ago.' He was writing in 1955. (*A History of Worship in the Church of Scotland*, 146 and note 1).
47 Robert Robinson (1735-90), introductory, 'Brief Dissertation on Publick Preaching' in his edition of Jean Claude's *An Essay on the Composition of a Sermon*, Cambridge, 2 vols., v.2, 1779, lix.
48 The Latin text of both letters may be found in *Ioannis Calvini opera quae supersunt Omnia* (Corpus Reformatorum, 59 vols., Brunswick, 1863-1900), V, 369-416. The English translation of both letters used here is by Henry Beveridge, found in *A Reformation Debate*, ed. John C. Olin, 1966.
49 Boethius (480?-524) was one of Sadoletto's most illustrious predecessors as bishop of Carpentras.
50 *A Reformation Debate John Calvin and Jacopo Sadoletto*, ed. Olin (1966), 65.
51 Ibid., 75-6.
52 Ibid.,
53 See chapter 3 and Appendix B for what James Boswell understood by the term.
54 MacCulloch, *Reformation*, 585-6.
55 In MacCulloch-speak the Protestant Reform churches were 'noisy' in contradistinction with e.g. monasticism and, more especially, the Quakers who felt able to dispense with the pulpit altogether having applied the principle of 'inner light' to congregational worship. See MacCulloch's ingenious study, *Silence A Christian History* (2013), especially 144-150.
56 Chadwick, *The Reformation*, 418, 420.
57 Carolyn Muessig, 'Audience and Preacher: Ad Status Sermons and Social Classification', in *Preacher, Sermon and Audience in the Middle Ages* (2002), 255-76.
58 See *The Calvin Handbook*, C.1, 'Work, Sermons', 'Calvin as preacher', 173-181.
59 The title of the work in Knox's manuscript – and as used in the first edition of 1587 printed and published in London by T. Vautrollier, a Huguenot refugee – is *The history of the reformation*

of religion within the realm of Scotland, with the running titles reading *The historie of the Church of Scotland*. The extremely complex bibliographical history of the work is explained in detail by William Croft Dickinson in volume 1 of his 1949 edition of the *History*, lxxxviii-cix. All that we need to note here is that the Vautrollier version consists of a mix of printed and Ms. material with only Books I-III letterpress printed and Book IV printed as Ms. and, at that, only 'about 2/3ds. of ye 4th Book, at p. 370 of ye Edition in fol. An. 1644' is supplied. [From a note in an unknown hand appended to the last leaf of the British Library copy. The reference to the 1644 edition is to the David Buchanan version.] The Buchanan 1644 edition originally printed in London (John Raworth) was reprinted in the same year in Edinburgh (Robert Bryson). Book V, covering the period from July 1564 to July and August 1567 was published for the first time by Buchanan in 1644 and may well have been written by Buchanan himself since, to use Croft Dickinson's phrase, it 'never came from Knox's pen'. (Dickinson, *John Knox's History of the Reformation in Scotland* v. 1, xciii).

60 'Ephphatha' – 'Be opened'. An Aramaic word which Mark's gospel (7, v. 34) has Jesus utter when, beside the Sea of Galilee, he performed one of his miracles. Jesus singled out from the crowd a deaf man with a speech impediment, 'and put his fingers into his ears, and he spit and touched his tongue:/ And looking up to heaven, he sighed, and saith unto him, Ephphatha, that is, Be opened./ And straightway his ears were opened, and the string of his tongue was loosed, and spake plain.' (AV). But Buchanan's description of the impact of Knox's preaching on his followers also relates the stirring words of Psalm 24, v. 7 – Lift up your heads, O ye gates; and be ye lift up, ye everlasting doors; and the King of glory shall come in – the metrical version of which is to this day solemnly sung at the Sacrament of the Lord's Supper (Communion) in the Church of Scotland.

61 In the Preface to his only published sermon Knox writes: '... to compose bokes for the age to come, seeing that so much is written (& that by men of most singular condition) and yet so little well observed: I decreed to contain my selfe within the bondes of that vocation, whereunto I founde myselfe especially called.'– *A Sermon preached by Iohn Knox Minister of Christ Iesus in the Publique audience of the Church of Edenbrough, within the Realme of Scotland, upon Sonday, the 19. of August. 1565. For the which the said Iohn Knoxe was inhibite preaching for a season.* ([London]: Henry Denham? 1566). Buchanan prints the whole of the sermon, complete with the preface, as an appendix to his edition of 1644.

62 From his preface 'To the Reader' in his published sermon of August 1565.

63 As in Buchanan. The original 1587 rubric reads: 'The first vocation by name of Iohn Knox to preach.'

64 i.e. Knox expounded on a passage of scripture. For the difference between the 'lecture' and the 'sermon' see Maxwell, *A History of Worship in the Church of Scotland*, 97-8, 102-3, 128.

65 Buchanan = 'Rowgh' or 'Rawgh'.

66 c. 1486-1555. Lindsay was the author of the famous morality play, *Ane Satyre of the Thrie Estaitis* – expressing a desire for reform in church and state that was 'widespread in Scotland by the mid-century'. Lindsay is also remembered for his long poem, The Historie of Squyer Meldrum. See *Longer Scottish Poems*, Edinburgh, Scottish Academic Press, v. 1, ed. Bawcutt and Riddy, 248-9 and C. S. Lewis, *English Literature in the Sixteenth Century, Excluding Drama*, (Oxford History of English Literature, 1954), 102-3.

67 Dickinson, v. 1, 83.

68 Ibid.

69 The passage cited in the History is a rendering of Rowland Hall's English version of the Geneva Bible of 1560, in the translation of which Knox may have played a part while he was in Geneva in 1558. The extensive marginal notes may have been inspired by Knox's writings and doctrines.
70 Dickinson, v.1, 85.
71 Ibid., 86.
72 Parliament opened on 26 May and closed on 6 June, thus dating the sermon.
73 Dickinson, v. 2, 63, note 8: 'These "Dukes, brethren to Emperors, and Kings", who were spoken of for Mary's hand were Don Carlos, son of Philip II of Spain; the Archduke Charles of Austria, a younger son of the Emperor Ferdinand I, and brother of Maximilian II; Robert, Lord Dudley, later Earl of Leicester; James, Duc de Nemours; and Henry, Lord Darnley, whom Mary eventually married in 1565.'
74 Ibid., 81.
75 It is also important to note that either the author or the printer, Henry Denham [?], has got the scriptural citation wrong in the title-page motto: the text is not from '1 Timoth. 4.', but from the second of Paul's letters to Timothy, verses 2 - 3. Rowland Hall's Geneva Bible of 1560 renders the passage: 'Preach the worde; be instant in season, out of season; improve, rebuke, exhort with all long suffring and doctrine. For the time will come, when they will not suffer wholsome doctrine; …'. I have been forced to concede defeat in attempting to identify the biblical translation used by Knox in his epigraph and conclude that he employed a mixture of invention and artifice to get his message across, especially in the phrase 'Sermon of veritie.' By contrast, the passage he cites from *Isaiah*, 26, 13-20 (immediately after the Preface, occupying one and a half pages), as the text moderating the theme of the sermon, is word for word from Hall's Geneva Bible. The first verse immediately and dramatically sets the scene for Knox's message: 'O Lorde our God, other Lordes beside thee have ruled us, but we will remember thee onely and thy name.' The reference to Mary and 'King' Henry [Darnley] is obvious.
76 Jane Dawson, while supplying no concrete examples, confirms that Knox generally was cavalier in his approach to citing scripture in an academic sense: 'Convinced he understood the sense of Scripture, Knox often ignored a humanist precision over linguistic meaning or variants within the text and happily ranged between different biblical translations or supplied his own. [RLC's italics] For him, theology was never confined to an intellectual activity.' – *John Knox* (2015), 314.
77 *A Sermon preached by Iohn Knox, Minister of Christ Iesus*, 6, 10-11, 18, 25.
78 Ibid., 'To the Reader'. – '… from my bed I was called before the Council; and, after long reasoning, I was by some forbidden to preach in Edinburgh, so long as the King and Queen were in town.'
79 A good example is to be found in Blair's fast-day sermon, *On the Love of Our Country*, which was never published on its own and not included in his collected *Sermons* until after his death. It was preached in April 1793. Blair's title is intentionally borrowed from Richard Price's *A Discourse on the Love of Our Country* (London, 1790). In his sermon Blair steers well clear of criticising radical organisations preferring to praise the historic liberties of the British constitution. See chapter 7.
80 Neither Henry Meikle in *Scotland and the French Revolution* (1912) nor Bob Harris in *The Scottish People and the French Revolution* (2008) makes specific mention of Carlyle's controversial loyalist sermon of 1794.

81 Ivo Clark points out that in the Reformed 'Order of Excommunication and of Public Repentance' of 1569, the church is shown as determined to put down the sin of child-life or potential child-life: '... it is to be noted, that all crymes that be the law of God deserve death, deserve also excommunication from the society of Christ's Church, whether the offender be Papist or Protestant ... thairfor wilful murtherars, adulteraris (lauchfullie convict), sorcerars, witches, conjurars, charmars, and gevars of drinks to destroy children, – such, we say, aucht to be 'Excommunicat from the society of Christes Church,' ...'. *A History of Church Discipline in Scotland* (1929), 101.
82 Crawford, *The Bard* (2009), 168.
83 Brown, *Robert Burns's Tours of the Highlands and Stirlingshire 1787* (1973), 53.
84 The Form of Process would stand, virtually unaltered, for almost three hundred years until the Act of 1902, which 'legalised and regularised changes and modifications that by this time were becoming customary, and so prevented worse irregularities.' – Clark, *A History of Church Discipline in Scotland* (1929), 141.
85 Ibid., 179.

Chapter 1

1 The incident to which Boswell refers took place while he and Johnson 'drank tea with Mrs. Williams' on Saturday, 1 May 1773. Johnson responded to Boswell's question with one of his impromptu 'oral essays'.(See also chapter 3, 97-99). James Boswell became the patron of Auchinleck parish on the death of his father, Alexander Boswell, Lord Auchinleck, in 1782, and in 1793 he presented John Lindsay as minister of the parish.
2 John Erskine was minister at Kirkintilloch in the Presbytery of Glasgow from 1744 until 1753 when he was 'transported' to Culross (1753-58), and thence to New Greyfriars, his final move to Old Greyfriars occurring in 1767.
3 Roger L. Emerson, *Professors, Patronage and Politics* (1993) and *Academic Patronage in the Scottish Enlightenment* (2008).
4 Ronald M. Sunter, *Patronage and Politics in Scotland, 1707-1832* (1986).
5 *Church and University in the Scottish Enlightenment* (re-issued 2015), 58.
6 *The Moral Culture of the Scottish Enlightenment, 1690-1805* (2014), 67.
7 *The Present State of the Church of Scotland*, 12.
8 Grant actually names a *third* grouping 'which I am loath to describe ... a very small one I hope, of such as are not acted by any regards to Religion or their Country, but influenced by little mean hopes of being made King's Chaplains. ... Some great Men who are elders instigate Ministers of this sort on both sides. Both sides I include under the Name of the Political Clergy.' (*The Present State*, 13).
9 Ibid., 14.
10 Ibid., 16.
11 Ibid., 29.
12 Ibid., 31.
13 'The patronage of a vast number of parish-churches accrued to the crown, by abolition of popery, and thereafter of episcopacy, and which at present, as to many of them, belong to subjects, by grants to the crown'. – McDouall, *An Institute of the Laws of Scotland*, v. II, Book II, Tit. VIII, §99, 36. (Stair Society ed., 1993).

14 'The right of patronage imports Honour, Interest, and Burdens. The honourable part consists in the right of presentation.' Ibid., §61, 23.
15 'His career seems to have been rather uneventful', wrote D. M. Walker, 'He is recorded as having been married five times.' (*Scottish Jurists*, 1985, 195, cited by W. M. Gordon – see note 16 below).
16 From Professor Gordon's Foreword to the Stair Society reprint of 1993, v. 1, iii-iv. Gordon points out that 'No new edition was called for in Bankton's own lifetime and no-one has since undertaken the massive task of re-editing the *Institute* in the fashion of Stair, Erskine, Bell or Hume. Choice of an edition to reprint has therefore posed no problem.'
17 The other, of course, being Henry Dundas. See Emerson, *Academic Patronage in the Scottish enlightenment: Glasgow, Edinburgh and St. Andrews Universities* (2008), Introduction, 6-7.
18 McDouall, *An Institute of the Laws of Scotland*, v. I, 'The Preface', ix.
19 Ibid., v. II, Book II, Tit. VIII, §68, 26.
20 Cited in *The Early History of Church Patronage* (Anon., by 'A Member of the Faculty of Advocates', Edinburgh, 1833), 2.
21 Ibid., 7.
22 Ibid., 10-11.
23 Michael Lynch, *Scotland A New History*, (1991), (revised 1992), 304.
24 Ibid., 321.
25 *Act 10, Q.Anne, ch. 12, 1711*.
26 'Simony' was 'The act or practice of buying or selling ecclesiastical preferments', *etc. (OED)*.
27 *An Account of Lay-Patronages in Scotland*, 13.
28 *A Church History of Scotland*, 283.
29 McDouall, *An Institute of the Laws of Scotland*, v. II, Book II, Tit. VIII, §102, 37.
30 In the case of the Inverkeithing case, however, the Act of Assembly cited by the five ministers who had explained their reasons for not attending the admission of Richardson to the vacant charge on the day appointed (21 May 1752) was an Act of 1736 that stated that 'no minister shall be intruded into any parish contrary to the will of the congregation'. It is this Act that is cited by the Popular party authors of the *Answers to the Reasons of Dissent* given in to the 1752 Assembly at the height of the Inverkeithing case. It should be noted that the 'appointed day' was the day immediately before the date of Gillespie's deposition.
31 Ibid., §103, 38.
32 Morren, *Annals 1752-1766*, Preface, iii-iv.
33 Sher and Murdoch have analysed disputed presentations in the General Assembly over the period 1751-1800 and have shown that the high watermark for such cases lay in the five years between 1771 and 1775 when no less than 21 were reported. From 1751 to 1775 a grand total of 73 cases were dealt with by the Assembly; from 1776 to 1800, by contrast, the number had dropped to 31 cases. ['Patronage and Party in the Church of Scotland, 1750-1800', in *Church, Politics and Society: Scotland 1408-1929* (1983), 197-220.]
34 *A Serious Apology* (1763), Dedication, iii-iv – *WJW*, 3, 265-8. Witherspoon is here referring to the Campbeltown/Southend case and specifically to a petition on behalf of the ministers of these parishes, respectively John Macalpin and David Campbell, who, against their better judgment and contrary to the desire of their congregations, had for a time carried out the instruction of the Synod of Argyll not to continue with the old practice of preaching sermons on every night of the communion season. On pressure from their 'people', however, they relaxed the previous injunction and were censured by the Synod for having done so, resulting

in their appealing to the Assembly. 'After long reasoning', the Assembly upheld their appeal 'for the interest of religion and the ends of edification.' See Morren, *Annals 1752-1766*, 256-7.
35 *WJW*, 3, 269-70.
36 Ibid., 270.
37 Ibid. Footnote. But later in his pamphlet Witherspoon appears to contradict himself : 'What very much contributed or rather indeed, what chiefly brought me to a resolution of publishing the *Characteristics* was a pamphlet published a few months before it called *A Just View of the Constitution of the Church of Scotland*. This universal fame attributed to the late Dr. H——n [*John Hyndman]: and the express purpose of it is to represent a certain set of ministers as agitators of the people, and in general as not acting upon conscience, even where they pretend it, but from a love of popularity.' – *WJW*, 3, 277.
   * John Hyndman (1723-62) served as Moderator of the General Assembly in 1761; in his speech to the Assembly he appears to regret his minor role in opposition to Gillespie. See Morren, *Annals 1752-1766*, 244.
38 E.g. see Sher, *Church and University in the Scottish Enlightenment*, Chapter Two, 'The Moderate Revolution', 45-64; and McIntosh, *Church and Theology in Enlightenment Scotland* (1998), Chapter Three, 'The Problem of Patronage', especially 103-7.
39 By the Moderator of the 1752 General Assembly, Patrick Cuming, in his closing address (Morren, *Annals 1752-1766*, 290).
40 'I believe I might have spared myself the trouble of inserting this maxim [*'Maxim V'*], the present rising generation being of themselves sufficiently disposed to observe it. This I reckon they have, either constitutionally, or perhaps have learned it from the inimitable Lord Shaftesbury, who in so lively a manner sets forth the evil of universities and recommends conversation with the polite Peripatetics as the only way of arriving at true knowledge.' (*Ecclesiastical Characteristics*, *SWJW*, ed. Miller, 78).
41 Morren, *Annals 1752-1766*, 227.
42 *A Short History of the late General Assembly of the Church of Scotland* (1766), 11. (In GUL Special Collections, Murray and Robertson series – multiple copies including Mu43-d.21 and Bf66-i.17).
43 From George F. S. Elliot, *The Border Elliots and the Family of Minto* (1897), 333, cited by Sher in *Church and University in the Scottish Enlightenment*, 50.
44 Sher and Murdoch, 'Patronage and Party in the Church of Scotland, 1750-1800', in *Church, Politics and Society: Scotland 1408-1929*, 213.
45 Ibid., 16. See also Morren, *Annals 1752-1766*, 311.
46 See note 44 above.
47 *Church and Theology in Enlightenment Scotland*, 99.
48 'There is no Law in *Scotland*, no Practice or Precedent for any Action before the Lords of the Session, to compel a Presbytery to ordain the Presentee: no *Quaere impedit* lies against them'.– Anon. (William Grant of Prestongrange), *The Present State of the Church of Scotland. With respect to Patronages* (London, 1736), 3.
49 Adams had been Moderator of the General Assembly in 1744.
50 Morren, *Annals 1752-1766*, 208.
51 Scott, *Fasti*, New Edition, v. V, 44.
52 Ibid., 188.
53 Paton (1690-1768) was minister of Renfrew in the Presbytery of Paisley and, therefore, a colleague of John Witherspoon. He died in the year Witherspoon left Paisley for New Jersey.

54 The letter is published in full in Morren, *Annals 1739-1752*, 190-4.
55 Ibid., 224.
56 Leven served as High Commissioner for the period 1741 to 1753 inclusively.
57 Morren, *Annals 1739-1752*, 261.
58 'When signing the *Confession of Faith* he took exception to chapter xxiii, in which are defined the powers of the civil magistrate.' (Scott, *Fasti*, New Series, v. V, 10).
59 *Principal Acts of the General Assembly* Sess. 8, May 22, 1752: 'Act Deposing Mr Thomas Gillespie, Minister at Carnock, from the Office of the holy Ministry within this Church, and appointing the Presbytery of Dunfermline to admit Mr Andrew Richardson as Minister of the Parish of Inverkeithing.'
60 Subsequently, three ministers were suspended for a period of thirteen years. See also chapter 3, 'Bribery and Corruption', note 1.
61 Morren, *Annals 1739-1752*, 289-90.
62 Scott, *Fasti*, New Series, V, 11.
63 See 'To the Reader' prefacing *Principal Acts of the General Assembly* (1733), iii-v, and the appendix containing 'Passages of Mr. Ebenezer Erskine's Sermon upon which the Sentence of the Synod of Perth and Stirling against him was founded, copied from the Minutes of that Synod', 14-16.
64 'If a late calculation be right, 120,000 of the people of this country have left the established church; and, it cannot be denied, chiefly on account of patronages.' (Anon. [John MacLaurin], *Considerations on the Right of Patronage*, 1766, 9).
65 *The Stone rejected by the Builders*, 14.
66 Ibid.
67 The majority of presbyteries had sent in opinions hostile to the proposal that when a presentation was disputed and thus fell to be resolved by a presbytery, *jure devoluto*, the presbytery, after meeting with heritors and elders, should propose a settlement for approval or otherwise, but in the event of disapproval being expressed it was still competent for the presbytery to have the last word. The main bone of contention was that a majority of presbyteries had opposed the proposal, yet the Barrier Act of 1697 had not been implemented, which required the 'opinion and consent' of presbyteries before any Act of Assembly became binding. See Bankton, *An Institute of the Laws of Scotland in Civil Rights*, v. II, 25, §66: 'A settlement, *tanquam jure devoluto*, by the presbytery.'
68 *The Stone rejected by the Builders*, 39, 41.
69 Not to be confused with another George Logan (1723-54), minister of Ormiston, friend and intimate of William Robertson, Alexander Carlyle and other Moderates, before his untimely death from cancer.
70 There are two versions of this work, quaintly with variant titles, *viz. A Modest and Humble Inquiry* (1732) and *The Humble and Modest Inquiry* (1733).
71 Logan's untitled General Assembly sermon (1741), 10.
72 Ibid., 27.
73 Ibid., 28.
74 Ibid., 34-5.
75 Ibid., 35.
76 Ibid., 36.
77 Ibid., 37-8.
78 Ibid., 38-9.
79 Cf. Jonathan Yeager, *Enlightened Evangelicalism. The Life and Thought of John Erskine* (2011).

80 Erskine had entered Edinburgh University in order to study law and had taken law classes there before switching to divinity.
81 *Doctrinal and Occasional Sermons* (1800?), 38.
82 Ibid., 65.
83 Ibid., 73.
84 Thomas Gillespie, *A Treatise on Temptation* (1774), 'Chusing a Minister', 145-6.
85 Ibid.
86 ESTC speculates it may have been printed in Edinburgh.
87 *Corruptions in the Church to be Eradicated*, 86.
88 Cf., for example, MacLaurin's outrageous *The Keekeiad* (London, 1760). Maclaurin (later the judge, Lord Dreghorn) was (more soberly) author of *Considerations on the Right of Patronage* (1766).
89 *The Kirkiad*, 35.
90 *The Catechism Modernized and Adapted*, 36.
91 Ibid., 36-7.
92 To some extent Peebles got back at Burns *in sepulchro* with *Burnomania* (Edinburgh, 1811). Chapter VII is entitled 'Old and New Light – Dr M'Gill'.
93 E.g. see *The Holy Fair*, stanza 16, *Canongate Burns*, ed. Noble and Hogg, 32.
94 It reads: "William Peebles in Newton upon Ayr, a Poetaster, who among many other things, published an Ode on the Centenary of the Revolution in which was this line – 'and bound in liberty's endearing chain'. R.B." The note refers to this stanza: 'Poet Willie, Poet Willie, gie the Doctor [McGill] a volley,/Wi' your 'Liberty's chain' and your wit:/O'er Pegasus' side ye ne'er laid a stride,/Ye but smelt, man, the place where he shit, &c.' The poem was first printed in 1789 as an anonymous broadside sheet. (*Canongate Burns*, ed. Noble and Hogg, 438).
95 Peebles, *The Great Things which the Lord hath done for this Nation*, 'Sermon II', 43.
96 Thomas Randall (1711-80) was minister at Inchture (1739-70), then of the East Church, Stirling (1771-80). He is remembered for having been 'one of the leaders of the Presbytery of Stirling in its seven-year defiance of the Moderate-controlled General Assembly in the St. Ninian's case of 1766-74, for which he was rebuked at the bar of the Assembly.' (McIntosh, *Church and Theology*, 242).
97 Peebles, 'Sermon II', 44-5 (footnote).
98 Wodrow-Kenrick correspondence, Dr. Williams's Library, London, MS 21157, fol. 241.
99 McGill, *The Benefits of the Revolution*, 17-18.
100 For more on Walker see chapter 5, note 4.
101 The doctrine of Christ's 'substitution', or the Atonement, was (and continues to be) considered fundamental to the Reformed church. The notorious passage in McGill's treatise, *A Practical Essay on the Death of Jesus Christ*, to which Peebles and others took exception occurs in a long footnote at pp. 339-40, where McGill relates an account of a meeting between the British Governor of the American colonies of South Carolina and Georgia and an Indian chief by way of illustration of his belief 'that the custom of sacrificing men and other animals, by way of compensation for the forfeited life of the offerer, or of others, obtained among the Heathen Nations, seems to be an unquestionable fact.' Peebles responds to this 'ridicule' in his 'Sermon II', 35-6.
102 The 1789 General Assembly reversed a decision of the Synod of Glasgow of Ayr requiring the Presbytery of Ayr to pursue the matter, while directing the Presbytery to take steps to 'purify

the doctrine of the church' and the authority of its doctrinal standards. The incident was finally settled at a meeting of the Synod on 14 April 1790 on McGill offering an explanation and apology for that which 'may appear improper' and this was accepted by a majority vote.

103 The full title is *Socinianism Unmasked in Four Letters to the Lay-Members of the Church of Scotland, and especially to those of the Collegiate Church of Ayr: occasioned by Dr M'Gill's Practical Essay on the Death of Jesus Christ* (Edinburgh, 1787).

Chapter 2

1 Thomas Ahnert expresses the view that in his satire on Moderatism, *Ecclesiastical Characteristics* (Glasgow, 1753), Witherspoon may have been the first to apply the term 'Moderate' to a distinct grouping within the Kirk (*The Moral Culture of the Scottish Enlightenment 1690–1805*, 67). But credit for that honour belongs to William Grant (1701-1764), the future Lord Prestongrange, in his pamphlet on patronage, *The Present State of the Church of Scotland* (London, 1736). See chapter 1, 28-29.

2 *The Lost World of John Witherspoon* [*LWJW*], 59, note 26.

3 (Baron) David Hume (1797) comes very close to the nature of Witherspoon's complaint against John Snodgrass *et al* in his definition 'Scoffing at Religion': 'The act 1661 [The Sunday Act], c. 38. applies the same penalties, as in case of cursing and swearing, to all "who shall be mockers or reproachers of piety, and the exercise thereof." Which words seem to reach all reviling, scoffing at, and reproaching of the Established Church, its ordinances, discipline or worship. The same thing is mentioned as a known offence in these statutes, 1690, c. 25; 1696, c. 13; 1701, c. 11. Indeed it is not to be doubted, that even at common law, all speeches or practices which favour of blasphemy, *or are to the plain contempt and mockery of religion* [italics added], fall under the cognisance of the Magistrate as scandalous indecencies; and are punishable with the same censures as those which the statutes against cursing and swearing have appointed.' (*Commentaries on the Law of Scotland*, v. II, II. 'Prophanity', XXIX, 520). Erskine, on the other hand, in *An Institute of the Law of Scotland*, 3rd ed., (1793), Bk. IV, Tit. IV, 16, 756-7, contrasts two kinds of blasphemy: 'In blasphemy, doctors distinguish between that kind [of blasphemy] which ascribes any thing to God inconsistent with his perfections, as injustice, cruelty, resentment, &c.; and those oaths and imprecations, which, without any deliberate design of exposing the divine attributes, *tend to throw contempt upon religion*. [do.] It is the first sort only which is punishable by death; the last escapes with an arbitrary punishment proportioned to the circumstances and aggravations of the crime.' See also Walker, *A Legal History of Scotland*, V, *The Eighteenth Century*, 'The Sabbath and the profanation of it', 260.

4 Dated at Edinburgh 22 November 1753. (Morren, *Annals 1752-1766*, 33-4).

5 The case of 'Captain Moodie' in August 1712. Hume, *Commentaries*, v. II, XXIX, 523.

6 In 1763 John Bryce of Glasgow published an edition of *The Form of Process in the Judicatories of the Church of Scotland; with relation to Scandals and Censures*. Subjoined to the main work are several other 'Acts and Overtures of the General Assembly', including the 'Act against Prophaneness' of 1697 and the 'Act against Prophanation of the Lord's Day' of 1705.

7 The printed version in *WJW*, 2, 485-507 includes the notorious 'prefix' 'To the Public', but omits the 'Advertisement'.

8 For an explanation of a minister 'lecturing' his congregation on a passage of scripture, and how the 'lecture' differed from the 'sermon', see Maxwell, *A History of Worship in the Church of Scotland*, 97-8, 113-14. Having gone out of favour for most of the seventeenth century,

lecturing was revived from the 1690s and was not officially denounced by the General Assembly until 1856.
9   *WJW*, 2, 489.
10 Ibid., 492-3.
11 Ibid., 493.
12 Ibid. By referring to the 'poison of infidel writings' JW has specifically in mind the works of Hume and Kames. He reiterates what he had already said several times before about 'infidel writers' in, notably, his *Essay on Justification* (1756) and in his sermon, *The Absolute Necessity of Salvation through Christ* (1759). After he went to America he softens his stance: there, he would famously abandon his prejudices relating to Hume and Kames, recommending to his students at Princeton both 'David Hume's *Essays*' and the 'essays' and 'political essays' of Kames in the reading lists he drew up for them in his 'Recapitulation', at the close of the *Lectures on Moral Philosophy.* – *SWJW*, 230).
13 Ibid.
14 *LWJW*, 242, note 14.
15 Ibid., 243. (Dalrymple's *Answers for JW* dated 9 December 1775).
16 *WJW*, 2, 495.
17 Ibid., 498.
18 Ibid.
19 Ibid., 499.
20 Ibid., 500.
21 Ibid., 500-501.
22 Ibid., 501.
23 Ibid., 503.
24 Ibid., 505.
25 Ibid., 506.
26 Ibid., 507.
27 '... he the said Mr. John Wetherspoon [sic] ... before or immediately upon the Rising of the Assembly published and Dispersed the foresaid Sermon and libel prefixed thereto.' (From the Court of Session *Summons* served on Witherspoon, dated 21 August 1762. – NRS, CS29/1776/3). From an advert in the *Caledonian Mercury* of 29 May announcing that the sermon was 'just published' it seems most likely, however, that the date of publication was while the Assembly was sitting and *before* it rose on 31 May.
28 In 1762, that is – excluding the Antiburgher meeting-house – the Abbey Church, the Laigh and the High churches.
29 It is never made clear if any of the accused were members of Witherspoon's own Laigh Church congregation. One strongly suspects, however, that John Snodgrass himself (and possibly also Robert Hunter) were members of the High Church (which would serve, in part, to explain the Reverend James Baine's persistent ambivalence towards the case as it took its course through the Kirk Session and the Presbytery). See *LWJW*, 64-5.
30 *LWJW*, 66.
31 Finlay writes: 'Writers might usefully be placed in three categories: the urban writer, the country writer and the local procurator.' (*The Community of the College of Justice: Edinburgh and the Court of Session, 1687-1808*, 159). At this juncture in his career Snodgrass would have fallen into the last of these categories, since he served as Procurator Fiscal at Paisley from 1759 until his enforced resignation from that office in 1764. For more on Snodgrass's chequered career see *LWJW*, 302.

32 M'Croachit dropped out of the Court action in its early stages and is not heard of again.
33 The Chalmers brothers were weavers. Both emigrated to America long before the determination of the case.
34 *LWJW*, 66-8 and note 37. Robert Cantwell, in his biography of the Paisley weaver-poet and ornithologist, Alexander Wilson (1961), has an altogether grimmer 'take' on the episode; that the revellers were re-enacting so-called 'Medmenham' rites associated with members of the Hellfire Club. Such an interpretation is inventive, but completely without foundation. James McCoist (see note 74 below), however, takes a similar line in his *Scottish Philosophy* (1875), 171.
35 *LWJW*, 67.
36 See *LWJW* 112-135 for an account of 'Snodgrass 2'.
37 ALSP, Arniston Collection, v. 150, no. 13 and Miscellaneous collection, ser. 7, v. 5 (1782-85), respectively *Replies for James Kibble and others To the answers for John Snodgrass, sheriff-clerk of Renfrew, and Robert Walkinshaw his depute*, 1 Jan. 1783, p. 14; *The Petition and complaint of James Kibble and others*, 20 November 1782, p. 6; and *The Petition of John Snodgrass sheriff-clerk of Renfrewshire*, 24 November 1784, p. 1. See Finlay, *Legal Practice in Eighteenth-Century Scotland* (2015), 98, 275-6.
38 James Baine (1710-90) published his sermon: *A sermon preached at the translation of the Rev. Mr. Wotherspoon, from Beith to the Laigh Church of Paisley, June 16, 1757* (Glasgow, M.DCC.VII [1707 – a misprint for 1757]). From both a bibliographical and intellectual point of view Baine's sermon is a shambolic mish-mash. Poorly edited – if any of his added notes, he states in a preface, 'have assum'd a spirit and colour different from the original discourse' he hopes no offence will be taken by the 'more grave reader' – Baine ranges chaotically from the doctrine of original sin to the threat to public morality from the theatre and the stage, the latter a theme he further developed in a sermon he published in Edinburgh in 1770, *The Theatre Licentious and Perverted. Or, a sermon for reformation of manners*. In perhaps the only area where the two men appeared to share any kind of common view, Witherspoon, too, had contributed to anti-theatre literature in his early work, *A Serious Enquiry into the Nature and Effects of the Stage* (Glasgow, 1757). Baine's desertion of the High Church for the Relief congregation rocked the General Assembly of 1766.
39 *LWJW*, 87. [All Kirk Session minutes cited here inside double quotation marks, and with italic script intact, are from David Dalrymple's printed *Answers for The Reverend Doctor John Witherspoon, late Minister of Paisley* dated 'December 9. 1775.', although the references given here for the sake of convenience are to my book *LWJW*.]
40 Ibid., 88.
41 Ibid., '*Dramatis Personae*', 306-7. Dalrymple was later elevated to the bench as Lord Westhall. Of potential confusion, there were two David Dalrymples, distant cousins, both advocates practising at the Scottish bar at the same time; the 'other' Dalrymple (always known as Sir David Dalrymple, later, on his elevation, as Lord Hailes) similarly participated in the Snodgrass-Witherspoon process, albeit in a more peripheral role.
42 *LWJW*, 90.
43 Ibid., 95.
44 Ibid., '*Dramatis Personae*', 313-14.
45 *LWJW*, 95-6.
46 Ibid., '*Dramatis Personae*', 312-13.
47 Ian D. L. Clark, *Moderatism and the Moderate Party in the Church of Scotland, 1752-1805*, unpublished PhD thesis, University of Cambridge, 1964.

48 The full account of the proceedings before the Presbytery will be found in *LWJW*, 97-107.
49 Ibid., 101.
50 Hay's *Petition of John Snodgrass Sheriff-clerk of Paisley* [et al.] of 25 November 1775, 5. (*LWJW*, 101).
51 Ibid., 106.
52 The minutes of the meeting of the Presbytery of Paisley of 10 June 1762 record that the Witherspoon/Kirk Session protestation that had been lodged with the Depute Clerk of Assembly was 'null and void and deserted'. – *LWJW*, 108.
53 See Morren, *Annals 1752-1766*, 261-2.
54 Ibid., 108-112.
55 Ibid., 110.
56 Ibid., 329. For the career of Rae (later the judge Lord Eskgrove) see *LWJW*, 'Dramatis Personae', 310-11. See also note 59 below.
57 Ibid., 'Dramatis Personae', 309-10.
58 Ibid., 308.
59 The original Ms. of Rae's *Representation* of 1763 has been lost but can be reconstructed from the Extract Decreet of 1776. See *LWJW*, 166, and Appendix C, 'Commentary on the Extract Decreet', 329. Montgomerie's *Answers* of the same year are in NRS CS29/1776/3. The bound volume containing the 298 page long Extract Decreet is referenced CS/1776/6/663.
60 Such determination on the part of Snodgrass and the others is illustrated [by David Dalrymple, in his printed *Answers* of 9 December 1775] by the 'plumb bond' they executed in the Edinburgh Commissary Cour in 1762, by means of which, under oath, they became 'bound and obliged' not to drop out of the process 'until the final conclusion thereof, either before the said commissaries, or before Court of Session, or British parliament.' The bond also committed all of them to share equally the expenses of the action, and for any one of them resiling from the terms of the bond to forfeit their contribution towards its cost of £50 sterling. See also *Appendix C* for an explanation of Dalrymple's analogous reference to the notorious 'black bond' of Stirling.
61 For a detailed explanation of '*Snodgrass 2*' see *LWJW*, 112-135.
62 For an explanation of legal processes 'falling asleep' and 'wakening', see *LWJW*, 175-7 and 323.
63 Scots law, a statement of particulars. See *LWJW*, xviii and 320.
64 In NRS CS29/1776/3. These Mss. are not to be confused with the printed submissions, a *Petition* (Hay) and *Answers* (Dalrymple) of 1775.
65 *LWJW*, 'Dramatis Personae', 311.
66 For an account of Garden's *Replies* of 1764 – we do not know the precise date – see *LWJW*, 173-4.
67 Ibid., 234. See also 278-80.
68 Ibid., 282-3.
69 Crosbie's *Replies* of 11 January 1776, 27.
70 Ralph Ketcham, 'James Madison and Religion – A New Hypothesis', 179, in *James Madison on Religious Liberty*, ed. Robert S. Alley (1985), cited by Morrison in *John Witherspoon and the Founding of the American Republic*, 14.
71 E.g. McGinty (2012) and Mailer (2017) seem blissfully unaware of the Court case. Both rely exclusively on Collins (1925), and especially Butterfield (1953), for the facts surrounding JW's coming to America.

72 *The Letters of Benjamin Rush 1761–1792* (Princeton University Press, for the American Philosophical Society, 1951).
73 The contents of both almanacs – and, in particular, their relevance to the Court process – are discussed in two 'interludes' in *LWJW*, 137-150 (1763) and 197-222 (1768).
74 Savage hits the nail on the head: '[Collins'] besetting sin – a venial one – is to curtail his recital of some of the happenings in the Doctor's career, or even to pass over them. He does not squeeze out all the juice from the orange.' – Ashbel Green's *Life of the Revd John Witherspoon*, ed. Savage (1973), 'Introduction', 9.
75 'The full manuscript report of the case is in the archives of His Majesty's Register House at Edinburgh …'. Collins goes on to make particular mention of the Tartuffe reference [cited by the advocate, Francis Garden] and says of it that 'the reader (if there ever be another) who struggles through the reams of legal foolscap, will find at least one bright spot in the closing sentence of the plaintiffs' argument which quotes in extraordinary French a sentence from Molière's *Le Tartuffe* wherein is distinguished the character of true and false zeal.' (*President Witherspoon*, 1, 61-2).
76 James McCosh (1811-94) was a farmer's son from Patna in Ayrshire who, after serving as professor of logic and metaphysics at Queen's College, Belfast for seventeen years, accepted an invitation to become president of the College of New Jersey and played a key part in its transition from provincial college to a great national university (Princeton). The McCosh quotation is from his best-known work, *The Scottish Philosophy, Biographical, Expository, Critical, from Hutcheson to Hamilton* (1875), 172.
77 Green's *Life*, 79.
78 October, 1829, vol. 28.
79 For references to David Dale (1739–1806) and Dale's role in easing Witherspoon's financial problems arising from the Court process, see *LWJW*, 201 (and note 11), 202 (and note 15), 298-9. My 'Concluding Essay' also reveals that contrary to the accepted notion of the purpose of Witherspoon's return to Scotland in 1784 – i.e. to raise funds for the College of New Jersey, a venture which he stubbornly refused to be talked out of by Benjamin Franklin and others – the underlying motivation was really to discharge his debts to Dale and others. (ibid., 297-9).
80 Crichton wrote Ewing a long letter dated at Paisley 1 June 1835 which Green cites in extract (*Life*, ed. Savage, 81-3). That letter confirms Dale's remarkable record of financial help to Witherspoon, the facts behind which I was able to supplement from other sources (especially the Wodrow–Kenrick correspondence in Dr. Williams's Library, Ms. 24.157 – 86) in the section of my 'Concluding Essay' entitled 'Repaying his debts'. (ibid., 298-9 and note 18).
81 Green's *Life*, 101.

Chapter 3

1 Minutes of the Presbytery of Dunfermline for 1775-76 reveal that Alexander Dalling, minister of Cleish and John Spence of Orwell (both parishes within the neighbouring Presbytery of Kinross) contrived to raise the issue with a view to censuring Thomson but failed in their efforts to do so. (NRS CH/105/10, ff. 194-6, 250-2 and 261-3). See also the *Scots Magazine*, xxxviii, May 1776, 277-8. It is not without interest that both Dalling and Spence (with one other, David Hunter, minister of Saline) had absented themselves at the admission and ordination of Andrew Richardson to the much disputed settlement of Inverkeithing in 1752, following the highly controversial deposition of Thomas Gillespie of Carnock earlier in the

same year and were consequently suspended for thirteen years (See Morren, *Annals 1739-52*, 274-5; *Annals 1752-66*, 308, and chapter 1 above).
2 From his choice of scripture it seems clear that in his first sermon Thomson did not set out to launch an oral attack on Robert Scotland, but only did so in an angry 'digression' – as confirmed by David Rae's *Petition* of 14 July 1775, 3: '... he [Thomson] made a digression ...'.
3 Boswell had been 'fully intoxicated' the evening before – the day of the declaration of the election result – and for the second time in his life had joined with the mob in breaking windows. See his journal entry for Monday 31 October 1774 in Ryskamp and Pottle, eds., *Boswell: The Ominous Years 1774-76* (1963), 31-2 and note 2.
4 Ibid., 31.
5 Boswell probably borrowed this description of the sermon as 'curious' from the *Caledonian Mercury* report of it in its issue of 2 November
6 Rae's *Petition* 3-4.
7 Ibid., 4.
8 The Reverend James Thomson (1699-1790) was a St. Andrews graduate and served as minister of the first charge of the Abbey church in Dunfermline from 1743 to his death in 1790. Thomson succeeded the great Ralph Erskine, after Erskine was deposed from his charge following the 1733 'great secession'. He saw service as a chaplain for fourteen years to the 26th Regiment of Foot ('commonly called the Cameronian Regiment') and was with them in Gibraltar as a young man. Hew Scott writes: 'He preached regularly in his turn till his eighty-ninth year, and delivered an Action sermon lasting two hours when he was ninety.' (*Fasti*, New Series, V, 32). In James Boswell's unpublished *Memorial* of 15 February 1775 (see p. 90 and Appendix B) Boswell affirms (f. 1) that Thomson 'had the Honour of being well Esteemed by the Officers, while at the same time he maintained a decency of character'.
9 The Reverend Thomas Fernie (1715-90), also a St. Andrews graduate, was minister of the second charge in the same church as Thomson from 1744 to 1789. It was apparently his weak voice that earned him his nickname. (ibid., 35).
10 Rae (and other counsel who cite parts of the sermon) would have used the *Caledonian Mercury* text, 'improving' on it as they thought appropriate.
11 *Caledonian Mercury*, 4 February 1775, 3.
12 c. 1710-81. Dundas was created a baronet in October 1762, having requested the honour in a letter he had written to Shelburne only that summer. See Edith Haden-Guest, *History of Parliament: The House of Commons 1754-1790*, I. Constituencies, 'Stirling Burghs', 509-510, and II. Members, 'Sir Lawrence Dundas 1st Bt.', 357-361.
13 At least that is the traditional view. To be fair to Dundas, of late a more benevolent view has emerged, articulated by G. E. Bannerman, which lays much more stress on Dundas's ingenuity, hard work and know-how as the secret of his success in his government contracting years: 'Perhaps the financial rewards were greater than the effort required, but Dundas was rarely criticized for the performance of his contracts.' ('The "Nabob of the North": Sir Lawrence Dundas as government contractor', *Historical Research* (Institute of Historical Research), v. 83, no. 219, February 2010, 122.
14 Anon., *The Humours of the Town, a dramatic interlude, in one act* (dated *Edinburgh, Oct. 1. 1776*), 11. The last line quoted parodies Chatham's famous claim that America was conquered in Germany.
15 1715-77. Masterton was the member for Stirling Burghs from 1768 until his defeat by Campbell in 1774.

16 Haden-Guest, 'James Masterton (1715-77), of Newton, Stirling', in Namier and Brooke, *The History of Parliament: the House of Commons 1754-1790 III. Members*, 118-9.
17 d. 1799. Edgar in later life became a prosperous customs official in Edinburgh and a member of the Poker Club. See Richard B. Sher's Oxford *DNB* article on the Poker Club.
18 Shelburne served in the army in Germany on Lord Granby's staff and distinguished himself at Minden (1759) and Kloster Kampen (1760). He was subsequently promoted colonel and appointed *aide-de-camp* to the new king, George III, thereby transforming his prospects.
19 Bannerman, *op cit*, 106 and notes 30 and 32.
20 In his entry for 11 Dec 1762 James Boswell seriously underestimated the scale of Dundas's profits in Germany, claiming that he would 'bring home a couple of hundred thousand pounds'. – *Boswell's London Journal 1762-1763*, ed. Pottle, 75.
21 Shelburne to Fox, 19 Aug. 1762. – *Letters to Henry Fox, Lord Holland*, ed. Earl of Ilchester, 157.
22 In 1794 Lawrence Dundas's son, the MP Sir Thomas Dundas of Kerse (1741-1820), 'won the peerage long coveted by his family', in return for abandoning his electoral interests in Stirlingshire and elsewhere. – Fry, *The Dundas Despotism*, 187. See also Haden-Guest, *op cit*, *Members II*, 'Thomas Dundas of Castlecary, Stirling and Aske, nr. Richmond, Yorks.', 364-66.
23 In 1756-7 Boswell and Erskine were enrolled in Professor John Stevenson's class in logic and metaphysics at the University of Edinburgh. See page 95 below.
24 Haden-Guest, *op cit*, 'Edinburgh', *Constituencies I*, 502-3.
25 October 1774, v. xxxvi, 556. Extracts from the letter were printed in the *Caledonian Mercury* for Saturday 15 October and the full letter in the same paper for 2 November.
26 The whole episode of the 1774 Edinburgh election, Dundas's part in it and the parallel Dunfermline controversy, is described in the *Scots Magazine*, xxxvi, October 1774, 554-8.
27 Anon., *A Rhapsody. By a Freeman*, 10. The pamphlet, published in Edinburgh, bears the date 9 Sept. 1777. It carries the same style and adopts a similar hostility towards Dundas as the four-page broadsheet entitled *A Letter to a Certain Baronet*, dated 2 September 1777. The latter is thought to have been the work of Sir Hew Dalrymple, 2[nd.] baronet, of North Berwick.
28 See note 32 below.
29 Anon., *A Letter to a Certain Baronet*, 2.
30 Letter dated 8 Oct. 1781, cited in Holden Furber, *Henry Dundas First Viscount Melville 1742-1811*, 196.
31 Haden-Guest, *op cit*, 'Stirling Burghs', *Constituencies I*, 509-510.
32 Later General Sir Archibald Campbell (1739-91) of Inverneil. He was a prisoner of war in America in 1776-8. See also the postscript to this chapter.
33 Campbell secured control of three burghs – Culross, Inverkeithing and Dunfermline. Boswell was celebrating not just the result but his enormous relief that he was not called on to swear the 'Formula', requiring (on the authority of an Act of 1700) those to whom it was administered to declare that they were not Roman Catholic and 'denied, disowned, and abhorred' certain tenets assumed to be peculiar to that faith. Why this matter had disturbed Boswell is explained by Hugh M. Milne in the introduction to his edition of *Boswell's Edinburgh Journals 1767-1786*, 19-20. See also Ryskamp and Pottle, eds., *Boswell: The Ominous Years 1774-76*, 25 note 1.
34 In the sense intended here, the president of an incorporated society of trades in any Scottish town or city.
35 *Boswell: The Ominous Years*, 22 and note 5. Boswell later records that his suspicions about Fergusson were well-founded: he was arrested and imprisoned for forgery, then escaped but was later recaptured. (ibid., 27-9).

36 Morison, *Decisions of the Court of Session*, IV, Appendix, Part 1, 'Delinquency', No 3, 9: 'August 8. John, Robert, and David Scotlands, *against* The Rev. Mr. James Thomson, Minister of Dunfermline.' See also *Decisions*, XVI, 'Reparation', 'No 21. A clergyman found liable in damages for defamatory language undecently used in the pulpit.', 13934-5.
37 *The Life of Samuel Johnson*, ed. Womersley, 548.
38 NRS CS21/1776/1009/ff.2-3.
39 Almost certainly this is the same George Bean who, in 1788, was threatened to be struck off the List of the Society of Advocates in Aberdeen if he failed in six months to make good arrears which he owed. See Finlay, *Legal Practice in Eighteenth-Century Scotland*, 160. Professor Finlay explains that Bean (originally an Aberdeen writer who was admitted as a notary in 1749) at one point served as sheriff clerk in Inverness. He died on 17 March 1798. [NRS CS228/A/5/1*]
40 James Grant WS (1743-1835), admitted advocate in 1767. See F. Grant, *The Grants of Corrimony* (1895), 25-6.
41 *Boswell: The Ominous Years*, 47-8. For the key papers in the *Shaw v Bean* process – it is not listed by Morison – see the Bibliography at the end of this study under NRS and Advocates Library. Advocates involved in the process included Henry Dundas, Ilay Campbell and Bannatyne W. Macleod.
42 NRS CS21/1776/1009/1/1.
43 NRS CS21/1776/1009/14. 'James Boswell for Mr Ilay Campbell' is written on the last page of the Ms. on f. 64, but not, of course, on the printed version. Evidence of Campbell's partial cannibalisation of Boswell's *Memorandum* is fairly extensive when the texts are compared.
44 Boswell's *Memorial*, f. 5.
45 *I Thessalonians* 5:7.
46 Sir Robert Atkyns (or Atkins) (*bap.* 1621-1710). See Weston and Greenberg, *Subjects and Sovereigns: the grand controversy over legal sovereignty in Stuart England* (1981).
47 'Demurrer' – a technical term in English law meaning 'a pleading which, admitting the facts as stated in the opponent's pleading, denies that he is legally entitled to relief, and thus stops the action until this point be determined.' (*OED*).
48 Atkyns, *Parliamentary and Political Tracts*, second edition, London, 1741, 16-17.
49 For an explanation of the distinction at this time between judges of the Court of Session sitting in the 'Inner' and 'Outer' House, see Finlay, *The Community of the College of Justice*, 11: 'The Court of Session had fourteen lords ordinary and a president. Important decisions were taken by "the hail fifteen", sitting in the Inner House, while a lord ordinary of the week was appointed to sit in the Outer House, dealing with ordinary and extraordinary actions.' Finlay goes on to make a highly relevant point in the context of this action: 'Since Scots procedure favoured fairness over speed, it was possible to reclaim against interlocutors and to do so repeatedly. Lords ordinary were regularly called upon to review their own decisions, as were the judges in the Inner House, and cases could continue for several years without a final resolution'.
50 All printed papers in the process *Scotlands v. Thomson* are found in Signet Library Session Papers series (SLSP), vol. M 6 and vol. M 7a (Kennet Collection).
51 This statement and the near-identical wording in Dundas's *Answers* (see note 52 below) refer, of course, to the *Snodgrass et.al. v Witherspoon* case of 1762-1776.
52 The date of the interlocutor given in the extract Decreet and in the later printed submissions. Boswell, however, gives the date as the previous day, Tuesday 19 December (*The Ominous Years*,

202), which is when he would have learned of the decision.
53 Ibid., and note 9.
54 Here Campbell is referring to the Court's interlocutor prohibiting any proof of the *veritas convitii non excusat* principle, presumably on the grounds that it was not considered relevant to the circumstances of the case and, in any event, was not in the interests of natural justice as then understood.
55 In the course of the process Henry Dundas, having been Solicitor General since 1766, had become Lord Advocate in the previous year, an office he would hold until 1783.
56 Note, again, the near-identical wording of the same point in Rae's *Petition* as cited above. (See note 49 above).
57 See page 93 above.
58 *Answers*, 31.
59 'Decreet' means the final determination of a process in Scots law; not to be confused with the 'Extract Decreet' which is the extracted record of the entire process from summons to determination.
60 I refer to Ryskamp and Pottle's long note 3 on page 61 of their *Boswell: The Ominous Years* (1963) where they summarise the *Scotlands v Thomson* process.
61 All references to Thomson's appeal are to *House of Lords Journal*, v. 35, Nov. 1776, 11-20, online.
62 Finlay, 'Scots Lawyers and House of Lords Appeals in Eighteenth-Century Britain', in *The Journal of Legal History*, v. 32, No. 3, Dec. 2011, 262. In an appendix to his article Finlay records a total of 83 reported Scottish appeals to the House of Lords over the period 1770 to 1779.
63 *The Ominous Years*, 61, note 3. The journal editors' view is most likely based on a misreading of the four elements of the 'Case' as laid before Thurlow – i.e. the brief drawn up by Boswell – including Johnson's oral essay, even though it is made clear by Boswell that none of the four stated items presented to him included Johnson's work. See *The Life of Samuel Johnson*, ed. Womersley, 551-2.
64 *Life*, ed. Womersley, 552.
65 Ibid. The whole of Johnson's oral essay is to be found at 548-51. Boswell notes that 'When I read this to Mr. Burke, he was highly pleased and exclaimed, "Well; he does his work in a workman-like manner."'
66 Morison, *Decisions of the Court of Session*, (1811), v. xxiii-xxiv, sect. 12, no. 72, 9530-1.
67 In Scots law a process calling on the defender to produce a statement of his accounts and to pay any balance due. See Bell's *Dictionary and Digest of the Law of Scotland*, rev. ed., (ed. George Ross), 1861, 231.
68 See Lord Kames's *Elucidations* (1777) for a contemporary explanation of 'intrinsic' / 'extrinsic' qualities in Scots law: 'When in a process a fact is referred to the oath of a pursuer or defendant, he who gives the oath may have occasion to qualify it by the addition of circumstances. Where the circumstances added are intimately connected with the fact acknowledged, so as to require no proof but the oath itself, they are termed *intrinsic qualities*: where they require other proof, they are termed *extrinsic qualities*.' (*Elucidations respecting the Common and Statute Law of Scotland*, Art. 25, 158).
69 For the general reader I have simplified the wording of the judgment. Morison's summary is as follows: '... as the receipt of the money rests on the acknowledgment of the defender, the *causa dandi* is an intrinsic quality, and cannot be separated from the other parts of it.'

70 The case against the *Advertiser* collapsed at the early stages, on the ground that it merely copied material published in the other paper. The *Caledonian Mercury*, which was being sued by the Scotland faction for a 'card' they had inserted allegedly libelling Robert Scotland (reprinted in the *Scots Magazine* in February 1775), was defended by Ilay Campbell and John MacLaurin. The outcome of the action is not known. See *Boswell: The Ominous Years 1774-76*, 60 note 8.

Chapter 4

1 The Select Society (active in Edinburgh, 1754-64). See note 77 below.
2 Morren, *Annals of the General Assembly 1752-1766*, Assembly of 1755, 54.
3 Two editions were published in 1733, the second a 'corrected' version. Anderson's preface to his second ed. refers in a footnote to [Ramsay's] *Some Few Hints in Defence of Dramatical Entertainments*.
4 See chapter 5 for John Anderson's synodical sermon of 1712.
5 Ibid., 58.
6 George Anderson had published that year *An Estimate of the Profit and Loss of Religion, personally and publicly stated: Illustrated with references to Essays on morality and natural religion* (Edinburgh, 1753).
7 McIntosh, *Church and Theology in Enlightenment Scotland*, 85, 90-1.
8 Chapter II, Book III, 'Of the Stage', 364-78.
9 Arnot's *History of Edinburgh*, 366 and footnote marked †.
10 The bibliography is unusually confusing. Originally published in London in 1675 as *A Practical Exposition of the X Commandements* [t.p. variant 'Ten'], Durham's posthumous work came out as a second ed. 'revised and corrected' under the title *The Law Unsealed* in both Edinburgh (2 eds.,1676) and Glasgow (1677). To complicate matters further the work was re-issued in Glasgow by the same publisher in 1676 as a 'second Addition' [sic], but reverting to the original London title.
11 *Fasti*, v. III, 456. See also Burleigh, *A Church History of Scotland*, chapter V, 'From the Restoration to the Revolution', 233-257.
12 'Thou shalt not commit adultery'. (*Exodus* 20, 14).
13 The anonymous writer has been referring to the writings of James Ussher (1581-1656), Church of Ireland Archbishop of Armagh, in support of his argument.
14 'Address', 'To the Christian Reader', in Durham's *Ten Commandments* – the Glasgow (John Bryce) reprint of 1777, 22. 'Mr. Pryn' is, of course, the Lincoln's Inn lawyer, William Prynne (1660-69), whose literary output was phenomenal. Though he does not cite it specifically, the author of the 'Address' is 'beholden' to Prynne's huge work, *Histrio-Mastix. The Players Scourge, or, Actors TragÆdie* (London, 1633), which drew its inspiration from a play of the same name, published in 1610 and doubtfully attributed to John Marston, which satirised professional actors.
15 Ibid., 'Postscript', 33.
16 The same argument is developed in the concluding paragraphs of Chapter 5, 'Heresy'.
17 'Ministerial Fidelity' (the 'Farewell sermon'), *WJW*, 2, 549-50.
18 Walker, *Sermons on Practical Subjects*, v. 1, Third Edition, 1777, Sermon XVIII, 'Preached on the day of national thanksgiving, Nov. 29. 1759.' The sermon is included in the very rare 1st ed. of Walker's sermons published by Kincaid and Bell in Edinburgh in 1765.
19 Erskine, *Ministers of the Gospel Cautioned Against Giving Offence. Preached before the Synod of Lothian and Tweeddale, at Edinburgh, November 8. 1763.* (1764), 12. The sermon is also included in the

collection *Doctrinal and Occasional Sermons* (Creech and Constable, 1800?) which, according to the 'Advertisement', Erskine proposed to supplement with a further volume of sermons 'chiefly on practical subjects' if his 'life and health allowed'. No further volumes appeared.
20 *A Serious Apology for the Ecclesiastical Characteristics*, *WJW*, 3, 288.
21 'Written by Mr. Shakespear, with Alterations by Mr. [Nahum] Tate.' Tate (1652-1715) 'improved' several of Shakespeare's plays, including, most notoriously, when he gave a happy ending to *King Lear* with Cordelia surviving and marrying Edgar.
22 Taylor's (or Tailor's) Hall partially survives as no.139 Cowgate, Edinburgh, a listed building under the care of Historic Environment Scotland.
23 *The Caledonian Mercury*, 12 June 1733. Other numbers carrying news of theatrical performances in Edinburgh in 1733 include those for 4 June, 1 November and 27 December.
24 Carrubber's Close is one of several closes on the Royal Mile (High Street) in the old town of Edinburgh. A modern brass plaque indicates that the name derives from a 'William Carriberis', merchant, who circa 1450 'had his mansion here'. The plaque also discloses that Allan Ramsay was a resident there and in 1736 'launched a theatre which the Magistrates closed.'
25 Dibdin, *The Annals of the Edinburgh Stage*, (1888), 43. Jackson, *The History of the Scottish Stage* (1793), has nothing to say of Ramsay or the Carrubber's Close theatre.
26 *The Recruiting Officer*, an 'ingenious' comedy by the Irish playwright George Farquhar (1676/7-1707), first opened on 8 March 1706 in the new Queen's Theatre in the Haymarket. It was first published in 1707 and editions came out in Glasgow (Robert and Andrew Foulis) in 1755 and Edinburgh (A. Donaldson) in 1759. It was one of the most regularly performed comedies in the eighteenth century. Henry Fielding's *An Old Man taught Wisdom; or, The Virgin Unmask'd* was described as a 'farce' but its true genre is as a ballad-opera; it opened in the Theatre Royal, Drury Lane on 6 January 1735.
27 Dibdin (p. 48) has 'Mrs. Bridges'. The actor cannot be identified.
28 Phillipson points out in his biography of Adam Smith that precisely at this time it was accepted that it was a 'relatively common humanist technique in the more avant-garde schools of central Scotland' for the stage and the performing of plays to be regarded as a 'vehicle of civic education'. He instances the High School of Dalkeith and Perth Grammar School as examples. Smith's own teacher at Kirkcaldy burgh school, which he attended from 1731/2 to 1737, David Miller, wrote plays, one of which – *The Royal Command for Advice* – was put on while Smith was a pupil. – *Adam Smith An Enlightened Life* (2010), 18.
29 Though published anonymously, there is no longer any reason to doubt that Ramsay is the author of *Some Few Hints, in Defence of Dramatical Entertainments* (1728), which he wrote in answer to William Law's *The Absolute Unlawfulness of the Stage-Entertainment Fully Demonstrated* (1726), a work which was, in turn, answered by the literary critic John Dennis in his *The Stage Defended* (1726). Law (1686-1761) was a non-juror whose best-known work, *A Practical Treatise upon Christian Perfection* (1726), incorporates a version of *The Absolute Unlawfulness*. [He is not to be confused with another William Law* who was appointed professor of philosophy at Edinburgh in 1708 by minute of the Town Council of Edinburgh dated 16 June. (Bower, *History of the University of Edinburgh*, v. II, 73).] Further, as early as 1720 – integrated (with a separate title page and imprint bearing the date 1721) within the very rare first edition of *Poems. By Allan Ramsay* (Edinburgh, 'Printed for the Author', 1720) – Ramsay published 'an Heroi-Comical Poem' entitled *The Morning Interview*. The 'Epilogue' begins: 'The Curtain's drawn: Now gen'rous Reader say,/Have ye not read worse Numbers in a Play?/Sure here is *Plot, Place, Character, and Time*,/All smoothly wrought in good firm English Rhime.'

*Thomas Ahnert cites this man's Edinburgh undergraduate thesis of 1705: *Theses philosophicae, quas favente numine. Generosi aliquot & ingenui juvenes, Universitatis Jacobi Regis Edinburgenae alumni, hac vice cum laurea emittendi, eruditorum examani subjicient; ad 27 diem Aprilis, H. Lq. S. Praeside Gulielmo Law* (Edinburgh, 1705). [NLS shelfmark 1943.12(19)] – *The Moral Culture of the Scottish Enlightenment, 1690-1805*, 20-1, 149 and note 18).

30 There does not appear to have been a 'Volume I'. The BL ESTC confirms that the 1728 title is a reissue of the 1721 edition with a cancelled title-page.

31 That is, it is absent from the 1727 edition of the 'Fourth Edition' of the *Poems* which does, however, contain a different poem entitled 'The 'Address of Allan Ramsay to the Right Honourable, The Town Council of Edinburgh' (pp. 328-30).

32 Geo. II, cap. xxviii, June 24, 1737. The statute is reproduced in J. Raithby, ed., *Statutes at large*, v. 5, 266-8. The Act applied to 'any interlude, tragedy, comedy, opera, play, farce, or other entertainment of the stage, or any part, or parts therein'; in its scope it covered 'any part of Great Britain, except in the City of Westminster and within the liberties thereof, and in such places where His Majesty, his heirs or successors, shall in their royal persons reside, and during such residence only'. In the case of Scotland, jurisdiction was vested in 'the Court of Session or Judiciary there'.

33 *Pasquin. A dramatick satire on the times: being the rehearsal of two plays, viz. A Comedy call'd The Election; and a Tragedy call'd The Life and Death of Common-Sense.* (London, M.DCC.XXXVI.) (1736)

34 For the full extraordinary story of the background to the *Golden Rump* controversy see Kinservik, 'The Dialectics of Print and Performance after 1737', in *The Oxford Handbook of the Georgian Theatre 1737-1832*, eds. Swindells and Taylor (2014), 126-7; and Battestin, Martin C., *Henry Fielding A Life* (1989), 225-7.

35 ' Neither one thing nor another', i.e. 'nonsense' (*OED*).

36 *The Gentleman's Magazine*, August 1737, 507.

37 NRS CH2/121/13/509.

38 NRS CH2/121/13/529. The minutes of a meeting of the Presbytery of 7 February record that 'the agent of the Church did commence and carry on a Process against them before the Lords [of Session], and at Last after a Proof led obtained Decreet against Eight of the said Actors in Terms of Law finding each of them Lyable in fifty pounds sterling ... which Decreet was Extracted.'

39 Carlyle, *Anecdotes and Characters of the Times*, ed. Kinsley (1973), 1746, 101.

40 See Chapter 3.

41 M. A. Stewart, 'George Anderson', in Oxford *DNB*, online ed., 2004-15, accessed 10 October 2016.

42 Peter King, first Baron King of Ockham (1669-1734). King was Lord Chancellor from 1725 to 1733. He assisted at the impeachment of the political preacher, Henry Sacheverell, in 1710. Sacheverell was found guilty and suspended from preaching for three years.

43 The correct title is *Some Few Hints, in Defence of Dramatical Entertainments*. The pamphlet lacks a proper title page and there is no imprint, though the BL ESTC lists the provenance as '[Edinburgh?, 1728']. In the first edition of the sermon Anderson omits all footnote references to Ramsay's pamphlet in the sermon itself, though they are included in the Appendix.

44 Anderson calls the anonymous author of *Some Few Hints* 'Our City-hinter' (Appendix, 54, footnote).

45 *The Use and Abuse of Diversions*, 'To the Reader', iv.

46 Defiant ministers regarded acquiescence in the reading of the Act as 'an Erastian heresy'. George Wishart's pamphlet is entitled *A Letter to the Author of a Pamphlet* [George Logan, second charge minister of Trinity Church, Edinburgh] *intituled Lawfulness and Necessity of Ministers, their reading the Act of Parliament for bringing to justice the murderers of Captain John Porteous* [Edinburgh, 1737]. Wishart would become Moderator of the General Assembly in 1748.
47 See note 29 for more on William Law.
48 This is a reference to §XXII.1 of the *Westminster Confession of Faith* – 'A lawful oath is a part of religious worship', etc..
49 James Drake (*bap.*1666-d.1707). Drake's *Historia Anglo Scotica* (1703), purportedly based on a manuscript by an unknown author, made him very unpopular in Scotland. The book was publicly burned at the Mercat Cross on 30 June 1703. Drake's plays included *The Sham Lawyer, or, The Lucky Extravagant* (1697), based on *Wit without Money* by John Fletcher and *The Spanish Curate* by Fletcher and Massinger.
50 *Use and Abuse of Diversions*, 6.
51 The more familiar of the two variants of the same theme is found in Matthew's gospel, 25, 14-30. One 'talent' equalled 60 'minas'.
52 *Use and Abuse of Diversions*, 11.
53 Ibid., 12.
54 Ibid., 14.
55 Ibid., 15-16.
56 Though he does not mention Anderson's sermon, Thomas Ahnert cites the example of Henry Scougal (1650-1678), professor of divinity at King's College, Aberdeen, whose classic work *The Life of God in the Soul of Man* (1677) takes up the theme of the role of divine grace, good works and the conditions that could influence access to the afterlife. Scougal proclaimed that doctrinal orthodoxy played only a 'minor, subordinate role, if any' in his own notion of religion. That view, Ahnert maintains, was in contrast to the standard orthodox position which grounded religious faith in doctrine and salvation through grace, the 'new covenant ... by which humans were able to reverse the effects of the Fall.' – *The Moral Culture of the Scottish Enlightenment, 1690-1805*, 23-4, 28-9.
57 *Use and Abuse of Diversions*, 19.
58 Ibid., 23.
59 Ibid., 25-6.
60 Ibid., 36.
61 The Appendix occupies pages 39 to 59 (the end) of the published sermon.
62 Ibid., 57 note (a). The quote is from the *Symposiacs*, Lib. VII, Question 8. A modern translation has it: 'Concerning new comedy there is no need of any long discourse. It is so fitted, so interwoven with entertainments, that it is easier to have a regular feast without wine, than without Menander.' Anderson could have gone on to the next sentence: 'But its phrase is sweet and familiar, the humour innocent and easy, so that there is nothing for men whilst sober to despise, or when merry to be troubled at.' (*Plutarch's Morals*, v. 3, trans. W. W. Goodwin, Boston, 1878, Online Liberty ed. unpaginated). Menander (born c. 342, died c. 292 BCE) was an Athenian dramatist and the author of more than a hundred comedies. He influenced the Roman writers Terence and Plautus and, through them, the development of European comedy from the Renaissance.
63 Ramsay, *Some Few Hints*, 2-3.
64 'Wilks', 'Mills' and 'Aston' are of course strolling players. 'Wilks' is Robert Wilks (c. 1665-

1732), and 'Aston' is Anthony (Tony) Aston (c.1682-1753?), while 'Mills' may be the same man who is identified in Rosenfeld, *Strolling Players & Drama in the Provinces 1660-1765* (1939), as having been part of a company from Drury Lane who, in June 1747, played in the White Swan, Norwich. Ramsay's description of Aston's apparently blameless life may be true, but that is not the usual picture of either him or his like. E. D. Cook (rev. Terry Enright) says of Aston that he 'was probably seen, like most wandering players, as an untrustworthy rogue'. – Oxford *DNB*, online ed., accessed 28.10.2016. See also note 89 below.

65 *Some Few Hints*, 21.
66 Glasgow, John Bryce, 1757. The work was reprinted in Witherspoon's *Essays on Important Subjects* (London, Edward and Charles Dilly, 1765). It is significant that unlike Adam Ferguson, who preferred the authorship of his pamphlet, *The Morality of Stage-Plays Seriously Considered* (also 1757), to remain anonymous, JW is content that his name appear on the title page; by this time, of course, he was widely known as the author of *Ecclesiastical Characteristics* (1753).
67 Robert Craigie (c.1685-1760) of Glendoick, Perth. Craigie was appointed deputy solicitor general to Robert Dundas in 1719 and Lord Advocate in 1742 after Lord Ilay was ousted by the Squadrone on Walpole's fall that year. In 1754 Craigie became Lord President of the Court of Session.
68 *An Estimate of the Profit and Loss of Religion*, 251.
69 In the first ed. of *Church and University in the Scottish Enlightenment* (1985), 71, Sher wrongly attributes to Anderson authorship of the pamphlet *Infidelity a Proper Object of Censure* (Glasgow, 1756), but correctly re-assigns the title as the work of the Reverend Thomas Walker of Dundonald in the re-issued 'Classic Edition' of his study (2015), xxxiv.
70 Wesley, *Journal*, ed. Curnock, Part 10, v. 4, 218.
71 Home was minister of Athelstaneford in the Presbytery of Haddington from 1746 until 1757. Hew Scott writes: 'Many of his brethren in the ministry strongly disapproved of his having this connection with the stage, and a libel was about to be served upon him in 1757 when he resigned his charge.' (*Fasti*, New Series, v. 1, 354). See also Morren, *Annals 1752-66*, 118.
72 It is not entirely clear how many performances of *Douglas* were given in its first run, but in spite of its success, not many were given – and very few by modern standards. Dibdin suggests there were no more than four consecutive 'playing' evenings (*Annals of the Edinburgh Stage*, 91).
73 *An Enquiry concerning the Principles of Morals* (London, A. Millar, 1751), 87-8. The *Enquiry* was subsequently reprinted by Andrew Millar in Hume's *Essays and Treatises on Several Subjects*, v. III, 91-2. Hume attracted ridicule and scorn from several of his most scathing critics (including John Witherspoon and even John Home) for his assertion elsewhere in the *Enquiry* that 'health, cleanliness, taper legs, and broad shoulders' were 'capital virtues' and 'a running sore' a pardonable crime. See *The Moderator. Number II*, p.7 [there is no 'Number I'], attributed by Mossner to Witherspoon, but now generally attributed (including by BL ESTC) to Home.
74 *Four Dissertations* (London, A. Millar, 1757), Dedication, iii-vi. See the very useful note in the BL ESTC for help in tracking the extremely complicated bibliographical background to Hume's publication.
75 The BL ESTC identifies a fourth pamphlet as 'attributed to John MacLaurin', *viz.* a humorous poem entitled *The Stage or the pulpit: a sermon. Sung By the Reverend author of Douglas, the first night he went to see his own play represented. To the tune of Gill Morice*. [1757?] [*Note by RLC* In the light of its style and other factors, I think it unlikely to have been MacLaurin's work and for that reason have chosen to ignore it here.]
76 See chapter 1, 'Patronage', 33-42.

77 Roger L. Emerson, 'The Social Composition of Enlightened Scotland: The Select Society of Edinburgh, 1754-1764', *Studies in Voltaire and the Eighteenth Century* 114 (1973): 291-329.
78 Coryphaeus was the leader of the chorus in ancient Greek drama.
79 *Apology for The Writers*, 15.
80 Although Carlyle became Moderator in 1770 he was defeated in a competition in 1789 for the vacant post of Principal Clerk of Assembly.
81 Probably a reference to John Erskine's SSPCK sermon of the previous year, *The Influence of Religion on National Happiness* (1756).
82 Meaning, of course, Anderson's *An Estimate of the Profit and Loss of Religion* (1753).
83 Almost certainly a satirical reference to the Reverend Dr Alexander Webster's celebrated sermon first published in 1740, *The Wicked Life, and Fatal but Deserved Death of Haman*.
84 Carlyle's *Argument* (1757), 12-13.
85 Alexander Carlyle, *Anecdotes and Characters of the Times*, ed. Kinsley (1973), 157-67. Carlyle's avowed position throughout the case was, he affirms, 'not to Yield, but to Run every Risk, Rather than Furnish an Example of tame Submission not merely to a Fanatical, but an Illegal Exertion of Power, which would have stamped Disgrace on the Church of Scotland, kept the younger Clergy for half a Century Longer in the trammels of Bigotry or Hypocrisy, and Debar'd every Generous Spirit from entering into Orders.' (ibid., 160). See also Morren, *Annals of the General Assembly 1752-1766*, 122-130. Richard B. Sher, in *Church and University in the Scottish Enlightenment* (1985, re-issued in 'Edinburgh Classic Editions', 2016, 82-5) skilfully analyses the Carlyle case in terms of its relevance to the aims and aspirations of the 'Moderate *literati*' in their heyday. See also Michael Brown's fine essay, 'Alexander Carlyle and the Shadows of Enlightenment', in *Scotland in the Age of the French Revolution* (2005), ed. Harris, 226-46.
86 Ibid., 160.
87 Ibid., 160 and long starred footnote at 161. Carlyle explains that he provides this information about the conduct of Arniston on the grounds that 'it accounts for that animosity, which arose against him among my friends of the Moderate Party, and the Success of Certain Satirical Ballads and Pamphlets which were published some Years after.'
88 BL ESTC 006424743. .
89 The play which offended the Presbytery was probably the enormously successful comedy *Love for Love* (first published in 1695) by William Congreve which the manager of a touring company known as Tony Aston (or Ashton) had put on in Edinburgh in November 1727; the date of the Presbytery *Admonition* is 30 November. See Dibdin, 37. Editions of the play were published in Glasgow (Robert & Andrew Foulis) in 1751 and in Edinburgh (G. Hamilton and J. Balfour) in 1755. See also note 64 above.
90 John Home (1722-1808) was licensed by the Presbytery of Edinburgh in April 1745 and ordained at Athelstaneford in July 1746. It was in the light of his awareness that a libel was about to be served on him by the Presbytery of Haddington in 1757 that he chose to resign his charge. (Scott, *Fasti*, v. I, 354).
91 Morren prints the whole text of the 1757 version (*Annals 1752-1766*, 112-15).
92 The Presbytery's 1757 *Admonition and Exhortation* was expressly directed to be read 'from all Pulpits within their bounds, on the last Sabbath, being the thirtieth day of this Month, immediately after divine Service before Noon.'
93 In 1746 Ferguson was appointed principal chaplain to the Black Watch but left the army and the church in 1754 yet retained his military commission and his ministerial ordination.

Mossner notes that Hume refers to him in 1758 as 'The still Rev. Adam Ferguson' (*Life of David Hume*, 392).
94   *Morality of Stage-Plays*, 15.
95   Ibid., 26-7.
96   Ibid., 15-16.
97   Ibid., 28. In support of the contention in the last sentence Ferguson cites the Church of Scotland's rule-book on all matters affecting discipline procedure as exercised by Kirk judicatures, the *Form of Process* of 18 April 1707, and in this instance specifically, § 1. 84.
98   The letter is dated 'Edinburgh, December 29, 1756.' Morren prints it in full in *Annals 1752-1766*, 116-17.
99   Ibid., 119.
100 The Synod of Glasgow and Ayr had appointed 9 December 1756 as the date upon which Witherspoon's call to Paisley should be moderated but in the event it took six months more to negotiate his release from Beith. *Douglas* was first performed in Edinburgh on 14 December 1756.
101 Witherspoon, *A Serious Inquiry*, 57: 'Since writing the above, I have met with a pamphlet just published, entituled, *The Morality of Stage-plays seriously considered*.' He was not yet, of course, in a position to attribute authorship of the pamphlet to Adam Ferguson.
102 Ahnert, *The Moral Culture of the Scottish Enlightenment*, 117.
103 McIntosh, *Church and Theology in Enlightenment Scotland*, 88.
104 *Morality of Stage-Plays*, 18.
105 Ibid., 27.
106 Ibid., 16-17.
107 The identity of the 'late, very elegant writer' is interesting. In Joseph Warton's *An Essay on the Writings and Genius of Pope* (*v.1, London, 1756), 182 we read: '... we may rest secure, if the observation of an acute writer be true, who says, "Europe will perhaps behold ages of a bad taste, but will never again relapse into barbarism. The sole invention of printing has forbidden that event."' The 'acute writer' Warton (and thus Witherspoon too) has in mind is the French Protestant author of *Mes Pensées*, Laurent Angliviel de Beaumelle (1726-1773); an English translation of his best known work was published in London in 1753, though it is the Warton translation that Witherspoon appears to use here.
   * A second volume was not issued until 1782.
108 *A Serious Inquiry*, 69.

Chapter 5

1   Scott records that he was made D.D. 'source and date unknown'. (*Fasti*, III, 202).
2   Princeton University, Firestone Library Ms. CO 199, 1141. (The leaves are unpaginated). See Crawford, *LWJW*, 147-9 and notes 28-31. Modern West Kilbride is on the coast, a mere seven miles south of Largs, where Witherspoon 'preached in' the Reverend Patrick Wallace in 1748 with his sermon 'Ministerial Character and Duty'.
3   Located in Ayrshire, and within the Synod of Glasgow and Ayr, Witherspoon's former charge of Beith belonged to the Presbytery of Irvine.
4   Walker was older brother to Witherspoon's mother, Anne (or Anna) Walker who married James Witherspoon, minister of Yester, in 1720. Her father was David Walker (1690-1737), minister of Temple parish church, near Edinburgh, in the Presbytery of Dalkeith.

5   *Ecclesiastical Characteristics* ('generally ascribed to the same author') is included in the volume of Witherspoon's *Essays on Important Subjects* published in London by the Dilly brothers in 1765. His *Serious Apology for the Ecclesiastical Characteristics* (1763) is also included in the same volume.
6   'The author's manner of thinking, may, in some points, be esteemed bold and new.' (From the 'Advertisement' to Kames's *Essays on the Principles of Morality and Religion*, Edinburgh, 1751).
7   *WJW*, 3, 201: 'To the Departed Ghost, or Surviving Spirit, of the late Reverend Mr. – , Minister in – .'
8   For the origin of Church parties, and the earliest use of the term 'Moderate' see chapter 1, 28-29.
9   Adam, *How a minister should approve himself unto God*, 14-15.
10 Anderson's *Sermon*, 52.
11 Ibid., 34
12 Thomas Ahnert, *The Moral Culture of the Scottish Enlightenment, 1690-1805*, 'Moderatism, Orthodoxy, and Reason', 129-135. Colin Kidd goes markedly further than Ahnert, arguing that 'While noticing a few cracks in the façade of polite Presbyterianism, not least the enduring debate over patronage, historians have concluded that there was no major *theological* fissure in the Kirk of the Enlightenment.' Kidd then proceeds to adumbrate an important regional exception to this line: various serious theological disputes, culminating in the Fergusson affair and the later McGill heresy case, involving 'Auld Licht' and 'New Licht' ministers in Renfrewshire and Ayrshire. ('Enlightenment and anti-Enlightenment in eighteenth-century Scotland: an Ayrshire-Renfrewshire microclimate', in Dunyach and Thomson, ed., *The Enlightenment in Scotland*, 2015).
    * Yet one certain fundamental theological 'fissure' dividing the Kirk factions was, for example, the doctrine of original sin – as it happened, the issue on which Witherspoon would finally part company with Thomas Paine after the latter had ridiculed it in his pamphlet, *Common Sense*. See *The Dominion of Providence over the Passions of Men*, in *WJW*, 3, 23-24 and long footnote; and note 44 below.
13 John R. McIntosh calls Anderson's *Defence of the Church-Government* 'one of the ablest justifications of Presbyterianism ever published' [Oxford *DNB*, John Anderson (1671-1721), online ed., 2014-15, accessed 10 October 2016]. Anderson wrote his *Defence* in answer to Thomas Rhind's *Apology* (1712).
14 Anderson's *Sermon*, 8.
15 Adam is probably referring here to none other than William Leechman (1706-1785), a disciple of Francis Hutcheson and Witherspoon's predecessor as minister of Beith until Leechman's appointment to the chair of divinity at Glasgow in 1744. While at Beith Leechman would have made the acquaintance of Adam's father – and, conceivably, of young John as well – since both charges, (West) Kilbride and Beith, lay within the Presbytery of Irvine. Leechman served as moderator of the General Assembly in 1757. None of the other candidates who were moderators 'a very few years ago' seems to fit the bill. If it *was* Leechman who had remarked to Adam that 'patronage would be the ruin of the church of Scotland', his comment offers important insight into church politics of the time. In later life, when principal of Glasgow University, Leechman famously fell foul of the Reverend John Anderson's grandson, the eccentric and litigious Professor John Anderson (1726-96), then professor of natural philosophy at Glasgow.

16 Adam, *How a minister should approve himself unto God*, 34-5.
17 Chapter XXX, § 3, '*Of Church Censures*'.
18 Ibid., 8-9.
19 Anderson's *Sermon*, 38-9.
20 Ibid., 30-31.
21 Anderson does, however, deal with some of the doctrinal implications of the Articles of Faith (e.g. free-will and predestination) in Chapter III of his *Defence of the Church-Government*, 196-227.
22 These are the opening words of 'Maxim III' of *Ecclesiastical Characteristics* – *WJW*, 3, 216.
23 General Assembly of 1690, *Acts of the General Assembly of the Church of Scotland 1638-1842* (British History Online, Institute of Historical Research, University of London, School of Advanced Study).
24 J. H. S. Burleigh, *A Church History of Scotland*, 287.
25 Colin Kidd, 'Subscription, the Scottish Enlightenment and the Moderate Interpretation of History', in *Journal of Ecclesiastical History*, v. 55, No. 3, July 2004, 502-519. See also notes 12 above; 53 and 84 below.
26 John R. McIntosh, *Church and Theology in Enlightenment Scotland: The Popular Party, 1740-1800*, 25.
27 Kidd, *op. cit.*, 506. Sher, *Church and University in the Scottish Enlightenment*, 35.
28 The tortuous history of the Kilwinning debate is unravelled in John Graham's long Preface to his anonymous *The Religious Establishment of Scotland*. Relevant issues of the *Scots Magazine* are April, May, July and October 1767 (v. xxix) and January and March 1768 (v. xxx).
29 The date of the original of A.B.'s letter to Adam is supplied as 'October 6, 1766'.
30 The names include those of merchants, writers [solicitors], customs and excise officers and surgeons. Intriguingly, one of the writers named in support of publication of A.B's letter is 'Jo. Snodgrass' who can be identified as none other than the pursuer of John Witherspoon in the Court of Session in an action for defamation and damages. (See chapter 2 *pass.*; and Crawford, *LWJW*, 8 and note 10).
31 Baine, minister of the High Church in Paisley, who had 'preached in' Witherspoon to his new charge in Paisley in June 1757, deserted his charge on 10 February 1766 on which date he wrote to the Presbytery of Paisley informing them of his inability to continue to sustain such an 'intolerable load'. On 13 February Baine was admitted minister of the newly opened Relief Church in Nicolson's Park, Edinburgh. See Morren, *Annals 1752-1766*, 313-329. See also note 64 below.
32 *Scots Magazine*, April 1767, v. xxix, 172.
33 Morren, *Annals 1739-1752*, 387.
34 NRS CH2/197/4/511.
35 See also note 53 below. The *Second Warning* is unseen. Hew Scott lists both pamphlets in his entry for Fergusson in *Fasti*, III, 117, but refers to the earlier as a *Warning against Divisive Courses*. In the introduction to the *Display* Fergusson relates the full story of the various responses to his original *Warning*. Scott notes that Fergusson's successive 'warnings' provoked two sets of 'answers', both purporting to be the work of one 'David M'Lerie', a weaver, but in reality probably written by James Ellis (or Alice), minister to the flourishing Antiburgher congregation in Paisley (and a former friend and colleague of John Witherspoon). Crawfurd (Semple) notes that James Ellis was 'ordained their minister' (*i.e.* to the rapidly expanding Antiburgher congregation in Paisley) on 21 September 1756. – *The History of the Shire of Renfrew*, Part II, (1782), 308. At the end of his letter of 18 May 1768, written on board

the *Peggy* about to sail from Greenock for the Delaware, Witherspoon touchingly asks the moderator of Paisley Presbytery and minister of the High Church, George Muir, to convey to 'Brother Alice' that he thinks of him 'and all other friends'. – Collins, *President Witherspoon*, v. 1, (1925), 95; and Crawford, *LWJW*, 32-3 and note 59.

36 *Act, Declaration and Testimony* (Edinburgh, 1737), 44. See also note 54 below.
37 *A Display of the Act and Testimony*, 21-2.
38 *The Grounds of the Process*, 'Introduction', 1.
39 The author is quoting without attribution from *Jeremiah*, 9, v. 3: *'And they bend their tongues like their bow for lies: but they are not valiant for the truth upon the earth; for they proceed from evil to evil and they know not me, saith the Lord.'*
40 *The Grounds of the Process*, 'Introduction', 1.
41 Ibid., 4. Again unattributed, the words are from *2 Kings*, 8, v. 13.
42 Fergusson's wife Katherine (daughter of an Edinburgh lawyer) died on 2 May 1766, just three weeks after Adam preached his sermon. His own condition towards the end of his life was so fragile that Hew Scott notes he was 'assisted by five probationers in succession, to whom he gave the whole stipend.' (*Fasti*, III, 117).
43 *Scots Magazine* (*SM*), April 1767, xxix, 172; *The Grounds of the Process* (*GOP*), 11; *The Religious Establishment of Scotland* (*RES*), Appendix, 342.
44 Even in his 'enlightened' American career Witherspoon never lost his implicit belief in the Calvinist doctrine of original sin. In a long footnote to Robert Aitken's first edition of Witherspoon's famous sermon preached at Princeton on 17 May 1776, *The Dominion of Providence over the Passions of Men*, (later discussed in chapter 8, 212-216) JW rebukes and takes serious issue with Thomas Paine for what he considered Paine's casual dismissal of the doctrine in the latter's iconic pamphlet of January that year, *Common Sense*. Witherspoon concludes: 'Is there so little to be said for the doctrine of original sin, that it is not to be refuted, but despised? Is the state of the world such, as to render this doctrine not only false, but incredible?' – *WJW*, 3, 23-24. See also note 12 above.
45 In *RES* (London, 1771) – a substantial anonymous work now known to have been written by the Reverend John Graham (minister of Dunlop in the Presbytery of Irvine before his translation to Kirkinner in the Presbytery of Wigtown in 1779) – the author has added a footnote at this point : '*Supposed to be Dr. Witherspoon.' The footnote does not appear in either of the transcripts of the letter in *The Scots Magazine* or in *The Grounds of the Process*.
46 *SM*, 175; *GOP*, 17-18; *RES*, 139-41.
47 *SM*, 172; *GOP*, 12; *RES*, 345-6.
48 *SM*, 173; *GOP*, 13-14; *RES*, 349.
49 Adam's sermon, 31.
50 The tendency for fines to supplement, or even on occasion replace censures became increasingly common as the eighteenth century progressed. Ivo Clarke cites a Farnell & Kinnaird [villages near Brechin, Angus] kirk session minute of 30 September 1787: 'He ['a man guilty of fornication', having been 'rebuked and dismissed'] gave of penalty for the use of the poor twelve pounds Scots.' And Clarke notes that 'there are similar instances in subsequent years.' (*A History of Church Discipline in Scotland*, 157-8).
51 *SM*, 173-4; *GOP*, 14-15; *RES*, 350-1.
52 *SM*, 174; *GOP*, 15; *RES*, 351-2.
53 In *A Warning relating to the Present Schism* (1759) Fergusson, who, according to the title page actually read it out in his pulpit, accused seceding ministers of being authors of 'contentious

divisions, disorderly courses, erroneous Principles, and false Notions of Religion'. See Colin Kidd, 'The Fergusson affair: Calvinism and dissimulation in the Scottish Enlightenment', *Intellectual History Review*, 26:3, 2016, 341-2; and James Kennedy's excellent online publication, *Antiburghers to the End – The Kilwinning Original Secession Church (1738-1956)*.

54   Kennedy *op cit* explains in detail the full history of the (considerable) Antiburgher tradition in the town. The *OSA* entry for Kilwinning (v. 4, 1794) merely reports that 'an Antiburgher minister, ordained in 1762, died about 3 months ago.'

55   *SM*, 174; *GOP*, 15; *RES*, 352-3.

56   Witherspoon's views on patronage are often misunderstood. To be clear, in his speech he leaves one in no doubt that the chief abuse he is attacking is not so much the principle of patronage itself, as that of 'open solicitation' of settlements on the part of ministerial candidates: 'In the history of the Church we find no character more odious, or more unclerical, if I may speak so, than ambition and open solicitation of ecclesiastical preferment.' (Morren, *Annals 1752-1766*, 206). The historian of the Popular party, John R. McIntosh, confirms that 'it is difficult to find an eighteenth-century publication from an identifiable [Popular party] minister, after the secession of Ebenezer Erskine, who actually ascribed to the congregation, or heads of families, the sole right of calling a minister.' – *Church and Theology in Enlightenment Scotland*, 94-5.

57   *SM*, 174; *GOP*, 16; *RES*, 354-5.

58   *SM*, 175; *GOP*, 17-18; *RES*, 140-1.

59   *Scots Magazine*, May 1767, v. xxix, 255.

60   Ibid., July 1767, v. xxix, 346. From the internal evidence of his references to the Council of Trent and the Koran it is entirely possible that, despite the provenance supplied, 'a well-wisher' is none other than Thomas Walker, minister of Dundonald, who would use the *nom de plume* 'Philalethes'.

61   Ibid., October 1767, v. xxix, 526.

62   The contribution to the debate by 'Philanthropos' attracted a published response in the form of a 24-page pamphlet by 'Philorthodoxus' [lover of orthodoxy], printed in Glasgow by the religious printer John Bryce – *Kilwinning Divinity Weighed and found Wanting*, Glasgow, 1768. The pamphlet contains two letters originally published in the *Glasgow Journal*. Bryce had published some of Witherspoon's early works and in 1761-3 brought out a tome of 645 pages containing *The Confessions of Faith*, together with numerous other Acts and Ordinances relating to the Church of Scotland.

63   Ibid., 534.

64   In 1767 a pamphlet had appeared in Glasgow: *Observations on the letters published by the Rev. Mr. James Baine*, referring to the case of Baine's desertion to the Relief congregation debated at the General Assembly of the year before. The third letter is signed *Philalethes*. This pamphlet, however, is the work of Thomas Randall, at that time minister of Inchture. [Witherspoon's predecessor at the Laigh Church, Robert Findlay, minister of the North-West Church (the Ramshorn), and later professor of divinity at Glasgow, published two pamphlets in 1762 and 1778 under the same *nom de plume* of *Philalethes*.]

65   And he names it: *A Display of the Act and Testimony* (Glasgow, 1761).

66   *Scots Magazine*, January 1768, v. xxx, 11-12. Walker's letter is at pp. 9-20.

67   The Princeton University copy of the *Display* (Wit. 0099.695 v. 59) is Witherspoon's own copy, bearing his signature 'J. Witherspoon.' on the blank leaf after p. 47.

68   With typical crankiness, Fergusson uses the imprint on his title page to make a point, the point here being that he 'dedicates' his *Display* of 1761 to the great historian of the Church of

Scotland in its years of acute crisis – Robert Wodrow (1679-1734), minister of Eastwood and author of *The History of the Sufferings of the Church of Scotland from the Restoration to the Revolution*, ([1721]-1722). In the 'Advertisement' (printed on the *verso* of the title page) Fergusson states that the editions from which he cites extracts are: of the *Act [Declaration] and Testimony* – the Lumsden and Robertson Edinburgh edition of 1737 – and of the three *Acts of the Associate Presbytery*, the Ruddimans' Edinburgh edition of 1744. James Wodrow, Robert's ninth son, served as a probationer under Fergusson at Kilwinning for almost four years from 1753.

69 *Scots Magazine*, January 1768, v. xxx, 12.
70 Ibid., 15.
71 I. D. L. Clark notes that from his analysis of the composition of Presbyteries in the years 1755, 1780 (the nearest, of course, to the legal process against Fergusson) and 1805, he concludes that 'only very occasionally (as for example in the proceedings concerning Fergusson and McGill in the Presbyteries of Irvine and Ayr) did the Moderates enjoy a substantial majority in the lower courts of the Church.' Clark also observes that Ayrshire was one of only three areas in Scotland (the others being 'Fife and the east coast burghs as far north as Aberdeen', and 'the Lowlands, from the Synod of Lothian & Tweedal across the Borders to Galloway') where the Moderates 'were at their strongest'. – *Moderatism and the Moderate Party in the Church of Scotland, 1752-1805* [1964], 166-7, 182. See also Clark's chapter 9 'From Protest to Reaction: The Moderate Regime in the Church of Scotland, 1752-1805', in *Scotland in the Age of Improvement* (1970; re-issued 1996), ed. Phillipson and Mitchison, in which (pages 213-4) he expands on the same point, noting that 'The presbytery of Ayr has always been regarded as a hotbed of Moderatism, yet in 1780 only twelve out of the twenty-nine clergy can be identified as active and consistent supporters of Moderate measures.'
72 McConnell's pamphlet of 29 pages – *Some Remarks on a Book, lately come abroad into this Nation* – is directed against Graham's *Religious Establishment*. The place of publication is not listed.
73 See note 84 below.
74 A blow-by-blow exposition of the entire legal process is set out in the preface to John Graham's *Religious Establishment*, 8-70.
75 *The Happiness of Dead Clergymen* (1769) and *A Vindication of Doctor Tail from the Charge of Heresy* (1770).
76 Cf. *Fasti*, New Edition (1917), v. II, 366 with the same entry in older editions.
77 Ibid., 365.
78 *The Religious Establishment*, 58.
79 Ibid., 265.
80 Ibid., 290.
81 *The Terms of Ministerial and Christian Communion*, (Glasgow, 1753), 121. Walker probably 'borrowed' the title from *The True Terms of Christian and Ministerial Communion … A Sermon By the late Reverend Robert Craghead, M.A.* (Dublin, 1739). According to his *DNB* entry by A. W. Godfrey Brown, Craghead, who studied at Glasgow, Edinburgh and Leiden, 'wrote in support of the non-subscribers in the controversy over subscription to the Westminster confession and attempted to reconcile the two parties'. (Oxford *DNB*, 2004-16; accessed 10 November 2016).
82 Walker's *Vindication*, Preface, xvi.
83 Ibid., xxi.
84 Colin Kidd, 'The Fergusson affair: Calvinism and dissimulation in the Scottish Enlightenment', *Intellectual History Review*, 2016, vol. 26, No. 3, 339-354, p. 351.

Chapter 6

1 Scott, *Fasti*, 'New Edition', v. III, 483. Dunn had briefly appeared in the limelight at the General Assemblies of 1778 and 1779 when he had supported (i) a failed motion of Dr John Gillies and a few other members of the Popular party (including Charles Nisbet of Montrose), the purpose of which was to re-convene the Assembly Commission if events made it necessary to do so (1778); and (ii) a further unsuccessful overture in the following year to appoint a series of committees to co-ordinate the Church's response to any proposal to extend Catholic relief to Scotland (1779).

2 'Stability', it need hardly be pointed out, is not, however, the precise antithesis of 'discord' or 'disaffection'. The point is that the Scottish sedition trials of 1793-94 and, perhaps above all, the guilty verdict passed on Robert Watt on a charge of high treason at the High Court in Edinburgh in September 1794 (and Watt's subsequent public hanging, swiftly followed by the decapitation, drawing and quartering of his corpse) all tend to put things into their proper context. Significantly, at Watt's trial one of the witnesses (Fairley) is quoted as having reported 'Paisley to be in a state of great readiness, but did not know what that meant.' (Howell, *State Trials*, v. XXIII, 1272). Reports of these trials show that similar tensions were equally evident in other known radical hot-spots in Scotland at the time, as Meikle and Harris have shown. The issue is discussed in Harris's 'Conclusion' to *The Scottish People and the French Revolution*, especially at p. 227, where he contrasts Brims' emphasis on the 'moderation of Scottish radicalism' with the evidence presented in his own study to the effect that 'more ideologically extreme currents of radicalism ... took a hold in many [sic] communities in parts of lowland Scotland', but for a strictly limited period, until roughly mid-1794.

3 Ian D. L. Clark, *Moderatism and the Moderate Party in the Church of Scotland, 1752-1805*, unpublished PhD thesis, University of Cambridge (King's College), 1964, Chapter 4, 'The Moderates and Politics'. See also Clark's Chapter 9, 'From Protest to Reaction: The Moderate Regime in the Church of Scotland, 1752-1805', in Phillipson and Mitchison, *Scotland in the Age of Improvement* (1970), 200-224.

4 James Finlayson (1758-1808) held the chair of Logic at Edinburgh from 1787 to 1808 and was Moderator of the General Assembly in 1802. His 'short account' of the life of Hugh Blair, dated 'Edinburgh, March 13th, 1801', is appended to volume five of Blair's collected *Sermons* (1801), 455-75.

5 Cited by Clark in *Moderatism and the Moderate Party*, 139, note 24.

6 Fry, *The Dundas Despotism* (1992, reprinted 2004), 181.

7 *The Principal Acts of the General Assembly of the Church of Scotland* (1793), 10. The Moderator for 1793 was Thomas Hardy, whose sermon *Fidelity to the British Constitution, The Duty and Interest of the People* is discussed later in this chapter. For a different slant on Hardy, preaching on 'Slavery', see chapter 10.

8 'On the Danger of Political Innovation, from a discourse delivered on the 28th. November 1794, before the Literary Society in Glasgow College, by Dr. Reid.' – included in *Sketch of the Character of the late Thomas Reid, D.D.*, published by the *Glasgow Courier*, a loyalist newspaper.

9 Colin Kidd, 'The Kirk, the French Revolution, and the Burden of Scottish Whiggery', in *Religious Change in Europe 1650-1914: Essays for John McManners*, 224, 227.

10 With its exponential population growth and ingrained weaving traditions, allied to a reputation for self-enlightenment, Paisley is a case in point. I point out in my PhD thesis of 2011 that the Paisley *Declaration of Rights* (quite possibly the work of the weaver-poet, Alexander Wilson)

was a key Crown production at the trial of Thomas Muir. See *Scotland, America and Tom Paine: ideas of liberty and the making of three Americans – John Witherspoon, Robert Aitken and Alexander Wilson. A study in bibliographical history*, 92-5, and Appendix C, 407-8. Wilson himself was deeply involved in radical politics, leading directly to his flight from Scotland to America in May 1794 (ibid., 290-344).

11 *The Scottish People and the French Revolution*, 226.
12 See Pentland, *The Spirit of the Union* (2011), Chapter 4, 'The General Rising of 1820', 89-108.
13 E.g. as evidenced by the growth of circulating libraries, one of which was run by Robert Aitken, then a bookbinder in Paisley, before his emigration to America. For more on Aitken's career as a distinguished post-colonial printer and bookstore proprietor in Philadelphia, see Crawford, unpublished PhD thesis, University of Strathclyde (2011), chapter 5, 'Robert Aitken (1735-1802) – Conduit of Liberty'.
14 Meikle notes that the sederunt prefacing the minutes of the proceedings of the first General Convention has one 'James Alcie' [sic] attending as one of two representatives from Paisley, but prints a question-mark after his name; almost certainly this is the old minister of the extensive and rapidly growing Antiburgher congregation in the town. – *Scotland and the French Revolution*, Appendix A, 240.

James Ellis (*aka* Alice) had been an intimate friend of John Witherspoon who, in his last letter written in Scotland prior to his departure for Princeton, dated 18 May 1768, asked to be remembered to 'Brother Alice.' – Crawford, *The Lost World of John Witherspoon*, 32-3 and note 59. There is an account of Ellis's remarkable life and career in W. Ferrier, *Two Discourses: - The first preached June 17. 1798, before the Associate Congregation in Paisley, on occasion of the death of the Rev. James Alice, their senior pastor* (Paisley, 1798).

15 *Statistical Account of Scotland*, v. 2, 'Number XXI. Parish of Kirkintilloch' (Edinburgh, 1791), 275-284. Dunn's facts were assembled in 1791, the date of publication of this volume.
16 Erskine's Kirkintilloch ministry lasted from 1744 to 1753 in which year he was called to Culross.
17 *The fatal consequences and the general sources of anarchy. A discourse, the substance of which was preached in the Old-Greyfriars Church, before the magistrates of Edinburgh, 2^d September 1792. By John Erskine, D.D. one of the ministers of Edinburgh* (Edinburgh, 1793).
18 Ibid., 5.
19 'Take the sermons of Dr. Blair, deservedly the most popular, the most approved and which seem to come the nearest to perfection of any that we have. … Who can avoid profiting by the vivacity and solidity of his remarks, by the force and precision of his arguments, by the judicious and lucid order in which they are arranged? … I am of opinion that Dr. Blair's Sermons, taking them all in all, considering their number, the variety and novelty of their subjects, form the best Collection for practical purposes, for reading in the parlour or the closet, of any at present extant in any language.' – John Gardiner, *Brief reflections on the eloquence of the pulpit*, Taunton, [1796], 58-9 and note.
20 See chapter 7 for an analysis of Blair's posthumously published sermon, 'On the Love of our Country'.
21 Cited by Sidney Pollard in his chapter 'Labour in Great Britain' in *The Cambridge Economic History of Europe. VII. The Industrial Economies: Capital, Labour, and Enterprise. Part 1*, ed. Mathias and Postan (Cambridge, 1978), 120.
22 Dunn, Old Statistical Account for Kirkintilloch, 280-1.
23 Ibid., 283.

24 Ibid., 284.
25 Boog, minister of Paisley Abbey Church, contributed his piece on the Abbey Parish of Paisley, leaving his colleague, the Reverend Dr. John Snodgrass of the Middle Church, to supply the parallel entry for the Town of Paisley.
26 *Statistical Account of Scotland*, v. 7, 'Number V. Parish of the Abbey of Paisley' (Edinburgh, 1793), 74-98. The passage quoted is at 88-9. Boog's information applies, of course, to 1791.
27 See Edith Haden-Guest, 'William Adam (1751-1839), of Woodstone, Kincardine and Blair-Adam, Kinross', in *The History of Parliament The House of Commons 1754-1790*, ed. Namier and Brooke, 8-10. He is described there as 'a warm-hearted, popular man, exceptionally able in business management'.
28 Cobbett's *Parliamentary History of England*, v. xxx, cols. 1486-1576
29 i.e. (Sir) James Mackintosh (1765-1832), *Vindiciae Gallicae. Defence of the French Revolution and its English admirers against the accusations of the Right Hon. Edmund Burke* (London, 1791). By the following year a fourth edition had appeared.
30 *The Glasgow Courier*, November 6, 1792, no. 186.
31 Originally a Platonic concept, the notion of *'punctum stans*, as the 'schoolmen' [medieval philosophers and scholars, e.g. Thomas Aquinas] express it' is directly borrowed by Dunn from George Berkeley's *Siris*, a work first published in 1744: '... instead of a temporary succession of moments, there is one eternal now, or punctum Stans, as it is termed by the Schoolmen.'– *Siris: a chain of philosophical reflexions and inquiries concerning the virtues of tar water ... by G.L.B.O.C.* [George, Lord Bishop of Cloyne], Dublin 1744, 248.
32 Dunn's synodical sermon of 1792, 9.
33 Ibid., 10-11.
34 Ibid., 11.
35 Ibid., 13.
36 Ibid., 13-14.
37 Clark calculates that over the period 1755 to 1805 the Presbytery of Glasgow (easily the largest in the Synod of Glasgow and Ayr) had 'a perennial Popular majority which is reflected in the measures it passed and the exasperated comments of its Moderate members.' In the 1780s the Moderates had a large majority in the Presbytery of Ayr while their opponents enjoyed a majority in the Synod. Clark points to the Moderatism of 'many of the Ayrshire clergy' being well known from the 'acrimonious charges and counter-charges of the contemporaries of Robert Burns'. By the beginning of the nineteenth century, it appears that there were about as many Popular ministers in the Synod of Glasgow and Ayr as Moderates. Clark also states that 'in a Presbytery where the Popular ministers had a majority there was also a majority of Popular elders.' – *Moderatism and the Moderate Party*, 166-7, 180-4.
38 Keane, *Tom Paine A political life* (New York, 1995), 327.
39 Typical is *The Paisley Weaver's letter to his neighbours and fellow tradesmen* (Glasgow, *Courier* office, William Reid, 1792). As Harris notes, this pamphlet is almost certainly 'the product of official encouragement or intervention.' (*The Scottish People and the French Revolution*, 133). In 1793 William Creech brought out the government-subsidised loyalist comic dialogue *Look before ye loup* by 'Tam Thrum', in reality an Aberdeen printer by name of William Brown who was paid £50 per annum by government for agreeing to move to Edinburgh where he set up a new newspaper, the *Patriot's Weekly Chronicle* in opposition to the *Edinburgh Gazetteer*. For more on Brown see *The Scottish People and the French Revolution*, 63, 133. A second ed. of *Look before ye loup* came out with Brown's name in the imprint in 1794.

40 The royal proclamation of 21 May 1792 against seditious writings, however, gives, deliberately, little clue on what is intended by the term, having been drafted with Paine's *Rights of Man Parts 1 and 2* specifically (though not exclusively) in mind. In his 94-page Introduction to his posthumously published *An Examination of the Trials for Sedition which have hitherto occurred in Scotland* (1888) Lord Cockburn quotes Lord Brougham in his evidence before the Commons Committee in 1834: 'I have never yet seen, nor have I been able myself to hit upon anything like a definition of libel, or even of sedition, which possessed the qualities of a definition; and I cannot help thinking that the difficulty is not accidental, but essentially inherent in the nature of the subject.' Even so, Cockburn attempts a definition of the crime of sedition which must, he states, include 'disrespect towards the authority of the State' and that 'the mischief must be done, or attempted, *malo animo*.' (v. I, 8, 10). Elsewhere in the same volume he writes: 'My notion of sedition then is, that it is the publication of any sentiment intended and calculated materially and speedily to obstruct or weaken the legal authority of the State.' (*ibid.*,14). By the application of Cockburn's strict definition, Dunn's published sermon signally fails to pass muster.

In the same work, dealing this time with the trial of Margarot, Cockburn returns to the issue of how most appropriately to define the crime of sedition: 'This doctrine, *viz.*, that the guilt of sedition may be incurred by the mere remote tendency of the acts composing it, to create a dissatisfaction which may end in rebellion, *though this was not in the view of the accused at the time,* is one of the most monstrous that has been uttered [in this instance, by the Lord Advocate, Robert Dundas] from any modern British bench.' (*ibid.*,16).

41 Dunn's sermon, 14-15.
42 Ibid., 18.
43 Ibid., 20
44 Ibid., 21.
45 Ibid., 22-3.
46 Ibid., 23-5.
47 J. D. Brims is careful to exclude farm servants and general labourers from those who supported, or were even remotely interested in the cause of reform; these workers, Brims maintains, 'remained, politically impassive throughout the 1790s, neither siding with the radicals nor actively supporting the defenders of the constitution.' (*The Scottish Democratic Movement in the Age of the French Revolution*, unpublished PhD thesis, University of Edinburgh, 1983, v. 1, 214.)
48 Draft 'Address to the Public from the Friends of the People' in NRS JC 26/230. Cited by Brims, *ibid.,* 200 and note 108. Skirving suffered the same fate as Muir, being sentenced to 14 years' transportation at the High Court on 7 January 1794. Braxfield mused on Skirving's sentence: 'Mr Muir was transported for fourteen years; and the only hesitation in that case was whether it should be limited to fourteen years or not. I have no inclination to go beyond it in this case; but I think it is impossible we can, consistently with the justice of the country, pronounce a less sentence upon this panel than we did upon Mr. Muir.' – Howell, *State Trials*, v. xxiii, 601. And Cockburn quotes Lord Abercromby on Skirving's sentence: 'I think that no man – I THINK THE PANEL HIMSELF – cannot think that this punishment is too severe' [ibid., 600], and with grim humour adds: 'No criterion, certainly, could be more fair than this. But it is not recorded that the panel intimated his concurrence.' – *Examination of the Trials for Sedition*, 1, 291.
49 Dunn's sermon, 25.

50 Ibid., 26. This is almost certainly a thinly disguised reference to the Reverend James Lapslie, minister of Campsie, the neighbouring parish to Kirkintilloch. It is unlikely that Dunn would have used the sentence in his original spoken sermon but, despite his prefatory note to the effect that he is 'certain' the printed text is 'very little different from what it then was,' it was probably inserted as an afterthought into the published version. Lapslie's role as a paid government informer is discussed in chapter, 6 pp. 176-181.
51 Ibid., 29.
52 Ibid., 31-2.
53 William Moodie was Moderator of the General Assembly in 1799.
54 By Henry Scougal (1650-78), a King's College, Aberdeen graduate and minister of Auchterless parish in Aberdeenshire for a short time until his appointment as professor of divinity at his *alma mater* in 1674. Tragically, Scougal died of consumption in 1678, aged just twenty-eight. Scougal's *Life of God*, first published anonymously in the year before his death, became immensely popular throughout the eighteenth century in numerous successive editions.
55 *Political Preaching* (1792), 23-4.
56 Hardy, *Fidelity to the British Constitution*, 15.
57 Not, of course, to be confused with one of the Crown productions in Thomas Muir's indictment of the same name which Harris identifies as a Sheffield radical periodical 'which was being sold by Alexander Guthrie in Edinburgh from April 1792.' (*The Scottish People and the French Revolution*, 98). In support of this claim Harris cites an advert placed by Guthrie in the *Edinburgh Evening Courant* of 30 April 1792. From the record of the trial evidence, however, it seems clear that the publication forming part of the Crown's case against Muir was *The Patriot: or, political, moral, and philosophical repository* (London, 1792-3). Guthrie specifically advertises *this* title in the very first number of the *Edinburgh Gazetteer* of 16 November 1792. See Crawford, *Scotland, America and Tom Paine*, unpublished PhD thesis, University of Strathclyde, 2011, 133, note 56.
58 Lord Advocate to Henry Dundas, January 13, 1793. Meikle also notes that a copy of *The Patriot* had been forwarded to Pitt for inspection on January 4. (*Scotland and the French Revolution*, 117 and note 3). See also Kay, *Original Portraits*, v. 2, 50, 'The Reverend Patriot.'
59 Colin Kidd, 'The Kirk, the French Revolution, and the Burden of Scottish Whiggery', 224.
60 Lord Daer to Charles Grey in 1793: Home Office Papers SRO RH 2/4/66/254 cited in Fry, *The Dundas Despotism* (John Donald edition, 2004), 165.
61 Cockburn, *Examination of the Trials for Sedition*, v. I, 183.
62 Section 51 of the Criminal Justice and Licensing (Scotland) Act 2010 abolished the common law offences of sedition and leasing-making [in England 'lese-majesty', interpreted as any offence against the sovereign power] with effect from 28 March 2011. Similar legislation was passed in England at around the same time.
63 Hume's *Commentaries on the Law of Scotland, respecting the description and punishment of Crimes* (2 vols., Edinburgh, 1797), v. II, 484-98.
64 Ibid., 485-6. Hume has clearly written this with Muir's case in mind which he later (490-1) discusses and notes that Muir was tried on a charge that included 'forming associations, for the purpose of constraining, and accomplishing, of their own authority, an alteration of the Government of this country.' Muir had denied that specific charge in his written 'defences': '... so far from exciting the people to riot and insurrection, it can easily be proved ... that, upon every occasion, the panel exhorted them to pursue measures moderate, legal, peaceable, and constitutional.' – *State Trials*, XXIII, col. 129.

65 In Scots law the preliminary examination of, and/or a statement taken from, a witness for the purpose of obtaining, with a view to trial, an understanding of the available evidence.
66 NLS LC 1133 (16).
67 In such circumstances, therefore, the 'decreet' (final judgment or sentence) could be pronounced by the Lord Commissioners of Justiciary trying the accused in the absence of a jury.
68 NLS LC 1133 (17). The *Answers* have an Appendix attached containing the copy Declaration.
69 Admitted WS 28 June 1787, died 1808. Dunn had been shown the minute-book of the reform society in the house of a Mrs Oswald of Springfield, Kirkintilloch, whose family affairs, after her husband's death in 1787, had been 'under the respondent's [i.e. Dunn's] charge.' The 'agent of that family' and 'the respondent's agent in this case' was Grant. (*Answers*, 2).
70 It is likely that the wording of the vote of thanks in the minute book would have been identical to that contained in the published notice in the Glasgow press of 6 November 1792.
71 In addition to Lord Braxfield and Lord Swinton, Lords Henderland, Dunsinnan and Abercromby would sit at the trial of Thomas Muir. The Special Commission of Oyer and Terminer that tried Robert Watt for high treason in August-September 1794 consisted of nine judges headed by the Lord President of the College of Justice (Ilay Campbell) and included all five sitting on the bench in consideration of the charge against Dunn. Braxfield (Robert Macqueen) and Eskgrove (David Rae) in particular have earned an unenviable reputation for their cold injustice and hardline conduct in the course of the sedition trials, meriting the scorn of Cockburn in his forensic analysis of the conduct of each of them in his *Examination of the Trials for Sedition* (posthumously published in 1888).
72 NRS JC 7/48 ff. 212-15 (High Court Minute Book): dated 11 March 1793; signed on each page 'Robert M'Queen [Lord Braxfield] I.P.D.' (*In Presentia Dominorum*).
73 The case of John Morton, James Anderson and Malcolm Craig, journeymen printers (8, 9 and 11 January 1793), who were found guilty of having uttered seditious speeches and having drunk a toast in a 'canteen' in Edinburgh Castle to 'George the Third and last, and damnation to all crowned heads', along with other utterances held to have been made 'with a seditious and wicked design'. They were imprisoned for nine months 'and thereafter, until they should find security to the extent of 1000 merks each for their good behaviour for three years,' a punishment Cockburn found 'not too severe'.
74 Cockburn, *Examination of the Trials for Sedition*, v. I, 107.
75 Glasgow: printed by A. Duncan and R. Chapman, for Brash and Reid, 1793. Now extremely rare.
76 *An Address by a Scotsman*, 16.
77 For the trial proceedings see *State Trials*, XXIII, cols. 117-238, and 'Addenda', 1405-1408.
78 Gilbert Innes (1751-1832) in 1780 inherited from his father the large estate known as Stow, near Lauder in Berwickshire. He became a director of the Royal Bank of Scotland in 1787 and deputy governor – the second most senior post in the Bank (next to that of cashier) – in 1794. At the time of his death in 1832 Innes was said to have been the richest commoner in Scotland, but died intestate, his fortune passing to his sister Jane. Claims relating to his estate revealed that he was the father of 'at least 67 illegitimate children.'
79 More usually known as 'John Balfour junior' (1740-1814), second son of James Balfour of Pilrig (1705-95), professor of moral philosophy at the University of Edinburgh from 1754 until 1764 when he was translated to a professorship of 'the law of nature and nations'. Young Balfour's uncle, also John Balfour (1715-95), was a prominent bookseller and papermaker.

80 In Scots law the proprietor of a modest plot of land forming a portion of what originally would have been a larger estate; more simply, a small landowner.
81 William Dalrymple (1747-94) was cashiered by the king on 3 December 1792 on account of his connections with the Friends of the People and the reform movement in Scotland. See Harris, *The Scottish People and the French Revolution,* 97, citing the Minute Book of the Society for Constitutional Information, National Archives TS 11/962, f.94r.
82 Not to be confused with another William Muir of 'Fisher-row, Paisley', who was cited by Thomas Muir though not called.
83 *The Scots Magazine* account of the trial puts it: '... it was against his principles, as he was a Mountaineer.' (Sept., 1793, v. 55, 423). The 'Cameronian' sect is named after its founder, Richard Cameron (d. 1680), a covenanter field preacher who was ordained in the Scots Church in Rotterdam in 1679. Cameron became a martyr to the anti-Erastian cause when he and some of his followers were hunted down and killed by government troops in Ayrshire in the following year. The term applied to Muir's church in the trial – 'the mountain' – is intended to be derogatory and probably derives from the description (*la Montagne*) bestowed on the extreme Jacobins by virtue of their elevated seating position high up at the back of the chamber of the National Convention in Paris in the early days of the Revolution. In time, the Cameronians became known as the Reformed Presbyterian Church and to this day are still strong in Ireland and especially in America where they were the first church to deny membership to slave-owners. See Drummond and Bulloch, *The Scottish Church 1688-1843*, 25-6, and Burleigh, *A Church History of Scotland*, 250-1.
84 i.e. cited by the accused.
85 *The Scots Magazine* trial report (see note 56 above) has it that William Muir's scruples were 'removed by the Rev. Mr. Dunn in prison'.
86 Not, of course, to be confused with the Reverend Thomas Hardy's loyalist polemic of the same name. See note 57 above.
87 Unusually the Robertson-Berry-Callender trial took place over five days – in February and March 1793. Callender failed to appear, was held to have 'fugitated' and was declared an outlaw. The verdict was controversial in that the activities of the Court descended into a forensic interpretation of what the accused had actually done to imply their guilt. In the event Robertson's role was adjudged the more serious in that he had *printed* as well as *published* Callender's book, whereas Berry had only *published* it. The distinction was reflected in the judgment which meted out six months' imprisonment to Robertson and three to Berry, with a fine of £100 each payable on the expiry of three years on caution or surety relative to their good behaviour over the period.
88 See Paine's *Rights of Man, Part One*: 'The town of old Sarum, which contains not three houses, sends two members; and the town of Manchester, which contains upwards of sixty thousand souls, is not admitted to send any. Is there any principle in these things? Is there anything by which you can trace the marks of freedom, or discover those of wisdom?' (Penguin Classics edition, ed. Foner, 74).
89 A 'precognition' is a term in Scots law defined as a preliminary statement from a witness in order to obtain, with a view to trial, a general appreciation of the available evidence.
90 Scots law 'voluntarily'.
91 *State Trials*, XXXIII, col. 141. *The Scots Magazine* trial report states that 'Mr. Muir called three witnesses, who proved that Mr. Lapslie was present at the taking of their precognitions. – Whereupon the Lord Advocate agreed to pass from Mr. Lapslie's examination.'

92 Only the west gable of Lapslie's former St Machan's church still stands in Clachan of Campsie (2015).
93 Murray Armstrong, *The Liberty Tree*, 21. These few lines later inspired a much longer satirical poem, entitled 'Black coats and gravats sae white' [sic], by the radical poet Alexander Rodger (1784–1846), himself imprisoned for suspected seditious activities at the height of the 'Radical War' of 1819–20. The poem is included in Rodger's posthumously published *Poems and Songs*, ed. Robert Ford (1897). Cameron prints Rodger's variant stanza on Lapslie in *The Parish of Campsie*, 11.

The anonymous author in John Kay's *Original Portraits* prints a variant: '*My name is Jamie Lapslie/I preach and I pray/And as an informer/Expect a good fee.*'– *Biographical Sketches*, II, 113. In the text accompanying Kay's uncompromising portrait of him Lapslie is said to have been 'distinguished for his active hostility to Sunday schools', an aversion he shared with many others, including the Reverend William Moodie.
94 (1759-1836). Suttie, who in 1818 took the forename of Grant, attended classes in Glasgow University in 1777 and became an advocate in 1781. He was called to the bar in 1785. Grant-Suttie became the member for Haddingtonshire in East Lothian (1818-26) and quickly earned a reputation for stern opposition to parliamentary reform and, indeed, to any 'progressive' legislation. See R. G. Thorne's article on him in the online *History of Parliament, House of Commons 1790-1820*, maintained by the Institute of Historical Research.
95 On Lapslie, see John Cameron, *The Parish of Campsie* (1892), 3-26.
96 Ronald M. Sunter, *Patronage and Politics in Scotland, 1707–1832*, 71-2 and note 53.
97 The Reverend William Dunn is named as witness number 11.
98 ['Old'] *Statistical Account of Scotland*. Lapslie's expansive account of the parish of Campsie is in volume XV (1795), number XIX, 314 – 386.
99 The Kirkintilloch society had been formed on 3 November.
100 E.g. Colin Kidd, in 'Conditional Britons: The Scots Covenanting Tradition and the Eighteenth Century British State' (*English Historical Review*, 474, 2002, 1147-76), and Harris, *The Scottish People and the French Revolution*, 29-30. See also Meikle, *Scotland and the French* Revolution, 198, 200, who is particularly helpful on the radical leanings of some ministers of the Relief church.
101 *SND*: 'Blue Gown' = 'a licensed beggar whose badge of office was a blue gown.' They were sometimes known as 'bedesmen' or 'gaberlunzies'. Scott's character, Edie Ochiltree, in his novel *The Antiquary* refers to himself as wearing the blue gown.
102 Meikle, *Scotland and the French Revolution*, 196 and note 3. The earlier of Lapslie's two letters to Dundas (27 June 1798) concerns remuneration that was outstanding to the local schoolmaster in relation to his duties as a result of the passing of the Scottish Militia act in June 1797. For a description of the duties of local schoolmasters in this context see Meikle, *op cit,* 179. But it is the later letter of August 1799 that is easily the more important. Here, incredibly, Lapslie offers himself as a candidate for appointment, first, to the chair of astronomy at the University of Glasgow, but if that were not forthcoming, to the soon to be vacant chair of church history in the same university, whose present incumbent fancied the astronomy chair, having 'too long been a mere sinecure.' (Laing Mss. ref. LA. 500, 2143-4, 2266-7, II, University of Edinburgh, Centre for Research Collections).
103 The 'Pension List of Scotland' was published in the *Scots Magazine* at the end of 1792 (and, of course, is too early for either Hardy's or Lapslie's names to figure). A total of 176 names are on the list (often, however, listing more than one beneficiary within a family), with a total expenditure of almost £25,000. Notable names on the list include those of 'Dr Hugh

Blair' (£200), 'Dr William Robertson' (£200), 'Dr Adam Fergusson' [sic] (£200) with separate pensions totalling £100 listed for *'Mrs Katherine Burnet, spouse to the said Dr Adam Fergusson [sic], and Isabella, Mary, and Margaret Fergusson, his daughters', and the judge 'Francis Garden of Gardenston, Esq'. One may speculate on the reasons for pensions to have been awarded to such individuals: in the case of Ferguson, for example, it is well known that he came to the attention of the government at the outset of the American war and that his adversarial attitude towards the American cause may serve to explain not only why the state bore the expense of publication of his 1776 pamphlet criticising Richard Price's pro-rebel stance, but that his pension may have been a reward for services rendered when he had acted as secretary to the ill-fated Carlisle Commission of 1778.

A report to the House of Commons by a Select Committee on Pensions of 24 July 1838 makes the following caustic comments on government pensions in Scotland in the period covered in this chapter: 'In Scotland, until 1810, an unrestricted power existed of charging the hereditary Revenue; no provision was made to afford adequate security in this respect through the responsibility of the Ministers, or to allow public opinion to pronounce a judgment upon the advice given to the Sovereign. ... Pensions were granted for life or for lives, in possession or in reversion, without restriction in amount or in the duration of the grant.'

*Katherine was the favourite niece of Adam Ferguson's relative, the chemist Joseph Black. She bore Ferguson four sons and three daughters.

104 Laing Mss. ref. LA. 500, II, 2170, University of Edinburgh, Centre for Research Collections.
105 Scott, *Fasti*, 'New Edition', III, 484.

Chapter 7

1   Scott, *Fasti*, 'New Edition', v. I, 68.
2   Ibid., 326-7.
3   Alexander Broadie, *The Scottish Enlightenment* (2001), 146.
4   Ann Matheson, 'Preaching in the Churches of Scotland', in *The Oxford Handbook of the British Sermon 1689-1901*, 158.
5   Ibid., 162.
6   F.P. Lock, *Edmund Burke. Volume II: 1784-1797*, 285.
7   Ibid.
8   Sher, *Church and University in the Scottish Enlightenment* (Edinburgh Classic Editions) (2016), 262.
9   Ibid., 189 note 75. See Anand Chitnis, *The Scottish Enlightenment: a social history* (1976), 241.
10 McIntosh, *Church and Theology in Enlightenment Scotland*, 218.
11 'The only Popular writer to raise the issue', according to McIntosh, was the Reverend John Dun (1752-92), minister of Auchinleck, tutor to James Boswell.
12 *The Charge of Sedition and Faction against Good Men, especially Faithful Ministers, considered and accounted for* (Glasgow, Bryce and Paterson, 1758; reprinted Belfast, 1759), 31.
13 The passage to which Witherspoon had taken exception in Paine's pamphlet begins: 'Yet I should be glad to ask how they suppose kings came at first?' See *WJW*, 3, 23-4 – the long footnote to the sermon, *The Dominion of Providence over the Passions of Men* (1776); and *Common Sense* in *The Thomas Paine Reader*, eds. Foot and Kramnick, 76-7. See also chapter 8, 214.
14 *John* 3, 3.
15 Snodgrass's SSPCK sermon is entitled *Leading Doctrines of the Gospel Stated and Defended* (Edinburgh, 1794) and was preached in the High Church of Edinburgh (Hugh Blair's charge) on 29 May that year. See *Church and Theology in Enlightenment Scotland*, 198-9.

16 *Leading Doctrines of the Gospel Stated and Defended*, 19.
17 See chapter 2, 73-76, and also Crawford, *LWJW* (2014), especially my 'Concluding Essay', 287-300.
18 John Snodgrass's Middle Church did not exist in the Paisley of Witherspoon's day, having opened its doors in 1781. Yet it is likely that the two knew each other since Snodgrass was born in Paisley (in 1744) and conceivably attended the Laigh Church as a boy. In 1784, on the occasion of Witherspoon's return to Scotland, when he had preached before packed congregations in Paisley, it is almost certain they would have met. See Scott, *Fasti*, New Series, v. III, 179.
19 Colin Kidd, 'Enlightenment and anti-Enlightenment in eighteenth-century Scotland', in Dunyach and Thomson, *The Enlightenment in Scotland. National and International Perspectives* (2015), 62-3.
20 Ibid., 63.
21 Maxwell describes himself in many of his titles as 'Poet in Paisley' and/or 'S.D.P.' ('Student of Divine Poetry'). His versifying at times rivals that of William McGonigall at his worst, yet his comments on contemporary issues, including in 'On the French Revolution' and 'A Touch on the Times', offer insight into the presence of right-wing loyalist views existing inside a radical hotspot, the town of Paisley, at a key period in its history.
22 Kidd (2016) refines and updates his Kilwinning hypothesis in a later essay discussed in chapter 5.
23 My unpublished PhD thesis contains a chapter on Wilson (290-344) and sections on Kennedy (293-5; 331-7). For more on Wilson and Kennedy see Hook, *Scotland and America. A study of cultural relations 1750-1835*, Second Edition (2008), 140, 158, 241-2 (Wilson) and 240-1 (Kennedy); on Wilson in particular see Meikle, *Scotland and the French Revolution*, 120-1. Much more remains to be discovered about Kennedy's post-Paisley career.
24 See extracts from Wilson's political poem *Address to the Synod of Glasgow and Ayr* (1792) in the Postscript to this chapter.
25 Clark's table gives *estimated* membership (where it can safely be identified) of presbyteries within the Synod of Glasgow and Ayr in three base years: 1755, 1780 and 1805. In the quarter-century between 1780 and 1805 a steady increase of Popular party ministers is revealed until, by 1805, out of a total of 19 parishes in the presbytery only one Moderate minister can be identified (though from an admittedly low sample of 7, where the affiliation of the minister is not in doubt). (*Moderatism and the Moderate Party in the Church of Scotland, 1752-1805*, 182).
26 The Burgess Roll held in Paisley Central Library records the admission of twelve members of the 'Associate' (or Antiburgher) congregation to burgess status on 8 February 1760. Names of those signing the Roll include those of their minister, James Ellis [sic], and the circulating bookshop proprietor and bookbinder, Robert Aitken (1735-1802), who emigrated to Philadelphia in 1771 and set up business there as a printer, publisher and binder, retaining his Antiburgher beliefs. It was Aitken who first introduced Witherspoon to Paine, both of whom supplied articles for Aitken's *Pennsylvania Magazine*.
27 See chapter 5, note 35 and chapter 6, note 14 for more on Alice (*aka* Ellis) in both a political and ministerial context. For the list of representatives of urban societies of Friends of the People at their first General Convention, see Meikle, *Scotland and the French Revolution*, Appendix A, 240, where Alice's name is rendered 'Alcie (?)'.
28 According to a letter published in the *Glasgow Courier* on 23 January 1796 signed by Archibald Morison, 'weaver, Broomlands' and five other weavers in Paisley. The letter is reprinted in a

pamphlet published in Ayr in the same year, *Review of a paper published in the Glasgow Courier, on the 23 January, 1796, called a Deed of the Relief Congregation of Paisley*. See also Crawford, *Scotland, America and Tom Paine*, 90-1.
29   'Mountaineers' were members of the religious sect known as 'Cameronians'. See also chapter 6, note 83.
30   Maxwell ('J.M.'), *Issachar, the strong ass, over-burdened; or, the Groans of Brittannia* [sic] *from the Pitt. A poem descriptive of the times. Part II.* (Paisley? 1795?), 7.
31   *Lectures on Rhetoric and Belles Lettres*, v. I (1783), 114.
32   Ibid., 108.
33   'On Gentleness', Sermon VI, in *Sermons*, v. I, 1794, 155-6.
34   Ibid., 'On the Death of Christ', 143.
35   'On Sensibility', in *Sermons*, v. III, 1794, 35-6.
36   'On the Disorders of the Passions', 'Sermon VII' in the first (Creech) edition of 1777 of *Sermons, by Hugh Blair D.D.* The book was published in Edinburgh on 8 February and in London on 15 April.
37   v. I, 1794, 194-5.
38   Blair's footnote gives the source of the italicised phrase as '* 1 Kings, xviii, 44.'
39   v. I, 1794, 202-3.
40   *The wicked life, and fatal but deserved death, of Haman, Ahasuerus's prime minister: A Sermon, preached before the Magistrates of Edinburgh, on the day of election, in the year 1740. By Alexander Webster, A.M. one of the ministers of Edinburgh ... The Second Edition*, (Edinburgh, 1797), 'The Preface', vi. See also the *Postscript* to this chapter for an extract from Alexander Wilson's poem *Address to the Synod of Glasgow and Ayr* (1792) who similarly uses the story of Haman for political purposes.
41   See *Boswell in Extremes, 1776-1778*, ed. Weiss and Pottle, 56, 88, 359-60; and Richard B. Sher, 'Scottish Divines and Legal Lairds', in *New Light on Boswell*, ed. Clingham, 39-40.
42   Ann Matheson, 'Hugh Blair's Sermons', in *The Edinburgh History of the Book in Scotland*, v. 2, *Enlightenment and expansion*, eds. Brown and McDougall, 473.
43   See note 4 above.
44   See chapter 6, note 57.
45   'On the Love of our Country', 'Sermon VI', in Blair's *Sermons*, v. V (1791), 115.
46   'On the Love of our Country', 117.
47   Diderot, *Oeuvres complètes*, ed. Assevat and Tourneaux, V, 812. Cited in Pagden, *The Enlightenment and why it still matters*, (2013), 273 and 387, note 88.
48   Pagden, *The Enlightenment and why it still matters*, 275.
49   E.g. by Nigel Leask in 'Thomas Muir and *The Telegraph*: radical cosmopolitanism in 1790s Scotland', *History Workshop Journal*, no. 63, Spring, 2007, 48-69.
50   'On the Love of our Country', 120.
51   See note 57 below.
52   Ibid., 123.
53   Cf. Article 10 of the French Declaration of the Rights of Man and of the Citizen, as approved by the National Assembly on 26 August 1789: 'No one shall be disquieted on account of his opinions, including his religious views, provided their manifestation does not disturb the public order established by law.' See Grayling, *Towards the Light. The story of the struggles for liberty & rights that made the modern west* (2007), Appendix 3, 287.
54   'On the Love of our Country', 134-5.
55   Ibid., 126.

56 Price, *A Discourse upon the Love of Our Country* (1789), 3.
57 Despite, that is, the royal proclamation of 21 May 1792 against seditious writings. 'Is there a single man amongst you', Thomas Muir asked the jury at his trial, 'who has not read the works either of Paine or of Burke?' (Howell, *State Trials*, v. xxxiii, 206). See also chapter 6, note 40.
58 'On the Love of our Country', 127.
59 *Rights of Man. Part One* (1791), ed. Foner, 119.
60 'On the Love of our Country', 128.
61 Ibid., 129.
62 Ibid., 130-1.
63 Ibid., 135.
64 *An Address to the Public from the Friends of the Liberty of the Press*, attributed to Erskine (1793), 10.
65 'On the Love of our Country', 138.
66 *The Moral Culture of the Scottish Enlightenment*, 138.
67 *National Depravity*, 2.
68 *John*, 3, 19.
69 *National Depravity*, 9-10.
70 Ibid., 11.
71 Ibid., 13.
72 Ibid., 15-16.
73 Ibid., 18.
74 *National Depravity*, 19.
75 Ibid., 19-20.
76 Ibid., 21-22.
77 *The Sentiments and Conduct Becoming Britons in the Present Conjuncture* (1794), 2-3. This Robert Walker (1755-1808), sometimes known as the 'skating minister' after the famous painting of him attributed to Raeburn, is not to be confused with the Reverend Robert Walker (1716-83), first charge minister of the High Church in St. Giles, author of *Sermons on Practical Subjects* (1765), a leading member of the Popular party and a staunch opponent of patronage; his sermons were published under the editorship of Hugh Blair.
    For the full text of Pitt's great speech, and the circumstances in which he made it, see Hathaway ed., *The Speeches of the Right Honourable William Pitt, in the House of Commons*, v. II (1806), 166-179.
78 Cockburn, *An Examination of the Trials for Sedition which have hitherto occurred in Scotland*, v. 2 (1888), 41.
79 Vincent, 'The Responses of Scottish Churchmen to the French Revolution, 1789-1802', *Scottish Historical Review*, v. LXXIII, 2: No. 196: October 1994, 191-215.
80 Sinclair, *OSA*, v. 16 (1795), 44.
81 *National Depravity*, 22-3.
82 1726-92. This David Dalrymple is not to be confused with his distant cousin, contemporary and namesake, the future Lord Westhall (1719-84). Both Dalrymples were involved as defence counsel in the Court of Session action against John Witherspoon lasting fourteen years from 1762 to 1776 – the so-called Snodgrass affair, discussed in chapter 2.
83 Dalrymple was the author of *Annals of Scotland*, 2 vols., 1776-79.
84 *Sermon on the death of Sir David Dalrymple*, 25, 27.
85 Ibid., 28-9.
86 Ibid., 29-30.

87 Ibid., 31.
88 Ibid., 32.
89 Meikle, *Scotland and the French Revolution*, Appendix A, 270.
90 Henry Scott, third Duke of Buccleuch and fifth Duke of Queensberry (1746-1812). As a young man Adam Smith had served as his tutor on a tour of Europe which had begun in 1764; after that the two men were friends for life. Buccleuch married Lady Elizabeth Montagu in 1767; she outlived her husband, surviving to the ripe old age of 84.
91 *The Love of Our Country Explained and Enforced*, 2.
92 Ibid.
93 Ibid.
94 Ibid., 10.
95 Ibid., 19.
96 Ibid., 19-20.
97 Ibid., 27. For an account of the landing by three French frigates of 1,500 troops on the Welsh coast near Fishguard on 22 February 1797 see Rodger, *The Command of the Ocean. A naval history of Britain, 1649 to 1815* (2004), 438: 'In military terms the expedition was pure comic opera, but its consequences for the government in London were not at all funny. The news that French troops were ashore on the British mainland caused a run on the banks.' Curiously, another version of the same event denies that no landings were made. See Knight, *Britain against Napoleon. The organisation of victory, 1793-1815* (2013), 85-6; and Thomas, *Britain's Last Invasion. Fishguard 1797* (2007).
98 We can date the poem to November, 1792 from the dedication 'To James Wardrop of Spring Bank, Esq.' See Grosart, ed., *The Poems and Literary Prose of Alexander Wilson, the American Ornithologist* (2 vols., Paisley, 1876), v. 2, 70-75 (extract stanzas, 74-5).
99 In *Treason! or Not Treason! alias The Weavers Budget. By James Kennedy, Scotch Exile* (1795), 19-20.
100 'Crimp' = 'an agent who procures seamen, soldiers, etc., *esp.* by decoying or impressing them' (*OED*).

Chapter 8

1 *Correspondence of Adam Ferguson*, ed. Merolle (1995), v. 1, 227. For more on the 'redress of grievances' in the context of the mission of the doomed Carlisle Commission of 1778 see Hartley, *Letters on the American War* (1779), Sixth Edition, Letter IV, 93 f.
2 Anderson's letter and enclosures are transcribed in *The Papers of George Washington, Presidential Series*, v. 13, 1 June-31 August 1793, ed. Christine Sternberg Patrick (2007), 547-552. See also Crawford, *Professor Anderson, Dr Franklin and President Washington* (2014), Appendix C, 81-3.
3 *Scotland and America A Study of Cultural Relations, 1750-1835*, 47-8.
4 Ibid., 69.
5 Cited by Devine (*To the Ends of the Earth*, 136) from Boyd, *The Declaration of Independence and the Evolution of the Text* (1945), 34-5.
6 Witherspoon was by no means alone in considering the time ripe for political sermons. Benjamin Rush wrote that Paine's *Common Sense* (1776) in the year of its publication was, 'instead of a sermon', delivered from the pulpit by 'a clergyman in Connecticut': cited in *Liberty & the American Revolution. Selections from the Collection of Sid Lapidus*, Exhibition Catalogue, Princeton University Library (2009), 68.
7 *The Charge of Sedition and Faction against Good Men* (1758), *WJW*, 2, 438. Witherspoon did not always, however, conform to his own rule in that regard. See, in particular, the sermon *A*

Prayer for National Prosperity (London, 1758) in which he castigates the poor performance of the British and allied 'fleets and armies' to date, before the victories in the *annus mirabilis* of the following year.

8   This sermon is lost. JW says that it was preached in Paisley in August 1758 on a text from *Psalms* 74, 22.
9   *WJW*, 4, 297-299.
10 Collins, *President Witherspoon* (1925), 2, 163.
11 *WJW*, 3, 30.
12 Ibid., 33-4.
13 Ibid., 36.
14 Ibid., 23-4. See chapter 7, note 13 for an explanation of JW's footnote on original sin and its relevance to Paine.
15 Ibid., 2, 437 ff. The sermon, *The Charge of Sedition and Faction against Good Men*, was preached on 7 September 1758 and subsequently published in Glasgow by Bryce and Paterson. The ordinand was the Reverend Archibald Davidson (d. 1803) who, after a ministry at Inchinnan, would serve as Principal of the University of Glasgow from 1785 to 1803.
16 *John*, 3:3.
17 *WJW*, 3, 46.
18 The Reverend Ezra Stiles (1727-95) was seventh president of Yale College. His best known published work is probably the sermon *The United States elevated to Glory and Honor* (New-Haven, 1783).
19 Stiles, *Literary Diary*, 2: 185, cited by Gideon Mailer in 'Anglo-Scottish Union and John Witherspoon's American Revolution', *The William and Mary Quarterly*, Vol. 67, No. 4 (October 2010), 744. Mailer notes: 'For Stiles the responsibility for the bloody battle that America fought with Britain lay with nationalistic Scots such as Witherspoon.' (ibid.)
20 For an account of the backlash in Scotland and elsewhere in Britain roused by JW's sermon see Sher, 'Witherspoon's *Dominion of Providence* and the Scottish Jeremiad Tradition', in Sher and Smitten, ed. *Scotland and America in the Age of the Enlightenment* (1990), 58-61.
21 In the 'Advertisement' prefacing the 1778 London edition of *Dominion of Providence* it is claimed that 'the discourse contains many admirable hints of advice, which, if properly regarded, will tend to the prosperity of both countries'. The title page incorrectly gives the date of the sermon as 'May 17, 1775'.
22 *An Address to the Natives of Scotland*, (separate) London ed., 1778, 2-3.
23 For an explanation of the significance of *North Briton* no. XLV see Robin Eagles, 'The treaty of Paris, John Wilkes and North Briton Number 45', in *The History of Parliament*, online blog, posted 23 April 2013. Alternatively (and more conventionally), see Thomas, *George III King and Politicians 1760-1770* (2002), 98-100.
24 There are numerous contemporary published examples that may be cited in evidence of the prevalence of anti-Scottish sentiment in England at this time, including the anonymous *A North Briton Extraordinary: Written by a young Scotsman, now a Volunteer in the Corsican Service* (London, 1769): '... the present taste of political writing, is, at all events, to revile the poor Scots.' (p. 14). Hook thinks the pamphlet was 'probably by Boswell'. (*Scotland and America*, 63).
25 Hook, *Scotland and America*, 64. See also Devine, *To the Ends of the Earth*, 135-9.
26 Devine, ibid., 137 and note 51, p. 342, citing Wallace Brown, *The King's Friends* (1965), 51. It is disappointing that the latest study of loyalism and its aftermath once the American war ended, Maya Jasanoff's *Liberty's Exiles The Loss of America and the Remaking of the British Empire*

(2011), has little to add to Brown's work in relation to the Scottish context of her otherwise excellent book.
27 The Hugh Simm papers are in the Firestone Library, Princeton University (see Bibliography). See also Crawford, Strathclyde University PhD thesis, *Scotland, America and Tom Paine* (2011), 243-6; De Wolfe, *Discoveries of America* (1997), 122-148; and Butterfield, *John Witherspoon Comes to America* (1953), 83. Simm died in 1810 and an obituary of him appears in the *Glasgow Sentinel* of 19 July that year.
28 Edward Dilly, the older brother, came to Paisley in 1761 probably at the invitation of Witherspoon, who was then engaged in writing his *Practical Treatise on Regeneration* which the Dilly brothers published in 1764. In the course of his visit Dilly was admitted an honorary burgess of Paisley and signed the Burgess roll. See Crawford, *LWJW*, 33-4 and note 62.
29 *Life of Samuel Johnson* ed. Womersley (2008), 555.
30 Franklin was the most active member of the Committee which was set up by the Continental Congress on 29 November 1775. See *Journals of the Continental Congress* (online) (Library of Congress), v.3, 392.
31 The Franklin Papers at Yale website records hundreds of exchanges involving Franklin and Lee over the period 1771 to 1787.
32 *Wealth of Nations Books IV-V*, ed. Skinner, Book IV, VII, Part Third, 199. [1st. (London) ed. of 1776, v. II, 223.]
33 Ibid., 194. [1st. (London) ed. of 1776, v. II, 217.] The italics are Lee's own; Smith continues the sentence beyond 'Colonies' to read: ', without in the least increasing, but on the contrary diminishing that of the country in whose favour it is established.'
34 Letter dated 'London, August 13, 1776', v. 1: 929, American Archives Collection, Northern Illinois University.
35 Hutcheson, *A System of Moral Philosophy* (1755), v. II, Book III, Chapter 5, 227.
36 David Fate Norton, 'Francis Hutcheson in America', in *Studies on Voltaire and the Eighteenth Century*, 154 (1976), 1547-68.
37 Hutcheson, *A Short Introduction to Moral Philosophy* (1747), 316-17; Liberty Fund edition, ed. Turco (2007), 265. Hutcheson makes a similar defence of the rights of colonists in his *System* v. II, Book III, 8, 306-9.
38 'I made that Man my Enemy', wrote Franklin, 'by doing him too much Kindness. 'Tis the honestest way of acquiring an Enemy.' See *Benjamin Franklin Writings* (1987), 798: letter to Mary Stevenson, March 25, 1763.
39 *Op. cit.* note 36 above.
40 *Correspondence of Adam Smith*, ed. Mossner and Ross (1977), 151.
41 *Wealth of Nations Books IV-V*, ed. Skinner, Book IV, VII, Part Third, 208. [1st. (London) ed. of 1776, v. II, 234.] As a strictly non-economist myself I express here my gratitude to the late Professor Andrew S. Skinner FBA (1935-2011), formerly Adam Smith Professor of Economics at my *alma mater*, the University of Glasgow, for presenting me a year or two before his untimely death with a copy of an unpublished paper of his entitled 'Francis Hutcheson and Adam Smith: visions of America', on which some of the ideas in this section of the chapter are based (and which I found helpful in my PhD research), especially the links between Hutcheson and Smith and their relevance to the American question. See also Winch, *Adam Smith's Politics* (1978), Chapter 3, 'Hutcheson and Smith: Real Whig versus sceptical Whig', 46-69; and Chapter 4, 'Commerce, liberty and justice', 70-102.
42 *Ibid.*, (Skinner), 209. [1st. (London) ed. of 1776, v. II, 235.] Also, see note 62 below for a similar sentiment expressed by William Thom.

43 Ibid., (Skinner), 197. [1st. (London) ed. of 1776, v. II, 221.]
44 'Of the First Principles of Government', in *David Hume Selected Essays*, ed. Copley and Edgar (2008), 28.
45 Ibid., 25. In an affectionate letter of 8 December 1775 to his nephew and namesake, the future Baron David Hume, then a student of Professor John Millar at Glasgow, Hume tells him that while he 'cannot but agree' with Millar that 'the Republican Form of [Government] is by far the best', it is 'only fitted for a small State; and any Attempt towards it can in our [Country], produce only Anarchy, which is the immediate forerunner of Despotism.' He ends his letter referring to Harrington as 'an Author of Genius; but chimerical.' [*Letters*, ed. Greig, v. II (1932), letter 512, 305-7.]
46 *Letters*, v. II, letter 307, 21.
47 Ibid., letter 321, 42.
48 Ibid., letter 509, 300-01.
49 Ibid., 301, note 1.
50 Ibid., letter 511, 304-05.
51 Ned C. Landsman, Oxford *DNB* contribution on William Thom, OUP, online ed., 2016. (Accessed 15 November, 2016).
52 Morren, *Annals 1739-52*, 102, 106, 361.
53 Near the close of 'this unusual sermon' Thom makes it clear that it was preached over a forenoon and afternoon. (*Works*, 221).
54 In 1770 Thom made a further verbal assault on Traill, *A Vindication of Doctor Tail, from the Charge of Heresy*.
55 Thom, *Works* (1799), 163.
56 Thom, *Works*, 165.
57 I am grateful to my good friend of many years, and *nonpareil* Burnsian, Dr Andrew Noble, who having read a draft of this chapter, drew my attention to the similarity in sentiment between (especially this section of) Thom's sermon and Burns's caustic anti-American war posture in his *Address of Beelzebub*. See the *Postscript* to this chapter.
58 Ibid., 182.
59 Ibid.
60 Ibid., 195.
61 Ibid., 196.
62 See reference to Smith's *Wealth of Nations*, note 42 above.
63 This is obviously the one 'advantage' from Thom's list that is grossly exaggerated. Thom preached his sermon in 1770. Just two years before, the *Peggy*, out of Greenock, with John Witherspoon and family aboard, took eleven weeks to sail from Greenock to the Delaware. She was a brigantine, a two-masted ship with square rigging on the foremast and fore-and-aft rigging on the mainmast. Other lighter ships, built for speed (e.g. Royal Navy frigates), could make the crossing (depending on the tides, time of year, wind and state of the sea) in perhaps six to eight weeks.
64 Thom, *Works*, 198-210.
65 Ibid., 199.
66 Modern Corkerhill is located in Glasgow G52, just a few miles from Govan and the eastern boundary of Paisley.
67 De Wolfe, *Discoveries of America* (1997), 109.

68 De Wolfe's source is the collection known as the 'James Whitelaw Papers' held by the Vermont Historical Society at Montpelier, VT. For the identification of Thomson's correspondent as William Thom of Govan, see William Whitelaw to James Whitelaw, March 25 1774, Whitelaw Papers MS 29. (Ibid., 88 note 1, 109 note 48).
69 See Bibliography under 'Primary sources – Manuscripts'.
70 For more on Simm see Crawford, *LWJW*, 207 and note 25.
71 *Scots Magazine*, xxx (June 1768), 300, in a footnote to a long extract from JW's 'Farewell Sermon', comments that 'he departed from Paisley, and imbarked [sic] at Greenock, for New Jersey, in May last, with his wife, children, and servants.' The 'servants' have never been identified.
72 E.g. his 'Advertisement' entitled *'Lands to be settled in North America'* in the *Scots Magazine*, v. xxxiv, Sept. 1772, 482-3.
73 See Yeager, *Enlightened Evangelicalism* (2011), Chapter 7, 'Friend to America', 141-63.
74 Ross, *The Life of Adam Smith*, Second Ed., (2010), 154.
75 For more on John Anderson *primus* see chapter 5, 'Heresy'.
76 For Anderson's extensive American associations see Crawford, *Professor Anderson, Dr. Franklin and President Washington* (2014).
77 Robert Kent Donovan, 'Evangelical Civic Humanism in Glasgow: The American War Sermons of William Thom', in *The Glasgow Enlightenment*, ed. Hook and Sher (1995), 227-45.
78 Thom, *Works*, 79.
79 The doctrine of passive obedience and non-resistance was at its height among Tory churchmen in the period from the Restoration to the Glorious Revolution during which time it was declaimed from pulpits and extolled in pamphlets in order to bolster the notion of royal absolutism, *e.g.* by Robert South, Gilbert Burnet and Edward Stillingfleet among others. In his posthumously published *Patriarcha* (1680) Sir Robert Filmer held that the laws were the expression of the king's will and that virtually everything he did was lawful and unable to be resisted. To a more limited extent, the doctrine persisted into Queen Anne's reign and in 1712 Berkeley published his own thoughts on the issue, insisting repeatedly that 'no act of rebellion against a *de facto* ruler (here he means Queen Anne) can be justified.' (See Ross, 'Was Berkeley a Jacobite?', in *Eighteenth-Century Ireland*, v. 20 (2005), 17-30). The controversy was briefly revived in Scotland as late as 1754 by the judge and Jacobite sympathiser, Lord Dun (David Erskine), whose *Friendly and Familiar Advices* (1754) was scathingly answered in the same year by the Reverend Robert Wallace in his *The Doctrine of Passive Obedience and non-Resistance Considered* (Edinburgh, 1754). Hume, too, dealt with the issue, from a different viewpoint, and with different conclusions, in the *Treatise of Human Nature* (1739-40) and *Essays* (1760). Of more immediate interest here, however, is that in addition to Thom, George Campbell and Alexander Carlyle also refer to passive obedience and non-resistance in their 1776 fast day sermons: *Duty of Allegiance*, 17; *Justice and Necessity*, 10.
80 Thom, *Works*, 79.
81 *WJW*, 3, 437, *Lectures on Moral Philosophy*, Lecture XII, 'Of Civil Society'.
82 Thom, *Works*, 78.
83 *Epistle of James* 2,6.
84 Thom, *Works*, 117.
85 Ibid., 112.
86 See Cobbett, *Parliamentary History of England*, v. XIX, 1777-78, 317.
87 Thom, *Works*, 118-9.

88 George Campbell cites the same text in his *Duty of Allegiance* sermon, second edition (1778), 10.
89 The quotation is from *Jeremiah* 8, 20.
90 Thom, *Works*, 153.
91 Ibid., 147.
92 Ibid., 147-8.
93 Donovan, *op cit*, 237.
94 While his reference to 'imperfect' and 'perfect' rights has its origin in the Aristotelian theory of justice – with its divisibility into 'corrective' (or 'commutative') and 'distributive' justice – it is more than likely that Thom learned the theory sitting at the feet of Francis Hutcheson (*A Short Introduction*, 113-4; *System*, 2.3.3, v. I, 257) while a student at Glasgow. In that regard, Thom has at least something in common with Adam Smith who similarly cites the notion of two kinds of rights and two notions of justice: 'We may here observe the distinction which Mr Hutchinson [sic], after Baron Puffendorf, has made of rights. He divides them into *jura perfecta* and *imperfecta*, i.e. perfect and imperfe(c)t rights.– ... The common way in which we understand the word right, is the same as what we have called a perfect right, and is that which relates to commutative justice. Imperfect rights, again, refer to distributive justice. The former are the rights which we are to consider, the latter not properly belonging to jurisprudence, but rather to a system of moralls as they do not fall under the jurisdiction of the laws. We are therefore in what follows to confine ourselves entirely to the perfect rights, and what is called commutative justice.' [*Lectures on Jurisprudence*, ed. Meek, Raphael and Stein (1978), 9.] See also Fleischacker, *A Short History of Distributive Justice* (2004), especially 1.1 'Two kinds of justice.'
95 *WJW*, 3, Lecture VIII, '*Lectures on Moral Philosophy*', 407-8.
96 Ibid., 'Recapitulation', 472.
97 Thom, *Works*, 157.
98 In May 1771 Elliot had acquired the premises and stock of the bookseller, William Sands, on the east side of Parliament Square. On Elliot's death from 1791 onward the shop was run by Bell & Bradfute. The titlepage of the Edinburgh *Common Sense* merely states that Elliot and Stirling 'sold' the title in their bookshops but it is likely that they co-published it.
99 Anderson was an importer of illegal Irish reprints. See Sher, *The Enlightenment & the Book*, 356.
100 One edition was printed by the entrepreneurial Paine at his own expense and delivered by him to the Bradfords at eight pence halfpenny each to be sold by them at 'one shilling each, or tenpence by the dozen.'– Keane, *Tom Paine A Political Life* (1995), 109-110.
101 Gimbel, *A Bibliographical Check List of "Common Sense" with an Account of its Publication* (1956), 79-80.
102 The Reverend Dr Alexander Webster (1707-84), minister of the Tolbooth Church in Edinburgh from 1737 until his death, was 'one of the main leaders' of the Popular party in the mid-eighteenth century (McIntosh, 243). See frontispiece illustration of Webster in action in his pulpit.
103 The Reverend Robert Walker (1716-83), minister of the High Kirk (St Giles') from 1754 until his death, was an evangelical preacher and a leading opponent of patronage. (McIntosh, *Church and Theology*, 242-3).
104 The Reverend David Johnston (1734-1824) was minister of North Leith Church from 1765 to 1799. He received an honorary D.D. from Edinburgh in 1781 and was appointed one of His Majesty's Chaplains in Ordinary in 1793. Scott notes that he declined a knighthood in 1812. (*Fasti*, New Edition, v. 1, 156).

105 Boswell wrote to Blair on 24 February conveying his concern that Blair had preached against the Americans and prayed for their defeat, whereas he maintained their resistance was 'not rebellion'. He goes on to ask, 'If Nation may pray against Nation, may not Individual pray against Individual?' (Pottle, Abbott and Pottle, *Catalogue of the Papers of James Boswell at Yale University* (1993), v. 1, L59, 146).
106 Donaldson (1727-94) probably bought his way into the partnership with Alexander Kincaid to form the celebrated book trade business they ran for seven years from 1751. Donaldson went his separate way in 1758 and 'made a fortune in the reprint trade'. (Sher, *The Enlightenment and the Book* (2006), 313-16).
107 John Maclaurin (1734-96), advocate, elevated to the bench in 1789 as Lord Dreghorn. He was the author of several anonymous satires and clever, if occasionally naughty, lampoons. See chapter 4, 119-121.
108 *Boswell's Edinburgh Journals 1767-1786*, ed. Milne (2013), 278.
109 Erskine, *Shall I go to War with my American Brethren?* (Edinburgh, 1776), 'Preface', v.
110 *The Equity and Wisdom of Administration, in Measures that have unhappily occasioned the American Revolt, tried by the Sacred Oracles*; and *Reflections on the Rise, Progress, and probable Consequences, of the Present Contentions with the Colonies. By a Freeholder.*
111 Johnston, *The signal Deliverances which have been wrought for these Kingdoms, and the most probable means of obtaining a like Divine Interposition in the present conjuncture of public affairs* (Edinburgh, 1779).
112 Campbell was principal of Marischal College, Aberdeen and author of *The Philosophy of Rhetoric*, 2 vols., (1776), a work that 'stresses the power of the orator'. [Broadie, *The Scottish Enlightenment An Anthology* (1997), 685.]
113 Both titles were extensively reprinted in America and their popularity was largely responsible for Price receiving an invitation to visit America in order to address Congress, an invitation which he declined. The invitation was delivered personally to Price by Benjamin Franklin, Arthur Lee and John Adams. *Observations* was reprinted in Edinburgh in 1776. Price wrote to Franklin, with whom he had a fairly steady correspondence, on 14 October 1779: 'The clouds gather frightfully over this country. I am waiting for the issue with anxiety, but at the Same time with much complacency in the reflexion, that at this most important period I have endeavoured to act the part of a faithful and good citizen.' (Founders Online; original MS. in American Philosophical Society).
114 Footnote (a) of the second edition of Campbell's published sermon (1778), 24-5. A reprint of the eighth edition of Price's *Observations* had been published by Wood and Dickson in Edinburgh in 1776.
115 In his prefatory 'Advertisement' Carlyle says that his sermon 'should have been published some time ago', a delay which accounts for his ability to take note of Campbell's published sermon in his citation, together with references to Roebuck and the anonymous author of *The Rights of Great Britain Asserted – Justice and Necessity*, footnote, 10.
116 Ibid., 21.
117 Ibid., 36-7.
118 Ibid., 49-50. Cf. 'Life, Liberty and the pursuit of Happiness' in the Declaration.

Chapter 9

1. Reprinted by the Stair Society for the Law Society of Scotland, 1993. John Millar described Bankton's *Institute* as gathering together 'a most laborious Collection of Facts' containing many things not found in Erskine or Stair, but 'Collected with little Judgement.' – Cited by John W. Cairns in '"Famous as a School for Law, as Edinburgh … for medicine': Legal Education in Glasgow, 1761-1801", *The Glasgow Enlightenment*, ed. Hook and Sher (1995), 148.
2. Reprinted in Falkirk in 1779 'for W. Burns, *Preacher*, the Publisher'.
3. Blair was second charge minister of the Canongate from 1743 to 1754 before accepting a call to Lady Yester's Church – his successor there was William Robertson – where he served for four years until his translation to St. Giles' (his admission to Trinity Parish having been delayed). See Scott, *Fasti*, New Edition, v. I (1915), 29, 68, 82.
4. Previously minister of Kirkintilloch, 1744-53; Culross, 1753-8; New Greyfriars, 1758-67.
5. Originally preached 'before the Synod of Perth and Stirling at Perth' on October 16, 1754, and subsequently printed by Robert Foulis of Glasgow for Robert Banks, 'bookseller in Stirling' in 1758. The London version of 1779 contains an 'Advertisement' by Fordyce and is almost a different work from his synodical sermon of twenty-one years previously.
6. 'Reverend' Daniel Macarthur (d. 1808) was a master in the Grammar School in Glasgow for 25 years (according to his tombstone inscription, Ramshorn churchyard, Ingram Street), and is probably the same man who acted as tutor to young Thomas Muir and gave evidence at his trial. See *State Trials*, v. 23, col. 178.
7. *A Legal History of Scotland*, V, 'The Eighteenth Century' (1998), chapter 9, 'The Church', 271. At the same time, Walker notes that a Catholic bishop (Hugh McDonald) having evaded his pursuers for a lengthy time was arrested in 1755 and tried in the High Court for being 'by habit and repute a Popish priest' (ibid). He was 'merely banished and took refuge in the Cabrach district of Banffshire'. See also William Forbes Leith, *Memoirs of Scottish Catholics during the XVIIth and XVIIIth Centuries*, v.2 (1909), 354.
8. The Society of Jesus, the Jesuit order, was 'extinguished' and 'suppressed' by papal edict in 1773.
9. Stat. 33 Geo. III. c. 44 (3 June 1793). This legislation prescribed 'a certain form of oath of abjuration and declaration' to be sworn by Catholics, relieving them from certain, but by no means all the 'pains, penalties and disabilities' imposed on them in 1700. See John Erskine, *An Institute of the Law of Scotland*, ed. James Ivory, V. I (1824), Bk. II, Tit. III, 264-5, footnote †.
10. *Ferguson v Glendonwyne*. See Morison, *Decisions of the Court of Session*, v. XXI-XXII, 'Member of Parliament', February 17, 1803, No. 122, 8733.
11. Stat. 10 Geo. IV. c. 7 (13 April 1829). See William Bell, *Dictionary and Digest of the Law of Scotland* (1838), 'Roman Catholics', 868-70.
12. [Baron] David Hume, *Commentaries on the Law of Scotland, respecting the Description and Punishment of Crimes*, v. II (1797), 'Offences against Religion', 'V. Popery', XXIX, 535.
13. *Principal Acts of the General Assembly*, 1746, 8.
14. Morren, *Annals 1752-1766*, 257-8.
15. The annual *Principal Acts of the General Assembly* specify these regions over many years as 'South Uist, Small-Isles [Eigg, Muck, Rum and Canna], Glenco[e], Harris, the Countries of Moidart, Glengairie [Glengarry], and Lochaber, and the other Parishes of the Synods of Glenelg and Argyle'.
16. Clotilde Prunier, 'Representations of the 'State of Popery' in Scotland in the 1720s and 1730s', *Innes Review*, 64.2 (2013), 120-226.

THEODORUS:
A
DIALOGUE
CONCERNING
THE ART OF
PREACHING.
BY
Mr. *DAVID FORDYCE,*

Late Professor of PHILOSOPHY in the Marischal College of *Aberdeen*, and Author of the DIALOGUES on EDUCATION.

Duo sunt, quæ, bene tractata ab Oratore, admirabilem Eloquentiam faciunt: quorum alterum est quod *Græci* ἠθικὸν vocant, ad Naturam, & ad Mores, & ad omnem *Vitæ Consuetudinem* accommodatum; alterum quod Iidem παθητικὸν nominant, quo perturbantur Animi & concitantur; in quo Uno regnat Oratio. CIC.

THE SECOND EDITION.

To which is added,

A SERMON on the ELOQUENCE of the PULPIT.

By the Rev^d Mr. *JAMES FORDYCE.*

LONDON:
Printed for R. DODSLEY in *Pall-Mall*.
MDCCLIII.

Theodorus completed by David Fordyce in 1750 but published posthumously in 1752, and in successive editions thereafter incorporating his brother's sermon, *Eloquence of the Pulpit*.

17 Noel MacDonald Wilby, 'The "Encreasce of Popery" in the Highlands 1714-1747', *Innes Review*, 17 (1966), 91-115.
18 Robert Kent Donovan, 'Voices of Distrust: The Expression of Anti-Catholic Feeling in Scotland, 1778-1781', *Innes Review* 30 (1979), 62-76. See also the same author's *No Popery and Radicalism. Opposition to Roman Catholic Relief in Scotland, 1778-1782* (New York, 1987).
19 Christine Johnson, *Developments in the Roman Catholic Church in Scotland, 1789-1829* (Edinburgh, 1983).
20 Daniel Szechi, 'Defending the true faith: Kirk, State and Catholic missioners in Scotland 1653–1755', *Catholic Historical Review*, 82 (1996), 397-411.
21 E.g. Prunier who reproduces a key document which 'definitely belongs to the 1730s', entitled 'Memoire de l'etat de la Mission d'Ecosse en l'Annee 1735' (the date being suspect). The original is in Vatican City Historical Archives 'de Propaganda Fide' (Congregation for the Evangelization of Peoples) [APF], *Congregatio Particularis Super Rebus Scotiae*, vols. 86, 87. For a note on the latter organisation see Fuller, *Alexander Geddes 1737-1802* (Sheffield, 1984), 165.
22 Prunier (see note 16 above), 192.
23 Hyndman, *A Sermon on Proverbs xiv. 34. Preached before The Society in Scotland for propagating Christian Knowledge, At their Anniversary Meeting, in the High Church of Edinburgh, On Monday, February 23.1761.* (1761), 29.
24 Lachlan Shaw, *The History of the Province of Moray* (Edinburgh, 1775), 380-1.
25 Modern Wroclaw in Poland. Breslau was then the capital of Silesia.
26 Morren [*Annals 1739-52*, 343, note] states that William Hogg died on 22 December 1766. In his 'Scottish Journal', compiled while he was a medical student at Edinburgh, Benjamin Rush records that on January 7, 1767 he was invited to attend Hogg's funeral: '… this venerable Gentleman died in the 72nd year of his age after a Life spent in the most uninterrupted Services of mankind …'. [University of Indiana Ms, ff. 25-28.]

Hogg's bank failed in 1769. See Forbes, *Memoirs of a Banking House* (1860), 43. Hogg's daughter Annie had rejected John Witherspoon's proposal of marriage while JW was a divinity student at Edinburgh, though the two continued to correspond even long after Witherspoon's departure from Scotland in 1768. See Collins, *President Witherspoon* (1925), v. 1, 20.
27 For more on Samuel Chandler (1693-1766) see Wilson, *The History and Antiquities of the Dissenting Churches and Meeting Houses* (1808), v. II, 360-84.
28 Robertson's speech to the 1779 General Assembly as reported in the *Scots Magazine*, v. 41, August 1779, 413.
29 Wishart, *Publick Virtue recommended* (1746), 13.
30 Blair, *The Wrath of Man praising God* (1746), 20.
31 The king's letter is dated 16 May, the Assembly's 'Answer' 17 May, and the 'Congratulatory Address' 19 May. The afterthought of a 'Congratulatory Letter' to Cumberland is dated 20 May.
32 *Principal Acts of the General Assembly* (1746), 11.
33 Matheson, 'Preaching in the Churches of Scotland', in *The Oxford Handbook of the British Sermon 1689-1901* (2012), 156.
34 The sermon first appears in Blair's collected *Sermons*, v. II, (1780), 396-426.
35 A second and third edition of the sermon, 'with elucidating remarks', intended to discredit JW, were published in Glasgow in 1777.
36 *The Importance of Religious Knowledge to the Happiness of Mankind* (1750), 25-6.
37 The same title (1780), in Blair's collected *Sermons*, v. II, (1780), 451-2.

38 Yet, without attributing his source, Scott cites the common view of Willison that 'there was no asperity in what he said or wrote'. (*Fasti*, New Series, v. 5 (1925), 321).
39 *Church and Theology in Enlightenment Scotland: The Popular Party, 1740-1800* (1998), 243.
40 Scott, *Fasti, op cit*.
41 In 1797 the parish of Falkirk boasted of 'one chapel for the Burghers, two for the Antiburghers, and one belonging to the Relief interest'. The explanation for the existence of two Antiburgher meeting places is 'a difference subsisting between the two congregations … which arose chiefly from the manner of setting apart the elements in the Lord's supper.' (Reverend James Wilson, *OSA*, v. 19, 75).
42 The NLS Scottish Book Trade Index lists Reid in business in Glasgow in 1772 and latterly in Falkirk, 'near Carron', from 1773 to 1786. He is described in the SBTI as 'one of the most important of the Scottish chapbook printers'. Thomas Johnston was a printer, newspaper printer and bookseller in Falkirk from 1797 to 1831 and, again, we learn from an 1801 imprint that 'chapbooks must have formed a principal part of his business.'
43 John Robertson's name is omitted from the Falkirk imprint.
44 *Britain's Remembrancer* (1746), Edinburgh ed., 41.
45 Gaskell 350 (1758), 221-2.
46 For an assessment of David Fordyce's influence on the educational thought of Benjamin Franklin, see Crawford, *Professor Anderson, Dr Franklin and President Washington* (2014), 35-7 and notes 70-71. Returning home from a continental grand tour, David Fordyce (*bap*. 1711-51) drowned at sea in September 1751 when his ship, out of Rotterdam heading for Leith, foundered off the Dutch coast. See also chapter 10, 'Slavery', 275.
47 *The Life of Samuel Johnson*, ed. Womersley (2008), 210. The sixth and last of Fordyce's *Addresses to the Deity* (1785) is entitled 'On the Death of Dr. Samuel Johnson'.
48 Aberdeen, 1752. The same 'ordination sermon' was reprinted in a fourth edition in Glasgow in 1755. James Fordyce edited his late brother David's *Theodorus: A Dialogue concerning the Art of Preaching* (London, R. Dodsley, 1752), within the second edition of which he included his sermon (1753).
49 For invaluable information relating to the Protestant Association petition and its signers from Monkwell Street I am hugely indebted to *The Gordon Riots. Politics, Culture and Insurrection in Late Eighteenth-Century Britain*, ed. Haywood and Seed (Cambridge, 2012), and especially Part 1, chapter 3, 'The Fall of Romish Babylon anticipated: plebeian Dissenters and anti-popery in the Gordon riots', by John Seed, pp. 76-7, in particular. The history of the Monkwell Street dissenters is comprehensively documented in Wilson, *The History and Antiquities of Dissenting Churches and Meeting Houses*, v. III (1810), 185-217.
50 *The Delusive and Persecuting Spirit of Popery* (London, 1779), from the 'Advertisement', vi-viii.
51 Ibid., 28, 32.
52 Ibid., 34.
53 Originally anonymous when it first came out in 1766, Fordyce's work was a runaway bestseller, going through no less than seven editions within a year of its first publication and continuing to be published up to 1800 (12th ed.).
54 *Sermons to Young Women: in two volumes*, v. I (1766), 'Preface', iii.
55 For more on Erskine in the specific context of America, see Chapter 8.
56 Yeager, *Enlightened Evangelicalism The Life and Thought of John Erskine* (2011), especially chapter 6, 'The Controversialist', 113-139.
57 31 Geo. III. c. 32.

58 *Caledonian Mercury*, Wednesday January 6 1779, page 3, col. 1.
59 Walker is described as a 'merchant in Edinburgh' and a Bailie. In the 1780 *Universal Scots Almanac* he is listed as a 'manager' of the SSPCK.
60 For a list of these see the postscript to this chapter.
61 *Scots Magazine*, 'Account of the Public Life and Character of the Late Dr Erskine, of Edinburgh', v. 65, February, 1803, 81 (cited in Sher, *Church and University in the Scottish Enlightenment*, 284, note 87).
62 Three of these have survived among Robertson's papers.(NRS, 3943, 85-89) See also Sher, *op. cit.*, 289, note 113.
63 It is Erskine's normal practice meticulously to name his sources in his discourses and sermons; e.g. in the early *The People of God consider'd as Righteous* (1745) he acknowledges his indebtedness 'in composing the first of these Discourses' to Jonathan Edwards' 'Sermons published at Boston 1738' [*Discourses on Various Important Subjects*, Boston, 1738, reprinted as the first five sermons in Edwards' *Sermons on Various Important Subjects*, Edinburgh, 1785]; and to a Manuscript 'Essay on Prejudices against the Gospel, by a Minister of this Church.' [i.e. the Reverend John Maclaurin (1693-1754) of the Ramshorn Northwest) Church, Glasgow] published posthumously under that title in *Sermons and Essays by the late Reverend Mr. John M'Laurin, one of the Ministers of Glasgow* (1755). The volume is edited by Maclaurin's son in law, the Reverend John Gillies, minister of Blackfriars Church (the College church), Glasgow, and both the Reverend John Adams of Falkirk and John Erskine (then of Culross) supply testimonial frontispieces.
64 *Shall I Go to War With My American Brethren?* (1769 ed.), 34-5; (1776 ed.), 18.
65 Erskine is referring here to their SSPCK sermons preached in 1761, 1762 and 1748 by, respectively, the Reverends John Hyndman (West Kirk), Robert Dick (Trinity College Church) and Robert Walker (South Leith, and from 1754, the High Church – St Giles').
66 Ibid., (1769 ed.), 39; (1776 ed.), 20.
67 Ibid. The reference to the House of Savoy as claimants to the throne of Great Britain is explained by the fact that the king of Sardinia, Charles Emmanuel III (1701-73) – 'his Sardinian majesty'– was the grandson of Henrietta Anne Stuart, youngest daughter of Charles I and Henrietta Maria.
68 Ibid., Preface, (1776 ed.), v-vi. Erskine's contention that his pamphlet antagonised some of his friends is borne out in the note accompanying the news of its re-issue in the *Scots Magazine* for May 1776 (v. xxxviii, 265): 'A correspondent, who expresses the highest regard for Dr Erskine, is under melancholy apprehensions, that this discourse may have an effect directly the reverse of what the humane author intended; for that it may induce the colonists to reject the plan of reconciliation which is to be proposed to them, and so protract the unnatural war ... and therefore he earnestly requests the justly-esteemed author to consider, whether a desire of independence in the colonists be not a more evident sign of a judicial infatuation in them, than a desire of continuing the supremacy of the mother-country over them is in the people of Britain.'
69 *Scots Magazine*, v. 41, February 1779, 108. In the same issue the *Magazine* printed a pastoral letter from the 'Bishop of Daulis' – an alias for George Hay – designed to comfort all Catholics in his charge and describing in detail what had occurred.
70 Ibid., 62-3.
71 Ibid., August 1779, 409.
72 E.g. in 1745 he had written in the 'Advertisement' prefacing his *Three Sermons*: 'I never yet

esteemed the Pulpit a fit Place for Slander and Defamation, and I hope shall never be left to prostitute it to so base a Purpose.' (p. iv)
73 *Prayer for those in civil and military offices recommended* (1779), 5.
74 In the eighteenth century orthodox ministers commonly used the term 'depravity' to connote man's original sin, the sense intended here.
75 Erskine, *Prayer* (1779), 5.
76 Ibid., 11, 13-14.
77 Ibid., 24-5.
78 Ibid., 25-6.
79 Ibid., 28-9.
80 Ibid., 30.
81 *Scots Magazine*, v. 40, May 1778, 269.
82 *Church and University in the Scottish Enlightenment*, 281.
83 Scott's biography of Grant is tantalisingly brief: *Fasti*, New Series, v. VII (1928), 50.
84 Unlike the modern practice of moderators being elected up to a year in advance of the meeting of Assembly over which they will preside, in the eighteenth century the identity of the moderator was known only when the Assembly convened. One presumes that candidates were 'sounded out' beforehand.
85 This is the rarest pamphlet by far of any cited in this study. It is not mentioned in the BL ESTC and, according to WorldCat, just one copy exists anywhere in the UK and North America – in the Library of the University of Guelph, Canada, to whose Librarian and imaging staff I am most grateful for permitting me to acquire a digitised copy. Is its rarity conceivably related to the controversial nature of its content, and/or to the obscurity of its author, one wonders?
86 *The Spirit of Moderation*, 1-2.
87 Ibid., 4-6.
88 Ibid., 6.
89 Ibid., 8-9.
90 Ibid., 11.
91 Ibid., 18.
92 Ibid., 26-7.
93 Ibid., 28.

Chapter 10

1 Only this volume was published.
2 Further editions of the sermon were published in Edinburgh in 1759, 1775 and 1791; and in Dublin in 1773
3 Hardy was first called to the High Church in 1784 but was translated two years later because of ill health to the 'less demanding' West Church of St Giles. He had begun his ministry at Ballingry in Fife (1774-84).
4 As evidence of the extent to which the abolition issue tended to become entangled in the wider issue of popular radicalism, see Somerville, *My Own Life and Times 1741-1814* (1861), 263-4: 'A sermon I preached at this time [*A Discourse ... for the Prospect of the Abolition of the African Slave-Trade* (1792)] gave great offence to some of the gentlemen in the country, who uncharitably imputed it to those spreading seditious principles, which at that time were the occasion of just alarm to all the friends of order and peace.'
5 MacCulloch, *Silence A Christian History* (2013), 212-16.

6   The first (1771) and second edition (1773) of the work is entitled *Observations concerning the Distinction of Ranks in Society*. Easily the most comprehensive study of Millar's great work in the context of its contribution to the slavery debate is 'John Millar and Slavery' by John W. Cairns, chapter 3 of *MacCormick's Scotland*, ed. Walker (2012), 73-106. I am much indebted to Professor Cairns for his generous help in readily making available to me some of his numerous and distinguished publications in the general area of slavery, the law and the Scottish Enlightenment.
7   *The Origin of the Distinction of Ranks* (text based on the fourth ed.), ed. Garrett (2006), 271.
8   Israel, *Democratic Enlightenment*, 423-4.
9   'Feudalism and slavery may have been discredited for the most part, but Scots Enlightenment did much to erect potent new hierarchies based on stages of development, sentiment, cultural properties, as well as tentative racial theories.' Ibid., 256.
10 Barbeyrac (1672-1744) was the 'outstanding authority on natural jurisprudence in the early eighteenth century'. – James Moore, *Natural Rights on the Threshold of the Scottish Enlightenment: The Writings of Gershom Carmichael*, ed. Moore and Silverthorne (2002), Foreword, xiv.
11 *WJW*, 3, 420-1, Lecture X, 'Of Politics'. See much the same point in Israel, *A Revolution of the Mind* (2010), 41-2.
12 Reported briefly as '*Robert Sheddan* [sic] *against a Negro*' in Morison, *Decisions of the Court of Session*, v. XVII, 'Slave', no. 1, 14545. See also Cairns, 'Freeing from Slavery in Eighteenth-Century Scotland', in *Judge and Jurist: Essays in Memory of Lord Rodger of Earlsferry*, ed. Burrows, Johnston and Zimmermann (2013), 367-81. The papers relating to 'Shedden v Montgomery' are in the file NRS CS234/S/3/12.
13 Cairns, 'Freeing from Slavery in Eighteenth-Century Scotland', 378.
14 See chapter 5, 'Heresy', notes 12 and 44.
15 But Israel follows Douglas Sloan in believing that while JW 'admired Hutcheson up to a point, he was particularly an enthusiast for Common Sense, especially Reid.' (*Democratic Enlightenment*, 268 and note 166). ['Sloan' is author of *The Scottish Enlightenment and the American College Ideal* (1971), 110-112.] See also Phelps, *John Witherspoon and the Transmission of Common Sense Philosophy from Scotland to America*, unpublished Oxford University DPhil thesis, 2002.
16 Wallace's *System* (1760), 97 and footnote.
17 In 1762 the French Huguenot Quaker abolitionist, Anthony Benezet, published in Philadelphia *A Short Account of that part of Africa, inhabited by the Negroes; with respect to the fertility of the country; the good disposition of many of the natives; and the manner by which the slave trade is carried on. … With a quotation from George Wallis's* [i.e. Wallace's] *System of the Laws &c.* Witherspoon's unlikely connection with Benezet, slavery in America (and Thomas Paine) is explained in Crawford, *LWJW* (2014), 306. See Millar, *The Origin of the Distinction of Ranks* 4th ed. (1806), Liberty Fund, ed. Garrett (2006), 265 and footnote. It is credible that Benezet was as early in the field as 1759, with the pamphlet attributed to him, *Observations on the inslaving, importing and purchasing of Negroes* (Germantown [Pa.] 1759).
18 John W. Cairns, 'Slavery without a *Code Noir*: Scotland 1700-78', in *Lawyers, the Law and History: Irish Legal History Society Discourses and Other Papers, 2005-2011* (2013), ed. Larkin and Dawson, 156.
19 'Man was born free, yet he is everywhere in chains.' The most celebrated modern apostle of 'liberty' as a political idea is Sir Isaiah Berlin in works such as 'The Idea of Freedom', in *Political Ideas in the Romantic Age*, ed. Hardy (2006), 88-154; and 'Five Essays on Liberty', in *Liberty*, ed. Hardy (2002), 3-2.

20 Wallace, *A System of the Principles of the Law of Scotland* (1760), 'Vol. I', Bk. III, Tit. II, 89-90.
21 Ibid., 96.
22 Thus, 'God' is referred to by Wallace as the 'Deity', the 'Creator', or most usually, the 'Divinity'.
23 B. Barnett Cochran, article on Robert Wallace, 2004, Oxford *DNB* online, accessed 23 August 2016.
24 But see the Bibliography for Hamilton and Balfour's French ed. of *De L'Esprit des Loix* of 1750.
25 'Where Rousseau has virtually nothing to say about the black and brown peoples, not even ending the slave trade, the *Histoire Philosophique* carries anti-slavery on to a new level of mobilization and combat.' – Israel, *Democratic Enlightenment*, 416.
26 Leslie's list was seized by the authorities for use as a crown production at his trial but, although he was arrested in late 1797, he fled on bail rather than face a trial for treason in the following year. See Harris, *The Scottish People and the French Revolution*, 161. The list survives in NRS JC26/293.
27 Marischal College, Aberdeen enjoyed independent university status from 1593 until 1860 when it merged with King's College (a fully accredited university from 1495) to form the unified University of Aberdeen. The University of St. Andrews (Scotland's oldest) 'made little impact' upon the Scottish Enlightenment, perhaps in part because it 'was not surrounded by a bustling commercial, legal or ecclesiastical life with which it could interact'. (Broadie, *The Scottish Enlightenment*, 25-6).
28 Carmichael had published an earlier edition of the same abridgement in Glasgow in 1718. An English translation of the work, based on the second (Edinburgh) ed., is provided in Moore and Silverthorne, *Natural Rights on the Threshold of the Scottish Enlightenment: The Writings of Gershom Carmichael* (2002).
29 Gerhard Gottlieb Titius (1661-1714), Pufendorf's editor.
30 *The Writings of Gershom Carmichael*, 144-5.
31 Hume, *Selected Essays*, ed. Copley and Edgar, 'Of the Populousness of Ancient Nations', 229.
32 Hutcheson, *Philosophiae Moralis Institutio Compendiaria with A Short Introduction to Moral Philosophy*, ed. Turco (2007), 231.
33 Hutcheson, *A System of Moral Philosophy* (1755), v. I, ch. 5, 'The Private Rights of Men ... and the natural Equality of Men', III, 301.
34 Thomas D. Kennedy, Liberty Fund ed. of Fordyce, *The Elements of Moral Philosophy*, (2003), x.
35 Fordyce's own footnote reference to Hutcheson is to the *'Moral Instit. Phil. Lib. iii. Cap. 3.'* Kennedy's reference is to Turco's Liberty Fund ed. of the work (2007), *'Philosophiae Moralis'*, 230-4.
36 Ibid., 90. Kennedy fails to identify the 'fine Writer' whose words had so clearly appealed to Fordyce.
37 Rundle, *A Sermon preached at St. George's Church Hanover Square* (1734), 15. Less than two years after the sermon was published John Wesley arrived in Georgia where he would remain until December 1737. As his diaries reveal, Wesley too would have problems with Oglethorpe.
38 In his *System* Wallace *fils* cites his father without attribution.
39 Founded in 1731. Apart from Robert Wallace, Henry Home was a founder member. David Hume became its joint secretary in 1751.
40 *The Life of David Hume, Second Edition* (1980), 260-8.
41 'In the long history of speculation on the question, David Hume was the first to maintain, however sceptically, the superior populousness of the modern world over the ancient world.' – Mossner, *Life*, 263.

42 Hume, *Selected Essays*, ed. Copley and Edgar, 'Of the Populousness of Ancient Nations', 229.
43 Ibid.
44 Wallace, *Dissertation on the Numbers of Mankind* (1753), 'Appendix', 207-8.
45 E.g. Mirabeau in *L'Ami des Hommes* (1756) who supported Wallace's views, while the Marquis de Chastellux, in *De la félicité publique* (1772), upheld Hume's. See Mossner, *Life*, 268.
46 Smith, *Theory of Moral Sentiments*, ed. Raphael and Macfie (1976), 206-7.
47 Israel, *Democratic Enlightenment* (2011), 240. The passage he cites from Smith is from *The Wealth of Nations*, Book III, Penguin Classics, ed. Skinner (1986), 489.
48 Ibid.
49 Smith, *Lectures on Jurisprudence*, ed. Meek, Raphael and Stein (1978), 'Report of 1762-3', 186-7.
50 Cairns, 'John Millar and Slavery', 76. See note 6 above.
51 Ibid., 75-6; and Whyte, *Scotland and the Abolition of Black Slavery, 1756-1838* (2006), 78, 91.
52 Millar, *The Origin of the Distinction of Ranks*, ed. Garrett (2006), based on the fourth ed. of 1806, 275.
53 Ibid.
54 Ibid., 269: footnote† by Garrett *op. cit.* citing Christopher A. Whatley, 'The Dark Side of the Enlightenment? Sorting out Serfdom', in *Eighteenth-Century Scotland: New Perspectives*, ed. Devine and Young (1999), 259-74. Conditions were marginally improved for 'colliers, coal-bearers, and salters' by an Act of Parliament of Scotland of 1775 (15 Geo III c. 28). Millar had anticipated the legislation in the fourth ed. of *The Origin of the Distinction of Ranks*, trusting that 'such regulations have been made as, in a short time, will probably abolish the remains of that servitude to which this order of men have been so long subjected.' (ibid., 277), but it was not until an amending Act of 1799 (39 Geo III c. 56) that real improvements began to take effect. See also Erskine, *The Principles of the Law of Scotland* (1754), I, 1.7.39, 102; Erskine compares the 'coal-hewers, coal-bearers, and salters' to the '*adscriptii glebae* [serfs] of the Roman law'.
55 Ibid., 278-9.
56 See Cairns, 'John Millar and Slavery', 94; and the same author's '*Knight v Wedderburn*' in *The Oxford Companion to Black British History* ed. Dabydeen, Gilmore and Jones (2007), 244-6.
57 3rd ed. (1779), 361-2.
58 *A Church History of Scotland* (1960), 415.
59 See the 'Postscript' to this chapter.
60 Reverend Andrew Robertson, who was minister of Gladsmuir from 1728 until his death in 1743. [Scott, *Fasti*, New Series, v. I (1915), 366.] Easily the most authoritative study of Robertson's career, however, is Jeffrey R. Smitten's *Life of William Robertson Minister, Historian, and Principal* (2017).
61 *Edinburgh Review*, no 1, 39-43. Jardine had been translated from Lady Yester's Church – where his successors were Hugh Blair (1754-58), and William Robertson (1758-61) – to the second charge of the Tron Kirk, Edinburgh in 1754. (Scott, *Fasti*, New Edition, v. 1, 140-1).
62 For Maconochie's acknowledgment of his debt in the course of his pleading in the *Knight v Wedderburn* action of 1776-78 – not only to Robertson the minister in *The Situation of the World*, but also to Robertson the historian in *The History of the Reign of the Emperor Charles V.* – See Whyte, *Scotland and the Abolition of Black Slavery*, 29-30; and Morison, *Decisions*, XVII (1804), 'Slave', 14545-49.

*E.g. 'The gentle spirit of the Christian religion, together with the doctrines which it teaches, concerning the original equality of mankind, as well as the impartial eye with which the Almighty regards men of every condition, and admits them to a participation of his benefits, are inconsistent with servitude.' [*Charles V*, v. I (1769), 'Note XX. Sect. I p. 41', 268.]

63 In 'Freeing from Slavery in Eighteenth-Century Scotland' (see note 12 above), 380, Cairns cites the jurist and biblical scholar David Daube (1909-99) on the same issue. Daube believed that, for Paul, Onesimos's [sic] baptism had 'a realistic, supernatural effect of conversion', as credited by the Rabbis: 'It has long been noticed,' wrote Daube, 'that, though not asking Philemon to manumit Onesimos, yet he does ask him to receive him not as a slave but as a brother. The explanation is that a manumission would be superfluous, if not offensive. The baptized Onesimos, by virtue of the baptism, is no longer he that was owned by Philemon. The latter, himself guided into the faith by Paul, would understand.' – Daube, *Appeasement or Resistance and Other Essays on New Testament Judaism* (1987), 62. The story of Onesimus, and its relevance to the slavery issue generally, is also highlighted by John Millar in Chapter VI, ('The Authority of a Master over His Servants') Section III ('Causes of the freedom acquired by the labouring people in the modern nations of Europe') of *The Origin of the Distinction of Ranks*, ed. Garrett, 264-5, and Millar's footnote.
64 *The Situation of the World* (1755), 8.
65 Ibid., 11.
66 Ibid., 25. Nicholas Phillipson, Colin Kidd and Geoffrey Carnall have all drawn attention to Robertson's near-obsession with the baleful impact of *superstition* upon nations, empires and civilisations, detectable throughout all his histories – *Scotland* (1759), *Charles V* (1769), *America* (1777), and even his much briefer last work, the *Historical Disquisition Concerning the Knowledge Which the Ancients Had of India* (1791). Thus, Phillipson: 'What is so interesting about Robertson's treatment of the history of the Western world since the Reformation and Counter-Reformation is his suggestion that its religion was still rooted in a necessarily imperfect understanding of the Word and was still deeply penetrated by superstition, Protestant as well as Catholic.'; Kidd: 'The ideas of the Reformers instilled in the people of Scotland a new spirit of liberty. By "overturning the established system of superstition", the reformers had "weakened the firmest foundations of civil tyranny"'.; and Carnall: 'Robertson's main reservations about Indian civilisation related ... to the Hindu religion, which he described as "a regular and complete system of superstition, strengthened and upheld by every thing which can excite the reverence and secure the attachment of the people."' See *William Robertson and the expansion of empire*, ed. Stewart J. Brown, 70-1 (Phillipson), 140 (Kidd) and 214 (Carnall).
67 *The Situation of the World*, 27.
68 Ibid., 28.
69 Ibid., 33, 35,36. These sentences have been seized on by Iain Whyte who accuses Robertson of having 'glossed over' 'the flourishing of slavery in many Christian lands and the acceptance of the trade within Britain'. – *Scotland and the Abolition of Black Slavery*, 55. In Robertson's defence, however, it should not be lost sight of that he was speaking these words in 1755 (by a curious slip Whyte assigns the year '1775' to the sermon), at a time when relatively scant facts were known (at least by the public at large) about the full extent and ghastliness of the modern trade, or even of the comprehensive nature of Britain's role in it.
70 Ibid., 36.
71 In editions after the first, the word in the footnote is rendered 'permission'.
72 Ibid., 37, footnote.
73 Ibid., 39.
74 Ibid.
75 Nevertheless, for John Wesley writing in his journal of Robertson's *History of America*, which he had just finished reading, 'I cannot admire ... a Christian Divine writing a History, with so very little of Christianity in it.' (*Journal XVIII*, 6 December 1778).

76 Sher sees Robertson's sermon, along with Blair's SSPCK sermon, *The Importance of Religious Knowledge to the Happiness of Mankind* (1750), as examples of how both ministers 'sought to reconcile Christian principles with those of the Enlightenment.' – *Church and University in the Scottish Enlightenment* (Classic ed., 2015), 63-4.
77 'William Robertson (1721-1793) and the Scottish Enlightenment', in *William Robertson and the expansion of empire*, ed. Brown (1997), 17.
78 See chapter 9, 'Popery', 248-251.
79 Blair, 'On Gentleness', in *Sermons* v. 1 (1777), 154.
80 See Roscoe, *Reports of Cases argued and determined in the Court of King's Bench*, v. III (1831), 'Gregson v Gilbert' (1783), 232-5. The case was heard by, among others, the Lord Chief Justice, the Earl of Mansfield, a Scot (William Murray), whose role in the determination of the milestone Somerset case of 1772 had been widely reported in Scottish newspapers. Mansfield's opinion was that 'a master could not compel or force his servant or slave to leave England.' George Wallace prefaces his *The Nature and Descent of Ancient Peerages* (1785) with a 'Discourse' addressed to Mansfield. See *State Trials*, vol. 20, cols 1-6, 79-82 (1816).
81 Ramsay later qualified as a surgeon and entered the Royal Navy in 1757. His ship the *Arundel* intercepted a British slave ship *Swift* in November 1759 and, on boarding her, Ramsay found indescribable conditions, 'a scene of human degradation which remained forever in his memory'. His two pamphlets, both published in 1784, *Essay on the Treatment and Conversion of African Slaves in the British Sugar Colonies* and *An Inquiry into the Effects of Putting a Stop to the African Slave Trade* were influential in the lengthy abolition campaign that followed.
82 *A Sermon on the subject of the Slave Trade; delivered to a society of Protestant Dissenters, at the New Meeting, in Birmingham; and published at their request* (Birmingham, 1788).
83 Whyte, *Scotland and the Abolition of Black Slavery* (2006), 71.
84 Emma Vincent Macleod in her Oxford *DNB* article on Hardy, online ed., accessed 29 August 2016.
85 Hardy had started his ministerial career at Ballingry in Fife where he had languished for ten years from 1774 until called to the 'plum' pulpit of St Giles. He was there for barely two years, however, when he was permitted on health grounds to accept the less arduous charge of the New North Parish (or West St Giles *aka* 'Haddo's Hole'). In 1788 he was appointed professor of ecclesiastical history at Edinburgh, though he continued with his ministry concurrently.
86 Somerville, *My Own Life and Times 1741-1814* (1861), 301 (note).
87 For more on Hardy and his personal opposition to popular reform, see chapter 6, 168-169
88 Hardy, *The Progress of the Christian Religion* (1794), 13.
89 See note 66 above.
90 Phillipson, 'Providence and progress: an introduction to the historical thought of William Robertson', chapter 3 of *William Robertson and the expansion of empire*, ed. Brown (1997), 62.
91 Herder's enormous study of race, *Izeen zur Philosophie der Geschichte der Menscheit* (1784-91), was not available in English translation until 1800. Bernasconi and Lott comment: 'It was Herder [Kant's student], not Kant, who maintained that every people or every nation contributed to humanity and thereby provided the framework from which to argue that any action such as forced baptism, the imposition of an alien culture, colonialism, or the slave trade, that interfered with that people's capacity to fulfil its historical mission is destructive of humanity as a whole.' – *The Idea of Race* (2000), Introduction, ix. But Hardy is obviously speculating much more generally, while conceivably having in mind the views of an eccentric Scottish controversialist, John Pinkerton (1758-1826), whose *A Dissertation on the Origin and*

Progress of the Scythians or Goths (1787) had stated a belief in the intellectual inferiority of Celts; and/or those of a blatant advocate of slavery, Edward Long (1734-1813), himself a former sugar planter, whose *The History of Jamaica* (3 vols., 1774) had attempted to justify the slave trade on the grounds it was actually benevolent since the transportation of Africans to the Caribbean brought discipline into the lives of an inferior, sub-human species.

92 In the essay 'Of National Characters' – it first appeared simultaneously in 1748 in the *Three Essays* and in the 3rd edition of *Essays, Moral and Political* – Hume added to the version in the 1753 edition of *Essays and Treatises on Several Subjects* a notorious 'racist' footnote beginning: 'I am apt to suspect the negroes to be naturally inferior to the whites. There scarcely ever was a civilized nation of that complexion, nor even any individual, eminent either in action or speculation. No ingenious manufactures amongst them, no arts, no sciences. ... Not to mention our colonies, there are Negroe slaves dispersed all over Europe, of whom none ever discovered any symptoms of ingenuity'.' There has been speculation that, partly on account of stinging criticism from James Beattie ('that bigoted silly Fellow'), Hume later sought to water down (slightly) his comments, but this has been disputed. See John Immerwahr, 'Hume's Revised Racism', in *Journal of the History of Ideas*, 53.3 (1993), 481-6; Aaron Garrett, *Hume Studies*, XXVI, No 1 (April 2000), 171-8; and Garrett's chapter 'Human Nature' (particularly section IV, 'Race and Natural Character') in *The Cambridge History of Eighteenth-Century Philosophy*, ed. Haakonssen, v. I, 195-7.

93 *The Progress of the Christian Religion*, 14.
94 Ibid., 15.
95 Ibid., 16-17.
96 Ibid., 18-19.
97 Ibid., 38.
98 Ibid., 39.
99 Ibid., 40-1.
100 Ibid., 42-3.
101 Ibid., 43-4.
102 See Bibliography. Sir William Jones (1746-94) had translated this work, which Michael J. Franklin describes as 'a revolutionary contribution to orientalism'. It went into six editions between 1790 and 1807 and, in the century following it was published in 'no fewer than forty-six translations in twelve different languages.' (Oxford *DNB* online article by Franklin on Sir William Jones; accessed 5 September 2016).
103 Volume I (Calcutta, India, 1788-89). The series ceased publication with volume 20 in 1839.
104 *The Progress of the Christian Religion*, 52-3.
105 *The Principal Acts of the General Assembly of the Church of Scotland* (1792), May 24, Session 7.
106 *My Own Life and Times 1741-1814* (1861), 263-4.
107 Somerville was married to Martha Charters, Samuel Charters' first cousin.
108 Particularly those on pp. 35-36 (Dale, Wilberforce, Raikes); 107 (Frossard on Slavery); 122-4 (Wilberforce); 124-8 (Quakers and slavery; act for emancipating slaves 'has just been passed in America').
109 Thomas Firmin (1632-97), businessman, philanthropist and prison reformer; Firmin was a founding member of the Society for the Reformation of Manners. David Dale (1739-1806), born in Stewarton, Ayrshire, was similarly a wealthy evangelical businessman who gave away much of his fortune to the hard-pressed poor. Dale founded New Lanark in 1784. Professor John Anderson (1726-96) of the University of Glasgow named both Dale and his son (also

David Dale) in his will of 1795 as a trustee of his putative 'Anderson's University', now the University of Strathclyde. Dale is credited with the authorship of an *Address to the Inhabitants of Glasgow, Paisley, and the Neighbourhood, concerning the African Slave, by a Society in Glasgow* (Glasgow, 1795), although the extent of Dale's personal hand in the pamphlet must remain uncertain.

110 Charters, *A Sermon on Alms* (Third Edition) (1795), 64.

111 There are two versions of this pamphlet, the titles bearing minor variants: reproduced here is the title and wording of the Glasgow version, printed by Robert Sanders, 'One of His Majesties Printers 1699.' The Edinburgh version, printed by George Mosman, has (in the ESTC copy) part of the title page and pp. 1-6 missing.

Endnote

1 Alexander Bruce, *The Kirkiad* (1774), 2.
2 *Letters on Dr Blair's Sermons* (Edinburgh, 1779). Cited by Stewart J. Brown in 'Hugh Blair, the sentiments and preaching the enlightenment in Scotland', in *Intellectual History Review*, vol. 26, No. 3, 2016, 422 and note 91.
3 That is, <u>both</u> *'bonum commune hominis'* ('the common good of man') <u>and</u> *'bonum commune communitatis'* ('the common good of the community').

Appendix B

1 Andrew Crosbie, Ilay Campbell and James Boswell for the defender; David Rae, Henry Dundas and Bannatyne W. Macleod for the pursuers.
2 See *The Life of Samuel Johnson*, ed. Womersley, 547-52; and *Boswell's Edinburgh Journals*, ed. Milne, 188.
3 Boswell's submission is in manuscript and bears a date '8 February' [1776]; Crosbie's printed *Answers* is dated 'October 14. 1775.'
4 '... however entertaining these anecdotes may be, it is believed, your Lordships will not think they afford any authority, or justification of what is now complained of.' (David Rae, printed *Petition* for the pursuers ('John, Robert, and David Scotlands [sic], Merchants in Dunfermline' dated 'July 14. 1775.').
5 Crosbie, printed *Answers for the Reverend James Thomson*, 14 October 1775, 7. The MS version is referenced NRS CS21/1776/1009/12/ff.1-33.
6 Ibid., 4. For Knox's own description of the impact of his sermon on Mary in his *History* see 'Introduction', 18-20.
7 Macleod's *Memorial* is undated but a note by the Lord Ordinary, Lord Gardenstone, written on the paper, indicating he is 'making avizandum to himself with the Memorials for both partys', bears the date 24 February 1775, so one can safely assume a date earlier in the same month.
8 Macleod's *Memorial* (undated) NRS CS21/1776/1009/15/f.39.
9 Ibid., ff.42-43.
10 Ibid., ff.44-45.
11 1485?-1555. See William Gilpin's *The Lives of Hugh Latimer, Bishop of Worcester, and of Bernard Gilpin* (London, 1780).
12 Crosbie, *Answers*, 4.
13 See the excellent essay on Latimer by Susan Wabuda in the Oxford *DNB*, 2004 (online 2009-2016). Accessed 6 June 2015.

14 The sense of the word 'bocardo' is sometimes intended as a mnemonic in the language of logic. But here what Latimer probably specifically intends is the old prison at the North Gate in Oxford, pulled down in 1771. Though only much later (from the early eighteenth century) used in its generic sense as 'prison', *simpliciter*, it is also just possible that this is how Latimer really intends it to be understood in his sermon.
15 Latimer, *Fruitfull Sermons* (1635), 106. (Boswell's given page no. is out by one page). See Boswell's *Memorial* for Thomson, 15 February 1775, NRS CS21/1776/1009/14/ff.6-7.
16 *Fruitfull Sermons*, 104-5.
17 1516-1584. For accounts of this remarkable preacher's life see George Carleton, *Vita Bernardi Gilpini* (London, 1628) and William Gilpin, *Life of Bernard Gilpin* (London, 1752). Crosbie fails to make it clear that Gilpin's outburst happened in the midst of a largely extempore sermon at Chester-le-street when at the last moment he was 'required' to preach. One senses that Thomson's case might have been served a little better had he done so.
18 Crosbie, *Answers*, 4-5. William Gilpin, *The Life of Bernard Gilpin*, Second Edition (1753), 186.
19 Ibid., 187-8. William Gilpin borrowed the story from the popular *Vita Bernardi Gilpini* by George Carleton, Bishop of Chichester.
20 The anecdote cited by Crosbie and related by Wilson is from pp. 144-45.
21 *Fasti*, New Series, II, 185.
22 Crosbie, *Answers*, 5.
23 Ibid., 5-6. I have to concede defeat in trying to trace the source of this anecdote. This is frustrating given that the minister concerned is almost certainly the Reverend Robert Douglas (1594-1674), four times Moderator of the General Assembly. On 1 January 1651 Douglas officiated at the coronation of Charles II at Scone, and preached a sermon reminding the king of his covenanted responsibility to establish presbyterianism in all three of his kingdoms. In July of the same year Douglas was elected moderator of the 'pretended' general assembly at St Andrews and Dundee, which saw the kirk irreparably divided between 'resolutioners' and 'protesters'.
24 NRS CS18/1776/421 (Dalrymple office - volume). The extract decreet is dated 8 August 1776.
25 Presumably Alexander Henderson (1583?-1646) is meant, though he died long before the Restoration.
26 See *The Acts and Monuments* [Foxe's title from 1563] *of John Foxe A new and complete edition*, ed. Cattley, v. 1, 372-376.
27 The circumstances of the Wray/Coke/Popham citations are conveniently summarised in a long footnote in *The Jurist* for December 19, 1840, 1133. See also Matthew Bacon ['a Gentleman of the Middle Temple'], *A New Abridgment* [sic] *of the Law*, v. III, Third Edition (London, 1768), 'Libel', 493.
28 Rae comments on the Bacon quotation: 'This last case proves that where a preacher maliciously slanders any person from the pulpit, an action will lie against him as for a libel, and malice must be presumed from such circumstances as occur in the present case.' (NRS CS21/1776/1009/f. 34; printed version pp. 13-14). Macleod's *Memorial* at f. 49-50 and Dundas's printed *Answers*, 20, cite exactly the same passage from Bacon's *New Abridgment* cited here.
29 NRS CS 21/1776/1009/ ff. 49-51.
30 Ibid., 50-51.
31 Robert South (1634-1716) was a clergyman and theologian who, in 1660, as the result of his 'Laudian railings against the Presbyterians', came to the attention of Edward Hyde,

Earl of Clarendon, Lord Chancellor and chancellor of the University of Oxford who made him the university's public orator and his own domestic chaplain. Following the landing of William of Orange in 1688 South delivered sermons 'which offered ecumenical jeremiads but conclusively evinced a more passionate hatred of protestant rebels than of Catholics.' By 1691-92, however, South had 'fully finessed his transition into compliance with William and Mary.' (Burke Griggs, Oxford *DNB*, online ed., 2004-2016; accessed 14 October 2016).

32 Boswell specifically mentions the *Shaw v Bean* case as having been 'lately very fully considered' in the context of 'Liberty of the Bar'. It involved 'a charge of defamation for expressions thrown out in a paper before the sheriff' (Bean). See *Boswell's Edinburgh Journals*, ed. Milne, for Friday 23 December 1774, 181.

33 Boswell's *Memorial* for Thomson, 15 February 1775, NRS CS21/1776/1009/14/ff.14-15.

34 *A sermon preached at Lambeth-Chappel on the 25th. of November, upon the Consecration of the Right Reverend Father in God Dr John Dolben Lord Bishop of Rochester* [not 21 November as indicated by Boswell] ([London] Savoy, 1666).

35 Boswell's *Memorial* for Thomson, NRS CS21/1776/1009/14/ff.5-6.

36 Johnson's *Journey* was first published in 1775 but Boswell's *Journal of a Tour* not until ten years later.

37 Boswell's *Memorial* for Thomson, 15 February 1775, NRS CS21/1776/1009/14/f.16.

38 In the year the play first opened (1760) Boswell had published in Edinburgh a humorous pamphlet entitled *Observations, good or bad, stupid or clever, serious or jocular, on Squire Foote's dramatic entertainment, intitled, The minor. By a genius*. He frequently saw the play in London (as well as, of course, later in Edinburgh: *e.g.* 'At night I went to the opening of Mr. Foote's Little Theatre in the Haymarket for this season, with *The Minor*, in which I saw Wilkinson for the first time, a most admirable mimic.' (*Journal* for Monday 20 June, 1763).

39 *Observations, good or bad, stupid or clever, serious or jocular, on Squire Foote's dramatic entertainment, intitled, The minor. By a genius.* (Edinburgh, 1760), 7.

40 In the NLS copy, shelfmark Ry II d. 34.

41 Boswell's *Memorial* for Thomson, 15 February 1775, NRS CS21/1776/1009/14/f.17.

42 Johnson regarded Hugh Blair (1718-1800) as a 'very pleasing man', though by his much publicised and stinging criticism of the poetry of 'Ossian' – which Blair had defended as authentic in his pamphlet *A critical dissertation on the poems of Ossian* (1763, reprinted in an edition of *The Works of Ossian* (1765) – the Englishman had offended the Edinburgh minister. In his letter to Boswell of 7 February 1775 Johnson, smug in the knowledge that James Macpherson's claims in the 'Ossianic controversy' were now seen as false,* refers to Blair as 'deceived'. (*Life of Samuel Johnson*, ed. Womersley, 421). In a long encomium on Blair in the *Life* Boswell describes Johnson's role in the publication (by William Strahan) of Blair's first collection of *Sermons*, and notes the large sums paid Blair by Strahan for the right to publish successive editions, such was their continuing success. Boswell himself regarded Blair's *Sermons* as 'one of the most successful theological books that has ever appeared.' (ibid., 571). Elsewhere in the *Life* Johnson is found expressing the sentiments 'I wish Blair would come over to the Church of England.' (ibid., 707); and 'I love *Blair's Sermons*. Though the dog is a Scotchman, and a Presbyterian, and every thing he should not be, I was the first to praise them.' (ibid., 817).

*Johnson himself, however, was of course wrong to claim that no Gaelic poetry was older than one hundred years.

43 Sher, 'Scottish Divines and Legal Lairds: Boswell's Scots Presbyterian Identity', in *New Light on Boswell*, ed. Clingham, 31. The 'New Kirk' was, strictly, the name given to the choir of

St. Giles' Church, the section to the east of the building referred to as the 'Old Kirk'. (*Fasti*, I, New Series, 48). St. Giles' became a 'cathedral' when Charles 1 restored bishops to the church. In 1688 it lost its bishop though its entitlement to the description thereafter was never in doubt.
44 The House of Lords made judgement in the case on 27 February 1769, allowing the appeal, and thus reversing the outcome reached by the Court of Session on 15 July 1767.
45 *Romans*, 6, v. 21.
46 Boswell's *Memorial* for Thomson, 15 February 1775, NRS CS21/1776/1009/14/f.17.
47 In 1909, as part of the *Notable Scottish Trials* series, A. Francis Steuart in *The Douglas Cause* edited the fifteen speeches made in the Court of Session relating to the case, prefaced by a useful summary of the process. Also worth consulting, though it reads at times like a novel, is *The Heir of Douglas* by Lillian de la Torre (1953).
48 *Life of Samuel Johnson*, ed. Womersley, 382.
49 Lord Bankton (Andrew MacDouall) and Viscount Stair (James Dalrymple) are two of the greatest authorities on Scots law; their best known works are *An Institute of the Law of Scotland*, 4 vols., (Edinburgh, 1751-53), and *The Institutions of the Laws of Scotland*, 2 vols. in 1 (Edinburgh, 1681).
50 John (Keyse) Sherwin (*bap.* 1751, *d.* 1790), Edward Cocker (1631/2-1676) and Nicholaus Alexander Mair, *aka* Mair von Landshut (c. 1455-1520), were all outstanding engravers and illustrators.
51 The Roman code of the 'Twelve Tables' formed the basis of Roman law and as a written code applied across the social scale from patricians to plebeians. Only extracts have survived into modern times, the original stone tablets having, according to legend, been lost in 390 BCE.
52 In other words, Boswell is saying, the case goes on and on, constantly enlarging itself.
53 *Scots Magazine*, v. xxix, March 1767, 119.
54 These are: *The Douglas cause*, a song ridiculing the *Memorial* for the Duke of Hamilton in the Court of Session process (also published in the *Scots Magazine*, v. 29, March 1767, 119); *Dorando: a Spanish tale* in which Boswell cleverly creates a fictionalised pastiche of the case; *The essence of the Douglas case*, a straightforward analysis of the issues at stake; and (as their editor) *Letters of the Right Honourable Lady Jane Douglas*. See Milne, ed., *Boswell's Edinburgh Journals 1767-1786*, 48 and note 27, 55.
55 Alexander Boswell was Sheriff-Depute of the shire of Wigtown from 1748 until his resignation in 1750. Milne comments: 'The *Sheriff-Depute* in each sheriffdom, notwithstanding the contrary impression conveyed by the title, was the principal sheriff there and had power to appoint Sheriffs-Substitute to act for him.' (*Boswell's Edinburgh Journals 1767-1786*, 13). See also Finlay, *Legal Practice in Eighteenth-Century Scotland*, 122 and note 58: 'After 1748, many sheriff courts were staffed largely by substitutes appointed by the sheriff, and although they presided personally on occasion, the role of sheriff-depute bore some similarity to the role of sheriffs principal in modern practice.'
56 Evidence that Boswell's father was Provost of Wigtown in 1748-49 or 1750 is found in Pottle, Abbott and Pottle, *Catalogue of the Papers of James Boswell at Yale University*, 3 vols., (Edinburgh and New Haven, 1993), v.3, 1017: Wigtown Council/Baillies to Alexander Boswell, 25 Jan. 1749: '... it is hoped that Boswell as their provost will be able to get generous subscriptions from the Earls of Galloway and Selkirk.' (ref. C3087.5). Interestingly, another member of the bench who had served Wigtown as Sheriff (in 1750) was *Andrew Pringle, Lord Alemore, admitted advocate 1760, so it is just possible that Boswell's joke concerned Pringle if, as seems

likely, the post of sheriff and provost of the burgh was then a conjoint one. [I am most grateful to James Caudle, Associate Editor, Boswell Editions at Yale University, for this information.]
* Died 1776. See *Boswell's Edinburgh Journals 1767-1786*, 48, note 33; and Brunton, G. and Haig, D., *An Historical Account of the Senators of the College of Justice, from its institution in MDXXXII* (Edinburgh, 1832), 523.
57   1 Thessalonians 5, v.7.
58   Boswell's *Memorial* for Thomson, 15 February 1775, NRS CS21/1776/1009/14/ff.17-18.

Appendix C

1   Alexander Wedderburn, Andrew Crosbie and James Boswell represented the respondents.

Appendix D

1   Morren, *Annals of the General Assembly 1739-52*, 387 and footnote.
2   For an explanation of the distinction between the 'Lesser' and 'Greater' Excommunication as regulated by the Church of Scotland at this time see Crawford, *LWJW*, 257-8 and note 33.
3   Scott, *Fasti*, New Edition, v. III, Synod of Glasgow and Ayr, 117.
4   'Mr Logan', an elder in membership of the Kilwinning Kirk Session, later identified as 'David Logan.'
5   A 'penny wedding – sometimes known as a 'penny bridal' – was characterised by each guest contributing financially or by providing food towards the dinner and then paying for their own drink. By the end of the festivities (which often went on for several days) a tidy sum could have been raised for the newly-weds. Penny weddings were especially popular in rural Scotland 'despite the disapproval of the Kirk.' (NLS note to its copy of *A Scottish penny wedding*, Belfast, 1840?). [By permission of the National Library of Scotland.]
6   Not to be confused with 'Writer to the Signet' (WS). The term 'writer', as Finlay has pointed out, 'had many popular synonyms (doer, law agent, man of business, solicitor) but all of them referred simply to anyone who held himself out as sufficiently expert to manage the legal affairs of others. The title implied no authorisation by any public authority.' (*Legal Practice in Eighteenth-Century Scotland*, 2).
7   'Generally a procurator was any lawyer admitted to practise in any court where he would be expected to plead.' (Finlay, *Legal Practice in Eighteenth-Century Scotland*, xii).
8   General Assembly *Act approving a Form of Process in the Judicatories of the Church, with relation to Scandals and Censures*, passed on 18 April 1707. The full text was published on a subscription basis by John Bryce of Glasgow in 1763.
9   A reference to a procedural issue in one of two cases involving John Simson (1667-1740), professor of divinity at Glasgow University from 1708 until his suspension from all teaching duties in 1729. At the Assembly of 1717 Simson was cleared of making statements in his lectures of an Arian tendency, and a committee of the Assembly arrived at a compromise decision to suspend but not depose him. It has been said that the two cases made the secession of 1733 inevitable – that is, by virtue of the dismay caused members of the more extreme orthodox faction of the church over what they viewed as Simson's lenient treatment.
10   In Scottish church law 'a prevalent report of scandalous or immoral conduct by a church member'. (*SND*).
11   See the helpful NRS online introduction to Old Parish Register Deaths and Burials where it is explained that 'mortcloth entries' are common in the OPR, either recording the person's

name and date of burial (or interment) or date of (or fee paid for) the hiring of the mortcloth which covered the coffin at a funeral.
12 Like David Logan (see note 4 above) Cunninghame was an elder in Fergusson's Kirk Session.
13 Reverend Robert Dow (1707-87), minister of Ardrossan. John Witherspoon notes in his almanac for 1763 that on 7 July that year he was 'at Saltcoats' (the neighbouring seaside village to Ardrossan]) and 'preached for Mr Dow'. The two would have known each other from JW's Beith days when they were colleagues in the Presbytery of Irvine for the whole of Witherspoon's twelve-year ministry in the Ayrshire town. See Crawford, *LWJW* (2014), 147 and note 28.
14 Scot is almost certainly the shoemaker who was the one man who had come forward to support Leitch in his original complaint to the Presbytery.
15 Cockfighting was commonplace in Britain throughout the eighteenth century and not banned in Scotland until 1895, whereas it had been banned in England and British overseas territories by the Cruelty to Animals Act 1835.
16 We learn later (from Fergusson's exculpation) that she had previously been a servant in his manse.
17 Fergusson's near obsessive hatred of secessionism is described in chapter 5. At one point in his exculpation he states: '... tho he [Leitch] and his associates have been at great pains to publish calumnious stories to create disaffection in my parishioners against me, to this good hour there has not been the least offence taken, or so much as one deserted my Ministry; on the contrary severals [sic] who had seceded from the Church have returned to my Ministry, which shows that it is the sense of my parishioners that their stories and lybels are false and malicious.'
18 The Presbytery met at Glasgow to coincide with the meeting there of the Synod of Glasgow and Ayr on the same day. This was normal practice.
19 'mealling' or 'maling' is 'the action of letting or taking for rent; renting, letting, leasing. Also the management of the letting of a property.' (*DOST*)
20 The patronage of the parish of Kilwinning was traditionally vested in the Montgomeries of Eglinton.
21 A further example of Fergusson airing his knowledge of the technicalities of Scots law. See Stair, *Institutions of the Law of Scotland* (Second ed., 1693), Tit. 41, '*Diligences* Pendente Processu', 1, 683. Applying the terms to 'Precepts direct to Messengers at Arms, commanding Parties, Witnesses, or havers of Writs, to Compear before the *Lords* [the Court]', Stair defines '*Executorials*' – so named 'because they are for putting the Acts to effect, by Execution' – and 'are also called *Compulsators* for the same reason.'
22 The five apologies received include William Leechman of Beith who would demit office there in January 1744 on his appointment as professor of divinity at Glasgow.
23 See note 2 above.
24 Reverend John Fullarton (*primus*) (d. 1761), minister of Dalry from his ordination in 1717 until his death in 1761. He had been a schoolmaster in Irvine prior to his licensing as a minister. His son, also John Fullarton, succeeded him in the charge in 1762. (*Fasti*, New Series, v. III, 85).
25 Reverend John Montgomery (or Montgomerie) (d. 1757), minister of Stewarton from his ordination in 1713 until his death. (*Fasti*, New Series, v. III, 126).

Bibliography

Primary sources

1 Manuscripts and printed Court of Session papers

National Records of Scotland (NRS)

Church records

(a) Papers relevant to chapter 2, 'Profaneness':
Snodgrass et al v Rev. John Witherspoon
See Crawford, *LWJW*, 349.

(b) Papers relevant to Appendix D, 'Alexander Fergusson and James Leitch':
Records (Minutes) of the Presbytery of Irvine, 1742-1744: CH2/197/4-5 (digitised).

(c) Papers relevant to chapter 4, 'The Stage':
Records (Minutes) of the Presbytery of Edinburgh, 1738: NRS CH2/121/13/509, 529; (digitised).

Legal records

(a) Papers relevant to chapter 2, 'Profaneness':
Snodgrass et al v Rev. John Witherspoon
CS26/1776/663 Extract Decreet: Mackenzie office [volume]
For other legal records relating to the process held by NRS see Crawford, *LWJW*, 349.

(b) Papers relevant to chapter 3, 'Bribery and corruption':
Scotlands v The Rev. James Thomson
CS18/1776/421/ Extract Decreet: Dalrymple office [volume]
CS21/1776/1009/1-18 documents relating to the process (box)
'Memorial for the Reverend Mr James Thomson Minister of the first Charge of Dunfermline Against John Scotland Merchant in Dunfermline and Robert Scotland and David Scotland his Sons also merchants there.' [Unpublished MS, signed 'James Boswell' on f. 30; NRS CS21/1776/1009/14/ff.1-30]
[James Boswell's *Memorial* is discussed in chapter 3 and Appendix B]

(c) Papers relevant to chapter 3, 'Bribery and corruption' and, in particular, to Boswell's concern in his unpublished *Memorial* for the 'liberty of the bar' noted in (b) above:

Shaw v Bean (1774-75)
CS235/B/6/4
CS226/8679
CS221/7

(d) Papers relevant to chapter 6, 'Reform':
JC7/48 ff. 212-215: Minute book of High Court of Justiciary for 11 March 1793.

National Library of Scotland (NLS)

(Printed) papers relevant to chapter 6, 'Reform':
LC 1133 (16) *Petition and Complaint of Robert Dundas upon the Reverend Mr William Dunn* (dated 'February 25. 1793.'
LC 1133 (17) *Answers for Mr William Dunn, Minister of Kirkintulloch* [sic] (dated 'March 6. 1793.')

Signet Library, Edinburgh

(a) Papers relevant to chapter 2, 'Profaneness':
Snodgrass et al v Rev. John Witherspoon
SLSP Printed Session Papers, v. 593, 1775-76, case 15.

(b) Papers relevant to chapter 3, 'Bribery and corruption':
Scotlands v The Rev. James Thomson
M6/7a (Kennet Collection).

Advocates Library, Edinburgh

(a) Papers relevant to chapter 2, 'Profaneness':
Snodgrass et al v Rev. John Witherspoon
Pitfour collection 1767, v. 38, 23;
Arniston collection 1775-6, v. 121, 12

(b) Papers relevant to chapter 3, 'Bribery and corruption' and, in particular, to Boswell's concern in his unpublished *Memorial* for the 'liberty of the bar' noted under 'NRS *Legal Records*' above:
Shaw v Bean
Pitfour collection 1774, v. 57, 11.

Paisley Central Library

Paisley Burgess Records 1756-68

Princeton University (Firestone) Library, New Jersey

(a) Almanacs (pocketbooks) dated 1763 (CO199, 1141) and 1768 (CO199, 1140) belonging to John Witherspoon

(b) Hugh Simm papers (C1201)

Dr. Williams's Library, London

James Wodrow-Samuel Kenrick correspondence, MS 21.157-186

University of Indiana Library

Benjamin Rush's *Scottish Journal*.

2 Books and pamphlets (excluding printed Court of Session papers)

[*NB* names of authors inside square brackets indicate that the work was originally published anonymously.]

ADAM, John. *How a Minister should approve himself unto God. A sermon, preached at the opening of the Synod, in the High Church of Glasgow, on Tuesday April 9. 1765.* (Glasgow, for John Gilmour, 1765).

ANDERSON, George. *The Use and Abuse of Diversions. A Sermon on Luke xix. 13. With an Appendix, shewing that the Stage in particular is an Unchristian Diversion* (Edinburgh, R. Fleming and Company, 1733).

– *A Reinforcement of the Reasons proving that the Stage is an Unchristian Diversion* (Edinburgh, R. Fleming, 1733).

[—] *An Estimate of the Profit and Loss of Religion, personally and publicly stated: Illustrated with references to Essays on morality and natural religion* (Edinburgh, s.n., 1753).

– *Remonstrance against Lord Viscount Bolingbroke's Philosophical Religion. Addressed to David Mallet Esq; the Publisher* (Edinburgh, s.n., 1756).

– *The Complaint made to the Presbytery of Edinburgh verified* (Edinburgh, for Gray and Peter, 1756).

ANDERSON, John. *A Sermon Preach'd in the Church of Air. At the opening of the Synod. On Tuesday the First of April 1712. By John Anderson Minister of the Gospel in Dumbarton. Published at the desire of the Synod of Glasgow and Air* (Glasgow, Hugh Brown, 1712?).

– *A Defence of the Church-Government, Faith, Worship & Spirit of the Presbyterians* (Glasgow, Hugh Brown, 1714).

[ANON.] *The Confession of Faith, Together with The Larger and Lesser Catechismses. Composed by the Reverend Assembly of Divines, Sitting at Westminster, Presented to both Houses of Parliament. Again Published with the Scriptures at large, and the Emphasis of the Scriptures in a different Character. ... [The second Edition.]* (London, E[dward]. M[ottershed]. for the Company of Stationers, 1658).

– *Some Remarks upon the Rev*^{d.} *Mr. Anderson's Positions Concerning the Unlawfulness of Stage-Plays* (Edinburgh, R. Fleming, 1733).

– *Ignorance, Falshood [sic], and Malice exposed: or, Remarks upon a Pamphlet, intituled A Warning, &c. Read by Mr. Alexander Ferguson to his Congregation at Kilwining [sic]. Being a Letter from a Seceder in P—y to his Friend in K—w—g.* (Glasgow, John Bryce, sold by Robert Aitken 'at Buchanan's Head in Paisley', 1759).

— *Kilwinning Divinity Weighed and found Wanting: or, The Grand Secret of the New Kilwinning Lodge, concerning Subscription to the Confession of Faith, Tried and Cast* (Glasgow, John Bryce, 1768).
— *The Grounds of the Process set on foot by the Synod of Glasgow and Ayr against Mr Alexander Ferguson, Minister at Kilwinning; As the same is represented in a Series of Letters, published in the Scots Magazine, on both Sides of the Question* (Glasgow, s.n., 1769).
— *A North Briton Extraordinary: Written by a young Scotsman, now a Volunteer in the Corsican Service* (London, J. Knox, 1769).
— *The Humours of the Town, a dramatic interlude, in one act* (Edinburgh, s.n., 1776).
— *A Letter to a Certain Baronet* (Edinburgh, s.n., 1777).
— *A Rhapsody. By a Freeman.* (Edinburgh, s.n., 1777).
— *Asiatick Researches: or, Transactions of the Society, instituted in Bengal, for inquiring into the History and Antiquities of the Arts, Sciences, and Literature, of Asia* (Calcutta, Manuel Cantopher, 1788-89). [The series continued to vol. 20, 1839.]
ARNOT, Hugo. *The History of Edinburgh* (Edinburgh and London, W. Creech and J. Murray, 1779).
[ASSOCIATE PRESBYTERY?] *A Testimony to the Doctrine, Worship, Government and Discipline of the Church of Scotland* (Edinburgh, Thomas Lumisden and John Robertson, 1734).
ASSOCIATE PRESBYTERY. *Act, Declaration and Testimony for the Doctrine, Discipline, Worship and Government of the Church of Scotland; ... By some Ministers ... With an Introduction, containing the grounds of their associating into a Presbytery* (Edinburgh? s.n., 1736).
— *Acts of the Associate Presbytery: viz. I. Act concerning the Doctrine of Grace ... II. Act for renewing the National Covenant, and the Solemn League and Covenant of the three Nations, in a Way and Manner agreeable to our present Situation and Circumstances in this Period.* (Edinburgh, T. W. and T. Ruddimans, 1744).
ATKINS (*aka* ATKYNS), Sir Robert. *Parliamentary and Political Tracts* (Second Edition) (London, Dan. Browne, 1741). [First published London, R. Gosling, 1734.]
BAINE, James. *A sermon preached at the translation of the Rev. Mr. Wotherspoon, from Beith to the Laigh Church of Paisley, June 16, 1757* (Glasgow, Archibald McLean, 1757).
— *The Theatre Licentious and Perverted. Or, a sermon for reformation of manners.* (Edinburgh, J. Reid, 1770).
— *The Case of the Reverend Thomas Gillespie, reviewed. In a Letter to The Reverend Dr W—R* (Edinburgh, J. Reid, 1770).
BAXTER, Richard. *A Christian Directory: Or, A Summ of Practical Theologie, and Cases of Conscience* (London, Robert White for Nevill Simmons, 1673).
BENEZET, Anthony. *A Short Account of that Part of Africa, inhabited by the Negroes. With respect to the Fertility of the Country; the good Disposition of many of the Natives, and the Manner by which the Slave Trade is carried on. ... With Quotations from the Writings of several Persons of Note, viz. George Wallis, Francis Hutcheson, and James Foster, and a large Extract from a Pamphlet, lately published in London, on the Subject of the Slave Trade* (Philadelphia, s.n., 1762). [A second ed. published in the same year is printed by W. Dunlap.]
BERKELEY, George. *Siris: a chain of philosophical reflexions and inquiries concerning the virtues of tar water ... by G.L.B.O.C.* [George, Lord Bishop of Cloyne] (Dublin, Margt. Rhames, 1744).
BLACKBURNE, Francis. *Considerations on the Present State of the Controversy between the Protestants and Papists of Great Britain and Ireland* (London, for A. Millar and T. Cadell, 1768).
[BLACKLOCK, Thomas.] *Protestant Interest Vindicated. In a series of letters to Edmund Burke, Esq.; and other eminent persons. By Valerius Corvinus* (Edinburgh, for William Creech, 1789 [sic]) [The date

in the imprint is '1789', and ESTC gives the date as '1789', but this must be in error for '1779', since the pamphlet is reviewed in the *Scots Magazine*, v. 41, May 1779, 264-66.]

[BLAIR, Hugh.] *The Importance of Religious Knowledge to the Happiness of Mankind. A Sermon preached before The Society for propagating Christian Knowledge: At their Anniversary Meeting in The High Church of Edinburgh, on Monday, January 1. 1750* (Edinburgh, R. Fleming, 1750; re-issued with amendments as Sermon XV, 'On the Importance of Religious Knowledge to Mankind', in *Sermons by Hugh Blair*, etc. v. II, 1780.

[—] *Objections against the Essays on Morality and Natural Religion Examined* (Edinburgh, 1756).

— *A Sermon preached in the High Church of Edinburgh, May 18th, 1746. Before His Grace the Lord High Commissioner to the General Assembly of the Church of Scotland. By Hugh Blair, A.M. One of the Ministers of Canongate. Published by Desire of the Lord High Commissioner* (Edinburgh, R. Fleming for A. Kincaid, 1746).

— *Sermons, by Hugh Blair, D.D. F.R.S. Ed. One of the Ministers of the High Church, and Professor of Rhetoric and Belles Lettres in the University, of Edinburgh* (London, various imprints, 5v., 1777-1794). [*Note* The BL ESTC lists over eighty discrete editions and sets published in London, Dublin and Edinburgh — excluding American editions — from 1777 to 1800. V. 5 in the 'Second Edition' was published in 1801 posthumously by Strahan for Cadell, Davies and Creech and contains an appreciation of Blair by the Rev. Professor James Finlayson (1758-1808).]

— *Lectures on Rhetoric and Belles Lettres* 2v. (London, for W. Strahan, T. Cadell; and W. Creech in Edinburgh, 1783).

— *On the Love of our Country* 'Sermon VI' in *Sermons by Hugh Blair* v. V., 114 -139.

BOSWELL, James. *The Life of Samuel Johnson, LL.D* (London, Charles Dilly, 2v., 1787). ed. David Womersley (London, Penguin Classics, 2008).

— (Yale Editions of Private Papers) *Boswell's London Journal 1762-1763* ed. Frederick A. Pottle (London, William Heinemann, 1950).

— do. *Boswell: The Ominous Years 1774-1776* ed. Charles Ryskamp and Frederick A. Pottle (London, William Heinemann, 1963).

— do. *Boswell in Extremes, 1776-1778* ed. Charles McC. Weis and Frederick A. Pottle (London and New York, McGraw-Hill, 1970).

— *Boswell's Edinburgh Journals 1767-1786* ed. Hugh M. Milne (revised ed., Edinburgh, John Donald, 2013).

— *The Legal Papers of James Boswell Volume 1 29 July 1766 to 11 November 1767* ed. Hugh M. Milne (Edinburgh, The Stair Society, 2013).

— *The Legal Papers of James Boswell Volume 2 12 November 1767 to 11 November 1769* ed. Hugh M. Milne (Edinburgh, The Stair Society, 2016).

[BRUCE, Archibald.] *The Kirkiad: or, Golden Age of the Church of Scotland. Canto I.* (Edinburgh, s.n., 1774).

— *Corruptions in the church to be eradicated. A sermon preached at the opening of the Associate Synod. At Edinburgh, 1778. By A. Bruce, Minister in Whitburn* (Whitburn or Edinburgh, s.n., n.d.).

[—] *The Catechism Modernized and Adapted to the Meridian of Patronage and Late Improvements* ('Eleutheropolis' [Edinburgh?], s.n., 1791).

[BURGH, James.] *Britain's Remembrancer: or, The Danger not over* (London, for M. [Mary] Cooper, 1746).

BURKE, Edmund. *Reflections on the Revolution in France, and on the proceedings in certain societies in London relative to that event. In a letter intended to have been sent to a gentleman in Paris* (London, for J. Dodsley, 1790).

BURNS, Robert. *The Canongate Burns The Complete Poems and Songs of Robert Burns* ed. Andrew Noble and Patrick Scott Hogg (Edinburgh, Canongate Classics, 2001).

CALVIN, John. [trans. Thomas Norton] *The Institution of the Christian Religion: in four books* (Glasgow, John Bryce and Archibald M'Lean, Junior. 'For Alexander Irvine, Printer.' 1762).

— [trans. Beveridge, H.] *Institutes of the Christian Religion* (Peabody, Mass., 2008).

CAMPBELL, George. *The Philosophy of Rhetoric* 2v. (London, for W. Strahan and T. Cadell, and W. Creech 'at Edinburgh', 1776).

— *The Nature, Extent, and Importance, of the Duty of Allegiance: a Sermon, preached at Aberdeen, December 12, 1776, being the Fast Day appointed by the King, on account of the Rebellion in America* (Aberdeen: J. Chalmers and Cº., 1777) [first ed. published, without apparatus.] *The Second Edition, with Notes and Illustrations* (Aberdeen, Chalmers, 1778).

— *Address to the People of Scotland, upon the alarms that have been raised in regard to Popery* (Aberdeen, J. Chalmers and Co., 1779).

CARLYLE, Alexander. *Anecdotes and Characters of the Times* ed. James Kinsley (Oxford and London, OUP, 1973); text also published as *The Autobiography of Dr. Alexander Carlyle of Inveresk 1722-1805* ed. John Hill Burton (London and Edinburgh, T. N. Foulis, 1910).

— *A Full and True History of the Bloody Tragedy of Douglas, As it is now to be seen acting at the Theatre in the Canongate* (Edinburgh, s.n., 1757?).

— *Argument To prove that the Tragedy of Douglas Ought to be Publickly burnt by the Hands of the Hangman* (Edinburgh, s.n., 1757).

— *The Justice and Necessity of the War with our American Colonies Examined. A Sermon, Preached at Inveresk, December 12. 1776, being the Fast-Day appointed by the King, on Account of The American Rebellion. By Alexander Carlyle, D.D. Minister of Inveresk, and Almoner to his Majesty* (Edinburgh, for J. Murray, London, and J. Dickson, Edinburgh, 1777).

— *A Sermon on the death of Sir David Dalrymple, Bar^t Lord Hailes; from Eccles. VII. 3. Preached in the Church of Inveresk, on Sunday the 9th Day of December, 1792. By Alex^r Carlyle, D.D. F.R.S.E. Chaplain to His Majesty, & Minister of that parish. With an address to the Congregation suited to the circumstances of the times* (Edinburgh, John Balfour, 1792).

— *National Depravity The Cause of National Calamities, A Sermon from Jeremiah vi. 8. Preached in the Church of Inveresk, on Thursday Feb. 25 1794; Being the day appointed by his Majesty for a General Fast* (Edinburgh, John Ogle, 1794).

— *The Love of Our Country, Explained and Enforced in a Sermon from Psalm CXXXVII, 5. 6. Preached in St. Andrews Church Edinburgh, March 19 and in Dalkeith Church, April 2. 1797. By Alex. Carlyle, D.D. F.R.S. Edin. Minister of Inveresk, and one of His Majesty's Chaplains* (Edinburgh, William Creech, 1797).

CARMICHAEL, Gershom. *S. Puffendorfii De Officio Hominis et Civis. Juxta Legem Naturalem. Libri Duo.* etc. trans. by Carmichael's modern editors (see next entry) as *Supplements and Observations upon the Two Books of Samuel Pufendorf's On the Duty of Man and Citizen according to the Law of Nature composed for the use of students in the Universities by Gershom Carmichael Professor of Philosophy in the University of Glasgow* the *second edition with additions and amendments (Edinburgh, John Mosman 'and Partners', 1724).

[*The first ed. came out in Glasgow (Donald Govan) in 1718.]

— *Natural Rights on the Threshold of the Scottish Enlightenment: The Writings of Gershom Carmichael* ed. James Moore and Michael Silverthorne, (Indianapolis, Liberty Fund, 2002).

CHARTERS, Samuel. *A Sermon on Alms. ... The Third Edition* (Edinburgh, George Caw, 1795).

[The sermon, preached for the SSPCK, was first published in 1788, without notes].

[CHURCH of SCOTLAND] *The First and Second Booke of Discipline* (London, 1641).
— *Principal Acts of the General Assembly* (Edinburgh, various printers, published annually from 1691, virtually without interruption throughout the eighteenth century and beyond).
— *Letter from the Commission of the General Assembly, of the Church of Scotland to the Honourable Council and Inhabitants of the Scots Colony of Caledonia in America. Dated at Glasgow, July 21, 1699* (Glasgow, Robert Sanders, 1699; same title with minor variants published in Edinburgh in 1699 by George Mosman).
— *The Confession of Faith, larger and shorter catechisms, agreed upon by the Assembly of Divines at Westminster, with the Assistance of Commissioners from the Church of Scotland* (Edinburgh, Thomas Lumisden and John Robertson, 1725).
— *The Form of Process In the Judicatories of the Church of Scotland; With relation to Scandals and Censures* (Glasgow, John Bryce, 1763).
CLAUDE, Jean. *An Essay on the Composition of a Sermon* (Cambridge, Francis Hodson, 2 v. 1778-79).
COBBETT, William ed. 36v. *The Parliamentary History of England 1066-1803* (London, T.C. Hansard, 1806-1820). (see also under Online Databases).
COCKBURN, Henry, Lord. *An Examination of the Trials for Sedition which have hitherto occurred in Scotland* 2v. (Edinburgh, David Douglas, 1888). [Published posthumously; the 'prefatory note' by Cockburn is dated '17th August 1853'.]
COLLIER, Jeremy. *A Defence of the Short View of the Profaneness and Immorality of the English Stage &c. Being a Reply to Mr. Congreve's Amendments, &c. And to the Author of the Relapse* (London, for S. Keble, R. Sare and H. Hindmarsh, 1699).
CRAWFURD, George and SEMPLE, William. *The History of the Shire of Renfrew* (Paisley, Alex. Weir, 1782).
CRICHTON, Thomas. *Memoir of the Life and Writings of John Witherspoon, D.D. LLD. late President of the College of Princeton, New Jersey* in the *Edinburgh Christian Instructor*, October 1829, xxviii, no. x, 674-94. [signed 'A Presbyterian of the West']
[CROSBIE, Andrew.] *Thoughts of a Layman concerning Patronage and Presentations* (Edinburgh, Sands, Murray, and Cochran, 1769).
[DALE, David.?] *Address to the Inhabitants of Glasgow, Paisley, and the Neighbourhood, concerning the African Slave, by a Society in Glasgow* (Glasgow, Alex. Adam, 1791).
[DALRYMPLE, Sir David.] *An Account of Lay-Patronages in Scotland, And of the fatal Differences They have occasion'd betwixt the Church and Lay-Patrons, with Observations on the Arguments for restoring them* (London, s.n., 1712).
DENNIS, John. *The Stage Defended from Scripture, Reason, Experience, and the Common Sense of Mankind, for Two Thousand Years. Occasion'd by Mr Law's late Pamphlet against Stage-Entertainments. ... By Mr. Dennis* (London, for N. Blandford, 1726).
[DRAKE, James.] *The Antient and Modern Stages survey'd. Or, Mr Collier's View of the Immorality and Profaneness of the English Stage set in a True Light* (London, for Abel Roper, 1699).
— *Historia Anglo-Scotica: or an Impartial history of all that happen'd between the Kings and Kingdoms of England and Scotland, from the beginning of the Reign of William the Conqueror, to the Reign of Queen Elizabeth.* (London, for John Hartley, 1703).
DUNN, William. *A Sermon, preached at the opening of the Synod of Glasgow and Air, at Glasgow, 9. October, 1792* (Glasgow, Brash & Reid, 1792).
[—] *An Address by a Scotsman, to his Countrymen and Fellow Citizens, respecting the situation of public affairs, the reform, and the war impending from France* (Glasgow, A. Duncan and R. Chapman, for Brash and Reid, 1793).

DURHAM, James. *The Law Unsealed, or a Practical Exposition of the Ten Commandments* (London, Dorman Newman, 1675). See chapter 4, note 10 for the complex bibliography of this title.

EDWARDS, Jonathan. *Sermons on Various Important Subjects* (Edinburgh, 'Boston printed. Edinburgh reprinted', for M. Gray, 1785).

ERSKINE, David (Lord Dun). *Lord Dun's Friendly and Familiar Advices. Adapted to the various stations and Conditions of Life, and the mutual Relations to be observed amongst them* (Edinburgh, for G. Hamilton and J. Balfour, 1754).

ERSKINE, Ebenezer. *The Stone rejected by the Builders, exalted as the Head-Stone of the Corner. A Sermon preach'd at the Opening of the Synod of Perth and Stirling, at Perth, October 10. 1732. To which is subjoin'd a Sermon preach'd June 4th 1732, on the Sabbath Evening after the Sacrament, from Isa. 1x.6. – The Government shall be upon his Shoulder* (Edinburgh, for David Duncan, 1732).

ERSKINE, John (of Carnock). *The Principles of the Law of Scotland. In the Order of Sir George Mackenzie's Institutions of that Law* 2v. (Edinburgh, Hamilton, Balfour and Neill, 1754).

– *An Institute of the Law of Scotland. In Four Books. In the Order of Sir George Mackenzie's Institutions of that Law* 2v. (Edinburgh, for John Bell, 1773).

– The same, in a 'New Edition with additional notes. By James Ivory, Esq.' 2v. (Edinburgh, Bell & Bradfute, 1824-28).

ERSKINE, John. *The People of God Consider'd as all Righteous; In Three Sermons preach'd at Glasgow, April 1745.* (Edinburgh, T. Lumisden and J. Robertson, for John Traill, 1745).

– *The Qualifications Necessary for Teachers of Christianity*, preached before the Synod of Glasgow and Ayr at Glasgow, October 2. 1750 (Glasgow, Robert Urie, 1750).

– *The Influence of Religion on National Happiness* (Edinburgh, s.n., 1756).

– *Ministers of the Gospel Cautioned against Giving Offence. A sermon by John Erskine, M.A. One of the Ministers of Edinburgh* (Edinburgh, Sands, Murray, and Cochran for William Miller, 1764).

[—] *Shall I Go To War With My American Brethren? A Discourse from Judges the xxth and 28th. Addressed to all concerned in determining that important question* (London, for G. Kearsly, 1769; re-issued in Edinburgh in 1776 (s.n.), with a new preface and with Erskine credited as author on the title page).

[—] *The Equity and Wisdom of Administration, in Measures that have unhappily occasioned the American Revolt, Tried by the Sacred Oracles* (Edinburgh, s.n., 1776).

[—] *Reflections on the Rise, Progress, and probable Consequences, of the Present Contentions with the Colonies. By a Freeholder.* (Edinburgh, s.n., 1776).

– *Considerations on the Spirit of Popery* (Edinburgh, Murray & Cochran, 1778).

– *Prayer for those in civil and military offices recommended, from a view of the influence of Providence on their characters, conduct, and success: a Sermon. Preached before the election of the Magistrates of Edinburgh, Oct. 5. 1779, And published at the request of the Magistrates and Town-Council* (Edinburgh, for W. Gray, 1779).

– *The Fatal Consequences and the General Sources of Anarchy* (Edinburgh, M. Gray, 1793).

– *Doctrinal and Occasional Sermons. Preached by John Erskine D.D. One of the Ministers of the Old Grayfriars* [sic] *Church Edinburgh.* (Edinburgh, for W. Creech and 'Ar. Constable', 1800?).

ERSKINE, Thomas. (attr.) *An Address to the Public from the Friends of the Liberty of the Press; Assembled at the Crown and Anchor on Saturday Jan 19. 1793* (London, C. Stalker, 1793).

FERGUSON, Adam. *The Morality of Stage-Plays Seriously Considered* (Edinburgh, s.n., 1757).

[FERGUSSON (*aka* FERGUSON), Alexander.] *A Warning Relating to the present Schism in the Church of Scotland* (Glasgow? s.n., 1759).

[—] *A Second Warning* [unseen; cited by Scott in *Fasti*, III, 117; not in ESTC under this title.]

— *A Display of the Act and Testimony published by Mr. Ebenezer Erskine and his Associates who separated from the Church of Scotland in the year 1740* (Glasgow, James Knox for 'Mr. Robert Wodrow', 1761).

FERRIER, William. *Two Discourses:-The first preached June 17. 1798, before the Associate Congregation in Paisley, on occasion of the death of the Rev. James Alice, their senior pastor* (Paisley, Neilson & Weir, 1798). [*Crawford* 206-98]

FIELDING, Henry. *Pasquin. A dramatick satire on the times: being the rehearsal of two plays, viz. A Comedy call'd The Election; and a Tragedy call'd The Life and Death of Common-Sense* (London, for J. Watts, 1736).

FILMER, Sir Robert. *Patriarcha: or the Natural Power of Kings* (London, Walter Davis, 1680).

— *A Defence of Plays: or, The Stage vindicated* (London, for Jacob Tonson, 1707).

FINLAYSON, James. *A Short Account of the Life and Character of Dr. Hugh Blair*, in *Sermons by Hugh Blair, D.D. F.R.S.Ed.* v.5, 1801, 455-75. (See above under Blair, Hugh).

FORDYCE, David. *The Elements of Moral Philosophy in Three Books ... By the late Rev. Mr. David Fordyce* (London, for R. and J. Dodsley, 1754). [A modern ed. (Indianapolis, Liberty Fund, 2003) is edited by Thomas Kennedy.]

FORDYCE, James.

— [Version A] *The Delusive and Persecuting Spirit of Popery. A Sermon preached before the Synod of Perth and Stirling at Perth , October 16, 1754.* (Glasgow, R. & A. Foulis [Gaskell 350], 1758).

— [Version B] *The Delusive and Persecuting Spirit of Popery: A Sermon, preached in Monkwell-street, on the 10th of February last, Being the Day appointed for a General Fast* (London, T. Cadell, 1779).

— *The Eloquence of the Pulpit, an Ordination Sermon* (Aberdeen, for A. Thomson, 1752; reprinted in Glasgow as a fourth ed. for R. Banks of Stirling, 1755).

— *An Essay on the Action thought proper for the Pulpit* (London, for R. and J. Dodsley, 1753).

[—] *Sermons to Young Women* 2v. (London, for A. Millar and T. Cadell, 1766).

GERARD, Alexander. *Liberty the cloke of maliciousness, both in the American Rebellion, and in the manners of the times. A Sermon, preached at Old Aberdeen, February 26. 1778, Being the Fast-Day appointed by Proclamation, on account of the Rebellion in America* (Aberdeen: J. Chalmers & Co., 1778).

GILLESPIE, Thomas. *An essay on the continuance of immediate revelations of facts and future events in the Christian church ...With a letter ... by the late Reverend Mr James Cuthbert, Minister of Culross. And a preface; – by John Erskine D.D. one of the Ministers of Edinburgh.* (Edinburgh, A. Murray and J. Cochran for W. Gray, 1771).

— *A Treatise on Temptation* (Edinburgh, for W. Gray, 1774).

[GRAHAM, John.] *The Religious Establishment of Scotland examined upon Protestant Principles: a tract occasioned by The late Prosecution against the late Reverend Mr. Alexander Fergusson, Minister in Kilwinning* (London, for T. Cadell, 1771).

GRANT, Patrick. *The Spirit of Moderation in Religion Recommended. A Sermon, Preached on the 20th of May 1779, In the High Church of Edinburgh, Before His Majesty's High Commissioner, At the opening of the General Assembly of the Church of Scotland* (Edinburgh, Balfour & Smellie, 1779).

[GRANT, William.] *The Present State of the Church of Scotland. With respect to patronages; and the Bill now depending before the Parliament* (London, for J. Roberts, 1736).

GREEN, Ashbel. *The Life of The Revd John Witherspoon D.D., LL.D. with a brief review of his writings: and a summary estimate of his character and talents* ed. Henry Lyttleton Savage (Princeton, Princeton University Press, 1973).

HARDY, Thomas. *Fidelity to the British Constitution, The Duty and Interest of the People. A Sermon, preached in the New North Church, Edinburgh, On Thursday, February 27. 1794, being the day appointed by His Majesty for a General Fast* (Edinburgh, David Willison, 1794).

— *The Progress of the Christian Religion. A Sermon, preached before the Society in Scotland for Propagating Christian Knowledge, at their Anniversary Meeting in the High Church of Edinburgh, Thursday, May 30. 1793. By Thomas Hardy, D.D. One of the ministers of the City, and Regius Professor of Divinity and Ecclesiastical History in the University of Edinburgh* (Edinburgh, John Paterson, 1794).

HERDER, Johann Gottfried von. *Ideas on the Philosophy of the History of Humankind (Izeen zur Philosophie der Geshichte der Menscheit)* (v. 1, 1784) Extract in English in *The Idea of Race*, ed. Robert Bernasconi and Tommy L. Lott (Indianapolis, Hackett, 2000), 23-26.

HILL, George. *A View of the Constitution of the Church of Scotland* 3rd. ed. (Edinburgh, John Waugh, 1835).

HOME, Henry (Lord Kames). *Essays on the Principles of Morality and Natural Religion* (Edinburgh, R. Fleming for A. Kincaid and A. Donaldson, 1751).

— *Elucidations respecting the Common and Statute Law of Scotland* (Edinburgh, for William Creech, 1800): a 'new edition' of Creech's first ed. of 1777.

HOWELL, T. B. *A Complete Collection of State Trials ... From the earliest period to the year 1783 ...* [v.1 to v. 21, 1809-1814] *and continued from the year 1783 to the present time: By Thomas Jones Howell* [v. 22 to v. 33, 1815-1826] (London, T. C. Hansard, 1809-26).

HUME, David. *Three Essays, Moral and Political: Never Before Published* [containing the essay, 'Of National Characters'] (London, for A. Millar, and A. Kincaid in Edinburgh, 1748).

— *Essays, Moral and Political* (Third Edition) [containing this same essay] (London, for A. Millar, and A. Kincaid in Edinburgh, 1748).

— *Enquiry concerning the Principles of Morals* (London, for A. Millar, 1751).

— *Political Discourses* [containing the essay, 'On the Populousness of Antient Nations'] (Edinburgh, R. Fleming, 1752).

— *Essays and Treatises on Several Subjects* 4v. [v. I contains an added footnote to the essay, 'Of National Characters'] (London, for A. Millar, and A. Kincaid and A. Donaldson in Edinburgh, 1753).

— *Four Dissertations. I. The Natural history of Religion. II. Of the Passions. III. Of Tragedy. IV. Of the Standard of Taste.* (London, William Bowyer for A. Millar, 1757).

— *Selected Essays* ed. Stephen Copley and Andrew Edgar (Oxford and New York, OUP, 1993).

— *The Letters of David Hume* 2v. ed. J.Y.T. Greig (Oxford, OUP, 1932).

HUME, (Baron) David. *Commentaries on the Law of Scotland, Respecting the Description and Punishment of Crimes* 2 v. (Edinburgh, Bell & Bradfute, 1797).

HUTCHESON, Francis. *Philosophiae Moralis Institutio Compendiaria* (Glasgow, Robert Foulis [Gaskell 22], 1742; and rev. second ed. [Gaskell 62], 1745); Indianapolis, Liberty Fund (with the next work listed below), ed. Luigi Turco, 2007).

— *A Short Introduction to Moral Philosophy* (Glasgow, Robert Foulis [Gaskell 85], 1747).

— *A System of Moral Philosophy in Three Books; written by the late Francis Hutcheson, L.L.D ... To which is prefixed Some Account of the Life, Writings, and Character of the Author, by the Reverend William Leechman, D.D.* 3v. (London, A. Millar, 1755).

[HYNDMAN, John.] *A Just View of the Constitution of the Church of Scotland* (Edinburgh, s.n., 1753).

ILCHESTER, Earl of. *Letters to Henry Fox Lord Holland with a few addressed to his brother Stephen, Earl of Ilchester* ed. The Earl of Ilchester (London, Roxburghe Club, 1915).

[JAMIESON, John.] *Socinianism Unmasked in Four Letters to the Lay-Members of the Church of Scotland, and especially to those of the Collegiate Church of Ayr: occasioned by Dr M'Gill's Practical Essay on the Death of Jesus Christ* (Edinburgh, W. Creech, 1787; re-issued in 1790 as a second ed. 'corrected and enlarged').

JOHNSON, Samuel. *Taxation no Tyranny; an Answer to the Resolutions and Address of the American Congress* (London, T. Cadell, 1775).

JOHNSTON, David. *The signal Deliverances which have been wrought for these Kingdoms, and the most probable means of obtaining a like Divine Interposition in the present conjuncture of public affairs, illustrated, in a Sermon, Preached on occasion of the General Fast, Feb. 9. 1779* (Edinburgh, Murray and Cochran ,1779).

[JONES, William. (translator)] *Sacontalá; or, The Fatal Ring: An Indian Drama. By Cálidás. Translated from the original Sanscrit and Pracrit* (Edinburgh, for J. Mundell, 1796).

[KENNEDY, James.] *Treason!!! or, not treason!!! Alias The Weavers Budget* (London, for Daniel Eaton, 1795).

KNOX, John. *A Sermon preached by Iohn Knox Minister of Christ Iesus in the Publique audience of the Church of Edenbrough, within the Realme of Scotland, upon Sonday, the 19. of August. 1565. For the which the said Iohn Knoxe was inhibite preaching for a season.* (London, Henry Denham? 1566).

[—] *The Historie of the Reformation of the Church of Scotland* (* London, John Raworth for George Thomason and Octavian Pullen, 1644).

* reprinted in the same year in Edinburgh by Robert Bryson. See 'Introduction', note 59.

– do. ed. William Croft Dickinson (Edinburgh, Thomas Nelson, 1949).

LAW, William. *The Absolute Unlawfulness of the Stage-Entertainment Fully Demonstrated* (London, W. and J. Innys, 1726).

[LOGAN, George.] *A Modest and Humble Inquiry concerning the Right and Power of Electing and Calling Ministers to Vacant Churches. By a minister of the Church of Scotland.* (Edinburgh, Gavin Hamilton, 1732; re-issued in a revised ed. in 1733 as *The Humble and Modest Inquiry* etc.).

[—] *An Overture for a Right Constitution of the General Assembly* (Edinburgh, R. Fleming, 1736).

— *A Sermon preached at the Opening of the General Assembly of the Church of Scotland, in the High-Church of Edinburgh, on the 14th of May 1741; before His Majesty's High-Commissioner* (Edinburgh, R. Fleming and A. Allison, 1741).

[LONG, Edward.] *The History of Jamaica* 3v. (London, for T. Lowndes, 1774).

MACARTHUR, Daniel. *The Church of Rome, the Mother of Abominations: A Sermon delivered in the Black-Friars Church, on Monday, 16th November, 1778* (Glasgow, Alex. Adam, 1778).

'M'CONNEL, James, Indweller in Beith'. *Some Remarks on a Book lately come abroad into this Nation, Intitled The Religious Establishment of Scotland, examined on Protestant Principles, &c.* [Edinburgh] [s.n.] (1772).

McCULLOCH, William. *A Sermon against the Idolatrous Worship of the Church of Rome. Preach'd in the New-Church of Glasgow, the Fifth of November, 1725* (Glasgow, Robert Sanders, 1726).

[McDOUALL, Andrew (Lord Bankton).] *An Institute of the Laws of Scotland in Civil Rights: with observations upon the Agreement or Diversity between them and the Laws of England. In Four Books.* 3v. (Edinburgh, R. Fleming for A. Kincaid and A. Donaldson, 1751). (Re-issued by the Stair Society, Edinburgh, with Foreword by W. M. Gordon, 1993).

McGILL, William. *A Practical Essay on the Death of Jesus Christ* (Edinburgh, Mundell and Wilson, 1786).

– *The Benefits of the Revolution. A Sermon, preached at Ayr, on the 5th of November, 1788, by William McGill, D. D. To which are added, Remarks on a sermon, preached on the same day, at Newton upon Ayr; very necessary for all the Readers of said Sermon.* (Kilmarnock, J. Wilson, 1789).

MACLAURIN, Reverend John. *Sermons and Essays by the late Reverend Mr. John M'Laurin, one of the Ministers of Glasgow* (Glasgow, James Knox, 1755).

[MACLAURIN, John (later Lord Dreghorn).] *Apology for The Writers against the Tragedy of Douglas. With some remarks on that Play.* (Edinburgh, s.n., 1757).

[—] *The Philosopher's Opera* (do.)

[—] *The Deposition, or Fatal Miscarriage: a Tragedy* (do.)

[—] (attr.) *The Stage or the pulpit: a sermon. Sung By the Reverend author of Douglas, the first night he went to see his own play represented. To the tune of Gill Morice* (do.)

[—] *Considerations on the Right of Patronage* (Edinburgh?, s.n., 1766).

MACLEOD, (*aka* McLeod), Bannatyne W. (later Lord Bannatyne). *Memorial for George Bean, writer in Inverness, Defender, against Angus Shaw, merchant in Inverness, Pursuer.* [dated 'July 5. 1774.'] (Edinburgh? 1775).

[MACPHERSON, James.] *The Rights of Great Britain Asserted Against the Claims of America: Being an Answer to the Declaration of the General Congress* (London, for T. Cadell, 1776).

MAXWELL, James. *On the French Revolution. A Moral Essay on the Rights of Man. By James Maxwell, Poet in Paisley* (Paisley, J. Neilson, 1792). [Crawford 138-92]

– *Issachar, the Strong Ass Over-Burdened; or, The Groans of Brittannia* [sic] *from the Pitt. A poem descriptive of the times. Part II. By J.M. author of the first part* (Paisley, s.n., 1795?). [Crawford 172-95]

MILLAR, John. *The Origin of the Distinction of Ranks: or, an inquiry into the circumstances which give rise to influence and authority, in the different members of society* (Third ed., London, J. Murray, 1779). [The title of Millar's first ed., published by Murray in 1771 and printed by W. and J. Richardson, is *Observations concerning the distinction of ranks in society*. A fourth ed. was published posthumously in 1806 in Edinburgh by William Blackwood; it is this ed. that is used for the Liberty Fund ed. (Indianapolis, 2006), ed. Aaron Garrett.]

MOIR, James. *A Distinct and Impartial Account of the Process for Socinian Heresy against William M'Gill. D.D. one of the ministers of Ayr.* (Edinburgh, for J. Laing, 1790).

[MONTESQUIEU, Charles de Secondat, Baron de.] *De L'Esprit des Loix.* (' A Edinbourg, Chez G. Hamilton & J. Balfour.', 1750). [*NB* As published in this 'Nouvelle Edition', the work is unattributed, yet the English version published in London in the same year by J. Nourse and P. Vaillant bears Montesquieu's name on the title-page.]

MOODIE, William. *Political Preaching: or the meditations of a well-meaning man, on a sermon lately published; in a letter addressed to the Rev. Mr. William Dun* (Glasgow, Brash and Reid, 1792).

– *Sermons by the late Reverend William Moodie* (Edinburgh, C. Stewart, 1813).

MORISON, Archibald. *Review of a paper published in the Glasgow Courier, on the 23 January, 1796, called a Deed of the Relief Congregation of Paisley, also of a handbill industriously circulated ... with observations respecting lawful authority, and the only method of having petitions and addresses answered. By Archibald Morison, one of the Paisley Volunteers* (Air [sic], J. and P. Wilson, 1796).

MORISON, William Maxwell. *The Decisions of the Court of Session, from its first institution to the present time, digested under proper heads, in the form of a Dictionary* (Edinburgh, Bell & Bradfute, 22 v., 1801-15). [v. 22 is a supplementary volume – *Dictionary of the Decisions of the Court of Session* (Edinburgh, for John Anderson, 1815).]

MORREN, Nathaniel. *Annals of the General Assembly of the Church of Scotland from the Final Secession in 1739, to the Origin of the Relief in 1752* (Edinburgh, John Johnstone, 1838).

– *Annals of the General Assembly from the Origin of the Relief in 1752, to the Rejection of the Overture on Schism in 1766* (Edinburgh, John Johnstone, 1840).

PAINE, Thomas. *Common Sense: Addressed to the Inhabitants of America* ('Philadelphia, Printed: ['To promote the traitorous purposes therein set forth.] ... 'Edinburgh, re-printed', s.n., 1776).

– *Rights of Man: being an Answer to Mr. Burke's Attack on the French Revolution* [Part I] (London, for J. Johnson, 1791).

— *Rights of Man: Part the Second. Combining Principle and Practice* (London, 'printed for the booksellers', 1792).
— [both Parts] with an intro. by Eric Foner (London, Penguin Classics, 1985).
—*The Thomas Paine Reader* ed. Michael Foot and Isaac Kramnick (London, Penguin Classics, 1987)
PEEBLES, William. *The Great Things which the Lord hath done for this nation, illustrated and improved; in Two Sermons preached on the 5th of November, 1788, the day appointed by the General Assembly of the Church of Scotland, for a National Thanksgiving, in Commemoration of the Revolution, 1688. To which is subjoined an Ode to Liberty.* (Kilmarnock, J. Wilson, 1789).
PINKERTON, John. *A Dissertation on the Origin and Progress of the Scythians or Goths. Being an Introduction to the Ancient and Modern History of Europe* (London, John Nichols, 1787; also bound in with v. 2 of Pinkerton's *An Enquiry into the History of Scotland*, 1789).
PITT, William. *The Speeches of the Right Honourable William Pitt, in the House of Commons* 4v. ed. W. S. Hathaway (London, Longman, 1806).
PRICE, Richard. *Observations on the Nature of Civil Liberty, the Principles of Government, and the Justice and Policy of the War with America* (London, for T. Cadell; 'and re-printed and sold by David Bruce in Charlestown, South-Carolina', 1776).
— *Additional Observations on the Nature and Value of Civil Liberty, and the War with America* (London, for T. Cadell, 1777).
— *A Discourse on the Love of Our Country, delivered on November 4, 1789 at the Meeting-House in the Old Jewry, to the Society for Commemorating the Revolution in Great Britain* (London, George Stafford for T. Cadell, 1789).
PRIESTLEY, Joseph. *A Sermon on the subject of the Slave Trade; delivered to a society of Protestant Dissenters, at the New Meeting, in Birmingham; and published at their request* (Birmingham, Pearson and Rollason, 1788).
PRYNNE, William. *Histrio-Mastix. The Players Scourge, or, Actors TragÆdie*
RAITHBY, John and TOMLINS, Sir Thomas E. [v. 1-2 ed. Tomlins, v. 3-20 ed. Raithby.] *The Statutes At Large, of England and of Great Britain : from Magna Carta to the Union of the Kingdoms of Great Britain and Ireland* 20v. (London, G. Eyre and A. Strahan, 1811).
[RAMSAY, Allan.] *Poems. By Allan Ramsay* (Edinburgh, for the Author, 1720).
[—] *Some Few Hints, In Defence of Dramatical Entertainments* (Edinburgh? s.n., 1728?).
— *The Gentle Shepherd; a Scots Pastoral Comedy. By Allan Ramsay. The Seventh Edition with the Sangs.* (Glasgow, Robert Foulis, 1743). [The Foulis Press printed a total of seven editions of Ramsay's most popular work between 1743 and 1796 (Gaskell, 417).]
RAMSAY, James. *An Essay on the Treatment and Conversion of African Slaves in the British Sugar Colonies* (London, James Phillips, 1784).
— *An Inquiry into the Effects of Putting a Stop to the African Slave Trade, and of Granting Liberty to the Slaves in the British Sugar Colonies* (London, James Phillips, 1784).
[RANDALL, Thomas.] *Observations on the letters published by the Rev. Mr. James Baine entitled Memoirs of Modern Church Reformation: or, The History of the General Assembly 1766* (Glasgow, James Duncan, 1767).
— 'A candid inquiry into the constitution of the church of Scotland, in relation to the settlement of ministers', in *Tracts concerning Patronage, By some Eminent Hands.* (Edinburgh, W. Gray, 1770). [Randall, it is supposed, edited the compilation.]
RHIND, Thomas. *An Apology for Mr. Thomas Rhind. Or An Account of the Manner how, and the Reasons for which he separated from the Presbyterian Party, and embraced the Communion of the Church* (Edinburgh, Robert Freebairn, 1712).

ROBERTSON, William. *The Situation of the World at the Time of Christ's Appearance, and its Connexion with the Success of his Religion, considered. A Sermon preached before the Society in Scotland for propagating Christian Knowledge, At their Anniversary Meeting, In the High Church of Edinburgh, On Monday, January 6. 1755. ... By William Robertson, Minister of the Gospel at Gladsmuir* (Edinburgh, Hamilton, Balfour, and Neill, 1755).

— *The History of the Reign of the Emperor Charles V* 3v. (London, W. and W. Strahan for W. Strahan and T. Cadell, and J. Balfour, Edinburgh, 1769).

— *The History of America* 2v. (London, W. Strahan and T. Cadell, and J. Balfour, Edinburgh, 1777).

— *The History of Scotland, during the reigns of Queen Mary and of King James VI, till his Accession to the Crown of England* 2v. (London, for A. Millar, 1759).

[ROEBUCK, John.] [A 'new edition' in the same year attributes the work to him.] *An Enquiry, whether The Guilt of the Present Civil War in America, ought to be imputed to Britain or America* (London, for John Donaldson, 1776).

ROSCOE, Henry. *Reports of Cases argued and determined in the Court of King's Bench in the 19th, 20th, and 21st years of Geo. III* v.III (London, S. Sweet and Stevens and Sons, 1831).

RUNDLE, Thomas. *A Sermon preached at St. George's Church Hanover Square, On Sunday February 17, 1734. To recommend the Charity for establishing the New Colony of Georgia* (London, for T. Woodward and J. Brindley, 1734).

RUSH, Benjamin. *The Letters of Benjamin Rush* ed. L. H. Butterfield, 2v. (Princeton, Princeton University Press, for the American Philosophical Society, 1951).

'SCOTUS AMERICANUS' [sometimes attr. to William Thom] *Informations concerning the Province of North Carolina, addressed to Emigrants from the Highlands and Western Isles of Scotland. By an impartial hand* (Glasgow, for James Knox, and Charles Elliot, Edinburgh, 1773).

[SCOUGAL, Henry (attr.)] *The Life of God in the Soul of Man* (London, for Charles Smith and William Jacob, 1677).

SHAW, Lachlan. *The History of the Province of Moray* (Edinburgh, William Auld, 1775).

SINCLAIR, Sir John. *The Statistical Account of Scotland. Drawn up from the communications of the ministers of the different parishes.* 21v. (Edinburgh, William Creech, 1791-99). [See also below under 'Online databases'.]

SMITH, Adam. *The Theory of Moral Sentiments* (London, for A. Millar, 1759; ed. D. D. Raphael and A. L. Macfie, Oxford, OUP, 1976).

— *Lectures on Jurisprudence* ed. R. L. Meek, D. D. Raphael and P. G. Stein (Oxford, OUP, 1978).

— *Lectures on Rhetoric and Belles Lettres* ed. J. C. Bryce (Oxford, OUP, 1983).

— *An Inquiry into the Nature and Causes of the Wealth of Nations. By Adam Smith, LL.D. and F.R.S. Formerly Professor of Moral Philosophy in the University of Glasgow* 2v. (London, for W. Strahan and T. Cadell, 1776; also in Penguin Classics, Books 1-III, ed. Andrew S. Skinner, 1986, Books IV-V, ed. Skinner, 1999).

— *The Correspondence of Adam Smith* ed. Ernest Campbell Mossner and Ian Simpson Ross (Oxford, Clarendon Press, 1977).

'SMITH, William'. [sometimes attr. to William Thom] *Information to Emigrants, being the Copy of a Letter from a Gentleman in North-America* (Glasgow, Morrison and Mcallum [sic], 1773).

SNODGRASS, John. *Leading Doctrines of the Gospel Stated and Defended. A Sermon, preached before the Society in Scotland for Propagating Christian Knowledge, at their Anniversary Meeting in the High Church of Edinburgh, Thursday, May 29. 1794* (Edinburgh, John Paterson, 1794).

SOMERVILLE, Thomas. *A Discourse on our Obligation to Thanksgiving, for the Prospect of the Abolition of the African Slave-Trade, with a Prayer. Delivered in the church of Jedburgh on April 15* (Kelso, J. Palmer, 1792).

— *My Own Life and Times 1741-1814* (Edinburgh, Edmonston & Douglas, 1861).
THOM, William. [see also under Smith, William.] *An Enquiry into the Causes of the Decline of Religion* (Glasgow, Robert Urie, 1761).
[—] *A Short History of the late General Assembly of the Church of Scotland, shewing the rise and progress of the schism overture, the reasonableness or necessity that some restriction be put to the exercise of the Patronage-Act, and the means which the Church hath in its own power to mitigate or remove that grievance* (Glasgow, James Duncan, 1766).
[—] *The Happiness of Dead Clergymen, Provided they die in the Lord. A Funeral Sermon. Preached in the L—gh K—k of Gl—g—w, on the Death of the C—m—tee which sat there. By the R—v—d D—T–* (Glasgow, 'Typis Academicis', 1769).
[—] *A Vindicatio[n] of Doctor Tail, from the Charge of Heresy; Being A Defence of a Sermon entitled, The Happiness of Dead Clergymen, &c. By the Reverend Doctor Tail.* (Glasgow, 'Typis Academicis', 1770).
[—] *Seasonable Advice to the Landholders and Farmers in Scotland. A sermon, on Exod. iii. 7, 8. ... By a minister of the Gospel* (Edinburgh, J. Robertson, 1770).
[—] *A Letter of Advice to the Farmers, Land-Labourers, and Country Tradesmen in Scotland, concerning Roups of Growing Corn, and of Tacks* (Glasgow, James Duncan, 1771).
— *The Revolt of the Ten Tribes. A Sermon, preached in the Church of Govan, on the Forenoon of the Public Fast, December 12th, 1776. By the Reverend William Thom, A.M. Minister of Govan* (Glasgow, Robert Chapman and Alexander Duncan, 1778).
— *Achan's Trespass in the Accursed Thing considered. A Sermon, preached in the Church of Govan, on the Public Fast. February 26th, 1778. By the Reverend William Thom, A.M. Minister of Govan* (Glasgow, James Duncan, 1778; reprinted by John Robertson of Edinburgh in 1779).
— *From whence come Wars? An Enquiry into the Origin, with a View of the Progress and Effects, of War. A Sermon, preached in the Church of Govan, on the Public Fast, February 9th, 1779. By the Reverend William Thom, A.M. Minister of Govan* (Glasgow, Robert Chapman and Alexander Duncan, 1782).
— *The Works of the Rev. William Thom, Late Minister of Govan* (Glasgow, James Dymock, 1799).
'THRUM, Tam' (i.e. William Brown). *Look before ye loup: or, a healin' sa' for the crackit crowns of country politicians. By Tam Thrum, an auld weaver* (Edinburgh, s.n., 1793).
— do. *Part second, or anither box of healin' sa' for the crackit crowns of country politicians* (Edinburgh, William Brown, 1794).
WALKER, Robert (1716-83). *Sermons on Practical Subjects* (Edinburgh, for A. Kincaid and J. Bell, 1765).
WALKER, Robert (1755-1808). *The sentiments and conduct becoming Britons in the present conjuncture* (Edinburgh, for William Creech, 1794).
[WALKER, Thomas.] *The Terms of Ministerial and Christian Communion imposed on the Church of Scotland by a Prevailing Party in the General Assembly, in Opposition to the Great Bulk both of Office-Bearers and private Christians, considered in some Conferences between two Neighbouring Ministers.* (Glasgow, s.n., 1753).
— *Infidelity a Proper Object of Censure* (Glasgow, John Bryce and David Paterson, 1756).
— *A Vindication of the Discipline and Constitutions of the Church of Scotland, for preserving Purity of Doctrine: in reply to a Book, intitled, The Religious Establishment of Scotland* (Edinburgh, W. Gray, 1774).
WALLACE, George. *A System of the Principles of the Law of Scotland. By George Wallace, Advocate. Vol. I* (Edinburgh, for A. Millar, D. Wilson and T. Durham in London; and G. Hamilton and J. Balfour, Edinburgh, 1760). [No further volumes were published.]
WALLACE, Robert. *A Dissertation on the Numbers of Mankind in antient and modern Times: in which The superior Populousness of Antiquity is maintained* (Edinburgh, for G. Hamilton and J. Balfour, 1753).

— *The Doctrine of Passive Obedience and Non-Resistance Considered … Published on occasion of Lord Dun's Friendly and Familiar Advices* (Edinburgh, Hamilton, Balfour and Neill, 1754).

[WARTON, Joseph.] *An Essay on the Writings and Genius of Pope* (London, for M. Cooper, 1756). [A note on the last page states that this is a first v.; Warton published a second v. in 1782.]

WASHINGTON, George. *The Papers of George Washington, Presidential Series*, v. 13, 1 June-31 August 1793, ed. Christine Sternberg Patrick (Charlottesville and London, University Press of Virginia, 2007). (also online)

WEBSTER, Alexander. *The Wicked Life, and Fatal but Deserved Death of Haman, Ahasuerus's Prime Minister. A Sermon preached before the Right Honourable Lord Provost, Magistrates and Town-Council of Edinburgh, at their Election, on Tuesday 30th September, 1740. By Mr. Webster.* (Edinburgh, for John Traill, 1740). [A second ed. was issued in the same year. The title was subsequently reprinted in 1797 in Edinburgh by J. Guthrie and J. Ogle.]

WESLEY, John. *A Calm Address to our American Colonies* (London, R. Hawes, 1775).

— *The Journal of the Rev. John Wesley, A.M.* ed. Nehemiah Curnock (London, Robert Culley [v. 1 only; v. 2-8 Charles H. Kelly], 8 v., 1909-16).

WILLISON, John. *Popery another Gospel: or, A Demonstration that the Romish Religion is not the Gospel that Christ hath left his Church, but what Anti-Christ hath since devised, to the Destruction of Christianity and the Souls of Men. In Six Sermons from Gal. i. 8 Preached in the Time of the Rebellion, Anno 1745* (Edinburgh, Thomas Lumisden and John Robertson, 1746). [Reprinted in Falkirk in 1779 'for W. Burns, *Preacher*, the Publisher'.]

WILSON, Alexander. *The Poems and Literary Prose of Alexander Wilson, the American Ornithologist* 2v. ed. Alexander B. Grosart (Paisley, Alex. Gardner, 1876).

WILSON, Gabriel. *The Trust. A Sermon, At the Opening of the Provincial Synod of Mers and Teviotdale, at Kelso, October 17, 1721* (Edinburgh? 1723).

WISHART, George. *A Letter to the Author of a Pamphlet intituled Lawfulness and Necessity of Ministers, their reading the Act of Parliament for bringing to justice the murderers of Captain John Porteous* (Edinburgh, s.n., 1737).

WISHART, William. *Publick Virtue recommended. A Sermon preach'd in the High-Church of Edinburgh, On Thursday, May 8th, 1746. At the Opening of the General Assembly of the Church of Scotland* (Edinburgh, R. Fleming for A. Kincaid, 1746).

WITHERSPOON, John. *The Works of the Rev. John Witherspoon* with an introduction by L. Gordon Tait (Bristol, Thoemmes Press, 2003), based on the 4 v. set (Philadelphia: William W. Woodward, 1800-1802).

— *The Selected Writings of John Witherspoon* ed. Thomas Miller (Carbondale and Edwardsville, Southern Illinois University Press, 1990).

[—] *Ecclesiastical Characteristics: or, the Arcana of Church Policy. Being an humble Attempt to open up the Mystery of Moderation* (Glasgow, s.n., 1753).

— *A Serious Enquiry into the Nature and Effects of the Stage* (Glasgow, J. Bryce and D. Paterson, 1757).

— *The Charge of Sedition and Faction against Good Men, especially Faithful Ministers, considered and accounted for* (Glasgow, J. Bryce and D. Paterson, 1758).

— *Seasonable Advice to Young Persons: A Sermon on Psalm i. 1. Preached in the Laigh Church of Paisley, On Sabbath, Feb. 21st, 1762. To which is prefixed, An Authentic Narrative of the disorderly and riotous Meeting, on the Night before the Celebration of the Lord's Supper in that Place, which gave occasion to the Discourse.* (Glasgow, Robert Urie, 1762).

[—] *A Serious Apology for the Ecclesiastical Characteristics by the Real Author of that Performance* (Edinburgh, William Gray, 1763).

— *Essays on Important Subjects* (London, 3v., for Edward and Charles Dilly, 1765).
— *The Dominion of Providence over the Passions of Men. A Sermon preached at Princeton, on the 17th of May, 1776. Being the General Fast appointed by the Congress through the United Colonies. To which is added, An Address to the Natives of Scotland residing in America. By John Witherspoon, D.D. President of the College of New-Jersey* (Philadelphia, Robert Aitken, 1776).
— *Lectures on Moral Philosophy*, in *WJW*, 3, 365-472; and in *SWJW*, 152-230.
WODROW, Robert. *The History of the Sufferings of the Church of Scotland, from the Restauration to the Revolution* 2v. (Edinburgh, James Watson, 1721-22).

3 Newspapers and serials

The Scots Magazine
The Gentleman's Magazine
The Caledonian Mercury
The Edinburgh Christian Instructor
The Edinburgh Evening Courant
The Edinburgh Review
The Glasgow Journal
The Glasgow Courier

4 Online databases

Acts of the General Assembly of the Church of Scotland 1638-1842 (British History Online, Institute of Historical Research, University of London, School of Advanced Study)
Eighteenth Century Collections Online (ECCO) (JISC Historical Texts)
English Short Title Catalogue (British Library)
Founders Online (US government National Records and Archives Administration in partnership with the University of Virginia Press)
History of Parliament: The House of Commons 1754-90 (British History Online)
House of Lords Journal v. 35 1776-1779 (British History Online)
Journals of the Continental Congress online (Library of Congress *American Memory*)
'Old' Statistical Account of Scotland 1792-1798 online (EDINA)
Oxford Dictionary of National Biography online ed. [*DNB*] (Oxford University Press)
(Cobbett's) Parliamentary History of England (Oxford University Digital Libraries online)
Scottish Book Trade Index (National Library of Scotland)

Secondary sources

1 Books

AHNERT, Thomas. *The Moral Culture of the Scottish Enlightenment, 1690-1805* (New Haven and London, Yale University Press, 2014).
[ANON.] *The Early History of Church Patronage ... By a Member of the Faculty of Advocates* (Edinburgh, John Waugh, 1833).
ARMSTRONG, Murray. *The Liberty Tree The stirring story of Thomas Muir and Scotland's first fight for democracy* (Edinburgh, Word Power Books, 2014).
BATTESTIN, Martin C. (with Ruthe R. Battestin) *Henry Fielding A Life* (London, Routledge, 1993).

BAWCUTT, Priscilla and RIDDY, Felicity, eds. *Longer Scottish Poems Volume One 1375-1650* (Edinburgh, Scottish Academic Press ,1987).

BELL, William. *Dictionary and Digest of the Law of Scotland* (Edinburgh, John Anderson and Bell & Bradfute, 1838; revised edition, ed. George Ross (Edinburgh, Bell & Bradfute, 1861).

BERLIN, Isaiah. *Liberty* (Oxford and New York, OUP, 2002).

– *Political Ideas in the Romantic Age* (Princeton and Oxford, Princeton University Press, 2006).

BOYD, Julian P. *The Declaration of Independence and the Evolution of the Text* (Princeton, Princeton University Press, 1945; revised ed., Library of Congress, 2000).

BRIMS, John D. See 3 below.

BROADIE, Alexander. ed. *The Scottish Enlightenment An Anthology* (Edinburgh, Canongate, 1997).

– *The Scottish Enlightenment* (Edinburgh, Birlinn, 2001).

– ed. *The Cambridge Companion to the Scottish Enlightenment* (Cambridge, CUP, 2003).

BROWN, Callum G. *The Social History of Religion in Scotland since 1730* (London and New York, Methuen, 1987).

BROWN, Michael. See 2 below.

BROWN, Raymond Lamont. *Robert Burns's Tour of the Highlands and Stirlingshire 1787* (Ipswich, Boydell Press, 1973).

BROWN, Stewart J., ed. *William Robertson and the Expansion of Empire* (Cambridge, CUP, 1997). [See also under Phillipson, N.; Kidd, C.; and Carnall, G. in section 2 below, 'Journal articles and book chapters'.]

BRUNTON, George and HAIG, David. *An Historical Account of the Senators of the College of Justice, from its institution in MDXXXII* [1532] (Edinburgh, Thomas Clark, 1832).

BURLEIGH, J. H. S. *A Church History of Scotland* (London, OUP, 1960).

BUTTERFIELD, L. H. *John Witherspoon Comes to America A documentary account based largely on new materials* (Princeton, Princeton University Press, 1953).

CAMERON, John. *The Parish of Campsie* (Kirkintilloch, D. Macleod, 1892).

CARRUTHERS, Gerard and MARTIN, Don eds. *Thomas Muir of Huntershill: Essays for the Twenty First Century* (Edinburgh, Humming Earth, 2016).

CHADWICK, Owen. *The Reformation* (Harmondsworth, Penguin Books, 1964).

CHITNIS, Anand C. *The Scottish Enlightenment: a social history* (London, Croom Helm, 1976).

CLARK, Sir George. *The Later Stuarts 1660-1714* Second ed. (Oxford, Clarendon Press, 1956).

CLARK, Ian D. L. See 3 below.

CLARK, Ivo Macnaughton. *A History of Church Discipline in Scotland* (Aberdeen, W. and W. Lindsay, 1929).

CLINGHAM, Greg. ed. *New Light on Boswell Critical and Historical Essays on the Occasion of the Bicentenary of 'The Life of Johnson'* (Cambridge, CUP, 1991).

COLLINS, Varnum Lansing. *President Witherspoon A Biography* 2v. (Princeton, Princeton University Press, 1925).

CRAWFORD, Robert. *The Bard Robert Burns, a Biography* (London, Jonathan Cape, 2009).

CRAWFORD, Ronald Lyndsay. *Professor Anderson, Dr Franklin and President Washington* (Glasgow, University of Strathclyde, 2014).

– *The Lost World of John Witherspoon Unravelling the Snodgrass affair, 1762 to 1776* (Aberdeen, Aberdeen University Press, 2014).

– See also 3 below, 'Unpublished higher degree theses'.

DABYDEEN, David, GILMORE, John and JONES, Cecily. *The Oxford Companion to Black British History* (Oxford and New York, OUP, 2007).

DAUBE, David. *Appeasement or Resistance and Other Essays on New Testament Judaism* (Berkeley, University of California Press, 1987).
DAWSON, Jane. *John Knox* (New Haven and London, Yale University Press, 2015).
DEVINE, T. M. *The Scottish Nation 1700-2000* (London, Allen Lane, 1999).
– *Scotland's Empire 1600-1815* (London, Allen Lane, 2003).
– *To the Ends of the Earth Scotland's Global Diaspora 1750-2010* (London, Allen Lane, 2011).
– and YOUNG, J. R. ed., *Eighteenth-Century Scotland: New Perspectives* (East Linton, Tuckwell Press, 1999).
De WOLFE, Barbara ed. *Discoveries of America Personal accounts of British emigrants to North America during the Revolutionary Era* (Cambridge, CUP, 1997).
DIBDIN, James C. *The Annals of the Edinburgh Stage* (Edinburgh, Richard Cameron, 1888).
DONALDSON, Gordon. *Scottish Church History* (Edinburgh, Scottish Academic Press, 1985).
DONOVAN, Robert Kent. *No Popery and Radicalism. Opposition to Roman Catholic Relief in Scotland, 1778-1782* (New York, Garland Publishing, 1987).
DRUMMOND, Andrew L. and BULLOCH, James. *The Scottish Church 1688-1843 The Age of the Moderates* (Edinburgh, Saint Andrew Press, 1973).
ELLIOT, George F. S. *The Border Elliots and the Family of Minto* (Edinburgh, David Douglas, 1897).
ELTON, G. R. *Reformation Europe 1517-1559* (Glasgow, Collins, 1963).
EMERSON, Roger L. *Professors, Patronage and Politics Aberdeen Universities in the Eighteenth Century* (Aberdeen, Aberdeen University Press, 1993).
– *Academic Patronage in the Scottish Enlightenment Glasgow, Edinburgh and St. Andrews Universities* (Edinburgh, Edinburgh University Press, 2008).
FINLAY, John. *The Community of the College of Justice: Edinburgh and the Court of Session, 1687-1808* (Edinburgh, Edinburgh University Press, 2012).
– *Legal Practice in Eighteenth-Century Scotland* (Leiden and Boston, Brill, 2015).
FLAVELL, Julie. *When London was Capital of America* (New Haven and London, Yale University Press, 2010).
FLEISCHACKER, Samuel. *A Short History of Distributive Justice* (Cambridge, Mass. and London, Harvard University Press, 2004).
FRANCIS, Keith A. and GIBSON, William, eds. *The Oxford Handbook of the British Sermon 1689-1901* (Oxford, OUP, 2012).
FRUCHTMAN, Jr., Jack. *Thomas Paine Apostle of Freedom* (New York, Four Walls Eight Windows, 1994).
FRY, Michael. *The Dundas Despotism* (Edinburgh, Edinburgh University Press, 1992; re-issued by John Donald, 2004).
FULLER, Reginald C. *Alexander Geddes 1737-1802 Pioneer of Biblical Criticism* (Sheffield, Almond Press, 1984).
FURBER, Holden. *Henry Dundas First Viscount Melville 1742-1811* (Oxford and London, OUP, 1931).
GIMBEL, Richard. *Thomas Paine: A Bibliographical Check List of "Common Sense" with an account of its publication* (New Haven, Yale University Press, 1956).
GRAYLING, A. C. *Towards the Light The Story of the Struggles for Liberty & Rights that Made the Modern West* (London, Bloomsbury, 2007).
GREEN, V. H. H. *Renaissance and Reformation* (London, Edward Arnold, 1952).
HAAKONSSEN, Knud. 2v. *The Cambridge History of Eighteenth-Century Philosophy* (Cambridge, CUP, 2011).
HARRIS, Bob. *The Scottish People and the French Revolution* (London, Pickering & Chatto, 2008).

— ed. *Scotland in the Age of the French Revolution* (Edinburgh, John Donald, 2005). [See also Brown, Michael below under 'Journal articles and book chapters'.]

HETHERINGTON, W. M. *History of the Church of Scotland* (Edinburgh, J. Johnstone, 1842).

HOOK, Andrew. *Scotland and America A Study of Cultural Relations, 1750-1835* (Second ed., Humming Earth, Glasgow, 2008).

— and SHER, Richard B. *The Glasgow Enlightenment* (East Linton, Tuckwell Press, 1995).

ISRAEL, Jonathan. *A Revolution of the Mind. Radical Enlightenment and the Intellectual Origins of Modern Democracy* (Princeton and Oxford, Princeton University Press, 2010).

— *Democratic Enlightenment Philosophy, Revolution, and Human Rights 1750-1790* (Oxford and New York, OUP, 2011).

JACKSON, John. *The History of the Scottish Stage, from its first establishment to the present time* (Edinburgh, for Peter Hill, 1793).

JAYANOFF, Maya. *Liberty's Exiles The Loss of America and the Remaking of the British Empire* (London, Harper Press, 2011).

JOHNSON, Christine. *Developments in the Roman Catholic Church in Scotland, 1789-1829* (Edinburgh, John Donald, 1983).

KAY, John. *A Series of Original Portraits and Caricature Etchings* 2v. (Edinburgh, Hugh Paton, 1837; re-issued Edinburgh, Birlinn, 2007).

KEANE, John. *Tom Paine A Political Life* (London, Bloomsbury, 1995).

KENNEDY, James. *Antiburghers to the End — The Kilwinning Original Secession Church (1738-1956)* (online publication).

KNIGHT, Roger. *Britain against Napoleon The Organization of Victory 1793-1815* (London, Allen Lane, 2013).

KNOX, R[onald]. A. *Enthusiasm A Chapter in the History of Religion* (Oxford, Clarendon Press, 1950).

LEITH, William Forbes. *Memoirs of Scottish Catholics during the XVIIth and XVIIIth Centuries* 2v. (London, Longmans, Green, 1909).

LOCK, F. P. *Edmund Burke Volume I: 1730-1784; Volume II: 1784-1797* (Oxford and New York, OUP, 1998-2006).

LYNCH, Michael. *Scotland A New History* (London, Pimlico, 1992; revised 2011).

McCOSH, James. *The Scottish Philosophy, Biographical, Expository, Critical, from Hutcheson to Hamilton* (New York, R. Carter, 1875).

MacCULLOCH, Diarmaid. *Reformation Europe's House Divided 1490-1700* (London, Allen Lane and Penguin Books, 2003).

— *Silence A Christian History* (New York, Viking, 2013).

McDANIEL, Iain. *Adam Ferguson in the Scottish Enlightenment* (Cambridge, Mass. and London, England, Harvard University Press, 2013).

MACDOUGALL, Norman. ed. *Church, Politics and Society: Scotland 1408-1929* (Edinburgh, John Donald, 1983). See also Sher, Richard and Murdoch, Alexander below under 'Journal articles and book chapters'.

McGINTY, J. Walter. *'An Animated Son of Liberty' A Life of John Witherspoon* (Bury St. Edmunds, Arena Books, 2012).

McINTOSH, John R. *Church and Theology in Enlightenment Scotland: The Popular Party, 1740-1800* (East Linton, Tuckwell Press, 1998).

MAILER, Gideon. *John Witherspoon's American Revolution* (Chapel Hill, University of North Carolina Press, for the Omohundro Institute of Early American History and Culture, Williamsburg, Virginia, 2017).

MAXWELL, William D. *A History of Worship in the Church of Scotland* (Oxford, OUP, 1955).
MEIKLE, Henry. *Scotland and the French Revolution* (Edinburgh, James Maclehose, 1912; reprinted London, Frank Cass, 1969).
MORRISON, Jeffry H. *John Witherspoon and the Founding of the American Republic* (Notre Dame, Ind., University of Notre Dame Press, 2005).
MOSSNER, E. C. *The Life of David Hume* Second ed. (Oxford, Clarendon Press, 1980). See also under 2 below, 'Journal articles'.
NAMIER, Sir Lewis and BROOKE, John. eds. *The History of Parliament The House of Commons 1754-1790* 3v. (London, Secker & Warburg, 1985).
OLIN, John C., ed. *A Reformation Debate John Calvin and Jacopo Sadoletto* (Grand Rapids, Baker Books, 1976).
OSBORNE, Brian D. *Braxfield the hanging judge?* (Glendaruel, Argyll Publishing, 1997).
OVERTON, J. H. *John Wesley* (London, Methuen, 1891).
PAGDEN, Anthony. *The Enlightenment and why it still matters* (Oxford, OUP, 2013).
PENTLAND, Gordon. *The Spirit of the Union: popular politics in Scotland 1815-1820* (London, Pickering & Chatto, 2011).
PHILLIPSON, Nicholas (or N. T.). *David Hume The Philosopher as Historian* (London, Penguin Books, 2011; originally published in 1989 by Weidenfeld & Nicolson as *Hume*).
– and MITCHISON, Rosalind. ed. *Scotland in the Age of Improvement Essays in Scottish History in the Eighteenth Century* (Edinburgh, Edinburgh University Press, 1970; re-issued 1996).
POTTLE, Marion S., ABBOTT, Claude Colleer, and POTTLE, Frederick A. 3v. *Catalogue of the Papers of James Boswell at Yale University* (Edinburgh, Edinburgh University Press; New Haven, Yale University Press, 1993).
RODGER, Alexander. *Poems and Songs* ed. Robert Ford (Paisley and London, Alexander Gardner, 1897).
RODGER, N. A. M. *The Command of the Ocean. A naval history of Britain, 1649 to 1815* (London, Allen Lane, 2004).
ROPER, Lyndal. *Martin Luther Renegade and Prophet* (London, The Bodley Head, 2016).
ROSENFELD, Sybil Marion. *Strolling Players & Drama in the Provinces 1660-1765* (Cambridge, CUP, 1939).
SCOTT, David. *Annals and Statistics of the Original Secession Church: till its disruption and union with the Free Church of Scotland in 1852* (Edinburgh, Andrew Elliot, 1886).
SCOTT, Hew. *Fasti Ecclesiae Scoticanae*, New Edition, 7 v. (Edinburgh, Oliver and Boyd, 1915 -1928).
SELDERHUIS, Herman J., ed. *The Calvin Handbook* (Grand Rapids, Mich., 2009).
SHER, Richard B. *Church and University in the Scottish Enlightenment The Moderate Literati of Edinburgh* (Edinburgh, Edinburgh University Press, 1985; re-issued with new preface, 2015).
– *The Enlightenment and the Book Scottish Authors and Their Publishers in Eighteenth-Century Britain, Ireland, and America* (Chicago and London, University of Chicago Press, 2006).
   [See also under HOOK, Andrew above.]
– and MURDOCH, Alexander. See 2 below.
– and SMITTEN, Jeffrey R. ed. *Scotland and America in the Age of the Enlightenment* (Princeton, Princeton University Press, 1990).
SLOAN, Douglas. *The Scottish Enlightenment and the American College Ideal* (New York, Teachers College Press, Columbia University, 1971).
SMITTEN, Jeffrey R. *The Life of William Robertson Minister, Historian, and Principal* (Edinburgh, Edinburgh University Press, 2017).

SUNTER, Ronald M. *Patronage and Politics in Scotland 1707-1832* (Edinburgh, John Donald, 1986; re-issued 2003).
SWINDELLS, Julia and TAYLOR, David Francis ed. *The Oxford Handbook of the Georgian Theatre 1737-1832* (Oxford, OUP, 2014).
TAIT, L. Gordon. *The Piety of John Witherspoon Pew, Pulpit, and Public Forum* (Louisville, Geneva Press, 2001).
THOMAS, J. E. *Britain's Last Invasion Fishguard 1797* (Stroud, Tempus, 2007).
THOMAS, Peter D. G. *George III King and politicians 1760-1770* (Manchester and New York, Manchester University Press, 2002).
WALKER, David M. *Scottish Jurists* (Edinburgh, W. Green, 1985).
– *A Legal History of Scotland* 7v. (Edinburgh, W. Green/T. and T. Clark, 1988-98); v. V *The Eighteenth Century* (Edinburgh, Clark, 1998).
WESTON, Corinne Comstock and GREENBERG, Janelle Renfrow. *Subjects and Sovereigns The Grand Controversy over Legal Sovereignty in Stuart England* (Cambridge, CUP, 1981).
WILLIAMS, Basil. *The Whig Supremacy 1714-1760* Second ed. rev. by C. H. Stuart. (Oxford, Clarendon Press, 1962).
WILSON, Walter. *The History and Antiquities of the Dissenting Churches and Meeting Houses in London, Westminster and Southwark* 3v. (London, for the author, s.n., 1810).
WINCH, Donald. *Adam Smith's Politics* (Cambridge, CUP, 1978).
WHYTE, Iain. *Scotland and the Abolition of Black Slavery, 1756-1838* (Edinburgh, EUP, 2006; reprinted with corrections 2007).
YEAGER, Jonathan. *Enlightened Evangelicalism: The Life and Thought of John Erskine* (Oxford and New York, OUP, 2011).

2 Journal articles and book chapters

BANNERMAN, G. E. 'The "Nabob of the North": Sir Lawrence Dundas as government contractor', *Historical Research* (Institute of Historical Research), v. 83, no. 219, February 2010.
BREKKE, Luke. 'Heretics in the Pulpit, Inquisitors in the Pews: The Long Reformation and the Scottish Enlightenment', *Eighteenth-Century Studies*, XLIV (2010).
BROWN, Ian. 'Public and Private Performance 1650 to 1800', in *The Edinburgh Companion to Scottish Drama* ed. Ian Brown (Edinburgh, Edinburgh University Press, 2011).
BROWN, Michael. 'Alexander Carlyle and the Shadows of Enlightenment', in *Scotland in the Age of the French Revolution* ed. Bob Harris (q.v.).
BROWN, Stewart J. 'Hugh Blair, the sentiments and preaching the enlightenment in Scotland', *Intellectual History Review*, vol. 26, No. 3, 411-427, 2016.
CAIRNS, John W. 'Stoicism, slavery and law', in *Grotius and the Stoa*, ed. H. W. Blom and L. C. Winkel (Assen, Royal van Gorcum, 2004).
– 'John Millar and Slavery', in *MacCormick's Scotland*, ed. Neil Walker (Edinburgh, Edinburgh University Press, 2012).
– 'After Somerset: The Scottish Experience', *Journal of Legal History*, 33:3 (2012), 291-312.
– 'Freeing from Slavery in Eighteenth-Century Scotland', in *Judge and Jurist: Essays in Memory of Lord Rodger of Earlsferry*, ed. Andrew Burrows, David Johnston and Reinhard Zimmermann (Oxford, OUP, 2013).
– 'Slavery without a *Code Noir*: Scotland 1700-78', in *Lawyers, the Law and History: Irish Legal History Society Discourses and Other Papers, 2005-2011* (Dublin, Four Courts Press, 2013), ed. Felix M. Larkin and Norma M. Dawson.

CARNALL, Geoffrey. 'Robertson and contemporary images of India', in *William Robertson and the Expansion of Empire* (Cambridge, CUP, 1997).
CLARK, Ian D. L. 'From Protest to Reaction: The Moderate Regime in the Church of Scotland, 1752-1805', in *Scotland in the Age of Improvement*, ed. Phillipson and Mitchison (q.v.).
DONOVAN, Robert Kent. 'Voices of Distrust: The Expression of Anti-Catholic Feeling in Scotland, 1778-1781', *Innes Review* 30 (1979), 62-76.
EMERSON, Roger L. 'The Social Composition of Enlightened Scotland: The Select Society of Edinburgh, 1754-1764', *Studies in Voltaire and the Eighteenth-Century* ed. T. Besterman, 114 (1973): 291-329.
GARRETT, Aaron. 'Hume's Revised Racism Revisited', in *Hume Studies,* XXVI, No 1 (April 2000), 171-8.
– 'Human Nature' (particularly section IV, 'Race and Natural Character'), in *The Cambridge History of Eighteenth-Century Philosophy*, II.8, ed. Knud Haakonssen, v. 1, 195-7.
IMMERWAHR, John. 'Hume's Revised Racism', in *Journal of the History of Ideas*, 53.3 (1993), 481-6.
KETCHAM, Ralph L. 'James Madison and Religion – A New Hypothesis', in *James Madison on Religious Liberty* ed. Robert S. Alley (Buffalo, NY, Prometheus Books, 1985).
KIDD, Colin. 'The Kirk, the French Revolution, and the Burden of Scottish Whiggery', in *Religious Change in Europe 1650-1914: Essays for John McManners* ed. Nigel Aston (Oxford, OUP, 1997), 213-47.
– 'The ideological significance of Robertson's *History of Scotland*, in *William Robertson and the Expansion of Empire* (Cambridge, CUP, 1997).
– 'Conditional Britons: The Scots Covenanting Tradition and the Eighteenth-Century British State', *English Historical Review*, 474, 2002, 1147-76.
– 'Subscription, the Scottish Enlightenment and the Moderate Interpretation of History', *Journal of Ecclesiastical History*, v. 55, No. 3, July 2004, 502-519.
– 'Enlightenment and anti-Enlightenment in eighteenth-century Scotland: an Ayrshire-Renfrewshire microclimate', in *The Enlightenment in Scotland. National and international perspectives*, ed. Jean-Francois Dunyach and Ann Thomson (Oxford, Voltaire Foundation, 2015).
– 'The Fergusson affair: Calvinism and dissimulation in the Scottish Enlightenment', *Intellectual History Review*, vol. 26, No. 3, 339-354, 2016.
KINSERVIK, Matthew J. 'The Dialectics of Print and Performance after 1737', in *The Oxford Handbook of the Georgian Theatre 1737-1832*, ed. Swindells and Taylor (see above).
LEASK, Nigel. 'Thomas Muir and *The Telegraph*: radical cosmopolitanism in 1790s Scotland', *History Workshop Journal*, no. 63, Spring, 2007, 48-69.
MAILER, Gideon. 'Anglo-Scottish Union and John Witherspoon's American Revolution', *The William and Mary Quarterly*, Vol. 67, No. 4 (October 2010), 709-746.
MATHESON, Ann. 'Preaching in the Churches of Scotland', in *The Oxford Handbook of the British Sermon 1689-1901* ed. Keith A. Francis and William Gibson, (Oxford, OUP, 2012).
– 'Hugh Blair's Sermons', in *The Edinburgh History of the Book in Scotland*, v. 2, *Enlightenment and expansion 1707-1800*, eds. Stephen W. Brown and Warren McDougall, (Edinburgh, Edinburgh University Press, 2012), 471-474.
MOSSNER, E. C. 'Hume's Four Dissertations: an essay in biography and bibliography', *Modern Philology*, 48:1 (August, 1950), 35-57.
MUESSIG, Caroline. 'Audience and Preacher: *Ad Status* Sermons and Social Classification', in *Preacher, Sermon and Audience in the Middle Ages* ed. Muessig (Leiden, Brill, 2002).

NORTON, David Fate. 'Francis Hutcheson in America', in *Studies on Voltaire and the Eighteenth Century*, ed. T. Besterman, 154 (1976), 1547-68.

PHILLIPSON, Nicholas. 'Providence and progress: an introduction to the historical thought of William Robertson', in *William Robertson and the Expansion of Empire* (Cambridge, CUP, 1997).

POLLARD, Sidney. 'Labour in Great Britain' in *The Cambridge Economic History of Europe. Vol. VII. The Industrial Economies: Capital, Labour, and Enterprise. Part 1, Britain, France, Germany and Scandinavia* ed. Peter Mathias and M. M. Postan (Cambridge, CUP, 1978), 97-179.

PRUNIER, Clotilde. 'Representations of the 'State of Popery' in Scotland in the 1720s and 1730s', *Innes Review*, 64.2 (2013), 120-226.

SHER, Richard (and MURDOCH, Alexander). 'Patronage and Party in the Church of Scotland, 1750-1800', in *Church, Politics and Society: Scotland 1408-1929*, ed. Norman Macdougall (q.v.).

– 'Scottish divines and legal lairds: Boswell's Scots Presbyterian identity', in *New Light on Boswell Critical and Historical Essays on the Occasion of the Bicentenary of 'The Life of Johnson'* ed. Greg Clingham (q.v.).

SKINNER, Andrew S. 'Francis Hutcheson and Adam Smith: visions of America' (unpublished; see chapter 8, 'America', note 41).

SZECHI, Daniel. 'Defending the true faith: Kirk, State and Catholic missioners in Scotland 1653–1755', *Catholic Historical Review*, 82 (1996), 397–411.

TODD, William Burton. 'David Hume: a preliminary bibliography', in *Hume and the Enlightenment: essays presented to Ernest Campbell Mossner*, (Edinburgh and Austin, Edinburgh University Press; University of Texas Humanities Research Center, 1974).

VINCENT, Emma. 'The Responses of Scottish Churchmen to the French Revolution, 1789-1802', *The Scottish Historical Review*, v. LXXIII, 2: No. 196: October 1994, 191-215.

WHATLEY, Christopher A. 'The Dark Side of the Enlightenment? Sorting out Serfdom', in *Eighteenth-Century Scotland: New Perspectives*, ed. T. M. Devine and John R. Young (East Linton, Tuckwell Press, 1999), 259-74.

WILBY, Noel MacDonald. 'The "Encreasce of Popery" in the Highlands 1714-1747', *Innes Review*, 17 (1966), 91-115.

3 Unpublished higher degree theses

BRIMS, John D. *The Scottish Democratic Movement in the Age of the French Revolution* (PhD thesis, University of Edinburgh, 1983).

BREKKE, Luke G. *'In an age so enlightened, enthusiasm so extravagant': popular religion in Enlightenment Scotland, 1712-1791* (PhD thesis, University of Minnesota, 2009).

CLARK, Ian D. L. *Moderatism and the Moderate Party in the Church of Scotland, 1752-1805* (PhD thesis, University of Cambridge, 1963).

CRAWFORD, Ronald L. *Scotland, America and Tom Paine: Ideas of Liberty and the Making of Three Americans – John Witherspoon (1723-94), Robert Aitken (1735-1802) and Alexander Wilson (1766-1813)* (PhD thesis, University of Strathclyde, 2011).

PHELPS, Matthew. *John Witherspoon and the Transmission of Common Sense Philosophy from Scotland to America* (DPhil thesis, University of Oxford, 2002).

Index

1. References to successive pages in the text are separated by commas; to notes in the same chapter by a forward slash. Thus:
'Collins, Varnum Lansing, Ch.2 n.71/74/76, 73, 74'

2. Entries in **Bold** refer to authors/sermons assigned prominence in the text.

A

Aberdeen, 273
  King's College, Ch.4 n.56, 286
  Marischal College, 253, 275
Abertarf, 246
'Academy' movement, 3, 228, 296
Achadrom, 246
Adair, Dr. James, 23, Introduction n.83
Adam, Rev. John (West Kilbride; Greenock Middle): 51
  How a Minister should approve himself unto God, 129-145
Adam, William (M.P.), 161, Ch.6 n.27
Adams, John (second President of the United States), Ch.8 n.113
Adams, Rev. John (Dalrymple; Falkirk): 37-38, 129
Addison, Joseph, 111
Ahnert, Thomas, 3, Introduction n.14, 28, Ch.1 n.6, Ch.2. n.1, Ch.4 n.29/56/102, 125, Ch.5 n.12, 133, 198
Aitken, Robert (printer, bookbinder, publisher & circulating library proprietor), Ch.5 n.44, Ch.7 n.26, 209
Alice (*aka* Ellis), James (Antiburgher minister in Paisley), Ch.5 n.35, 158, Ch.6 n.14, 189, Ch.7 n.26-27
Allan, David (artist), *cover* ill., 23, 324
Allison, Rev. Francis, 219
Alloa, 253
American Civil War, 276
American Philosophical Society, Ch.8 n.113
American Revolutionary War, 211, 243, 252, 259

Carlisle Commission (1778), Ch.6 n.103, 221
  Alexander Carlyle on, 200
Anderson, Professor John, Ch.5 n.15, 227, Ch.8 n.76, Ch.10 n.109
Anderson, Rev. George, Introduction n.18/19, 103
  The Use and Abuse of Diversions, 103-104, Ch.4 n.6, 108, 112-118
Anderson, Rev. John (Dumbarton; Glasgow North-West – the 'Ramshorn') 129, Ch.4 n.4/5, 227, Ch.8 n.2/75
  A Sermon Preach'd in the Church of Air, 129, 132-135
  A Defence of the Church-Government, 133
Anderson, William (bookseller in Stirling), 234, Ch.8 n.99
Anderson's University, Ch.10 n.109
Anne, Queen, 32, 43, Ch.8 n.79
Anstruther, Captain Philip, 38
Antiburghers (or Associate congregation), 49, 175, 189, Ch.7 n.26
'Application' (in a sermon) 9, Introduction n.32
Argyll, 3rd. Duke of, 30
Aristotle, Ch.8 n.94, 275
Armstrong, Murray, Ch.6 n.93
Arnot, Hugo, 104, Ch.4 n.8/9
'Associate Presbytery', 43
Aston, 'Tony' (actor), Ch.4 n.64/89
Athelstaneford, 125, Ch.4 n.71
Atkyns (or Atkins), Sir Robert, 89, Ch.3 n.46/48
Atonement, Christian doctrine of the, 53
Atterbury, Francis, 316
'Auld Licht', Ch.5 n.12
Ayr, Presbytery of, 131, Ch.5 n.71

B

Bacon, Matthew, 315, App. B, n.27-28
Baine, Rev. James (Paisley High; Edinburgh Relief congregation): 65, Ch.2 n.29/38, 89, 138, Ch.5 n.31/64, 144, 316-317
Balfour, Elphingston, 287
Balfour, John, the younger (of Pilrig), 174, Ch.6 n.79
Ball, Father John, 14
Balnaves, Henry, 16
Bannerman, G. E., Ch.3 n.13, 19
Baptisms of premature babies, 327
Barbeyrac, Jean, 271-272, Ch.10 n.10
Bean, George (writer) (see *Liberty of the bar*)
Beattie, James, 272, Ch.10 n.92
Beaumelle, Laurent Angliviel de, Ch.4 n.107
Beccaria, Cesare, 274
Beith (Ayrshire), 130, Ch.5 n.3, 147
Bell, Robert (Scots émigré publisher in Philadelphia), 234
Bell, William (legal historian), Ch.9 n.11
Bell, Rev. William (Campsie): 177-178
Benezet, Anthony, Ch.10 n.17
Berkeley, George, Ch.6 n.31, Ch.8 n.79
Berlin, Sir Isaiah, Ch.10 n.19
Berry, Walter, 176, Ch.6 n.87
Beza, Theodore, 15
Black, Joseph, Ch.6 n.103
Blackburne, Francis, 258
Blacklock, Thomas ('Valerius Corvinus'), 260
Blair, Rev. Hugh (Collessie; Edinburgh Canongate; Edinburgh Lady Yester's; Edinburgh High, or 'New', St. Giles's): (see also under S.S.P.C.K.), 2-3, 21, 89, 121, 137, 156, 159, Ch.6 n.19, 189-197, 199, 201, 235-236, Ch.8 n.105, Ch.9 n.3, 249, 256, 287, 300, Endnote, n.2
'Douglas cause', and the, 317-318
Gardiner, Rev. John, on HB's sermons, 19
his enlightened Moderatism, 251
introduced by James Fordyce (q.v.) to Samuel Johnson, 254, App. B, n.42
'Ossianic controversy, his role in, App. B, n.42
political preaching, attitude to, 286
Works cited:
Lectures on Rhetoric and Belles Lettres, 190, Ch.7 n.31-32, 254
On the Love of Our Country, 21, Introduction n.79, 103, 183-184, 189-197, Ch.7 n.45-46/50/58/60-63, 200
'On the Death of Christ', Ch.7 n.34
'On the Disorder of the Passions', 191, Ch.7 n.36
'On the Divine Government of the Passions of Men', 250, Ch.9 n.34
'On Gentleness', 190, Ch.7 n.33-34, 286, Ch.10 n.79
The Importance of Religious Knowledge to the Happiness of Mankind, 250-251, 286, Ch.10 n.76
'On Sensibility', 191, Ch.7 n.35
Sermons, 183, 250, 286
The Wrath of Man praising God (one of two 're-cycled sermons by Blair noted), xiv (ill.), 241-242, 248-251, Ch.9 n.30
as the 'Scottish Tillotson', 249
Blasphemy, the crime of, 56, Ch.2 n.3
'Blue gown' beggars, 180, Ch.6 n.101
Boethius, 12, Introduction n.49
Boog, Rev. Robert, Ch.6 n.25
Boston ('the Younger'), Rev. Thomas, 42
Boswell, Sir Alexander (Lord Auchinleck), 72, 318-319, App. B, n.55
Boswell, James, (see also under *Liberty of the bar* etc.), vii, 1, 2, Introduction n.10/14/ n.53, 21, 25, Ch.1 n.1, 30, 31, 78, Ch.3 n.20 /23, 86-87, 94, 193, Ch.7 n.41, 217, 235-236, Ch.8 n.29/105/108, App. B, n.38-39
'Douglas cause', his pamphlets relating to, 318, App. B, n.54
Edinburgh Journals, Ch.3 n.33, Ch.8 n.108
Life of Samuel Johnson, 21, Introduction, n.10, 25, Ch.1 n.1, 86-87, Ch.3 n.37/63/64-65, 94, 95-97, 217, Ch.8 n.29, 254, Ch.9 n.47, App. B, n.2/42/48
London Journal, Ch.3 n.20
Memorial for the Reverend James Thomson, 88-90, 92, 94-100, Ch.3 n.41-44, App. B, 310-319, n.1-58
The Minor, pamphlet on, App. B, n.38-39
The Journal of a Tour to the Hebrides, with Samuel Johnson LL.D., App. B, n.36
Bowles, John, 165

Boyd, Julian P., Ch.8 n.5
Bradford, W. and T., 234
Brechin, 253
Breslau, Reformed Church of, (see also under Church of Scotland, Breslau collection), 246-247
Brims, J. D., Ch.6 n.2/47-48
Broadie, Alexander, 2-3, Introduction n.13, 21, Ch.7 n.3, Ch.8 n.112, 278
Broughton, 38
Brown, Dr. David, ix
Brown, George (Lord Coalston), 71
Brown, Michael, Ch.4 n.85
Brown, Stewart J., 286, Ch.10 n.66/77/90, Endnote, n.2
Brown, Wallace, Ch.8 n.26
Bruce, Archibald (secessionist minister), 158, 299
Corruptions in the Church to be eradicated, 27, 49-51
The Kirkiad, Endnote, n.1
Bryce, John (printer and publisher), Ch.2 n.6, Ch.4 n.66, Ch.5 n.62, 226
Buccleuch, 3rd. Duke of, 84, 205, Ch.7 n.90
Buccleuch, Duchess of, 205
Buchanan, David, 16, Introduction n.62/63
Bullinger, Henry (Heinrich), 12
Burgh, James
Britain's Remembrancer, 253, Ch.9 n.44
Burke, Edmund, 161, 260
Reflections, 185
Burlamaqui, Jean-Jacques, 233
Burleigh, J. H. S., Ch.5 n.24, 137, 280, Ch.10 n.58
Burnet, Gilbert, Ch.8 n.79
Burns, Robert, 22-24, 51, Ch.1 n.92/93, Ch.6 n.37, 188, 299
Alloway museum, 23
Address of Beelzebub, Ch.8 n.57
Burns, W., ('preacher of the Gospel'), 252
Butler, Bishop Joseph, 258
Butterfield, Lyman H., Ch.2 n.71, 73/74, Ch.8 n.27

C

Cadder parish, 158
Cadell, Thomas, 254, 258
Cairns, John W., ix, Ch.10, 12-13/18/50-51/56/63, 271-272
Caledonia, Scots colony of, in America, 297, Ch.10 n.111
Caledonian Mercury, 78-81, Ch.3 n.11/25/70, 88, 99, 107-108, Ch.4 n.23, 121, 257
Callender, James Thomson, 176, Ch.6 n.87
Calvin, John (Jean), xix, 8, 11-14
Institutes, 9, Introduction n.33, 11, Introduction n.41-43
Ordinances, 10
Calvinism, 4, 11, 97, 133, 159, 186-187, 227
'Cambusland Wark' (1742), 242
Cameron, John, 177
'Cameronians' (religious sect; or, the 'Mountain'), 175, Ch.6 n.83, Ch.7 n.29
Campbell, Colonel Archibald (later General Sir Archibald), 78-81, 85-87, Ch.3 n.32/33, 97-98
Campbell, Rev. Professor Archibald, 130
Campbell, Rev. George, 210, Ch.8 n.112/114
Address to the People of Scotland, 260
The Nature, Extent, and Importance, of the Duty of Allegiance, 210, 236, 238, Ch.8 n.79/88
Campbell, Ilay (Sir), of Succoth (advocate), 88, Ch.3 n.41/43/54/70, 92-93, Ch.6 n.71
Campsie, 176, 178-179
Canna, island of, Ch.9 n.15
Carlyle, Rev. Alexander (Inveresk): 21, 35, Ch.1 n.69, 112, 121-122, Ch.4 n.80, 156, 183-184, 198-206, 221, Ch.8 n.79, 256, 287, 300
Works cited:
Anecdotes and Characters of the Times (Carlyle's Autobiography), Ch.4 n.39/85, 184
A Sermon on the death of Sir David Dalrymple, 183, 203-205
National Depravity, 21, 183-184, 198-201, 202-203
The Love of Our Country, 184, 205-206
The Justice and Necessity of the War with our American Colonies, 210, 238-239, Ch.8 n.79/115-118
Carmichael, Gershom, 271, Ch.10 n.10/28/30, 274
Carmichael, James, 83
Carnall, Geoffrey, Ch.10 n.66
Carnock, 40-41

Carpentras (France), 12
Catholic Church in Scotland, Roman, 32, 45, 97, 237 (ill.),
  anti-Catholic riots in London, Edinburgh and Glasgow, 254, 256
  anti-Catholic sentiment ('Popery'), 241-267 *passim*, 294
  charge of superstition made against, 195
  numbers of Catholics in the Scottish population, estimated, 247
Catholic Emancipation Act (1829), 243, Ch.9 n.11
Catholic Relief Act in England (1793), Ch.9 n.9, 255-256
Catholic Relief Bill in Scotland, proposed, (see also Henry Dundas), 243, 247, 256, 262-264, 295
Caudle, James, ix, App. B, n.56
Chadwick, Owen, 6, Introduction n. 26/56, 14
'Chair of Verity' (as a metaphor for the pulpit), *Frontispiece* ill., vii, 7-9, 19, 72,87, 197, 328
Chandler, Samuel (English nonconformist pastor), 247, Ch.9 n.27
Charles II, King, 314
Charters, Rev. Samuel, 296, Ch.10 n.107/110
Chastellux, François-Jean de Beauvoir, Marquis de, Ch.10 n.45
Chitnis, Anand C., 185
Church of Scotland, xviii, 4
  Acts of the General Assembly, Ch.5 n.23, Ch.9 n.13/15, 249
  American War of Independence, reaction to 211
  attendance at, decline of, 299
  Breslau collection (and similar initiatives), 244, 246-247, Ch.9 n.25-27
  Confession of Faith, and ministerial subscription to, 7, 28, 53, Ch.4 n.48, 114-115, 130, 134, 136-137, 144-145, Ch.5 n.62, 150
  'Darien letter' of 1699, 280, 297
  discipline within, 4, 9-12, 130, 134-136, 142, Ch.5 n.50
  First Book of Discipline, 12, 23, 31
  Second Book of Discipline, 7, 23, 31, 91
  evolution of parties within, 28-29 [see also under William Grant (Lord Prestongrange)], 55, Ch.2 n.1
  excommunication, 12, Introduction n.81, 323, 333
  Form of Process, 7, 12, 23, Introduction n.84-85, 57, Ch.2 n.6, Ch.4 n.97, 147, 325, 330
  Moderates/Moderatism (heterodox party), 4, 21, 28-29, 53, 106, 126, 130, 132-133, 140, 147, 156, 189, Ch.7 n.25, 264
  Moderator of the General Assembly, office of, Ch.9 n.84
  patronage, 4, 25-53, *passim*, 133-134, App. A, 303-308, 321-322
  Patronage Act, 47, 133-134, Ch.7 n.77, 264, 321
  people, the, C. of S. becoming aloof from, 300
  'Popery', measures to combat, 244-247
  Popular (orthodox) party of, 4-5, 28-29, 106, 121, 126, 130, 131, 156, 180, 189, Ch.7 n.25
  'protesters' and 'resolutioners', 105
  radical movement, attitude towards, 155-181 *passim*
  Royal Bounty granted to, 244-245
  secession from, 37, 42-44
  settlements, disputed, 33-42 *passim*
  slave trade, attitudes towards abolition of, 294-297
'citizen of the world', (see Stoic cosmopolitanism)
Clark, Ian D. L., 67, Ch.2 n.47, Ch.5 n.71, 156, Ch.6 n.3/5/37, 189, Ch.7 n.25
Clark, Iwo, 11, 22-24, Introduction n.81/84, Ch.5 n.50
Clarkson, Thomas, 270
Claude, Jean, Introduction n.47
Clerk, Sir John, of Penicuik, 174
Clyde, Firth of, 130
Cobbett, William
  Parliamentary History of England, Ch.6 n.28, Ch.8 n.86
Cockburn, Alexander, 16
Cockburn, Henry (Lord Cockburn), 169, Ch.6 n.74, 202, Ch.7 n.78
  on a definition of sedition, Ch.6 n.40/48
Cocker, Edward (engraver), App. B, n.50
cockfighting in Scotland, 328, App. D, n.15
Coke, Sir Edward, 314
Colier, Rev. Thomas, 42
Colladon, Nicolas, 15
Collier, Jeremy, 114
Collins, Varnum Lansing, Ch.2 n.71/74/75, 73, 74, 213, Ch.8 n.10, Ch.9 n.26

Colquhoun, Sir James, of Luss, 172
'combinations' (early trade unions), 158
Congress, Continental (of the American colonies), 217, 221, Ch.8 n.30
Congreve, William, 114, Ch.4 n.89
Conquistadores, 288
Cooper, Mary (London printer), 253
Corkerhill, Ch.8 n.66
Coulton, G. G., 14
'Counter-Enlightenment', 187
Court of Session (Scotland), 20, 104, 142
  Action of 'Count and Reckoning', 97, Ch.3 n.67, 100
  Colonel Campbell and his Trustees v Robert Scotland, 97-98
  'Decreet', definition of, Ch.3 n.59
  'Douglas cause', 317-318
  'Dunfermline case', 20
  Ferguson v Glendonwyne, Ch.9 n.10
  John Snodgrass and Others v Witherspoon, 20, 69-73, 142, 187
  Judges sitting in 'Inner' and 'Outer' House of, Ch.3 n.49
  Knight v Wedderburn, 280, Ch.10 n.6
  'Paisley case', 20
  Presbytery of Edinburgh brings private prosecution against strolling players (1739), 111
  Scotlands v The Rev. James Thomson, 20, 86-94 passim, Ch.3 n.50/60, App. B (James Boswell's unpublished *Memorial*), 309-319
  Shaw v Bean, 88-89, Ch.3 n.39/41, App. B, n.32
  Shedden v Montgomery [aka *Montgomery v Sheddan* (sic)], Ch.10 n.12, 271-272, 282
Craigie, Robert, 118, Ch.4 n.67
Crawford, Rev. James, 178
Crawford, Robert, 22, Introduction n.82
Crawford, Ronald L.
  The Lost World of John Witherspoon, 2, Introduction n.18, 55-76 passim, Ch.5 n.2, Ch.6 n.14, Ch.7 n.17, Ch.8 n.28, App. D, n.2
  PhD thesis, Ch.6 n.57, Ch.7 n.23, Ch.8 n.27
  Professor Anderson, Dr. Franklin and President Washington, Ch.8 n.2/76, Ch.9 n.46
Creech, William, Ch .6 n.39, 174, 184, 260
Crichton, Thomas, 74, 76, Ch.2 n.80
Cromwell, Oliver, 213

Cromwell, Thomas, 6, 192
Crosbie, Andrew (advocate), 30, 66, 68, 72, 91-92
Cullen, Francis (Lord Grant), 30
Culloden, Battle of (1746), 248-249
Culross (Fife), 47, 78, Ch.6 n.16
Cumberland, Duke of, 82, 249, Ch.9 n.31
Cuming, Rev. Patrick, 41

D

Dale, David, 76, Ch.2 n.79, 296, Ch.10 n.108-109
Dalkeith, High School of, Ch.4 n.28
Dalling, Rev. Alexander, Ch.3, n.1
Dalrymple, Sir David Bt. (1726-1792) (Lord Hailes), 30, 32-33, 52, Ch.2 n.41, Ch.7 n.82-83
Dalrymple, David (1719-1784) (Lord Westhall), 30, 39, 59, 66, Ch.2 n.39/ 41, 68, Ch.7 n.82
Dalrymple, Sir Hew Bt., Ch.3 n.27
Dalrymple, James (Viscount Stair), 32, App. D, n.21
Dalrymple, William, of Fordell, 175, Ch.6 n.81
Darnley, Lord (Henry Stewart), 19
Daube, David, Ch.10 n.63
Davidson, Rev. Archibald (Inchinnan): 186, Ch.8 n.15
D'Avray, D. L., 14
Dawson, Jane, 8, Introduction n.45
Deane, Silas, 217
Dennis, John, Ch.4 n.29
'depravity', 198, Ch.9 n.74
Devine, T. M. (Sir Tom Devine), 157, 216, Ch.8 n.5/26, Ch.10 n.54
De Wolfe, Barbara, 226, Ch.8 n.27/67-68
Dibdin, James C., Ch.4 n.25/27/89, 110-111
Dick, Rev. Robert, 258, Ch.9 n.65
Dickinson, H. T., 157
Dickinson, William Croft, Introduction n.67-68/70-71/73-74
Diderot, Denis, 193-194, Ch.7 n.47
Digges, West (actor-manager), 121
Dilly brothers, Edward and Charles (booksellers in London), 217, Ch.8 n.28, 252
Diogenes ('the Cynic'), 194
Doddridge, Philip, 52, 228, 296
Donaldson, Alexander (Edinburgh printer and bookseller), 118, 235, Ch.8 n.106

Donaldson, Gordon, 10, Introduction n.38
Donaldson, James (secessionist minister), 158
Donovan, Robert Kent, 228, 233, Ch.8
  n.77/93, 245, Ch.9 n.18
Douglas, Francis, 16
Douglas, George, 16
Douglas, Rev. Robert, App. B, n.23
'Douglas, a minister in the name of', 314, App.
  B, n.23
Douglas, Neil (secessionist minister), 158
'Douglas cause', the, 318, App. B, n.44/47/54
Dow, Rev. Robert, 131, 326, App. D, 13
Drake, James, 114, Ch.4 n.49
Drummond, George (benefactor of an
  'Infirmary at Edinburgh'), 296
Dumas, Charles-Guillaume-Frédéric, 217
Dumbarton, 132
'Dundas despotism', 169
Dundas, Henry, 5, 21, 69, 71, 322
  attempt to introduce Scottish version of
  English Catholic Relief Bill, 243, 247, 256,
  263, 266, 287, 295
Dundas, Robert (Lord Arniston) (1713-1787),
  122, Ch.4 n.87, 318
Dundas, Robert (1758-1819) (Lord Advocate at
  time of Thomas Muir's trial), 156, Ch.6 n.40,
  171, 175, 180
Dundas, Sir Lawrence, 82-86, Ch.3 n.12/13
Dundas, Sir Thomas, Ch.3 n.22, 177
Dundee, 22, 252
Dundonald, 4, 131, 188
Dunfermline, xviii, 20, 23, 57, 77-101 *passim*,
  Ch.3 n.33, 97
Dunn, Rev. William (Kirkintilloch), 5, 151,
  155-181 *passim*, Ch.6 n.1
  *A Sermon, preached at the opening of the
  Synod of Glasgow and Air*, 160-169
Durham, James, 104-106, Ch.4 n.10

E

Eaton Constantine (Shropshire), 14
Eaton, Daniel Isaac (radical bookseller and
  publisher), 189
Edgar, James, 83, Ch.3 n.17
Edinburgh, 5, 44, 135, 157, 264, 273
  Arnot's *History of Edinburgh*, 104, Ch.4 n.8-9
  Canongate playhouse, 103, 108, Ch.4 n.24,
  112, 118

Carubber's Close, 108-109
Goldsmiths' Hall Association, 174
'Haddo's Hole' (West St. Giles' Church),
  Frontispiece, 155, 269, 287, Ch.10 n.85
MP for Edinburgh, 82
'New Theatre', 107, 109
Philosophical Society of, 276
Presbytery of, 104, 111, 122-124, Ch.4 n.92
St. Giles' Church, 19, 281, App. B, n.43
Shakespeare's plays performed in, 107-108
  (see also under *Macbeth*)
Taylor's Hall, 107, Ch.4 n.22, 112
Town Council, 109
Trinity Church, Ch.4 n.46
Tron Church, 113
University of, 38, 112, 247
Edinburgh Advertiser, 80, 88, Ch.3 n.70
Edinburgh Christian Instructor, 74, Ch.2 n.78
Edinburgh Evening Courant, Ch.6 n.57, 293
Edinburgh Gazetteer, Ch.6 n.39, 202
Edinburgh Review, 281, Ch.10 n.61
Eigg, island of, Ch.9 n.15
Eglinton, Earl of, 144, App. D, n.20
Elliot, Charles (Edinburgh bookseller),
  234-235, Ch.8 n.98
Ellis, James (see 'Alice, James')
Elphinstone, Lord (Charles), 161, 180
Emerson, Roger L., 27, Ch.1 n.3, Ch.4 n.77
'Enlightenment, Religious', 289, 300
Enlightenment, Scottish, characteristics of, 2-3,
  27-28, 36, 88, Ch.5 n.12, 166, 185, 276, 282
Epicurus, 44
Episcopal Church in Scotland, 32
Erastianism, 4, 49
Erskine, David (Lord Dun), Ch.8 n.79
Erskine, Rev. Ebenezer (Portmoak, nr.
  Kinross; Stirling - third charge; co-founder of
  the Associate Presbytery)
  The Stone rejected by the Builders, 25,
  42-44, Ch.1 n.63/ 68, Ch.5 n.56
Erskine, Henry, 30
Erskine, Captain James-Francis, of Forrest 83,
  Ch.3 n.23, 86
Erskine, Colonel John, of Carnock, 40
Erskine, Professor John (jurist), of Carnock,
  Ch.9 n.9, Ch.10 n.54
Erskine, Rev. John, (Kirkintilloch; Culross;
  New Greyfriars; Old Greyfriars): vii, 3, 5,

26 (ill.), Introduction n.21, Ch.1 n.2/79-83, 106-107, Ch.4 n.19/81, 159, Ch.6 n.16, 190, 227, 235, 240 (ill.), 256-263 *passim*, 264, 300-301
Works cited:
The Equity and Wisdom of Administration, 236, Ch.8 n.110
Prayer for those in civil and military offices recommended, 260-263, Ch.9 n.73/75-80
The Qualifications Necessary for Teachers of Christianity, 25, 47-49
The fatal consequences, 159, Ch.6 n.17
Reflections on the Rise, Progress, and probable Consequences of the Present contentions with the Colonies, 236, Ch.8 n.110
Shall I go to war with my American brethren? (1769 & 1776), 235, 238, Ch.8 n.109, 257-258
Three Sermons, Ch.9 n.72
Considerations on the Spirit of Popery, 262
Erskine, Mary, 40
Erskine, Rev. Ralph, Ch.3 n.8
Erskine, Thomas
 Crown and Anchor speech (*Address to the Public*) (1793), 197, Ch.7 n.64
Eskgrove, Lord (*see* David Rae)
Estienne, Robert ('Robertus Stephanus'), 8, Introduction n.29
euthanasia, 6
Ewing, Dr. Greville, 74, 75

F

'Faithometer, Doctor Tail's' [William Thom's], 152 (ill.)
Falkirk, 37, 252, Ch.9 n.41-42
Farquhar, George, Ch.4 n.26
Fasti Ecclesiae Scoticanae (Scott)
 I, Ch.10 n.61
 II, 148, Ch.5 n.76-77, Ch.6 n.1
 III, Ch.4 n.11, Ch.5 n.1/35/42, Ch.6 n.105, Ch.7 n.18, App. D, n.25
 V, Ch.1 n.62, Ch.3 n.8, Ch.9 n.38/40
 VI, Introduction n.25
 VII, Ch.9 n.83

Ferguson, Adam, 21, Ch.4 n.93, 137, Ch.6 n.103, Ch.8 n.1, 272
 The Morality of Stage Plays Seriously Considered, Ch.4 n.66/94-97, 123-125
Fergusson, Rev. Alexander (Kilwinning), 51, 129-130, 221
 'A.B' in the *Scots Magazine*, Ch.5 n.29-30/71, 137-146, 188
 Leitch affair, App. D, 323-333
Fergusson, William, ('schoolmaster'), 86
Fernie, Rev. Thomas ('peep sma'), 79, Ch.3 n.9
Fielding, Henry
 Pasquin, 109, Ch.4 n.33
 The Golden Rump controversy, 130, Ch.4 n.34
Fills, Robert, 9-10, Introduction n.35/36
Filmer, Sir Robert, 114, Ch.8 n.79
Findlay, Rev. Robert, Ch.5 n.64
Finlay, John, ix, 64, Ch.3 n.39/49/62, App. B, n.55, App. D, n.6-7
Finlay, Richard, ix
Finlayson, Rev. James, 156, Ch.6 n.4
Firmin, Thomas, 296, Ch.10 n.109
Fishguard, French landing at (1797), 206, Ch.7 n.97
Fleischacker, Samuel, Ch.8 n.94
Fleming, Robert (printer), 118
Fletcher, Andrew (Lord Milton), 122
Fletcher, Archibald, 30
Fletcher, John (playwright), Ch.4 n.49
food banks, 22
Foote, Samuel (playwright)
 The Minor, 89, 316-317, App. B, n.38
Forbes, Duncan, of Culloden, 110
Fordyce, David, 228, 253, Ch.9 n.46, 275, 279
 Dialogues Concerning Education, 253
 The Elements of Moral Philosophy, 253, 275
 Theodorus, Ch.9 n.48, 429 (ill.)
Fordyce, Rev. James (Brechin; Alloa; minister to the dissenting congregation, Monkwell Street, London)
 introduces Hugh Blair to Samuel Johnson, 254
 Works cited
 Addresses to the Deity, Ch.9 n.47
 Addresses to Young Men, 255
 The Character and Conduct of the Female Sex, 255
 The Delusive and Persecuting Spirit of Popery, 242, 253-256
 The Eloquence of the Pulpit, 254

An Essay on the Action proper for the Pulpit, 254
Sermons to Young Women, 254-256, Ch.9 n.53-54
fornication, crime of, 22-24
Fort Augustus, 113
Fort William, 113
Foulis, Robert and Andrew, 108, Ch.4 n.26/89
Fox, Henry (Lord Holland), 83
Foxe, John, 310
Martyrology (aka 'Book of Martyrs'), 314
Franklin, Benjamin, 217, 219, Ch.8 n.30/113
Franklin Papers at Yale, x, Ch.8 n.31
free-will, Christian doctrine of, Ch.5 n.21
French Declaration of the Rights of Man, Ch.7 n.53
French Revolution, 159, 185, 200, 270
Friars, preaching, 15
Friends of the People, 21, 158, Ch.6 n.14/48, 163, 189, 202-206
Frossard, Benjamin Sigismond
La Cause des esclaves nègres et des habitans de la Guinée (1789), Ch.10 n.108
Fry, Michael, Ch.3 n.22, 156, Ch.6 n.6, 169-170
Fullarton, Rev. John *primus* (Dalry), 333, App. D, n.24
Fullarton, Rev. John Fullarton *secundus* (Dalry), App. D, n.24
Furber, Holden, Ch.3 n.30

G

Galen, Bishop (later Cardinal) Clemens von, 6, Introduction n.27
Garden, Francis (Lord Gardenstone), 21, 71, Ch.2 n.66, 88, 90, 94
Gardiner, John (on Blair's sermons), Ch.6 n.19
Gay, John
The Beggar's Opera, 90, 107, 111
Gentleman's Magazine, 110
Geneva, 8, 12, 15
Geneva Bible, Introduction n.69/ 75
George III, King, 196, 201, 273
Georgia, American colony of, 276
Gerard, Rev. Alexander, 236
Gerrald, Joseph, 174, 202
Gibson, Thomas, 86
Gillespie, Rev. Thomas, 41-42, Ch.1 n.84-85, 47-49
Gillies, Rev. John, Ch.6 n.1, 252, 263-264
Gilmour, Sir Alexander, 86
Gilpin, Bernard, 312-313, App. B, n.17-20
Gimbel, Richard, Ch.8 n.101
Gladsmuir, 281
Glasgow, 1, 3-4, 264, 273
Blackfriars (the College) Church, 242, 263
Presbytery of, Ch.6 n.37
University of, 105, Ch.5 n.15, 161,186, 221-222, 227, Ch.8 n.94, 254, Ch.10 n.109
Glasgow and Ayr, Synod of, Ch.4 n.100, 129, 138, 145, 172, Ch.6 n.37, Ch.7 n.25, 333, App. D, n.18
Glasgow Courier, 162, Ch.6 n.30, 171, Ch.7 n.28
Glencoe, Ch.9 n.15
Glengarry, Ch.9 n.15, 246
Glenmoriston, 246
'Glorious Revolution', 51, 280, 294
Goldie, John, 188
Gordon, Hon. Alexander (Lord Rockville), 235
Gordon, Lord George, 254
Gordon, W. M., 30, Ch.1 n.15-16
Gordon (anti-Catholic) riots, 254
'Goudie's Bible', 188
Govan, 222
'Grace', Christian doctrine of, 115
Graham, Rev. John, Ch.5 n.28/45, 148
Grant, Alexander (writer), 172, Ch.6 n.69
Grant, James (of Corrimony), 88, Ch.3 n.40
Grant, Rev. Patrick (Urray and Tarradale):
The Spirit of Moderation in Religion Recommended, 242, 264-267 *passim*, Ch.9 n.86-93
rarity of his printed sermon, Ch.9 n.85
Grant, William (Lord Prestongrange)
The Present State of the Church of Scotland, 28-29, Ch.1 n.7-12, 30, Ch.2 n.1
Gray, William (Edinburgh publisher), 149, 260
Grayling, A. C., Ch.7 n.53
Green, Ashbel, Ch.2 n.74/77, 76, 187
Green, James N., ix
Green, V. H. H., 9, Introduction n.34
Greenock, 130, Ch.8 n.63
Grotius, Hugo, 233, 271-272
Guelph, Canada, University of, Ch.9 n.85
Guthrie, Alexander, (radical bookseller in Edinburgh), Ch.6 n.57

H

Haden-Guest, Edith, Ch.3 n.12/16/22/24/31
Haddington Grammar School, 108
Hall, Rowland, 10, Introduction
   n.36/18-19/69/75
Haman and Ahasuerus, Biblical story of,
   according to Hugh Blair, 191
   do. John Skip, 6, Introduction n.24, 192
   do. Alexander Webster, 192
   do. Alexander Wilson, Ch.7 n.40
Hamilton, Duke and Duchess of, 111
Hamilton, James, ix
Hamilton, William, 112
Hampden, John, 213
handloom weaving, 158
Hanway, Jonas, 296
Hardy, Rev. Thomas (Ballingry; Edinburgh
   High, St. Giles'; Edinburgh North – West
   St. Giles' ('Haddo's Hole'): 155, 157,
   Ch.6 n.7/56-57/86, 180, 184, 193, Ch.10
   n.85/87, 300
   Works cited
   Fidelity to the British Constitution, 155,
   168-169
   The Progress of the Christian Religion,
   269, 287-294, Ch.10 n.93-101/104
Harrington, James, 220
Harris, Bob, 21, Introduction n.80, 156-157,
   Ch.6 n.2/39/57
Harris, island of, Ch.9, n.15
Harvard University, 275
Hay, Bishop George (*aka* Bishop of Daulis), 257,
   259, 261
Hay, Charles (Lord Newton), vii, 59, 68, 71-72
Helvétius, Claude Adrien, 271, 274
Henderson, Rev. Alexander, App. B, n.2
Henry VIII, King, 6, 16
Herder, Johann Gottfried von, Ch.10 n.91
heresy, 4, 129-153 *passim*
High Court of Justiciary (Edinburgh), 163, 202,
   318
   Special Commission of Oyer and Terminer
   (1794), Ch.6 n.71
Hindu culture and religion, 291, 294, Ch.10
   n.66
Hobbes, Thomas, 44, 274
Hogg, Annie (correspondent of John
   Witherspoon), Ch.9 n.26

Hogg, William (Edinburgh banker), 247, Ch.9
   n.26
d'Holbach, Paul-Henri Thiry, Baron, 271
Home, Rev. John (Athelstaneford): 21, 35, 121,
   Ch.4 n.90
   Douglas, 103, 112, 118-124, Ch.4 n.100
Hook, Andrew, ix, Ch.7 n.23, 212, Ch.8
   n.3-4/24-25
   and Sher, Richard B., Ch.8 n.77
Hooker, Richard, 274
Hopetoun, Earl of, 281
House of Commons, 161, Ch.6 n.103,
House of Lords, 21, 57, 94, Ch.3 n.61, 161,
   230, 295, 322, App. B, n.44
Howard, John (penal reformer), 296
Hume, David, 2, 4, Ch.2 n.12, 104, 112,
   118-120, 130-131, 186, 194, 272, 299
   Works cited:
   [Correspondence], Ch.8 n.45-50
   Enquiry concerning the Principles of Morals, 118,
   Ch.4 n.73
   Essays (1760), Ch.8 n.79
   Four Dissertations, Ch.4 n.74
   History of Great Britain. Vol. I, 120
   Of the First Principles of Government, 219-220,
   Ch.8 n.44
   Of National Characters (Footnote), 288, Ch.10
   n.92
   On the Populousness of Ancient Nations, 274,
   276-277, Ch.10 n.31/41-43, 279
   Treatise of Human Nature, Ch.8 n.79
Hume, (Baron) David (jurist), Ch.2 n.3, Ch.8
   n.45
   on the crime of sedition, 170, Ch.6 n.63-64
   on 'offences against religion', 244, Ch.9 n.12
Hunter, Andrew, (benefactor of the Orphan
   Hospital in Edinburgh), 296
Hunter, Rev. David, Ch.3 n.1
Hutcheson, Francis, 52, 131-132, Ch.5 n.15,
   218, 233, Ch.8 n.35-37/41/94, 272, 274
Hutchison, Patrick (secessionist minister), 158,
   189
Hyndman, Rev. John, 246, Ch.9 n.23, 258,
   Ch.9 n.65

I

India (see under 'Hindu')
Indiana, University of, Ch.9 n.26
Innes, Gilbert (of Stow), 174, Ch.6 n.78
'intrinsic' and 'extrinsic' in Scots law, definition of, Ch.3 n.68
Inveresk, 22
Inverkeithing, 33-42 *passim*, Ch.3 n.33, 86
Ireland, 1
Irvine, Presbytery of, 131, Ch.5 n.15/71, 138, 147
Israel, Jonathan, 271, Ch.10 n 8-9/11/15/25/47, 278

J

Jack, Rev. James, 181
Jackson, John, Ch.4 n.25
Jacobin dogma, 194
'Jacobin societies', 179
Jacobitism, 139, 248, 252-253
Jamieson, John (secessionist minister), 53
Jardine, Rev. John, 281, Ch.10 n.61
Jasanoff, Maya, Ch.8 n.26
Jefferson, Thomas, 212, 218
Jesuits (Society of Jesus), 243, Ch.9 n.8
Johnson, Christine, 245, Ch.9 n.19
Johnson, Samuel, 2, 21, 86, 217, 254, 256
   meets Hugh Blair, 254, 315
   'Oral essay' on pulpit censure, 95-97, Ch.3 n.64-65
   Preface to James Fordyce's *Sermons to Young Women*, 254
   Taxation no Tyranny, 2
Johnston, Rev. David, 235-236, Ch.8 n.104/111
Johnston, John ('writing-master in Edinburgh'), 296
Johnston, T. (printer in Falkirk), 252, Ch.9 n.42
Jones, John Paul, 216
Jones, Sir William ('Selim'), 291, 294, Ch.10 n.102-103
Junius's letters, 262
Jusserand, J. J., 14
justice, 'commutative' (or 'corrective') and 'distributive', Ch.8 n.94

K

Kames, Henry Home, Lord, 4, Ch.2 n.12, 104, 118, 130, 186, 272
   Essays on the Principles of Morality and Religion, Ch.5 n.6
Kant, Immanuel, Ch.10 n.91
Keane, John, Ch.8 n.100
Keith (Banffshire), 6
Kelso, 295
Kennedy, James (radical poet), 188-189, Ch.7 n.23/99
   Treason, or not Treason, 207
Kenrick, Samuel, 52
Ketcham, Ralph, Ch.2 n.70
Kidd, Colin, ix, Ch.5 n.12/25/27/84, 133, 137, 149-150, 157-158, Ch.6 n.9/59/100, 169, 187-189, Ch.7 n.19-20/22, Ch.10 n.66
Kilbride (Ayrshire) (modern West Kilbride), 130, 144
Kilconquhar settlement, 143
Kilwinning (Ayrshire), 138
Kilwinning
   James Leitch affair, 323-333
Kilwinning 'heresy', Introduction n.39, 51, 53, 129-153 *passim* (esp. 135), 188
Kincaid, Alexander (Edinburgh bookseller and printer), 118, Ch.8 n.106
King, Peter (Lord King of Ockham) (Lord Chancellor), 113, Ch.4 n.42
Kininmonth, Rev. William, 6
Kircudbright, 216
Kirkintilloch, 5, 22, 155, 158-160, 171, 180
Knight, Roger, Ch.7 n.97
Knox, John, vii, 8, 15-20, Introduction n.59/61-64, 133, 310
   and the 'six Johns', Introduction n.45
   History of the Reformation, 16, 19
   Sermon (1565), 17 (ill.), Introduction n.77-78
Knox, Ronald A., 1
Koran, The, 144, Ch.5 n.60

L

Landsman, Ned C., 221, Ch.8 n.51
Lapslie, Rev. James (Campsie), 151, Ch.6 n.50/92/93, 175, 176-181 *passim*
Largs, Ch.5 n.2

Latimer, Bishop Hugh, 310, 311 (ill.), 312, App. B, n.13-16
Law, William (1686-1761) (writer against the stage), Ch.4 n.29, 114
Law, William (professor at Edinburgh), Ch.4 n.29
Lawrence, Samuel (English dissenter), 254
Leask, Nigel, Ch.7 n.49
Lee, Arthur, 217, Ch.8 n.113
Leechman, Principal William, 130, Ch.5 n.15, 227, App. D, n.22
Leibniz, Gottfried Wilhelm, 187
Leitch, James (wright), affair of, Introduction n.39, 138, App. D, 324-333
Leith, William Forbes, Ch.9 n.7
Leslie, Alexander (radical Edinburgh bookseller), 274, Ch.10 n.26
Leven, Seventh Earl of (Alexander Leslie), 40, 44, 248
lex talionis, 72
'Liberty of the bar', 87-88, 315
   Shaw v Bean, 88-89, Ch.3 n.39/41
'Liberty of the press', 87, 239, 315
'Liberty of the pulpit', 14, 21, 87, 89, Ch.3 n.44, 97, 315
'liberty, natural' (according to Francis Hutcheson), 275
Licensing Act (to control theatres and performances) (1737), 104, 109-110
Lindsay, Dr. Alison, ix
Lindsay, Sir David, 16, Introduction n.66
Lindsay, James, 254
Linlithgow, 252
Loch, David, 83
Lochaber, Ch.9 n.15
Lock, F. P., 185, Ch.7 n.6
Locke, John, 218, 274
Logan, Rev. George (1678-1755) (Lauder; Sprouston; Dunbar; Edinburgh Trinity): Ch.1 n.70-78, Ch.4 n.46
   A Sermon preached ... on the 14th of May 1741, 25, 44-47
Logan, Rev. George (1723-1754), Ch.1 n.69
Lollards, 14
Long, Edward, Ch.10 n.91
Longson, Andrea, ix
Lothian and Tweeddale, Synod of, Ch.5 n.71, 156

Luddism, 165
Lynch, Michael, 32, Ch.1 n.23-24

Mac/Mc

Macarthur, Daniel ('preacher of the Gospel'), 242, Ch.9 n.6
Macbeth (performed in Edinburgh in 1731), 107
Mackintosh, Sir James, 161, Ch.6 n.29
McConnell, James (town drummer in Beith), 147
Maconochie, Allan, 281, Ch.10 n.62
McCosh, James, 74, Ch.2 n.76
MacCulloch, Diarmaid, 10-12, 14, Introduction n.40 and 54-55, 270
McCulloch, Rev. William, 242
McDonald, Bishop Hugh, Ch.9 n.7
McDouall, Andrew (Lord Bankton), 30-31, Ch.1 n.13-16/18/67, 241, Ch.9 n.1, 243
McEwan, James (secessionist minister), 158
McFarland, E. W., 157
McGill, Rev. William (Kilwinning – assistant; Ayr – second charge): 130, Ch.5 n.12/71, 188
   The Benefits of the Revolution ... in Two Sermons, 27, 51-53, Ch.1 n.99/101-103
McGinty, Walter, Ch.2 n.71
McIntosh, John R., 37, Ch.1 n.47, 104, Ch.4 n.7/103, 125, Ch.5 n.13/56, 137, Ch.7 n.10-11, 185-186, 189, Ch.8 n.102, 252, Ch.9 n.39/41
Mackenzie, Rev. John, 148
MacLaurin, John (Lord Dreghorn), 30, Ch.1 n.64/88, Ch.3 n.70, 103, 119-121, Ch.4 n.75, 235, Ch.8 n.107
Macleod, Bannatyne W. (later Lord Bannatyne), Ch.3 n.41, App. B, 315
Macleod, Emma Vincent, 202, Ch.7 n.79, Ch.10 n.84
'M'Lerie, David' ('weaver in Paisley'; see James Alicc)
Macpherson, James
   Rights of Great Britain, 217-218, 238, Ch.8 n.115
Macqueen, Robert (Lord Braxfield), 88, 90, 98, 172-173, Ch.6 n.71/72

M

Madison, James, 73
Mailer, Gideon, Ch.2 n.71, 215
Mair, Nicholaus Alexander (*aka* Mair von Landshut) (engraver), App. B, n.50
Malplaquet, Battle of (1709), 113
Malthus, Thomas Robert, 277
Margarot, Maurice, Ch.6 n.40, 202
Marischal College, Aberdeen, 228
Marlowe's *Tamerlane*, 108
Massachusetts, 217
Massinger, Philip, Ch.4 n.49
Masterton, Lieut. Colonel James, 83-86, Ch.3 n.15-16
Matheson, Ann, Ch.7 n.4/42, 193, Ch.9 n.33
Maxton (Selkirkshire), 8, 43
Maxwell, James (poet in Paisley), 188-189, Ch.7 n.21/30
Maxwell, William, Introduction n.46, Ch.2 n.8
Meikle, Henry, 21, Introduction n.80, Ch.6 n.2/102, 157, 205, Ch.7. n.89
Melville, Andrew, 7
Methodism, 1, 118, 242, 317
Millar, Andrew, 254, 258
Millar, John, 180, Ch.8 n.45, 270, Ch.10 n.6-7/17/50-56
on slavery, 279-280
Milne, Hugh M., Ch.8 n.108, 322
Milton of Campsie, 160, 179
Mirabeau, Honoré Gabriel Riqueti, Comte de, Ch.10 n.45
Mission, Christian, weakness of (according to Thomas Hardy), 291, 300
Moderatism (see Church of Scotland)
Moidart, Ch.9 n.15
Moir, James (secessionist minister), 53
Molière
Le Tartuffe, 71, Ch.2 n.75
Monkwell Street, London (dissenting congregation), 254, Ch.9 n.49
Montesquieu, Charles de Secondat, Baron de, 271, 274, 277
Persian Letters, 273
Spirit of the Laws (*De l'Esprit des Loix*), 272-273, Ch.10 n.24, 292 (ill.)
Montgomery, (Sir) James (Bt.) (advocate), 70
Montgomery, Rev. John, 333, App. D., n.25

Montrose, Marquis of (James Graham), 6
'Moodie, Captain' case, Ch.2 n.5
Moodie, Rev. William, 5, Introduction n.20, 151, 156, 168, Ch.6 n.53
moral corruption, 160-161
'moral sense' (according to Francis Hutcheson), 275
Moray, 246
Morison, Archibald (weaver in Paisley), Ch.7 n.28
Morison, Rev. James, 145
Morison, William M.,
Decisions of the Court of Session, 87, Ch.3 n.36/66/69, 97, Ch.9 n.10, Ch.10 n.12/62, 322
Morren, Nathaniel
Annals of the General Assembly 1739-1752, Ch.5 n.33, Ch.8 n.52, Ch.9 n.26
Annals of the General Assembly 1752-1766, 3, Introduction n.17, 33-34, Ch.1 n.32/39/41, 37-38, 56, Ch.2 n.4, Ch.4 n.2/71/91, Ch.5 n.56, Ch.9 n.14
Morrison, Jeffry, 73
mortcloths (at funerals), 325-326, App. D, n.11
Morthland, John, 175
Morton, Earl of, 277
Mossner, E. C., 276, Ch.10 n.40-41/45
Muck, island of, Ch.9 n.15
Muir, Rev. George, Ch.5 n.35
Muir, Thomas, of Huntershill, (advocate), 5, 158, 161-163, Ch.9 n.6
his trial before the High Court, 156, Ch.6 n.57, 170, 174-176, 197
Paisley Declaration of Rights, 188
his radical cosmopolitanism, 194
on the writings of Thomas Paine, 57
Muir, William (witness at Thomas Muir's trial), 175-176
Muessig, Carolyn, 15, Introduction n.57
Murray, Alexander (Lord Henderland), 172-173, 322
Murray, William (Earl of Mansfield), Ch.10 n.80
Münster, 6

N

National Covenant, 135
National Library of Scotland, Scottish Book Trade Index, Ch.9 n.42

New Jersey, College of, 74, 187
New Lanark, Ch.10 n.109
'New Licht', Ch.5 n.12
Newton, John, 270
Newton, Lord (see Hay, Charles)
Nisbet, Rev. Charles, Ch.6 n.1, 264
Noble, Andrew, x, Ch.8 n.57
non-resistance (see passive obedience)
North, Lord, 177, 221, 229
Northampton, 228
Norton, David Fate, 218-219, Ch.8 n.36
Nova Scotia, 226

O

'Onesimus', (in Paul's letter to the *Colossians* and *Philemon*), 282
    David Daube on, Ch.10 n.63
    John Millar on, Ch.10 n.63
'original sin', Christian doctrine of, Ch.5 n.12/44, Ch.7 n.13, 186-187, 198 (see also John Witherspoon; relations with Thomas Paine; and John Taylor)
Oglethorpe, James, 276
Ohno, Kate Mearns, x
'Ossianic controversy', App. B, n.42
Otway, Thomas, 119, 127
Owst, Gerald Robert, 14

P

Pagden, Anthony, 194, Ch.7 n.48
Paine, Thomas, 21, Ch.6 n.40, 166, 168, Ch.7 n.13/26/57, 196, 299, 301
    Works cited
    The Age of Reason, 299
    Common Sense, Ch.5 n.12/44, 186, 214, 231 (ill.), 234-235, Ch.8 n.6/98/100-101, 272
    Rights of Man Part I, 164, Ch.6 n.88, 185, 196
    Rights of Man Part II, 21
Paisley, xvii, 20, 22, 77, 91, 106, 142-143, 158, 160, Ch.6 n.39, 188, 202, 226, Ch.8 n.8, 301
    Burgess Roll, Ch.7 n.26
    Central Library, Ch.7 n.26
    Paisley Declaration of Rights, 188
    Presbytery of, 189
    Relief congregation in, 189
Palmer, Rev. Thomas Fyshe, 158, 161

'Papists Act, The' (1778), 243
Paris, 184
passive obedience, doctrine of, and non-resistance, 228-229, Ch.8 n.79
Paton, Bernadette, 14
Paton, Elizabeth, 22
Paton, Rev. Robert, 39
Patriot, The, 169, Ch.6 n.57/58
patriotism, 183-207 *passim*
Patriot's Weekly Chronicle, Ch.6 n.39
Patronage Act (1712), 32, 134
Peebles, Rev. William (Dundonald – assistant; Newton upon Ayr): Ch.1 n.92/94/97
    The Great Things which the Lord hath done, 27, 51-53, Ch.1 n.95
Peggy, The, Ch.8 n.63
Pennsylvania, Protestant emigrants in, 247
Pennsylvania Magazine, Ch.7 n.26
'penny weddings', 324, App. D, n.5
Pension List, Scottish, 180, Ch.6 n.103
Perth, 1, 43, 255
    Grammar School, Ch.4 n.28
Phelps, Matthew, Ch.10 n.15
Phillipson, Nicholas, Ch.4 n.28, 288, Ch.10 n.66/90
Pinkerton, John, Ch.10 n.91
Pitt, William, 5, 184, 202, 205, Ch.7 n.77
'Pitt's Terror', 165
'plumb bond', Ch.2 n.60
Plutarch
    Morals, Ch.4 n.62
    Symposiacs, 117, Ch.4 n.62
Pocock, J. G. A., 220
Poker Club (Edinburgh), Ch.3 n.17
Pollard. Sidney, Ch.6 n.21
Pope, Alexander, 49
'Popery' (see Roman Catholic Church in Scotland)
Popham, Sir John, 314
'popularity', ministers cultivating, 46
Porteous murder and its aftermath, 114, Ch.4 n.46
Porteous, Rev. William (Glasgow Wynd), 180
Port Glasgow, 271
predestination, Christian doctrine of, Ch.5 n.21
Price, Richard, 236, 239, Ch.8 n.114
    Works cited
    A Discourse on the Love of Our Country, 185, 195

Observations on the Nature and Value of Civil Liberty, 236, Ch.8 n.113
Additional Observations, 236, Ch.8 n.113
'Prick, Parson', 314
Priestley, Joseph, 286, Ch.10 n.82
Princeton, NJ, 56, Ch.5 n.44/67, 186, 226, Ch.8 n.6, 301
Pringle, Andrew (Lord Alemore), App. B, n.56
'profaneness', the crime of, 55-76 *passim*, Ch.2 n.3, 272
Protestant Association, 254, Ch.9 n.49
Prunier, Clothilde, 245, Ch.9 n.16/21-22
Prynne, William, 105-106
Pufendorf, Samuel, 233, Ch.8 n.94, 271-272, 274
'punctum stans', concept of, Ch.6 n.31

Q

Quakers, 270, Ch.10 n.17
Queen's Theatre, Haymarket, London, Ch.4 n.26

R

radical movement in Scotland in the 1790s, 155
Radical War of 1819-1820, 158
Rae, David (Lord Eskgrove), vii, 21, 69-70, Ch.2 n.56/59, 80-81, Ch.3 n.10, 86-87, 90-91, Ch.6 n.71
Raeburn Sir Henry, 182 (ill.), 268 (ill.), Ch.7 n.77
Raguenier, Denis, 15
Raikes, Robert, 296, Ch.10 n.108
Ramillies, Battle of (1706), 113
Ramsay, Allan (poet and playwright), Ch.4 n.3/24-25/29/31/63/64, 102 (ill.), 107-113, 117
The Gentle Shepherd, 108-109
Ramsay, Allan (artist), 102 (ill.)
Ramsay, Rev. James, 286, Ch.10 n.81
Randall, Rev. Thomas, 52, Ch.1 n.96, Ch.5 n.64
Raynal, Abbé, 273-274
'reason' in religious belief, 132-133, 141-142
rebellions of 1715 and 1745, 248
Reeves, John, 165
Reevesian 'placemen', 158
Reform, Parliamentary and political, 155-181 *passim*, 166

Regeneration, Christian doctrine of, 187, 215, 301
Reid, Daniel (printer in Falkirk), 252, Ch.9 n.42
Reid, Thomas, 157, Ch.6 n.8, 272
Relief Church (or Presbytery of Relief), 138, 142-143, 178, 316
'religion, universal', 287
repentance, stool of, cover ill., 23, 92
Republicanism, 196-197
revelation, divine, 132-133
Rhind, Thomas, Ch.5 n.13
Richardson, Rev. Andrew, 38-40, Ch.3 n.1
Richardson, Samuel, 111
Ridley, Nicholas, 310
rights, concept of 'perfect' and 'imperfect' (see also John Witherspoon), 233, Ch.8 n.94
Robertson, Rev. Andrew, Ch.10 n.60
Robertson, James, 176, Ch.6 n.87
Robertson, Rev. Principal William (Gladsmuir; Edinburgh Lady Yester's; Edinburgh Old Greyfriars): 35, 42, Ch.1 n.69, 121, 137, Ch.6 n.103, 247, Ch.9 n.28, 250, 256-257, 260-262, 273, 287, Ch.10 n.60-62
Works cited
The Situation of the World at the Time of Christ's Appearance, (see also under slavery), 270, 281-286, 288, Ch.10 n.64-74/76
History of the Reign of the Emperor Charles V (and other histories), Ch.10 n.62/66/75
Robinson, John, 85
Robinson, Robert, Introduction n.47
Rodger, Alexander (poet), 181, Ch.6 n.93
Rodger, N. A. M., Ch.7 n.97
Roebuck, John, 238
Ross, Ian Simpson, Ch.8 n.74
Rough, John, 16, 18
Rousseau, Jean-Jacques, 271-272, Ch.10 n.19/25
Row, Rev. John, 313
Rum, island of, Ch.9 n.15
Rundle, Thomas (as cited by David Fordyce), 275-276, Ch.10 n.37
Rush, Benjamin, 74, Ch.2 n.72, Ch.8 n.6, Ch.9 n.26

S

Sadoletto, Cardinal Jacopo, 12, Introduction n.50-52
St. Andrews (Fife), 16, 18
 University of, 105
St. John, Henry (Viscount Bolingbroke), 118
St. Kitts, 286
St. Petersburg, 184
Saltcoats (Ayrshire), 131
Sardinia, Ch.9 n.67
Savage, Henry Lyttleton, 73
Scotland, John, Robert and David (of Dunfermline) (see Court of Session)
Scots Magazine, The, 84-86, Ch.3 n.26/70, 99, 130, Ch.5 n.28/43/46-48/51-52/55/57-59/66/69, 137-146, 150, Ch.6 n.83/85/91, Ch.8 n.71, 257, 260, Ch.9 n.69-71/81, 322, App. B, n.53
Scots Greys, 113
Scott, Alexander (newspaper proprietor), 202
Scott, Rev. Hew Scott (see *Fasti etc.*)
Scougal, Henry, Ch.4 n.56, Ch.6 n.54
Seceders and Secessionism in Scotland, 138-139, 159, 189, 194, 252, 329
Sedition, crime of, Ch.6 n.40, 170, 174, Ch.7 n.57 (see also Lord Cockburn)
Select Society, (of Edinburgh), 103, Ch.4 n.1/77
Shakespeare (Home's *Douglas* favourably compared with), 119, 127
Sharp, Granville, 286
Shaw, Angus, (merchant) (see under *Liberty of the bar* and Court of Session)
Shaw, Rev. Lachlan, 246, Ch.9 n.24
Shelburne, William Fitzmaurice, Earl of, 83, Ch.3 n.18/ 21
Sher, Richard B., (see also Hook, Andrew), ix, xvii, 3, Introduction n.18, 21, 28, Ch.1 n.5, Ch.3 n.17, Ch.4 n.69/85, Ch.5 n.27, Ch.7 n.8-9, 185, 189, Ch.8 n.20/106, 264, Ch.9 n.82, 286, Ch.10 n.76, App. B, n.43
Sher, Richard B. and Murdoch, Alexander, 37, Ch.1 n.44
Sher, Richard B., and Smitten, Jeffrey R., Ch.8 n.20
Sheriffs-Depute, App. B, n.55
Sheriffs-Substitute, App. B n.55
Sherwin, John (Keyse) (engraver), 50

Sierra Leone, 296
Simm, Hugh (loyalist Scot in America), 216, Ch.8 n.27/70
Simpson, Rev. Patrick, 313-314
Simson, Professor John, 130, 147, 325, App. D., n.9
Sinclair, Sir John
 'Old' Statistical Account (*OSA*), 158-159, Ch.6 n.15/22-24/26/98, 161, 178, 203, Ch.7 n.80
Skinner, Andrew, 219, Ch.8 n.41
Skip (or Skyppe), John, 6
Skirving, William, Ch.6 n.48, 175, 202
slavery, 250-251, 269-297 *passim*, 273-274
 abolition of slave trade, 294-297
 in Africa, 291
 in ancient times (dispute between David Hume and Robert Wallace), 276-277
 in the American colonies (according to William Robertson), 285
 Frossard on, Ch .10 n.108
 Knight v Wedderburn, 280, Ch.10 n.62
Sloan, Douglas, Ch.10 n.15
Smith, Adam, Ch.4 n.28, 217-218, Ch.8 n.34/94, 296
 Correspondence, Ch.8 n.34/40
 'rights' and 'justice', views on, Ch.8 n.94
 slavery, views on, 277-279
 Lectures on Jurisprudence, Ch.8 n.94, 278, Ch.10 n.49
 The Theory of Moral Sentiments, 278, Ch.10 n.46
 Wealth of Nations, 217-219, Ch.8 n.32-33/41-43/62, Ch.10 n.47-48
Smith, William, 219, Ch.8 n.38
Smitten, Jeffrey R., Ch.10 n.60 (see also Richard B. Sher)
Snodgrass, John (writer in Paisley), 55, 62-64, Ch.5 n.30, 187
Snodgrass, Rev. John, 187
Socinianism, 53, 188
S.S.P.C.K. (Society in Scotland for Propagating Christian Knowledge), 187, Ch.7 n.15, 250, Ch.9 n.65, 287, 296
 as an instrument of anti-'Popery', 246
 Hugh Blair's 're-cycled' sermon, 250
Somerville, Rev. Thomas, 287, 295, Ch.10 n.107
South, Robert, Ch.8 n.79, 315, App. B, n.31
Spence, Rev. John, Ch.3 n.1

Stage, The, 103-127 *passim*
Stair Society, Ch.9, n.1
Stamp Act, 220, 257
Steuart, A. Francis, App. B n.47
Stewart, Henry (see Darnley, Lord)
Stewart, M. A., 112-113, Ch.4 n.41
Stewarton (Ayrshire), Ch.10 n.109
Stiles, Ezra, 215, Ch.8 n.18-19
Stillingfleet, Edward, Ch.8 n.79
Stirling
   '*Black bond*', Ch.2 n.60, App. C, 321-322
Stoic cosmopolitanism, 194
Strahan, William, 220-221, App. B, n.42
Strathclyde, University of, Ch .10 n.109
Strathglass, 246
Stuart, Mary (Mary, Queen of Scots), 18-20
subscription, ministerial (to the Confession of Faith), (see Church of Scotland, *Confession of Faith*)
Suttie (Grant), Sir James, 177
Sunter, Ronald M., Ch.1 n.4, 177, Ch.6 n.96
superstition, 283-284, 290, Ch.10 n.66
Swift, Jonathan,
   Jure Divino, 131
   Tale of a Tub, 131
Szechi, Daniel, 245, Ch.9 n.20

T

'Tam Thrum', Ch.6. n.39
Tarbolton (Ayrshire), 22
Tate, Nahum, Ch.4 n.21
Taylor, John (English dissenter)
   The Scripture-Doctrine of Original Sin, 187
Thayer, Anne, 14
theatre, the, (see 'The Stage')
Thom, Rev. William, 3, Introduction n.15-16, 35, Ch.1 n.42, 36, 129, 148, 201, 221, Ch.8 n.3/94, 301
   Works cited:
   Letters of Advice to the Farmers, Land-Labourers, and Country Tradesmen, 223
   Seasonable Advice to the Landholders and Farmers in Scotland (aka *The Task-Masters*), 210, 222-226, Ch.8 n.53/62-63
   The Revolt of the Ten Tribes, 210, 228-229

Achan's Trespass, 210, 229-230
From whence come Wars? 210, 232-234
A Vindication of Doctor Tail, from the Charge of Heresy, 148, 152 (ill.), 153
Works, Ch.8 n.55-56/58-61/64-65/78/80/82/84-85/87/90-92/97
Thomson, Alexander, 226
Thomson, Rev. James
   '*virtual' sermon of*, 20, 77-101*passim*, Ch.3 n.8, 112
'theodicy' (Leibniz), 187
Thomas, J. E., Ch.7 n.97
Thurlow, Edward (Lord Chancellor), 57, 94
Tillotson, John, 249, 316
Titius, Gerhard, Gottlieb, Ch.10 n.29
'tolerance, religious', principle of (as applied to Moderate ministers), 264
Toleration Act (1712), 32, 43
Torphichen controversy, 35
Torre, Lillian de la, App. B, n.47
Traill, Professor Robert, 148, 152 (ill.), 153
Trent, Council of, 144, Ch.5 n.60
Turnbull, George, 228
'Twelve Tables', Roman code of, 318, App. B, n.51

U

Uist, South, Ch.9 n.15
Union of Parliaments (1707), 29
Universities, Scottish, in the eighteenth century, 274, Ch.10 n.27
Urray and Tarradale (*aka* Urray and Kilchrist) (Presbytery of Dingwall), 264
Ussher, James (Archbishop of Armagh), Ch.4 n.13

V

Vatican archives, Ch.9 n.21
Vermont Historical Society, 226
Volney, Constantin François de Chasseboeuf, Comte de, 274
Voltaire, François-Marie Arouet, 274

W

Walker, David M., Ch.1 note 15, Ch.2 n.3, 243, Ch.9 n.7
Walker, Rev. Robert (1716-1783), 3, 106, Ch.4 n.18, 207, 235, Ch.8 n.103, 258, Ch.9 n.65
Walker, Rev. Robert (1755-1808), 202, Ch.7 n.77
Walker, Rev. Thomas, 4, Introduction n.18, 53, Ch.1 n.100, Ch.4 n.69, 131, Ch.5 n.4/60, 146-147, 149-150, 188
Wallace, George (advocate), 70, 122, 272-273, Ch.10 n.80
A System of the Principles of the Law of Scotland, 270, 272-273, Ch.10 n.16/17/20-22
Wallace, Rev, Robert, 122, Ch.8 n.79, 273, Ch.10 n.23/44-45, 276-277
Walpole, Sir Robert, 104, 109
Warburton, Bishop William, 258
Warner, Rev. John ('The Abbot'), 67
Warton, Joseph, Ch.4 n.107
Washington, George, 221, Ch.8 n.2
Watt, Robert, Ch.6 n.71, 197
weaving (see handloom weaving)
Webster, Rev. Alexander, *frontispiece ill.*, 235, Ch.8 n.102
Wesley, John, 1, 118, 254, Ch.10 n.75
Journal, 1, Introduction n.3/5-7/9, Ch.4 n.70
A Calm Address, 1
Whatley, Christopher A., Ch.10 n.54
Whitburn, 49
Whitefield, Rev. George, 242, 252, 317
'Whyte, Adam' (Rev. William Moodie *q.v.*), 168
Whyte, Ian, 287, Ch.10 n.51/62/69/83
Whyte, Rev. Thomas, 124
Wigtown, 318, App. B, n.56
Wilberforce, William, 270, 295-297, Ch.10 n.108
Wilby, Noel MacDonald, 245, Ch.9 n.17
Wilkes, John, 216-217
The North Briton, 217, Ch.8 n.23-24, 262
Wilks, Robert (actor), Ch.4 n.64
William III, King, 32
Willison, Rev. John (Brechin; Dundee South): 237 (ill.), 241, 252-253, Ch.9 n.2
Popery another Gospel ... In Six Sermons, 252-253
Wilson, Alexander (poet and ornithologist), 188-189, Ch.7 n.23-24/98, 202

Address to the Synod of Glasgow and Ayr, 207
Wilson, Rev. Gabriel, 8, Introduction n.30-31, 43, 313-314
Wilson, Rev. James, Ch.9 n.41
Wilson, James (Scottish signatory to the Declaration of American Independence), 212
Wilton (Presbytery of Jedburgh), 296
Wishart, Rev. George, 18, 113-114, Ch.4 n.46
Wishart, Rev. Principal William (*secundus* Scots Church, Founder's Hall, London; Edinburgh New Greyfriars; Edinburgh Tron – second charge): 38, 241, 248-249, Ch.9 n.29
Publick Virtue recommended, 241, 248-249
Witherspoon, Rev. John (Beith; Paisley Laigh): xvii, 2-3, 5-6, 34-35, 55-76 *passim*, 106-107, Ch.5 n.45, 147-149, 198, 212, Ch.8 n.6/8/9-17, 301, 316
almanacs (pocketbooks) at Princeton University Library (for 1763 and 1768), 74, Ch.2 n.73, 130-131, Ch.5 n.2, 226
America, his coming to, 73-4, 76, 142, Ch.5 n.35, 146, Ch.6 n.14, 187, Ch.8 n.63
America, his role in Scots emigration to, 226, Ch.8 n.72
baptizes the slave, James Montgomerie, 272, 293 (ill.)
Colin Kidd on, 188
Dundee, called to be minister at, 68
Fergusson, Alexander, his lack of regard for JW, 142-143
London and Rotterdam (1768), visits, 71
'rights' – 'natural' and 'acquired', 233
Snodgrass affair and Court judgment, 55-76 *passim*, 91, 93, 272
its impact on JW's decision to quit Scotland, 73-76, Ch.2 n.76-81, 146
parallels with 'Dunfermline case', 78
Thomas Paine, relations with, Ch.5 n.12/44, Ch.7 n.13/26
Tusculum, JW's death at, 187
Works cited:
Address to the Natives of Scotland residing in America, 215, Ch.8 n.22
The Dominion of Providence over the Passions of Men, Ch.5 n.44, 186, 212-216, Ch.8 n.21, 250, Ch.9 n.35

Ecclesiastical Characteristics, 28, 35, Ch.1 n.40, 49, 55, Ch.4 n.66, 130, Ch.5 n.5/22, 136-137
Essays on Important Subjects, Ch.4 n.66
A Serious Apology for the Ecclesiastical Characteristics, 34, Ch.1 n.34-37, 107, Ch.4 n.20, Ch.5 n.5
A Serious Inquiry into the Nature and Effects of the Stage, 117-118, 125-127, Ch.4 n.101
The Charge of Sedition and Faction, 6, Introduction n.22, Ch.7 n.12, Ch.8 n.7/15
Lectures on Moral Philosophy, 233, Ch.8 n.79/95-96, 271-272, Ch.10 n.11
Ministerial Fidelity (the 'Farewell sermon', 106, Ch.4 n.17, Ch.8 n.71
Practical Treatise on Regeneration, Ch.8 n.28
Prayer for National Prosperity, Introduction n.23, Ch.8 n.7
Seasonable Advice to Young Persons, 55-76 *passim*
Thoughts on American Liberty, 213
Wodrow, Rev. James, 52, Ch.5 n.68
Wodrow, Rev, Robert, 145, Ch.5 n. 68
Wollstonecraft, Mary, 161
Wray, Sir Christopher, 314
Wroclaw, Poland (formerly, Breslau), Ch.9 n. 25

Y

Yeager, Jonathan M., Ch.8 n. 73
Young, John R., Ch.10 n. 54

Z

zeal, religious, 71-72, Ch.2 n. 75, 265
Zong (slave ship), scandal of, 286
Zwingli, Ulrich, 12

www.ingramcontent.com/pod-product-compliance
Lightning Source LLC
Chambersburg PA
CBHW051107230426
43667CB00014B/2468